Gerard DeGroot is Professor of Modern History at the University of St Andrews, where he has taught since 1985. An American by birth, he came to Britain in 1980 to do a PhD at Edinburgh University. He is the author of ten highly acclaimed books on twentieth-century history and has published widely in academic journals and in the popular press. His study of the atomic bomb, *The Bomb: A Life*, won the RUSI Westminster Medal, awarded in Britain to the best book published in the English language on a war or military topic, and *The Sixties Unplugged*, his acclaimed account of that dazzling decade, was published by Macmillan in 2008.

Also by Gerard DeGroot

The Bomb: A Life

The Dark Side of the Moon

The Sixties Unplugged

THE SEVENTIES UNPLUGGED

A KALEIDOSCOPIC LOOK AT A VIOLENT DECADE

Gerard DeGroot

PAN BOOKS

First published 2010 by Macmillan

First published in paperback 2011 by Pan Books
an imprint of Pan Macmillan, a division of Macmillan Publishers Limited
Pan Macmillan, 20 New Wharf Road, London N1 9RR
Basingstoke and Oxford
Associated companies throughout the world
www.panmacmillan.com

ISBN 978-0-330-45578-7

1 3 5 7 9 8 6 4 2

A CIP catalogue record for this book is available from
the British Library.

Typeset by Ellipsis Digital Limited, Glasgow
Printed in the UK by CPI Mackays, Chatham ME5 8TD

To three friends from my 1970s:

Rick, Jeff and John

living proof of what a wonderful time it could be

Picture Acknowledgements

Page 1 – *top* © CSU Archives / Everett Collection / Rex Features, *bottom* © Rex Features. 2 – *top* © AFP / Getty Images, *bottom* © AP / Press Association Images. 3 – *top* © Getty Images, *bottom* © CSU Archives / Everett Collection / Rex Features. 4 – *top* © AFP / Getty Images, *bottom* © Getty Images. 5 – *top* © Time & Life Pictures / Getty Images, *middle* © Feri Lukas / Rex Features, *bottom* © Redferns. 6 – *top* © Getty Images, *bottom* © CSU Archives / Everett Collection / Rex Features. 7 – *top* © Getty Images, *bottom* © ITV / Rex Features. 8 – *top* © AFP / Getty Images, *middle* © Getty Images, *bottom* © Popperfoto / Getty Images.

CONTENTS

INTRODUCTION

In music, the term 'unplugged' originally referred to concerts in which rock musicians played only acoustic instruments, leaving their electric equipment in the trailer. The term has since come to mean something unprocessed – without synthetic enhancement. That is the aim here. The first plug I'm pulling belongs to ABBA, the band that embodied nearly every tired Seventies cliché. It's hard to come to terms with the decade if, in the background, four Swedes dressed in phosphorescent spandex sing 'Dancing Queen'. While we're at it, let's pull the plug on David Essex, the Bee Gees, Donna Summer and Gary Glitter. Granted, some of those artists produced noteworthy music. But if we want to get to grips with the 1970s, we need to peel away the polyester.

So, what lies beneath? Or, as a student asked when I announced I was writing a sequel to *The Sixties Unplugged*: 'What's the thrust this time?' I was momentarily flummoxed because, unlike the Sixties and the Eighties, for which themes abound, the Seventies seems a decade in-between, a black hole of meaning. Indeed, Peter Carroll titled his history of America in the 1970s: *It Seemed Like Nothing Happened.*

The operative word is, however, 'seemed'. I started with the purpose of rehabilitating the decade by showing that something meaningful *did* happen. I sold the book to my publisher on that premise, promising a chronicle of notable, even noble, achievements. I aimed to show that much of the progress commonly associated with the Sixties actually occurred in the Seventies.

I still believe that – to an extent. The decade was packed with profound achievement. Dictatorial regimes ended in Portugal, Spain,

Nicaragua, Rhodesia and Greece. Accord between nations was established at Camp David, Beijing, Moscow, Geneva and Brussels. For feminists, environmentalists and homosexuals, the Seventies was *the* decade of hope. In cultural terms, it brought the Sydney Opera House, Monty Python, *Annie Hall*, David Hockney and *M*A*S*H*. The music, with or without ABBA, was simply brilliant. For sheer diversity of output (not to mention talent) the decade outshines the much-celebrated Sixties.

But there's always a 'but'. Despite my efforts to rehabilitate the decade, I couldn't escape what Jonathan Coe, in *The Rotters' Club*, called 'the ungodly strangeness . . . the weird things that were happening all the time'. By any calculation, Marabel Morgan, the Christian fundamentalist who encouraged women to titillate their husbands by wrapping themselves in cling film, was weird. So too were Jim Jones, Idi Amin, Bobby Fischer, Anita Bryant, Sid Vicious and Bobby Riggs, not to mention pet rocks, shag carpets, platform shoes and the AMC Gremlin. Don't even ask what I wore to my senior prom.[1]

The weird might have been wonderful if not for the fact that it was so often violent. As time passed, that theme dominated. That was a rude epiphany, since the Seventies was my golden decade. Looking back, it seems that the mellow harmonies of Carole King and James Taylor, when combined with a lot of acrid smoke, obscured much of the terrible violence. True to the spirit of the 'me' decade, most of us retreated into the best worlds we could construct. We knew something of Jonestown, Vietnam, Palestine and Belfast, but the bloodletting in the Philippines, Chile, Zaire, Uganda and Bangladesh largely escaped our notice. The truth about Cambodia emerged only after the skulls were stacked away. Even today, ignorance remains endemic. How many people are aware that 8,000 acts of terrorist violence occurred in Italy during the 1970s?

The brutality of nations is a constant throughout history, but what is striking about the 1970s is the way perfectly ordinary people easily surrendered to violence. Linda Hager Morse, formerly a model child and A-student, explained to a court in Chicago that she had bought a gun and learned karate because the police riot at the 1968 Democratic convention had changed her 'from being a pacifist to the realization that we had to defend ourselves'. She had decided that 'a nonviolent revolution was impossible'. Where, indeed, had all the flowers gone? 'We're not trying to end wars!' shouted a Weatherman during the 1969 Days of Rage. 'We're starting to fight war.' The educational psychologist Kenneth Keniston diagnosed an epidemic:

> Nominally opposing violence and suffering violence from others, some fringes of the counterculture became infected by the very violence it opposed. The shouted obscenity calculated to offend the policeman was . . . a form of violence; so, too, was the categorization of the opponents of the student movement as subhuman – as pigs. And above all, that ideological argument which led a few members of the youth movement to consider their fear for violence a 'bourgeois hang-up' to be overcome by the practice of terrorism – this was no less a symptom of . . . pathological violence . . . than were the police riots . . . in Chicago in 1968 or our indiscriminate bombing in Southeast Asia.

The Times commented on the 'extent to which the terrorist bomb has developed into the standard international protest during the last decade'. Violence had become fashionable, a point driven home with peculiar irony when the Angry Brigade bombed a boutique. In Paris, a petrol bomb was left at the home of a member of the committee entrusted with selecting the Prix Goncourt literary prize.[2]

Nor was violence confined to the usual suspects – armies, terrorists, psychopathic dictators, cocaine barons and radical students. It was everywhere. Punk, whatever its musical merit, was violent sound. Skinhead style was aggressive even when its practitioners were not actually fighting. The Seventies was the decade of football hooliganism, hardhat riots, gays running amok and the National Front fighting the Anti-Nazi League. Much of the violence was simply gratuitous – an expression of nothing more substantial than nihilism. The British teenager Jayne Casey liked Bowie, salmon pink trousers and boys who wore make-up. She was neither punk nor skinhead, football hooligan, fascist or anti-fascist. She was simply angry. 'We were well prepared to have a fight because we'd all grown up fighting. We weren't soft kids, we came from heavy working class backgrounds and we knew how to fight . . . We'd shock them . . . and [then] we'd batter them! We attracted violence, every night, which was good; we hated the world and expected the world to hate us.' Joe Strummer of The Clash used to strut on stage wearing a T-shirt with the slogan 'Hate and War' – proof indeed that the decade of peace and love was over. Hate proved a much more durable social glue than love ever had.[3]

The Sixties was wonderful, the Seventies dire – or so it seems. To believe the Sixties heavenly requires ignoring its horror. Likewise, to judge the Seventies horrible requires ignoring its abundant good. Problems arise when we insist on seeing one decade as the antithesis of the other; in searching for contrast, we neglect continuum. Memory has been kind to the Sixties. So, too, has coincidence: so much of what was rotten about the decade did not surface until after 1970. It is perhaps best to see the Seventies as a time when Sixties chickens came home to roost, a decade when dreams died, hope was thwarted, problems long ignored finally exploded, and optimism repeatedly crushed gave way to frustration. No wonder, then, that macro turned into micro and grandiose dreams gave way to small pleasures. Surrounded by the detritus of forlorn ambition, people quite understandably turned inward, to family and individual fulfilment.

The Seventies Unplugged is not meant to be an international history of the decade, but it is more international than most Seventies books. The great problem with breadth, however, is lack of depth; in trying to cover everything one inevitably sacrifices substance. In an attempt to address that problem, I have taken the pointillist approach – fifty separate stories together provide an intriguing, albeit incomplete, portrait of the decade. Some are predictable, others not. There are notable gaps, but that is inevitable with this approach and the tyranny of a word limit. I hope, however, that the book will be judged by what it includes, not by what it neglects. In some cases, big issues are purposefully examined through small lenses. Thus, instead of Nixon goes to China we have Ping-Pong diplomacy; instead of Microsoft we have Pong. The stories are like parables, though readers can draw their own grand moral conclusions.

As I wrote in the introduction to *The Sixties Unplugged*, the metaphor of the kaleidoscope is useful. A brilliantly simple invention, it consists of a tube, a lens, some bevelled mirrors and some coloured pieces of glass. Look through the lens and a complex pattern appears. Twist it and a different pattern, a reality equally logical, emerges. That is the effect I have tried to achieve here. My short sections are designed to stand alone, without linking narrative. They are the shiny pieces of glass capable of being arranged into myriad patterns. How they are arranged depends in large part on how the reader manipulates the kaleidoscope.

Books make enemies, but also, thankfully, friends. As a result of *The Sixties Unplugged*, I met (in cyberspace) a man called Rebel. He is a former student radical, Vietnam vet, reader of history and biker. I'm delighted we met, if only for the way he has challenged my conformist prejudices. I wasn't aware that bikers read the *Journal of American History* or the novels of Stephen Crane. I'm also delighted that we agree on so many of the events of our youth. But the fact that we agree does not mean we are right. History, no matter how carefully crafted, cannot completely banish perspective.

I'm told that since the eyes of two people cannot occupy the same point in space at the same time, each observer sees a different rainbow. The same, I think, could be said of the past. The past is what happened, history the way we remember. Rebel once reminded me of something Friedrich Nietzsche said about the way we look back. 'I have done that,' says memory. 'I cannot have done that,' says pride. The conflict between memory and pride made writing about the Sixties a hazardous endeavour, especially when baby boomer critics took aim. I suspect that the Seventies does not inspire the same passion, but I am prepared to be surprised.

1

OMENS

Los Angeles: Manson is Innocent!

On the evening of 9 August 1969, the heavily pregnant Sharon Tate, a B-movie actress, invited friends round to her home at 10050 Cielo Drive in Los Angeles. The property belonged to the record producer Terry Melcher, son of Doris Day, who leased it to Roman Polanski, Tate's husband. Keeping Tate company that evening were the coffee heiress Abigail Folger, her lover Wojciech Frykowski, and Jay Sebring, a Hollywood hairstylist.

Shortly after midnight, a car drew up. Out stepped Charles Watson, Patricia Krenwinkle, Susan Atkins and Linda Kassabian, all high on psychotropic drugs, all on a mission to murder. Steven Parent, a passer-by, unfortunately witnessed their approach. He begged for mercy; they shot him. Reacting to Parent's murder, Kassabian lost her nerve and retreated to the car. The other three then barged into the house. 'I am the devil!' Watson shouted; 'I'm here on the devil's business.' When Sebring tried to defend Tate, he was shot, then kicked repeatedly about the head. Amidst the chaos, Folger and Frykowski escaped. They were caught on the front lawn, and stabbed to death. Their work nearly complete, the murderers turned on Tate, who pleaded for her unborn child. 'Look, bitch, I don't care about you,' Atkins bellowed. 'I don't care if you're going to have a baby . . . You're going to die, and I don't feel anything about it.' She was stabbed repeatedly until her screams quietened. Atkins then wrote 'PIG' on the front door, using Tate's blood.[1]

The following night Leslie Van Houten joined Watson and Krenwinkle on a second murder mission, their victims this time the supermarket magnate Leno LaBianca and his wife Rosemary. Accompanying the group was their spiritual leader, Charles Manson, a thirty-eight-year-old psychopath who wanted to make sure the murders were carried out correctly. Police gave up trying to count the stab wounds. This time, the message in blood read: 'DEATH TO PIGS'.

Manson had spent most of his adult life behind bars. Prison reports from as early as 1950 described his intense need for attention and his uncanny ability to manipulate. Psychologists judged him totally incapable of rehabilitation. After being released from prison in 1967, he went to Haight-Ashbury where he worked as a pimp and drug dealer, preying on the innocence of hippies who thought they had discovered Shangri-La. Like moths to a shining light, a group of drug-addled misfits were drawn to Manson and became his Family. For them, he was Jesus Christ, or sometimes the Devil. On first encountering the Family, the journalist David Dalton noticed how 'their heads swiveled in synch when anything . . . caught their attention. Their pupils were dilated and they stared like the children in *Village of the Damned*.' Most came from stable middle-class backgrounds – former campfire girls, Boy Scouts, cheerleaders, honour students.[2]

The Family eventually settled at the Spahn ranch in the foothills of the Santa Susana mountains, north of Los Angeles. They consumed copious quantities of drugs, participated in robotic orgies, and dutifully acted out Manson's bizarre fantasies. He told them that a hole in the desert provided entry into a secret world where they would find serene refuge during the impending Armageddon. Long hours were spent looking for that hole. Manson drew cosmic revelations from The Beatles – his Four Horsemen of the Apocalypse. He became convinced that the *White Album* – songs like 'Rocky Raccoon', 'Revolution 9', 'Piggies' and 'Helter Skelter' – was an oracle written for him. 'Helter Skelter' supposedly foretold a race war that would escalate into nuclear apocalypse. It would be 'all the wars that have ever been fought, piled on top of each other'. 'Revolution 9' referred to 'the battle of Armageddon' foretold in Revelations chapter 9. 'It's the end of the world,' he explained. 'It predicts the overthrow of the Establishment. The pit will be opened, and . . . a third of all mankind will die. The only people who escape will be those who have the seal of God on their foreheads.'[3]

During the Tate–LaBianca trials, which lasted from June 1970 to January 1971, the Family laid claim to some thirty-five killings. They might have been boasting but, then again, they might not have been. Horror of that magnitude was not beyond Manson's capability. 'There's no need to feel guilty,' he confessed in 1987. 'I haven't done anything I'm ashamed of. Maybe I haven't done enough; I might be ashamed of that, for not doing enough . . . Maybe I should have killed four or five hundred people, then I would have felt better. Then I would have felt like I've really offered society something.'[4]

The Manson murders, impossible to forget, have too often been perversely remembered. For nearly forty years, thousands of people (ranging from normal to seriously disturbed) have spent far too much time trying to make sense of the crimes. Since psychopaths exist in every era, one might ask why the story deserves telling here. The answer lies not in its macabre allure, but in the fact that the murders were a portentous moment at the cusp between two eras. They mark the point at which the Sixties turned into the Seventies.

Elements of the story give it a Sixties feel. Without the evil, the Family resembles a hippie commune. 'He played the guitar, he sang, he preached love and peace and all that' went the standard refrain. There were orgies, drugs, flowers with power. Within Hip Nation, Manson and his acolytes were accepted and trusted because weirdness was shibboleth. Dalton explains:

> The only credentials you needed were long hair, a liking for drugs and the peace sign. Charlie easily infiltrated the far too gullible counterculture and began assembling his demonic crew from the

> counterculturalwreckage – those shattered by the mind-crunching disorientations of psychedelic drugs, radical politics, mystical aspirations and a dissolving sense of reality. As if playing some satanic poker game, he took our fantasies and turned them into phantasmagoric realities.

The laid-back lifestyle was built on a foundation of trust – hippies were incapable of evil. In the mellow of marijuana, vigilance relaxed, and wickedness slithered inside. 'Manson lucked into a situation where the elements around him allowed him to get away with that stuff,' Pamela Des Barres, quintessential rock chick, recalled. 'He couldn't have done it in the 50s and he couldn't have done it in the 70s.'[5]

In the LA canyons, money, music, drugs and sex were blended like margaritas. Sometime in 1968, Beach Boy Dennis Wilson, feeling lonesome and horny, was cruising Malibu in his Rolls-Royce Silver Shadow. He picked up two girls hitchhiking, took them to his mansion, told them to make themselves at home, and then went to a recording session. When he returned early in the morning, his guests had multiplied like a fungus. A dozen strange freaks greeted Wilson, among them a bearded character named Charlie who insisted on kissing his feet. Like a voracious parasite, the group doubled in size over subsequent months, despite Wilson's persistent hints that they had outstayed their welcome. Unable to lever the Family out of his home, he decided instead to move out. For his troubles, he ended up with a trashed house, a wrecked Mercedes and the 'largest gonorrhea bill in history'. He nevertheless reckoned that he was 'the luckiest guy in the world, because I got off only losing my money'.[6]

The Family's ready supply of drugs made it easy to overlook their faults. Back then, the connection between drugs and evil was not firmly established; in fact, a fondness for pot, acid and even heroin was proof of virtue. The counterculture was deeply embedded in a short and tragic love affair with outlaws, people whose goodness was measured by their badness, since their badness seemed the fault of the 'establishment'. As the rock critic J. Marks explained, Manson was the offspring of 'the marriage of two outlaw cultures: the hood and the head . . . it was inevitable that the Charles Mansons would appear in our image and enact insane rituals in our name. It is even inevitable that we would then embrace them, defend them and care about them since it is our prime virtue and prime weakness to love and to protect the foundlings of our parents' cruel society.'[7]

Fancying himself a rock star, Manson tried to use the Wilson connection to launch his musical career. The Beach Boys recorded a Manson song, but when they changed the lyrics Dennis got a silver bullet in the mail. Though Wilson thought 'Charlie never had a musical bone in his body', that didn't stop him from introducing him to friends in the business, among them Neil Young, who initially thought Manson was 'great'. 'He was unreal. Really, really good – scary.' That scariness eventually proved too hard to ignore; Young decided to 'get out this guy's way before he explodes'. Like a deadly game of 'pass the parcel', Young sent Manson to Mo Ostin at Warner Brothers. When Ostin failed to recognize Charlie's genius, Manson's grudge against the industry grew toxic.[8]

Melcher, another Wilson friend, was likewise briefly charmed by Charlie. '[Melcher] told me about this exotic, charismatic guy who lived out . . . in the Valley,' the rock guitarist, Ned Doheny recalled. 'There were all these girls hanging around, and they were living out of dumpsters. Terry said we should go out and visit.' Like Ostin, Melcher soon discovered that Manson was a distinctly average musician – and a lunatic. He thought Charlie 'sounded like a man relating a grotesque, incomprehensible nightmare'. When Melcher gave the thumbs down, Manson's grudge metastasized. 'Charlie got pissed off that they didn't think he was a fucking genius,' Denny Doherty, of the Mamas and Papas, concluded. 'His attitude was, "Who the fuck is *Terry Melcher*? He can't even *sing*."' Police later speculated that the Tate murders might have been revenge against Melcher. In truth, that's probably too logical.[9]

When Dalton heard of Manson's arrest for the Tate–LaBianca murders, he smelled a rat. He'd been out to the Spahn ranch and had grown fond of the Family. Granted, they seemed weird, but murderers? No way. 'He looked just like one of us. He had long hair and a beard and, although skinnier, resembled Jim Morrison or maybe Jerry Garcia. We knew that anybody who looked like that could never have done these horrible things . . . It was just the Pigs picking on some poor hippie.' Many a Sixties radical joined the chorus of disapproval, including Phil Ochs and Jerry Rubin, both of whom visited Manson in prison. 'I wanted to believe that the charges against Manson were an FBI frame-up,' Rubin confessed in 1989. 'I was so into romanticizing outlaw behaviour that I looked for any possible explanation to find something good in the outlaw . . . And that attitude was part of the madness of the times.'[10]

Intent on rescue, Dalton phoned Jann Wenner at *Rolling Stone*. 'I said I thought there was more to the Charles Manson story than was being told. I felt the whole counterculture was on trial here and we needed to tell our side of the story. Jann, in his characteristically enthusiastic way, said: "Let's do it! We'll put 'MANSON IS INNOCENT!' on the cover."' For Dalton, this was more crusade than commission; he was 'fight[ing] for the life of the counterculture itself – one of our own was being martyred, our most cherished beliefs were being trashed by the cynical establishment and their lackeys, the LAPD'.[11]

Dalton interviewed Manson in jail. 'He seemed a little more slippery (and creepier) than I had imagined, but this might be accounted for by the fact that he had been touched by some terrible truth, been struck by some divine lightning.' He grew more convinced than ever that Manson was being crucified for the entire counterculture. 'It was just like Charlie had told us, "Anything you see in me is in you. If you want to see a vicious killer that's who I'll be . . . If you see me as a brother that's what I'll be . . . I am you and when you admit that you will be free. I am just a mirror."'[12]

While waiting to see the prosecutor, Vincent Bugliosi, Dalton was shown some photos from the LaBianca murder scene. 'The moment of truth came for me when I saw "HELTER SKELTER" written in blood on the LaBiancas' refrigerator,' he recalls. Charlie had earlier explained to Dalton the revelations hidden within the *White Album*.

'I now knew they had done it. I may have thought that the LAPD stormtroopers were capable of almost any kind of sleazy frame-up but daubing Beatle lyrics in blood on a refrigerator was a little beyond their imagination.'[13]

Realization stabbed like a knife in the gut. While Dalton was being shown incontrovertible proof of Manson's guilt, his girlfriend was out at the Spahn ranch riding horses and getting stoned. Dropping everything, he rushed out to the ranch and somehow managed to spirit her away. 'Seeing the Spahn ranch recede through the rear-view mirror it felt as if we were rowing furiously away from the Isle of the Mutants in a small dinghy as a pack of zombies wailed their anguished cries from the dock. We had escaped from Dr. Manson's fiendish experiments just in the nick of time.'[14]

Perhaps because he had drawn so close to the psychotic centre of the Manson saga, Dalton noticed something others missed, or have ignored. We conveniently forget that the yearning to kill 'pigs' was frequently expressed by radicals of the late 1960s. 'Kill all the rich people,' Billy Ayers once told the Weatherman faithful. 'Bring the revolution home, kill your parents, that's where it's really at.' At a Weatherman rally in 1970, Bernardine Dohrn paid tribute to Manson – his willingness to kill white pigs and spread honky fear seemed admirable. 'Dig it!' she shouted. 'Manson killed those pigs, then they ate dinner in the same room with them, then they shoved a fork into a victim's stomach.' The Sixties radical Tom Hayden likewise felt pulled by the 'charisma of violence'. 'The mystery of what was out there, beyond normal experience,' he wrote, 'was magnetic to some from bourgeois backgrounds.' As Dalton recognized, however, Manson was different. Unlike Dohrn or Ayers, he acted on his fantasies. 'The children's crusade of the late sixties dreamed terrible dreams not that dissimilar to the ones Charles Manson dreamed. White radicals routinely planned such atrocities . . . But due to our inhibitions . . . we were powerless to carry them out.'[15]

Because the Manson story smells like the Sixties, it has often been made into a morality tale – the inevitable consequence of all that hedonism and idolatry. While that is probably unfair, there is nevertheless no denying that a fin de siècle feeling existed at the end of the 1960s, to which Manson provided an exclamation mark. 'Perhaps the one thing that most determines the way we think about Manson was his timing,' Dalton thought. 'When you need a monster one will appear . . . He is a demon of the zeitgeist, immaculate in his terror and confusion. It's as if he were summoned up out of the churning wells of our own fear and doubt. Appearing with almost supernatural precision in the last months of the '60s, he seemed to call into question everything about the counterculture. His malign arrival synchronized so perfectly with America's nervous breakdown that it is hard not to bestow occult meanings on him.' The composer Van Dyke Parks agreed that the killings were a 'collective sin' that 'forced everyone to think about the idealism that had gotten us to that point.' 'We were dying,' J. Marks concluded. 'Dying of our own massive appetite for humanity: the act of faith which had directed us not only to imbibe mysterious potions which changed our heads, but also directed us to engulf and to absorb huge, fatal doses of derelict humanity . . . antisocial psychopaths were . . . turning into mad dogs and destroying those who had welcomed them.'[16]

The new decade would be different. The fact that the horrors were revealed in a trial that took place in 1970 drove home the sense of before and after. Manson had demonstrated that Sixties naivety could be fatal. Innocence, previously glorified, suddenly seemed dangerous. 'Perhaps the most unsettling thing about pulling away from the Spahn Ranch that afternoon,' Dalton concluded, 'was that we were also leaving behind part of ourselves, our Edenic others who had once believed we could create a new heaven and a new earth.' Paranoia and distrust, those terrible establishment traits, now seemed sensible. Long hair and faded jeans were no longer proof of righteousness.[17] Hitchhikers suddenly found it difficult to get rides.

Before the Manson murders, the television series *Hawaii Five-O* seemed like just another assembly line cop show, its only redeeming feature being its paradise location. After the murders, the show suddenly went psychedelic, with its criminals frequently taken from the hippie underworld. Drugs provided a recurrent subtext. As the show demonstrated, hippies had become public enemy number one. Book 'em, Danno.

'It just destroyed us,' writes the record producer Lou Adler. 'I mean, everyone was looking at everyone else . . . And then no one trusted hippies any more. It was a very paranoid time, and the easiest thing was to get out of it. Everybody went behind closed doors.'[18]

London: Jimi was Murdered!

'Jimi Hendrix died under circumstances which have never been fully explained.' That short sentence has inspired a multitude of sordid conspiracy theories. Suspicion, like a virus, easily replicates itself in the hospitable environment of the Internet. It has been said of John Kennedy that a life so large requires a death of equal magnitude – he was too important to be eliminated by a mediocrity. The same applies to Hendrix. The idea that the greatest rock guitarist in history choked on his own vomit in a seedy London hotel lacks the magnitude worthy of the man.[19]

The facts seem incontrovertible – except to those who wish them otherwise. At 11.18 on 18 September 1970, an ambulance was called to a flat in the Samarkand Hotel in Notting Hill. The call was probably made by Monika Dannemann, one of Hendrix's girlfriends. The ambulance arrived nine minutes later. The two crewmen, Reginald Jones and John Saua, found the door to the flat wide open and the caller gone. In the bedroom, they discovered Hendrix, fully dressed and lying in a pool of vomit. 'We felt his pulse,' Jones recalled, 'pinched his earlobe and nose, showed a light in his eyes, but there was no response at all. I knew he was dead as soon as I walked in the room.'[20]

Attempts were nevertheless made to revive him, both at the scene and during the journey to the hospital. 'We knew it was hopeless, nothing would have worked,' Jones recalled. Dr John Bannister, Surgical Registrar at St Mary Abbots Hospital, confirmed that conclusion. 'On his admission, he was obviously dead. He had no pulse, no heartbeat and the attempt to resuscitate him was merely a formality.' Bannister saw no mystery, correctly suspecting that Hendrix had mixed sedatives with alcohol, to disastrous effect. 'I recall vividly the very large amounts of red wine that oozed from his stomach and his lungs, and in my opinion there was no question that Jimi Hendrix had drowned.' An autopsy revealed that Hendrix had taken nine sleeping pills. That by itself might not have been fatal, but, combined with the wine, it was. 'My own feeling,' Bannister reflected, '[was] that it was a tragic loss of a young person to the effects of alcohol.'[21]

In other words, Hendrix died a typical rock star's death. But since he wasn't typical, some find that explanation inadequate. The story is clouded by the testimony of Dannemann, who claimed that Hendrix was alive while she rode with him to the hospital. That tiny fissure in the account, caused by a 'witness' who was not actually present and who maintained a tenuous grip on reality at the best of times, has been turned into a chasm of conspiracy by those who want to believe that Hendrix fell victim to foul play. On the Internet, videos re-enact how he was murdered by having alcohol forced down his throat. 'Experts' argue that a person with his deep experience of drugs was incapable of overdosing. Cue the usual suspects: the CIA, the FBI, white supremacists and the Mob.

To believe in the conspiracy requires accepting the claims of those (like Dannemann) who had motive to lie, while rejecting the accounts of those (like Bannister, Jones and Saua) who did not. The fact that so many people easily negotiate such a precarious leap of logic demonstrates the sheer power of the cult of Jimi. As one critic argued, his concerts were like 'religious rites', with Hendrix the 'high priest'. No wonder, then, that some of the devout believe he was crucified. The conspiracy theory enables one to imagine a world still blessed by this shaman; it allows the transformation of a banal story of self-destruction into a glorious tale of martyrdom. Instead of Hendrix providing a metaphor for the sad end of the swinging Sixties, he provides evidence of how the 'establishment' conspired to bring the heavenly decade to an end. A single parable of tragic waste becomes instead the entire gospel.[22]

Hendrix perfectly embodied the Sixties counterculture – the outrageousness, decadence, innocence, fun, music and drugs. Those elements were, however, dangerous when imbibed in a single cocktail, as Hendrix enjoyed doing. For his fans, he was more than a brilliant guitar player; through him, they could live vicariously the culture of excess without having to suffer its consequences. Unfortunately, he was (despite claims to the contrary) a mere human being, a man who could not for ever ignore the limits that physiology and psychology imposed. His characteristic exuberance inevitably conflicted with his other defining feature, namely his fondness for drugs. More fundamentally, his reputation as a wild man threatened to smother his genuine sensitivity, intelligence and emotional depth. He was a troubled soul who had to perform in front of fans who revered a two-dimensional stereotype. 'Very early, it seemed that Hendrix had been almost captured by his audience . . . and he was never given room to grow,' the rock journalist Lenny Kaye reflected. His manager, Michael Jeffrey, agreed: 'His stage image halted him . . . and that was frustrating for him. That old ghost from the past – the humping the guitar, the "Foxy Lady" stuff . . . that wasn't the true Jimi Hendrix.' 'All his audiences wanted to hear were the four big songs that they knew,' his friend Deering Howe reflected. 'It was like he was trapped . . . forced to play what someone else told him. He didn't feel he could break free of that.'[23]

'I don't want to be a clown anymore,' Hendrix told Sheila Weller of *Rolling Stone* in 1969. 'I don't want to be a rock and roll star.' Weller found that revelation worrying. 'The forces of contention are never addressed but their pervasiveness has taken its toll on Jimi's stamina and peace of mind. Trying to remain a growing artist when a business empire has nuzzled you to its bosom takes a toughness, a shrewdness . . . it isn't a question of selling out but of dying, artistically and spiritually . . . I wonder just where he will be and what he will be doing five years from now.' Rock stars, it is often said, can cope with failure; it is success that throws them. 'Success means . . . remorseless pressure . . . to do better and better and better, till every past achievement is a yoke,' the critic Michael Gray feels. Throw in the 'deluge of excesses . . . more money, more drugs, more women' and it is 'no wonder the more sensitive people fall'. Hendrix, despite the raunchy exterior, was a very sensitive soul. The more successful he became, the more he felt alienated. His torment was magnified exponentially by Jeffrey, a leech determined to suck him dry. Drugs masked and temporarily anaesthetized his pain, but that was a zero sum game he played against himself. 'One of the things he'd do was to get real stoned, really high; didn't want to talk to anyone,' said Buddy Miles, his last drummer. 'He used the drugs to put up a barrier.'[24]

The demons caught up during the last year of his life. 'I've had no time off to myself since I've been in this scene,' he complained. He hinted at a longing to retire and 'just disappear from the scene', but felt that 'there's still things I'd like to say. I wish it wasn't so important to me. I wish I could just turn my mind off.' During a long European tour in the winter of 1968–9 he was criticized as 'listless and tired', a terrible transgression for an artist whose trademark was exuberance. When a concert at the Albert Hall was ruined because he was too stoned to play, his fans concluded that that was simply Jimi, rather than a man in trouble. He, however, had become convinced that he would not live to see his thirtieth birthday. In late July, at his last concert in the United States, the music was arrhythmic and his audience unsympathetic. 'Fuck you! Fuck you!' he shouted. At the Isle of Wight on 31 August 1970, he was brilliant, but not in the way admirers expected. He stood stock still, lost in convoluted chords, exploring his own murky emotions. He did not smash his guitar, nor set it on fire, nor play it with his teeth, nor simulate sex with it. He just played it. Richard Neville, aristocrat of the British counterculture, saw depressing portents: 'Farewell to the joy of Jimi, farewell to the fun at the funfair . . . Jimi failed because we all failed . . . we've created nothing, nothing.' Eighteen days later Hendrix made his last recording – on an answer machine. 'I need help bad, man' was the message muttered to his producer Chas Chandler. Within hours, he was dead.[25]

For Charles Shaar Murray, a precocious eighteen-year-old, the Isle of Wight Festival seemed a long death rattle. 'Over the course of the six-day festival I'd had most of my noble hash-pie-in-the-sky ideals burnt out of me . . . by the petty rip-offs and violence and bozos throwing coke cans at each other while the likes of John Sebastian prattled on about how *rilly rilly byootiful* everybody was.' Omens abounded. 'Young Liberals and Hells Angels and all kinds of strangeos were fighting pitched battles with the security men . . . and I was having to realise that the counterculture was prone to all the ills of the parent culture and maybe more.' Then came Hendrix to deliver the final soliloquy. 'The P.A. system was in its death throes and it ground the sound up like a cement mixer and spat the pieces contemptuously into the crowd while Hendrix sweated like a bull on the stage . . . his flight of doves crashed rotting to the ground and I knew it was all over now, baby blue, and that if any of us had contingency plans it was about time we activated them.'[26]

To Shaar Murray, it seemed that there was no place for Hendrix in the new world dawning.

> I knew it was over even before Hendrix finished his set with that weird sad speech about how he wanted to thank us for a great four years and that he will see us all again . . . somewhere, sometime. I smelled death on him and on us when I saw that he didn't have the power any more, and I knew that even the most beautiful thing in my world – the music of Jimi Hendrix – could be destroyed . . . I blundered out of there crying like a baby . . . The last thing I remember that night was pissing against a fence, still crying, while Joan Baez sang 'Let It Be'.

Because the end of Jimi coincided so perfectly with the end of the Sixties, his death was packed with meaning. Some saw it as glorious escape: an individual who embodied so quintessentially the Sixties ethos could not possibly survive in the polyester decade. The Sixties seemed over not just temporally but spiritually; Kennedy had given way to Nixon, Martin Luther King to the Black Panthers, Rudi Dutschke to the Red Army Faction, Woodstock to Altamont, the

Summer of Love to Charles Manson. Jimi's death was like a handful of dirt thrown on a coffin containing a decade full of dreams. 'The 60s ended for me in 1970 when they announced on the radio that Jimi Hendrix was dead,' John Marsh recalled. 'My first reaction was I knew the 1970s were going to fuck it all. And by God they did.'[27]

Marsh's retrospective reaction is a perfect manifestation of the human tendency to compartmentalize time and experience. Decades, neatly bound packages of ten diaries, are casually assigned cultural significance more appropriate to eras. Thus, the death of Hendrix was the terminus at the end of a glorious railway journey; all passengers were required to disembark and board a less comfortable train headed in a less picturesque direction. 'I was just old enough to pick up on the vague sense of disillusionment at the start of the Seventies,' the novelist Jake Arnott recalls. 'I remember my oldest sister Deborah's disappointment when she came back from the Isle of Wight festival . . . Jimi Hendrix had been so stoned that she hadn't bothered to stay to watch all of his set. Three weeks later he was dead. All of the hope and excitement of the Sixties was coming to an end. I was just beginning to become interested in music and fashion but it seemed that the party was already over. I wasn't yet 10 and already I was feeling disappointed.'[28]

Hendrix, by swallowing those pills and that wine, had inadvertently given those who wanted portents an appropriate event of solemn meaning. It seemed there were omens aplenty. Altamont was the day the music died. Janis Joplin exited just sixteen days after Hendrix, the victim of heroin. That drug was itself symbolic of sordid end, a far cry from the frivolity of pot and LSD. Meanwhile, Bob Dylan, in contrast to Hendrix, chose survival, which for him meant a family and a white picket fence. As for the Beatles, they survived, but not as a group. The Fab Four were now four separate individuals who did not like one another. After the break-up, John Lennon provided a depressing precis of a decade that had once seemed magical, meaningful and revolutionary. 'The people who are in control and in power, and the class system and the whole bullshit bourgeosie is exactly the same . . . nothing happened,' he told *Rolling*

Stone's Jann Wenner in 1971. 'We all dressed up, the same bastards are in control, the same people are runnin' everything. It is exactly the same.' The Who said essentially the same thing in 'Won't Get Fooled Again'. The new boss was the same as the old boss; the times were not a'changin'.[29]

The greater the disillusionment, the more important Jimi's death seemed. No wonder, then, that some insist on conspiracy: the icon becomes confused with the era, with the result that the destruction of the former is believed to have caused the demise of the latter. That might seem preposterous, but not to those who still worship Hendrix the god. Others take solace in the assumption that he committed suicide, in other words that he saw what was coming and decided to leave. 'He made his exit when he wanted to,' his friend Eric Burdon concluded. 'His death was deliberate. He was happy dying . . . and he used the drug to phase himself out of this life and go someplace else.' Burdon later retracted that conclusion, but for many it remains a refuge.[30]

The flip side of this mournful song is that Hendrix's death is made into a watershed, and everything that flows downstream is tainted. As Marsh attested, the new generation would 'fuck it all'. Because the Sixties was so wonderful, the Seventies would automatically be crap. That perhaps explains why the Seventies usually brings to mind ABBA, disco and Gary Glitter, instead of the more sublime Jethro Tull, prog rock, Led Zeppelin and Joni Mitchell. While most people can recall a busload of Sixties heroes, their memories of the Seventies are crowded by Richard Nixon, Pol Pot and Idi Amin. The new decade had hardly begun before it was written off as antithesis – the price paid for dreaming. While this does not quite qualify as self-fulfilling prophecy, it does seem to be wilful pessimism. When rock critic J. Marks was lamenting the carnage at Altamont, a hippie friend offered consolation: 'Ah, yes, it's true, there were some terrible things that went down in 1970. But just think of it – just think what a bright, strong light it took to cast such a dark shadow!' The Sixties generation was nothing if not possessive: ownership of an ethos was asserted by placing a strict limit on its duration.[31]

What some saw as watershed, others perceived as breaking point – Jimi's death was the moment when Sixties optimism suddenly seemed unwarranted, and a crushing sense of futility took over. Flower children who once wore rose-tinted spectacles switched to dark sunglasses when the new decade began – the better to block out the harsh light. That sense of desolation annoys Hendrix's one-time drummer Mitch Mitchell, who feels that too much meaning has been assigned to his death. 'I think people are trying to make it like some kind of Judy Garland syndrome. It's getting too fucking theatrical. All I hope for is the man is in peace at last. All he ever wanted to do was play his guitar.'[32]

St-Tropez: Mick gets Married

For millions of parents, the Rolling Stones seemed like an outpost on the road to hell. Their lyrics seemed confrontational, their lifestyle debauched. For most of the Sixties, the Stones capitalized on that image. A drug bust, combined with rumours of Mars Bars used as sex toys, provided exclamation point to insurrectional message. Ersatz rebellion was sold for the price of a 45-rpm disc. The subversiveness was, however, purely cultural, rather superficial, and mostly contrived. 'I like my house and horses and land,' drummer turned country squire Charlie Watts confessed. 'I wish things were more capitalistic, less restrained,' confessed Mick Jagger in an accidental moment of honesty. If there was political message to any of their songs, it was drowned out by the raucous rhythm of enjoyment. The Stones perfectly embodied the sell-out central to rock music. In 1968, Jagger joined the protesting hordes outside the American Embassy in Grosvenor Square, and then made millions by recording 'Street Fighting Man'.[33]

Towards the end of the decade, the Stones gave up on the pretence of rebellion. They crossed to the other side, flipping the bird at blinkered fans who desperately insisted on seeing Ned Kelly in Mick Jagger. They moved to France, mainly to escape Britain's punishing tax laws.

Fans found that disappointing, since money was not supposed to matter. Worse still, when they got to France, they lived like royalty, paying far too much attention to designer clothes, yachts and fine wines, while hobnobbing with Camilla, Chloe and Reginald. Instead of rolling, they were flying with the jet set. The tragic farce of Altamont, Jagger's misbegotten attempt to recreate the Elysian garden of Woodstock, underlined what seemed a terminus. Afterwards, Marks wrote: 'we began to recognise the sheer helplessness of our great pop super-fathers and prick-deities who could not turn back the sea with a single command so that we might safely stride uninterrupted toward the magic milieu of their music'.[34]

The final straw came when Jagger got married. Sex gods were not supposed to pledge themselves to one woman. To make matters worse, his betrothal to Bianca Pérez Morena de Macías, a Nicaraguan beauty from an ambassadorial family, seemed a calculated insult to the underground. They were married in the town hall in St-Tropez on 12 May 1971 in front of a star-studded array of guests. She wore an Yves Saint Laurent trouser suit which flatteringly disguised her pregnancy. Hippies on bicycles tried to crash the wedding, but they were shoved aside when they attempted to cross a cordon of police. Two years earlier, Jagger had pelted cops with stones. Now he demanded their protection.

Jagger – for whom publicity was oxygen – got in a nasty row with the press when he protested that he did not want to get married 'in a goldfish bowl'. After a short delay, the ceremony went ahead and, in a stroke, destroyed the pretence of Rolling Stone radicalism. Background music was taken from the film *Love Story*. After the vows, a fleet of Rolls-Royces took the guests to a reception on a seventy-five foot yacht, the *Romeang*. The bill for champagne and caviar rivalled the GNP of Zaire. Later, the happy couple, along with a six-man crew, sailed off on a honeymoon cruise around Corsica and Sardinia, taking the illusions of millions with them. As an end to the Sixties it was pathetic; as a harbinger of the Seventies it seemed perfect.[35]

2

REMNANTS FROM THE REVOLUTION

London: Fashionable Anger

On May Day 1971, a bomb exploded in Biba, the celebrated fashion emporium owned by Barbara Hulanicki. The bomb – an attack upon the consumer society – was itself a fashion statement since bombs had become de rigueur on the militant left. It was planted by the Angry Brigade, a small group of anarchists responsible for perhaps twenty-five explosions over the previous year. The Brigade's Communiqué No. 8, paraphrasing Dylan, proclaimed:

> 'If you're not busy being born you're busy buying'.
> All the sales girls in the flash boutiques are made to dress the same and have the same make-up, representing the 1940s. In fashion as in everything else, capitalism can only go backwards – they've nowhere to go – they're dead.
>
> . . .
>
> Life is so boring there is nothing to do except spend all our wages on the latest skirt or shirt.
> Brothers and Sisters, what are your real desires?
> Sit in the drugstore, look distant, empty, bored, drinking some tasteless coffee? Or perhaps BLOW IT UP OR BURN IT DOWN.

> The only thing you can do with modern slave-houses – called boutiques – IS WRECK THEM. You can't reform profit capitalism and inhumanity. Just kick it till it breaks.
> REVOLUTION.[1]

'The bombing,' claims Jean Weir, unofficial Brigade spokesperson, was an attempt to destroy 'the stereotyping and alienation of the spectacle of consumerism.' Biba was targeted because it was a prominent icon of the consumer society. The Brigade objected to the hypocrisy of a store that sold 'revolutionary' clothes produced in sweatshops. For radicals of the 1970s, consumerism was the opiate of the people. Those who clung desperately to Marxism agonized over a phenomenon Marx failed to anticipate, namely ever-rising standards of living. Workers, so the dialectic went, were being bought off with things. The ability to purchase an endless range of frippery was sapping the revolutionary will of the masses, giving them a false sense of contentment and a desire to get ahead in order to get more. Radicals grew increasingly frustrated at the refusal of the workers to accept truth and act like a proletariat. Out of frustration grew desperation, and a turn to violence.[2]

Radicals agonized over the way clothes blunted the sharp edges of class consciousness. Identity was increasingly determined not by work, but by commodities consumed. In other words, Biba shoppers colluded in their own enfeeblement. Oppression of this sort was much more complex than the tyranny of a dead-end job, a nasty boss and low pay. It was difficult to explain to the worker that a purple velvet jacket was a new version of Marx's chains.

As an opiate, fashion was doubly narcotic because it provided the illusion of individuality. Style gurus liked to claim that anything goes, but that was nonsense. In the Seventies, straight-legged trousers, conservative skirts, twin-sets, beiges and greys definitely did not go. Shiny paisley-patterned polyester, massive cuffs and collars, huge flares, lots of velvet and corduroy, platform shoes and rich colours definitely did. Style was a badge of belonging. 'We were all posers,' one former fashion slave confessed. 'When bands like Mott the Hoople became really popular people used to walk around with those stupid jackets Ian Hunter used to wear . . . And loon pants, I mean, God almighty! Skin-tight loon pants, bright red, bright yellow. What were we thinking?' Unfortunately, with weirdness as standard, the outrageous ceased to cause outrage and became instead banal. Everyone tried to shock, but no one did. For agonized rebels, the flamboyant clothes of the early 1970s symbolized the demise of the Sixties dream; they were style without substance, rebellion without pain – the perfect expression of a generation in love with itself and in thrall to display.[3]

Fashion, briefly a tool of countercultural expression, had been hijacked by the High Street. The Mods of the early 1960s had invented their own style and had worn it with rebellion in mind. But that rebellion was blunted when Mod styles started appearing in King's Road boutiques. Originality died with mass-production. In fact, the very phenomenon of the 'boutique' was invented to keep pace with rapidly changing clothing styles. The boutique pioneers Mary Quant and John Stephen boasted of being able to get an original street style onto the racks within a fortnight.

Later in the decade, hippie fashion suggested a rejection of mainstream society. No self-respecting hippie would be caught dead in Quant's Bazaar. Their clothes were instead culled from granny's attic, or from thrift stores. Old clothes made of rich antique fabrics expressed the romantic, millenarian nature of the hippie movement, a cult devoted to self-fulfilment and sensation. Before long, however, the boutiques, with Biba leading the way, began offering watered down versions of hippie fashion. Hulanicki, a marketing genius, could sense what the people wanted long before they knew they wanted it. *Time* magazine described Biba as 'revolutionary' – a revolution not simply in style, but, more importantly, in commerce: 'Biba overthrew the rules of retailing. [It] recast shopping as entertainment. Fans lingered on the shop floor and . . . spent whole days reveling in the Art Deco-infused Biba experience.'[4]

Biba was indeed an experience – an important word back then. It was 'a theme park devoted to elegantly wasted decadence,' writes Alwyn Turner, the store's biographer.

> Drawing on Art Deco, Nouveau, Victoriana and the golden age of Hollywood, it was more than just fashion: it was a whole world, a lifestyle choice. At the height of the store's glory, the committed shopper could buy not only a new wardrobe, fully co-ordinated from head to toe, but also a complete range of cosmetics and soft furnishings, together with the washing powder to care for her clothes, and food for both herself and her pets, all presented in the distinctive Biba packaging. Alternatively she could just hang out . . . sipping cocktails upstairs amongst the flamingos that lived in the Roof Garden, or in the Rainbow Room, where on a good night there might be a live performance by the likes of the New York Dolls, Liberace or the Manhattan Transfer.

'It took girls out from being second-class citizens, secretaries and shop girls, to being stars,' the Biba designer Steve Thomas once boasted. That is, of course, tripe, but the British, back then, were still fond of tripe. Those stars still had to go to work on Monday morning, with their bank balance depleted.[5]

Biba was decadent and unapologetically escapist. Shoppers had fun fantasizing. For po-faced radicals, however, the fantasy was dangerous. They were perhaps right: a woman decked out in Biba fashions, believing herself suddenly special, does not make good raw material for the revolution. The boutique effect was noticed by Anthony Lewis of the *New York Times*, who remarked rather disapprovingly in 1966 that the atmosphere in London 'can be almost eerie in its quality of relentless frivolity. There can rarely have been a greater contrast between a country's objective situation and the mood of its people.' In other words, fun blunts the sharp edges of oppression. Those searching for an explanation for why Britain lagged so far behind in the political revolution of the 1960s might want to ask whether it was mere coincidence that she was so far ahead in the style revolution. The most influential movement in Sixties Britain was not the crowd of protesters outside Grosvenor Square, but the crowd of shoppers on Carnaby Street. In the febrile world of revolutionary politics, an entirely logical conclusion emerged: decadence needed to be corrected – with a bomb.[6]

Into this heady cocktail of revolution add a splash of feminism. Radical feminists protested at the way fashion objectified women. Quant had argued that short skirts were empowering, and to an extent they were. But they also titillated, offering men the opportunity to leer. Men delighted in the demise of the bra. The American journalist John Crosby, whose article in the *Daily Telegraph* started talk of 'Swinging London', took lascivious delight in describing a 'kaleidoscope of young English girls who were appreciative, sharp tongued and glowingly alive, who walk like huntresses, like Dianas, and who take to sex as if it's candy'. According to Andrea Adam, who worked at *Time*, that magazine's iconic issue celebrating swinging London was inspired not by 'a fascination with a socio-cultural phenomenon, it was the fascination amongst the senior editors for mini-skirts . . . Any opportunity to put legs, tits or bums in the magazine and they would do it.'[7]

Feminists accepted that fashion had recast the role of women, but they did not necessarily see progress in that development. Style by itself did not seem empowering. The goal of women was still to be adored by men. Furthermore, women, by enthusiastically accepting their defined role as avid consumers, were colluding in their own debasement. There is some evidence that the Biba bomb might have come at the insistence of women within the Angry Brigade who resented the manipulative powers of fashion. The journalist Rosie Boycott recalled getting her 'first whiff of feminism' when she met the Angries Angela Weir and Hilary Creek in the summer of 1971. 'Their aggravation with everything irritated me, the fact that they didn't see any fun in anything, that there was very little joy in their lives and that they were extremely bitter about the general state of the world. There was this endless talk about the masses, the oppressed masses, without being very specific.' The frustration felt by Weir and Creek was compounded because they had the great misfortune of being very good-looking, which made it nearly impossible for anyone to take their message seriously. The press, instead of paying heed to their feminism, delighted in the erotic image of girls with guns.

'Nothing happened except that we all dressed up,' John Lennon famously told Jann Wenner in 1971. 'There are a lot of middle-class kids with long hair walking around London in trendy clothes.' That verdict undoubtedly prompted nods of agreement from the Brigade of Angries. The shallow nature of Seventies radicalism is beautifully satirized in Malcolm Bradbury's *The History Man*, in which the protagonist, Howard Kirk, busily acts out the role of a Marxist sociology lecturer, always unaware of his deep hypocrisy. His wife dresses in kaftans, the compulsory uniform of the hip intelligentsia, and regularly goes to London for 'Biba weekends', where she meets her lover for the obligatory affairs that define her 'open' marriage. Radicalism had been reduced to a fashion statement. Feelings had given way to things.[8]

Confident that they could speak for the working class, the Angries proclaimed: 'We are bored . . . poor . . . and very tired of keeping the peace.' The great battles of the 1960s, it seemed, had been lost, leaving nothing but the empty gestures of Howard and Barbara Kirk. As an antidote to this assumed malaise, the Brigade offered a weird amalgam of Marxism, anarchism and libertarianism, interlaced with elements of Situationism. Traditional Marxists had blamed the debacle of 1968 on a failure of leadership. Situationists, on the other hand, felt that the proletariat had been bought off by a consumerist 'spectacle' – tricked into believing that life was sweet. 'Behind the glitter of the spectacle's distractions,' wrote the Situationist guru Guy Debord, 'modern society lies in thrall to the global domination of a banalising trend.' True to the Situationist dialectic, the Angries were fond of 'guerrilla theatre' in which propaganda was communicated through highly visible violence. 'Our role is to deepen the political contradictions at every level. We will not achieve this by concentrating on "issues" or by using watered down socialist platitudes.' The violence was, however, largely symbolic. Bombs were desirable not for what they destroyed, but for the attention they received and the mood they inspired. 'It wasn't the bombs themselves that [politicians] . . . were worried about,' argued Creek. 'It was the fact that it exposed the vulnerability of the system . . . It wasn't so much the criminal damage, it was the fact that it made them look stupid.' Bombs, it was thought, would coerce the government and the media to convey, unintentionally, the Angry Brigade message. They would destroy what Herbert Marcuse called 'the policeman in all our heads', the taken-for-granted beliefs in stable society and trustworthy government. They would spread confusion and cause people to question the status quo.[9]

The Angries tried to graft themselves onto the rampant trade union unrest of 1971, which they assumed was motivated by political goals, not material ones. They thought the workers wanted to overthrow the system, when in fact most wanted more money to spend at Biba. Lovers of the pronoun 'we', the Angries easily imagined solidarity with the workers.

> People's sweat and blood is used and exploited. They make us produce shit . . . they give us next to nothing while their class pockets huge profits . . . Then, when we put the overalls aside, we clean up the muck from our faces and we take the boring bus or train home and they suddenly transform us into consumers. In other words when we are not working they make us buy . . . the same shit we produced. The miserable wage packet they gave us they make us spend on useless food, on machines specially designed to break down and on houses we know look and feel like prisons.
>
> . . . Producers of shit – consumers of shit.

Never mind that none of the Angries had ever worn overalls. 'We have started to fight back and the war will be won by the organised working class, with bombs', one of their communiqués boasted. Many of their actions, including the bombing of the home of Employment Minister Robert Carr, were intended as attacks upon the government's treatment of workers, and particularly on the Industrial Relations Bill, which placed limitations on the right to strike.[10]

Tariq Ali – leader of the 1968 Grosvenor Square protests – was once approached by an Angry Brigade member who wanted to plant a bomb at the American Embassy. 'I told them it was a terrible idea. They were a distraction. It was difficult enough building an anti-war movement without the press linking this kind of action to the wider Left.' Like Ali, most radicals did not welcome this new troupe of actors on the revolutionary stage. To working-class Marxists, they were the 'big-head brigade' – a bunch of middle-class university dropouts who thought they could lead a revolution without ever having to look over their shoulders. 'They were on the fringes,' the political activist, Nina Fishman remarked. 'I'd always been enough of a good Marxist, a good Leninist, to know that terrorism will get you nowhere. There was definitely the feeling that there was no point whatsoever to what they were doing.' *Red Mole*, a Trotskyite paper, expressed qualified support, wrapped in serious misgivings. The Angries were 'potentially very good comrades', but they needed to realize that 'bomb-throwing is an easy option that does not deal with the problem of helping to change the political understanding of millions of people'. Even more scathing was the anarchist paper *Freedom,* which argued that the bombing campaign 'achieved absolutely nothing because, in direct contradiction with their spoken ideals, they were trying to act as an elite vanguard leaving ordinary people as passive spectators of their actions. Far from this resulting in an "awakening" of the masses it resulted in a fear of anarchism . . . which has significantly contributed to our current impotence.'[11]

Unlike their counterparts in Germany or the United States, Brigade members cultivated anonymity. They had no desire to be revolutionary celebrities. This harmonized with the libertarian nature of the movement, and had the added benefit of sowing confusion. 'We are not in a position to say whether any one person is or isn't a member of the Brigade,' one communiqué claimed. 'All we say is: the Brigade is everywhere.' Anonymity allowed them to pretend to be bigger than they were. 'The AB is the man or woman sitting next to you. They have guns in their pockets and anger in their minds . . . We are getting closer.' Ironically, however, the abhorrence of celebrity probably limited their effect. Both the Weather Underground and the Baader–Meinhof gang cleverly played to the cult of radical chic. Andreas Baader was a part-time model and Gudrun Ensslin made a porn film. They stole fast cars. Bernardine Dohrn wore thigh-high boots and intentionally forgot to button her blouse. In contrast, the Angry Brigade's disapproval of display limited their exposure, with the effect that most people did not have a clue what they were about.[12]

Reflecting on her days as an urban guerrilla, Creek confessed that: 'There was a lot going on and each of us had our own particular area. But there was no organisation . . . It was just people helping and supporting each other.' John Barker is slightly less respectful of the memory: 'For one thing we were libertarian communists believing in the mass movement and for another we were not that serious . . . what I mean is that like many people then and now we smoked a lot of dope and spent a lot of time having a good time.' Jake Prescott, the only genuinely working-class member, found the anger contrived. Having emerged from a life of orphanages, crime, drug addiction and prisons, he had reason to feel irate. 'When I look back on it, I was the one who was angry and the people I met were more like the Slightly Cross Brigade.'[13]

The Brigade was enormously successful in its mission to embarrass. Whether they actually committed the twenty-five actions attributed to them is beside the point, since they certainly gave that impression. The public saw a terrorist group acting with impunity, making a mockery of the police by delivering bombs to the back doors of prominent politicians. That success brought an inevitable backlash; using the excuse that political stability was threatened, the government dispensed with legal niceties. On 21 August 1971, a raid on a flat in Amhurst Road in Stoke Newington yielded four suspects (Barker, Creek, Jim Greenfield and Anna Mendelson), 2 sub-machine guns, an automatic pistol, 81 rounds of ammunition and 33 cartridges of gelignite. Over the next two days, four other suspects – Stuart Christie, Christopher Bott, Angela Weir and Kate McLean – were also taken into custody.

The trial began on 30 May 1972. Lacking the evidence to connect any of the accused to a specific bombing, the prosecution instead went for a conspiracy conviction. This in effect meant guilt by association – the prosecution had only to prove proximity to a plot. Over the course of 109 days, more than 200 witnesses were called by the prosecution, 688 exhibits were produced and approximately 1,000 pages of evidence were submitted. The defence insisted that the weapons taken from Amhurst Road had been planted, that the forensic evidence was inconclusive or flawed, and that the accused had been randomly selected for a political show trial. That argument was sufficiently convincing for charges against Christie, Bott, Weir and McLean to be dropped. The others, however, were found guilty on a majority verdict and sentenced to ten-year jail terms for conspiracy, to run concurrently with fifteen-year sentences for possession of explosives. 'We will never know all the answers,' Ian McDonald QC, one of the defence counsels, concluded. 'But there's no doubt [that] . . . those weapons and explosives were planted.' That said, those who stood in the dock were the Angry Brigade and they had exploded bombs. As John Barker subsequently admitted, 'In my case, the police framed a guilty man.'[14]

After the convictions, the bombings stopped, which is not mere coincidence. Occasional communiqués recycled tired slogans. 'It is not possible for the Angry Brigade to "re-form",' a message from the deep proclaimed in 1983. 'It wasn't an organisation, nor was it a single grouping – but an expression of the anger and contempt many people up and down the country had for the State and its institutions. In this sense the Angry Brigade is with us all the time.' To an extent, that was true. While the Brigade eventually disappeared, its politics and methods have thrived, manifesting themselves most notably in the anti-globalization protests of recent years.[15]

The *Guardian* would later remark that it was 'some kind of macabre tribute' that Biba should be targeted 'to protest the rising tide of capitalist female deco-decadence'. The store was indeed a spectacle, the archetype of shallow commercialism. The attack 'was a Situationist reprisal against the "spectacle of society",' writes the novelist Jake Arnott. 'Retro and reactionary, [Biba] was the epitome of commodity fetishism. But what the bombers failed to grasp was that it was fabulous. Kids needed some sort of sparkle to brighten up the already drab new decade . . . The adolescent glitter rockers didn't want to blow it up, they just wanted to shoplift from it.' And that is what they did. When the bomb exploded, enterprising customers took the opportunity to fill their shopping bags with free merchandise. Shoplifters caused far more damage than did the Angry Brigade. In other words, they wanted what Biba sold – a simple fact no bomb could alter.[16]

It is said that sales of BMW cars got a significant boost in the 1970s when it was revealed that Andreas Baader looked for BMW 2002s when choosing which car to steal. Revolution is fashionable, but fashion is the enemy of revolution. As has been argued, the clothes of the 1960s and 1970s were rebellion without pain – the perfect expression of a generation in love with itself and in thrall to display. The same, however, could be said of the Angry Brigade. It, too, was a dedicated follower of fashion, namely the fashion for violence. The Brigade's bombs were revolutionary symbols – style without substance. This particular suit of clothes provided the illusion of action and commitment, and as such meant that the Angries did not have to get down among the working class and engage in the hard work of political organization. Yet violence is only ever effective if it takes place within a context of general social revolt, it cannot by itself create that context. In other words, the Angry Brigade was as shallow as Barbara and Howard Kirk. Strip away the violence and we find an emperor without any clothes. If fashion was the opiate of the people, violence was the opiate of the Angry Brigade.

With opportunism typical of the fashion industry, the designer Craig Stuart used the furore of the Biba bomb to launch a set of trousers called 'Angry pants'. Rather like the group that inspired its name, and indeed all fashion, the trousers enjoyed a brief period of popularity and then disappeared.

Chicago: Eight Men and a Culture on Trial

'Political trials are trials of people for their political views,' Mr Justice James argued during the Angry Brigade trial. 'We do not have them in this country.' A similar claim might have been made by Judge Julius Hoffman in the Chicago Eight Trial – with an equal lack of credibility. No matter how much a nation prides itself on liberty and justice, the temptation to use the courts for political purpose is sometimes irresistible. In Chicago, the court was used as an instrument of moral condemnation directed against the Sixties counterculture.[17]

On 20 March 1969, Tom Hayden, Rennie Davis, Abbie Hoffman, David Dellinger, Jerry Rubin, Bobby Seale, John Froines and Lee Weiner were indicted on conspiracy charges arising from their involvement in demonstrations at the Democratic Convention the previous year. The defendants constituted a sampler of Sixties radicals – a handful of New Left politicos, some peaceniks, a couple of Yippies, and a token Black Panther. Hayden, Davis, Dellinger, Hoffman and Rubin had indeed been involved in organizing the demonstrations, as they fully admitted. Froines and Weiner, however, had no real involvement. They were indicted on the basis of allegations that they had openly discussed attacking the police and had collected gasoline, bottles and rags for Molotov cocktails. As for Seale, he played no part in the organization and was not on familiar terms with the other 'conspirators'. His arrest arose from a speech in Lincoln Park in which he openly advocated violence. His status as a Black Panther also made him fair game for any miscarriage of justice. The idea that the Eight had conspired was simply ridiculous. 'Conspire?' Hoffman sneered. 'Hell, we couldn't agree on lunch.'[18]

The Chicago protest brought together two groups usually distrustful of each other. The first was the National Mobilization Committee to End the War in Vietnam, or Mobe. Davis, the national coordinator, saw the convention as an opportunity to show the world 'that there are thousands of young people in this country who do not want to see . . . another four years of Lyndon Johnson's war'.

The venue also seemed attractive to a second group, the Yippies, for different reasons. Hoffman and Rubin, while both anti-war, were more interested in showcasing the counterculture through a great Yippie event.[19]

At a Mobe meeting in March 1968, a strategy was agreed. Organizers aimed for a crowd of 100,000. The event would offer something for everyone, including teach-ins, marches and anarchic street theatre, but, it was stressed, no violence. Rubin and Hoffman were invited to join in the planning because the Yippies were the acknowledged experts at theatricality and promotion. That invitation bothered Mobe's old guard – those concerned about respectability. Their fears were quickly confirmed when it became apparent that the two Yippie clowns were determined to go their own way. 'A Statement from Yip' invited all-comers to:

> Join us in Chicago in August for an international festival of youth, music and theater. Rise up and abandon the creeping meatball! Come all you rebels, youth spirits, rock minstrels, truth-seekers, peacock freaks, poets, barricade-jumpers, dancers, lovers and artists! . . . The threats of LBJ, Mayor Daley, and J. Edgar Freako will not stop us. We are coming! We are coming from all over the world! The life of the American spirit is being torn asunder by the forces of violence, decay, and the napalm-cancer fiend. We demand the Politics of Ecstasy! We are the delicate spores of the new fierceness that will change America. We will create our own reality, we are Free America!

Over subsequent months, almost every bizarre suggestion was endorsed, as long as it was calculated to shock. Rubin dreamt up the idea of nominating a pig for president. Hoffman advocated a mass public orgy, what he called a 'fuck-in'. A pamphlet promised that 'Two-hundred thirty rebel cocksmen under secret vows are on a 24-hour alert to get the pants off the daughters and wives and kept women of the convention delegates.' Putting LSD in the city water supply was openly discussed.[20]

As the convention drew near, cracks in the radical edifice became apparent. Hoffman committed the cardinal sin of Yippiedom: he began to take himself seriously. A violent anger overcame him, expressed in an obsessive desire to do battle with the police. Mobe's steadfast adherence to non-violence seemed an annoying obstacle in the way of aggressive self-discovery. Rubin was likewise intoxicated by the supercharged atmosphere. 'Kill the pigs, kill the cops!' he shouted to a group of supporters. Hayden, in a similar mood, told a crowd: 'Make sure that if blood is going to flow, let it flow all over the city. If we're going to be disrupted and violated, let the whole stinking city be disrupted. I'll see you in the streets!'[21]

The violent talk persuaded genuine pacifists to avoid Chicago, leaving the streets clear for those who heard music in the sound of breaking glass. 'Watching these kids gather sticks and stones, I realized how far we have come from that mythical summer when everyone dropped acid, sat under a tree, and communed,' wrote Richard Goldstein in the *Village Voice*. 'If there were any flower children left in America, they had . . . stayed home. Those who came fully anticipated confrontation.' Dellinger shared Goldstein's disappointment. 'I wish that there had been a greater turnout of people experienced in militant non-violence,' he reflected. 'More, for example, who do not think it is revolutionary to taunt the police by screaming "oink, oink" or "pig" at them.'[22]

The mayhem would previously have been the business of the Chicago police, the district attorney and the Illinois courts. However, in response to incessant anti-war demonstrations, new federal laws had been passed making it illegal to cross state lines for the purpose of inciting riot. Johnson's Attorney General, Ramsay Clark, a sensible man, had no desire to use Chicago as a test case for the new law, especially since he felt that the police were mainly to blame for the ugly events. That view, however, annoyed Chicago mayor Richard Daley, who was determined to punish the hippies for ruining his party. He persuaded his friend, the federal judge William Campbell, to summon a grand jury. On 20 March 1969, indictments were returned against the Eight. By this time, Clark had been replaced by the Republican hardliner John Mitchell, who was attracted to the idea of punishing nonconformity.

The trial began on 24 September 1969. Defence attorneys William Kunstler and Leonard Weinglass tried to challenge the jury selection by submitting a list of fifty-four questions, including whether the jurors had heard of Janis Joplin or Jimi Hendrix, whether their daughters always wore bras, and whether they would object if their son or daughter married a Yippie. Judge Hoffman, however, rejected nearly all of the questions as immaterial, in the process ensuring that the resultant jury was a collection of Ozzie and Harriet clones. 'I felt as if I were at a convention of the silent majority,' wrote Hayden.[23]

'Our identity is on trial,' Hayden argued. On that point, he was absolutely right. The trial was much more than an attempt to prosecute those responsible for the riots; it sought to punish the Sixties generation for going astray. Hayden wanted to play it straight, using the system to defeat the system, and in so doing make a legitimate point about oppressive conformity. 'We were not interested simply in denying that Jerry Rubin threw paint, that Dave Dellinger meant something else in a speech, that undercover agents were distorting and lying; we wanted to go beyond the narrow terms of the prosecution to the larger picture of what was going on in America.' He confidently assumed that the prosecution would crumble under rational rebuttal. His plan was, however, thwarted by Rubin and Hoffman who delighted in the opportunity to take Yippie philosophy into the high temple of orthodoxy. Though secretly worried, Rubin approached the trial with typical bluster. 'This is the greatest honor of my life,' he told a press conference. 'I hope that I am worthy of this great indictment, the Academy Award of Protest . . . It is the fulfilment of childhood dreams.' For he and Hoffman, the trial provided an opportunity to continue the bizarre theatrics of convention week. They dressed in judicial robes or other outlandish costumes, brought a birthday cake, blew kisses to the jury, sang, farted and told jokes. Behind the bedlam lurked a legitimate aim: they wanted to help an absurd process make a mockery of itself. In doing so, however, they embroiled themselves in an ever-escalating challenge. Each day's bizarre behaviour had to be bettered the following day. What began as outrageous soon became blasé. When their shock value wore off, Hoffman and Rubin grew exasperating, then boring.[24]

Judge Hoffman seemed determined to outdo the Yippies in the strangeness stakes. Contempt sentences were handed out like candy – the defendants and their attorneys were charged 159 separate times, for offences as innocent as smiling. Hoffman clearly wanted a quick conviction on all counts and had no qualms about trampling over constitutional rights. Evidence that seemed to suggest violent intent was freely admitted, no matter how trivial, while that suggesting a pattern of non-violence was quashed on grounds that it was 'self-serving'. Since the judge had decided, even before the trial, that the defendants were beneath contempt, he felt no need to show respect to their witnesses, who were badgered, bullied and gagged.[25]

Seale suffered the worst of Hoffman's wrath. The Black Panther had originally wanted to be represented by attorney Charles Garry, but he was hospitalized on the eve of the trial. Hoffman refused a delay until Garry's return. When Seale then asked permission to represent himself, the judge denied that request. Seale, with good reason, judged Hoffman's behaviour racist and began hurling ever more strident abuse, calling him a 'fascist dog', a 'pig' and other choice epithets. On 29 October, Hoffman lost patience and ordered Seale bound and gagged. When that did not sufficiently quieten him, he severed him from the case, sentencing him to four years in prison for contempt. The Eight became seven.

The conspiracy charge was as unstable as a two-legged stool. Some of the defendants had worked together closely; others hardly knew one another. In any case, the prosecution could provide no evidence that the seven had actually met as a group prior to the convention. Even if they had met, they would not have been able to agree on anything, given that they had different political philosophies and contradictory goals. As Norman Mailer, a defence witness, proclaimed: 'Left-wingers are incapable of conspiracy because they're all ego-maniacs.' Judge Hoffman answered that problem by telling the jury that actual collusion did not need to be proved. 'The substance of the crime was a state of mind,' he said.[26]

The jurors were initially split, with eight wanting conviction and four acquittal. Judge Hoffman then demanded a verdict, rejecting the possibility of a hung jury. A deal was struck which acquitted all on the conspiracy charge, while finding Hayden, Hoffman, Rubin, Dellinger and Davis guilty of crossing state lines for the purpose of inciting riot. 'I think we just gave in,' Jean Fritz, one of the four dissenters, confessed. 'We were scared.' Other jurors expressed dismay at the lesser convictions; they were so outraged by the weird behaviour that they felt comfortable ignoring matters of law. One juror felt that the defendants 'should be convicted for their appearance, their language and their lifestyle', while another regretted that the Eight had not been 'shot down by the police', thus saving everyone a lot of bother.[27]

Sentences were delivered on 20 February 1970. Hoffman gave each of the guilty five years in prison and a $5,000 fine. Nine months later, all convictions were overturned by the appeal court, which also quashed the contempt convictions. The judge was criticized for not allowing lawyers to probe the cultural bias of jurors and for maintaining a 'deprecatory and often antagonistic attitude toward the defense'. It also became apparent that FBI agents had, with the full knowledge of the judge and prosecutors, bugged the offices of the defence attorneys, Kunstler and Weinglass, thus rendering the convictions dubious.[28]

Hayden later argued: 'we became the architects, the masterminds, and the geniuses of a conspiracy to overthrow the government – we were invented'. That seems a fair assessment, but amidst all the pandemonium one important truth was obscured: Hayden, Rubin, Hoffman and Davis were guilty, though perhaps not of conspiracy. They had wanted a riot, and they had crossed state lines to incite one. 'We were not just innocent people who were victimised by the police,' Rubin later admitted. 'We came to plan a confrontation.' The justice of the laws they violated might be debated, but there is no doubt that they violated them. More important than laws broken, however, was their cynical manipulation of impressionable youths. In his summing up, the prosecuter Thomas Foran confessed that he felt sympathy for those young people who 'feel the lights have gone out in Camelot'. But, he added, pointing to the defendants, 'these guys take advantage of them. They take advantage of it personally, intentionally, evilly . . . they use them . . . for their purposes and for their intents.' It was not just right-wing authoritarians who felt that way. 'They called all those kids together to be extras in a piece of "police theatre",' actor Peter Coyote, a founder of the Diggers, said of the Eight. 'And they did that to present themselves . . . to America as the new leaders of the radical left. That was as manipulative and conniving a piece of bullshit as anything Lyndon Johnson ever did.'[29]

Dellinger bitterly lamented the events in Chicago. Alone among the Eight, he regretted his involvement. 'Because "they" are vicious and wrong and "we" are humane and right, it is easy to conclude that whatever we do is justified,' he later wrote. He recalled talking with a friend who, in the heady aftermath of the riot, boasted: 'We have won a complete victory at Chicago. The day of non-violence is dead. I've already got my gun.' Dellinger disagreed with those who argued that non-violence had run its course. That logic, he argued, would inevitably degrade the movement. 'We will begin to lose sight of our objectives and develop a Movement style which attracts lovers of violence rather than lovers of justice.' In fact, that had already happened.[30]

Barnard College: Let's Live Together

In the 1960s, a single street in New York separated two very different worlds. On one side of Broadway stood Columbia, the elite, modern, progressive men's college. On the other stood its affiliate, Barnard, the women's college determined to remain old-fashioned. While Barnard had long attracted highly intelligent female students, the college remained uneasy about the role they should play in society. In 1959, President Millicent McIntosh signalled this unease during a convocation address when she first urged her girls to prepare themselves for a fulfilling career, and then advised them to adjust 'without regret' to the most rewarding career of all – their families.[31]

Double standards again arose the following year during the Bermuda Shorts Affair. In keeping with Barnard's progressive charade, students were allowed to wear slacks and even tasteful shorts. But this caused unrest at Columbia, where they were allowed to take classes, since male students were distracted by shapely calves. President Grayson Kirk complained to McIntosh, demanding a more stringent dress code. Suitably obedient, she ruled that women would be allowed to wear shorts while on the Barnard campus, but had to cover themselves with a long coat the minute they crossed Broadway.

The Bermuda Shorts Affair was tiny in comparison to the Linda LeClair scandal eight years later. In March 1968, newspapers across the United States became obsessed with LeClair, who upset Barnard authorities by living with her boyfriend. The scandal emerged when the *New York Times* ran a puff piece on student life, highlighting the new phenomenon of males and females sharing accommodation. LeClair and her boyfriend, Peter Behr, spoke to reporters, under an agreement of anonymity. She confessed that they had decided to live together in lieu of wedlock because marriage seemed 'too serious a step'. That arrangement contravened Barnard regulations which stipulated that non-commuting students under the age of twenty-one were required to live in college housing. LeClair confessed that, in order to sidestep that rule, she had supplied a false address to college authorities.[32]

The college, which did not appreciate being made to look foolish in the *New York Times*, easily identified LeClair as the guilty party. Barnard's president, Martha Peterson, wanted to expel her, if only to satisfy the college's conservative benefactors. Such an action would have been immensely popular. Peterson's office received nearly 500 letters and phone calls demanding expulsion. One correspondent suggested that Barnard should be renamed 'Barnyard', while another concluded that the scandal proved that a 'bunch of glorified whores go . . . to eastern colleges'. The term 'alley cat' proved popular. So, too, did the word 'flaunt' – as in LeClair 'openly flaunting rules of civilized society' – though most writers probably meant 'flout'. David Abrahamson, M.D., on the other hand, understood the correct meaning of 'flaunt'. He judged LeClair an exhibitionist – 'her tendency . . . to be in the limelight . . . clearly indicates some emotional disturbance'. An entirely more mundane issue bothered a female correspondent to *Time*: 'I don't know what kind of student Linda LeClair is or what kind of a mistress she makes, but judging from the picture of her apartment, she makes one lousy housekeeper. Doesn't Barnard College have a Home Economics department?'[33]

We need to remind ourselves that this was 1968, a year after the Summer of Love, when hippies danced naked and copulated in Golden Gate Park. While the nation was getting terribly agitated about LeClair's desire to live with her boyfriend, John Sinclair of the rock group MC5 was arguing that 'all people must be free to fuck freely, whenever and wherever they want to . . . fuck whoever wants to fuck you and everybody else do the same. America's silly sexual "mores" are the end-product of thousands of years of deprivation and sickness, of marriage and companionship based on the ridiculous misconception that one person can "belong" to another person . . . and all that shit.'[34]

The LeClair scandal reveals how little sexual revolutionaries like Sinclair had actually achieved. Mainstream attitudes had hardly changed. Barnard College, for instance, still believed in its role *in loco parentis*; its duty was not just to teach, but to chaperone. To that end, a curfew of midnight at weekends and ten o'clock on weeknights was strictly maintained. Estelle Freedman, class of 1969, recalls 'having to sign out of the dorms at night, meet curfews, and limit male visitors to certain hours'. When a man visited a female's room, the door had to be kept open to the width of a book. 'People remember the protests and the hippies and this and that, and I don't think they remember what a conservative time it was,' Behr reflected. 'The idea that someone was having sex out of marriage was still pretty titillating.'[35]

For LeClair, the issue was not sex, but civil rights. She was a feminist, though she did not use that label. For her, the physical juxtaposition of Barnard and Columbia graphically illustrated the gender double standard. 'Barnard students had to live at the dormitories, and there were . . . stringent curfews, and Columbia students could do whatever they wanted. The media coverage made it into a story about sex . . . but really what it was about was power and equality. There was a lot of unhappiness about the . . . patronizing attitude toward the college women.' Though the doctrine of *in loco parentis* had come under severe attack in the 1960s, when victories were won, it was male students who had benefited. LeClair demanded that *all* students should be treated like adults regardless of gender. 'I'm old enough by law to live anywhere and with anyone without my parents' permission,' she argued.[36]

Armed with a mimeograph machine, LeClair and Behr went to war against Barnard hypocrisy. Leaflets entitled 'A Victorian Drama' were distributed on both campuses in an attempt to cast light upon the double standard. Students were urged to picket the administration building and to demand attendance at LeClair's hearing. Returns from questionnaires revealed that at least 300 Barnard women were living in similar arrangements to LeClair. Sixty agreed to sign affidavits stating: 'I am a student of Barnard College and I have violated the Barnard Housing Regulations. In the interest of fairness I request that an investigation be made of my disobedience.'[37]

When Barnard's Judicial Council convened on 11 April, LeClair showed up in a matronly, knee-length pastel dress. In cross-examination, she forced the Housing Director to admit that, if a student's family home was within the 50-mile commuting limit, no questions were asked about her actual living arrangements. She also supplied testimony from a philosophy professor and two college religious counsellors who argued that Barnard's assumption of *in loco parentis* had no basis in ethics or law. After a five-hour deliberation, the Judicial Council was forced to admit that housing rules needed a 'thorough revision' in order to remove 'any suggestion of discriminatory practice'. The Council could not, however, bring itself to ignore the fact that LeClair had lied. For that misdemeanour, she was banned from use of the college cafeteria, a measure the Columbia student newspaper described as 'suitable non-punishment'. Disgusted with that verdict, one anonymous correspondent complained to Peterson about 'the kow-tow to female "students" who practice prostitution, PUBLICLY!'[38]

While LeClair had won, she'd gone cold on Barnard. 'I decided not to go back,' she later explained, 'because what I had thought Barnard was – namely a place to support feminism, to support the empowerment of women . . . wasn't . . . true.' Peterson welcomed that decision and, tongue firmly in cheek, confessed to journalists that 'recognizing sexual intercourse would cause embarrassment to the ladies that give money to the college'.[39]

In a year hardly devoid of momentous events, it is astonishing how often the LeClair story occupied the front pages, with journalists exploring every angle, no matter how insignificant. Yet, for all that attention, papers consistently got the story completely wrong. Blinded by sex, journalists carelessly concluded that the central issue was carnality. 'It got trivialized by making it be about the fact that I was living with my boyfriend, and about sex and speculation and innuendo,' LeClair recalled. Yet she was not indulging in wild orgies, she was simply living with the man she loved. The arch-conservative William F. Buckley was the most prominent example of a misfiring critic. Railing against the 'delinquency of this pathetic little girl, so gluttonous for sex and publicity', he argued:

> There isn't anyone around who seems prepared to say to Miss LeClair: Look, it is wrong to do what you have done. Wrong because sexual promiscuity is an assault on an institution that is central to the survival of the hardiest Western ideal: the family. In an age in which the *Playboy* philosophy is taken seriously, as a windy testimony to the sovereign right of all human appetites, it isn't

> surprising that the LeClairs of this world should multiply like rabbits, whose morals they imitate.

Buckley obviously hadn't been paying attention, since almost everyone was shouting just that to LeClair, as the letters to Peterson attest. All missed the point, however, since LeClair wasn't attacking the family; she was trying to create one. 'Peter is my family,' she told one reporter. 'It's a very united married type of relationship; it's the most important one in each of our lives. And our lives are very much intertwined.' At a time when the Weather Underground was trying to 'smash monogamy' by forcing its members to take part in compulsory orgies, she was trying to enshrine the principle of one guy for one gal. Behr and LeClair were not eroticists; they were romantics.[40]

'Free love!' the papers screamed. That approach is understandable, since sex sells, while romance does not. The sex angle nevertheless caused journalists to miss the real importance of this story. Because almost everyone was obsessed with sex, the LeClair scandal was interpreted as the logical extension of the sexual revolution and therefore quintessentially Sixties. In fact, it was a reaction to that revolution, and therefore a harbinger of the Seventies. One of the few journals to get the story right was *Life*, despite trying desperately to get it wrong. The magazine went looking for carnality, but couldn't find any. 'History will often have its little joke,' the writer began in determinedly condescending fashion. 'And so it was this spring when it found as its symbol of this revolution a champion as staunch, as bold and as unalluring as Linda LeClair.' Continuing in that vein, the author confessed that LeClair's revolt was rather 'dull', especially when judged against the orgies advocated by rebels like Sinclair. 'Love still makes the world go square,' the magazine concluded. The young people interviewed seemed to be 'less indebted to Playboy than Peanuts'. One 'California girl' confessed: 'Besides being my lover, Bob is my best friend in all the world.' A depressingly prosaic young man maintained: 'We are not sleeping together, we are living together.'[41]

The Seventies is supposed to be the decade of sex. The keys went in the bowl and jealousy out the window. 'The rock and roll dopers of the Sixties,' writes Richard Zacks, 'had spread the legs of a generation and now, as the new decade progressed, we could *all* get laid more easily, even if we weren't that cool.' That makes for good gonzo journalism, but not very good social science. Sexual revolutionaries made a lot of noise, but they were hardly numerous. A sex survey conducted by Albert Klassen of the Kinsey Institute in 1989 found that the typical male born in the 1940s had six sexual partners during his lifetime, or double what his grandfather experienced. That seems entirely explainable by reference to better health standards, increased longevity, greater social mobility, a tendency to stay longer in education, more reliable birth control, and easier treatment of sexually transmitted diseases. In other words, it is not necessary to assume a revolution in order to explain the greater number of sexual liaisons. That said, attitudes were changing. In 1963, 80 per cent of American women thought premarital sex was wrong. By 1975, only 30 per cent did. This did not, however, mean rampant orgies – as the papers liked to suggest. Monogamy remained the goal, even if it was often premarital and sometimes serial. Sexual restraint was still prized, especially if love entered the equation.[42]

'There was an awful lot of sex not happening, then being talked about afterwards as if it did happen,' one baby boomer recalled. 'The great sexual freedom of the 60s was not as great as it would appear in retrospect.' The illusion of free love nevertheless put a lot of pressure upon women, who were expected to conform to the nonconformist model of the 'liberated chick'. 'Free love', built on the foundation of the Pill, was a dream world largely constructed by men. For them, liberation meant freedom from responsibility. For women, however, free love could be frightening, depressing and sometimes dangerous. 'In spite of all the scientific advances,' the novelist Beryl Bainbridge reflected, 'there wasn't a pill invented, and we women knew it, that could stop one's heart from being broken.'[43]

The LeClair revolt needs to be seen in this context. She tried to graft Sixties liberation onto old-fashioned monogamy in an effort to find a domestic arrangement which would be honest and companionate but, most of all, sensitive to the needs of women. Educated middle-class girls from her generation had witnessed the way traditional marriage often handcuffed women, forcing them into prescribed roles – a problem given prominence by Betty Friedan in *The Feminine Mystique* (1963). In keeping with their belief that they could change the world, young women tried to re-invent monogamy. They wanted *partnership* – an ideal of togetherness, mutuality and respect sensitive to the progress women had made. The solution seemed to be 'living together' – an idea attractive not just in the limited sense of a 'trial marriage', but, more importantly, as something devoid of the patriarchal baggage that burdened traditional marriage. One of LeClair's witnesses at her hearing, Rabbi A. Bruce Goldman, testified that Barnard's residency rules 'cause a great deal of guilt because everybody breaks them'. The same could be said of marriage vows. So often disillusioned after witnessing their parents merely endure, young people thought they could construct something better than marriage.[44]

Living together wasn't the only solution proposed. For those who clung to notions of nonconformity, communes seemed the perfect solution. 'Living our lives communally is a choice that we once made and now cannot abandon,' wrote a member of the Rainbow Farm. 'We live the exhilarations and the ambiguities of the style.' Communes proved especially popular in the early 1970s among hippies and political radicals disenchanted by their failure to change the world. Not yet ready to abandon the quest for Utopia, they switched from macro to micro. The new rebel, one enthusiast argued, 'creates his freedom here and there and now and then, and by diligence winds up with as much as any conscious man anywhere. His landscape is small and patterned, but there are discoveries to be made on it, discoveries that can feed his own life at the same time they are important to the culture.'[45]

Communes, however, proved a poor substitute for old-fashioned monogamy. Communities that genuinely adhered to the ideal of free love frequently became machines for the sexual exploitation of women. Patriarchy proved hard to eradicate. The goal, Rosie Boycott recalled, was a society that was 'meant to be equally beneficial to everybody. But for a long time even the communes felt that it was right that Sue bakes bread and Bill brings in the cows.' Tom Hayden, disillusioned with radical protest after the Weatherman hijack of Students for a Democratic Society (SDS) and the ordeal of the Chicago trial, retreated into a Berkeley commune called the 'Red Family'. 'What I really wanted was a home,' he said, by which he meant a house with a family contained within. He was eventually asked to leave because he acted too much like 'an oppressive male chauvinist'. Perhaps significantly, he moved from there to marriage – to Jane Fonda.[46]

While communes were undoubtedly common, they were not nearly as popular as living together. According to the US Bureau of Census, the number of couples cohabiting in 1960 was 439,000. That rose slightly to 523,000 in 1970, but then increased threefold by 1980, to 1,589,000. This trend was duplicated in most Western countries and would continue for the rest of the century. By the mid-Seventies, surveys at American universities regularly showed that 20 to 30 per cent of students had tried cohabitation. Nevertheless, while living together was popular, so too was marriage, further proof that free love had not taken hold. In the 1970s, 34 per cent of adult males were married, up from 30 per cent in the previous decade. Thirty-nine per cent of females were married, a 5 per cent rise on the 1960s. Among those who legally tied the knot, an increasing percentage lived together beforehand. In the US, only 11 per cent of marriages occurring between 1965 and 1974 were preceded by cohabitation, while the figure for those who married between 1975 and 1979 was 32 per cent.[47]

These trends threw the self-appointed guardians of society into moral apoplexy. 'Living together', or what was derogatively called 'shacking up', would eventually be blamed for a long list of social ills, including the rise in the divorce rate, the increase in the number of single parent families, and child abuse. A White House Conference on Children concluded that 'America's families are in trouble – trouble so deep and pervasive as to threaten the future of our nation.' That played into the hands of right-wing commentators who insisted that the behaviour of individuals within relationships would be improved by the strengthening of the marriage contract. It was also argued that those who lived together before marriage were more likely to get divorced than those who did not, a statistic that only proves that two different groups of people behave differently. To some critics of cohabitation, condemnation was mixed in equal parts with envy. 'You have to understand, things were very different when I was dating,' one Christian fundamentalist woman confessed. 'Today, all these kids living together and not married . . . All these new things. Orgies and couples that switch off and girls having careers and living with their boyfriends. It's not for me. But you wonder about it.' She then paused a moment as the gears turned. 'Still, if I were doing it all over again, I wouldn't get married quite so soon.'[40]

Many critics decided that cohabitation was typical of the 'me' decade – an emphasis upon selfish pleasure without entangling responsibility. It was lumped in with all the detritus of the sexual revolution that clutters the Seventies. Cohabitation, like the porn star Linda Lovelace, *The Joy of Sex*, *Open Marriage*, *Oh Calcutta!* and the 1971 decision by editors of *Penthouse* to include photos of female genitalia, seemed to presage moral ruin. What few critics realized was that the vast majority of people who embarked upon cohabitation were genuinely looking for stability and happiness, not to mention sexual honesty and fulfilment, something they feared marriage would not provide.

What the cohabiters failed to realize was that marriage without the piece of paper was easier to escape, but was still essentially marriage. LeClair can take pride in scoring a point for feminism, but she did so by fighting for something that already existed. Looking back on her revolt, the law professor Ann Althouse, a child of the Sixties, disparaged the 'tendency of young people to limit their freedom by setting up a marriage-like living arrangement with the person they happen[ed] to be having sex with'. As she pointed out, 'keeping house together is [not] something excitingly modern. It's just common law marriage and it's the most boring, stodgy, stunting thing in the world. Linda LeClair is not hip. She's a housewife. And she doesn't even know it.' 'We didn't mean to set the world on fire,' Peter Behr admitted. Nor did they.[49]

Nyack: A Change in the Weather

On 20 October 1981 Kathy Boudin left her baby son Chesa with a sitter and went off to rob a bank. This was no ordinary heist, but an important battle in a revolution. By the end of the day, three people were dead and Boudin was starting a twenty-two-year stretch behind bars.

Boudin ingested her revolutionary politics while still in nappies. The fact that she was born on 19 May, the same birthday as Ho Chi Minh and Malcolm X, was celebrated by her radical parents. Her father, Leonard Boudin, an aristocrat of the American left, was an attorney whose client list included Paul Robeson and Alger Hiss. Her uncle was the radical journalist I. F. Stone, her mother a poet and self-confessed 'parlor revolutionary'.[50]

Kathy went to Bryn Mawr, where she met Diana Oughton, with whom she practised revolution by agitating for every left-wing campus cause. After graduation, she tried to bring her radical inheritance into harmony with the chaotic world of the 1960s. She had no intention of emulating her mother by hosting debates over Marxism while sipping Chablis on soft couches. She wanted action, which explains why she ended up in the Weather Underground. Kathy and Diana saw themselves as 'this country's executioners'.[51]

The first major step in that direction was a nail bomb intended for soldiers at Fort Dix. A slip of a screwdriver caused the bomb to detonate prematurely on 6 March 1970, destroying a townhouse in Greenwich Village and taking the lives of Terry Robbins, Ted Gold and Oughton. Boudin has always maintained that she was unaware her friends were making a bomb. Those who might contradict that claim are either dead or stubbornly silent. After the explosion, she and her Weather colleagues backed away from the kind of violence that actually killed people. 'It was a terrible tragedy,' Billy Ayers reflected, 'but also a . . . moment to stop and think and pull back from what might have been a . . . really disastrous course.' His sister-in-law Melody agrees: 'If we hadn't killed ourselves, we would have killed others. Deep down, we knew that the townhouse saved us.'[52]

If the Weatherman dialectic lacked logic before the bomb, it was Cloud Cuckooland after it. The faithful still insisted they could topple the system, but were not prepared to kill to do so. They also decided it would be a good idea to go underground, thus separating themselves from the masses they were trying to convert. This meant purging members who could not be trusted to keep quiet. Weatherman ranks were culled from a couple hundred to a couple dozen, a process called 'purification'.

Over the next seven years, the Weather Underground furthered the revolution by blowing up toilets in government and corporate buildings. Perhaps a dozen bombs were detonated. A flurry of fear followed each, but in truth The Man was unaffected by the ant on his shoe. 'It's not a revolution,' the radical journalist Andrew Kopkind complained. 'Universities have not ground to a halt. Draft boards have not shut down, the war . . . has not ended. The resources of the corporations and the government that make public decisions and social policy are complete.' Boudin's uncle I. F. Stone struggled to make sense of the madness: 'It sounded like the Children's Crusade come back to life, a St Vitus's dance of hysterical politics.'[53]

Life underground was an adult version of hide and seek. Imagination was directed toward clever disguises, new identities and grand plots that never materialized. Whenever one identity grew boring, another was constructed. Most members were sufficiently well connected to have friends willing to loan them a yacht or mountain cabin in which to hide. It was all terribly Seventies – the rebels could pretend they were making revolution when in truth all they were doing was looking after themselves. When life grew dull, a bomb injected momentary drama.

As time passed, the ranks of the Weather faithful dwindled due to arrests, second thoughts and purification. Commitment eroded as members found it increasingly difficult to recall the point of it all. This was especially true after American troops came home from Vietnam in 1973 and the anger that had punctuated the Sixties proved hard to sustain. Mark Rudd, the radical firebrand who once led the revolt at Columbia, was one of the first to fall victim to good sense. 'What are we accomplishing?' he repeatedly asked his friends, who could not provide a plausible answer. The revolutionary army had deteriorated into a gaggle of fugitive celebrities.[54]

Ayers recalls waking up every day thinking: 'I wonder how many times I'll be nervous today.' After bitter fights with old comrades (particularly Boudin) about the future of the revolution, he and his partner, Bernardine Dohrn, came to the conclusion that they were stuck in a cycle of diminishing return. There was nothing to achieve because nothing had been achieved. Hiding out was a pain, especially with children in tow. Being parents 'gave us something to think about besides our fucked-up selves', Ayers recalled. The 'kids were getting . . . older and older' and it seemed wrong that they were not allowed to bring their friends home. Fed up with their 'strange life', Dohrn and Ayers decided to surrender. The fact they were no longer attracting attention must also have weighed heavily, since massive egos do not take well to being ignored.[55]

The great irony of life underground was that Weather people were forced to act normal in order to avoid being noticed. They got jobs, formed monogamous relationships and usually stayed on the right side of the law. 'You could always tell a Weatherman,' Ayers reflected. 'He was the only person who paid his bills on time and obeyed the traffic laws.' The pretence eventually grew pleasant – conformity apparently had its virtues.[56]

When Dohrn and Ayers were preparing to give themselves up in 1980, they tried to persuade Boudin to join them. Though pregnant with Chesa, she refused, certain that there were still causes to fight. She and her partner, David Gilbert, had begun to devote their energies to the Black Liberation Army, a nasty bunch of proto-revolutionaries who wrapped their drug-dealing in the camouflage of political commitment. She signed up to that cause because, she explained, she felt 'guilty about being white'.[57]

On that fateful day in October 1981, Boudin and Gilbert drove the getaway van in a planned BLA hold-up. It was assumed that a middle-aged white couple would not arouse suspicion. The target was a Brinks truck carrying $1.6 million in cash. While carrying out the robbery, the bandits shot and killed one of the guards. They escaped in two cars, then rendezvoused with Boudin and Gilbert several miles away. Contrary to expectation, the van was stopped at a roadblock near Nyack. Boudin got out, her arms raised. Seconds later, the BLA gunmen sprang from the back of the van and shot Sergeant Edward O'Grady and Officer Waverly Brown, killing both. The latter was the first black policeman hired in Rockland County. That should not have been significant but, given Boudin's politics, it was.

Boudin got a life sentence, with the possibility of parole after twenty years. Gilbert remained defiant, siding with his black co-defendants and refusing to accept a plea bargain. He got seventy-five years to life. A prison sentence was perhaps inevitable for Boudin given the life she had chosen. Since her revolution never had a hope of realization, martyrdom behind bars was the next best thing. In Boudin's weird worldview, there was something beautifully noble about futility.

Ayers and Dohrn had meanwhile carefully prepared their coming out. Newspapers, fed leaks, announced that the King and Queen of the Weather Underground were about to emerge. Dohrn, a lawyer by training, had a fair idea of the legal consequences of surrender. In the end, she got three years' probation and a fine of $1,500 for crimes committed during the Days of Rage in 1969. All charges against Ayers were dropped. As for the dozen or so bombs that the Weather Underground proudly exploded, not a single one was linked to the golden couple. This was partly because the FBI had acted illegally in gathering evidence.

While Boudin was mired in prison, Ayers and Dohrn joined the mainstream, always pretending not to do so. The one-time leaders of the Smash Monogamy campaign found happiness in a stable, loving marriage. To those ignorant of their past, they looked like typical bourgeois baby boomers embracing life in the late twentieth century. Their two boys, Malik Geronimo and Zayd Osceola, not to mention their foster son Chesa, were constant sources of pride. They enjoyed fine wines, soft couches and balsamic vinegar on their radicchio.

They remained stubbornly unapologetic. 'To apologize for militantly opposing racism . . . is a perversion,' Ayers argued in 1996. Dohrn echoed that sentiment: 'Resistance by every means necessary is happening and will continue to happen within the United States as well as around the world, and I remain committed to the struggle ahead.' A generation raised on CDs, MP3s and iPods won't appreciate how much that sounds like a scratched phonograph record first pressed in 1969.[58]

Their reflections on their past life form an intricate weave of moral relativism, self-justification, forgetfulness, prevarication and denial. 'I don't regret setting bombs,' Ayers confessed in 2001. 'I feel we didn't do enough.' In his memoirs, he admits what is safe to admit and dissembles about the rest. 'Is this, then, the truth?' he asks himself. 'Not exactly. Although it feels entirely honest to me . . . Obviously, the point is it's a reflection on memory . . . It's true as I remember it.' 'Memory is a motherfucker,' he maintains with contrived radical bombast. As for his call to his comrades to kill their parents, he claims he doesn't remember saying such a thing, but 'it's been quoted so many times I'm beginning to think I did'. If he did say it, it was 'a joke about the distribution of wealth'. Dohrn was likewise only joking when she voiced her homage to Charles Manson. Over the years, she has alternated between denying the remark and offering an incomprehensible explanation for it. In 2001, she claimed: 'It was a joke. We were mocking violence in America.'[59]

Dohrn still defends the turn to violence. 'There's no way to be committed to non-violence in the middle of the most violent society that history has ever created,' she argued. 'I'm not committed to non-violence in any way.' Ayers admits to being 'embarrassed by the arrogance, the solipsism, the absolute certainty that . . . we alone knew the way'. Weatherman's 'rigidity and . . . narcissism' do occasionally rankle his conscience. But, when asked if he would do it all again, he replies: 'I don't want to discount the possibility . . . I don't think you can understand a single thing we did without understanding the violence of the Vietnam War.' 'I didn't kill innocent people,' he argues. While that is true, his defence rests more on accident than intent. Nail bombs have only one purpose.[60]

'I feel like we came into our adulthood at a moment in time where we had the opportunity to have purpose to our lives,' Dohrn explains. 'I feel completely fortunate to have been a part of that. I want to still be a part of that . . . I have many personal apologies to give to people for things I said and hurts that I did, and of course, I wish we'd done better . . . but don't we all wish that about our lives? In that sense, I feel lucky and unapologetic.' That faux repentance irks her former colleague Mark Rudd, who eventually saw her for what she was. He recalls running into Dohrn in 1977 and being astonished at how she seemed untroubled by doubt.

> I couldn't believe the rhetoric. The same old shit. Later on, it occurred to me how her ego was still totally involved with all that dead history. How little she had looked at herself all those years. She should have had to confront what she really did to people – manipulated, maneuvered, and isolated them, fucked them up; she should have had to admit how wrong her ideas were, how meshuga her self-conception was. A great revolutionary leader! She had no great revolutionary ideas. None of us did.

Rudd, now a teacher in Albuquerque, feels genuine shame about his past and the fact that innocent people might so easily have died. 'Just like the passive Americans we derided, I acquiesced to this terrible demented logic . . . I cherished my hate as a badge of moral superiority.' Rudd castigates himself for having chosen 'the stupid, losing strategy of "revolutionary" violence . . . The Weather Underground was a huge fuck-up! We did the work of the FBI by destroying SDS. . . . We split and undermined the larger anti-war movement . . . the importance of the Weather Underground was that it was a total disaster.' Tom Hayden, present at the beginning in 1962, mourned the way 'an organization that at its birth believed in thinking and acting in new ways to change the world . . . had in just seven short years fallen victim to every dire and cynical prediction ever made about revolutionary movements'.[61]

Who is Bernadine Dohrn? 'There's no right answer,' she contends. 'Am I the militant in black leather, shouting slogans, or am I . . . a suburban matron[?]' She insists that her comfortable home should not be seen as evidence of a sell-out to Seventies values. 'This is where we raised our kids and are taking care of our aging parents,' she argues. 'We could live much more simply, and well we might.' As for her surrender to monogamy, she struggles hard to make conformity seem radical. 'You're always trying to balance your understanding of who you are and what you need, and your longing and imaginings of freedom.' Ayers adds: 'We have to learn how to be committed, and hold out the possibility of endless reinventions.' Coming from two former revolutionaries, that's supposed to sound radical. In fact, it's not unlike the emotional challenges every baby boomer faced in the 1970s.[62]

Ayers and Dohrn, who had once scorned 'white skin privilege', eventually used it to their advantage. Their reintegration was made infinitely easier by the fact that they returned to the milieu of white, middle-class respectability in which they were raised. Friends in the legal profession smoothed their re-emergence. Their black colleagues in the revolution did not enjoy such easy re-entry. But, leaving that aside, there remains the question of how to interpret the radical couple's return to respectability. Is it a reluctant acceptance of painful inevitability – proof of the tyranny of conformity? Or is it instead evidence that traditional ways of living have their origins in genuine human need – we make what we instinctively require?

And what of Kathy Boudin? She was released from prison in 2003 at the age of sixty, having served twenty-two years. Her parole was vigorously opposed, for understandable reasons. She was, however, always more a symbol than a criminal. The court in New York incarcerated an idea by jailing an individual. Kathy Boudin did time for the Weather Underground, for all the slippery characters like Ayers and Dohrn who were well-versed about statutes of limitation.

She absorbed America's wrath with considerable dignity. A model prisoner, she ran literacy programmes, AIDS awareness campaigns and counselling sessions for inmates whose children had been taken into foster care. She was, according to one observer, 'an entirely transformed human being', who displayed a great deal more remorse than was ever expressed by Dohrn or Ayers. 'Do I feel what I did was wrong?' she wrote.

> Yes. I want to be clear. I know that I am responsible for a terrible thing. I feel nothing but remorse and shame about my involvement. I will live with this for the rest of my life.
>
> Three people died; others suffered physically and emotionally; families were ripped apart; a whole town shaken. Now in spite of my dream of helping to create a more humane society, I am forever connected to the deaths of innocent people. This connection has changed me. I will never be associated again with any act that places human lives at risk.

Three points require emphasis. First, Boudin, unlike Ayers or Dohrn, understood what violence really means – the destruction it causes. Secondly, the worst punishment meted out to her was not prison itself, but separation from her son. Thirdly, she achieved a great deal more for the revolution as a prisoner of war than she could ever have achieved as a soldier.[63]

The Sixties saw a rebellion against the conformity and hypocrisy of the older generation. Yet by 1970, the vast majority of rebels were ready to join the mainstream. The Seventies is the decade of their maturity. Conformity, they discovered, was simply a derogatory way of describing the things that most people love. And as for hypocrisy, most rebels would eventually try to enforce rules of behaviour upon their children that they rudely defied during the decade of revolution. Dohrn and Ayers underwent this process of maturation later than most, but did so nonetheless. They eventually discovered that their children were more important than their self-centred political fantasies and that growing old with someone you love (monogamy) was actually quite nice. Boudin undoubtedly would have enjoyed the opportunity to make that discovery. Though the veterans of the Weather Underground might never admit it, they have quite a bit in common with the parents they once wanted to kill.

3

OLD ARGUMENTS, NEW DEATHS

Bangladesh: 'We can kill anyone for anything'

Pakistan was formed so that Muslims in the former colony of India could have a nation of their own, free from Hindu oppression. After partition, however, ethnicity supplanted religion as a source of conflict. Pakistan soon demonstrated that Muslims were fully capable of oppressing other Muslims.

Pakistan was the deformed offspring of a botched settlement. Two largely Muslim regions, separated by 1,600 kilometres of Indian territory, were made into a single nation. The two regions differed markedly in language, ethnicity and culture. There was no logical capital city, no established bureaucracy of government. The workforce was rent asunder when thousands of skilled Hindus decanted to India. Administration of the two separate 'wings' was dependent upon the fickle goodwill of India. The economy was heavily reliant upon jute production at a time when worldwide demand was in decline.

East Pakistan had the larger population, but was dominated by the more developed West, where government, banking and commercial interests were concentrated. With dominance went a sense of ethnic superiority; easterners justifiably complained of racial prejudice by politicians and employers. The mongrel state limped from crisis to crisis, with regional disharmony punctuated by violence. Given the weakness of democratic institutions, it is entirely understandable that Pakistanis developed a taste for military rule.

In October 1958, with easterners in rebellious mood, Governor General Iskander Mirza placed Pakistan under martial law and appointed General Mohammed Ayub Khan prime minister. Keen for 'a clean break with the past', Ayub promptly exiled Mirza to London – a military coup in all but name. Martial law continued until 1962, enough time for Ayub to purge civilians from key government positions, replacing them with hand-picked soldiers. His solution to regional animosity was a highly centralized government. To this end, a new constitution vested immense authority in the executive, while hobbling the legislature. Antagonism nevertheless continued to fester. Political parties, deprived of influence, turned into organs of discontent. In East Pakistan, the Awami League was the mouthpiece for Bengali anger. Ayub, realizing that the region was a powder keg, made some conciliatory gestures, promising not to import 'foreign' administrators and reserving half of his Cabinet for easterners. In addition, Dacca was made a 'second capital' and seat of the National Assembly. To Bengalis, however, this smacked of tokenism reminiscent of colonial days.[1]

In 1963, the Awami League chairman, Huseyn Suhrawardy, died, opening the way for the firebrand separatist Sheikh Mujibur Rahman. Mujib, as he was known, turned the party into a vehicle for Bengali liberation. He argued that Pakistan's recent economic growth, achieved by the sweat of easterners, had benefited westerners alone. That claim held enough truth to constitute a powerful rallying cry. There was no escaping the fact that Bengalis were desperately poor. Foreign aid, administered from Karachi, was spent mainly in the West. While maldistribution had more complex causes than simple animosity, the fact that the animosity existed made disparities all the more corrosive. Mujib, the quintessential populist, loved simple explanations. The word 'colony', however inappropriate, peppered his diatribes.

In 1966, Mujib threw down the gauntlet by launching his Six Points programme, a form of autonomy so profound that only foreign and defence policy would remain the purview of central government. Equally alarming was the fact that the proposal did not refer exclusively to the division between East and West, but rather envisaged devolution wherever ethnic or religious diversity dictated. West Pakistanis rightly worried that it would lead to the fragmentation of their region, thus allowing the more homogenous Bengal territory to emerge as the most powerful unit. When the proposals were rejected, Mujib encouraged his followers onto the streets. After a general strike in January 1968, he was arrested, further ratcheting tension.

Ayub was simultaneously rocked by a threat from within his own government. The highly ambitious Zulfikar Ali Bhutto used his fiefdom at the foreign ministry to showcase his credentials as a nationalist determined to defend Pakistani integrity. His resignation from the government in June 1967, and subsequent establishment of the Pakistan People's Party (PPP), was a challenge both to Ayub and to Mujib. Bhutto's strident populism enflamed nationalist sentiment in West Pakistan, pressuring Ayub to be tough with the Bengalis. While Mujib's supporters rioted in support of local autonomy, Bhutto's agitated for exactly the opposite. The only thing the two movements had in common was their disdain for Ayub.

With the country spiralling out of control, Ayub resigned on 25 March 1969, handing power to General Yahya Khan. On assuming office, Yahya promised to hold elections on 7 December 1970. Eager to placate the Bengalis, he decided that 162 of the 300 seats in the National Assembly should be awarded to East Pakistan. Aware of the popularity of the Awami League in East Pakistan, westerners looked on with considerable trepidation.

While there is never a good time for a cyclone, November 1970 was certainly the worst possible moment. On the 12th, a devastating storm ravaged 8,000 square kilometres of Bengal's coastal lowlands, killing 250,000 people. Yahya's response was at best incompetent, at worst cynical. Only one military transport plane and three small aircraft were mobilized during the first week of the crisis. 'We have a large army,' Mujib complained, 'but it is left to the British Marines to bury our dead.' He questioned why emergency aid from abroad had arrived more quickly than from West Pakistan. Joining the chorus, Bengali newspapers complained of 'gross neglect, callous inattention, and bitter indifference'. 'There have been mistakes, there have been delays,' Yahya admitted, 'but by and large I'm very satisfied that everything is being done and will be done.'[2]

Bengalis found Yahya's satisfaction an insult. 'The feeling now pervades,' Mujib concluded, 'that we must rule ourselves. We must make the decisions that matter. We will no longer suffer arbitrary rule by bureaucrats, capitalists, and feudal interests of West Pakistan.' While there is no doubting Yahya's incompetence, it has to be said that Mujib was not above turning personal tragedy into political advantage. He was, after all, behind the Awami League's decision to launch a general strike during the crisis, which inevitably hindered relief efforts.[3]

Less than a month later came the election. Ayub's appeal for national unity fell on deaf ears in the East. Mujib won all but 2 of the region's 162 seats. In the West, Bhutto's PPP did well, winning 81 of 138 seats, but that still meant an outright majority for the Awami League.

Bhutto summarily announced that he would not countenance a Mujib government committed to implementation of the Six Point programme. On that issue, he had the formidable weight of Yahya behind him. Mujib countered by proposing a double premiership – he would rule the East, Bhutto the West. That proposal, tantamount to secession, was unacceptable to those who still believed in the integrity of Pakistan. When Mujib's proposal was rejected, rioting erupted throughout Bengal. In early March, Yahya postponed indefinitely the convening of the National Assembly, appointed General Tikka Khan military governor of East Pakistan and moved troops into the area. Undaunted, Mujib told his followers to turn Pakistan's 'Republic Day' (23 March) into their own 'Resistance Day'.

Bereft of solutions, Yahya opted for terror. 'Kill three million of them,' he told his generals, 'and the rest will eat out of our hands.' On 25 March 1971 three West Pakistani battalions attacked targets in Dacca. They had no strategic purpose other than slaughter. 'Killing on a mass scale is underway,' the *Daily Telegraph* reported. 'The shelling of the capital, Dacca, has been cold-blooded and indiscriminate although there was almost no sign of armed resistance.'[4]

Tikka's troops methodically worked their way through a shopping list of targets. At the top were Bengali soldiers, police and paramilitary forces. Next came potential soldiers – boys as young as fifteen were slaughtered. Then came those identified as leaders – officials of the Awami League, students, academics and professionals. Finally, there were Hindus – the 'vermin' blamed for polluting East Pakistan. Eliminating them would, it was thought, allow East Pakistanis to accept that their identity was Muslim, not Bengali. Racism gave justification to indiscriminate killing. East Pakistan '[is] a low lying land of low lying people', said the senior general A.A.K. Niazi. Since the sole purpose of the campaign was to kill, soldiers enjoyed immense freedom. 'We can kill anyone for anything,' one boasted. 'We are accountable to no one.'[5]

'It became a crime to be a Bengali,' one resident remarked. 'The soldiers would say "Are you Bengali" and if you were, you would be killed.' In order to conceal the barbarity, Tikka expelled foreign journalists from the country. Press reports had therefore to be scraped together from whatever information leaked out. Witnesses told journalists of 'a veritable bloodbath' conducted by 'utterly merciless' troops. While exaggeration inevitably resulted, the slaughter was undoubtedly enormous. 'The word massacre applies', *Time* reported on 12 April.

> Opposed only by bands of Bengali peasants armed with stones and bamboo sticks, tanks rolled through Dacca . . . blowing houses to bits. At the University, soldiers slaughtered students inside the British Council building. 'It was like Chengis Khan,' said a shocked Western official who witnessed the scene. Near Dacca's marketplace, Urdu-speaking government soldiers ordered Bengali-speaking townspeople to surrender, then gunned them down when they failed to comply. Bodies lay in mass graves at the University, in the old city, and near the municipal dump.

At the university, one witness hid in a tree and watched while students and lecturers were herded into an enclosure and then slaughtered. The soldiers then directed bystanders to carry the bodies to the football ground. 'They were ordered to dig a huge grave. The Pakistani soldiers told the eight or nine bearers to sit down. After a while they were ordered to stand and line up near the grave. The guns fired again and they fell next to the bodies of my friends.' At the jute mill where she worked, Ferdousi Priyabhashinee witnessed a diabolical method of execution. Victims were 'taken to a jute-cutting machine, which looks like a guillotine . . . [Soldiers] put the man under the sharp blade . . . and within a couple of seconds, he was beheaded. This barbaric act continued one after another.'[6]

Various reports suggest that 15,000 were slaughtered in Dacca within three days. In the face of international outrage, Yahya was unrepentant. The 'rebellion', he claimed, was the work of 'mischief-mongers, saboteurs and infiltrators' and had to be crushed. The purpose of the operation was to protect Bengali Muslims from their Hindu oppressors. 'When one fights, one does not throw flowers,' he added. Tikka chimed in, dismissing newspaper reports as 'wildly exaggerated', while claiming that the death toll in Dacca on the first day had not exceeded 150.[7]

After rampaging through Dacca, Pakistani forces spread out across the country. In July, a World Bank mission reported widespread devastation; villages had 'simply ceased to exist'. 'They're nothing but butchers,' one witness told a reporter for the *International Herald Tribune*. 'They wiped out whole villages opening fire at first light and stopping only when they got tired.' At Hariharpara, killing assumed a daily ritual. Victims from surrounding towns and villages were gathered to await execution at sundown. Lashed together in groups of six or eight, they were taken to the riverbank and forced to wade into knee-deep water. 'Then the rifles opened up. And the firing and the screaming shattered the hot night air until dawn.' In the morning, village boatmen were 'forced to . . . haul the bodies out to midstream, where they were cut loose to drift downriver'.[8]

At Shohagpur village, every adult male was killed. 'When the army was gone, there was not a single man left to bury the dead,' one woman recalled. In such situations, women became helpless prey. Concentration camps provided immense opportunity for sexual abuse. Rape was an assault not just against an individual woman, but a systematic attack upon her family and her village. Geoffrey Davis, an Australian doctor who arrived in Bangladesh shortly after the war, treated West Pakistani soldiers held in Comilla prison. They claimed that the order to rape had come from Tikka, 'so there would be a whole generation of children in East Pakistan that would be born with the blood from the West'. For six months, Davis performed as many as a hundred abortions a day.[9]

While the actual number raped is difficult to determine, partly because of the stigma attached, the lowest estimates range around 200,000. The journalist Aubrey Menen investigated one case involving a nineteen-year-old Hindu woman, recently married. A truckload of six soldiers arrived outside her home late one evening.

> Two went into the room that had been built for the bridal couple. The others stayed behind with the family, one of them covering them with his gun. They heard a barked order, and the bridegroom's voice protesting. Then there was silence until the bride screamed. Then there was silence again, except for some muffled cries that soon subsided.
>
> In a few minutes one of the soldiers came out, his uniform in disarray. He grinned to his companions. Another soldier took his place . . . And so on, until all of the six had raped the belle of the village. Then all six left, hurriedly. The father found his daughter lying . . . unconscious and bleeding. Her husband was crouched on the floor, kneeling over his vomit.

Menen eventually located the victim in a shelter for rape victims in Dacca. She doubted that she would ever be able to return to her village. Her husband had shunned her, and her father was too ashamed to see her.[10]

Separated from her family in the first few days of war, Ferdousi Priyabhashinee fell under the control of Bengalis wishing to bargain with their invaders. For nine months she was used as currency in the sexual exchange. 'I . . . felt that nobody in the world was more helpless than me . . . I felt that my body was not mine, and it seemed to be decomposed.' When soldiers discovered that her brother was a resistance fighter, she was brutally tortured. 'At one stage, I stopped replying to any of their questions. I told them, "Please kill me. Don't torture me in this way", but unfortunately it was not my fate to be killed by the Pakistanis.'[11]

The international community made a show of moral outrage, but otherwise stood aside. The big, constraining fear was that the conflict would escalate into a general war between India and Pakistan. That had Cold War implications, since the Indians were friendly with the Soviets, and the Pakistanis with China and the US. America's willingness to turn a blind eye – a policy officially called 'massive inaction' – annoyed her consul in Dacca. In a telegram headed 'Selective Genocide', Archer Blood complained: 'We are mute and horrified witnesses to a reign of terror.' When evidence of the slaughter evoked no suitable reaction in Washington, Blood again complained. 'Our government has failed to denounce the suppression of democracy. Our government has failed to denounce atrocities . . . we have chosen not to intervene, even morally.' A short time later he was removed from his post.[12]

The US had armed Pakistan in the interests of maintaining an ally in the area, but then had to watch while American arms were used to slaughter Bengalis. Nixon was reluctant to stop the shipments since the threat of Indian intervention remained. 'The Indians are no goddamn good,' he told his National Security Adviser Henry Kissinger on 4 June 1971. Kissinger agreed. 'Those sons-of-bitches, who never have lifted a finger for us, why should we get involved in the morass of East Pakistan? . . . if East Pakistan becomes independent, it is going to become a cesspool . . . they have the lowest standard of living in Asia . . . They're going to become a ripe field for Communist infiltration.' Nixon called the Indians a 'slippery, treacherous people' – what they really needed was 'a mass famine'. 'They're such bastards,' Kissinger added. The *International Herald Tribune* thought that White House policy 'defies understanding'. What the paper did not realize was that Yahya was America's unofficial link to Beijing. As Kissinger confided to Nixon, it was necessary to 'buoy up Yahya' until relations with China were formalized.[13]

The Awami League had meanwhile proclaimed the independent republic of Bangladesh. Western commentators, digesting stories of endless massacre, held little hope for the new nation's survival. What journalists failed to notice, however, was that the massacre sowed a ferocious desire for revenge. In the midst of the slaughter, the Mukti Bahini liberation forces managed to regroup. A vicious war of attrition ensued. Using their knowledge of the terrain and local support, guerrillas methodically recaptured rural areas, forcing the West Pakistanis back into the cities. Reprisals were swift and brutal. Captured soldiers, or those who had supported them, were publicly beheaded.

Some 10 million frightened Bengalis had by this point flooded into India, the largest refugee crisis in history. Prime Minister Indira Gandhi rightly complained that 'no prosperous country' or any of the 'upholders of democracy has tried to help the . . . refugees'. With the crisis threatening to overwhelm her country, she waited until early December and then struck with overwhelming force. On 4 December, Indian troops, backed by the Mukti Bahini, moved on Dacca. 'This is India's biggest and final war against us,' Yahya told his troops. 'So far Pakistan has acted with supreme patience. We have tolerated enough. The time has now come to give a crushing reply to the Indian aggressors.' Bluster, however, proved no substitute for military might. The far superior Indian Army swept the Pakistanis aside in just ten days. Before Dacca was surrendered, however, the Pakistanis indulged in one last act of barbarity. On 19 December, around a hundred physicians, professors, writers and teachers were murdered in a field outside Dacca. 'All the victims' hands were tied behind their backs and they had been bayoneted, garrotted or shot,' reported the *New York Times.*[14]

Yahya, having optimistically sent his troops to war, could not possibly survive their humiliation. He yielded to Bhutto, who in turn released Mujib from prison, where he had been held since the first days of the war. The latter became the first prime minister of Bangladesh in January 1972. One of his first acts was to declare the rape victims 'Beerangana' – war heroes. He urged that strictures pertaining to female chastity should be relaxed so that the women could be re-integrated into society. In particular, he hoped they might provide a ready source of brides for the Mukti Bahini. In fact, however, custom could not easily be erased. Freedom fighters argued that they deserved better than 'damaged' goods. Others demanded that the government should provide large dowries, since the women's families were not likely to do so. Because the government was too poor, good intentions dissolved into tragic neglect. Ostracized in their new nation, many rape victims emigrated to Pakistan, ending up amongst those who had once abused them. 'We know about the courage of the freedom fighters during the war,' Priyabhashinee reflected, 'but I did not see the same courage among them after the country was freed from the occupation forces.'[15]

The death toll during the 267 days of the Bangladeshi Liberation War probably exceeded 1 million, and might have been double that. An accurate figure remains elusive because every estimate carries the taint of politics. But who died, at whose hands, is difficult to determine. What is clear is that the war does not conform to the simple image of ruthless aggressor vs innocent martyr that journalists once reported. The conflict was multi-layered – East Pakistan vs West Pakistan, Muslim vs Hindu, secessionist vs loyalist, Pakistani vs Indian. At every level, atrocity occurred. The torment continues because no semblance of closure has been achieved. The vast majority of the perpetrators, especially those at the top, walked free. It is now a ritual in Bangladesh, acted out every March and December, to lament that evil went unpunished.

Belfast: Bloody Sunday

Northern Ireland is part of the United Kingdom, but culturally it is not English, nor Irish, nor British. It is a place divided against itself where two antagonistic ethnic groups struggle to coexist. Mutual distrust fuels a sense of distinctiveness, which in turn fuels distrust, in an ever-repeating pattern. Past is present, old scores are never settled and history is perpetually re-enacted in real time. With hatred deep and memory bitter, agreement until recently remained elusive and violence therefore inevitable. Time was measured by tragedy – the ever-lengthening list of dead.

Under the terms of the Government of Ireland Act of 1920, the six counties of Northern Ireland were granted a devolved government, consisting of a bicameral parliament which from 1932 was headquartered at Stormont, 6 miles east of Belfast. In truth, Stormont was an elected dictatorship, a Protestant quango loyal to the Crown, but, more importantly, dedicated to its own interests. The cohesiveness and dominance of Unionists in Northern Ireland ensured a stranglehold on power.

Cohesiveness was continually reinforced by the culture of Unionism. Protestants sensed not only a religious divide, but also an ethnic one. They felt themselves a different race. Catholicism seemed a 'foreign' religion, a popish plot that threatened to destroy the 'self-contained island of eternal existence' that Unionists had built. Antagonism was buttressed by exclusive organizations: the Unionist Party, the Orange Order and the Apprentice Boys. Rituals of differentiation, such as the annual Orange marches, reinforced the politics of separation. Like a tomcat marking territory, Orangemen marched to assert dominance.[16]

Bigotry kept the working class divided. Instead of devoting energy to trade unions or social welfare, Protestant workers concentrated instead upon hating Catholics. Orange organizations and rituals allowed them to feel a sense of superiority in relation to their Catholic counterparts. They had no wealth to pass on to their offspring, but they could bequeath bigotry. Thus, with each passing generation, feelings of exclusivity were distilled. Unionism brought empowerment – the more extreme the prejudice, the greater the sense of exclusivity. Protestant workers failed to realize that, by colluding in bigotry, they conspired in their own emasculation.

Stormont, the Unionist David Trimble eventually admitted, was 'a cold House for Catholics'. Between 1921 and 1972, Northern Ireland was ruled by six prime ministers, all of them Unionists and members of the Orange Order. All but three Cabinet ministers during that period were Orangemen. Catholics could vote, but votes never translated into power. They were effectively disenfranchised, not just because the government was always Unionist but because Unionist power was used to perpetuate Catholic subjugation. They were, in effect, outsiders living inside the province.[17]

Protestant dominance at Stormont was replicated at local levels, further enfeebling the Catholic minority. Due to a system of gerrymandering, political representation did not accurately reflect population. 'Derry . . . was roughly two-thirds Catholic; one-third Protestant,' the civil rights activist Eamonn McCann explained by way of example. 'But the Protestants were able to elect twelve people onto the Council, the Catholics only eight. The way this worked was simple: the city was divided very carefully into three wards. The vast majority of the Catholics were crowded into one ward which returned eight councillors.' To further the enfeeblement, only ratepayers could vote in provincial elections, thus leaving renters of private housing disenfranchised. Around 250,000 people fell into this category, most of them Catholic. To compound this iniquity, Unionist councils allocated public housing disproportionately to Protestants. Since council house tenants could vote, this further cemented Unionist hegemony.[18]

Political power was naturally translated into economic power. Businesses were disproportionately owned by Protestants, who favoured those of their faith when hiring. In 1967, 99 per cent of the workers at the Harland and Wolff shipyard in Belfast were Protestant. Similar discrimination affected the distribution of jobs controlled by local councils. For example, though Catholics outnumbered Protestants in Tyrone, they did not control the local council. As a result, less than 4 per cent of the staff employed at council offices in 1969 were Catholic. Northern Ireland Catholics were twice as likely to be unemployed as Protestants of the same class.[19]

Law enforcement buttressed the religious divide. The Royal Ulster Constabulary was essentially a Protestant paramilitary force that strengthened an iniquitous system of religious privilege. Its authority was enhanced by the Special Powers Act, a relic of the First World War which allowed arrests without warrants, internment without trial, draconian restrictions on political expression, and virtually unlimited powers of search. While the RUC was tacitly Protestant, the Special Constabulary (or 'B Specials') was officially so. Membership in the Orange Order was a prerequisite of selection.

For over forty years the Catholic minority passively endured disenfranchisement and poverty. The Irish Republican Army persistently tried to turn discontent into revolutionary fervour, but with little success. The pattern of passivity was broken, however, in February 1967 with the formation of the Northern Ireland Civil Rights Association. NICRA set out five broad aims:

1. To defend the basic freedom of all citizens.
2. To protect the rights of the individual.
3. To highlight all possible abuses of power.
4. To demand guarantees for freedom of speech, assembly and association.
5. To inform the public of their lawful rights.

None of these demands, nor the grievances that inspired them, were specific to Catholics. That was intentional – NICRA strove to break away from sectarian politics. It recognized that while Catholics were undoubtedly discriminated against, so too were all workers in Northern Ireland, whose quality of life suffered in comparison to the UK as a whole. The group believed that the best way to correct iniquities was to remove the religious identifications that confused them. Toward that end, NICRA refused to be drawn on the issue of sovereignty. 'We were very adamant that the national question, the constitutional question, would not be part of what we were about,' Ann Hope, the former NICRA secretary, reflected. 'We were not asking for the end of partition, what we were asking, very consciously asking for, was reform in Northern Ireland.'[20] This sense of unity was demonstrated when, in the early days, Catholics and Protestants marched side by side, carrying signs which read 'British Rights for British Citizens'.

Appearances were, however, deceptive. While NICRA's broad platform was non-sectarian, the same could not be said for its specific aims. Imbedded within the group's literature were five other demands peculiar to Catholics. These included the institution of 'one man one vote' in council elections, an end to gerrymandering, fair allocation of public housing, anti-discrimination legislation, and the repeal of the Special Powers Act. The granting of these demands, however justified, would imply a surrender of authority by the Protestant community. Despite its genuine attempt to appear non-sectarian, NICRA could not completely camouflage the Catholic nature of its grievances.

NICRA embodied the Sixties culture of protest, taking heart from the American civil rights movement. Another example of transnational resonance was People's Democracy (PD), a Sixties-style left-wing student movement that emerged at Queen's University Belfast. PD, like other European student groups, was Trotskyite and, like campus militancy everywhere, was impatient, volatile and often immature. The PD leader Michael Farrell recalled 'a real feeling of revolution'. It was 'just like Wordsworth and the French Revolution: "A joy to be alive, to be young was very heaven." . . . Things happened very, very fast.' In contrast to other Sixties student movements, however, grievances never became abstract – PD members lived the injustice they protested and therefore remained focused. Style never overwhelmed substance.[21]

Stormont reacted with calculated torpor to the pressure applied by NICRA and PD. The attorney general, Edward Warburton Jones, scornfully rejected demands for a human rights bill, because he 'quite simply did not believe that there was any discrimination worth talking about in Northern Ireland'. When Prime Minister Terence O'Neill proposed some rather superficial reforms, his friends accused him of appeasement and his Catholic enemies of condescension. The failure of his modest attempt at reform revealed how sturdy were the obstacles to progress. Change was alien to the Unionist community; reform proposals, no matter how mild, inspired deep paranoia, expressed in a tendency to dig trenches.[22]

A new mood of Protestant extremism was profoundly expressed in the emergence of the Reverend Ian Paisley. While the line between religion and politics had long been blurred in the province, Paisley erased it, using the pulpit to advance a bigoted political crusade and using politics to reinforce sectarianism. More than any Unionist before him, Paisley placed the social and political concerns of the Protestant working class of Northern Ireland into a religious context, convincing them that their hegemony conformed to God's wishes.

Paisley realized that hatred was more easily stoked if the religious divide was reinforced by ethnicity. He therefore encouraged followers to believe that Catholics were essentially sub-human. Lending support was the *Protestant Telegraph*, which missed no opportunity to report on the 'Roman hovels' of the Lower Falls area of Belfast. One report told of 'squalid' and 'verminous' housing and conditions so vile that an inspector, 'overcome by the stench of a room being used as an open lavatory', had to receive medical attention. 'The "great unwashed" is an epithet applicable hygienically and spiritually to the natives of the Lower Falls,' the paper concluded. Believing Catholics a lesser race justified their maltreatment. Often, a Paisley sermon would be followed by an orgy of Protestant violence, which perpetrators believed righteous. Neither the political nor the legal authorities intervened to curb Paisleyite provocation, for the simple reason that he served the cause of Unionism so perfectly. Stormont's power was all the more secure with Paisley as its Rottweiler.[23]

On 5 March 1968 a NICRA march in Derry met a brutal response from the RUC and B Specials, armed with batons and water cannon. In January 1969, at Burntollet, Paisleyites and B Specials ambushed a PD march from Derry to Belfast. The RUC, supposedly deployed to protect the marchers, joined in the attacks. Clearly, if peaceful protest had become dangerous, the prospects for change were bleak. Activism did not, however, wane. 'Baton charges and hosing machines do not kill the earnest desires of second-class citizens to promote their civil and human dignity,' the *Irish News* warned. That might have been true, but the policy of non-violence was difficult to maintain in the face of brutal reprisals. In July 1969, 15,000 Apprentice Boys announced their intention to march through Derry. Stormont, by its inaction, effectively sanctioned an act of provocation. Catholics in the city, still bitter about Burntollet, were no longer wedded to passivity. Crude barricades were erected around the Bogside ghetto and over 1,000 gallons of petrol were siphoned for the manufacture of Molotov cocktails. For two days, Derry burned.[24]

O'Neill had by this stage been forced from office by Protestant paranoia. The by-election in his Bannside seat was won by Paisley, who gained a new pulpit from which to preach. Meanwhile, the violence in Derry prompted the new prime minister, James Chichester-Clarke, to request the deployment of British troops in order to restore stability. The soldiers were at first welcomed by Catholics, on the assumption that they would protect them from Protestant violence. As the *Irish News* reported on 16 August 1969, the Catholic community 'knew that this force would be impartial'. Optimists hoped that British troops would provide the stability necessary for reform to proceed. The British, however, were less sanguine. Lieutenant General Sir Ian Freeland warned on 18 August that 'the honeymoon period could finish in a matter of hours'.[25]

An uneasy peace nevertheless prevailed for the first year of the deployment. Some clashes between Catholic protesters and British troops did occur, but these were isolated and easily contained. A change in mood, however, became apparent in June 1970 with the election of a Conservative government at Westminster. The fact that the Tories were generally sympathetic toward Unionism inspired new bravado among Orangemen and fresh despair among Catholics. On 3 July a curfew was imposed in the Lower Falls, coinciding with a search for weapons by the army. After some weapons were found, rioting broke out. CS gas, fired to disperse the crowd, instead acted like petrol on a bonfire. For thirty-six hours, violence ruled Belfast. By the time quiet was restored, five people were dead, all killed by British troops. The honeymoon was over.

The Catholic community concluded that Unionist bigotry was now being reinforced by British military power. In this situation, NICRA's non-violence seemed pointless. Frustration inspired a significant number of Catholics to look for salvation in the previously discredited IRA. NICRA deeply regretted but fully understood this development. The IRA offered a simple solution to a complicated problem. 'Violence,' it argued, 'had to be met with violence.'[26]

The IRA's renaissance allowed Stormont to act without pretence of restraint. Oppressing Catholics had required some circumspection; confronting terrorists did not. The new prime minister, Brian Faulkner, asked the Catholic community to understand that the state was 'at war with the terrorist and in a state of war many sacrifices have to be made and made in a cooperative and understanding manner'. In truth, this meant that Catholics were supposed to acquiesce in the trampling of their civil liberties. Under Operation Demetrius, the police and courts deployed the full force of the Special Powers Act. Internment was liberally used against those suspected of IRA involvement. The aim was to enfeeble the IRA. That failed, but the process was very effective in radicalizing ordinary citizens.[27]

Against an increasingly violent background, NICRA continued its campaign. On Sunday, 30 January 1972, a march in Derry's Bogside was met with a hail of bullets from trigger-happy British paratroopers. Why precisely they felt the need to fire upon unarmed, peaceful protesters has never been adequately explained. Fourteen men, half of them under the age of nineteen, were killed. The following day, the PD activist and MP Bernadette Devlin physically attacked Home Secretary Reginald Maudling in the House of Commons. 'It was our Sharpeville,' she remarked, 'and we shall never forget it.'[28]

In addition to the fourteen dead, Bloody Sunday had two other casualties. The first was non-violent protest. The Catholic community could no longer turn the other cheek when British soldiers were murdering peaceful marchers. Sympathy for the IRA increased massively, and recruitment rose accordingly. The province was now gripped by guerrilla war. As if to signal a new phase, three days after Bloody Sunday the British consulate in Dublin was burned to the ground.

The second casualty was Stormont. The British government decided that the province was incapable of self-government. The parliament was suspended and the affairs of the province were henceforward assumed by the Northern Ireland Office. Ulster became Britain's problem in a way that it had not been before. The violence was easily blamed on the IRA, for the simple reason that terrorists rarely have opportunity to explain. That was especially true after the IRA extended its campaign to the mainland. Fear of the IRA precluded an understanding of the Catholic predicament. The end of Stormont did not therefore mean the end of oppression.

Radicalized by injustice, frustrated by intransigence, Devlin demanded not change, but destruction. 'If we are serious – and I have never been more so – in our efforts to end the poverty, the greed, the hatred and fear within our society, then we must destroy the system that creates it, and build the Socialist Republic of Ireland.' Sentiments of that sort were spoken by many a Sixties radical, but seldom with such deadly intent. 'Today I realize that just as our present society is a way of life, so, too, is its destruction, and its destruction is my way of life . . . Yesterday I dared to struggle. Today I dare to win.'[29] However admirable and eloquent Devlin's defiance, it is hard to ignore the tragedy it wrought. In a struggle wedded to absolutes, every English person became an enemy. That logic inspired the bombs placed in two Birmingham pubs, which killed 21 people and injured 182 on 21 November 1974.

Historians don't usually speak of inevitabilities. A close examination of the provenance of any problem usually reveals roads not taken, crucial decisions not made, and errors committed. All those are apparent in the evolution of the Troubles, but it is nevertheless difficult to see real alternatives to what transpired. Northern Ireland is a mass of twisting roads, all leading to exactly the same calamity.

The Middle East: Yom Kippur

'We are fighting for the sake of peace,' claimed Egyptian President Anwar Sadat shortly after he launched a surprise attack on Israel in 1973. In the confused logic of the Middle East, it seemed entirely reasonable to go to war in search of peace.[30]

In the Six Day War of 1967, Israel swept aside Egypt, Syria and Jordan, taking the Sinai peninsula, the Golan Heights and the West Bank as the spoils of victory. David Ben-Gurion, first president of Israel, argued afterwards that all the conquered lands, except Jerusalem, should be returned to the Arabs, otherwise generations of Israelis would suffer terribly in defending them. Good sense, however, shrivelled in the bright sunshine of victory. Most Israelis equated land with security.

The reputation of Gamal Abdel Nasser, then the Egyptian president, suffered terribly as a result of defeat. He had cast himself as the leader of all Arabs, the man who would destroy Israel. Despite his failure, he remained determined to prove that this was a mere chapter in the Middle Eastern story, not its conclusion. The Israelis, on the other hand, were bent on proving the opposite. The war, therefore, settled little. Both sides continued to fight, by whatever means.

Nasser died in 1970 and was replaced by Anwar Sadat. He was 'Nasser's poodle', a man most Egyptians disparaged. Sadat believed that Nasser's policies had placed Egypt in a straitjacket, inhibiting the quest for peace and prosperity. Socialism was therefore jettisoned, as was Egypt's close relationship with the Soviet Union. The expulsion of 17,000 Soviet advisers was specifically calculated to impress the US, whose help Sadat craved. He was also prepared to break with other Arab nations over the question of Israel. An agreement was offered on the principle of land for peace – if Israel would withdraw from the occupied territories, Egypt would renounce war. The Israeli Cabinet summarily rejected that offer.[31]

Israeli intransigence placed Sadat in a cul-de-sac. The economic regeneration he desired could not be effected in an atmosphere of continuous conflict. In a meeting on 20 May 1973, Muhammad Ismail, Sadat's national security adviser, confessed to his American opposite number, Henry Kissinger, that, 'Every time we step forward . . . we are still in the middle of that morass, it is very frustrating.' According to one of Ismail's staffers, Kissinger replied: 'Don't expect to win on the negotiating table what you lost on the battlefield.' The Egyptians took that as a reminder of the Clausewitzian maxim that war is a continuation of policy by other means. While Kissinger denies that account, the Egyptians nevertheless came away feeling that something profound had to be done to alter the status quo. A sudden, dramatic victory in a limited war, Sadat decided, might force Tel Aviv and Washington to take seriously his desire to negotiate. As Major General Hassan El-Gretli, Egypt's chief of operations, later explained, the aim was 'to break the political stalemate in the Middle East . . . by . . . altering the strategic balance of power'.[32]

Sadat had reason to believe that he could succeed where Nasser had failed. Supplies of Soviet weaponry remained healthy but, more importantly, Egyptian forces had learned from their 1967 defeat. Incompetent generals had been cashiered, and tactical training had improved. Sadat could also draw comfort from the fact that Syria seemed a formidable ally. Her new president, Hafiz Assad, was determined to recover the Golan Heights. The Russian desire to maintain a toehold in the Middle East meant that Syria became the Soviets' new client state. A flood of weaponry eventually provided Assad with a significant material advantage on the Golan front.

Within Israel, opinion was deeply divided over the issue of land for peace. The prime minister, Golda Meir, felt that Israel should retain Gaza and East Jerusalem, but might negotiate over other areas. Hardliners like Menachem Begin of the Gahal Party and the warhorse Ariel Sharon, on the other hand, rejected any surrender of territory. Their intransigence was reinforced by a belief in Israel's military invincibility. Given Egypt's humiliation in 1967, it seemed unlikely to them that she would again resort to war. The Egyptian military, they assumed, remained in disarray and was further hobbled by the withdrawal of Soviet assistance. What the hardliners failed to appreciate, however, was that the 1967 victory had complicated Israel's strategic situation. Conquest had increased the points of vulnerability.

Israeli strategy depended on being able to anticipate, and therefore pre-empt, threats to her security. When questioned about the possibility of an Egyptian surprise attack, Director of Military Intelligence Major General Eli Zeira confidently told Meir: 'I am sure we will know about it ahead, and we will be able to [react] . . . a number of days in advance.' Hubris, however, clouded judgement. Because Israeli leaders refused to accept that Egypt posed a threat, they failed to recognize indications to the contrary. As one former intelligence official reflected: 'You cannot suspect a stupid enemy of deceiving you . . . because the mere fact that he can deceive you makes him smarter than you, an idea that was completely unacceptable.'[33]

The Arabs, Zeira argued on 24 April 1973, could not escape the logic of their own limitations. 'I think that in coming years . . . [they] do not estimate that they can win a war against Israel.' Evidence that Egypt was planning an attack was therefore rejected outright. Eleven clear-cut warnings of war were received during September and all were ignored. 'We simply didn't feel them capable,' Zvi Zamir, the chief of Mossad, later admitted. He did not change his mind until midnight on 5 October, when an intelligence source indicated attack was imminent. Instead of the few days' advance warning Israel required, she got just a few hours.[34]

At 08.05 on 6 October, Meir met Defence Minister Moshe Dayan and General David Elazar to discuss options. Dayan still doubted an attack. Elazar, on the other hand, advocated pre-emptive strikes.

Meir had to weigh the apparent sensibility of that advice against the likely reaction of the United States. 'If we strike first, we won't get help,' she warned. The room went quiet while she deliberated. 'No,' she concluded, 'I don't want . . . to spend the rest of my life explaining why we struck first . . . We will not strike first.' 'It was a hard decision,' the Israeli ambassador to Washington, Simcha Dinitz, later reflected. 'But it was right,' Kissinger told him. He later admitted that, if Israel had attacked, America would not have contributed 'so much as a nail'.[35]

In stark contrast to 1967, modest aims increased the likelihood of Egyptian and Syrian success. The goal was no longer to destroy Israel. Egypt wanted simply a limited victory which would eradicate the illusion of Israeli invincibility and force her to negotiate. Assad, likewise, wanted only the Golan Heights. Given the preparation that went into the attack, and the failure of Israel to take seriously the threat, both goals were eminently realizable.

On 6 October 1973 most Israelis were quietly observing Yom Kippur. Then, shortly after 14.00 hours, sirens screamed. In a perfectly orchestrated assault on the Sinai, 250 Egyptian aircraft hit Israeli airfields, SAM sites, radar installations, tank concentration areas, artillery positions and command posts. Around 95 per cent of targets were hit, at the loss of just five aircraft. At the same time, 2,000 Egyptian guns pounded Israeli positions in a fearsome barrage lasting fifty-three minutes. Bound for the airport when war erupted, Dinitz 'saw young boys taken from the synagogues. Right out of the synagogues. They were folding their talises, and getting their revolvers. It was a very dramatic sight.'[36]

Israeli hopes rested on the Bar Lev Line, a wall of concrete, sand and steel stretching 160 kilometres along the Suez waterline, designed to hold back an Egyptian onslaught until reserves could be mobilized. In the event of attack, oil was to be pumped into the canal and ignited, creating a wall of fire. Egyptian engineers had, however, come to terms with the Bar Lev Line. Prior to the attack, frogmen blocked the pipes through which oil was to be pumped. High pressure hoses then carved breaches in the wall of sand. Under cover of the artillery barrage, Egyptian commandos crossed the canal in rubber dinghies, armed with portable anti-tank weapons and guided missiles. Sharon later admitted that the Bar Lev was Israel's Maginot Line. It was 'a fundamentally wrong defense perception . . . no more than fortified bunkers with little ammunition. Due to their location and weakness, they had little value and were a dangerous burden.'[37]

'The attack on Sinai', *Time* reported, 'was carried out with a finesse and synchronization that not even most Arabs suspected that the Arabs possessed.' In less than four hours, Egypt moved 32,000 men across the canal, with fewer than 300 killed. In stark contrast to 1967, brand-new SAM air defences cut Israeli fighters to shreds. By the morning of the 7th, the Israelis had lost 300 tanks and 30 aircraft. The Egyptians advanced 4 or 5 kilometres, capturing the important town of Qantara on the 8th. Counter-attacks were brutally repulsed. 'The Egyptians were fighting well, not running away,' an Israeli tank colonel noted with conspicuous surprise. 'Our tactic the first two days was, as usual, to move forward, move forward. But as we advanced, we hit a wall of hundreds of missiles, tanks and heavy guns.'[38]

'We are heading for a catastrophe,' Dayan told Meir on the second day. He called for nuclear weapons to be readied, in the form of thirteen 20-kiloton battlefield devices. Debate still rages over whether Israel would actually have used the weapons – the move might simply have been designed to frighten the Americans into helping. If that was indeed the aim, it worked perfectly. The US responded with Operation Nickel Grass, a commitment to replace Israeli losses, to the tune of $2.2 billion. 'Without you, I don't know where we would have been,' Meir later told Kissinger. 'It was more than I could ever have dreamed.' The Americans paid dearly for their benificence – spurred by King Faisal of Saudi Arabia, the Arab petroleum-producing nations imposed an oil embargo on the United States which was not lifted until 17 March 1974.[39]

Israel's panic was exacerbated by her awareness that she was heavily outgunned on the Golan Heights. Against her 2 brigades, 11 artillery batteries and 180 tanks, Syria mobilized 5 divisions, 188 batteries and 1,300 tanks. Israelis fought with fierce determination, but could not achieve the impossible. Within six hours, the first line of defence was overrun, and a Syrian tank brigade was passing through the Rafid Gap, bound for Nafah, the Israeli Divisional Headquarters.

With Israeli reserves flooding into the Golan Heights, the tide began to turn on the 8th. By the 10th, all Syrian units had been pushed back to or beyond their original starting point. The Israelis now faced a dilemma: whether to transfer troops from the Golan Heights to the Sinai front or to use them for an offensive into Syria. Meir feared that, if she moved her troops, the war might end before they achieved anything positive. Feeling that Israel needed an undisputed victory to use as political leverage, she ordered a push into Syria. Over the next three days, the Israelis captured 50 square kilometres of Syrian territory and drew within artillery range of Damascus.

On the Sinai, Sadat had made his point. 'It doesn't matter if the Israelis eventually counter-attack and drive us back,' one Egyptian journalist remarked. 'What matters is that the world now no longer will laugh at us when we threaten to fight. No longer will it dismiss our threats as a lot of bluff and bluster. It will have to take us seriously.' Agreeing with that assessment, Sadat was inclined to call a halt, but the Syrian debacle forced his hand. Unwilling to let his ally fail, he ordered attacks to continue, in an effort to ease the pressure on the Syrians. This meant that Egyptian forces strayed beyond the range of their air defences, suddenly changing the temper of the fight. Israeli aircraft attacked Egyptian columns with impunity, cutting them to ribbons.[40]

Sharon counter-attacked on the 15th, quickly penetrating to the banks of the canal. A gigantic bridge was manoeuvred into position, allowing tanks to cross late on the 17th. With Israeli forces just 60 kilometres from Cairo, Sadat welcomed a UN ceasefire resolution, calling for the fighting to cease at 18.52 on the 22nd. That resolution arose from an agreement Kissinger had forged in Moscow the previous day. Since a technical problem prevented the Israelis from being informed of that agreement until four hours after the fact, Kissinger told Dinitz that 'we would understand if . . . [you] required some additional time for military dispositions before cease-fire takes effect'.[41]

Unbeknownst to Kissinger, the Israelis were bent on annihilation. They had the Egyptian Third Army trapped in an impossible position east of the Suez Canal. Under pressure from hawks hovering around her, Meir allowed her forces to violate the ceasefire. When Kissinger met her in Tel Aviv at 13.35 on the 22nd, he gave her the green light to do so. 'You won't get violent protests from Washington if something happens during the night, while I'm flying,' he said. 'Nothing can happen in Washington until noon tomorrow.' He did not realize that Meir had in mind the destruction of the Third Army. 'You . . . didn't tell me what you intended,' he later complained. 'I had no reason to think twelve more hours, twenty-four more hours, were decisive . . . Then you took on the Third Army after the cease-fire.'[42]

Sadat rightly felt betrayed. Kissinger had assured the Egyptians, on the 21st, that 'as the fighting ceases, the US will use its influence to secure a lasting peace in the Middle East on a basis just for all parties'. Yet here he was allowing the Israelis to continue fighting. 'We were asked to comply with the ceasefire resolution with the full understanding of the effectiveness of the joint guarantees,' Sadat complained to Nixon on the 23rd. 'The Egyptian Government will consider the US Government fully responsible for what is happening.' He urged the US to intervene, 'even if that necessitates the use of force'.[43]

The Soviets were meanwhile growing increasingly impatient with Nixon's inability to control his ally. 'We would like to believe that . . . everything will be done in order that the Security Council decision . . . will be implemented,' Brezhnev remarked on the 23rd. 'Too much is at stake, not only as concerns the situation in the Middle East, but in our relations as well.' In a note to Nixon sent late the next day, he called for a UN peacekeeping force, consisting of Russian and American troops, to be inserted between the opposing armies. 'I will say it straight that if you find it impossible to act jointly with us in this matter, we should be faced with the necessity urgently to consider taking appropriate steps *unilaterally*.' Seven Soviet airborne divisions were placed on alert. Under no circumstances could the US countenance such a development. 'We were determined to resist by force if necessary the introduction of Soviet forces into the Middle East regardless of the pretext on which they arrived,' Kissinger later explained.[44]

Nixon, in the depths of despair over Watergate, was drinking heavily and taking sedatives. The Brezhnev note arrived after he had dragged himself to bed. Kissinger and Alexander Haig, the chief of staff, briefly debated waking him. He was 'too distraught', they concluded; 'he would just start charging around'.[45] Instead, they sent a somewhat conciliatory response to Brezhnev in Nixon's name, while simultaneously urging Sadat not to push for Soviet help. Rather crucially, they also changed the Defense Condition (DefCon) from four to three, 'the highest stage of readiness for essentially peacetime conditions'. The Soviets, taken aback, decided the issue unworthy of global nuclear war. 'It was our strategy to deliberately overreact,' Kissinger aide Peter Rodman later admitted. 'You had to scare them off.'[46]

'Let's not broadcast this all over the place,' Kissinger advised Haig, 'otherwise it looks like we cooked it up.' When Nixon awoke the next morning and learned of the momentous decisions made in his name, he congratulated his aides on 'a hell of a job'. That was an accurate assessment. The US now found itself in the perfect position to derive diplomatic advantage from the war. With the Soviet Union effectively neutralized, the US was now the only power capable of preventing the Third Army's destruction. 'The events of the last two weeks have been on the whole a major success,' a smug Kissinger told his staff. 'We are really in the central position . . . the fact of the matter is that any rational Arab leader now has to know that whether he hates us, loves us, despises us, there is no way around us. If they want a settlement in the Middle East, it has to come through us.' Exercising that influence, Kissinger told Dinitz that under no circumstances should the Third Army be destroyed.[47]

Sadat was only too eager to play ball. His foreign minister, Ismail Fahmy, met Kissinger and Nixon on 29 October and made it clear that Egypt wanted improved relations with the US. As a measure of his sincerity, Sadat conceded that a resolution of the Palestinian issue would no longer be a precondition of peace. In other words, Egypt would not allow Nasser's illusion of Arab solidarity to impede progress.

Meir proved more cantankerous. When she visited Washington on 1 November, she protested that destruction of the Third Army was appropriate retribution for Egypt's aggression. Kissinger wanted a withdrawal to positions extant when the ceasefire went into effect, but she demurred. 'We didn't start the war!' she shouted. 'Nor did we lose. Now we get these demands.' In a subsequent meeting, Nixon gave Meir a blunt warning: 'If the ceasefire breaks down and we have another deadly round, how much we could do is very much open to question . . . Of course, I could leave you to the UN.' The next day, Kissinger and Meir reiterated the same arguments, with increasing bitterness. 'You're saying we have no choice,' Meir lamented, her voice shaking. Kissinger repeated that the US would cut Israel loose if she attacked. 'You're saying we have to accept the judgement of the US,' she grunted. 'I'm telling you to face the facts,' he retorted. That turned out to be enough. Kissinger realized that Meir needed to be able to tell the Knesset that her hand had been forced.[48]

After a whirlwind week of diplomacy, Kissinger saw Sadat in Cairo on 7 November and obtained his agreement to a six-point plan to end the war based roughly on UN proposals already tabled. The Israelis grudgingly accepted the plan on 11 November. A week later, both sides began to withdraw their forces. Negotiations with Assad proved much more complicated, extending well into the new year. It was, however, eventually agreed that Israel would retain the Golan Heights, but that a demilitarized zone would separate the two sides.

'It was a very difficult war,' Sharon later reflected. 'It was a great victory of the forces that fought in the battlefield.' Those forces were, however, hobbled by 'the failure of the higher command in the rear'. Losses, including around 2,200 dead, were heavier than for any conflict in Israel's history. Serious mistakes were made at every level of command and panic, heretofore unknown, had been apparent. A nation known for its vigilance had been caught unprepared. Some leaders paid dearly for their mistakes, but in truth failure was ubiquitous. The war shattered the myth of a nation so blessed as to be invincible.[49]

For Israel, the Yom Kippur War proved a rite of passage. The settlement revealed painful truths about her dependence upon America. The facts of failure were difficult to swallow, but swallowing them allowed a healthier realism to prevail. As Kissinger remarked, the war had resulted in 'a realization . . . that this cockiness of supremacy is no longer possible; that like other countries in history, [the Israelis] now have to depend on a combination of security and diplomacy'. Perhaps the most significant result of the war, for Israel, was the way opinion polls afterwards revealed a desire not for revenge, but for negotiated peace, even at the cost of territory.[50]

Sadat's war should be judged by its first two days, for in that time he gained precisely what he sought. 'However the battle might end,' *Time* commented, 'it was already clear that the Arabs had never fought better against the Israelis. No longer were they so likely to be dismissed as powerless and posturing giants too weak to defeat the tiniest of neighbors.' In place of Nasser's febrile bluster, Sadat had delivered hard results. His willingness to use his newly established credibility to make a clean break from the past showed admirable insight and courage. The Nasser era was clearly over, brought to an end by a man once considered a lightweight.[51]

Vietnam: Peace with Honour?

'There's no way to win the war,' Nixon privately confessed nearly a year before becoming president. 'But we can't say that, of course . . . we have to seem to say the opposite, just to keep some degree of bargaining leverage.' For four years, Nixon tried to fool the North Vietnamese into thinking he sought victory. Hanoi, however, was not easily duped. The politburo simply waited for Nixon to turn into the person he was elected to be: a peace president. While they waited, thousands died acting out Nixon's charade. 'How do you ask a man to be the last man to die for a mistake?' Lieutenant John Kerry asked the Senate Foreign Relations Committee on 22 April 1971. No one replied.[52]

The Tet Offensive of January 1968 was a turning point in the war, but did not hasten peace. Though communist strength was sapped, their will remained formidable. In contrast, the Americans still possessed the strength, but lacked the will. This dynamic implied protracted disengagement. Rather like two tired boxers in the final rounds of a match, both sides could still inflict pain but could not deliver a knockout blow.

The People's Liberation Armed Forces (PLAF, or Viet Cong) paid dearly for the Tet disaster. They expected a decisive victory but encountered instead annihilation. One veteran who defected in 1970 revealed that 'the men were tired of fighting, afraid of death, and felt they were losing the war'. A local party official confirmed that cadres had 'lost confidence . . . in the revolutionary capability of the people' and were 'doubtful of victory'.[53] Soldiers were told that victory would come 'not suddenly but in a complicated and tortuous way'.[54]

The depletion of the Viet Cong brought scant advantage to the United States, however, since the enemy was far from beaten. The communists could still rely on the crack troops of the People's Army of Vietnam (PAVN), professional soldiers from the North heretofore held in reserve. 'The North Vietnamese have access to sufficient manpower to meet their replenishment needs . . . for at least the next several years,' the National Security Council advised Nixon on 21 January 1969. The NSC warned that the North would still be able to 'launch major offensives'.[55]

Americans had lost faith in the war, but had no idea how to end it. Nixon insisted that the US could not simply cut and run. A humiliating withdrawal would, he feared, compromise America's ability to carry out her foreign policy goals. He wanted 'to end the war as quickly as was honorably possible', but honour and speed were contradictory. 'I've been saying, "an honorable end to the war", but what the hell does that mean?' he privately confessed during the presidental campaign. He nevertheless assumed he could master this dilemma. 'I'm not going to end up like LBJ, holed up in the White House afraid to show my face in the street,' he boasted. 'I'm going to stop that war. Fast.'[56]

Formal peace talks, mired in acrimony since March 1968, offered little hope of breakthrough. Nixon tried another route, sending Kissinger to Paris for secret talks with the North Vietnamese diplomat Le Duc Tho. Desperate to get these talks moving, he applied pressure in an unorthodox way. 'Measures of great consequence' would be taken, if progress was not apparent by 1 November 1969. Confident that his reputation preceded him, Nixon felt no need to elaborate. 'I call it the Madman Theory,' he told his aides. 'I want the North Vietnamese to believe I've reached the point where I might do *anything* to stop the war. We'll just slip the word to them that "for god's sake, you know Nixon is obsessed about Communism. We can't restrain him when he's angry - and he has his hand on the nuclear button" - and Ho Chi Minh himself will be in Paris in two days begging for peace.'[57]

Nixon intentionally encouraged the belief that he might actually push for complete victory. Operation Duck Hook drove this point home. A programme of retaliatory actions to be taken if negotiations stalled, it included intensive bombing of urban areas, destruction of dykes, mining of rivers and harbours, a ground invasion, and nuclear strikes. Though supposedly secret, the plan was carefully leaked to Hanoi. 'Once the enemy recognizes that it is not going to win its objectives by waiting us out,' Nixon told a press conference in September 1969, 'then the enemy will negotiate and we will end this war before the end of 1970.'[58]

Hanoi remained unimpressed. The politburo stuck to its own agenda, known as *danh va dam, dam va danh* ('fighting while talking, talking while fighting'). Pressure on the battlefield was designed to make Americans desperate for peace, while formal peace discussions eroded their will to fight. Nixon's troop withdrawals, more than his hollow threats, confirmed the wisdom of this strategy. By the end of 1969, cuts of 110,000 troops had been announced, with a promise that at least as many would leave during 1970. This sent a clear message to the communists that they need only wait patiently for the last American to leave. Annoyed that his bluff had been called, Nixon blasted Hanoi's 'absolute refusal to show the least willingness to join us in seeking a just peace . . . it is convinced that all it has to do is to wait for our next concession, and our next concession after that one, until it gets everything it wants'.[59]

That elusive honour complicated the peace process. 'A nation cannot remain great if it betrays its allies and lets down its friends,' Nixon warned Americans on 3 November 1969. To cut and run would 'result in a collapse of confidence in American leadership not only in Asia but throughout the world . . . Far more dangerous, we would lose confidence in ourselves . . . inevitable remorse and divisive recrimination would scar our spirit.' Nixon's solution was to buttress the South Vietnamese ally – a strategy called Vietnamization. Henceforth, 'the primary mission of our troops' would be 'to enable the South Vietnamese forces to assume . . . full responsibility for the security of South Vietnam'. If the Army of the Republic of Vietnam (ARVN) could be strengthened, while communist forces were weakened, a stalemate might result and a settlement similar to that forged in Korea might result. Privately, Kissinger admitted that the administration wanted a 'decent interval' between American withdrawal and ARVN defeat. Nixon, however, had difficulty abandoning his desire to destroy. As late as June 1971, he was still looking for ways to 'level that goddamn country'.[60]

Vietnamization had, in truth, been going on since November 1967. Nixon, however, took an existing policy and magnified it with money, to the extent that ARVN commanders called it the 'US Dollar and Vietnamese Blood Sharing Plan'. By the beginning of 1972, South Vietnam had 120 infantry battalions, 58 artillery battalions, 19 battalion-sized armoured units, 1,680 naval craft, over 1,000 aeroplanes, and 500 helicopters. Its air force was the fourth largest in the world. Police and militia units added another 670,000 men to overall troop strength. Bigger did not, however, mean better. The ARVN suffered from the same problems that had always plagued it, namely a lack of commitment, expressed in an alarmingly high desertion rate. The ordinary soldier's loyalty was steadily eroded by the corruption of his officers and government. It was difficult to serve leaders who cheated and stole from their people. A 1969 Senate report identified a classic Catch-22: Vietnamization was essential to keep the government of Nguyen van Thieu in power, but 'if [his] . . . government remains in power . . . Vietnamization will fail'.[61]

Vietnamization went hand in hand with pacification, which, put bluntly, meant killing communists, by whatever means. While Nixon, in his more lucid moments, accepted that a communist victory was inevitable, he still wanted them to pay dearly for it. This explains why the 'peace president' widened the war by sending troops into Laos and Cambodia, the aim being to root out Viet Cong sanctuaries and to cut the Ho Chi Minh trail. 'This is not an invasion of Cambodia,' Nixon insisted to those confused by the action. An illegal operation was justified by assigning it a noble purpose. 'If, when the chips are down, the world's most powerful nation . . . acts like a pitiful, helpless giant, the forces of totalitarianism and anarchy will threaten free nations and free institutions around the world.'[62]

Pacification brought an intensification of covert operations – assassination, torture and other 'black ops'. The most notorious programme was called Phoenix, an effort begun in 1967, with help from the CIA. It entailed paying the South Vietnamese to do things civilized Americans were not supposed to do. Trained agents were inserted into over 300 villages, in order to root out communists. Funding was provided by the Americans, but the agents answered to the Republic of Vietnam, which meant that Phoenix became yet another manifestation of Saigon venality. The sadistic thugs who administered the programme were more interested in financial reward than genuine counter-insurgency. Rewards of up to $11,000 for a live communist opened the floodgates of fraud. Entirely innocent villagers were kidnapped and offered a stark choice: pay a hefty ransom or face exposure as a communist. Communist cadres joined the fun by pretending to be supporters of the Saigon regime, informing on their enemies, and then collecting the reward. The official policy, namely that 'it was better to detain the suspect than to free the criminal', encouraged massive miscarriages of justice. Thousands were captured (and killed), but few were actually communists. The net effect was alienation – 'to create new Viet Cong rather than to "root out" established operatives', one CIA agent admitted. Critics pointed out that America was employing torture and assassination to pursue her moral mission. 'I sometimes think we would have gotten better publicity by molesting children,' an American official confessed in 1972.[63]

Pacification severely weakened the enemy, but it did not encourage confidence in the Saigon government. Peasants, as always, maintained an attitude of *attentisme* – they sat on the fence. An American study in 1972 concluded that less than 20 per cent of peasants wanted American troops to stay, even though it was widely understood that their departure would allow the communists to triumph. The communists of the National Liberation Front were hated, but so too was the Saigon regime. The two sides competed in cruelty and corruption, with peasants caught in the middle – exiles in their own country.

As the 1972 election approached, Nixon's boast about a quick end to the war seemed a cruel joke. Negotiations had stalled and Vietnamization was a sham. The only good news was troop withdrawals – only 50,000 Americans remained by June 1972. Withdrawals also heartened the North Vietnamese, however. They rightly concluded that, since the momentum was inexorable, there was no reason to cooperate at the peace talks. On 26 January 1972, Kissinger accused Hanoi of holding out for a peace settlement 'in which the probability of their taking over is close to certainty'. That was precisely the strategy, but complaining about it did not alter its effectiveness.[64]

Nixon's efforts to disengage had been unsuccessful because he found it impossible to give up on victory. 'If we fail,' he remarked in March 1971, 'this country will have suffered a blow from which it will never recover and become a world power again . . . You can't fail after staying through six years . . . We've got to win. And by winning . . . I mean assuring a reasonable chance for South Vietnam to live in peace.' Desperate and frustrated, Nixon shifted to great power diplomacy. He and Kissinger decided that, if deals could be struck with the Soviet Union and China, the importance of Vietnam to great power relations could be reduced and an acceptable settlement would be easier to achieve.[65]

Much to the dismay of Hanoi, the Chinese were susceptible to Nixon's flirtation. In March 1971, Zhou Enlai informed Hanoi that, since the war was nearly over, Vietnamese problems would no longer be allowed to impede an improvement of Sino-American relations. In July, Kissinger visited Beijing and told Zhou that the Vietnam war was 'history . . . our problem now is how to end it'. He added that, 'Our position is not to maintain any particular government in South Vietnam . . . If the government is as unpopular as you seem to think, then the quicker our forces are withdrawn the quicker it will be overthrown. And if it is overthrown . . . we will not intervene.' The Chinese responded by pressuring the Vietnamese to accept a compromise.[66]

Diplomacy with the Soviets was less fruitful. Nixon and Kissinger failed to take into account that they needed agreement more than the Russians did. This gave the USSR the upper hand, which they used cleverly. The Soviets gained some lucrative trade deals and, more importantly, détente made them feel more secure on their European frontier. The Americans, while benefiting from détente, did not get a solid commitment from the Soviets to pressure Hanoi to end the war. The main problem with the Nixon/Kissinger triangular diplomacy was that it did not take sufficient account of Sino-Soviet rivalries. Deals with both sides merely intensified the distrust each felt for the other. Hanoi benefited handsomely from this rivalry. While Nixon achieved improved relations with the Soviet Union and China, the aid both countries sent to North Vietnam actually doubled from 1971 to 1972. North Vietnam was like the spoilt child who cleverly manipulates his parents' messy divorce.

In March 1972, Hanoi decided its hour had come. With American troop levels severely reduced, the time seemed ripe for a final push. The Nguyen Hue (or 'Easter') Offensive, launched on 30 March, was a three-pronged attack on major South Vietnamese cities, involving 125,000 troops, supported by hundreds of tanks. On hearing of the attack, Nixon went ballistic. 'We are not going . . . [to] be defeated by this little shit-ass country,' he spat. 'I intend to stop at nothing to bring the enemy to his knees.' Kissinger agreed that the US should 'blast the living bejeezus out of North Vietnam'. Air squadrons and carrier forces, headed for home, were ordered back to implement Operation Linebacker, a bombing campaign that dwarfed anything previously inflicted on the North. 'The bastards have never been bombed like they're going to be bombed this time,' Nixon promised. While Hanoi and Haiphong were spared, other cities were literally wiped off the map. Most Americans, unable to summon Nixon's anger, struggled to understand.[67]

ARVN forces were initially forced to retreat, but then, in early May, the PAVN advance slowed. Devastated by American air power, the communists were pushed back, with prodigious losses. Probably 75,000 soldiers were killed, and 700 tanks destroyed. The result suggested that the ARVN could hold its own and that Vietnamization was working. That was certainly the message Nixon conveyed, but in truth the deciding factor in the battle was American air power, an asset that would soon disappear. Kept under wraps by Washington was the growing evidence that the South Vietnamese peasantry were abandoning *attentisme* and throwing their weight behind the revolution – out of self-preservation if nothing else. The Americans were powerless to stop that development, since they were headed for the door. In mid-August, just before the Republican convention opened in Miami, the last American combat soldier left Vietnam.

The combined effect of severe losses in the Easter Offensive and the certainty that Nixon would be re-elected made the Vietnamese more malleable in the peace talks. Hanoi accepted a proposal for a tripartite council, to consist of representatives of the Saigon regime, the communists and neutral elements. A euphoric Kissinger announced that 'peace is at hand'. An angry Thieu, however, vetoed the deal, accusing Kissinger of being more interested in a Nobel Prize than in the fate of South Vietnam. '[Thieu] has chosen to act the martyr', Kissinger screamed, 'but he hasn't got what it takes! If we have to, the United States can sign a separate treaty with Hanoi. As for me, I'll never set foot in Saigon again . . . This is the worst failure of my diplomatic career!' Nixon sympathized but felt he could not abandon his ally on the eve of the American election. Kissinger was ordered back to Paris, where talks soon stalled. He railed at the way 'a little fourth rate power like Vietnam' had treated him. 'They're just a bunch of shits. Tawdry, filthy shits.'[68]

Nixon, in agreement with that assessment, decided that the time had come to teach those 'shits' a lesson. His confidence magnified by his landslide election victory, he ordered airstrikes on 19 December. The notorious Christmas bombing, or Linebacker II, was designed to get a 'message through to Hanoi'. For twelve days, North Vietnam was attacked incessantly – by night with B-52s and F-111s, during the day with tactical strike aircraft. 'This is your chance to use military power to win the war,' Nixon told Admiral Thomas Moorer. 'If you don't, I'll consider you responsible.' In all, 1,369 sorties dropped around 20,000 tons of bombs in the Hanoi–Haiphong area. Anger carried high cost – the US lost twenty-six aircraft, including fifteen B-52s. Twenty-nine crewmen were killed, and thirty-three captured.[69]

Joan Baez was on a humanitarian mission to Hanoi, along with a group that included retired Brigadier General Telford Taylor. It seemed safe to go since the war was almost over. Then came the bombs. 'It was like thunder, the kind of thunder that rolls and rolls,' she later wrote. 'I realized with shame and horror that to pray for the planes to go away was to pray that they would drop their bombs somewhere else.' Just after Christmas, the group visited American prisoners at a POW camp. 'I don't understand,' one of them said, while holding up a large piece of shrapnel that had almost killed him during the night. 'What don't you understand?' Baez asked incredulously, since this man was, after all, a pilot. 'Kissinger said peace was at hand, isn't that what he said?' 'That's what he said,' a now tearful Baez replied. 'Maybe he didn't mean it. They lie a lot.'[70]

Nixon assumed that the American people would not 'give a damn' about his lies. He was wrong. At home, bewilderment blended with anger. The journalist James Reston dubbed Linebacker II 'war by tantrum', while the *Washington Post* argued that Nixon 'has conducted a bombing policy . . . so ruthless and so difficult to fathom politically as to cause millions of Americans to cringe in shame and to wonder at their President's very sanity'. Apparently, that was the image Nixon wanted to convey. An old strategy had been reprised. 'The Russians and the Chinese might think they were dealing with a madman,' he explained to a reporter. They would 'force North Vietnam into a settlement before the world was consumed by a larger war'. Granted, talks did resume, in part because of the bombing. In truth, however, the North Vietnamese returned to Paris because they knew they would get, at the very least, the terms offered in October. In other words, the bombing achieved nothing.[71]

On 9 January 1973, both sides agreed that reunification of Vietnam would be 'carried out . . . through peaceful means on the basis of discussions and agreements between North and South Vietnam, without coercion or annexation by either party, and without foreign interference'. The vague wording made the settlement acceptable to Washington and Hanoi, but not to Saigon. Thieu felt betrayed. He objected especially to the fact that PAVN troops would be allowed to remain in the south of Vietnam, with triggers cocked. Nixon had, however, given up on trying to please Thieu. All he would offer was his word that, if Hanoi violated the settlement, he would 'respond with full force' – a direct contradiction of what Kissinger had told Zhou. 'You can count on us,' the president insisted. Thieu was left with the cold comfort of a Nixon promise.[72]

Hanoi was delighted. Officials privately admitted that the settlement provided 'a great opportunity for revolutionary violence, for gaining power in South Vietnam . . . and for making great leaps in the balance of forces'. No one, certainly not the Americans, expected Hanoi to behave. The settlement was acceptable to Washington because it allowed that illusive 'peace with honour' Nixon had promised in 1968. Kissinger privately admitted that, with a little luck, the South Vietnamese might 'hold out for a year or two'. The original reason for the war, namely to maintain the integrity of a non-communist South Vietnam, had long been abandoned. All the Americans wanted was the 'decent interval' – a settlement that would allow them to withdraw while the Thieu government remained intact. Few really cared if his regime lasted. Nixon's greatest success lay in transforming Vietnam into a country of no real importance.[73]

The remarks of an American Legion commander aptly summarized American reaction. 'There's nothing to celebrate,' he said, 'and nobody to celebrate with.' The Nixon administration spent four years in search of peace with honour, sacrificing over 20,000 American lives in the process. Nixon hoped to preserve American dignity, yet that dignity was compromised by the methods he used – the lies, deceit, bullying, bombing and torture. He brought American troops home, but their homecoming was hardly joyous. Given the malaise which afflicted the US after Vietnam, it is not certain that the delay was worthwhile, nor that Nixon achieved his purpose. The extra years of war, and the additional sacrifice, did not establish a country at peace with itself.[74]

South Africa: Biko

'Why do you call yourself black, when your skin is brown?' a white South African judge once asked Steve Biko. 'Why do you call yourself white, when you are actually pink?' he shot back. That response perfectly encapsulated Biko's activism. His philosophy was rooted in the concept of internal oppression – that blacks were subjugated by their own sense of inferiority. The strength of apartheid, he believed, lay in the psychological effect it had in causing blacks to conform to racist stereotypes. He was the perfect person to instil confidence in his fellow blacks, since he had no lack of it himself. Being black, he insisted, 'is not a matter of pigmentation – being black is a reflection of a mental attitude'.[75]

The Bantu Education Act of 1953 was designed to prepare blacks for a life of back-breaking labour, not to offer them an escape from that fate. But while limits could be placed on what was taught, it was impossible to limit what might be learned. From an early age, Biko sought liberation through education. 'He read everything he could lay his hands on,' a fellow student recalled. 'As a medical student, he could debate with me, an English major, the finer points of literary criticism of Shakespeare and the novels of George Eliot. He understood the politics of decolonisation in Africa and India. He had insight into the anti-imperial wars throughout Africa and in Vietnam. And he had a critical understanding of the politics of the civil rights movement in the United States.' The journalist Donald Woods was immediately impressed by his 'quick brain, superb articulation of ideas and sheer mental force'. During his career, Woods interviewed many prominent political figures, but 'Steve Biko . . . was the greatest man I ever had the privilege to know'.[76]

Biko's participation in the apartheid education system did not imply surrender to its values. He was expelled from his first school because of 'anti-establishment behaviour' – or, more precisely, outspoken opposition to apartheid. That did not, however, stop him from gaining admission to the University of Natal Medical School – specifically, the segregated faculty designed to train black doctors for the black community. In Natal, his political activism continued, through the vehicle of the National Union of South African Students – a multiracial group. Before long, however, the domination of NUSAS by white liberals caused Biko to conclude that it had little to offer the black population. Blacks, he argued, 'are tired of standing at the touchlines to witness a game that they should be playing. They want to do things for themselves and all by themselves.' An unbridgeable chasm developed between white liberals and the blacks they hoped to help. 'It [became] increasingly difficult to find any common ground,' Raymond Whittaker, a NUSAS activist, recalled. 'To the horror of the well-meaning whites . . . their black counterparts began to accuse them of holding back the cause of black empowerment through paternalism and unconscious racism.' Biko resigned in 1969 and formed instead the South African Students' Organisation (SASO). Its slogan summed up his philosophy: 'Black man, you are on your own.'[77]

The apartheid system was perhaps never as formidable as during the 1970s. International condemnation was strident but ineffectual.

Economic prosperity gave South Africa the confidence to ignore protests, safe in the knowledge that the world would continue to want its cheap produce, minerals and wine. An efficient and heavily funded security system kept internal opposition in check, with occasional unrest sparking brutal repression. The dire poverty suffered by black workers sapped their will to resist, while middle-class blacks cleverly played the system.

'The most potent weapon in the hands of the oppressor', Biko argued in 1971, 'is the mind of the oppressed.' The strength of apartheid, he felt, lay in its ability to persuade blacks to accept subservience. The system produced 'a kind of black man that is man only in form'. As a result of this dehumanization, 'the black man has become . . . a shadow of man, completely defeated, drowning in his own misery, a slave, an ox bearing the yoke of oppression with sheepish timidity'. SASO trumpeted the new radical doctrine of Black Consciousness – what Biko called the 'cultural and political revival of an oppressed people'. Blacks were encouraged 'to judge themselves'. Freedom came in liberating oneself from white values. 'The first step,' he argued, was 'to pump back life into his empty shell; to infuse him with pride and dignity, to remind him of his complicity in . . . letting evil reign supreme in the country of his birth.' This meant being proud of blackness. 'By describing yourself as black,' he argued, 'you have started on the road to emancipation, you have committed yourself to fight against all forces that seek to use your blackness as a stamp that marks you out as a subservient being.'[78]

By 1971, Biko was ready to extend Black Consciousness beyond the universities and into the oppressed communities, where feelings of inferiority were cancerous. He figured prominently in the establishment of the Black Peoples Convention (BPC), which brought together around seventy activist groups, all concentrating on concrete social projects designed to energize the oppressed. This activism caused his expulsion from medical school, a not unexpected development that confirmed his destiny as a full-time rebel.

In contrast to white liberals and most middle-class blacks, Biko did not advocate integration. As his colleague Bennie Khoapa explained, 'integration is irrelevant to a people who are powerless'. Liberation was 'far more important than physical proximity to white people'. Consciousness had first to be improved – on both sides. 'Whites must be made to realise that they are only human, not superior,' Biko argued. 'Same with Blacks. They must be made to realise that they are also human, not inferior.' Only with mutual respect could meaningful integration proceed. This could not, however, be achieved if blacks continued to suffer an 'inferiority complex – a result of 300 years of deliberate oppression, denigration and derision'. The first prerequisite was the 'very strong grass-roots build up of black consciousness' which would allow blacks to 'learn to assert themselves and stake their rightful claim'.[79]

Working with (or rather under) white liberals merely reinforced that sense of inferiority. White liberals, argued Biko, 'vacillate between the two worlds, verbalising all the complaints of the blacks beautifully while skilfully extracting what suits them from the exclusive pool of white privilege. But ask them for a moment to give a concrete meaningful programme that they intend adopting, and then you will see on whose side they really are.' Liberation, in other words, could only come through a movement confined to those in need of liberating. 'The white man', Khoapa argued, 'is free to aid . . . liberation by contributing information, sweat, money and blood, but he is not free to join that struggle or to lead it.'[80]

White liberals objected that they had been transformed from allies into enemies. They rejected the separatism inherent in Black Consciousness, comparing it to the evil notion of white supremacy. Biko countered that white liberals insisted upon seeing black oppression as 'a problem that has to be solved' – something external to themselves. There was, he insisted, no 'black problem' in South Africa. 'There is nothing the matter with blacks. The problem is WHITE RACISM and it rests squarely on the laps of white society . . . White liberals must leave blacks to take care of their own business while they concern themselves with the real evil in our society – white racism.'[81]

The apartheid government of Prime Minister John Vorster delighted in the discomfiture Biko caused white liberals. He was therefore given a long leash, on the assumption that his calls for black power would split the anti-apartheid movement. That proved a mistake. While Biko did cause discord within the movement, that was inconsequential compared to the energizing effect he had upon ordinary blacks in the townships. Eventually alerted to the threat Biko posed, the Vorster government belatedly took action. He was prevented from travelling outside his hometown and was prohibited from speaking in public or publishing his thoughts. His ideas were effectively banned, with severe penalties imposed on those who quoted him.

Biko could not, however, be neutralized. His influence was readily apparent in June 1976, when black students in Soweto, fired by Black Consciousness, took to the streets in a demonstration against apartheid. The uprising began among students protesting against the compulsory use of Afrikaans in schools, but soon spread to townships across the country. While the demonstrations started peacefully, activists were by no means wedded to non-violence and in fact saw violence as a legitimate expression of black pride. The brutal response of the police in turn demonstrated just how far the apartheid regime was prepared to go to continue black oppression. This turn to violence worried Biko. 'There are alternatives,' he argued. 'We believe there is a way of getting to where we want to go through peaceful means.' He feared that violence played into the hands of the apartheid government by converting a theoretical argument into a physical one. 'We operate on the assumption that we can bring whites to their senses by confronting them with our overwhelming demands,' he argued. As he repeatedly stressed, 'ideas and men are stronger than weapons'.[82]

As time passed, the regime grew increasingly frustrated at its inability to silence Biko. On numerous occasions he was jailed and interrogated. He did not, however, fear for his life, since he believed that the government still retained a vestigial respect for the law. 'They're not completely fascist *yet*,' he maintained. That assumption proved misguided. On 21 August 1977, Biko was arrested on suspicion of fomenting unrest in the Port Elizabeth area and of distributing pamphlets urging 'violence and arson'. Two weeks later, during the course of his interrogation, he sustained a head injury. Doctors who examined him did not at first detect a neurological injury. On 11 September, however, he slipped into a semi-comatose state and a police physician recommended hospitalization. For reasons unknown, he was instead transported 1,200 miles to Pretoria Central Prison – a trip made while lying naked in the back of a Land Rover. Shortly after his arrival, on 12 September, Biko died. He was thirty years old.[83]

The government at first claimed that Biko had died in a Pretoria hospital as a result of refusing food and water. His condition had been closely monitored, but, after appearing 'unwell' on the seventh day of his strike, he died suddenly and unexpectedly. When that story failed to stand up to serious press scrutiny, the authorities abandoned it. An inquest concocted a new explanation. The chief magistrate of Pretoria, Martinus Prins, explained that, during a peaceful interrogation, Biko went 'berserk'. In the process of restraining him, he suffered a brain injury that proved fatal. Eastern Cape security police commander, Colonel Pieter Goosen, speculated that Biko must have 'bump[ed] his head' during the scuffle. In fact, a post-mortem revealed that he had suffered five major brain lesions, a scalp wound, bruising around the ribs, and various cuts and abrasions. The inquest nevertheless concluded that 'the available evidence does not prove the death was brought about by an act or omission involving any offence by any person'.[84]

Perhaps inevitably, Biko's funeral on 25 September was transformed into a powerful political demonstration against apartheid. Its impact was magnified by the rather clumsy attempts by security forces to contain the grief and anger. Heavily armed police set up roadblocks to prevent mourners from converging on the gravesite. Those from the Transvaal found that they were denied permits to travel on buses. In Soweto, police dragged mourners from buses and attacked them with truncheons. The ceremony, which lasted most of the day, was nevertheless punctuated by the cries of black mourners, who punched the air and shouted a single, simple word – 'Power!'

Biko's death sparked a huge outcry, both in South Africa and around the world. When the result of the inquest was announced on 2 December, 200 supporters held an impromptu demonstration, chanting 'They have killed Steve Biko. What have we done? Our sin is that we are black?' 'I'm just afraid that . . . reason may not prevail,' Woods warned. 'Since the death . . . was announced I have received gloating messages from white racists who rejoice in his death and believe it will aid their cause. They don't realize to what extent his moderation was preserving the brittle peace in this country.' Chief Gaisha Buthelezi, leader of the country's 6 million Zulus, who had frequently criticized Biko's militancy, likewise warned of ominous implications. 'I will not be able to curb my people, and indeed I soon may not want to curb my people, when they adopt an attitude of an eye for an eye and a tooth for a tooth.'[85]

The brutality of Biko's death, and the contempt shown by South African authorities in their cover-up, caused opposition to apartheid to coalesce in a way that had previously seemed impossible. A significant number of nations imposed economic sanctions against South Africa and, after sustained pressure, the United Nations Security Council finally agreed to an arms embargo. Biko became a potent symbol of the oppressiveness of apartheid and of the brutal determination by the white government to maintain it. That determination was further evidenced by the backlash against the anti-apartheid movement after Biko's funeral. A number of his associates (including Woods) were banned, as were many of the Black Consciousness groups he had inspired.

Two decades would pass before a truer picture of Biko's last days could emerge. Evidence uncovered by the Truth and Reconciliation Commission revealed that after his violent interrogation, Biko was left naked on the concrete floor of his cell, chained to a metal grate. As a result of his brain injuries, he lost control of his bodily functions and therefore had to sit in his own faeces and urine. As to the sequence of events leading up to his injury, however, the story remains cloudy. Police officers who took part have proved evasive. 'I am not sure who hit him and who got hit,' Major Harold Snyman told the

Commission. 'We knew of a previous occasion in which Biko had assaulted a member of the police and knocked his teeth out. He was a big and strong man.' He insisted that, 'It was not our intention to kill him.' The Commission nevertheless decided that Biko's death was 'a gross human rights violation . . . Despite the inquest finding no person responsible for his death, . . . in view of the fact that Biko died in the custody of law enforcement officials, the probabilities are that he died as a result of injuries sustained during his detention.'[86]

Within days of his death, Biko became an icon in the struggle against apartheid. But icons are often easier to tolerate than activists. On the twentieth anniversary of his death, Nelson Mandela summed up Biko's importance. 'It is the dictate of history', he said, 'to bring to the fore the kind of leaders who seize the moment, who cohere the wishes and aspirations of the oppressed. Such was Steve Biko, a fitting product of his time; a proud representative of the re-awakening of a people.' That was a respectful assessment, but not an entirely sincere one. Biko and Mandela represented two divergent and frequently antagonistic strands of the anti-apartheid movement. Black pride did not harmonize well with the interracial brotherhood envisaged by Mandela.[87]

On this occasion, however, it behoved Mandela to say something positive about Black Consciousness, which he had previously found distasteful. He insisted that, 'The driving thrust of black consciousness was to forge pride and unity amongst all the oppressed, to foil the strategy of divide-and-rule, to engender pride amongst the mass of our people and confidence in their ability to throw off their oppression.' Mandela's attempt to turn discord into harmony was admirable, but the mere fact that he was giving a speech in honour of Biko demonstrates that one approach had supplanted another. Biko, had he survived, would not be impressed with the South Africa that has emerged post-apartheid. Black Consciousness was co-opted by the ANC government, and neutered in the process. The fulfilment it promised has not been achieved. 'We do not want to be reminded that it is we, the indigenous people, who are poor and exploited in the land of our birth,' Biko once wrote. 'These are concepts which the Black Consciousness approach wishes to eradicate from the black man's mind before our society is driven to chaos by irresponsible people from Coca-cola and hamburger cultural backgrounds.' Poverty and exploitation did not end with the demise of apartheid. The social transformation Biko advocated has not been achieved by the ANC. Blacks might be free, and racism banished, but dire poverty remains a massive obstacle to liberation.[88]

4

TERROR

Munich: Black Olympics

The simple chain-link fence around the Olympic village in Munich was only two metres high. There was no barbed wire, the perimeter was not regularly patrolled, and there were no security cameras. Guards were trained for nothing more threatening than an athlete's drunken celebration. All this was deliberate. The Germans wanted the 1972 Olympics to be 'The Friendly Games', a calculated counterpoint to Berlin 1936.

The organizers did ask Georg Sieber, a police psychologist, to think about worst-case scenarios. Number 21 on his list of 26 envisaged an attack by Palestinian terrorists who would scale the fence at night, then make for the building housing Israeli athletes. After killing a couple of hostages, they would offer to exchange the rest for comrades held in Israeli jails. Since Israel would refuse to bargain, the terrorists would be forced to execute their hostages. Sieber's warning was rejected because it was too frightening – the precautions it implied contravened the spirit of the friendly games. The organizers wanted an occasion remembered for Waldi, the dachshund mascot, not for jackbooted security personnel.

Palestine, a nation that did not technically exist, was not invited to the 1972 Olympics. A group of Palestinians therefore invited themselves. 'If they refuse to let us participate, why shouldn't we penetrate the Games in our own way?' Abu Mohammed, of the Black September organization, asked his comrades on 15 July 1972. Black September was formed in late 1970, in reaction to King Hussein's decision to expel thousands of Palestinians from Jordan. They were a militant response to the issue of self-determination, a group of zealots who considered the Palestine Liberation Organization insufficiently aggressive. 'There was not an organisation,' Abu Daoud, one of the ringleaders of the Munich action, explained. 'There was a cause, Black September. It was a . . . state of mind.'[1]

When Daoud first visited Munich on the 17th to reconnoitre the site, he found the answer to his dreams: a pathetic fence, minimal security, and guards who acted like a welcoming committee. On a subsequent visit, he talked his way into the residence set aside for the Israelis by claiming to be a Brazilian with a passionate love for Israel. On 24 August, two days before the Games began, Abu Iyad and two others flew into Frankfurt with five bags packed with weapons. Customs officials opened only one bag – the one containing clothes.

Since the operation carried enormous risk, neither Iyad nor Daoud would take part. That privilege went to the young and expendable. The leader was Issa, a sensitive man whose devotion to Palestine permitted acts of cold-blooded barbarity. Directly under him was a quiet psychopath nicknamed Tony. Joining them were six faceless fedayeen – youngsters radicalized in Lebanese refugee camps and susceptible to promises of glorious martyrdom. 'We were convinced Palestine could only be liberated by its children,' Jamal al-Gashey confessed. 'For the first time, I felt proud and felt that my existence and my life had a meaning, that I was not just a wretched refugee, but a revolutionary fighting for a cause.'[2]

The fedayeen were trained in Libya, then sent to Munich. Not until the evening before the attack did they receive details of their mission. Each was given a duffle bag decorated with the Olympic symbol and containing a gun, ammunition, grenades, food, rope, first aid kit, nylon stockings for use as masks, and amphetamines.

Daoud told them: 'The operation for which you've been chosen is essentially a political one . . . It's not a matter of liquidating your enemies, but seizing them as prisoners for future exchanges. The grenades are for later, to impress your German negotiating partners and defend yourselves to the death.' Issa added: 'From now on, consider yourself dead . . . killed in action for the Palestinian cause.' Despite the imminence of death, al-Gashey felt 'pride and joy . . . My dream of taking part in an operation against the Israelis was coming true.'[3]

At 04.30 on 5 September, the fedayeen, dressed in tracksuits, arrived at a pre-selected point on the perimeter fence. The spot was popular among those returning late from unofficial trysts in Munich. The guards knew that athletes were scaling the fence, but decided to ignore the practice in the interest of goodwill. At the fence, the Palestinians encountered some Americans also sneaking in. Trading banter, the two groups helped one another over. 'Hey, man, give me your bag,' one American remarked. Weapons were hoisted over the fence in the spirit of Olympic camaraderie.[4]

The fedayeen then made for the Israeli apartments. Yossef Gutfreund, a wrestling referee, was awakened by the sound of someone tampering with the lock. When he saw the muzzle of a rifle poke in, he threw himself at the door while yelling at his housemates to escape. Gutfreund, a huge man, kept the attackers at bay long enough for Tuvia Sokolovsky to flee through a window. When the terrorists managed eventually to force their way in, Moshe Weinberg, a wrestling coach, jumped them. He was shot through the cheek.

The wounded Weinberg was forced to take his captors to the other Israelis. He took them past Apartment 2, claiming that it did not contain Israelis, on the slim hope that the wrestlers and weightlifters in Apartment 3 might be able to overpower their attackers. Unfortunately, they were still sound asleep and easily subdued. As they were marched back to the first apartment, Gad Tsobari broke loose and escaped amidst a hail of bullets. While the terrorists' attention was focused on Tsobari, Weinberg again attacked. This time, the Palestinians shot him dead. When they arrived back at the apartment,

Yossef Romano, a weightlifter, managed briefly to overpower one of the terrorists, but he too was killed.

The fedayeen now had nine hostages and two bodies. A cleaning woman, having heard gunfire, alerted the Olympic police at 04.47. Arriving at the scene, an unarmed officer encountered a hooded man on the balcony. Two sheets of paper were tossed down. These contained an ultimatum: the hostages would be released in exchange for 234 Palestinians held in Israeli jails. If the demands were not met by 09.00, one hostage would be killed with each passing hour. In a gesture of solidarity directed at the German radical left, Ulrike Meinhof and Andreas Baader of the Red Army Faction were included on the list. A short time later a more senior policeman arrived. 'What is the meaning of this?' he shouted, as if authority could melt terror. Issa ignored the question and nodded in the direction of the house. Two terrorists emerged carrying Weinberg's bloody corpse, which they dumped at the policeman's feet. Issa reiterated the ultimatum: 'One each hour.'[5]

A crisis team was formed, consisting of West German Interior Minister Hans-Dietrich Genscher, Munich police chief Manfred Schreiber and the Bavarian Interior Minister Bruno Merck. Since the Germans had refused to consider such a disaster, they were ill-equipped to handle it. Schreiber tried to buy the Palestinians' surrender, but they refused. Genscher pleaded with Issa not to allow Jews once again to be massacred on German soil, but that appeal got nowhere. Genscher, Schreiber and Merck then offered to take the place of the hostages, again to no avail.

Golda Meir, the Israeli prime minister, informed the Germans that under no circumstances would Israel agree to an exchange. That came as no surprise, but did nevertheless underline the fact that the problem facing the Germans was rescue, not negotiation. An attempt was made to get policemen in by disguising them as a food delivery team, but the fedayeen saw through that ruse. A similarly ill-conceived plan to invade through the heating ducts was called off when it became apparent that preparations were inadvertently being televised and undoubtedly watched by the Palestinians.

Competitions were run and victories celebrated while the Israelis awaited execution. Anxious athletes, uncertain about the fate of the Games, passed the time in grim imitation of normality. 'People played chess or ping-pong,' the American marathon runner Kenny Moore recalled. 'Athletes sunbathed by the reflecting pool. It seemed inappropriate, but what was one supposed to do?' Gerald Seymour of ITN found the atmosphere 'unpleasant, selfish, [and] slightly obscene . . . It seemed like people having a noisy picnic in a churchyard.' Gossip was traded on a rising wind. 'Rumors leaped and died,' Moore remembered. 'There were 26 hostages. There were seven. The terrorists were killing a man every two hours. They were on the verge of surrender.' At 16.00, the IOC belatedly suspended competition. A dejected Moore returned to his room. 'I experienced level after level of grief: for my own event . . . those years of preparation now useless; for the dead and doomed Israelis; and for the violated sanctuary of the Games.'[6]

The crisis team stalled by claiming that there were problems liaising with the Israeli government. The fedayeen proved tolerant, since delays increased the coverage their cause received. The deadline was extended three times, eventually to 17.00. This annoyed Olympic organizers, who pressured the Germans for a resolution. '[They] naturally wanted the Games to resume as soon as possible, which meant that the situation had to be resolved in one way or another,' Schreiber recalled. Unfortunately, haste is ill-advised in a hostage situation – the usual procedure is to prolong negotiations so as to wear down the captors. Munich was instead rushing to a conclusion.[7]

Just before the final deadline, the Palestinians changed tactics. They demanded a jet to fly to Cairo, on the assumption that Israel might prove more willing to negotiate if the hostages were held in an Arab country. The Germans welcomed the new demand, on the assumption that it would be easier to take out the terrorists on airport tarmac than in the rabbit warren of the Olympic village. While that was undoubtedly true, a commando operation at the airport required skills the Germans did not possess. One consequence of the revulsion against all things military after 1945 was that West

Germany did not possess an elite commando unit. Realizing this, Meir directed Mossad chief Zvi Zamir to ask the Germans for permission to use an Israeli force. Chancellor Willy Brandt was open to the idea, but Bavarian state officials, in whom constitutional authority rested, demurred.

The operation was therefore left to ordinary police officers. 'We were trained for everyday offenses, to be close to the people, unarmed – but not for an action against paramilitary-trained terrorists,' Schreiber later admitted. Five marksmen were selected simply by going through personnel files in search of those who had performed well on target practice. Buried within the official post-mortem is a stark admission from the man identified only as 'Sniper No. 2': 'I am not a sharpshooter.'[8] The ad hoc force was both blind and deaf, since neither walkie-talkies nor night vision goggles were provided.

'We were 99 per cent sure that we wouldn't be able to achieve our objective,' Schreiber later confessed. 'We felt like doctors trying to bring the dead back to life.' To make matters worse, a misunderstanding allowed his deputy, Georg Wolf, to assume that there were only five terrorists instead of eight. Five marksmen against five terrorists was frugal; five against eight was suicidal. Meanwhile, another set of police officers selected to pose as the flight crew on the jet decided among themselves to abort their operation because it seemed too dangerous. 'It was nothing more than a suicide mission which was cancelled unanimously,' one later explained.[9]

The helicopters carrying the hostages and their captors arrived at the airport at 22.35. Six Palestinians disembarked, along with four pilots. The hostages remained inside, along with one terrorist in each helicopter. Issa and Tony then went to inspect the jet. Their suspicions were aroused when they discovered no crew. As they walked back to the choppers, Wolf ordered his men to open fire. Only three heard the order, the other two joining in once the shooting began.

Two fedayeen were killed instantly, another was mortally wounded. The effectiveness of the marksmen was, however, limited by the fact that they had placed themselves in one another's line of fire. Confusion intensified when the surviving terrorists methodically shot out the airport lights, thus plunging the area into total darkness. With the situation now in stalemate, an eerie quiet descended. The Germans decided to call in a SWAT team, an option that had not occurred to them before. The team arrived by helicopter a full half hour after shooting had commenced and, for some reason, landed two kilometres from the jet. Six armoured personnel carriers were also mobilized, but their arrival was delayed because the roads to the airport were clogged with people eager to witness an Olympic tragedy. One of the APCs was delayed further because the driver mistakenly went to Munich's civilian airport.

The arrival of the APCs just before midnight convinced the terrorists that the jig was up. One opened fire inside the first helicopter, killing three of the hostages and wounding a fourth. He tossed in a grenade and then turned his gun on his attackers, before being cut down in a torrent of fire. The grenade turned the helicopter into an inferno, killing the remaining hostage. A similar scenario was played out in the second helicopter, where five hostages were huddled. When the shooting stopped at about 00.30 all the hostages were dead, as were five of the terrorists. The remaining three lay on the tarmac, two pretending to be dead. They were captured alive.

'Our greatest hopes and our worst fears are seldom realized,' Jim McKay, the veteran ABC sportscaster, told his American audience. 'Tonight our worst fears have been realized. They're all gone.' While he was uttering those words, morning was breaking in the Village. As news spread that the hostages were dead, thoughts turned to the fate of the Games. Willi Daume, chairman of the Munich organizing committee, felt it would be wrong to continue. The IOC commissioner Avery Brundage overruled him, on the grounds that terrorists could not be allowed to destroy the Olympics. 'The games must go on, and we must . . . continue our efforts to keep them clean, pure and honest,' he told the crowd gathered for a memorial service in the Olympic Stadium that morning. He referred to 'two savage attacks' on the Games: the other one being the 'naked political blackmail' of black African nations whose threatened boycott had resulted in the expulsion of Rhodesia. An astonished crowd was left wondering whether Brundage meant to suggest parity. He later apologized for 'any misinterpretation' his words might have encouraged.[10]

Reactions to Brundage's decision varied widely. 'Incredibly, they're going on with it,' Jim Murray of the *Los Angeles Times* wrote. 'It's almost like having a dance at Dachau.' Norwegian athletes stayed, but some registered their protest by not competing. Six Dutch athletes left, complaining of the 'obscene decision to continue'. In contrast, Tom Dooley, an American walker, thought that the Games should go ahead, simply because the athletes needed 'to stay together. Who wins or loses now is ridiculously unimportant, considered against these men's deaths. But we have to stay together.' The Egyptian, Kuwaiti and Syrian teams went home, fearing reprisals, but the Lebanese team stayed, in order to preserve the Olympic spirit. That sentiment was echoed by Steve Prefontaine, the American distance runner: 'These are our Games,' he insisted. 'Anyone who would murder us for some demented cause just proves himself incapable of understanding what we do.'[11]

In the immediate aftermath of the slaughter, Golda Meir promised the Knesset that 'we will smite them wherever they may be'. The opposition leader, Menachem Begin, goaded her, demanding 'a prolonged, open-ended assault against the murderers and their bases'. Meir then promised 'to strike at the terrorist organizations wherever we can reach them. That is our obligation to ourselves and to peace. We shall fulfil that obligation undauntedly.' Her determination for revenge increased exponentially when West German authorities released the three surviving Munich terrorists on 29 October 1972 after the hijacking of a Lufthansa jet. Daoud claims that the deal had been prearranged and that the hijacking was staged as a pretext.[12]

Meir, feeling 'physically sickened' by news of the release, gave the green light to two operations. The first, called Spring of Youth, was carried out by Israeli Special Forces on 9–10 April 1973 and hit several terrorist targets in Lebanon. A second operation, called Wrath of God, went to Mossad. Over the next six years, agents killed at least twenty Palestinians in cities around Europe and the Middle East. 'The people who were shot all had nothing to do with Munich,' Daoud later claimed. That was not strictly true, since Adnan al-Gashey (cousin of Jamal al-Gashey) and Mohammed Safady, two of the three Munich survivors, were eliminated, as was Ali Hassan Salameh, who had helped organize the operation. As for the rest, however, Daoud was essentially right: Wrath of God was simply a pretext for eliminating Palestinians that Israel wanted dead. David Kimche, former deputy head of Mossad, later admitted that, 'The aim was not so much revenge but mainly to make . . . [the Palestinians] frightened. We wanted to make them look over their shoulders and feel that we are upon them.' It did not really matter that the slain often had nothing to do with Munich. 'A terrorist is a terrorist is a terrorist,' a senior Mossad agent confessed. 'We don't check too much if he was or wasn't involved . . . If he didn't do it yesterday, he'll do it tomorrow. He's a terrorist.' That was not strictly true either, since in July 1973 agents gunned down a completely innocent Moroccan in Norway, mistaking him for Salameh.[13]

'I regret nothing,' Daoud later confessed. He insisted that the Olympic killings were a legitimate response to Israeli injustice. Palestinians would 'fight as long as it takes for Israel to recognize our rights'. 'The only aim', Adnan al-Gashey claimed, 'was to scare the world . . . during their "happy Olympic Games" and make them aware of the fate of the Palestinians.' By that standard, the operation was a success; as Daoud claimed, it 'brought the Palestinian issue into the homes of 500 million people who never previously cared about Palestinian victims'. Nevertheless, while the operation made the issue much more difficult to ignore, quite a few people managed to do so. Abu Iyad was astonished at Western priorities. 'A large segment of world opinion was far more concerned about the twenty-four hour interruption in the grand spectacle of the Olympic Games than it was about the dramatic plight endured by the Palestinian people . . . or the atrocious end of the commandos and their hostages.'[14]

The families of the slain hostages, unable to bring the perpetrators to justice, have instead focused blame on the German authorities who bungled the operation. 'They should have protected my husband and the other athletes and they didn't,' argues Ankie Spitzer, widow of fencer Andrei Spitzer. Her anger is understandable, but if the Germans were guilty of anything, it was of quaint naivety. They weren't the only ones who wanted to pretend that the Olympics could be kept free of political violence.[15]

Moore recalls feeling that 'we were . . . actors in the modern Olympics' great loss of innocence'. The Olympic Village had seemed to him 'a refuge . . . from a larger, seedier world in which individuals and governments refused to adhere to any humane code'. The spirit was contrived, but still important. 'For two weeks every four years we direct our kind of fanaticism into the essentially absurd activities of running and swimming and being beautiful on a balance beam. Yet even in the rage of competition we keep from hurting each other, and thereby demonstrate the meaning of civilization. I shook and cried as that illusion, the strongest of my life, was shattered.' In future, experts like Sieber would prove as important to pre-Games preparations as stadium architects. Munich spent $2 million on security; Athens in 2004 spent $600 million. However sensible modern-day precautions are, a sanctuary cannot be turned into an armed camp and still remain a refuge. Munich provides a cruel reminder of a moment when sport ceased to be sacred.[16]

Berlin: Baader–Meinhof

Benno Ohnesorg was a twenty-six-year-old literature student when he was fatally shot by a police officer during a demonstration in Berlin on 2 June 1967. An official inquiry concluded that Ohnesorg's shooting was accidental. Militant students concluded otherwise. For them, the incident demonstrated the lengths to which the government would go to stifle dissent. Afterwards, students found themselves on the banks of a moral Rubicon. Some concluded that violence had to be met with violence, since the state would not respond to a movement that posed no physical threat. 'It was a very strange time,' Hans-Georg Brum, a former activist, concludes. 'We were all very critical of society. The question was, how far can you go? Can you turn to violence?'[17]

Some found the answer easy – too easy. One radical student paper promised: 'If the police open fire on us again, we will shoot back.' This was not simply tit for every tat. Violence, it was believed, would provide the stimulus necessary to awaken a lethargic proletariat. For proof, the students looked to successful revolutions in Latin America and Asia, assuming that Third World truths could easily be transplanted to an advanced industrial society.[18]

For Andreas Baader, violence was neither tactic nor strategy but a way of life. Born in 1943, he lost his father in the war and developed into the stereotyped delinquent who drew sadistic pleasure from being the tough male in a household of fawning females. He stole cars, snatched purses, and was always ready for a brawl. He was not, however, an ordinary hooligan. Good looks, sharp clothes, charisma and intelligence made it difficult to dismiss him for the thug he was, and gave his violence erotic frisson.

Baader moved to Berlin in 1963 in order to avoid compulsory military service. The intense political climate in the divided city gave thugs like him revolutionary validity, effectively camouflaging their psychosis. In 1968, he fell under the spell of Gudrun Ensslin, a willowy beauty with a first-class mind. The daughter of a Lutheran minister, she had converted to radical socialism after attending college in the United States. For her, linking with Baader was a dramatic rejection of an inherited moral code. He was, she confessed, 'refreshingly close to reality', by which she meant that he preferred action to thought. As such, he offered her the opportunity to act upon fantasies of violence. 'They will kill us all,' she proclaimed when Ohnesorg was shot. 'You know what kind of pigs we are up against. This is the generation of Auschwitz we've got against us. You can't argue with people who made Auschwitz. They have weapons and we haven't. We must arm ourselves.'[19]

On 2 April 1968 Baader and Ensslin – two fashion-conscious terrorists – firebombed a Frankfurt department store. '[Their] idea was that they would throw something into the world of consumerism which was very similar but on a much smaller scale to what was being dropped on people in Vietnam,' their lawyer Horst Mahler later explained. 'So they could then say: "You are horrified by a little fire in a department store in which a few clothes go up in flames. You should see what goes on everyday in Vietnam. What kind of people are you? Are you human?"' Fortunately for the police, Baader and Ensslin were conveniently inept, and therefore easily captured. Arrest slaked their craving for attention, which came aplenty when their trial provided the perfect opportunity for radical theatre.[20]

Released on bail while awaiting the outcome of their appeal, Baader and Ensslin returned to revolution. He was re-arrested on 3 April 1970, at which point the journalist Ulrike Meinhof turned the cosy couple into a revolutionary ménage à trois. She had previously worked for the radical journal *Konkret*, earning a solid reputation for insightful commentary. In 1968, she left her husband and job and migrated to Berlin, where she met Baader and Ensslin. After working with young female delinquents, she became convinced of the futility of capitalism. The 'system', she decided, could not be reformed – it had to be smashed.

After Baader's re-arrest, Meinhof launched a plan to free him. On the pretext of collaborating with her on a book, he was regularly escorted to the Free University library under armed guard. On 14 May 1970, she and two accomplices smuggled guns into the library and, after a shoot-out, freed Baader. That was the symbolic starting point of the Red Army Faction, commonly known as the Baader–Meinhof gang. For Meinhof, springing Baader was a personal statement of commitment to revolution; she shed the last vestiges of bourgeois respectability and became an urban guerrilla. This meant jettisoning (on the advice of Ensslin) the excess baggage of her twin daughters, who were dumped in a commune in Sicily. She became obsessed by the need to erase her past life. 'Ulrike Meinhof and I had the same problem,' Horst Mahler reflected. 'She had a bourgeois career, too. She was very successful and . . . felt hemmed in by that. For this reason, Gudrun held a huge fascination for her. She looked up to Gudrun. She pushed herself to the front line of this struggle.' Beate Sturm, briefly a member of the gang, thought Meinhof's hunger for action was typical of the radical intellectual: 'One only has to explain to her that action is more important than her scribbling and that is sufficient.' She was captivated by Baader's 'great idea that criminal action is itself political action'.[21]

'Did the pigs really believe that we would let comrade Baader sit in jail for two or three years?' a Meinhof communiqué asked. 'Did any pig really believe that we would talk about development of the class struggle, the re-organisation of the proletariat, without arming ourselves? . . . Whoever does not defend himself will die. Start the armed resistance. Build up the Red Army.' She genuinely believed that Baader's release, by signalling that the war had begun, would stimulate a proletarian uprising. 'The release of Baader is only the beginning!' Members assured themselves that the working class, seething with anger, was a conscious revolutionary mass lacking only leadership.[22]

An urban guerrilla movement was constructed according to blueprints borrowed from Che and Mao, with jungle verities recklessly applied to the metropolis. 'What is now being launched here has already been launched in Vietnam, Palestine, Guatemala, in Oakland and Watts, in Cuba and China, in Angola and New York.' Since the war had already begun, to take up arms was sublime moral duty. Those who refused were by definition 'responsible for the crimes of capitalism'. That included left-wing reformists as well as those on the far right. State socialism was a dead end; it simply meant 'better means of discipline, better methods of intimidation, better methods of exploitation. That only breaks the people, it doesn't break what breaks the people!' A call to arms was issued: 'Don't sit around on the shabby, ransacked sofa and count your loves, like the small-time shopkeeper . . . Build up the right distribution apparatus, let the pants-shitters lie, the red-cabbage eaters, the social workers, those [who] only suck up . . . Get out where the homes are and the big families and the sub-proletariat and the proletarian women, who are only waiting to smash the right people in the chops.'[23]

'We despised what our parents had created,' Astrid Proll reflected. 'We were angry that we had to live with the past like that. Our generation was in love with revolution.' With the revolutionary path so clear, ideology seemed an obstacle to action. 'Whether it is right to organise armed struggle depends on whether it is possible,' the group blithely maintained. 'We affirm that . . . it is correct, possible, and justified.' Ensslin and Meinhof were millenarian fantasists for whom faith superseded theory.

> Not with cheap words, but with deeds, have we come to stand on the side of the overwhelming majority of the people, who today all over the world are taking up arms to free themselves from imperialist suppression and any kind of exploitation . . . This . . . is a world war – it will be the last and at the same time the longest and bloodiest war of history . . . It is not a war among nations but a war of classes, which will sweep all national, social, cultural, and religious boundaries and barriers forever from the stage of history.

Meinhof and Ensslin foresaw a cataclysm of biblical proportions from which the world would emerge transformed and through which individual redemption could be gained. Third World national liberation movements were attractive because of their purity – they involved revolutionaries uncorrupted by consumerism. Yearning for a condition of innocence, they saw peasants as living examples of humanity before the Fall. The revolution was felt and lived, not just conceived and planned. This explains the emphasis upon action and on action's dramatic expression – violence. Theory, in truth a cacophony of jargon, was picked up and pasted onto a great collage constructed to suit the millenarian mood. Each element in the collage could be carefully explained, but the picture itself was a mess, especially when viewed from detached distance. Meinhof, given her journalism background, should have been the one to explain the group's political ideas to sympathizers and critics, but, as Sturm explained, 'she couldn't do that because there were no ideas at all'.[24]

Blind faith encouraged a gargantuan self-righteousness, which provided a force field against doubt and made error inconceivable. The world was cleaved into black and white, good and evil, thus rendering a moral crusade both attractive and possible. The absolute certainty that they understood 'the people' led to an automatic assumption that they were popular and capable of leadership. RAF members saw themselves as an enlightened cadre: 'It is our task', Meinhof argued, 'to present the connection between the liberation struggle of the peoples of the Third World and the longing for liberation wherever it emerges in the metropoles.'[25]

The RAF's strength lay in the manipulative power of Baader, a demagogue who preyed on his followers' weaknesses. He was the macho stud who boasted that he suffered from 'revolutionary orgasm problems' – whatever that meant. Leadership was defined by the ability to down the most drugs, fuck the most women and spread the most hate. 'Everything was shit, arsehole, pigs, and it was like that all day long,' Ello Michel said of her former boyfriend. 'Full of hate against the whole society.' 'He had a great sense of self-belief,' Thorwald Proll recalled, with conspicuous understatement. 'He had this way of pushing everything to the limit.' Power was wielded partly through the psychological torture of female comrades who fell in love with him. 'I could not understand the way he insulted women all the time,' Mahler remarked. 'He called his girlfriend, Gudrun, "you silly bitch". He called Ulrike Meinhof "you really stupid bitch".' Self-criticism sessions turned acolytes into emotional wrecks, rendering them easier to manipulate. 'Everyone was criticized,' Margrit Schiller recalled. 'The only one who wasn't was Andreas.'[26]

After Baader's escape, the RAF prepared for a major offensive. Since terrorism was expensive, banks had to be robbed. A Robin Hood image was cultivated, but in truth it was paper thin. 'It was not about redistributing wealth,' Monika Berberich admitted. 'It was about getting money and we weren't going to mug grannies in the street.' Money bought weapons which were used to get more money.

Training was provided by the PLO, at a summer camp in Jordan. Most of it was irrelevant to the German context, but RAF members did learn to make bombs. Disagreements with their hosts quickly developed, however, because Baader insisted that men and women who trained together should be able to sleep together. The PLO also objected to Ensslin's fondness for sunbathing topless. Before long, the Germans were sent packing.[27]

With all the pieces in place, the RAF launched a wave of violence which peaked with the May Offensive of 1972. On 11 May, they bombed the American 5th Army Corps base and on the next day detonated three bombs at the Augsburg police headquarters. On the 15th, a car bomb in a vehicle belonging to the federal court judge Wolfgang Buddenberg seriously injured his wife, and four days later a bomb caused considerable damage at the headquarters of the Springer Press in Hamburg. The offensive ended on the 24th with the bombing of the Heidelberg headquarters of American armed forces in Europe.

The May actions were designed to provoke authoritarian repression and spark a mass uprising. The first aim was certainly successful; around 130,000 security personnel were mobilized to find and destroy the tiny gang. 'We could ask for anything we wanted,' Wolfgang Steinke of the German Federal Police Force recalled. 'We built crime-fighting technology which was the finest of the finest.' New computers 'collected information on a scale which would give any civil rights lawyer a heart attack today'. That effort resulted in the arrest of all the main players by 15 June 1972. Feeling smug, the government concluded that the RAF had been decapitated.[28]

Authoritarian force did not, however, inspire a mass uprising. The RAF was mildly popular on the student left, with perhaps 25 per cent of those under thirty expressing 'sympathy'. Frustrated by the failures of 1968, some leftists drew vicarious excitement from the May attacks and admired the concentration on 'praxis' – that wonderfully revolutionary word. In addition, shallow image inspired adoration: black leather, good looks and stolen sports cars suggested that revolution was cool. In contrast, the proletariat – those whose interests the RAF claimed to represent – reacted with nearly universal derision.

Imprisonment provided credence to claims about the evils of the authoritarian state. At Stammheim prison, gang members encountered a regime designed to break them. They were allowed books, newspapers and radios, but only limited human contact and few opportunities for exercise. This provoked accusations of torture by means of sensory deprivation. 'The political concept', one inmate argued, 'is the gas chamber. My image of Auschwitz became real . . . [We] are surprised that they haven't sprayed in the gas.' 'In not knowing what to do except torture when faced with revolutionary politics,' Baader argued, 'the state proves itself to be an imperialist state.' While that was perhaps true in theory, it was not a truth that elicited much sympathy. Most Germans agreed with Chancellor Helmut Schmidt that severity was entirely justified. As he told the German parliament: 'He who wishes to faithfully protect democracy must be fully prepared to go to the limit of what democracy permits.'[29]

The RAF trial, which began in May 1975, was held in a specially built courtroom in the grounds of Stammheim. The state, determined not just to gain a conviction but also to crush the movement, ran roughshod over civil liberties. The press was regularly leaked evidence for the purpose of creating the spectacle the state desired. That strategy worked, since the public became convinced that the RAF was a far greater menace than was actually the case, which in turn suggested that they had foreclosed on their right to justice. This conclusion was reinforced when the defendants acted like the demons they were supposed to be. They used the trial as an opportunity to preach rabid, often racist polemic, including one bizarre expression of solidarity with the Palestinian terrorists who had murdered Israeli athletes during the Munich Olympics. Israel, Mahler argued, 'has burned up its sportsmen like the Nazis did the Jews – incendiary material for the imperialist extermination policy.'[30]

On 9 May 1976, Meinhof was found dead in her cell, a makeshift noose around her neck. Sympathizers concluded that she had been murdered, or that she had been driven to suicide by the brutal

Stammheim regime. While the latter is possible, more compelling evidence suggests that the torment of prison was minor compared to the persecution meted out by Baader and Ensslin. 'Our self criticism took such a hard form we tortured ourselves with it,' Margrit Schiller admitted. 'Ulrike, the problem is that you, terribly confused pig that you are, have now become a burden,' Baader wrote. 'It's you who is driving us mad, something the legal system never managed to do. As it now stands, I've got nothing to say to you. So shut your trap until you change, or get lost.' Encouraged to believe that she was 'a hypocritical cow from the ruling class', Meinhof probably took her own life. 'They destroyed this woman,' Mahler felt.[31]

Meanwhile, government claims that the RAF had been eradicated proved false, as a second wave of attacks demonstrated. The new generation of activists included members of the Socialist Patients Collective, a gaggle of depressives and psychotics who became convinced (thanks to their psychiatrist) that their illnesses were caused by the injustices of capitalism and that a cure could be effected through violent revolution. 'The system has made us sick,' went the mantra; 'let us strike the deathblow at the sick system.' From his prison cell, Baader goaded the new revolutionaries, threatening to withdraw their right to call themselves RAF if they failed to prove themselves worthy. This culminated in the 'German Autumn' of 1977, a series of brutal kidnappings and murders. While the first wave of RAF actions had targeted institutions responsible for 'imperialist' crimes, this new offensive struck at individuals whose guilt arose from the simple fact that they were wealthy or powerful.[32]

On 5 September 1977, a woman pushing a baby stroller stepped in front of the chauffeur-driven car of Hanns-Martin Schleyer, president of the Federal Association of German Industries, forcing it to stop. She pulled a sub-machine gun from the stroller and, along with her accomplices lurking nearby, opened fire. Schleyer's bodyguards were killed and he was taken hostage. In exchange for Schleyer, the RAF demanded the release of eleven of its imprisoned members. When the government refused to negotiate, a Palestinian commando unit allied to the RAF hijacked a Lufthansa flight en route from

Palma to Frankfurt on 13 October, forcing the pilot to land in Mogadishu. The commandos demanded the release of RAF prisoners, along with two members of the Popular Front for the Liberation of Palestine held in Istanbul. Negotiations proceeded for the next four days, but they were just a stalling tactic designed to give GSG-9, the anti-terrorist unit formed in the wake of Munich, time to prepare a rescue. The commandos struck in the early hours of the 18th, killing three of the four hijackers. All hostages were rescued.

The hijack, according to Peter-Jürgen Boock of the RAF, 'was the moment of highest escalation and also the moment of . . . final failure'. Messages smuggled out of Stammheim presented a stark choice. 'They told us: "Either you manage to free us or we will decide our own fate." It was obvious to us what that meant – namely collective suicide.' Shortly after receiving the news from Mogadishu, Baader, Ensslin and Jan-Carl Raspe were found dead. Baader and Raspe had died of gunshot wounds that prison authorities claimed were self-inflicted. Ensslin had hanged herself. These 'suicides' seemed even more suspicious than that of Meinhof a year earlier. Sceptics questioned how Raspe and Baader had managed to get hold of a firearm in a high security prison. That said, the government had nothing to gain (and much to lose) from executing the leading lights of the RAF. It seems entirely possible that, faced with the choice of growing old in prison, or offering themselves as martyrs, Baader and his acolytes chose the latter. Thorwald Proll thought the suicide of Baader was a last act of manipulation: 'It was like he was saying . . . "Here's a riddle you'll never be able to solve. I am going to make it look like I was executed." Always the paradox, he played with truth and lies to unsettle other people.' Agreeing with that assessment, Mahler felt that Baader must have come to the conclusion that 'we are still left with our bodies. These we will now use as our ultimate weapon.'[33]

On the following day, the dregs of the RAF 'decided to put an end to the corrupt and miserable existence of Hanns-Martin Schleyer'. Boock admitted that this was 'simply revenge' for the deaths of Baader, Ensslin and Raspe. The group then went quiet until 25 June 1979, when it attempted to assassinate General Alexander Haig, commander-in-chief of NATO. Sporadic actions were staged in the 1980s and 1990s, but the carnage of the German Autumn was never replicated. Deprived of its revolutionary celebrities, the RAF could no longer pretend to be anything other than a group of psychopaths as sadistic as the imaginary enemy they hoped to destroy. In its final communiqué, released on 20 April 1998, the group proclaimed: 'Almost 28 years ago . . . the RAF was born from an act of liberation: Today we are ending this project. The urban guerrilla in the form of the RAF is now history.'[34]

Contrary to the febrile fantasies of its members, the RAF was not a beginning, but an end. It provides a rather familiar epilogue to the 1960s, one echoed by the Weather Underground and Angry Brigade. Frustrated with their inability to change the world by polite persuasion, a small group of militants turned to bullets and bombs. As Meinhof wrote from Stammheim, 'Nauseated by the . . . system, the total commercialisation and absolute mendacity . . . deeply disappointed by the actions of the student movement . . . [we] thought it essential to spread the idea of armed struggle.' In the hothouse of radical politics, a consciousness developed in which revolution, in order to have meaning, had to be total – powerful enough to overthrow not just government, but ethos. Reform was not enough, since that perpetuated and validated oppression.[35]

'We answered the violent conditions with the violence of revolt,' the group proudly boasted in its final communiqué. Violence was like snake oil – a cure to every ill. It was not only supposed to destroy the state and remove oppression, it would also transform the people into a true proletariat. The group thought they knew how to energize workers. 'A half dozen fighters who really put their backs into it . . . can fundamentally change the political scene, and provoke an avalanche,' the group claimed in 1972. The process seemed so beautifully simple. 'We said we would throw bombs into the consciousness of the masses,' Mahler recalled. 'We meant that those who are oppressed know it but they repress this knowledge because they identify with their oppressors as long as they believe their oppressors are invincible. The activities of the guerrillas were meant to generate an army of the people parallel to the army of the state. One day the masses would rise and say: "We want the old state to go away."'[36]

'In hindsight,' Berberich concluded, 'the revolution was impossible.' The RAF fostered that impossibility. Their gargantuan hubris prevented them from noticing how their actions alienated the proletariat. Instead of acting like a vanguard, they became outlaws. As was the case with the Angry Brigade, the RAF demonstrated that violence requires the context of a mass movement; it cannot by itself create that context. Nor is it possible to alert the people to the oppression of the 'police state' by physically attacking the state. Ordinary citizens who believe that the role of the police is to maintain social order do not suddenly abandon that belief at the onset of disorder. In fact, the opposite is much more likely. The massive mobilization of police resources in response to the RAF seemed, to most people, entirely logical and acceptable. In other words, violence is no substitute for organization. Granted, any attempt to organize the proletariat, no matter how sensitively conducted, would probably have failed. But the RAF did not even try. They decided instead that the proletariat lacked only a leader and that ordinary people would, on observing the state under attack, abandon their lives and follow this brave, violent Messiah.[37]

The only conspicuous success of the RAF came in spreading fear and paranoia. In response, German society became even more intolerant than it had once been. By attempting to defeat the state, they succeeded only in providing the rationale for its reinforcement. The self-proclaimed inheritors of the vision of 1968 were in fact its executioners.

California: Comrade Patty Hearst

They called themselves Cinque, Fahiza, Teko, Yolanda, Cujo, Bo, Gabi, Zoya and Osceola – names plucked from a beginner's guide to martyrdom. The Symbionese Liberation Army was a revolutionary force consisting of one field marshal, a handful of generals and no troops. They were the kind of activists Woody Allen might have created if he had turned his attention to urban guerrillas instead of making *Bananas*. This ridiculous band of militant dwarfs might never have been noticed if not for the fact that they kidnapped Snow White – a.k.a. Patty Hearst, a.k.a. Tania.

Like the RAF and the Angry Brigade, the SLA are the fag end of the Sixties dream, an example of fantasy turning to frustration. While most radicals were shaving beards, getting married and joining the workforce, a few turned to bombs and guns in the vain hope that violence could achieve what protest had not. Like the Weather Underground, the SLA was composed mainly of white, middle-class desperados riddled with 'white skin guilt'. Fulfilment, they came to believe, would come through joining a militant Black Power group and being told what to do by a black man – the badder the better.

The guilt of whiteness encouraged an uncritical chain of logic which held that, since all blacks were oppressed, crimes they committed were justifiable responses to oppression. Rapists, murderers, thieves and drug dealers – as long as they were black – were miraculously transformed into political prisoners. On college campuses, action groups were formed to bring together self-conscious white students and the black inmates they worshipped. Most of these started as noble efforts at prison reform, but some morphed into schemes more perverse. At Berkeley, a teaching assistant named Colston Westbrook took some of these ghetto groupies on regular visits to Vacaville prison, where they 'rapped' with members of the Black Cultural Association. The students obligingly provided pseudo-Marxist explanations for black incarceration. Validation of this sort appealed to Donald DeFreeze, a BCA member doing time for armed robbery. He set up a subgroup called Unisight, dedicated to the seven principles of Kwanza. Members took on African names, hoisted the tricolour black liberation flag at meetings, and perfected a rhetoric contemptuous of white honkies.

Within the ghetto community, DeFreeze was scum, a police informer notorious for mugging prostitutes. To the whites who visited him, however, he was a revolutionary prophet. Desperately seeking heroes, Angela Atwood, Nancy Ling Perry, Russ Little and Willie Wolfe fell hopelessly in love. For them, black prisoners provided the revolutionary vanguard they had failed to find at Berkeley. 'DeFreeze wasn't just some criminal,' Little explained. 'He couldn't live the American Dream, the thing you're seeing on TV, he couldn't do it just by working. So he also became a thief . . . I liked him.'[38]

DeFreeze escaped from prison in March 1973 and went straight to his white friends in Berkeley. They were delighted, since giving sanctuary to a black convict was the ultimate in radical chic. In a flash, he underwent a remarkable transformation: from petty criminal to romantic revolutionary, from Donald DeFreeze to Cinque Mtume. The new name was a reflection of his ambitious self-image: 'Cinque' was the leader of a 1839 slave revolt, while 'mtume' is Swahili for 'apostle'.

To the young white radicals who sat reverentially at Cinque's feet, he was 'not only a military genius to lead us but a spiritual prophet to save us'. By the end of the summer, the SLA had coalesced, committed to 'the most devastating revolutionary violence ever imagined'. Westbrook, the original catalyst, wanted nothing to do with the monster he had helped to create. He saw Cinque as a white-hating criminal who was being stage-managed by deluded white radicals. 'It's the same old thing. These people claim they're working for the good of the black community when really all they care about is their own ego.' In truth, however, manipulation went both ways.[39]

Russ Little discovered radical politics while studying engineering in Florida. When the Vietnam War ended, he watched in disgust as friends put down placards and returned to middle-class respectability. 'A lot of people were going, "Oh everything's over now, we'll go back to college" – and it wasn't over at all. The same stuff was still going on. The same criminals . . . were still running the government.' For him, the SLA offered an opportunity to act out boyhood fantasies of being Robin Hood. Another misfit drawn into the vortex was Bill Harris, a Vietnam vet who had difficulty finding purpose after demobilization. 'He got impatient when he found out other people hadn't read all the books he had,' a friend recalled. His wife, Emily, had already decided that she would 'never be free until there are no more rich people and no more poor people'. Together they headed to Berkeley in search of fulfilment, which they found in Cinque. 'I am in love with a beautiful black man,' Emily wrote. Equally in love, Bill adopted pathetic ghetto slang. Taking comfort in the refuge of absolutes, he proclaimed: 'White men . . . have only one avenue to freedom and that is to join in fighting to the death those who are and those who aspire to be the slave masters.' 'I'm a revolutionary now,' he proudly told his mother. 'The government . . . wants to kill me. That puts me in the same class with some pretty fantastic and beautifully courageous people.'[40]

'Symbionese' was an invented word suggesting symbiosis, or the cooperation between disparate elements. The SLA adopted as its emblem a seven-headed cobra, or *naga*, invoking the seven principles of Kwanza. 'Our forces are from every walk of life, from every religion, and of every race,' a manifesto proclaimed. They were united in the 'common goal for freedom from the chains of capitalism'. While that sort of rhetoric had been uttered by many a Sixties radical and was usually intentionally hyperbolic, with the SLA it was entirely sincere. When Emily Harris, or Yolanda, sent 'Greetings of profound love to all comrades in the concentration camps of fascist America', she meant precisely what she said.[41]

Members easily assumed their right to represent the oppressed. 'I am a black man and a representative of black people,' DeFreeze proclaimed. 'I'm that nigger you have hunted and feared night and day . . . I'm the wetback . . . the gook, the broad, the servant, the spick. Yes indeed you know us all, and we know you, the oppressor, murderer and robber. And you have hunted and robbed and exploited us all. Now we are the hunters that will give you no rest . . . Death to the fascist insect that preys upon the life of the people.'[42]

Like tinpot dictators, they awarded themselves grandiose titles. DeFreeze was 'General Field Marshal in the United Federated Forces of the Symbionese Liberation Army'. Atwood became Gelina, a general, the same rank held by Bill Harris, or Teko. An already minuscule cabal was subdivided into intelligence, medical, communications and logistics branches – in truth ministries of one.

DeFreeze used his underworld connections to buy weapons, while Harris, the former Marine, taught comrades to use them. Intense hours of political discussion provided a hothouse for radical fantasy. Spare time was spent demonstrating against monogamy – an invitation to Cinque's bed was equivalent to being anointed. All members eagerly anticipated the moment they might turn fierce rhetoric into real violence. 'We know that we have a long way to go to purify our minds of the many bourgeois poisons,' a manifesto proclaimed, 'but we also know that this isn't done through bullshitting and ego-tripping – it is done by fighting.'[43]

Cinque drew up a roster of 'slavemasters' requiring elimination, in truth a shopping list of his idiosyncratic hate. The first target was to be Charles O. Finley, the tyrannical owner of the Oakland As baseball team, but DeFreeze settled instead on Dr Marcus Foster, superintendent of Oakland schools. That seemed a strange choice, given that Foster, a black man, was adored by the African American community for his success in battling truancy. To Cinque, however, he was the 'black Judas of Oakland'. 'We're gonna waste that nigger,' he told his troops.[44]

Sure enough, on 6 November 1973, Foster was ambushed in a parking lot and shot with eight bullets dipped in cyanide. Little, who would eventually be convicted of the murder, struggled to understand. 'I remember saying to DeFreeze, why? Why would you kill a black guy?' Explanation came in a letter to the *San Francisco Chronicle* – Foster's 'fascist' policies, specifically a plan to introduce ID cards in public schools, warranted his assassination. In fact, he had withdrawn support for that proposal. Through one profoundly stupid act, the SLA leapt from utter anonymity to widespread scorn. Even Bernardine Dohrn, a paragon of senseless violence, confessed she could not 'comprehend the execution of Marcus Foster . . . who is not a recognized enemy of his people'. Condemnation was greatest amongst the blacks the SLA claimed to represent. 'They killed hope,' Paul Cobb, a local resident, recalled. 'They killed our opportunity to identify with a great educational leader. What Marcus Foster was to Oakland, . . . President Kennedy was to the country . . . hope and unfilled promise and endearment and opportunity crushed.'[45]

Two months later, Little and Joseph Remiro were stopped on a minor traffic offence and found with firearms used in the Foster killing. Police subsequently raided a house in Concord, forcing the gang into hiding. Out went any hope of indoctrinating the masses. 'The capture of our two comrades really hurt us and threw us into a panic,' Emily Harris reflected. 'Our changed situation compelled us to place primary importance on obtaining survival and military skills . . . We got ourselves into . . . a heavy military state of mind.'[46]

Blundering forward without a logical plan, on 4 February 1974 the SLA kidnapped the heiress Patricia Hearst. The kidnapping was punishment for 'crimes that her mother and father have committed against we the American people and the oppressed people of the world'. A communiqué explained:

> Randolph A. Hearst is the corporate chairman of the fascist media empire of the ultra-right Hearst Corporation, which is one of the largest propaganda institutions of this present military dictatorship of the militarily armed corporate state that we now live under . . . I wish to say to Mr. Hearst and Mrs. Hearst, I am quite willing to carry out the execution of your daughter to save the life of starving men, women and children of every race. And if as you and others so naively believe that we will lose, let it be known that even in death we will win, for the very ashes of this fascist nation will mark our very graves.

Little, awaiting trial in San Quentin, had begun to doubt his comrades' sanity. 'They did exactly what I, for one, didn't want to do . . . We heard this stuff . . . and we just couldn't believe it. The heat on us was bad enough. After that happened man it was . . . really a nightmare. We [were] now . . . the premier antigovernment terrorists.'[47]

The fact that the daughter of Randolph Hearst had been kidnapped led the FBI to assume that they were dealing with a formidable group. 'The FBI really didn't know what to do,' the journalist Tim Findley concluded. 'They didn't have a clue . . . who these people were.' Reporters were told that new recruits were enlisting every day, when in fact the entire SLA could fit inside a Chevy van. Dan Grove, a FBI agent, admitted that the Bureau had 'no idea whatsoever', but, given the circumstances of what seemed 'a terrorist investigation as well as a kidnap case', erred on the side of overreaction. What resulted was the biggest FBI manhunt in history, involving thousands of officers, all searching for eight confused fantasists. U-2 spy planes were deployed to search for hideouts in the mountains of the Sierra Nevada.[48]

Eight days after her capture, a message from Patty was delivered to the media. 'I'm OK,' she began. 'I'm with a combat unit that's armed with automatic weapons. And these people aren't just a bunch of nuts . . . they're perfectly willing to die for what they're doing. And I want to get out of here but the only way I'm going to is if we do it their way.' The group originally wanted to trade their 'prisoner of war' for Little and Remiro. When that proved impossible, DeFreeze improvised. He demanded that Hearst should feed the poor in California for one month, at a cost of around $6 million. This was the SLA's first and only clever move, in that it forced a very rich person to do something substantial for the poor and also placed Hearst in the uncomfortable position of having to put a monetary value on his daughter's life. 'I just want you to know that I'm going to do everything I can to get you out of there,' he assured her. 'It's a little frightening because the original demand is . . . one that's impossible to meet. However, in the next 24 to 48 hours I'll be trying my best to come back with some kind of a counter offer.'[49]

On 19 February, Hearst announced the formation of 'People in Need', a compromise that cut the number to be fed, lowering the cost to around $2 million. Within a few days, the first food packages were distributed. As part of the agreement, boxes were stamped with the seven-headed cobra, so that the poor would know who to thank. 'I hate to take advantage of what could happen to the young lady,' one woman remarked. 'But my children need food.' The programme made the SLA into real-life Robin Hoods. 'It was like a dream that you didn't want to wake up from,' said Mike Bortin, a sympathizer. 'There was thousands of poor Black people and poor Hispanics in line showing poverty in America, which is what we wanted to show for years.' Governor Ronald Reagan was not, however, impressed. 'It's too bad we can't have an epidemic of botulism,' he quipped.[50]

People in Need soon fell victim to its own limitations. With not enough food for everyone who wanted it, ugly scenes erupted at distribution centres. Angry at being excluded from Hearst's negotiations, the police and FBI willed the programme to fail. The state attorney general, Evelle Younger, attacked the scheme, promising that 'every crime committed in connection with the kidnapping will be prosecuted. And I'm including any persons who participated in any sort of a food distribution plan.' The SLA also expressed disapproval, using Patty Hearst as a mouthpiece: 'Mom, Dad . . . So far it sounds like you and your advisors have managed to turn [the food programme] into a real disaster. You said that it was out of your hands, what you should have said was that you wash your hands of it . . . most of the food is low quality. No one received any beef or lamb. Anyway, it certainly didn't sound like the kind of food our family is used to eating.'[51]

Hearst's subsequent promise to provide another $2 million worth of food in January 1975 made it seem like he was trying to buy his daughter back on an instalment plan. 'I felt my parents were debating how much I was worth,' she is alleged to have confessed. 'Like they figured I was worth $2 million but I wasn't worth $10 million. It was a terrible feeling that my parents could think of me in terms of dollars and cents. I felt sick all over.' When he again assured her that he was doing everything he could, she responded: 'You're not doing anything at all.' The nation was told that she was brainwashed, yet this sounded suspiciously like a spoilt child chastising her parents by way of the media. 'Should we be doing this?' the journalist John Lester asked himself. 'We're . . . being a mouth-piece for the family, we're recording what they have to say. We're recording what the bad guys are saying, . . . we're just sort of being messengers back and forth. Are we really doing our jobs?'[52]

Fifty-nine days after her capture came Patty's announcement that she was joining the SLA. 'I have chosen to stay and fight,' she explained. She railed against her parents and their shabby bargaining. 'The things which are precious to [them] are their money and power. It should be obvious that people who don't even care about their own children couldn't possibly care about anyone else.' Most SLA members had grown to respect Patty, but they still opposed her joining, on the grounds that her presence would make them infinitely more vulnerable. But DeFreeze, who saw Patty's conversion as proof of his power, was ecstatic, and he always got his way.[53]

'I have been given the name Tania after a comrade who fought alongside Che in Bolivia,' she announced. 'It is in the spirit of Tania that I say, "Patria o Muerte, Venceremos."' Tania proved perfect for communicating SLA fantasies, for the simple reason that the whole world was watching.

> Mom, Dad. Tell the poor and oppressed people of this nation what the corporate state is about to do. Warn Black and poor people that they are about to be murdered down to the last man, woman and child. Tell the people that the energy crisis is nothing more than a means to get public approval for a massive program to build nuclear power plants all over the nation. Tell the people that the entire corporate state is, with the aid of this massive power supply, about to totally automate the entire industrial state to the point that in the next five years, all that will be needed is a small class of button pushers.

She later elaborated: 'I [have] renounced my class privilege . . . And I would never choose to live the rest of my life surrounded by pigs like the Hearsts.' For good measure, she ridiculed her boyfriend, Steven Weed – an 'aging, sexist pig'.[54]

On the *Dick Cavett Show*, Weed replied that Patty was clearly brainwashed but would come to her senses once they were reunited. To that, Patty responded: 'Frankly, Steven is the one who sounds brainwashed. I can't believe those weird words he uttered were from his heart.' Little, following the soap opera from his prison cell, found the whole thing utterly bizarre. 'Joe [Remiro] and I would read this stuff and just look at each other and like, you know, "Is everybody stoned, what's going on over there?" . . . It was just like total Hollywood. But I guess the whole thing had turned into Hollywood so why shouldn't it be Hollywood for her too. "Yeah, I'll go join Robin Hood."'[55]

Meanwhile, Randolph Hearst, much to the annoyance of the FBI, pursued his own strategy. He welcomed to his home a ragtag collection of mystics, con-artists and delusionists who offered help, including a swami who sought inspiration from Patty's shoes. Joanna Harcourt-Smith promised to find Patty in exchange for the release of her boyfriend Timothy Leary. A shady character called Popeye provided a conduit to the Bay Area underworld, in exchange for Hearst helping out with his probation hearings. The FBI, feeling marginalized, paid the misfit Sara Jane Moore, who had earlier worked on the People in Need campaign, to spy on Hearst. She later gained notoriety when she attempted to assassinate President Gerald Ford.

On 15 April came a new twist: surveillance cameras showed 'Tania', armed with an automatic weapon, taking part in a robbery at the Hibernia Bank in San Francisco. Those who wanted to believe that she was brainwashed reiterated that argument with shrill frenzy. In her next communiqué, however, she offered a calm rebuttal: 'As for being brainwashed, the idea is ridiculous to the point of being beyond belief. I am a soldier in the People's Army.'[56]

A month later, Emily and Bill Harris stopped at Mel's Sporting Goods in Los Angeles to get supplies for the revolution. Bill, never the sharpest of outlaws, decided that since buying a rifle bandolier might raise suspicion, he would steal one instead. When a store clerk caught him, a scuffle ensued. Patty, waiting in a van outside, feared that the entire SLA would be exposed if Bill and Emily were arrested.

In order to create a diversion, she raked the storefront with rifle fire. In the ensuing panic, the three escaped.

In the abandoned van, police found clues leading them to a hideout in Compton. SWAT teams moved in, closely followed by the media. Viewers around the country watched as a fiery confrontation played out in real time. After a perfunctory warning, officers opened fire. Incendiary tear-gas canisters created an inferno that killed DeFreeze, Wolfe, Atwood, Ling Perry, Camilla Hall and Patricia Soltysik. 'They just went in and killed everybody,' Little later remarked. 'Joe and I heard the whole thing . . . And we figured, well, this is it. This is what we were afraid of and now it's happened.'[57]

Patty watched the massacre with the Harrises on television from a hotel a short distance away. Bill, the lone surviving male, quickly promoted himself to Field Marshal. At a loss over what to do next, the three limped back to the Bay Area, in search of supporters. Thanks to the massacre, the mood in Berkeley had shifted. Once dingbats, the SLA were now folk martyrs. The three hooked up with Kathy Soliah at a rally protesting the killings. She offered them shelter and introduced them to Bortin, who had been eager to join the cause. He found his new comrades distinctly unimpressive. 'I was kind of disappointed in how flat they were. They didn't seem to be that smart. There wasn't a fingernail of charisma among the three of them. That was kind of dawning on me, how middle class they all seemed.'[58]

On 7 June, three weeks after the massacre, Hearst released a new statement that poured cold water on claims that she was acting under duress:

> I want to talk about the way I knew our six murdered comrades because the fascist pig media have . . . been painting a typically distorted picture of these beautiful sisters and brothers. Cinque was in a race with time believing that every minute must be another step forward in the fight to save the children. Gelina [Atwood] was beautiful . . . Gabi . . . practiced until her shotgun was an extension of her right and left arms. Zoya [Soltysik], female guerrilla.

> Perfect love and perfect hate reflected in stone cold eyes. Fahizah [Ling Perry] taught me to shoot first and make sure the pig is dead before splitting. She was wise and bad. Cujo [Wolfe] was the gentlest most beautiful man I've ever known . . . Neither Cujo or I had ever loved an individual the way we loved each other . . . I died in that fire on 54th Street, but out of the ashes I was reborn. I know what I have to do.

Hearst's love for Cujo added a new twist to the guerrilla soap opera. It also severely damaged solidarity within the tattered remnants of the SLA. Since Harris's stupidity had led police to the house in Compton, Patty blamed her new field marshal for the death of her lover.[59]

Little, watching from prison, hoped the massacre would bring this sordid story to an end. 'To this day I can't understand why the need was felt to keep on with this kind of militaristic fantasy. Just end it and be done with it and good luck.' Harris, however, still clung to dreams of revolution. He decided that the group needed to escape the 'heavy scene' in the Bay Area, lie low and regroup. The radical sports journalist Jack Scott offered help, in exchange for cooperation on a book he was writing about the SLA. A farmhouse in Pennsylvania was found, where Scott and his wife Micki spent from July to October with the fugitives and a new recruit, named Wendy Yoshimura. At their rural idyll, they sunbathed, swam, did callisthenics, read Marx and shared each other's bodies. As autumn approached, the harmony began to unravel. Harris was desperate to 'give the pigs another defeat'. His dutiful wife agreed. Though Hearst and Yoshimura were fed up with Harris's machismo, they reluctantly agreed to accompany him back to the Bay Area.[60]

On their return, they hooked up with Soliah, Bortin and a new recruit named James Kilgore. They hoped to merge with the Weather Underground, but that group, busily disintegrating, had no room for additional lunatics. Hearst briefly stayed with the Harrises, but then moved into a house of her own, which she occasionally shared with her new lover, Steven Soliah. She jogged, played tennis, watched

B-movies at the local cinema, and cut coupons in order to make ends meet. The monotony was occasionally broken by hide and seek sessions in local malls, in preparation for eluding the police. Alienated from the Harrises, Hearst drew closer to Yoshimura. She adored Patty ('She is incredible!'), but found the others pathetic. 'They are victimized by the guilt they feel [for the] death of their comrades,' she told her brother, '[and the] guilt they feel for being born white.'[61]

Harris still had a hit list of candidates for assassination but seemed disinclined to act on it. The SLA concentrated instead on holding up banks, which made it difficult to distinguish its agenda from that of ordinary robbers. During a heist in Carmichael on 21 April 1975, Myrna Opsahl, who was depositing the collection plate money from her church, was gunned down. 'How's the woman who was shot?' Hearst asked Emily Harris as they fled from the scene. 'Oh, she's dead,' came the reply, 'but it really doesn't matter. She was a bourgeois pig.'[62]

Behind the bravado, the group was torn apart by the killing. Bortin recalls thinking, 'I have family in the world. I have friends in the world. I don't want to be thought of as a murderer. I don't want to be thought of as some fucking maniac that goes and shoots up a bank, acting like a radical, leave a woman to die like that.' Pretending to be revolutionaries was no longer fun, but alternatives were not readily apparent. On 18 September, the police finally caught up with the pathetic remnants of the SLA. Hearst, the Harrises, Yoshimura and Steven Soliah were arrested at separate locations. 'Please call it a rescue, not a capture,' Patty's mother instructed reporters. Only Kathy Soliah and Kilgore remained at large, as they would for the next twenty years.[63]

The great debate then ensued: was Patty victim or accomplice, brainwashed or lucid? She had earlier claimed: 'I've been brainwashed for twenty years, but it only took the SLA six weeks to straighten me out.' On her arrest, she gave her occupation as 'urban guerrilla' and defiantly thrust a fist into the air. A short time later, however, came a long statement from her attorney detailing a cruel process of indoctrination. 'She lived in a fog, in which she was confused, . . . unable to distinguish between actuality and fantasy.' Psychologists supplied a plethora of theories to support her innocence. She eventually settled on the explanation that compliance was her strategy of survival: 'I accommodated my thoughts to coincide with theirs.' The jury at her trial for the Hibernia Bank robbery was not, however, convinced. She was given seven years in prison, a sentence commuted after twenty-two months by President Jimmy Carter.[64]

'It was always a pipe dream,' Little admits. The constant repetition of revolutionary rhetoric – words like 'fascist', 'pig', 'struggle' and 'liberation' – wore a groove in their minds, to the point that they actually believed the nonsense they preached. Absolutes of hatred and extremism made life easy – faith smothered reason. In thrall to their fantasies, they became their own cult-masters – a collection of guerrilla gurus with no following. Badly drawn caricatures of themselves, they might have been hilarious if not for their ability to kill.[65]

The Symbionese Liberation Army was well-named, if only for the peculiar symbiosis between Hearst and her captor-comrades. 'All these naïve radicals [were] just hearing what they wanted to hear,' Bortin felt. 'They wanted a rich person to convert to their cause. She . . . just had a mutual agenda for a little while, that's all it was . . . We were all fooled.' That seems a good enough explanation. The mystery of Patty will never be solved for the simple reason that even she was baffled by it. No amount of sifting through ashes will reveal 'the truth' of the SLA or her involvement.[66]

The Hearst kidnapping changed the SLA's agenda in a way the group never intended. From that moment they found themselves on a media roller coaster that was impossible to control. The whole world was listening, but the group had nothing to say, except for the tired catchphrases of faux Marxism. The revolution was hijacked by Patty Hearst, and, because of the media, turned into caricature. The Hearsts, instead of conforming to the fascist pig image the SLA preferred, became instead loving parents living every family's worst nightmare. Meanwhile Patty, depending on the audience, became either romantic heroine or tragic victim – Tania or the Lindbergh baby. But the most serious and under-appreciated transformation pertained to the SLA itself, which became important because it kidnapped someone important. A group of silly fantasists was transformed into a frightening terrorist monster the entire country was encouraged to fear.

Rome: Time to Pick Up a Gun

In the early 1970s, the most articulate voice of opposition in Italian politics came not from a politician or journalist, but from a novelist. Leonardo Sciascia's mordantly sardonic novels exposed the festering miasma that was Italian government. No group was neglected – with equal venom Sciascia attacked bureaucrats, union bosses, Mafia hoods and terrorists of right and left. But his greatest wrath was directed against the plutocrats of the Christian Democratic Party (Democrazia Cristiana, DC) whose power was unassailable and therefore infinitely corruptible. In *Todo Modo*, the film based on Sciascia's novel, a satanic priest played by Marcello Mastroianni rails at an assembled group of party bosses: 'After thirty years in power, how much longer do you really think you have? You are all dead, can't you understand? Dead!'[67]

Sciascia was perceptive *and* disturbingly prophetic. On 9 May 1978, Aldo Moro, the DC president and former prime minister, was assassinated by terrorists of the Brigata Rossa (Red Brigade). That murder was foretold in *Todo Modo*, in which the character based on Moro falls victim to a dark plot engineered by the CIA. After Moro's murder, quite a few Italians suspected that life might be imitating art. Rejecting the simple explanation of a Red Brigade assassination, they imagined instead clandestine plots. The CIA, KGB, Mossad and secret Masonic cabals headed the list of likely culprits. Conspiracy theories, popular to this day, provided explanation to the otherwise incomprehensible, thus recasting this story in a style closer to a Sciascia novel.

The Christian Democrats were the most successful party in postwar European politics. For three decades, the question was not which party would govern, but which DC faction would dominate.

Lacking a credible opposition, Italy became what one journalist called 'a political unicycle without a spare tire'. With power taken for granted, complacency, cynicism and corruption thrived – the party served itself more than the country. While most members enjoyed this arrangement, a few sensitive souls worried about democratic legitimacy and complained of being 'doomed to govern'. 'It's the logic of the democratic system to go into opposition,' Industry Minister Carlo Donat-Cattin argued in 1976. 'That's how the system defends and regenerates itself.'[68]

The Partito Comunista Italia (PCI) regularly came second at elections but, because it was communist, was kept at arm's length by the DC. A coalition was unthinkable because, so the argument went, the PCI's loyalty was to Moscow, not to Rome. Voting communist was nevertheless becoming an increasingly popular way for Italians to express discontent with political stagnation. The PCI threat was enhanced further when the charismatic Sardinian aristocrat Enrico Berlinguer became General Secretary in 1972. His success in attracting support suggested that the PCI might soon supplant the DC as the dominant party. Christian Democrats watched helplessly as economic change edged their party closer towards impotence. Postwar industrial growth had increased the number of voters who considered themselves working class, and the DC found it difficult to reach them. 'Our problem is that we have no organization representing us in the factory shop, in the schools, wherever people are massed together – nothing to match the Marxist unions,' one DC politician complained. The PCI's growth also frightened Britain and the United States, both of whom treated Italy as an irresponsible child to be protected from itself. Italian anti-communists began lurking at the CIA office in Rome, where they received assurances that 'the United States would . . . [support] any initiative tending to keep the communists out of government'.[69]

To many, Italy seemed a stagnant pond unable to purify itself. Support for the Christian Democrats was haemorrhaging away, yet no viable alternative seemed apparent. Some Italians concluded that democracy itself had failed. Eager to hasten its demise, terrorists on the right and left used violence to create the conditions for revolution. Atrocity was more common than rain – nearly 8,000 terrorist attacks occurred during the 1970s. By far the most frightening and formidable faction was the militant right, whose *strategia della tensione* (strategy of tension) was designed to engineer a crisis so intense that it would provoke a military coup. Ordinary Italians, tortured by fear, watched their world disintegrate during the 'Anni di Piombo' (Years of Lead).

Right-wing atrocities were often carelessly blamed on the left, for the simple reason that the Red Brigade had a more clearly defined profile than other terrorist groups. When the clouds of Sixties idealism scattered, militant leftists in Italy saw a shining path toward revolution. Renato Curcio, Alberto Franceschini and Mara Cagol, who founded the Red Brigade in 1970, were Marxists who held the PCI in contempt for its belief in parliamentary change. As with so many leftist revolutionaries, they knew precisely what the proletariat wanted. A romantic notion of a Third World liberation front was easily imagined – without reference to political or social context. As with the RAF, the Brigade recklessly assumed that the workers could be roused by violent attacks upon the state. As one *brigatista* reflected: 'One does not make such a choice if one does not believe completely in Communism, if one does not believe in the armed struggle as the only way to bring it about, if one does not believe in victory.'[70]

The Brigade had some success recruiting young, disaffected factory workers around its base in Milan. Its first operations were modest, involving petty thuggery, sabotage and burglary. More ambitious actions became possible after clandestine aid arrived from the Soviet bloc, in the form of money and weapons. The Brigade thrived upon the obligatory respect the European left so often shows toward Marxist psychopaths, no matter how demented they might be. Buttressed by this support, the *brigatisti* avoided the steep descent into absurdity experienced by the Weather Underground. Their cult status allowed thousands of vicious crimes to be brushed under a mammoth rug of moral relativism. Left-wing philosophers like Jean Genet and Jean-Paul Sartre showed the way by cheering every explosion detonated in honour of Marx. Romanticism obstructed reason, which meant that the more desperate the violence, the more heroic it seemed. For sympathizers on the sidelines, violence became a measure of the Brigade's virility and legitimacy.

Bombs and bullets provided backing rhythm to the drama of the 1976 election. The very real possibility that the PCI might out-poll the DC caused panic in NATO. General Gianadelio Maletti, commander of Italy's military counter-intelligence unit, came to the conclusion that his American colleagues 'would do anything to stop Italy from sliding to the left'. A top secret CIA mission in Rome codenamed 'Gladio' organized meetings with other intelligence services, including Britain's MI5, in the hope of undermining the PCI. Maletti claims that the CIA tried to destabilize the Italian government by supplying right-wing terrorists with explosives. Meanwhile, Sir Guy Millard, British ambassador to Rome, warned that Berlinguer's entry into government would be 'catastrophic', and John Killick, Britain's NATO ambassador, feared that 'communist ministers' might leak military secrets to Moscow. A flurry of documents proposing military intervention, subversion, black propaganda and expulsion of Italy from NATO were circulated in Whitehall. 'Theoretically a coup could be promoted,' one Foreign Office paper suggested, while accepting that there was a risk of 'prolonged and bloody' civil war, not to mention adverse Soviet reaction. In the end, all options were strangled by their own impracticality. That suited Prime Minister James Callaghan, who found the very notion of 'interference in the internal affairs of a European ally' dangerous and distasteful.[71]

The election on 20 June gave the PCI slightly over 34 per cent, while the DC managed just 38 per cent. A PCI victory had been averted, but the potential remained. Reacting to the election, Moro began thinking the unthinkable. What he called 'the inevitable convergence of parallel lines' made a deal seem sensible. He hoped that by bringing the PCI into government, the communist juggernaut might be stopped. Participation in government would render the communists more vulnerable to public criticism and more inclined to moderation.[72]

The idea of a *compromesso storico*, or historic compromise, had originated with Berlinguer, who felt that a government of unity was the only way to tackle the political crisis. He was also desperate to reward his supporters with something more substantial than perennial opposition. In addition, mindful of how Salvador Allende's left-wing government in Chile had attracted the hostile attention of the CIA, Berlinguer thought that an alliance with Christian Democrats might offer protection against such a calamity. The deal he proposed called for cooperation on a programme of reforms, not, at this stage, actual Cabinet seats.

When Moro discussed the *compromesso storico* with Henry Kissinger during a visit to Washington in 1974, the latter allegedly shouted 'You will pay dearly for it.' While Kissinger vehemently denies that allegation, there can be no doubt that the US was bitterly opposed. That opposition, however, probably made Moro more determined to proceed, if only to assert Italian autonomy. He reached agreement with Berlinguer in early 1978 and on 16 March was scheduled to present the proposal to the House of Representatives. On the way to the House, however, his car was ambushed by *brigatisti* who took him hostage. The stated purpose of the kidnap was to exchange Moro for thirteen Red Brigade prisoners awaiting trial. That motive, however, ran parallel to a desire to sabotage the *compromesso storico* and kick off the revolution.[73]

Interviewed by *La Repubblica* a week after the kidnapping, Sciascia raised a point Italians feared to contemplate. Rejecting the idea that the Red Brigade was operating in isolation, he remarked: 'The . . . problem is to see with whom they communicate; that is, to raise the question . . . who benefits from this?' As Sciascia implied, the Brigade was not alone in desiring the destruction of the *compromesso storico*. The number of people who did not want Berlinguer and Moro to succeed could have filled the Coliseum many times over. The existence of so many powerful people who did not want this story to have a happy ending inevitably colours interpretations of it. Once raised, Sciascia's question for ever tormented. This tale of conspiracy is told in whispers, with 'allegedly' peppering the narrative.[74]

Moro was held for fifty-five days in an apartment in Rome. As long as there was hope that a deal could be struck, the *brigatisti* were happy for him to remain alive, since by doing so they prolonged their domination of the news. For eight weeks, other issues struggled for attention. The nation was essentially held hostage by a story which did not diminish but stubbornly refused to develop. Starved of hard news, the public gorged itself on rumour.

The government of Giulio Andreotti adopted a policy of *fermezza* – firmness. Negotiation was ruled out, on the grounds that it would set a dangerous precedent. In actual fact, precedent already existed, but Andreotti pretended otherwise. A government that had not previously shown much respect for principles suddenly discovered the convenience of integrity. The PCI, keen to demonstrate their credibility, echoed the Andreotti line. In contrast, the Socialists, led by Bettino Craxi, pushed hard for negotiation. Equally adamant was Pope Paul, a close friend of Moro's from university days. While he publicly demanded release 'without conditions', in private he worked hard to engineer a deal. On the Pope's urging, prison chaplains tried to establish a communication link with the Brigade. A ransom of up to $10 million was mooted. At one point, rumours circulated that the Pope was willing to take Moro's place, a preposterous offer which, if true, only demonstrates the Vatican's desperation.

The case for negotiation was presented most forcefully by Moro himself. In a letter to the Interior Minister, Francesco Cossiga, he argued that 'the principle according to which the demands of kidnappers should not be met . . . is not valid in political cases where inevitable and incalculable damage would ensue not to the victim alone but to the State'. That was a veiled hint that he might be forced to reveal state secrets. Mario Moretti, the ringleader in the kidnapping, found Moro's behaviour fascinating. 'We didn't know a thing about how the power game is played,' he later confessed. 'This was his universe, and he knew it to perfection.' While that might have been true, Moro's impeccable logic failed to pierce Andreotti's armour. Undaunted, Moro (according to Moretti) remained 'convinced that the hard-line bloc would be broken . . .

His friends and his party might not agree with his position, but how could they ignore it?'[75]

Andreotti and his cronies rudely dismissed Moro's pleas, publicly speculating that he had fallen victim to torture or mind-altering drugs. His credibility was further impugned in an open letter from fifty self-proclaimed 'friends', who argued that his pleas were not in keeping with 'the man we knew'. Increasingly perturbed at this betrayal, Moro replied: 'Let none of those responsible seek to hide behind the call of an imaginary duty. All things will come to light. Soon they will come to light.' To his Red Brigade captors, he dismissed Andreotti as 'cold, impenetrable . . . without a moment of human pity', yet at the same time he speculated that his party might have been neutralized 'by someone or something' – a hint of menace that intensified the whiff of conspiracy.[76]

On 2 April, a dozen esteemed academics (including the future prime minister Romano Prodi) were whiling away a rainy Sunday afternoon playing with a Ouija board, or so their story goes. They asked the board where Moro was being held and the board replied: 'Gradoli', along with the numbers 6 and 11. This information was then relayed to the police with a nod and a wink – everyone understood that the séance story was bogus but no one was pressed to reveal the true source. Three days later, 450 police and paramilitaries raided the village of Gradoli north of Rome, but found nothing. When Moro's wife suggested that Gradoli might refer to a street in Rome, Cossiga replied that no such street existed. A map quickly dispelled that misconception. As it turned out, Moretti was living in flat 96 at 11 Via Gradoli. Police had been alerted to suspicious activity there on the second day of the kidnapping, but did not follow it up, choosing instead to trust local advice that the residents were respectable. The revelation from the Ouija board should perhaps have warranted a second visit, but that didn't happen.[77]

As the affair suggests, Moro's chances of rescue were reduced significantly by police incompetence. Evidence was ignored, leads were not followed up, clues were simply lost – or never found. A performance so consistently dismal has convinced conspiracy theorists that what seems to have been ineptitude was in fact a clever plan – in other words, that police conspired to let Moro die. This has in turn fed suspicions that the clandestine organization Propaganda Due (P2) was involved. P2 was an ultra-secret right-wing Masonic lodge with members in the judiciary, secret service and police. The organization considered overtures to the PCI fundamentally abhorrent and might therefore have been interested in eliminating Moro. Tina Anselmi, a Christian Democrat who headed a parliamentary commission investigating P2, believes that lodge members would have had the inclination and ability to sabotage the search for Moro. Nevertheless, as was noted in the first trial of Moro's killers, an efficient and professional police investigation would have been even more surprising than a bungling one. As the historian Richard Drake has argued, mistakes 'cannot be redefined as crimes without a more solid basis of fact than has ever been unearthed'.[78]

Level-headed analysts like Drake do not, however, sell many books. Conspiracy theorists do. Dark revelations, like those of the maverick journalist Mino Pecorelli and the former judge Ferdinando Imposimato, always seem to surface when someone is trying to sell a book. That perhaps explains the disclosures of Steve Pieczenik, a Harvard-trained psychiatrist who was called to Rome the day after the kidnapping to take part in a crisis committee headed by Cossiga. Pieczenik claims that the purpose was not to effect Moro's release, but to manage the fallout from his death. He alleges that the government, worried that Moro might release state secrets, adopted a strategy designed to force the Brigade to kill him and thus to sabotage the *compromesso storico*. 'We sacrificed Moro for the stability of Italy,' he asserts. Pieczenik's collaboration with Tom Clancy on espionage thrillers might, however, raise suspicions of a tendency to confuse fact with fiction. Richard Gardner, American ambassador at the time, dismisses Pieczenik's version of events. 'After one month I asked . . . him to go back to America. He is not a reliable man.' Cossiga likewise feels the entire premise, as represented by Pieczenik, Imposimato, Pecorelli and others, lacks basic logic. 'Why would I have wanted Moro's death?' he asks. 'If I hadn't refused to negotiate the state would have collapsed and we would have found ourselves in a crisis, which it would have been very difficult to get out of.'[79]

Andreotti claims that he agonized 'almost every evening' over Moro's plight and did all he could to secure his release. The fact remains, however, that not much was done. Whether *fermezza* was principled or cynical remains open to debate. What is clear is that the Red Brigade had been playing for a deal all along and was left flailing when one did not materialize. The Brigade's point had been made the minute Moro was grabbed. 'We had wanted to demonstrate that we could attack the D.C. and make our accusations known,' Moretti recounts. 'In this we had succeeded. A solution could have been found – if it were wanted.' The refusal of the government to budge pushed the *brigatisti* toward a conclusion they dreaded, namely that Moro would have to be killed. Moro was fully aware of the approach of inevitabilities. Disgusted with his colleagues, he directed that 'neither State authorities nor Party members attend my funeral. I wish to be followed by those few who truly loved me and are therefore worthy of accompanying me with their prayers and their affection.' 'He knew nothing could save him,' Moretti feels. 'He knew he was going to die. Those final words to his party were written from the depths of his soul.'[80]

In Andreotti's dramatic scenario, Moro had been assigned the role of martyr. His death would provide tragic proof of the agony of courageous decisions. But he refused to play that role, choosing instead to scheme and plead. Fully aware of just how corrupt Italian politics was, he refused to provide it with ersatz dignity by dying a hero's death. He tried instead to play politics, but was defeated by a group who held better cards. In the end, his scheming looked sordid compared to Andreotti's synthetic resolve. The public, playing its assigned role, mistook the government's cynicism for principle. 'I felt infinite compassion for Moro,' Moretti recalls. 'Nobody in the world should ever have to feel as alone as he did. Here was a man who knew the most powerful people on earth . . . and not a single one of them lifted a finger to help him, or made the slightest move to step forward from the pack. This was what Moro could not accept.'

Other gang members argued for release, but Moretti felt that their arguments, though 'not unreasonable', were 'at that moment undoable'. To release Moro with nothing gained would make the Brigade seem weak and would validate Andreotti's tough line. Backed into a corner, the Brigade had but one option. 'When we decided to carry out the death sentence,' Moretti recalled, 'it was done with the awareness that from that moment forward our struggle would be one of desperation. I had a sense of doom.'[81]

'The time for reasoning had run out,' Moretti concluded. 'Now it was the time to pick up a gun and fire.' On 9 May, he delivered what the Brigade called 'proletarian justice'. '[Moro] knew it was over,' he recalled. 'You can't imagine what you feel. I told myself over and over that it was a political choice, that it was unavoidable, that it was taken collectively, that we're not the ones to blame for the failure to negotiate.' He shot Moro eleven times. Later that day his body was found in the back of a car, parked at a point midway between the offices of the DC and the PCI – symbolism that was lost on no one.[82]

The murder was 'a bloody mark which dishonours our country', the tearful Pope remarked. 'He was a good and wise man, incapable of doing harm to anyone . . . a man of high religious, social and human feelings . . . His premeditated and calculated slaying, carried out in hiding and without mercy, has horrified the city, all Italy, and has moved the entire world with indignation and pity.' Three days later, the Pope seemed to chastise God for the terrible murder 'of this good and gentle man . . . who was my friend'. Exhausted, demoralized and near death, he felt deserted. 'Lord Hear us. Who is it that can listen again to our lament if not you, oh God of life and death? You have not answered our prayers for the safe deliverance of Aldo Moro.'[83]

'To recall the collective fear of those long days still leaves me gasping,' writes the journalist Judith Harris. 'When Moro's body was found . . . I knew what had happened immediately because a thousand sirens were screaming at once . . . I was there to see the end of his personal drama – but not the end of Italy's, which is still recovering.'[84] The process of rehabilitation is obstructed by imagination of what might have been. 'Moro's assassination still conditions Italian life,' argues Rosy Bindi, a family friend. 'We . . . lost the architect of the project for a mature democracy . . . For 30 years we have been paying the consequences.'[85]

When a leader dies violently, he often becomes someone better, particularly if his passing leaves mysteries in its wake. That is the case with John Kennedy, a president loved even more deeply after Dallas. So, too, with Aldo Moro, the consummate Italian politician who has been assigned something close to sainthood. Conspiracy theorists live by the phrase 'if only' – they construct a better present by imagining a different past. We can never know if Moro would have successfully re-cast Italian politics, thus rendering men like Andreotti redundant. The *compromesso storico* might actually have proved historic only in its gargantuan folly. What we do know, however, is that anger over opportunities lost has fuelled a search for parties to blame. Italians are still obsessed with the question Sciascia once asked: 'Who benefits?'

Moro's political opponents, Andreotti chief among them, certainly benefited. So, too, did the United States and its loyal ally Great Britain. But advantage is not the same as guilt. There is no escaping the fact that Moro was killed by a bunch of sadistic terrorists who were convinced that a lunatic crime would bring closer the Marxist millennium. 'There are some who don't want to accept this one thing: that Aldo Moro was killed by the Red Brigades,' argues Cossiga. 'Some in the former Christian Democratic Party – who turned Moro into an icon, a left-winger, an enemy of the United States – they don't want to accept that Moro was killed by people from the left. It must inevitably be that he was killed by the right, by the Americans, by the CIA. Otherwise, it just doesn't work for them.' That is a valid point. The left is notoriously bad at recognizing and condemning the crimes of communists. In this case, however, Moretti admits he shot Moro. Andreotti's guilt, if it exists at all, lies in omitting to take action to prevent such a calamity. 'Conspiracy theories . . . thrive', writes Drake, 'because the truth hurts.'[86]

Fermezza might have been hypocritical, but it was successful. The outcry that followed Moro's death cured Italy of her bizarre love affair with left-wing radicalism. The Robin Hood masks were torn from the *brigatisti*, exposing the psychopaths beneath. The terrible 'Anni di Piombo' came to an end, though occasional acts of brutality offered painful reminders of just how awful the 1970s were. Those who indulge in counterfactuals might wish to consider the potential effects of a deal done to free Moro, and the damage a triumphant Red Brigade might subsequently have wreaked.

Guipúzcoa: ETA

Admiral Luis Carrero Blanco was a model of predictability. The Spanish prime minister, who had been hand-picked by Generalissimo Francisco Franco to be his successor, attended Mass at the same time every day at the San Francisco de Borja church, and then took precisely the same route back to his office. That predictability killed him. For five months, a group of young men, pretending to be art students, rented a basement flat on the street the admiral travelled along. From the flat they tunnelled under the road. They then packed the tunnel with 80 kilograms of explosives. On 20 December 1973, the explosives were detonated at the precise moment Carrero Blanco's car passed overhead. It seemed at first that car and passenger had completely disappeared. As it turned out, the blast threw the car over the roof of a four-storey building and into an internal courtyard, where it landed on the first-floor roof of a Jesuit college.

The assassins were members of the Basque separatist group Euskadi ta Askatasuna, or ETA. Because the odious Carrero Blanco promised *continuismo* – Francoism after Franco – his assassination was widely celebrated. Spaniards joked about Spain's first astronaut and, in the Basque country, a folk song with the chorus 'Whoops he goes' was popular on the streets. For a brief period, ETA enjoyed folk hero status. 'I was a bit of an ETA fan,' the journalist Christopher Hitchens confessed. 'Not only was the world well rid of another fascist, but, more important, the whole scheme of extending Franco's rule was vaporized in the same instant . . . If this action was "terrorism", it had something to be said for it. Everyone I knew in Spain made a little holiday in their hearts when the gruesome admiral went sky-high.' Ignorance, however, ran deep. The terrorists were judged on the basis of what they had achieved, not what they represented. 'We thought they were fighting Franco,' writes the former student radical Gotzone Mora, who openly supported ETA in the 1960s and 1970s, and now deeply regrets having done so. The vile nature of ETA's nationalism was conveniently ignored.[87]

The foundation of Basque identity is the ancient language of Euskara and the culture associated with those who speak it. Victor Hugo once observed that 'the Basque language is the land itself, almost a religion'. The fact that Euskara lacks Roman roots suggests that the Romans did not conquer Euskadi, the Basque homeland straddling the border between Spain and France. Indeed, Basques proudly assert that they have repelled successive waves of Carthaginians, Romans, Visigoths and Franks, all the while distilling their ethnic exceptionality. The fact that language is the essential indicator of ethnicity has made it easy for nationalists to identify those within and those beyond the pale. Euskara became the badge of belonging. This narrow definition of ethnicity complicated identity in the Basque territories, since at no time in the twentieth century did the percentage of the population who could speak Euskara exceed 50 per cent.[88]

Deeply chauvinistic Basque nationalists felt threatened when, beginning in the late-nineteenth century, workers from other parts of Spain migrated to Biscay for jobs in the steel mills. For the Basques, a predominantly agrarian people, the influx was unwelcome not just on racial grounds, but also because it represented evil modernity. Sabino Arana, the acknowledged father of modern Basque nationalism, condemned this 'invasion by Spanish socialists and atheists'. Arana, who gave Basque nationalism its distinctively racist cast, called for 'the salvation of the common fatherland and the race itself', while encouraging followers to see Spain as a 'foreign power'. In the interests of racial preservation, he advised followers not to teach Euskara to outsiders, nor to marry those unable to speak the language.[89]

A nation was imagined into being. 'We had to construct our nation to persuade our people, our culture, our economy to strengthen our consciousness, of belonging to one collectivity,' the prominent Basque nationalist José María Etxebarria confessed. Even the beloved Basque flag, the *ikurriña*, was a modern invention. Nationalists encouraged the belief that it dated to the Middle Ages, but in fact it was designed by Arana, using the Union Jack as a model. While sacred myths told of a Basque nation always united against Spanish oppression, the truth is that Madrid has consistently been able to depend upon a significant level of support within the Basque territories. In other words, resistance to the idea of a Basque nation is as deeply rooted as is support for ethnic exclusivity. Though a high percentage of Basques have traditionally had no truck with independence, that nuance has not altered the determination of extreme nationalists, who dismiss such people as unwelcome in Euskadi. Fierce paranoia has been the distinguishing feature of Basque nationalism. In contrast, the much more confident and cosmopolitan ethnic pride displayed by the people of Catalonia has rendered them more welcoming of outsiders. Those outsiders have, in turn, developed a deep pride in their adopted region, often learning the Catalan language and joining in sacred cultural traditions.[90]

Basque nationalism need not have become a serious problem, if not for the efforts of Franco to eradicate it. Instead of seeing ETA as a political problem meriting clever concession, Franco treated it as a disease to be eradicated. His obsessive pursuit of an indivisible Spain based upon Castilian hegemony meant that he banned expressions of ethnic identity, such as Sardana dancing in Catalonia, or the speaking of Euskara. By this means, everyday behaviour was transformed into rituals of defiance. Given the hatred of Franco among some Spaniards and most foreigners, the policy also had the effect of turning bigoted Basque nationalists into folk heroes.

ETA started in 1952 as a student discussion forum at the University of Deusto in Bilbao. It had loose affiliations with Euzko Gaztedi, the youth wing of the Partido Nacionalista Vasco (PNV; Euzko Alderdi Jeltzalea, in Basque), the main nationalist party founded by Arana in 1895. At that time, the group called itself EKIN, but seven years later reconstituted itself as ETA, and split from the PNV. Militants rejected the PNV preference for reform through established political channels, preferring instead direct action, not excluding violence. In common with so many revolutionary movements of the 1970s, ETA believed that violence would expose the repressive nature of the government and, in the process, raise the consciousness of otherwise apathetic Basques. Given that the opponent was Franco, a man devoid of subtlety, this was entirely possible. The opportunity for violence rendered ETA attractive to those who had grown impatient with the PNV's unfulfilled promises, especially urban youths of low education and unstable employment. For them, terrorism seemed a rational political choice – the only alternative in an environment otherwise resistant to change. Romantic fantasies derived from fairy tales of an invented history provided the downtrodden with pride and excitement otherwise lacking in their lives.

The dialectic of violence was tested on 18 July 1961, when ETA attempted to derail a train carrying civil war veterans to a remembrance ceremony. The action was not entirely successful, but it did provoke a suitably intemperate reaction from the government. Playing their role to perfection, Franco's police put up roadblocks, searched houses and arrested around 110 ETA suspects, who were then subjected to brutal interrogation. Emboldened by their success, an increasingly confident ETA executive declared that all Basques had a legal and moral duty to support the resistance, and therefore that ETA was morally entitled to force compliance. In practice, this meant extorting money from Basque businessmen, who were powerless to complain.

A faction known as ETA-Militar (ETA-m) meanwhile pushed resolutely for the commencement of armed struggle, a line officially adopted in 1965. For the next three years, the Basque country resembled the Wild West, with beatings, intimidation, bank robberies and extortion the common currency of daily life. Ordinary Basque workers contributed to the chaos by frequently downing tools – hours lost to strikes in the Basque region trebled during the 1960s, and nearly 40 per cent of Spanish strikes occurred there.

True to the revolutionary script, ETA adopted a Marxist–Leninist line, without properly assessing its applicability to Basque nationalism. This included manufacturing solidarity with Third World liberation movements. Since ETA had by this stage assumed the status of mythical freedom fighters, few noticed the utter nonsense of its revolutionary rhetoric. 'Our objectives', a manifesto proclaimed, 'are to favor . . . the organization of the working class and of the people, so that the latter, directed by the former, can carry out the revolutionary fight . . . revolutionary activities will be directed at dividing and isolating the oppressors, in an effort to radicalize the contradictions that exist in the breast of the exploiting classes.' ETA felt obliged to recite Marxist mumbo-jumbo, even though the dialectic of class struggle was ill-suited to their predicament. The basis for the Basque struggle was ethnic, not economic. Basques, among the most devout capitalists on the Iberian peninsula, hated Spain, not the 'oppressor class'.[91]

On 7 June 1968, a Guardia Civil officer was shot dead by an ETA operative at a routine roadblock. Keen on revenge, Melitón Manzanas, chief of the secret police in San Sebastián, instructed his forces to gun down the popular young activist Txabi Etxebarrieta, who became ETA's first martyr. Since even moderate Basques saw the Guardia Civil as the physical embodiment of Francoist repression – an occupying army – Etxebarrieta's funeral became a massive expression of nationalist anger. Crowds lined the streets shouting abuse at Manzanas and Franco. Few mourned when ETA avenged Etxebarrieta's death by shooting Manzanas, the group's first planned assassination.

Borrowing from the writings of Franz Fanon, ETA followed a clever strategy of action-repression-action, a cycle of violence made more effective by Franco's dependable brutality. In the aftermath of the Manzanas shooting, hundreds of Basques, not all of them ETA members, were taken into custody, beaten and tortured, thus providing the rest of Spain with a ready collection of martyrs. To disgruntled Spaniards, ETA seemed a shining example of active resistance. The government responded to the increasing tide of militancy by declaring a state of emergency from 24 January to 25 March 1969, in the process ratcheting up the cycle of repression. Summary arrests removed older ETA activists from the fray, thus offering opportunities to ambitious young militants eager to outdo their mentors.

In 1970, fifteen ETA members were tried by a military court in Burgos for conspiring in the killing of Manzanas. The *Proceso de Burgos* was in every sense a show trial – an attempt by Franco to impose his will. Government manipulation, obvious to everyone, guaranteed a guilty verdict. The trial nevertheless served as a megaphone for ETA. The accused did not deny membership, but pleaded innocent to involvement in the Manzanas killing. When questioned why their pleas contradicted 'confessions' obtained in jail, they were given a golden opportunity to tell the world about torture. Six members were sentenced to death, though their sentences were reduced to thirty years' imprisonment after a huge international outcry. The trial made ETA into revolutionary celebrities, with sympathy demonstrations taking place in most European capitals. Meanwhile, the cycle of assassinations, kidnappings and extortion continued, but these actions only rarely provoked condemnation.

The assassination of Carrero Blanco took the policy of action-repression-action to new heights. ETA justified the killing by claiming that 'Carrero more than anyone else symbolized . . . "pure Franquismo" . . . the Spanish oligarchy was counting on Carrero to ensure a smooth transition to a "franquismo" without Franco'.[92] This was a rather cynical attempt to court favour by connecting the Basque struggle to the anti-Franco movement across Spain. As another communiqué proclaimed, 'We . . . consider our action against the president of the Spanish government to be indisputably an advance of the most fundamental kind in the struggle against national oppression and . . . for the freedom of all those who are exploited and oppressed within the Spanish state.' That was bollocks. The Basque struggle was not against Franco, it was against Spain. In the eyes of ETA, Franco was simply the most recent manifestation of persistent Spanish oppression.[93]

The assassination was nevertheless an important step on Spain's road to democracy, since it eliminated the man assigned the task of continuing Francoism, and left a leadership vacuum eventually filled by the clandestine democrat King Juan Carlos. Effect should not, however, be confused with intent. According to the former ETA member Jon Juaristi, ETA's goal was not specifically to destroy Francoism, but to provoke a spiral of violence so intense that it would destabilize Spain. The resultant backlash by Franco's forces would leave no room for apathy, forcing the Basque people to choose between separatism or *continuismo*. Faced with that stark choice, most would presumably judge ETA the lesser evil. That was indeed what happened. As a *Time* correspondent found two years after the assassination, 'Silent support for [ETA's] bloody strategy seems to be rapidly growing . . . "No one is neutral any more," said one Basque lawyer . . . "Franco has polarized everyone here. You're either pro-E.T.A. or pro-Franco, and there aren't many of the latter."'[94]

In the aftermath of the assassination, Madrid seemed to act precisely as ETA predicted. The transition government of Adolfo Suárez, which followed Franco's death in 1975, was remarkably dexterous in most respects, but clumsy in dealing with Basque nationalism. ETA, for its part, kept fires stoked by continuing its terror campaign. Just eleven days after Franco formally ceded power to Juan Carlos, ETA exploded a bomb in a Madrid bar frequented by soldiers, killing twelve. Suárez reacted like Franco, treating the problem as a public order matter. He failed to recognize that what the Basque region needed most was devolution, in particular an indigenous security force. The brutality therefore continued. Suárez seemed a boon to ETA in that it appeared nothing had changed.

Subsequent months, however, demonstrated that the times were indeed changing. The speed with which democracy was introduced encouraged the Spanish to expect a wholesale transformation of their nation. Before long, the new government indicated that it would address the thorny problem of ethnic nationalism in Catalonia and the Basque region. A form of devolution was offered, along with a general amnesty extended to political prisoners. This strategy sought to neutralize regionalist movements by absorbing them into the party political system. The new constitution, while confirming the 'indivisible unity of the Spanish nation', acknowledged 'the right to autonomy of the nationalities and regions which form it'. That right was enshrined in law with the Basque Autonomy Statute, which gave devolved status to the regions of Alava, Guipúzcoa and Vizcaya.[95]

While this did not satisfy all Basque nationalists, it did seriously divide their ranks. For ETA, progress was disaster. In a pamphlet entitled 'ETA against Juan Carlismo', it proclaimed: 'We cannot postpone the struggle because liberal democracy is nothing more for us than a tactical objective . . . we have to create struggle organizations capable of winning over the power of the oligarchy, just as much if this power is exercised under dictatorial forms as if it is done under liberal forms.' Despite the bluster, ETA was clearly flustered at the prospect of sensible government. Madrid brutality was its oxygen – the policy of action-repression-action would not work if the government refused to repress. This explains why the worst period of ETA violence occurred after the new democracy was in place. Prior to the Carrero Blanco assassination, ETA only rarely resorted to murder, preferring instead bombings of important symbols of Spanish rule, like government offices and monuments. But from 1973 to 1982, the critical years of the transition, ETA was responsible for 371 deaths, 542 injuries, 50 kidnappings and hundreds of other explosions. Violence also grew more indiscriminate, contradicting ETA claims that only the guilty were targeted.[96]

The transition gave rise to a strange symbiosis between ETA and the fascist hardliners who still lurked in the military and police. Each needed the other to justify their existence. ETA wanted the fascists to gain ascendancy so that repression would resume, while the fascists needed ETA to provide proof that the transition was not working. 'I am convinced that some sectors in Madrid find ETA's existence convenient,' Xavier Arzalluz, head of the PNV, remarked. ETA pinned its hopes on a right-wing coup toppling Juan Carlos. As one Basque nationalist explained: 'It would only demonstrate what they already believe, that Spain is basically fascist, that they were right all along to continue fighting and that they have the people with them.'[97]

According to Arzalluz, Basque identity is intrinsically linked to 'its historic rights, the memory of which has never been lost. This has nothing to do with the ups and downs of the economy. It reflects an awareness of identity and history that is deeply felt.' As time passed, however, many Basques found it increasingly difficult to hang on to that manufactured certainty. Moderates grew tired of violence and increasingly disenchanted with ETA. This was especially true of the middle class, who craved a quiet life. For the first time in a generation, businessmen refused to pay when ETA extorted. Within ETA itself, a new faction called ETA politico-militar (ETA-pm) advocated the renunciation of armed struggle in exchange for political concessions from Madrid. Typical of the new attitude was the writer Angel Amigo, who had joined ETA in 1972 and had direct experience of torture. After the transition, he decided that violence was no longer justifiable. 'There has been a change in the scale of values among the young,' he reflected in 1981. 'Under repression, all life turned on politics. War was heroism, but all that is over now. Now there is political choice. It is possible to be constructive.'[98]

'The bringing of democracy was meant to divide us,' one ETA activist admitted. In that sense, the transition succeeded brilliantly. Though ETA still tried to sow chaos, the character of the struggle changed: instead of Basques fighting Spain, Basques increasingly fought other Basques. Radicals turned against moderates, including prominent members of the PNV. In July 1976, ETA-m kidnapped and then murdered Eduardo Moreno Bergaretxe (or 'Pertur'), a prominent ETA activist and theoretician who had committed the unforgivable sin of renouncing violence. A similar fault proved fatal for José María Portell, a journalist otherwise fiercely loyal to Basque independence. 'Suddenly, anyone and everyone became fair game,' reflected Eduardo Uriarte, one of the original fifteen defendants in the Burgos trial. He became a target of condemnation when he publicly endorsed the Autonomy Statute. 'Some in ETA argued that we had to go on after Franco's death, that nothing had changed,' he remarked in 1981. 'But clearly, that was not true. Since 1978, Madrid's legal reach over us here in the Basque Country is marginal at best.'[99]

The rug had been pulled from under ETA. Virtually overnight, folk heroes became pariahs. Instead of being defined by ideology, ETA would henceforth be defined by tactics. Whereas violence had once been seen as the only legitimate response to an oppressive state, it would now be seen as the defining feature of an intransigent terrorist group mired in the past. ETA did not, however, disappear, since it could always depend upon a small constituency in thrall to its warped logic. As one former member remarked: 'ETA is carried along by its own weight. They cannot give up the armed struggle because the families who have lost sons would feel their heroes had been betrayed.' For hardliners, Basque identity and ETA remained indivisible - the latter implied the former. 'ETA will not disappear until there are profound guarantees of rights for the Basque people,' argued Xabin Olaizola, the mayor of Rentería. 'It is better to take the gamble of having ETA. It is the guarantee that we can keep fighting for our rights.' That, however, was a self-fulfilling prophecy, since ETA would always be able to manufacture the conditions for its own oppression.[100]

On 19 June 1987 an ETA car bomb exploded in an underground parking lot in Barcelona, killing twenty-one and injuring forty-five. Among the victims were several small children. The action left all but the most militant of Basque nationalists completely mystified. With Franco removed from the equation, ETA had ceased to make sense. Yet as was the case with every terrorist group described in this chapter, an organization defined by terror needs to kill in order to keep mediocrity at bay. The past oppresses the future.

5

HOW THE MIGHTY FALL

Santiago: Making Chile Scream

In September 2003, a huge crowd gathered in the National Stadium in Santiago, Chile, for a concert marking the thirtieth anniversary of the coup that toppled President Salvador Allende. The concert, called 'The Dream Exists', was yet another manifestation of the deification of Allende which has occurred since his death in 1973. Among the artists was Shalil Shankar whose quartet performed a raga called 'Salvador Allende, Son of God'. The Cuban singer/songwriter Silvio Rodríguez who, six months earlier, had publicly supported his government's imprisonment of dissidents, delighted the crowd with his stinging rebuke of the 'tyrannical' United States. Plans for a commemorative DVD of the concert were dashed when performers failed to agree on royalties.

On one side sits Allende, the first communist leader to reach power by open election. Opposite him sits Augusto Pinochet, coup master, dictator and mass murderer. Careless assumption encourages the conclusion that the adversary of evil must be good. While there is no disputing Pinochet's venality, the world has been sold a fairy tale about Allende. That fairy tale casts the United States as wicked sorcerer, manipulating a sovereign nation. The real story is much more banal. The coup was very popular and distinctly local – most Chileans wanted rid of their mendacious president.

The US did interfere, but so, too, did the USSR. This was, after all, the Cold War. The striking fact about Chile, however, is that American manipulation was ineffectual. Chileans stubbornly refused to follow the script the CIA wrote. Allende became president in spite of American meddling, and he was toppled by Chileans, not the CIA. Pinochet was not an American creation – intelligence reports warned against using a man like him. The argument that this chapter of Chilean history was written by Nixon and Kissinger implies a decidedly condescending attitude toward the Chilean people, who proved fully capable of messing up their own affairs.

Chile, though a reasonably stable democracy, was burdened by a cumbersome system of proportional representation, which often resulted in no party winning a majority in presidential elections. When this occurred, the result was decided not by a run-off between the two top candidates, but rather by Congress deciding which candidate would be president. In such cases, the presidency usually went to the candidate with the largest share of the vote.

Throughout the 1960s, social tensions festered, due primarily to the maldistribution of income. A mere 3.2 per cent of the population owned around 42 per cent of wealth. Since the rich used their money to buy imported goods, this led to chronic balance of payments deficits and inflation that hovered around 30 per cent. Chile borrowed to make ends meet, her chief creditor being the United States.

In the 1964 election campaign, all parties agreed that something needed to be done about underdevelopment, debt and maldistribution of income. Parties on the left prescribed socialism, while in the middle the Christian Democrats offered social welfare, nationalization and income redistribution. Fearful of a socialist plurality, the Conservative Party threw its weight behind Eduardo Frei, the Christian Democrat, who gained 56 per cent of the vote, against Allende's 38.9 per cent.

For Allende, that result demonstrated the difficulty of achieving Marxist transformation through the ballot box. At the Congress of

Linares in July 1965, his Socialist Party came to the conclusion that 'Our strategy . . . rejects the electoral route as a way to achieve our goal of seizing power.' A similar inclination was expressed at the Congress of Chillán in November 1967, when the party resolved that 'revolutionary violence is inevitable and legitimate . . . Only by destroying the democratic-military apparatus of the bourgeois State can the socialist revolution take root.' In other words, while Allende's socialists were not above using the electoral process to gain power, they were not ideologically committed to democracy and did not trust capricious voters to keep them in power. 'The final phase of political struggle', Clodomiro Almeyda predicted, 'will most probably take the form of a revolutionary civil war.'[1]

In keeping with Sixties fashion, Allende worshipped the Cuban revolution, and in particular Che Guevara. Che's experiences were automatically assumed to be relevant to Chile. Allende's friend, the historian Claudio Véliz, felt that Che had 'a fundamental impact on his plans for Chile. After seeing Cuba, Allende thought that he could take a short cut. But the truth is that he went against Chilean tradition.' As for the Cubans, they found Allende suspiciously anachronistic. His taste for finery – tailored suits, vintage wines, expensive art, elegant women – may have been de rigueur in bourgeois Chile, but it clashed violently with Cuba's olive green austerity. Castro's inner circle thought the Chilean gallant a buffoon.[2]

By 1970, with a new election looming, Chilean politics was in turmoil. Frei's social revolution had raised expectations that remained unfulfilled. His willingness to tax the wealthy also shattered his alliance with conservatives. Debt and inflation had worsened due to Frei's fondness for foreign loans. He nevertheless still commanded significant support, and might have been able to win, if not for an electoral law that prohibited a second term. Lacking a leader, the centrist coalition flew apart. Christian Democrats settled on Radomiro Tomić, a man too meek to inspire enthusiasm. That calamity played into the hands of Allende. Most Chileans wanted Frei's reforms to continue, and therefore looked to the socialists to deliver. The obvious deserves emphasis: Chileans wanted a better life, not revolution – social welfare, not Marxism. They certainly did not want democracy dismantled.

The American State Department advised the White House that the chances of an Allende victory were slim. CIA warnings to the contrary did not trouble Nixon, who decided on an approach called Track I, involving subtle manipulation of the Chilean electorate, through entirely legal means. The CIA was denied a role, because the State Department did not want mountains being made from molehills. Around $400,000 of CIA money was spent on influencing the Chilean media, but that was pennies by agency standards. ITT, a US conglomerate with large holdings in the country, offered the CIA $1 million to stop Allende, but the offer was rejected.

The election on 4 September revealed deep fissures in Chilean society. Allende, at the head of a Popular Unity (UP) coalition which included his Socialist Party, the communists, social democrats, radicals and the Movement of the Revolutionary Left (Miristas), won 36.3 per cent. A whisker behind was the former president, Jorge Alessandri, the right's candidate, while the hapless Tomić managed 27.8 per cent. It bears noting that, despite coming first, Allende gained a smaller share of the vote in 1970 than he had in 1964, when he came a distant second.

Shocked by the results, the White House panicked. Since the Chilean Congress would meet to decide the outcome on 24 October, schemers figured they had seven weeks to stop Allende. 'We will not let Chile go down the drain,' Kissinger cautioned the CIA chief, Richard Helms, on 12 September. Helms agreed. When Kissinger warned Nixon that the State Department was inclined to 'let Allende come in and see what we can work out', Nixon angrily rejected that suggestion. 'Like against Castro? Like in Czechoslovakia? The same people said the same thing. Don't let them do it.' Nixon feared that, with socialist regimes in Cuba and Chile, Latin America would become a 'red sandwich'.[3]

Secretary of State William Rogers was uneasy about tampering with the election. 'We want to make sure the paper record doesn't look bad,' he remarked. 'No matter what we do it will probably end up dismal . . . we ought to encourage a different result . . . but should do so discreetly so that it doesn't backfire.' Despite the dithering, he had identified a central dilemma: 'After all we've said about elections, if the first time a Communist wins the US tries to prevent the constitutional process from coming into play we will look very bad.' Kissinger replied: 'The President's view is to do the maximum possible to prevent an Allende takeover, but through Chilean sources and with a low posture.' That satisfied Rogers.[4]

According to Kissinger, the administration felt that the US should not 'let a country go Marxist just because its people are irresponsible'. In an effort to correct the Chileans' misbehaviour, he called together the 40 Committee, which oversaw the conduct of covert actions abroad. They settled on a plan under which the Chilean Congress would be persuaded to name Alessandri the winner. He would then quickly resign, paving the way for a new election. The centre–right coalition would then be reconstructed, to stand against Allende in a two-horse race. The beauty of the plan was that it would allow Frei to run again, since he would not technically be serving consecutive terms. Alessandri had already agreed to the idea, but Frei found it distasteful.[5]

On 15 September, Nixon, in a foul mood, called together Kissinger, Attorney General John Mitchell and Helms. The latter's fractured notes reveal Nixon's desperation. 'One in 10 chance, perhaps, but save Chile: Worth Spending Not concerned risks involved No involvement of Embassy $10,000,000 available, more if necessary full-time job – best men we have game plan make the economy scream.' Despite Helms being pessimistic, Nixon thought that a one-in-ten possibility of saving Chile from Allende was worthy odds. When Helms warned that the CIA 'lacked the means' to achieve what the president wanted, Nixon remained adamant. 'Standing mid-track and shouting at an oncoming locomotive might have been more effective,' Helms reflected.[6]

Track II quickly took shape. Under the new plan, on the pretext of a national emergency, the Chilean military would declare the elections void, establish a ruling junta and then, after a short hiatus, restore democracy in conditions which would allow Frei (or someone like him) a favourable run at the presidency. Nixon was not particularly interested in details, as long as Allende could be stopped. The CIA's director of covert operations, Thomas Karamessines, was appointed to head the project. For reasons of clandestinity, the Departments of State and Defense were excluded, thus leaving the ambassador Edward Korry out of the loop. The remit, issued on 17 September, instructed covert units to begin 'probing for military possibilities to thwart Allende'. According to Helms, assassinations were not part of the plan – 'I . . . made that clear to my fellows.'[7]

The Americans seriously underestimated the probity of the Chilean military. While few commanders supported Allende, they were not willing to undermine democracy in order to stop him. With options limited, the agency reluctantly settled on General Roberto Viaux, an ambitious viper who had recently been dismissed from the army. While his enthusiasm for mischief suited CIA needs, his emotional stability left much to be desired. Korry had already warned against any 'attempt to rob Allende of his triumph', in particular any scheme involving Viaux, who was 'impossible'. Unaware of the existence of Track II, Korry warned that ignorant meddling might result in a disaster rivalling the Bay of Pigs. Since an Allende presidency was 'assured', the United States should just learn to adapt. That prompted Kissinger to conclude that Korry had 'lost his sanity'.[8]

Standing in the way of CIA plans was the Chilean commander-in-chief, General René Schneider, an annoyingly principled man. During the election, he publicly pledged not to interfere. 'The politicians are maneuvering to push the army into an adventure,' he told General Carlos Prats, his second in command. 'They should understand that we are not so stupid.' Schneider feared that the situation might be used as a 'trampoline' for Viaux. The Americans discovered to their dismay that Schneider would 'only agree to military intervention if forced to do so'. Revelation led inexorably to implication: Schneider would have to go.[9]

The CIA, under pressure from the White House, threw their weight behind Viaux. Within a matter of days, he managed to alienate those inclined to see the best in him. Agents on the ground found him 'too hot to handle'. 'Viaux has no military support,' they warned; he 'presents too great a risk . . . and offers very little in return'. The CIA station in Santiago cautioned that Viaux would 'split armed forces . . . Carnage would be considerable and prolonged, i.e., civil war.' Even worse, agents thought, would be if Viaux actually succeeded and it then emerged that the US had helped topple Chilean democracy and put in its place an unstable military dictator.[10]

That pessimism eventually caused those in Washington to see reason. The 40 Committee concluded that 'a coup climate does not presently exist', while Kissinger reluctantly decided that 'there presently appeared to be little the US can do to influence the Chilean situation'. He phoned Nixon, telling him that the situation 'looks hopeless. I turned it off. Nothing would be worse than an abortive coup.' The president replied: 'Just tell [Karamessines] to do nothing.'[11]

Viaux, however, was like a leaky tap – he could not be turned off. The Santiago station politely advised: 'Preserve your assets . . . the time will come when you with all your other friends can do something. You will continue to have our support.' That was far too subtle for one so stubborn and unstable as Viaux. By this stage, nothing short of a sledgehammer could have stopped him.[12]

On 18 October, Kissinger advised Nixon that the best course was to formulate 'a specific strategy to deal with an Allende government'. In truth, however, Kissinger had not finished plotting. He still believed that an Allende government 'poses for us one of the most serious challenges ever faced in this hemisphere'. Feelers were extended to disgruntled Chilean officers. The difficulty, however, was finding 'a general with b***s'. Ever hopeful, the CIA thought that General Camilo Valenzuela might satisfy that prerequisite. On the 22nd, a week after plotting had supposedly terminated, an American military attaché secretly passed three sub-machine guns and some tear-gas canisters to Valenzuela.[13]

Meanwhile, Viaux's loose cannon was about to fire. Late on the 22nd, his goons ambushed Schneider. Severely wounded, he died three days later. To the great relief of the White House, an investigation was unable to discover a connection to the Americans. A CIA cable immediately after the shooting reinforces the impression the agency did not know of the plot beforehand: 'Station unaware if assassination was premeditated or whether it constituted bungled abduction attempt . . . cannot prove or disprove that . . . attempt against Schneider was entrusted to elements linked with Viaux.'[14]

Despite CIA pessimism, a coup of sorts had materialized. Secretly delighted, the agency waited for Allende to be swept aside. First reports were, however, dismal. 'There has been thus far no indication that the conspirators intend to push on with their plans to overthrow the government,' agents revealed. Clearly, Chileans were in no mood for a coup. Viaux's desperados simply evaporated, while Allende urged the people to resist 'counter-revolutionary' plots. By his actions, Viaux had succeeded only in solidifying a popular desire for orderly, democratic change. Schneider became a martyr to the constitutional process, and Allende's accession seemed the most appropriate way to honour him. Congress duly elected Allende president, with 153 votes in favour and a mere 42 opposed or abstaining.[15]

'I am not going to do a thing for [Chile],' a spiteful Nixon shouted on 15 October, promising that Allende would be made to pay. In truth, however, the administration admitted that little could be done. A National Security Council memorandum of 9 November 1970 advised a 'correct but cool' approach, aimed at 'maximiz[ing] pressures on the Allende government to prevent its consolidation and limit its ability to implement policies contrary to U.S. and hemispheric interests'. Another paper outlined the need to 'give articulate support . . . to democratic elements in Chile opposed to the Allende regime' and underlined the importance of 'maintain[ing] effective relations with the Chilean military'. In other words, the US settled into a long game, with the focus on the 1976 election, by which time, it was confidently assumed, the people would have grown tired of Allende. While this still constituted meddling, it was hardly different from American action in scores of countries during the Cold War.[16]

Soviet meddling was, in contrast, more overt. Having hailed Allende's victory as 'a revolutionary blow to the imperialist system in Latin America', Moscow was determined that he should succeed. Contact was maintained not through legitimate embassy channels, but through Svyatoslav Kuznetsov, a KGB case officer assigned to 'exert a favourable influence'. Kuznetsov impressed upon Allende 'the necessity of reorganising Chile's army and intelligence services, and of setting up a relationship between Chile's and the USSR's intelligence services'. Cooperation was paid for with cash. In October 1971 Allende was given $30,000 to 'solidify . . . trusted relations'. When he asked for two precious Russian icons for his private art collection, these were duly supplied. Bribes were generously offered to key politicians and military commanders. Painfully aware of how unpopular the Marxist transformation might be and the obstacles democracy posed, Moscow urged Allende to curb democratic expression, hobble the media, and impose limits upon the powers of Congress. American attempts to encourage anti-Allende forces were, in other words, easily cancelled out by Russian efforts to neutralize them.[17]

External pressure upon Allende was, however, minuscule compared to the turbulence caused by his own people. Lacking a majority in Congress, he needed Christian Democrat support to pass his reforms. In most cases, this was easily had, since the party, wedded to redistribution, nationalization and social welfare, saw sense in being 'good *allendistas*'. Unfortunately, Allende's attempts to court the centre annoyed the left. Workers and peasants, impatient for change, reacted by seizing property, action Allende felt obliged to endorse. Miristas pressured Allende to move faster. They complained that Allende was insufficiently violent and too respectful of democracy. A power struggle raged within the UP between communists and Miristas, who acted upon doctrinal differences with beatings and murder.[18]

'Our objective is total, scientific, Marxist socialism,' Allende proclaimed in 1971. 'As for the bourgeois State at the present moment, we are seeking to overcome it. To overthrow it!' He sensed that bloodshed might be necessary in order to complete the transformation. 'We shall meet reactionary violence with revolutionary violence,' he proclaimed, 'because we know they are going to break the rules.' Nor would the law be allowed to stand in his way. 'The revolution will remain within the law as long as the law does not try to stop the revolution,' his minister of justice declared.[19]

Allende's first year in power was surprisingly successful. By the end of 1971, unemployment had dropped to 3.8 per cent, industrial production was up by 6.3 per cent, agricultural productivity by 5.3 per cent and real wages by 27 per cent. Success, however, brought fresh problems since the right concluded that progress had come at their expense, while the left decided that anything was possible. Statistics also deceive. What seemed like economic growth was actually a one-off windfall from nationalizing foreign assets. Chile was still heavily reliant on foreign loans, and lacked the capacity to repay them – in November 1971 loan payments were suspended. By the end of the year, shortages began appearing in the shops, causing housewives to protest in the 'March of the Empty Pots'. The financial crisis worsened when Nixon slashed aid, a move mirrored by other foreign powers. While that was undoubtedly politically motivated, it was also predicated by genuine fears of fiscal meltdown. The move was mirrored in the private sector, as foreign banks, wanting nothing to do with a failing socialist experiment, pulled the plug on loans.

In 1972, the economy went into nosedive. By the end of the year, the balance of payments deficit stood at $298 million; inflation had rocketed to 163 per cent; and real wages had dropped 7 per cent. Agricultural imports rose to $400 million, an increase of 84 per cent since the election. Food rationing was actively discussed. Powerless to control inflation, Allende printed money.

The crisis energized Allende's opponents. Congress blocked legislation in order to limit the damage Allende could do. Meanwhile, out of self-protection, the middle class sent capital out of the country, exacerbating the balance of payments crisis. A wave of strikes, some admittedly funded by the CIA, paralysed the nation. The UP reacted by sending paramilitary thugs onto the streets to punish striking workers. The mounting chaos did not go unnoticed in Moscow. KGB assessments of Allende's prospects turned increasingly bleak.

Moscow was reluctant to bankroll a president who seemed incapable of managing his own economy.

As the crisis deepened, Allende behaved ever more like the dictator he aspired to be. Opposition groups were harassed and journalists threatened. Businesses unsympathetic to the Marxist plan were closed down or nationalized. Lacking political subtlety, Allende failed to take advantage of Christian Democrat goodwill. No longer courting the party, he tried to destroy it by luring away leftists and persecuting the rest. Workers who professed Christian Democrat allegiance were beaten up or dismissed from jobs.

In the 1973 congressional elections, the UP won a surprising 43 per cent of votes, though voter intimidation was rife. Much more impressive, however, was the way Allende had destroyed the middle ground – the country was cleaved into those who supported him and those determined to block him. Chile seemed on the verge of civil war, with extremists on the right and left stockpiling arms. In late June, rightists from the Patria y Libertad movement pushed tanks and armoured cars into the centre of Santiago. The coup proved futile, but it did underline Allende's vulnerability. Warned in advance, he called upon his people to 'pour into the centre of the city'. They refused. 'You know I think that Chilean guy might have some problems,' a smug Nixon remarked on 4 July. 'Oh, he has massive problems,' Kissinger confirmed. 'He definitely has massive problems.'[20]

The knives were out. On 26 May, the Supreme Court formally objected to Allende's 'open and willful disregard for judicial verdicts'. With typical bluster, he responded that the law could not be allowed to stand in the way of socialist revolution. 'In a time of revolution, political power has the right to decide . . . whether or not judicial decisions correspond with the higher goals and historical necessities of social transformation.' Allende's friend Oscar Waiss responded even more aggressively, advising that, 'The moment had come to throw away all legalistic fetishism, to sack the military conspirators, to remove the Comptroller General, to intervene in the Supreme Court and the Judiciary, to confiscate the *El Mercurio* newspaper and the whole pack of counter-revolutionary journalistic hounds. We must hit first, since he who hits first hits twice.' Moderates like Frei despaired at the impossibility of removing Allende by regular means. 'Unfortunately, this problem can only be solved with guns,' he concluded.[21]

A massive truckers' strike, backed by the CIA, began on 26 July. Losses after two months were estimated at $100 million. With inflation topping 320 per cent, the Chamber of Deputies in August publicly censured Allende and called upon the military to remove him. The Christian Democrat Claudio Orrego justified the action on the grounds that 'the country is in a crisis that has no parallel in our national history'. A resolution listed twenty violations of the rule of law, including support of armed groups, illegal arrests, torture, muzzling the press, confiscating private property and usurping power. Action was necessary in order to preserve 'the constitutional order of our Nation and the essential underpinnings of democratic coexistence'. The Resolution was approved by 81 votes to 47. Allende responded with a familiar refrain: the law could not be allowed to stand in the way of socialism.[22]

The resolution was a huge gamble in that it called upon the armed forces to sort out a problem – namely the removal of Allende – which the Chamber of Deputies could not resolve. Allende objected that this was the equivalent of 'ask[ing] for a coup d'état'. That is precisely what the Deputies wanted, but their request was made with the constitutionalist tradition of the army in mind. In other words, Deputies assumed that the army would do what was asked and then quickly restore democracy.[23]

This time, the military was only too happy to oblige. Officers understood that if they did not act quickly they were very likely to fall victim to a left-wing coup, since leftist paramilitaries were busily preparing for a campaign of assassinations. Officers also understood that, given the deep discontent with Allende, their action was likely to be popular.

On 22 August 1973, General Carlos Prats, the interior minister and commander-in-chief, warned Allende that a coup was inevitable. Torn between his loyalty to Allende and to the constitution, he chose to resign. On hearing of his resignation, Allende asked Prats whether he could count on the loyalty of his replacement, General Pinochet. Prats thought Pinochet was loyal, but warned that support for a coup within the army was now so overwhelming that any officer who tried to resist would be swept aside.

The axe fell at 07.00 on 11 September. Pinochet played a clever game, pretending loyalty to Allende until it was clear that the coup would succeed. By 10.00, all of Chile was effectively under military control, except for the centre of Santiago. Instead of escaping, Allende stayed at the government palace, desperately trying to organize a counter-attack. Despite threats of an airstrike, he refused to surrender. His last words were devoted to making myth. 'Workers of my country,' he proclaimed, 'I want to thank you for the loyalty that you always had, the confidence that you deposited in a man who was only an interpreter of great yearnings for justice, who gave his word that he would respect the Constitution and the law and did just that.' The crisis was blamed on the usual enemies of socialism: 'foreign capital [and] imperialism'. As the cordon grew tighter, he concluded: 'I will always be next to you. At least my memory will be that of a man of dignity who was loyal to his country.' Shortly after those last words were uttered, air force jets bombed the palace. At some point during that attack, Allende stuck the muzzle of an automatic rifle beneath his chin and pulled the trigger.

The coup was a democratic act that led to the death of democracy. At the time, most Chileans assumed that the military had saved the country from socialist dictatorship. Reporting on 14 September, a *Guardian* journalist found individuals from all walks of life 'welcoming the patriotic gesture of our armed forces'. Unfortunately, public acclaim blinded Pinochet, causing him to forget his duty to the constitution. In the weeks that followed, he brutally excised all Allendistas. Thousands were murdered, huge numbers were imprisoned without trial, and many simply disappeared. The machinery of dictatorship was efficiently installed. The constitution was torn up, political parties outlawed, Congress disbanded and the press rigidly controlled. Murder, torture and intimidation would remain the hallmarks of Pinochet's regime for the next sixteen years.[24]

Allende, like so many heroes of the left, had the good fortune of dying before his perfidy could surface. Starry-eyed romantics have made a hero of him for supposedly trying, against all odds, to establish socialism by democratic means. But that is a fairy tale made no more valid by the frequency of its narration. Pinochet, Kissinger and Nixon inadvertently conspired in Allende's deification. Their malfeasance allowed the martyr myth to become transcendent. Today, Allende symbolizes sacred Chilean democracy, despite the contempt he held for the democratic process. In the accepted narrative of the Seventies, his goodness is non-negotiable. Likewise, CIA involvement is carelessly assumed to be absolute, up to and including the 1973 coup. Patricia Verdugo, a Chilean historian, blames American manipulation for the tragedy of the Pinochet years. 'The CIA's history in preparing the conflict makes the United States responsible for all that followed.' Given the derision that surrounds Kissinger and Nixon, hers is an easy brief to argue. But the US did not actually create Pinochet. Documentary evidence shows that the Americans wanted democracy preserved. 'Our hand doesn't show on this one,' Nixon remarked to Kissinger after the coup. 'We didn't do it,' Kissinger replied. As much as we might like to believe otherwise, that was true. The Allende story reveals the impressive capacity of the Chileans to control their own affairs, and also to make a mess of them.[25]

Washington: Watergate

Richard Nixon, despite his famous claims to the contrary, was a crook. That was plainly obvious long before Watergate. The nickname 'Tricky Dick' was not, after all, invented because of that scandal. Shady practices were evident as early as 1952 when he campaigned for the vice-presidency and called upon his dog Checkers to run camouflage for his duplicity. More recently, his actions during the 1968 presidential campaign and his conduct of the Vietnam War confirmed a pathological dishonesty. But while Americans were vaguely aware of his crookedness, they accepted him because he was their crook – a man dishonest on America's behalf. Deceit, it seemed, went hand in hand with toughness, and these were tough times.

What Americans did not realize, however, was the sheer scope of Nixon's perfidy. That was revealed because of Watergate, to the extent that the affair came to be seen not as a single crime, but as a metaphor of mendacity. That realization plunged the American people into a moral crisis much more serious than the affair itself.

The Democrats, in truth, had no chance of victory in the 1972 presidential election. The party had not remotely recovered from the bitter conflicts of four years earlier – in fact, turmoil had deepened. Edward Kennedy showed brief promise, but that was destroyed at Chappaquiddick in 1969, when poor judgement resulted in tragic death. The remaining contenders were a sorry lot which included Hubert Humphrey, who had yet to accept his lack of appeal; Senator Edmund Muskie, an inept, unlucky and boring campaigner; and George McGovern, a decent liberal out of touch with America. Starved of alternatives, the party settled on McGovern. In other words, Nixon did not need to cheat in order to win.

That said, Nixon's team did cultivate McGovern's selection. Donald Segretti, a slimy California lawyer, called the practice 'ratfucking', a term which encompassed bugging offices, spreading vile rumours, stealing secret files, and generally making mayhem in order to destroy stronger candidates. 'Let's have a little fun,' Nixon shouted as he encouraged his aides to ever more imaginative mischief. Muskie endured what he called a 'systematic campaign of sabotage', including bogus allegations that he had used a racial slur and forged letters accusing rival candidates of illicit sexual behaviour. In addition, the Internal Revenue Service was used to look for dirt in the tax files of prominent Democrats. 'Bob, please get me the names of the Jews, you know, the big Jewish contributors of the Democrats,' Nixon asked his chief of staff H.R. Haldeman on 13 September 1971. 'Could we please investigate some of the cocksuckers?' The day after George Wallace was shot while campaigning for the

Democratic nomination, Nixon and his aide Charles Colson discussed Wallace's assassin, Arthur Bremer:

NIXON: 'Is he a left-winger or a right-winger?'
COLSON: 'Well, he's going to be a left-winger by the time we get through, I think.'
NIXON: 'Good. [chuckles] Keep at that. Keep at that.'

E. Howard Hunt, a freelance spy, was subsequently instructed to plant pro-McGovern literature in Bremer's apartment. Unfortunately, the FBI got there first and sealed the place. When Nixon learned of this setback, he suggested that FBI Director L. Patrick Gray might be persuaded to help. 'Use him . . . you know, to sneak out things. I mean, you do anything. I mean, anything!'[26]

Nixon's philosophy was simple: 'Be ready. Lay in the bushes and then whack them.' He was a small man never satisfied with success. As the satirist Harry Shearer wrote, 'He never let the fact that he had reached the pinnacle of his aspirations distract him from his mission of vindictive resentment against those who failed . . . to stand in his way.' Consumed by hate and paranoia, he wanted not just to win, but also to humiliate his opponent. 'We're up against an enemy, a conspiracy,' he told aides nearly a year before the Watergate scandal broke. 'They're using any means. We are going to use any means. Is that clear?' Rejecting 'high-minded lawyers', he actively recruited the unscrupulous. 'I really need a son-of-a-bitch', he remarked, 'who will work his butt off and do it dishonorably.' As early as 1970, he directed his staff 'to come up with the kind of imaginative dirty tricks that our Democratic opponents used against us . . . in previous campaigns'. Since secrecy and deception allows small men the chance to feel big, Nixon never lacked a ready supply of rogues. An army of yes-men were infected with his warped view of the world. Given that they owed their elevation to him, they willingly did what he asked.[27]

With the outcome certain, the campaign was a non-event. The country had to endure a summer of McGovern preaching a platform written on Mars. He was probably the most liberal candidate ever to run for president, yet 'liberal' had become a dirty word. 'Every time he opened his mouth,' one former Democrat reflected, 'it came out irresponsible . . . So I voted for Nixon with no enthusiasm.' Because the nation tuned McGovern out, they failed to hear his one relevant message, namely that the Nixon administration was 'the most corrupt . . . in history'. Proof came on 17 June when five administration lackeys were caught prowling around the Democratic National Committee offices in the Watergate Building. News of the break-in, coming in the middle of a campaign, should have been monumental. In fact, few noticed, and fewer still cared.[28]

The idea originated within a sordid cabal aptly called CREEP, or the Committee to Re-Elect the President. CREEP collected illegal donations to fund dirty work dreamt up by men like G. Gordon Liddy, a thoroughly malevolent individual with a hooligan approach to politics. A former CIA agent, Liddy had previously been recruited as a 'plumber' to plug leaks of secret information from the White House. When CREEP was formed, he was enlisted, since his unscrupulous zealotry seemed just the ticket. In January 1972, Liddy proposed a comprehensive programme of dirty tricks with a price tag topping $1 million. John Dean, the White House counsel, found it 'the most incredible thing I have ever laid my eyes on: all in codes, and involv[ing] black bag operations, kidnapping, providing prostitutes to weaken the opposition, bugging, mugging teams'. John Mitchell, head of CREEP and formerly the attorney general, rejected the plan, but, ten weeks later, after pressure from Colson and Haldeman, commissioned Liddy to place wiretaps in the Watergate Building. That mission went ahead on 27 May, but was unsuccessful. A second attempt, on 17 June, resulted in the arrest of James McCord and four Cuban exiles.[29]

According to Colson, Nixon was so angry on hearing of the break-in that he threw an ashtray across the room. He 'thought it was the dumbest thing he had ever heard of and was just outraged that anyone even remotely connected with the campaign organization would have . . . anything to do with something like Watergate'. That seems doubtful. If Nixon was angry, it was not over the fact that the break-in had occurred, but rather that it had failed so abysmally. He had, after all, encouraged crimes of this nature fully a year before McCord's arrest. While it is entirely possible that Nixon knew nothing of this specific plan, there is no doubt that he created the climate that allowed its conception.[30]

Nixon's press secretary, Ron Ziegler, was quick to dismiss the break-in as a 'third-rate burglary'. That was true, but over subsequent months, it evolved into a first-rate scandal. Nixon was entirely to blame, for the simple reason that he decided on cover-up instead of *mea culpa*. The wisest course would have been to go before the country immediately after the arrests, blame the crime on rogue elements, apologize, fire a few scapegoats and promise a full investigation. Such a course would have allowed the White House, instead of journalists, to control the story. Nixon rejected that course, perhaps because he worried that full disclosure would cause more serious scandals to spread like a metastasizing cancer. Instead he chose cover-up, despite telling his aides, just a month after the break-in: 'The worst thing a guy can do . . . is to cover up . . . If you cover up, you're going to get caught.'[31]

The cover-up was designed to prevent any connection being made between the five burglars and the White House. To this end, hush money was distributed, with the fund for this purpose eventually reaching $500,000. As an extra precaution, just six days after the break-in, Haldeman suggested having Vernon Walters of the CIA tell Gray of the FBI to 'Stay the hell out of this . . . there's some business here we don't want you going any further on.' Nixon replied: 'Mm-hmm.' Both Haldeman and Nixon assumed that the involvement of the CIA would encourage the impression that national security was at stake and thus convince the curious to back off. Regardless of his original involvement, Nixon's mumbled assent automatically made him a conspirator in the obstruction of justice.[32]

For a while, the cover-up worked, partly because most journalists refused to get excited about the story at a time when news was dominated by events in Vietnam. Nixon's reputation for crookedness, however, meant that he could not completely escape attention when crimes were committed so close to the White House. The zeal with which the *Washington Post* reporters Carl Bernstein and Bob Woodward investigated was inspired by an assumption that a smoking gun would eventually be found on Nixon's desk. At first, however, their investigation seemed to many a silly vendetta. Feeling confident, the president decided to use the IRS to punish the paper, privately explaining: 'This . . . is war. They are asking for it and they are going to get it.'[33]

By November, there was still no indication that tiny sparks of scandal would ignite a conflagration. The lopsided election gave Nixon nearly 61 per cent of the vote and every state except Massachusetts and the District of Columbia. At his second inauguration on 20 January 1973, he had reason to feel triumphant. No mention was made in his inaugural address of misdeeds committed on his behalf. Then, a week later, came ceasefire in Vietnam, encouraging his belief in his own invincibility. But that development did not bring the gratitude Nixon anticipated, rather the opposite. With the war over, criticizing the president no longer seemed quite as disloyal as it had when guns were blazing. Worse still, the ceasefire coincided with awkward revelations relating to Watergate.

In January 1973 the five burglars were found guilty, along with two of the 'plumbers' – Liddy and Hunt. Mitchell had insisted from the beginning that 'McCord and the four men arrested . . . were not operating either in our behalf or with our consent'. But John Sirica, the presiding judge, refused to buy that line. Like a bloodhound, he followed the trail of complicity. Up to this point, administration strategy, articulated by Dean, Haldeman and John Ehrlichman (domestic policy coordinator) and supported by Nixon, had been to 'take a public posture of full cooperation, but privately . . . make it as difficult as possible to get information and witnesses'. Staffers were instructed that, if they were called to testify before the grand jury, they should not cooperate. 'I don't give a shit what happens,'

Nixon told his aides. 'I want you all to stonewall it, . . . plead the Fifth Amendment, cover-up.'[34]

Keen to cover up the cover-up, Nixon on 12 March asserted that the principle of executive privilege allowed him to prevent all current and past White House aides from testifying. He claimed that issues of national security would inevitably arise, therefore silence was essential. That justification provided a thin shield, however, since those determined to uncover the truth simply concluded that Nixon had much to hide. Nixon then ordered Dean on 16 March to release a statement claiming that his own internal investigation had revealed no complicity on the part of anyone in the White House – essentially it was an order to commit perjury. Dean, feeling increasingly uncomfortable, warned that, 'We have a cancer . . . close to the presidency, that's growing. It's growing daily. It's compounding. It grows geometrically now, because it compounds itself . . . it basically is because (1) we're being blackmailed; (2) people are going to start perjuring themselves very quickly . . . and there is no assurance . . .' 'That it won't bust,' Nixon interjected.[35]

Fearful that he might be forced take the rap for his bosses, McCord decided on 20 March to cooperate with Sirica. The information he supplied was taken up by Senator Sam Ervin, who headed the Senate committee formed to investigate. Unlike Sirica, Ervin did not have to contend with the slow pace of judicial process. Eager to get to the bottom of the matter, he conducted hearings at breakneck speed, which made them compulsive television drama. Thanks largely to the telegenic Ervin, the nation was now riveted to Watergate. 'Only Super Bowls, wars and the final episodes of beloved sitcoms', wrote Shearer, 'can bring us together . . . in the way that Watergate television did.'[36]

McCord's decision started a stampede. On the assumption that those who talked first might enjoy clemency, Jeb Stuart Magruder, Mitchell's assistant at CREEP, decided to cooperate, as did Dean. On 24 April, Ehrlichman warned Nixon that if Dean talked, the result might be impeachment. Nixon replied: 'Sometimes it's well to give them something and then they don't want the bigger fish.'

To that end, Haldeman and Ehrlichman were forced out, as was Richard Kleindienst, the attorney general, and Dean. On live television, Nixon told the nation on 30 April that Haldeman and Ehrlichman were 'two of the finest public servants it has been my privilege to know'. His refusal to extend the same praise to Dean was a ploy intentionally designed to encourage the assumption that while Haldeman and Ehrlichman were innocent victims, Dean was the arch-conspirator.[37]

While scapegoats might have saved Nixon in July 1972, by this stage they were useless. Once the powerful began to talk, the jig was up. Dean and Magruder fully realized they were more likely to gain favour if they supplied rich detail. Revelation inspired revelation in precisely the way Nixon had feared. Before long, attention strayed beyond the break-in. The Ervin committee heard about the plumbers, the dirty tricks played on Democratic candidates, the hush money, the wiretapping, and Nixon's attempt to use the CIA to block the FBI. In the midst of these revelations, Alexander Butterfield, an aide to Haldeman, shocked his questioners by revealing that Nixon kept tapes of Oval Office conversations. Ervin, Sirica and Archibald Cox, the independent special prosecutor, pounced like a pack of hungry dogs. The tapes proved a watershed. Up to this point, Watergate had seemed a bizarre affair shrouded in legal complexity. The tapes, however, reduced that complexity to a simple matter of evidence. Dean had accused Nixon, and Nixon had trashed Dean. The tapes would determine who was lying. If Nixon proved reluctant to release them, he clearly had something to hide.

Close on the heels of the tape controversy came news that Vice-President Spiro Agnew had received bribes from contractors while Governor of Maryland. In exchange for agreeing to resign, the Justice Department allowed him to plead *nolo contendre* on a single charge of tax evasion. He walked free with three years' probation and a minuscule fine, despite having committed crimes that sent lesser men to prison. Then came news that Nixon had used $10 million of federal money to improve two of his private homes and the homes of his daughters. That disclosure was followed, a few months later, by revelations of tax evasion to the tune of $467,000 – more than a lot of Americans made in a lifetime. Nixon, who had used the IRS to attack his opponents, was sliced open by the tax sword's double edge. 'You can't screw around . . . I mean, . . . you [can't] horse around with the IRS,' he had earlier warned Dean. The tax scandal demonstrated that Nixon, far from being a clever Machiavellian, was simply a petty thief. 'I am not a crook,' he told a news conference, while insisting that he had never benefited financially from public service and had 'never obstructed justice'. By this stage, however, most Americans were noticing how Nixon's nose seemed to grow longer with each passing day.[38]

Nixon tried desperately to block access to the tapes. When Cox proved a nuisance, Nixon decided to fire him, on the assumption that a more pliable prosecutor could be found. Nixon's aides, however, refused to do his dirty work. On 20 October, the new attorney general, Elliot Richardson, decided to jump ship rather than obey instructions to fire Cox. Richardson's second in command, William Ruckelshaus, also refused. After what the press called the 'Saturday Night Massacre', ordinary citizens jammed White House phone lines with complaints. On the following morning a man in a Nixon mask stood outside the White House and held up a sign reading 'Honk for Impeachment'. The cacophony of horns provided Nixon with potent indication of the national mood. *Time*, not usually given to direct attacks upon a sitting president, argued that Nixon had 'irredeemably lost his moral authority, the confidence of most of the country, and therefore his ability to govern effectively'.[39]

Acting Attorney General Robert Bork dutifully dismissed Cox, but the new special prosecutor, Leon Jaworski, proved as dogged as his predecessor. After some tapes were finally surrendered, a new twist appeared on 21 November, with revelations of a mysterious eighteen-minute gap in the recording of a conversation between Nixon and Haldeman three days after the break-in. When Nixon's secretary Rosemary Woods offered a completely implausible explanation for how the tape was 'accidentally' erased, the nation shuddered at the sight of a decent woman who had obviously been bullied into lying for her boss.

'One year of Watergate is enough,' Nixon proclaimed during his State of the Union Address on 30 January 1974. While that might have been true, he was beyond controlling the timetable of this unfolding drama. Jaworski, Sirica and the House Judiciary Committee slowly constructed their cases, carefully weighing what kind of charges the evidence might bear. On 1 March 1974, a grand jury issued indictments against seven White House aides, including Mitchell, Haldeman and Ehrlichman, while naming Nixon as an unindicted co-conspirator. The House Judiciary Committee was, meanwhile, considering the issue on everyone's mind, namely impeachment. While these discussions were progressing, Nixon continued to stall over the tapes. He did release 1,300 pages of edited transcripts, but these raised more questions than they answered. Since the cleaned-up version (peppered with 'expletive deleted') showed a foul-mouthed, vindictive president addicted to dirty tricks and obstruction, Americans naturally wondered what the unexpurgated tapes might reveal. The Republican congressman John Rhodes, House Minority Leader, judged the transcripts 'deplorable, shabby, disgusting and immoral'. In the wake of the transcripts, a Harris poll showed that a majority of Americans favoured impeachment.[40]

On 24 July the Supreme Court finally settled the tape issue, ruling unanimously that Nixon could not hide behind executive privilege. After a brief hesitation, he surrendered the tapes to Sirica. The surrender was by no means complete, however, since new gaps were discovered, and some tapes were mysteriously 'lost'. His compliance did not, in any case, affect the House Judiciary Committee's deliberations on impeachment. The general counsel to the committee, John Doar, accused Nixon of 'a pattern of conduct designed not to take care that the laws be faithfully executed, but to impede their faithful execution, in his political interest and on his behalf'. When formal votes were conducted between 27 and 30 July, on each occasion seven or eight Republicans joined Democrats in supporting impeachment.[41]

While the Judiciary Committee deliberated, lawyers for the president listened to their client destroy himself on tape. Particularly damning was the recording of the meeting on 23 June 1972 when Nixon ordered the CIA to prevent the FBI from investigating – the smoking gun. That by itself was enough to ensure a conviction on obstruction of justice, yet that was just one of Nixon's many crimes. His supporters in the House, having decided that their priority was to save their own careers, deserted the president in droves. Senior Republicans urged him to resign, in order to limit the damage to the party. Nixon stubbornly held out, but, on 8 August, finally surrendered. On the following day, he said goodbye to his White House staff in a rambling monologue peppered with cloying self-pity. He admitted making 'mistakes, yes. But for personal gain, never.' He insisted he was not a rich man, otherwise he would be able to pay his taxes. 'Always give your best,' he closed, 'never get discouraged, never get petty; always remember, others may hate you, but those who hate you don't win unless you hate them, and then you destroy yourself.' While that advice was undoubtedly wise, it was nestled in deep delusion.[42]

Nixon handed the presidency to Gerald Ford, who had earlier replaced Agnew as vice-president. Ford waited a month and then pardoned Nixon for all crimes committed, despite the fact that crimes had not yet been proven in a court of law. The pardon was hugely unpopular, but it was probably necessary in order to hasten closure. Ford understood that the nation would not benefit from a long trial of Richard Nixon. Most critics of the pardon understood that also, but were not about to pass on the advantage of complaint.

After Nixon's departure, Americans went looking for crumbs of solace. In an article ladled with self-congratulation, *Time* celebrated how the 'system' had worked. It was, the magazine argued, 'an extraordinary triumph'. A man in Brooklyn remarked: 'It's great. I can tell my senator to go to hell, the rights are mine. I'm proud of a country that can throw out a president . . . Democracy was strengthened by Watergate. It proved the Constitution works. The political system passed the test.' The system had not, however, passed with flying colours. Nixon's departure owed much to accident, not to mention stupidity. The system had allowed him to get away with a vast range of shady practices for a long time before he was caught and, but for the existence of the tapes, there might never have been grounds to dismiss him. On 18 April 1973, Nixon had told Haldeman to destroy the tapes. Had he carried out that instruction, it is unlikely that Nixon would have had to resign. The dominoes toppling within the White House would have stopped with Haldeman.[43]

Nor is it necessarily a good thing that an ordinary citizen can tell his senator to go to hell. Granted, Americans had reason to feel jaded. Watergate came in the midst of a long dark night during which they grew increasingly disdainful of those who governed them and increasingly doubtful of politics as a force for good. Healthy scepticism is a useful weapon against the duplicity of politicians, but contempt is the forage on which the populist feeds. In order for the system to work well, the people have to believe in it.

When Nixon followed his landslide victory in November 1972 with the notorious Christmas bombing of North Vietnam, a bumper sticker appeared on cars across America. It read: 'Don't blame me, I voted for McGovern'. When peace came in the spring of 1973, most people scraped the sticker off. Some, however, did not, either out of laziness or anger. The stickers that remained, faded and peeling at the edges, assumed ironic relevance in the summer of 1973, when the sordid Watergate revelations emerged. While that new relevance encouraged some citizens to feel smug, for most people the bumper sticker was a painful reminder of how bankrupt were the choices back in 1972. A crook had run against a decent but deluded liberal. The crook had eventually given way to Gerald Ford, the first non-elected president in history and a man stuck in a holding pattern. What was the future for America? 'Sometimes you get the feeling nothing has gone right since John Kennedy died,' one woman remarked. 'Before then you were used to America winning everything, but now you sometimes think our day might be over.' That assessment might not have been accurate, but it was widely expressed – and therein lay a problem.[44]

Athens: Metapolitefsi

The 1960s were the graveyard of revolution. In almost all cases, revolts by the left were brutally crushed by an organized and powerful right. One exception was Greece, where a vile seven-year military regime eventually fell victim to popular will. That said, Greece's Sixties revolution actually occurred in the 1970s – in 1974 to be precise.

The Sixties came late to Greece because the government was determined to hold back time. A clique of ultra-conservative colonels came to power in 1967 with the aim of placing Greece in a 'plaster cast' in order to 'set the bones' of the 'Hellas of Christian Hellenes'. The authoritarian regime led by Colonel George Papadopoulos, Brigadier Stylianos Pattakos and Colonel Nikolaos Makarezos was backed by a police force imaginative in brutality. The junta's 'revolution' banned most manifestations of the heavenly decade, including mini-skirts, long hair, rock music and student protest. It was neither popular nor competent, but was briefly tolerated because it seemed an improvement upon the chaos that preceded it and because, for a while, the economy cooperated.[45]

The colonels' desire to hold back time might have been comic if not for its viciousness. Papadopoulos, the strongman of the triumvirate, justified severity by arguing that Greece was in need of major surgery and, 'if the patient is not strapped to the table, the surgeon cannot perform a successful operation'. Parliament was abolished, the press rigidly controlled, 'dangerous' books banned, and nonconformity punished. 'Those . . . were dark days,' recalled Nick Michaelian, a Reuters correspondent.

> Plainclothes policemen from the dreaded ESA (Greek Military Police) arbitrarily arrested and beat up young people on street corners and threw them in cells and tortured them when they thought they belonged to some resistance group. Any left-leaning person was anathema. One day, two girls showed up at

> the Reuters office and . . . lifted their skirts to show us their thighs and genitals badly swollen from torture and broomstick insertions.

'Traitors' were sent to desolate prisons on remote islands. 'The brutal oppression which is now stifling my country has taught me a great deal, among other things the value of refusing to submit,' wrote Professor George Mangakis from prison.[46]

> As I sit in my cell thinking about these things, I am filled with a strange power . . . It is not expressed in a loud, insolent voice. It is the power of endurance – the power that is born of a sense of being right . . . I begin my day by uttering the word 'freedom'. This usually happens at daybreak. I emerge from sleep, always feeling bitterly surprised to find myself in prison, as on the first day. Then I utter my beloved word, before the sense of being in prison has time to overpower me.

The regime has commonly been called fascist, but that label is carelessly applied. In fact, the colonels were far too politically obtuse to espouse an ideology. They were simply opportunistic authoritarians who tried to bend an entire nation to their will.[47]

For a while the system worked, mainly because the rise of the colonels coincided with a period of prosperity. Greece, like Spain, benefited enormously from the emergence of the package tour industry, which injected much-needed foreign capital into the economy. But the junta's saving grace was also its nemesis. Tourists could not be told to cover up their bikinis or cut their long hair. Nor could the colonels do much about hippies, for whom the Greek islands provided a popular waystation on the pilgrimage from Marrakech to Kathmandu. Hippies brought with them the paraphernalia of cultural revolt, namely sex, drugs and rock 'n' roll. So, too, did the sailors from the American Sixth Fleet, who the colonels, keen to keep Washington happy, officially welcomed. Tourists, hippies and sailors foiled the junta's efforts to quarantine Greece.

Lacking a unifying ideology, the junta was riven with divisions and distrust. Members pursued selfish interests while Greece drifted. Utter ruthlessness allowed Papadopoulos to rise to the fore. He maintained power through a devil's pact with Colonel Dimitrios Ioannidis, the iceman who could call upon the loyalty of army units stationed around Athens. Papadopoulos mistakenly interpreted Ioannidis's aloofness from the nitty-gritty of government as evidence that he lacked political ambition. Feeling secure, he consolidated power, appointing himself prime minister, foreign minister, defence minister, minister of government policy and eventually regent and acting head of state. Greeks called him 'poly-Papadopoulos', a one-man Cabinet meeting.

The regime was always doomed because, in striking contrast to Spain, it failed to convince civilian politicians of its legitimacy. Most either left the country or went into self-imposed purdah, their silence the best expression of rejection. Politicians who broke ranks and cooperated with the junta were shunned. The most effective resistance to the regime came from its exiles – politicians like Andreas Papandreou and Constantine Caramanlis, the newpaper proprietor Eleni Vlachou, the actress Melina Mercouri and the banned composer Mikis Theodorakis. Their protests helped mobilize foreign opinion. Europe discovered unusual harmony in its hatred of the junta, but America's determination to hold on to its naval base meant that it ignored the regime's excesses. 'How can I fight the junta which has behind it the whole power of the United States, how can I hide anything from the omnipotence of the CIA?' a dissident complained.[48]

Politics was the favourite topic of conversation, even though talking about it was dangerous. An air of unreality prevailed, in the sense that most Greeks concurred that the regime had no future. Discussions therefore centred on when the end would come, and who would deliver the coup de grâce. This precarious state did not escape the notice of Papadopoulos, who repeatedly insisted that his was a revolution, not a regime – in other words that civilian government would soon evolve. Unfortunately, few believed him. In any case, every discussion of democracy revealed the limits of his power, since Ioannidis made clear his disapproval.

By 1970, the junta's honeymoon was over. Production could not keep pace with demand, leading to an increase in imports, crippling inflation and a rising balance of payments deficit. At the same time, tolerance for the colonels' puritanism wore thin, though displeasure was expressed in ad hoc defiance rather than organized dissent. Papadopoulos, aware that the junta had to change or perish, was by the end of 1972 meeting regularly with an 'inner cabinet' tasked with finding a smooth path to non-military rule. 'We must definitely leave office this year and surrender power to civilians!' he told colleagues in early 1973. His problem, however, had not changed: it was difficult to build a civilian government without the cooperation of civilians.[49]

Rumbling unrest underlined the urgency of change. In February, students at the law school in Athens staged a sit-in, the first indication that a protest movement was coalescing. Then, on 23 May, the crew of RNS *Velos* refused to return home after a NATO exercise. The commander, Nicholaos Pappas, hoped the mutiny would mobilize international opinion against the junta. Papadopoulos made light of the incident, though he knew full well how tenuous was the military support on which he depended. Addressing the nation on 1 June 1973, he announced his intention to establish a republic, with elections promised by the end of 1974. Keen to demonstrate his sincerity, he granted amnesty to 'enemies of the state', released some 300 political prisoners, relaxed censorship and lifted martial law. Ioannidis meanwhile fumed.

A plebiscite on 29 July approved the programme of change. The political elites, however, still remained aloof. The only prominent politician to cooperate was Spyros Markezinis, founder of the Progressive Party. Papadopoulos, who had named himself president, appointed Markezinis prime minister, with a mandate to oversee *metapolitefsi*, or regime change. The European Common Market countries welcomed the development and urged all Greek political parties to cooperate. Deaf to that call, politicians dismissed Markezinis as a quisling.

The Greek situation differs markedly from that of Spain, where political parties eagerly joined the 'transition' after Franco's death. The difference, of course, was that Papadopoulos was still alive and still ambitious. His presence rendered any new government automatically suspicious. 'The planned elections have a single purpose,' the centrist Georgios Mavros contended, '[namely] to legitimise the dictatorship covering it by a castrated Parliament which will not have the power to debate, let alone decide, any of the nation's vital matters.' Expressing rejection through ridicule, John Zigdis of the Centre Union Party argued that, 'Politics in Greece have for the moment lost their grimness represented by police tortures, and have taken on an atmosphere of vaudeville, with the arrival of the smiling juggler Markezinis.'[50]

Markezinis insisted that 'if I do not agree with the President, I shall resign . . . there is no other solution'. Interviewed by *Time*, he confessed his exasperation with those like Mavros, Zigdis and Papandreou. 'I don't fully understand [their] reaction. The worst political act is abstention. We must be realistic and reality is not always what we want it to be.' He claimed that he was motivated by 'the three Fs: forget, forgive and free elections'. His efforts were not, however, helped by Papadopoulos's repeated need to assert his dominance. 'Until the election of a Parliament,' he declared, 'the President is . . . the only source of power. The Premier-designate is accountable and responsible only to the President who makes the final decisions.' That statement encouraged doubters to continue doubting.[51]

Markezinis, though clearly sincere, was unfortunately tied to a president with a worse image problem than Attila the Hun. He nevertheless ploughed doggedly on. 'The top priority will be free elections,' he proclaimed. 'I will do my best to bring them as fast as possible. Greece needs to be governed by the will of its people.' He stressed that he was not motivated by ambition, since the voters would undoubtedly reject him. 'I . . . do not have any illusions. I will get 15 per cent. I hoped, however, that finally the old parties would participate and we could come to terms on forming a government.'

The consequences of failure, he warned, were dire. 'If I fail power will pass into the hands of a Greek Gaddafi!'[52]

Meanwhile, the liberalization Papadopoulos had introduced removed the lid from a can of worms. The effect was especially evident at the Polytechnic in Athens, where disgruntled students decided it was now safe to agitate. Repressive policing had, until then, kept Sixties-style student unrest in check. Following the example of Berkeley, Paris and Berlin, Greek students focused first on campus issues – the size and nature of classes, the rigid control of personal lives, the poor quality of facilities, the lack of job prospects after graduation. By 14 November, however, discontent had widened to the general state of politics in Greece, expressed through the slogan 'Bread, Education and Liberty'. Since that slogan tapped into the unease felt by the quiet multitude outside the campus, an alliance of sorts evolved. Quite suddenly, the people believed in their ability to destroy the junta.

Uncertain of the limits of government tolerance, students at first trod carefully. The government was likewise on unfamiliar ground: accustomed to the rigid maintenance of order, it too was unsure about the limits of tolerance. By the time Markezinis and Papadopoulos realized the seriousness of the situation, it was already out of control. With unrest spreading, Markezinis did his credibility as a reformer no favours by asking Papadopoulos to restore martial law.

On the 16th, thousands of Athenians crowded onto the streets to show solidarity with the students. Broadcasts from the campus radio station kept spirits high. 'This is the Polytechnic!' went the message. 'People of Greece, the Polytechnic bears the standard of our struggle and your struggle, our common struggle against dictatorship and for democracy!' Euphoria turned to apprehension in a flash. Panic boiled as the acrid smell of tear gas passed through the crowd. Pivoting on a dime, the march of righteousness became a stampede of fear.[53]

At midnight, around twenty-five tanks lumbered up to the Polytechnic gates. Students begged soldiers not to use force. 'You cannot do this,' they yelled, 'we are your brothers.' From the lead tank an officer emerged waving his pistol and ordered the students to disperse.

The army, he shouted, would not negotiate with anarchists. Out in the streets, those citizens still brave enough to remain outside knelt in prayer, pleading that a massacre might be averted. The students were given fifteen minutes to leave. Before ten minutes had passed, the first tank broke through the gate and opened fire. As bodies fell and blood drenched the pavement, protesters used bullhorns to call for help. Ambulances arrived quickly, but these contained not medical personnel, but gun-wielding police officers, some disguised in white coats. Not surprisingly, estimates of the dead vary widely, but it is safe to say that at least twenty, and probably twice that number, were killed.[54]

Brutality of this sort came as no surprise – the junta was nothing if not vicious. There was, however, something else at work in Athens; it was not just the students who came under attack. On the 17th, Markezinis was due to give a press conference at which plans for free elections were to be announced. It was cancelled because of the bloodshed at the Polytechnic. Those so inclined could smell a rat. Markezinis believes that Ioannidis used the unrest to justify a show of force so profound that it would stop democratization dead in its tracks. The students, by bravely testing the waters of reform, had unwittingly abetted tyranny.

A week later, tanks returned to the streets in order to complete the demolition of *metapolitefsi*. Since Papadopoulos had clearly gone soft, Ioannidis threw him out like a rotten piece of fruit. On the morning of the 25th, the streets crowded with military hardware, Papadopoulos received a note from the 'Revolutionary Committee'. 'On the demand of the Armed Forces,' it read, 'you, the vice-president and the Markezinis government have resigned. You will be informed of the developments from television.' A short time later came an announcement that the overthrow of the government had the support of the army, navy and air force – in other words, it was futile to resist. The communiqué promised a 'continuation of the revolution of 1967' and explained that Papadopoulos had been ousted because he had 'stray[ed] from the ideals of the 1967 revolution' and had 'push[ed] the country towards parliamentary rule too quickly'.[55]

The Dutch ambassador Carl Barkman concluded that 'it was [Papadopoulos's] misfortune . . . that the treachery of his own most trusted follower deprived him of the opportunity to undo the harm he had done to Greece'. That judgement depends, of course, on an assumption that Papadopoulos was sincere about democracy. He might simply have been planning cosmetic changes to the political system which would have allowed him to continue in power. The issue of sincerity will never be solved, but what can be said for certain is that the refusal of politicians like Caramanlis and Papandreou to cooperate with Markezinis made it easy for Ioannidis to shove Papadopoulos aside.[56]

Uncertain precisely what had occurred on the 25th, most Greeks welcomed the demise of Papadopoulos. 'I don't think anyone was so bitterly hated,' the exiled publisher Eleni Vlachos told the BBC. 'He humiliated the Greek people.' Most people assumed that whatever transpired, it could not be worse than Papadopoulos. The next eight months demonstrated how foolish that assumption was. Ioannidis was the 'Greek Gaddafi' Markezinis had warned of. Lieutenant General Phaedon Gizikis, the puppet president, became the mouthpiece for a sinister plan to subvert the public will. He claimed that he held no ambition for high office, but was simply doing his duty as a soldier. 'My only ambition is . . . the consolidation of tranquillity and unity among the Greek people.' If that was indeed his aim, he failed miserably.[57]

The 'junta nova' lasted a mere eight months. Ioannidis's most significant achievement came in the way he inspired nostalgia for Papadopoulos. He was the 'invisible dictator', a master puppeteer determined to set the clock back to 1967. While Papadopoulos had always claimed that the junta was a temporary measure, Ioannidis boldly asserted his faith in authoritarianism. 'We are not playing,' he confessed. 'We shall have a dictatorship, send all our opponents to exile on the islands and stay in power for thirty years!' The prison camps, so briefly closed, were immediately reopened, and instruments of torture taken out of storage.[58]

Ioannidis's big mistake was to embark upon a foreign adventure for which his people were neither prepared nor enthusiastic. On 15 July 1974, he launched a military coup in Cyprus, ousting the president, Archbishop Makarios. His aim was to annex the island, a goal that seemed in keeping with the greater glory of the nation. Most Greeks, however, thought the idea insane. Matters worsened when, five days later, Turkey invaded Cyprus on the pretext of protecting the Turkish Cypriot community. Full-scale war suddenly loomed.

While Ioannidis welcomed a war with Turkey, most sensible people considered it suicidal. The junta's announcement of full mobilization plunged the country into deep dismay. Chaos reigned as frightened citizens raided grocery stores in anticipation of economic collapse. A slide into anarchy seemed likely as turmoil deepened. On 23 July, however, Greece witnessed the strange spectacle of a government acting sensibly. Gizikis summoned military leaders to discuss how to escape the crisis Ioannidis had wrought. The iceman was not invited. The group decided to step down 'in view of the position in which the country finds itself'. While Greeks talked of rats and sinking ships, most realized that a sensible decision had been made.[59]

The last act of the junta was to invite the exiled Caramanlis to form a government of national unity. This time, he did not hesitate to take up his political duty. Ordinary citizens, on hearing that Caramanlis was on his way, crowded the streets to celebrate Metapolitefsi Mark II. 'Blue and white Greek flags and white banners suddenly sprouted from windows,' a journalist reported. '"Hellas! Hellas!" shouted the crowd every time another flag appeared. Groups of students locked arms, chanting, "The people have won!" "The junta is dead!" "Democracy! Democracy! Amnesty! Amnesty!"' 'It was a night unlike any other night,' recalled the journalist Mario Modiano. He rushed to the airport to witness the return of Caramanlis. Along the route were 'hundreds of thousands of jubilant Athenians . . . [there] to welcome their own Cincinnatus. Most of them held lit tapers as on Resurrection night.'[60]

Caramanlis arrived at 02.30 on 24 July. Emerging from the plane, he told the crowd: 'I have come to contribute to the best of my ability to the restoration of normal conditions and democracy. In the lives of nations there are crises which can be turned into a starting point for national regeneration and a better future. I am optimistic about the future.' He then made his way to Constitution Square, cheered all the way by countrymen who threw flowers in his path. From the balcony of the Parliament, he proclaimed, 'I am with you. Democracy is with you.'[61]

The power of the military was still formidable, but the soldiers had run out of ideas. They had simply to stand aside while civilians cleaned up the mess they had made. Change was immediately apparent. Political prisoners were released, exiles returned. Radios played musicians previously banned, instead of endless martial compositions. In a single moment, Greece leapt years ahead. It was suddenly the 1970s.

Well before his aborted experiment with reform, Markezinis wrote of the junta that 'this revolution will be judged by the way it ends'. Since it ended in utter failure, judgement seems easy. But the timing encourages equivocation. The regime of the colonels ended eight months later than it need have done. There was nothing inevitable about the reign of Ioannidis or the dreadful fiasco in Cyprus. With a little more imagination, selflessness and cooperation on the part of politicians in November, the tragedy at the Polytechnic, and the calamity that followed it, might have been averted.[62]

Vietnam: The Ho Chi Minh Offensive

The Paris Agreements of January 1973 were presented as a peaceful, political end to the Vietnam War. On the strength of that charade, Henry Kissinger and Le Duc Tho were awarded the Nobel Peace Prize. On the ground in Vietnam, however, peace was war in new packaging. 'There is no cease fire at all,' the South Vietnamese leader Nguyen van Thieu complained, while at the same time boasting that, during the six weeks that the guns were supposed to be silent, his forces had killed 5,218 enemy soldiers. 'Both the Communists and the government', the CIA analyst Frank Snepp recorded on 13 July

1973, 'are interpreting the new cease-fire agreement selectively, emphasizing . . . those parts of it which favor their respective interests and ignoring those that do not.' Each side manoeuvred for military advantage, all the while accusing the other of treaty violations. Neither Hanoi nor Saigon had faith in paper agreements. Both expected, and wanted, a decision on the battlefield.[63]

At the time the agreements were signed, Nixon had promised that the US would 'respond with full force should the settlement be violated by North Vietnam'. For some strange reason, Thieu believed Nixon, and, on the strength of that assurance, decided to go on the offensive, rather than using his troops to protect what he had. Realizing that Hanoi would continue its strategy of protracted war, Thieu went for broke, hoping to deal the communists a knockout blow that would settle the issue once and for all.[64]

At first, the strategy seemed to work. Within a year, Saigon had extended its authority over an additional 770 hamlets, seriously disrupting communist plans for the gradual political infiltration of the South. The Nixon administration was astonished - they had expected South Vietnamese forces to collapse once the American prop was removed. The success was, however, costly. Losses during the first year of 'peace' exceeded 26,000 for the ARVN and 39,000 for communist forces. Probably 15,000 civilians were killed.[65]

With the Americans gone, Thieu no longer felt any need to pay lip service to the laws of war. As had always been the case, military strategy was intertwined with personal vendetta. Now, however, the victims were not just communists, but also neutralists who refused obeisance. Club-wielding ARVN soldiers were brought in to beat up neutralist members of the National Assembly. Communists, of course, fared worse. If a suspect failed to produce a valid identity card, police were officially instructed to 'blow [their] brains out on the spot'. Those with suspicious papers were thrown in prison and left to rot - perhaps 80,000 were jailed that first year. Meanwhile, hamlets providing sanctuary to communists were starved into submission. Famine gripped the central provinces, with peasants forced to eat bark, cacti and banana roots.[66]

While progress was apparent, ARVN strength was spread desperately thin. Before long, half of the army was employed in holding on to territory already subdued. Thieu's 'no surrender' strategy meant that his soldiers were forced to defend the indefensible. All this meant that communist forces in secure sanctuaries could prepare for their offensive without fear of harassment. Thieu was able to hold on to territory conquered, but lacked the strength to push the communists back into North Vietnam.

Thieu possessed one of the largest militaries in the world, with some 450,000 regulars, 550,000 local militia, 51,000 air force personnel and around 45,000 in the navy. Those figures, however, easily deceive. In its development, the ARVN mirrored its American mentor, with bloated support services and less that half of the soldiers assigned to combat. In addition, desertion steadily drained strength – around 20,000 disappeared every month. Some 100,000 'flower soldiers' never reported for duty, bribing their commanders while remaining in civilian employment. 'Gold soldiers' paid others to fight, and 'phantom soldiers' were actually dead, their pay collected by larcenous commanders.

Just prior to the Paris Agreement, Nixon flooded the South with around $1 billion worth of military hardware. Feast then quickly turned to famine. Thieu, who had an insatiable appetite for weaponry, lacked the fortitude to diet. His troops, having been trained to fight like Americans (with the emphasis upon firepower), found it difficult to adapt to more parsimonious times. Consequently, by late 1974, stockpiles of artillery ammunition stood at 20 per cent of 1972 levels and eleven air force squadrons had to be disbanded for lack of fuel. At the front, ambulances were joined together in a train, pulled by a single truck.

Within the army, corruption remained high and morale low. Wounded soldiers often had to pay bribes in order to be rescued. Snepp watched as a 'chopper hovered for nearly an hour . . . as the pilot bickered with a hamlet chief by radio over the price of lifting out a bleeding militiaman. They finally settled on six ducks from the hamlet pond.'[67] Desertion was understandable given that pay often disappeared into the pockets of commanders. The problem worsened when soldiers were suddenly required to buy their own food. Before long, sturdy American boots gave way to flimsy sandals. As ammunition dwindled, insecurity increased and fear corroded loyalty. 'The morale of the ARVN soldier was adversely affected by so many factors', a Rand analyst reflected, 'that it is remarkable that he was able to fight at all.'[68]

The RVN economy was a delicate flower ill-equipped to survive outside the hothouse the United States had created. Some 250,000 South Vietnamese had been officially employed by the American war machine, with perhaps twice that number indirectly dependent. These workers were left high and dry when the Americans departed. While unemployment skyrocketed, so too did inflation, reaching 65 per cent. South Vietnam, an agrarian country, could no longer feed itself because so many peasants had fled to urban areas to escape the war. Once one of the largest rice producers in the world, Vietnam had become a net rice importer by 1972.

These problems had never been properly addressed because the US had always fixed them with dollars. After 1973, however, most Americans no longer wanted to spend money on Vietnam. Nixon, mired in the Watergate scandal, could no longer depend upon a friendly Congress to bankroll his plans for Vietnam. On 31 July 1973, Congress voted to cut off funds for American military action anywhere in Indochina. That meant that bombing of communist sanctuaries in Cambodia, which had continued unabated since the peace agreement, abruptly stopped. When Gerald Ford took over the presidency he warned that cuts would 'seriously weaken South Vietnamese forces during a critical period when Communist forces . . . are growing stronger and more aggressive'. In truth, however, few cared.[69]

When the flow of American money turned to a trickle, chaos descended in South Vietnam. Huge demonstrations of the hungry and jobless choked major cities. Corruption, reluctantly tolerated during times of plenty, now became a serious point of contention between people and government. The turbulence of the early 1960s returned. Even without the communist pressure, Saigon was ripe for revolution.

Hanoi, meanwhile, prepared for the final push. The Christmas bombing of 1972 had severely damaged the North's economy, rendering a full-scale offensive difficult. The alternative was a slow process of political infiltration, but the network of cadres essential to that strategy had been decimated by pacification. At the 21st Plenum of the Vietnamese Communist Party in October 1973, disagreement raged over the best course to take. The party eventually settled upon a cautious military offensive, designed to deliver victory sometime in 1976. This involved a gradual escalation of violence, simultaneous to political infiltration. When the time seemed right, a general offensive would be launched.

Immense energy went into the preparations. The Ho Chi Minh trail was widened and, in most areas, paved. Some 12,000 miles of new roads were built, a fuel pipeline was extended deep into the South, and a modern radio network was established. In addition, thirteen new airfields were constructed in South Vietnam, each with sophisticated anti-aircraft defences. While the construction proceeded, a propaganda offensive bombarded the American people with evidence of Thieu's brutality, in an effort to deepen American alienation with their former ally. Since this campaign occurred at the same time that President Nixon was being exposed as a liar, the administration's counter-claims about Hanoi's misdeeds fell on deaf ears.

The offensive began in early 1974, with small raids designed to test ARVN resolve and establish logistical corridors. While these raids met firm resistance, they were more successful than Hanoi appreciated at the time. The fighting sharpened the effectiveness of communist troops at the same time that they eroded ARVN morale. ARVN casualties and loss of weaponry were doubly significant since supplies were finite. By the autumn, the balance of power had clearly shifted.

Politburo opinion nevertheless remained divided on the best way forward. While one faction still insisted on caution, General Tran Van Tra argued vehemently that the ARVN stood on the brink of collapse. His plan for a bold offensive was initially rejected by the

General Staff but then approved, in a somewhat modified form, after Tra protested to Le Duan, the North Vietnamese leader since Ho's death in 1969. Keen to prove his point, Tran Van Tra attacked Don Luan with incredible ferocity on 22 December 1974. Though few realized it at the time, the end was near.

Don Luan fell within four days, whereupon a triumphant PAVN pushed relentlessly southward. The next important objective was Phuoc Long Province, where some bedraggled ARVN units were thrown in Tra's path, with predictable consequences. Air cover was pathetic since many South Vietnamese pilots simply refused to fly. Phuoc Long, situated just 75 miles from Saigon, fell on 6 January 1975. Hanoi took note of the fact that the Americans did nothing to prevent the catastrophe.

Impressed by the Phuoc Long result, on 8 January the politburo gave cautious approval to a general offensive. A plan to bisect South Vietnam through the Central Region was launched, with favourable results. Between the 4th and 8th of March, PAVN units cut transport routes, isolating Ban Me Thuot. The city fell on 12 March, prompting Thieu to order a counteroffensive. General Pham Van Phu left the task to his junior commanders, while he escaped to safety. The result was complete chaos, with units colliding on the roads to Ban Me Thuot. Over $250 million worth of equipment and munitions was left for the enemy to collect because no one thought to destroy it. The counter-attack soon dissolved into headlong retreat. Fear being contagious, civilians followed frightened troops, inevitably choking highways. 'No organization of any kind was set for the mass evacuation,' one refugee later complained. As the last plane left Pleiku, 'people grabbed for the tail, falling off as [it] . . . taxied'. That scene would become painfully common in subsequent weeks.[70]

The retreating mass of humanity was halted at Cheo Reo when engineers failed to bridge the Ea Pa River. PAVN troops discovered what it was like to shoot fish in a barrel. They made no attempt to distinguish between soldiers and civilians. The catastrophe was made worse by the fact that ARVN pilots, flying high in order to avoid flak, fired indiscriminately. Friendly fire tore through the ARVN ranks and killed hundreds of refugees. When the exodus finally came to a halt only one-third of the 60,000 troops survived, while one-quarter of the 400,000 refugees made it to safety. A South Vietnamese general called it 'one of the worst-planned and worst-executed withdrawal operations in the annals of military history'.[71]

On 19 March, PAVN struck again, this time capturing nearly the whole of Quang Tri Province in one day. This left Hué, the former capital, desperately vulnerable. Thieu reassured residents that the ARVN would protect them, but did nothing to act upon that promise. As the noose tightened, an attempt was made to evacuate by sea. PAVN troops responded by shelling the beaches. Refugees were cut to shreds, while others drowned in the red surf. On 25 March, Hué fell. Despite the obvious dangers of evacuation, many residents chose that option rather than staying put. The tide of exiles was living proof that Hanoi had failed to inspire popular revolution. While the evacuees were hardly enamoured of Saigon rule, they were frightened to death of Hanoi's grim authority.

By 29 March, Da Nang was surrounded. The city fell on the 30th, ten years and three weeks after American Marines first landed. President Ford meanwhile tried to rally Thieu by promising that the US would 'stand firmly [behind] the RVN at this critical hour'. He was considering 'actions which the situation may require and the law permit'. That was a roundabout way of saying that nothing could be done. Now confident of victory, the politburo gave orders to liberate Saigon before the monsoon arrived in June. The operation would be called the 'Ho Chi Minh Campaign'.[72]

While Saigon awaited execution, Ford tried to put together a rescue package. After an inspection tour of South Vietnam, General Frederick Weyand submitted a request for $722 million in military aid, a sum he admitted would only delay defeat. Ford added $250 million and shot the request over to Congress, with the message that it 'would at least allow the orderly evacuation of Americans and endangered Vietnamese'. 'We cannot . . . abandon our friends,' he pleaded. Legislators, however, were more impressed by the postbags full of letters from ordinary voters insisting that not another dime be wasted on Vietnam. Echoing popular opinion, the Senate Armed Services Committee killed the request. 'Those bastards!' the normally even-tempered Ford shouted. His CIA director, William Colby, concluded that 'South Vietnam faces total defeat, and soon'.[73]

On 20 April ARVN forces were driven back to Long Binh and Bien Hoa air bases, 12 miles from Saigon. The city was now surrounded by around fifteen communist divisions, supported by engineers, tanks, artillery and anti-aircraft units. In contrast, the ARVN managed to scrape together just four divisions plus some bedraggled forces evacuated from recent battles. A defensive plan was hastily improvised, but the real question was whether troops and commanders retained the will to fight. With supplies desperately short, and morale at rock bottom, the urge to surrender, or desert, was often irresistible.

Saigon was in a state of hysteria. At the American Embassy, the pool was rendered unusable because the water was choked with the ashes of documents hastily burnt. Few residents of the city failed to notice how the remaining Americans and their Vietnamese friends were leaving in a hurry. Diem Do, a schoolboy at the time, watched the trickle turn into a flood: 'One day a couple of guys would be gone, and then a couple more, and then the teacher wouldn't show up. Everybody was scared. They sensed that something tragic was about to happen.' Evacuation had begun in late March, with businessmen, politicians and orphans of mixed race airlifted from Tan Son Nhut. On 4 April, a C-5A Galaxy transport, with 243 orphans on board, crashed shortly after take-off. At the hospital where casualties were taken, a witness watched 'nurses . . . pass the children under the shower, saying, "This one's alive, this one's dead." . . . None of the babies had name tags, simply wristbands saying "New York", "New Jersey", and so on, the addresses of their new foster homes.' Over 200 children and 44 adults were killed.[74]

As communist troops rushed toward Saigon, Thieu somehow managed to find time for waterskiing and tennis. His belief in an eleventh-hour rescue did not waver, at least not until shells started falling on the city. Aware that the communists would never negotiate with him, he resigned on 21 April, in the vain hope that a new leader might be able to strike a bargain. 'The Americans abandoned us,' he complained. 'They sold us out. A great ally failed a small ally.' Thieu escaped to Taipei, taking 3½ tons of gold with him. In came General Duong Van Minh, who had tried to do a deal with the communists during his brief premiership in 1963–4. 'Accepting the responsibility of leading the country in such a moment is really not pleasurable,' he told his people. Two days later, Ford told students at Tulane University that the war 'is finished as far as America is concerned'. Robert Hartmann, Ford's speechwriter, noticed that, 'As soon as the students heard the word "finished" they almost literally raised the roof with whoops and hollers. They jumped up and down on the bleacher seats, hugging whoever popped up next.'[75]

Nam Pham was a college student living in Saigon. Every night he would climb onto his roof and watch the flashes of artillery fire draw closer, like a protracted sentence of death. 'It gave me kind of a weird feeling, watching something you love so much lost a little bit every day.' When Tan Son Nhut was attacked on the 29th, Ford implemented Operation Frequent Wind, the final evacuation. Helicopters from a task force in the South China Sea ferried refugees from rooftops. At the Embassy, an observer noted, 'the hordes of Vietnamese . . . were a collage of wasted hopes. Many were carrying all they owned in small brown paper bags. Some had dogs and cats underarm. The children stared in bewilderment at the chaos around them, and as the Embassy's air-conditioning system broke down, the stench and heat in the corridors became unbearable.' In order to gain permission to be evacuated, some Vietnamese women were married to their American sponsors while waiting in the queue. 'It was a quick thing,' an Embassy official recalled. '"Do you?" "I do." Then out.' The operation eventually evacuated 1,373 Americans, 5,595 South Vietnamese, 85 other nationals, and the American ambassador's poodle. The last helicopter, carrying the Marines who had supervised the evacuation, flew out on the 30th.[76]

That same day, PAVN tanks appeared on the streets of Saigon. ARVN soldiers quickly changed into civilian clothes and melted into the cheering crowds. Nam Pham recalls seeing some sheepish young men wearing only boxer shorts. Shortly after the last American Marine left, PAVN tank number 843 crashed through the gates of the presidential palace. Colonel Bui Tin raced inside and demanded Minh's surrender. 'I have been waiting since early this morning to transfer power to you,' an obsequious Minh told Tin. 'You cannot give up what you do not have,' Tin replied. W.D. Ehrhart, who had served in Vietnam eight years earlier, when Americans still believed in a noble mission, was overcome by a feeling of emptiness. 'The fall of South Vietnam', he later wrote, 'was reported on the six o'clock news with hardly more impact than the story of a bad fire in Cleveland. The lives of Americans were not altered in any way. Kids continued to play ball in the park, mothers and fathers went to work.'[77]

Madrid: After Franco

In 1959, the number of foreigners visiting Spain was just over 4 million. They came mainly for things old – the Prado and the Alhambra. By 1973, tourist numbers had risen to nearly 35 million. They came for things new – beachfront hotels and jugs of sangria. In fourteen years, income from tourism increased from $125 million to $3.1 billion, sparking an economic miracle. The growth rate was 7.1 per cent, second only to Japan, while national income rose by 156 per cent. Earnings from tourism allowed Spaniards to avoid the balance of payments problem that often brings modernization to a halt. Spain, in other words, was liberated by the bikini.

For Generalissimo Francisco Franco, those tiny pieces of cloth represented a huge dilemma. On the one hand, they seemed an offence to Christian decency, potent symbols of moral decay. In 1959, Pedro Zaragoza Orts, mayor of Benidorm, was slapped with an excommunication order by the local archbishop after he signed a municipal order authorizing the wearing of bikinis on local beaches. In the end, however, money shouted louder than morality. Franco despised the permissiveness that the bikini symbolized, but could not ignore the gold mines discovered on Spain's coast.

Franco eventually came to discover that the real problem on the beaches was not loose morals but loose change. A wealthy Spain proved difficult to control. Franco's ideologues had once assumed that prosperity would prove an acceptable substitute for liberalism – that the corporate state would be tolerated simply because it worked. But those ideologues did not understand progress. Prosperity rendered Spaniards more difficult to govern, not easier. They aspired to be like the Dutch, Germans and British who visited in droves. Bikini money bought televisions, cars and fashion, all very liberating possessions. In 1960, just 1 per cent of Spaniards had access to a television. By 1970, that figure had risen to 90 per cent. The economic miracle rendered Spain a modern country, yet one still saddled with a government that prided itself on being old-fashioned. Franco was an ailing dinosaur hopelessly fighting extinction.

Spain, like every country in the West, had its version of the 1960s. The young rebelled through long hair, outlandish clothing, sex, drugs and music – gestures which appalled the rigidly moralistic regime. The rebellion often had legitimate reason; when the young complained about authoritarianism they knew what the word meant. As Cardinal Angel Herrera warned in 1965, 'The one thing that has not developed is social justice.' Students, unlike their comrades in Berkeley, objected not to the flaws of liberalism, but to its absence. The government considered this rebellion threatening for the simple reason that – unlike in other Western countries – student unrest could not be dismissed as the selfish posturing of pampered middle-class youths. To make matters worse, student unrest coincided with agitation within the banned trade union movement and strident nationalist dissent in the Catalan and Basque regions. Still stuck in the 1930s, Franco argued that the unrest was 'all part of a Masonic leftist conspiracy of the political class in collusion with Communist-terrorist subversion in the social sphere'. His government reacted in the only way it knew: through unrestrained brutality, often carried out by right-wing vigilantes acting on Franco's behest.[78]

The government was Franco. Because he was an anachronism, it was difficult for him to engineer a transference of power that would ensure the survival of his system past his death. Perhaps realizing this, he decided to govern to the bitter end. In the 1960s, Spain found herself in weird limbo as she waited for Franco to die. The future seemed bright, but also precarious – no one quite knew what would follow the Caudillo's departure.

Prosperity had created a potentially powerful group of citizens who craved liberalization but feared radicalism. Their influence was rock-hard, built into the breeze-block towers that lined the beaches of the Costa del Sol. Having invested so much in Spain's future, they feared that prosperity might be jeopardized by a resumption of the political battles of the past. The Civil War of 1936–9 had essentially been a struggle between conservatism and modernity. Franco's victory settled the question, but did so in a way that rendered the nation a joke at best, a pariah at worst. In essence, his victory postponed the contest over modernity until his death. Pessimists feared that when he died that struggle would be renewed with the same hatred and violence that had marred the 1930s. The prime minister, Admiral Luis Carrero Blanco, counted himself among those pessimists who insisted that progress was antithetical to stability. To offer change to a Spaniard, he argued, was like offering a drink to an alcoholic.[79]

Though most people thought the Falange system doomed, Franco was determined that it should survive. To this end, he groomed Prince Juan Carlos for the succession, hoping that, if Falangism could be grafted onto the monarchy, it might have a better chance of survival. This was not technically a restoration, since Franco was not a monarchist, but rather a pragmatic attempt to create a legitimacy sufficient to ensure the continuance of Franquismo by other means.

In truth, the heir apparent was not Juan Carlos, but his father, Don Juan. Exiled in Switzerland, he remained committed to restoration, preferably in his person. His Lausanne Declaration, issued in 1945, asserted that, 'The regime set up by General Franco modelled on the totalitarian systems of the Axis Powers contradicts . . . the character and tradition of a people like our own . . . Only the traditional monarch is in a position to restore peace and harmony to the Spaniards.' Franco ignored that declaration, but eventually came to accept that a link to the royal line was advantageous, since otherwise Falangism would for ever be associated with the anachronistic regimes of Mussolini and Hitler. This explains his Law of Succession, promulgated in 1947, which proclaimed that 'Spain, as a political entity, is a Catholic, social and representative state which, in keeping with its tradition, is declared to be constituted as a monarchy'. The wording is significant, particularly 'declared' and 'constituted'. By these words, Franco emphasized that he was responsible for making Spain a monarchy. In order to reinforce that impression, he needed to make the monarch beholden to him. This could only be done by skipping a generation, since putting Don Juan on the throne implied a bona fide restoration – a briefly interrupted, but still continuous, line of succession from the Bourbon kings of the past. When a plebiscite resulted in 93 per cent of Spaniards backing his Law of Succession, Franco had the legitimacy he needed. Don Juan, outmanoeuvred, was forced to temper his opposition and seek accommodation with Franco, if only to ensure that his son might be favoured with the Caudillo's grace.[80]

Don Juan reluctantly agreed that Franco should supervise his son's education. Franco earnestly took to this task, hoping to create a worthy successor. Despite being pleased with the result, he was nevertheless reluctant to announce Juan Carlos as his heir apparent, since he did not want a competing focus for the people's loyalty. Spaniards were therefore kept waiting, while Franco repeatedly emphasized that 'God and Providence' had made him leader for life. Powerful supporters, however, urged him to name a successor. He finally relented on 22 July 1969, confirming that Juan Carlos would succeed him.

On the following day, Juan Carlos took an oath of loyalty to 'His Excellency, the chief of state, and to the basic principles of the National Movement as well as to the other fundamental laws of the state'. In other words, the oath reiterated that the monarchy answered to the state, not the other way around. Those hoping for change were bitterly disappointed when Juan Carlos asserted that, 'The work of setting [Spain] on the right road and showing clearly the direction it must go has been carried out by that exceptional man whom Spain has been immensely fortunate to have . . . as the guide of our policy.'[81]

A new term was invented to describe this strange hybrid: the monarchy had been 'reinstaured', not restored. 'The monarchy cannot be "restored" because of certain constitutional limitations and a traditional liberalism which would ensue,' the exiled academic Salvador de Madariaga remarked. 'It is "instaured", i.e. crafted by Franco so that his wishes are followed.' Pessimistic about the future, Madariaga added that 'Don Juan might have tried with some hope of success to restore a liberal monarchy. Juan Carlos cannot.' At the time, that seemed a sensible assessment. Most Spaniards saw Juan Carlos as a puppet whose strings would be pulled by Franco from beyond the grave. Santiago Carrillo, the communist leader, dubbed him 'Juan Carlos the Brief', a common appraisal of his likely fate. Most expected him to provide a turbulent interlude between Franquismo and democracy. Few took him seriously.[82]

Popular expectations were reinforced when, after Franco died on 20 November 1975, Juan Carlos dutifully reiterated his 'loyalty to the National Movement'. As it turned out, however, the new king proved more loyal to the monarchy than to Franquismo. He realized that if the monarchy was too closely associated with Franco, it would be rudely cast aside in the transformation that would inevitably follow the Caudillo's death. He also believed that change was more likely to proceed smoothly if it could be managed by the monarch. As he saw it, the monarchy was the one institution representing all of Spain, a focus of loyalty able to provide a moderating influence during a precarious period. In other words, Juan Carlos assumed a function few expected of him. He gave a hint of his intentions to *Newsweek* a few weeks before Franco's death:

> Juan Carlos . . . is determined to stand above party politics, to be king for everybody . . . The restoration of genuine democracy is one of the goals, but Spain should spare no effort to avoid disorder and chaos . . . He believes more in reform than repression, more

> in democratic evolution than revolution. He intends to form a modern government which will ensure the future of Spain, which does not want to hold on to the past.

In his first 'Crown Message', delivered on 22 November, he appealed for support:

> Today begins a new stage in Spanish history . . . The monarchy will be the loyal guardian of . . . [our] heritage and try at all times to retain the closest contact with the people . . . The institutions which I embody bind all Spaniards together, and today in this important hour I call on you, since it is the responsibility of all to serve Spain. Let us all in the spirit of magnanimity and dignity understand that our future is based on real national unity.

They were ambitious words, but most people saw them as mere rhetoric, not unlike what Franco had once uttered.[83]

Juan Carlos realized that if he did not deliver democracy, the monarchy would be destroyed. At the same time, he also understood that the *transición* had to be carefully managed since drastic, ill-conceived change would imperil both democracy *and* the monarchy. He therefore moved slowly, while realizing that gradualism would be interpreted as reluctance. Suspicions were raised further by the continued presence of the Francoist Carlos Arias Navarro in the office of prime minister. He wanted improvements to Franquismo, not its wholesale replacement. The tired rhetoric of the Franco era had worn a groove in his mind – tradition, he insisted, was the best defence against the communist conspiracy threatening the nation. Franco was the 'provident legislator' whose legacy needed to be preserved. What few realized was that Arias Navarro presented both problem and opportunity. He clearly stood in the way of change, but he also offered Juan Carlos the chance to demonstrate his reformist credentials. When the king let slip to *Newsweek* that Arias Navarro was an 'unmitigated disaster' who blocked reform and polarized Spanish politics, the implication was clear: the prime minister would be removed at the earliest possible opportunity.[84]

That came in June when Arias Navarro bungled legislation recognizing political parties. He offered his resignation, which Juan Carlos gladly accepted. Reformists demanded the appointment of José María Areilza, a prominent liberal. Fearing, however, that an outspoken liberal would polarize opinion, the king chose instead Adolfo Suárez y González, previously general secretary of the National Movement and, prior to that, director general of the state television network. While his close links to Francoism at first provoked widespread scorn, it soon transpired that the choice was astute. Suárez, though undoubtedly a conservative, was also a pragmatist who realized that progress could at best be managed – not stopped. His other advantage was his age – at forty-three, he was the youngest prime minister in Spanish history. This made him roughly the same age as Juan Carlos, which meant that the two together represented a clean break from the past. Some prominent liberals nevertheless remained suspicious, refusing to serve in the Cabinet. This, too, proved an opportunity, since it allowed Suárez to recruit a number of young men unconnected with past arguments. Suárez's conservative credentials also won him the trust of the military, which was essential to the success of reform.

The fact remained that Juan Carlos had so far done little to persuade reformists that he could satisfy them. His first significant overture came in a general amnesty of political prisoners – members of opposition groups who had not actually engaged in violent acts were pardoned. This was, one socialist admitted, 'the fruit of a desire to bury the sad, past history'. Another politician reflected that the amnesty was 'simply a forgetting . . . an amnesty for everyone, a forgetting by everyone for everyone'. With the past put neatly away, the task of building the future could begin.[85]

While the amnesty was enormously important, equally significant was the king's charismatic style. He often appeared in public with his fashionable wife, the two together giving the impression of modernity. He also acted upon the promise in his Crown Message that he wanted to 'be the king of all and at the same time of every individual in his own culture, history and tradition'. In other words, he would respect regional differences. To this end, he toured Catalonia in February 1976 and spoke Catalan. The gesture was hugely significant given the contempt toward cultural and linguistic autonomy Franco had shown. As a result of attitude as much as policy, Juan Carlos encouraged the impression that he could be trusted. A discernible shift of opinion became evident, with scepticism giving way to cautious support. Suddenly, the legitimacy of the king rested not in the Bourbon dynastic line, nor in his supposed allegiance to the Francoist past, but in the trust he engendered among his people and their desire for him to succeed.[86]

Good feelings were not, however, by themselves enough. The government also had to reassure the people that it could deliver a meaningful transition to democracy. In mid-September, Suárez announced a comprehensive programme of reform, which included a bicameral legislature elected on a system of proportional representation. While the proposals were generally welcomed, militant rightists objected that they went too far and democratic purists complained that they did not go far enough. A national referendum on 15 December 1976, however, showed overwhelming approval. With nearly 80 per cent of the electorate participating, 94.2 per cent voted in favour. The referendum demonstrated that government and people were now working in harmony toward the same goal.

The next step was the legalization of political parties banned during the Franco era. While this seemed to most a fait accompli, the stumbling block was the status of the Communist Party. Logic suggested that blanket approval should be extended, but legalization of the communists was bitterly opposed by the army. By this stage, however, Juan Carlos and Suárez felt sufficiently emboldened to ignore that obstacle. Legalization of all parties occurred on 9 April 1977. The army officially noted its discomfort but did not otherwise resist.

Though the *transición* had so far proceeded more smoothly than anyone had expected, political violence remained a problem. Between

Franco's death and the elections in June 1977, sixty-seven people were killed in terrorist attacks, most of them in the Basque country, but also in actions fomented by the extreme right and left. While the killings suggested a continuance of the dark days of Franco, in fact they were indicative of how much things had changed. Terrorist attacks during this period are best seen as an indication of the frustration felt by those who preferred revolution to reform. In addition, it bears emphasizing that the violence did not provoke the aggressive reaction on which the terrorist depends. The government made it clear that it would not be derailed from its mission to deliver democracy.

The people's determination to maintain a steady course can be measured by the overwhelmingly moderate election campaign. While some 200 parties existed by the end of 1975 and around 156 put up candidates, politicians willingly grouped themselves into broad coalitions in order to ensure stable government. Conservative forces coalesced around Suárez's Centre Democratic Union, while the left mobilized behind the charismatic Felipe González and his Spanish Socialist Workers Party. The proof of the pudding, however, came in the rhetoric employed during the campaign. The socialists' official platform was Marxist, but their behaviour remained steadfastly moderate, in line with European social democracy. The CDU, likewise, was a picture of restraint, pointedly ignoring the Francoist past and instead emphasizing a fresh start. Even the communists seemed determined not to offend. Shortly after their legal recognition, the party formally announced acceptance of the monarchy and, by implication, a willingness to work within the system. Spaniards were treated to the unusual spectacle of watching communists extol the virtues of liberalism – they campaigned under the slogan 'A vote for Communism is a vote for Democracy'. Much less in tune with the political mood was Manuel Fraga Iribarne's Popular Alliance, which sought to mobilize nostalgia for Franco.[87]

On 15 June, Spaniards went to the polls in an atmosphere of impressive calm. The election was notable for what did not happen: no intimidation of voters, very little violence, and no serious allegations of corruption. Despite their lack of experience, Spanish voters behaved like mature and enthusiastic democrats. Despite the plethora of choices, they chose options most likely to result in stable government. The CDU secured 34.7 per cent of the vote, the socialists 29.2, and the communists 9.2. The Popular Alliance proved the biggest losers, with just 8.4 per cent. The remaining votes were claimed mainly by regional parties in Catalonia and the Basque region.

Regardless of how each party fared, the result was essentially an expression of approval for what Suárez had achieved and what Juan Carlos represented. Suárez went on to form a government, but proved less adroit in running the country than he had been in managing the *transición*. Unrest in the Basque country and economic difficulties eventually got the better of him. What is important, however, is that his shortcomings did not inspire discontent with the new democracy. When their patience with Suárez ran out, the Spanish simply acted like mature democrats and voted in a new government. Indeed, the nature of that government indicates how far Spain had come. The victory of the socialists in 1982 did not lead to serious turmoil. In any case, while the new government called itself socialist, it was acutely aware that its supporters wanted moderate social democracy, not Marxist adventurism.

With breathtaking speed, Franco went from Generalissimo to f-word – something distasteful but seldom mentioned. The national anthem was retained, but the lyrics, written during the Franco era, were expunged, thus making Spain one of the few countries to have an anthem devoid of words. By agreeing not to talk about the Caudillo, Spaniards managed to avoid the recrimination that might otherwise have followed such a divisive regime. They were keen to forget not only the man, but also their own behaviour during his regime. An unofficial *pacto del olvido* – pact of forgetting – was followed. 'There was not sufficient strength to demand either justice or, even, any explanation for the past,' a somewhat regretful González reflected. The victims, writes Gregorio Morán, one of the few critics of the *transición*, were 'forced to forget as a condition for taking part in the new game'. The policy was disingenuous, but it worked.[88]

The *transición* provides a model to those nations seeking to rid themselves of authoritarian rule. In the space of a few years, Spain became a genuinely modern nation – not just stable, but dynamic. Her experience is especially fascinating since it contrasts sharply with the direction other Western nations were travelling in. In Germany, France and the United States, left-wing adventurism during the 1960s resulted in strident attacks upon the liberal heritage. This provoked an extreme reaction from the right, exactly what the rebels wanted. When the dust settled, however, radicalism was vanquished and liberalism lay mortally wounded. All three countries moved profoundly to the right.

In Spain, however, something very different happened. Because the people had grown tired of radicalism, they were determined to stay on the moderate road. They wanted nothing to do with political adventures, and were able to put aside selfish fantasies for clear, pragmatic goals. An indication of this pragmatism was the *Pactos de Montcloa*, essentially a social contract, signed in 1977 between the government, employers' organizations and trade unions to cooperate in order to consolidate democracy and to address economic problems. In other words, while other Western countries moved away from liberalism, Spain consolidated practical liberal goals. One of the most astonishing features of the *transición* is the breathtaking pace at which it was carried out. By the end of the 1970s, old-fashioned, authoritarian Spain had become one of the most stable, progressive and dynamic nations in Europe.

Nicaragua: The Sandinista Revolution

Between 1965 and 1975, the GNP of Nicaragua doubled. So, too, did the number of children under five suffering from malnutrition. Nicaragua was undoubtedly a poor country, but its main problem was the maldistribution of wealth, income and land. Between 1950 and 1977, the growth rate hovered at 6 per cent, but all that new wealth disappeared into the pockets of the rich. The wealthiest

5 per cent of the population shared 30 per cent of income, while the lower half divided up just 15 per cent. Voracious landowners gobbled up small farms, turning former owners into itinerant labourers or, worse, urban beggars. Nearly half of those dependent upon agriculture had no land at all. As a result of crippling poverty, half the population was illiterate, and life expectancy was just fifty-three years. In contrast, in neighbouring Costa Rica, by no means a wealthy country, the average adult lived seventeen years longer.

Nicaragua was a machine for exploiting the poor. Manning the levers was the Somoza family, a clan bred for tyranny that had ruled since 1932. The person in charge changed over time, but the name – Somoza – remained the same, a synonym for despotism. While the Somozas were essentially dictators, Nicaragua was technically a democracy. The family sometimes held the presidency, but sometimes did not. However, the person residing in the presidential palace was essentially a cipher, since power rested in the man who controlled the National Guard, and he was always a Somoza. Though elections were held, the Somozas made sure they were meaningless. 'I would like nothing better than to give . . . Nicaraguans the same kind of freedom as that of the United States,' Anastasio Somoza Debayle once remarked. '[But,] It is like what you do with a baby. First you give it milk by drops, then more and more, then a little piece of pig, and finally it can eat everything . . . You have to teach them to use freedom, not to abuse it.'[89]

Tyranny proved lucrative. By 1972, the family controlled at least one-quarter of GNP. When Anastasio Somoza García, a man of humble origins, died in 1956, he left his sons a fortune in excess of $100 million. Henry Kissinger, who showed great tolerance for corrupt right-wing dictators, once said that the Somozas 'gave new meaning to the term kleptocracy, that is, government as theft'. No wonder, then, that the family needed a private army. The National Guard, well-paid and heavily armed, kept protest at bay – an important asset since the people had much over which to complain. Political opponents were tortured, murdered or simply made to disappear.[90]

Brutality and fear closed the usual avenues of revolt. There seemed no point in protesting to a cloth-eared government that never hesitated to use force. For most people, therefore, apathy became a form of self-defence. The few rebels that did exist skipped the traditional first steps of non-violent resistance and moved straight to military insurgency. They were concentrated in the Sandinista National Liberation Front (Frente Sandinista de Liberación Nacional, or FSLN), which took its name from the nationalist hero Augusto César Sandino. He had managed to humiliate US Marines and the Nicaraguan National Guard during a six-year insurgency that ended in 1933. Sandino was hero *and* martyr; his value as a revolutionary saint was enhanced because he was assassinated, on the order of Somoza García, at his moment of triumph. To impoverished Nicaraguans, his example continued to resonate, since he had challenged the Somozas, the National Guard *and* the Americans – the very same triumvirate that blocked social justice in the 1970s.

The FSLN, founded in 1961, drew support mainly from student activists for whom nationalism went hand in hand with egalitarianism. They despised the brutal Somoza regime but felt that the real enemy was the United States which controlled Nicaraguan affairs through its proxies. 'They call [our] forces bandits,' Sandino had said. 'The real . . . bandits are in the caves of the White House in Washington, from which they direct the plunder and assassination of our Spanish America.' Given the nature of the movement, and the identity of its nemesis, it's no surprise that Sandinistas embraced Marxism and worshipped Che. 'Marxism . . . was a complete revelation – the discovery of a new world,' recalled Victor Tirado, a founding member. 'Through Marxism, we came to know Sandino, our history, and our roots.'[91]

Despite their deep commitment, the FSLN was no match for the Somozas' Guard, reinforced with American weaponry. For that reason, the lifespan of the average rebel was desperately short, and political cadres made little headway in their attempts to radicalize the workers and peasantry. As in other countries in the throes of revolution, ordinary people preferred to sit on the fence until the outcome of the contest became clear. The Sixties therefore proved lean years for

Sandinistas, who failed to build a peasant base. Through torture, assassination and brute military force, the Somoza government very nearly rid itself of the FSLN menace by the end of the decade.

The situation changed dramatically when a massive earthquake devastated Managua on 23 December 1972. The quake, followed by a catastrophic fire, killed perhaps 10,000 people outright and left 80 per cent of buildings damaged beyond repair. The United Nations judged 'the magnitude of the disaster . . . almost without precedent in recent world history'. The vast majority of the city's 400,000 residents were rendered homeless, while destruction of the economic infrastructure meant that most were also without jobs. 'Managua is a dying city,' the journalist Jay Mallin concluded. 'It can no longer support its population. It has neither water nor food nor electricity . . . one-third of its population . . . has already left and steady streams of people continue to pour out of the city.'[92]

The earthquake demolished the headquarters of the National Guard, causing a complete collapse in discipline. Guardsmen deserted their posts in order to join looters. For a short period, Somoza Debayle was deprived of the military might he depended upon to control the country. But authority was quickly re-established thanks to the help of his good friend Turner Shelton, the US ambassador, who arranged the despatch of 500 American paratroopers. President Nixon was only too happy to help, since he feared that the suffering might otherwise spark a communist uprising.

Once he regained his composure, Somoza discovered that the quake offered new opportunities for plunder. Over $32 million in disaster relief was donated by the United States, but half that amount was siphoned off by Somoza and his cronies. Pedro Joaquín Chamorro, the publisher of the daily newspaper *La Prensa*, described 'thousands and thousands of hands extended toward emptiness, asking for food, which was kept . . . under custody of the government tanks. They didn't give out the food.' Blood donated to quake victims was sold back to American hospitals, at huge profit. Somoza was so taken with this new line of business that he began exporting blood purchased at a pittance from Nicaraguans rendered destitute by the quake. He also decided that Managua needed to be relocated to safer ground. A new site was found, on land he happened to own but graciously sold back to the state.[93]

While the quake proved a financial boon for Somoza, it shook the foundations of his regime. Aftershocks would be felt for the rest of the decade. Rising unemployment, rampant inflation and unaffordable fuel exacerbated popular discontent. The anger of previously apathetic workers rendered them much more susceptible to FSLN agitation. The people's fear of the Guard was no longer enough, by itself, to keep protests and strikes at a manageable level. Nor was it just the workers who complained. Middle-class businessmen objected bitterly to the government's failure to rebuild the economy. The Church also became a stern critic, with clerics shining a bright light on government perfidy. On the first anniversary of the quake, a mass in memory of the victims turned into a huge protest against the regime.

As time passed, quake-related complaints coalesced into general discontent. It was not, however, the FSLN that rode the tide of dissatisfaction. Rather, middle-class organizations helped turn diffuse dismay into focused opposition. The Superior Council of Private Enterprise (COSEP), a union of business interests, became one of the fiercest critics of the government. Then, in 1974, the formation of UDEL (Democratic Liberation Union) brought together a diverse group of discontented people, including labour activists, entrepreneurs, professionals, academics and even conservative politicians. The front man was Chamorro, whose patriotic credentials were impeccable.

The FSLN, by comparison, remained a rather emaciated force, still nursing the wounds of the 1960s. As time passed, however, it was able to use the discontent to build a base among peasants, radical workers and students. By 1974, activists were sufficiently reinvigorated to launch a bold strike. On 27 December, thirteen commandos raided a party at the home of José María Castillo, a prominent Somoza supporter, taking the guests hostage. Among the captives were friends and relatives of Somoza. Since the Sandinistas were perfectly willing to die, they had the government in an armlock. After a few days of negotiation, they agreed to free their hostages in exchange for the release of twelve Sandinistas from prison, $1 million ransom and safe passage to Cuba. Under the agreement, the government was also obliged to broadcast Sandinista propaganda through various media. A huge crowd gathered at Managua airport to bid farewell to the Sandinistas on their departure for Cuba, thus underlining the government's humiliation.

Despite the setback, Somoza remained contemptuous of the FSLN. 'What is the political significance of this guerrilla organisation?' he spat. 'None whatsoever! This is a small group of youngsters who have been indoctrinated . . . But I know that they will die! There is no more than crust to this little pie!' In a fit of pique, he declared martial law, unleashing repression of a severity heretofore unseen even in his brutal country. FSLN militants were hunted down, murdered and often mutilated for good measure. Those who harboured them were sadistically tortured in order to send a message to would-be supporters. Around 2,000 people were slaughtered, with little attempt made to establish a direct connection to the rebellion. On one occasion, Guardsmen descended upon the village of Varilla, a suspected Sandinista enclave, and killed all the residents, including twenty-nine children. The conquerors then divided the land among themselves.[94]

While the Somoza regime thought the atrocities could easily be hidden in the remote mountains, a bush telegraph of Catholic clerics relayed news to the outside world. A letter from the Nicaraguan bishopric, detailing 'inhuman' abuse 'ranging from torture and rape to summary execution', was read out from pulpits around the country. While Somoza's backlash succeeded in cutting a swathe through the ranks of the Sandinistas, it turned otherwise apathetic peasants into enthusiastic supporters of the FSLN. It also alienated the US. The new ambassador, James Theberge, feared that Somoza's behaviour might affect the security of American interests in the area. 'We have reason to believe that some of the allegations of human rights violations are accurate,' he told reporters, 'and our concern has been made clear to the Nicaraguan government.' In early 1977, the Nicaraguan opposition pressured the new American president, Jimmy Carter, to act. He had promised 'a foreign policy that is democratic, that is based on fundamental values, and that uses power and influence . . . for humane purposes'. Somoza tested that promise. 'Nicaragua is a case where Carter can show that his advocacy of human rights is not just words,' one FSLN activist told *Time*. Carter, who had painted himself into a corner, responded by cutting military and financial aid. That, however, proved the limit of his commitment, since to go further implied support for an avowedly Marxist movement. 'We do not now contemplate asking Somoza to step down,' Secretary of State Cyrus Vance stated. Desperately trying to back-peddle, Carter argued that it was improper for the United States 'to intervene in the affairs of a sovereign country'.[95]

While fighting their bitter war with the Somoza regime, the Sandinistas somehow found time to argue among themselves over Marxist theory. The Prolonged Popular War faction, or GPP, were devotees of Che who advocated a protracted guerrilla campaign designed to politicize the peasantry. In 1975, that orthodoxy was challenged by Jaime Wheelock, who, while studying abroad, had become convinced that mainstream Marxist notions of a proletariat were perfectly applicable. A third group, formally known as the Insurrectionals, but popularly called Terceristas (or Third Way), was led by Daniel and Humberto Ortega, essentially Marxist-Leninists but with a distinctive pragmatic streak. They thought that Sandinistas should capitalize on widespread alienation by offering themselves as an alternative to, or adjunct of, UDEL. This implied temporarily toning down Marxist rhetoric in order to appeal to the bourgeoisie.

While the GPP and Wheelock's Proletarios argued, the Terceristas got on with the revolution. Somoza's reign of terror proved a boon to them, since its principal victims were the GPP cadres doggedly pursuing peasant revolution in the hills. In May 1977, the Terceristas released a new manifesto which proclaimed that 'the working class, represented and led by the Sandinista vanguard, the FSLN, will lead the revolution'. While policy documents did not skimp on Marxist rhetoric, Terceristas concentrated on broadening their appeal. A measure of their success came later in the year with the launch of the 'Group of Twelve', a committee of business, religious and cultural bigwigs who called for Somoza's immediate resignation and the inclusion of the FSLN in a provisional government. Terceristas meanwhile continued the armed struggle, launching lightning raids on National Guard posts around the country.[96]

Bad governments inevitably make bad decisions, often with peculiar aplomb. As the net tightened around the Somoza regime, someone – either the dictator himself, or one of his henchmen – decided it would be a good idea to assassinate Chamorro. His murder on 10 January 1978 provided further stimulus to anti-government feeling, with his funeral sparking mass protest. Angry mobs attacked businesses linked to the Somoza family or to America. UDEL then capitalized on the uproar by calling a general strike and demanding Somoza's resignation. The strike was widely supported, but had little effect upon the stubborn dictator who responded, as in the past, by unleashing the Guard. That force again demonstrated an impressive capacity for outrage – on one occasion Guardsmen sprayed mourners at a memorial service for Chamorro with tear gas.

With Nicaragua descending into chaos, the Terceristas decided to reprise the Castillo script, on a bigger scale. On 22 August 1978, forty commandos, disguised as Guardists, took control of the National Palace, taking hundreds of congressmen captive, including a cousin of Somoza. After another round of mediation, the result was essentially the same, except the ransom rose to $12 million. Again, Sandinista prisoners were released and given safe passage out of the country along with the commandos. This time, an even bigger crowd bade them farewell at the airport. The supposed invincibility of the Somoza regime had once again been seriously dented. More importantly, Nicaraguans were beginning to laugh at their dictator. A regime built on fear cannot long survive ridicule.

As a result of the Tercerista success, a movement sprang into being that was beyond Ortega's capacity to control. He was faced with a common revolutionary dilemma, summarized by the lament: 'There go my people, I must catch them, for I am their leader.' The FAO, or Broad Opposition Front, which had replaced UDEL, pressured him to organize a series of rolling strikes. These in turn inspired freelance demonstrations and random acts of violence. In an effort to take control, the Terceristas, reluctantly joined by the GPP and the Proletarios, launched simultaneous attacks on Guard posts in five cities during September 1978. The offensive was all the more impressive for the fact that it was suicidal: Sandinistas were able to mobilize hardly more than 150 armed insurgents. They enjoyed brief success, but were eventually swept aside by Somoza's forces. The Guards then went on the rampage, killing, raping, torching homes and even attacking schools, hospitals and Red Cross clinics. No distinction was made between rebel and innocent bystander. Boys in working-class areas were particularly vulnerable to summary execution, since it was assumed that any young man not in a Guard uniform must belong to the FSLN. '[Somoza] was born in power and he is wedded to it,' a bewildered Archbishop Miguel Obando remarked. 'Political tactics count for nothing, only pride, vanity. He is like a child with a toy. The majority of us underestimated the capacity for horror and destruction of this man and his National Guard. We never thought he was capable of levelling entire cities, as he has done . . . We never thought that the beast was so beastly.'[97]

Despite the annihilation, the desperate gamble brought dividends. The FSLN had demonstrated that it was the only opposition group willing to fight the Guard. While Sandinista ranks were depleted, the action mobilized the discontented of Nicaragua. Thousands of recruits rushed forward to take part in what was hoped would be a final offensive. With new strength came new unity, as the three factions formally set aside their differences. For the first time, rebels were also able to enjoy a steady supply of weaponry, thanks to donations from Venezuela, Cuba and other outside supporters.

What had been an insurrection became a full-scale war. In April 1979, a Sandinista force attacked in the north, capturing the city of Estelí with help from local insurgents. Somoza responded with extreme force, pummelling the city with bombs and shells prior to a massive ground attack. Estelí was virtually destroyed, with 1,000 dead, the vast majority civilians. The Sandinistas did not, however, back down. A steady flow of volunteers enabled losses to be overcome. Everywhere the insurgents went they found locals eager to lend support. While Sandinistas carried on the struggle militarily, the FAO intensified the pressure with a general strike, paralysing the economy. Progress came at huge cost, but there was no doubting its validity. Somoza was clearly doomed, the only uncertainty being when he might recognize that fact.

Acceptance came on 17 July 1979, when Somoza, his son and half-brother boarded a plane for Miami, leaving behind a caretaker administration. Tainted by its association with Somoza, that administration lasted two days, whereupon a government of national unity took over. It consisted of representatives of business and industry and, of course, the FSLN. For the Sandinistas, that arrangement provided the perfect platform for a gradual consolidation of power, made easier by the fact that they now possessed the only credible military force. While FSLN representatives slowly tightened their grip on central government, out in the countryside cadres implemented a programme of socialist indoctrination through a network of mass organizations.

Nicaraguans enthusiastically celebrated the fall of Somoza, but their nightmare was far from over. At first, all seemed well, with Sandinistas demonstrating their immense capacity for good. Land was redistributed, health care extended, diseases like polio eliminated, and illiteracy virtually eradicated. But then came the usual complaints of radical socialists everywhere: business interests were not cooperating, the bourgeoisie was bleeding the poor, the capitalist press was not sufficiently respectful, democracy stood in the way of progress. The solution was more power. 'The objectives of the Revolution are none other than to fight until it guarantees the well-being of all workers,' a party document proclaimed in 1980. That conviction validated a lorry-load of sins.[98]

The big mistake of the Sandinistas was to confuse victory with popularity and gratitude with support. They assumed that because they had bravely confronted Somoza, they had the right to shape the new Nicaragua. The bourgeoisie, in contrast, could be ignored because it was tainted with the evils of the previous fifty years. 'Our country's bourgeoisie – which liquidated and castrated itself as a progressive political force when it totally surrendered to the interests of Yankee imperialism and allied itself with the most reactionary Nicaraguan forces on 4 May 1927 – will not be a vanguard in the struggle against tyranny or in the revolutionary process,' a manifesto proclaimed. That was a prescription for a one party state. Within months of Somoza's fall, a new autocracy was taking shape. Elections, which were supposed to be held in early 1980, were delayed until 1983 and then delayed again until 1985. 'Nicaragua already has real democracy, brought about through social improvement, through our anti-illiteracy campaign,' a party leader explained. 'We do not reject the idea of going through the motions of formal democracy, but it is of course inconceivable that the Sandinistas would not win the elections.'[99]

The Sandinistas are not solely to blame for the terrible suffering of the Contra War of the 1980s. The Contras themselves, built from the dregs of the Guardists, were undoubtedly culpable. So, too, was Ronald Reagan, who insisted on turning Nicaragua into yet another Cold War struggle, instead of accepting that what the people really wanted was food, healthcare, education and peace. But, without indulging in counterfactuals, it seems clear that Nicaragua's suffering in the 1980s was avoidable. If the Sandinistas had accepted that Somoza had been brought down by a consensus, they might have turned that consensus into a formidable political movement. Instead, they insisted on radical socialist transformation, implemented through autocracy. Before long, Sandinistas and Contras were competing in the cruelty stakes. In 1987, the *New York Times* reporter James LeMoyne found a strange phenomenon in the mountains of Nicaragua. Peasants were supporting the Contras, their former oppressors, rather than the Sandinistas, their liberators. The Sandinistas were given a new nickname, 'piricuaco', which means rabid dog. 'The Government has thrown the army at us,' peasants complained. That, at least, seemed familiar.[100]

6

ENTER STAGE RIGHT

Merrie England: Rivers of Blood

The 'supreme function' of statesmanship, argued Conservative MP Enoch Powell on 20 April 1968, 'is to provide against preventable evils'. On this occasion, the 'evil' was immigration from non-white areas of the Commonwealth. 'We must be mad, literally mad, as a nation to be permitting the annual inflow of some 50,000 dependents . . . It is like watching a nation busily engaged in heaping up its own funeral pyre.' There followed the most inflammatory statement made by a British politician in the twentieth century. 'As I look ahead, I am filled with foreboding; like the Roman, I seem to see "the River Tiber foaming with much blood".'[1]

The 'flood' of immigrants, argued Powell, was making white people 'strangers in their own country'. He told of a constituent who had been repeatedly threatened because she refused to accept black tenants in her boarding house. 'She is . . . afraid to go out. Windows are broken. She finds excreta pushed through her letterbox. When she goes to the shops, she is followed by children, charming, wide-grinning piccaninnies. They cannot speak English, but one word they know. "Racialist", they chant.' To Powell, the issue was freedom, not prejudice. The private citizen was being denied 'his right to discriminate'.[2]

The 'Rivers of Blood' speech was delivered on the anniversary of Hitler's birth. That was mere coincidence, but it was nevertheless ominous that British neo-Nazis openly celebrated both the Führer's birthday and Powell's speech. Feeling decidedly uncomfortable with controversy of this sort, the Tory leader Edward Heath sacked Powell from the Shadow Cabinet. 'I consider the speech he made in Birmingham . . . to be racialist in tone and liable to exacerbate racial tensions,' Heath explained. The word 'tone' is significant, for it was in tenor, rather than substance, that Powell differed most markedly from his Tory colleagues. They, too, sought to curb immigration, but most were afraid to raise the subject.[3]

Labour's view was not altogether different. The party had officially opposed the Commonwealth Immigration Act of 1962, which limited the intake from Asian, African and Caribbean countries, but breathed a sigh of relief when it passed. A short time later, the Labour leader Harold Wilson admitted that his party did 'not contest the need for the control of Commonwealth immigration'. The official Labour strategy was to complain about the problem, while blaming it on the Tories. Thus, at the 1964 election, the Labour candidate in Wandsworth argued that, 'Large-scale immigration has occurred only under this Tory government. The Tory Immigration Act has failed to control it – immigrants of all colours and races continue to arrive here.'[4]

At that election, the Tory candidate Peter Griffiths, campaigning on the slogan 'If you want a nigger for a neighbour, vote Liberal or Labour', took the safe Labour seat of Smethwick. Afterwards, the Tories calculated that the race issue made around twenty Labour constituencies winnable. Shaken by Smethwick, a Labour Cabinet committee concluded that 'immigration can be the greatest potential vote-loser . . . if we are seen to be permitting a flood of immigrants to come in and blight . . . our cities'. Warming to the theme, Frank Soskice, the Labour Home Secretary, warned that, 'If we do not have strict immigration rules our people will soon all be coffee-coloured.'[5]

Powell had, in other words, touched a raw nerve. In the wake of his sacking, he received more than 100,000 letters of support. Over 1,000 dockers marched on Westminster chanting 'Enoch is right', and 400 meat-packers presented Heath with a 92-page petition protesting his dismissal. A Gallup Poll at the end of April 1968 found 72 per cent of Britons in sympathy. Sacking Powell nevertheless allowed the Conservatives to have their cake while eating it too. He had trumpeted his party's immigration policies, albeit rather too enthusiastically. By sacking him, Heath could claim that his party opposed racism, while at the same time benefiting from the exposure given to the issue.

Powell did not aspire to be a racist demagogue, but that is what he became. By voicing what he thought were consistent, logical principles, he provided validation to those inclined to hate. He had little in common with the workers who enthusiastically applauded his Birmingham speech, but that did not stop him from playing to their prejudices. While he saw complex problems of assimilation, they saw an alien invasion which threatened their neighbourhoods, jobs and culture. In Powell, they found a champion, an articulate man who put eloquent voice to raw emotion. As late as 1972, a *Daily Express* poll found him the most popular politician in Britain.

Meanwhile, on the fringes, an openly racist political party tried to capitalize on the furore. The National Front was founded on 7 February 1967, by A.K. Chesterton, cousin of the famous author. The NF was racist, anti-communist and isolationist, but not openly fascist. Affiliation with neo-Nazi groups was forbidden, though that did not stop prominent Nazis like John Tyndall from joining. Calculated avoidance of the fascist label allowed the NF to promote itself as ultra-nationalist and thus to broaden its appeal in a way that Oswald Mosley's British Union of Fascists had never managed. At first dismissed as a lunatic fringe group, the NF gained credibility because of Powell's speech. The NF cast itself as the party willing to act upon Powell's warnings.

NF leaders assumed they would attract Tories disillusioned with Heath's immigration policy, particularly after Powell's sacking. While some did jump ship, by far the greatest source of NF strength was the urban working class – natural Labour supporters. 'It was a vote for Great Britain, the Union Jack,' writes the skinhead spokesman George Marshall, 'and a protest vote against the Conservative and Labour parties who had done little in real terms for the British working classes who were now facing longer dole queues, shit housing and a country going to the dogs.' Brian Kelson recalled friends joining the NF: 'they said they wanted to make a point. It's all right for you, they'd say, living out in suburbia in a white community, but we live in the middle of Birmingham in a mixed race society. We didn't invite them here, the government invited them here, not us, and we don't want them here. They're taking our jobs and everything, and this is the only way we can make our voices heard.' Chris Brown, a skinhead, found the NF irresistibly attractive. 'The immigrants, the communists, the IRA, the ineffectual Labour government . . . were all our enemies. And they were all being orchestrated and manipulated by a world-wide Zionist plot. The only answer was to unite and fight and join the National Front. Of course, it was all bollocks, but regrettably I, and thousands of other gullible young whites . . . took it all in.' He eventually admitted that 'my pride and patriotism had been overtaken by my ignorance'.[6]

Marshall feels that the tendency to dismiss NF supporters as fascist reveals how ignorant most people were about what was really happening. He insists that, for the urban working class, the NF's appeal had little to do with fascism, since most supporters never read the party literature. They were instead

> kids looking to play the hard man, wanting to hit out at society. Life's a bastard, and kids will always cover up their own insecurities by hitting out at soft targets, whether that's a fat boy, the school smellies, the new girl, or the kid in the corner with a turban on his head. Chants of 'National Front!' echoed around playgrounds because it gave you a sense of belonging, a sense of power, a sense of defiance, and not because you had read the NF's manifesto and agreed with every word.

The main motivation, Marshall believes, was rebellion. 'Part of the National Front's attraction was the very fact that teachers, parents and other authority figures told you not to do it. Just like they told you not to smoke, drink bottles of cider . . . nick sweets from the corner shop, go looking for trouble at the football.' Brown agrees: 'Our involvement with the NF . . . was done purely to achieve maximum shock value. The political side of things was a secondary issue; the ability to dismay or even horrify our detractors was our main objective. If that meant saluting the air and paying lip-service to all things Nazi, then so be it.'[7]

While NF sympathizers fought Asians and blacks, the leaders fought one another. The party's effectiveness was severely limited by its fondness for coups and conspiracies. Chesterton was ousted in 1970 by John O'Brien, a former Conservative and supporter of Powell, who in turn left when Tyndall and his deputy Martin Webster took control. For most of the 1970s, formal NF membership hovered around 20,000. The best it could manage was third place at three parliamentary by-elections, and some 200,000 votes gained at the 1977 local elections. On only one occasion did it manage to save its deposit. Its only electoral victory came in a 1975 Carrickfergus Town Council by-election when the other candidate dropped out.

Nevertheless, the NF was important not for votes won, but for the fear it inspired. Its strength lay in what it could do on the streets – the graffiti daubed on walls, the loathsome posters plastered on hoardings, the menace suggested by jackbooted thugs with crude NF tattoos scratched on biceps or foreheads. Its success can be measured by the fear felt within black and Asian communities, fear made worse because the largely white police force too often failed to provide protection. Between 1976 and 1981, thirty-one black people were killed in racist attacks in Britain. While not all these murders were the work of NF supporters, it is fair to say that the perpetrators sympathized with what the NF represented.

On 5 August 1976, in Birmingham, the guitarist Eric Clapton interrupted his concert to shout 'I think Enoch's right . . . we should send them all back. Throw the wogs out! Keep Britain white!' He later explained that he was drunk, which was true, and that he was angry because an Asian man had 'pinched my missus's bum'. 'I just don't know what came over me that night,' he told an interviewer. When sobriety returned, however, racial tolerance did not. 'Enoch was . . . the only bloke . . . telling the truth, for the good of the country,' he reflected in 1978. 'I think Enoch is a prophet, see? . . . His ideas are right. You go to Heathrow any day, mate, and you'll see thousands of Indian people sitting there waiting to know whether or not they can come into the country . . . Enoch said six years ago, stop it, give 'em a grand, and tell 'em to go home.' Clapton was reassured by the fact that Powell was clearly 'a very religious man. And you can't be religious and racist at the same time. The two things are incompatible.'[8]

Meanwhile, David Bowie told German journalists that 'Britain could benefit from a fascist leader'. On his return to Britain, he apparently thought it funny to greet his fans with a Nazi salute. 'I think I might have been a bloody good Hitler,' he told *Rolling Stone*. 'I'd be an excellent dictator . . . I *do* want to rule the world.' The sudden prominence of reactionary rock deeply annoyed those who assumed that rock's rhythms were virtuously leftist. Shortly after the Birmingham incident, the rock photographer Red Saunders published an open letter in *Socialist Worker*, *NME* and *Melody Maker*, attacking Clapton. 'Come on Eric – Own up. Half your music is black. You're rock music's biggest colonist.' Saunders called for 'a rank and file movement against the racist poison music'. Joining the crusade, the journalist David Widgery wrote: 'We want Rebel music, street music. Music that breaks down people's fear of one another. Crisis music. Now music. Music that knows who the real enemy is.' What emerged was Rock Against Racism, a disparate group of musicians, radical politicos and rock fans whose aim, Widgery explained, was to 'rescue . . . rock and roll from . . . the record companies and use . . . [it] to change reality, as always had been intended. And have a party in the process.' Nostalgic for the Sixties, he imagined 'a real progressive culture, not a packaged mail-order stick-on nightmare of mediocre garbage'. Rock Against Racism, he later reflected, 'provided the creative energy and the focus in what became a battle for the soul of young working-class England'.[9]

Rock Against Racism was enthusiastically backed by the Socialist Workers Party and other leftists disillusioned with Labour's flaccidity on the immigration issue. That did not, however, mean that all RAR supporters were socialists. Because punk bands played at RAR concerts the audience often consisted of a large number of otherwise apolitical punks interested only in the music. In addition, some supporters saw RAR as a way to confront the establishment, not unlike supporters of NF. 'We naturally identified with other people getting harassed by the police,' Caroline Harper confessed. 'It was when the sus [stop and search] laws were at their heights. It didn't matter if you had green hair or were black, you would be stopped by the police, for any reason . . . We felt like victims of an authoritarian state.'[10]

'This ain't no fucking Woodstock,' Saunders shouted as he introduced a band at an RAR gig. 'This is the Carnival against the Fucking Nazis.' A central tenet of the anti-fascist front held that 'Where the political and physical circumstances are right, it can be correct to enter into a physical clash with fascists, to attempt to drive them off the streets and disperse and demoralise them.' In practice this meant that two anti-establishment mobs, each trumpeting a radical political platform but consisting of supporters whose political commitment was often weak, expressed their disillusionment with 1970s Britain by fighting in the streets. The worst violence occurred on 13 August 1977, when the NF attempted to march through Lewisham in order to 'reclaim the area from immigrants and blacks'. Blocking their route were thousands of anti-fascists. The 'Battle of Lewisham' was important to the anti-fascist struggle for three reasons: first because the NF was prevented from marching, second because the police seemed to side with the fascists, and third because press and politicians lumped both sides in the same basket of thuggery. The *Daily Mail* carried a front-page photo of a bedraggled policeman over the caption 'After the Battle of Lewisham, a question of vital importance: now who will defend him?', while the *Mirror* argued that the

SWP and NF were equally vile. Labour politicians accused the SWP of 'red fascism', and the left-wing MP Michael Foot protested that 'You don't stop the Nazis by throwing bottles or bashing the police. The most ineffective way of fighting the fascists is to behave like them.' All this convinced anti-fascists that, if the NF was to be stopped, it was up to them. That realization inspired the formation in early 1978 of the Anti-Nazi League, effectively the political wing of RAR. The agreed purpose was to drive the NF from the streets.[11]

ANL 'carnivals' began with a march and ended with a concert. This mix of politics and music pleased the crowd, but often resulted in a confusion of purpose. At the second great carnival on 24 September 1978, some 100,000 people gathered. The NF, rather cleverly, mobilized a march in East London to coincide with the event – effectively presenting anti-fascists with a test of loyalty: were they committed to politics or to music? The ANL failed that test. While anti-fascists were busily grooving, the NF dominated the streets. 'We collectively bungled it,' one ANL leader, Paul Holborow, later admitted. Angry left-wingers accused carnival-goers of 'scabbing' on the struggle and questioned the effectiveness of rock as an agent of political change. 'Potential action against racism', the ANL sympathizer Andrew Calcutt concluded, 'had been thwarted by the very organisers of Rock Against Racism, as we kids were invited to chill out and congratulate ourselves on our anti-racist feelings rather than do anything real to confront racism head-on. Thus were we demobilised, even depoliticised, by RAR.' The RAR formula, he feels, was to 'buy a badge, enjoy the carnival, stay with your right-on friends'.[12]

One-time activists in RAR and the ANL now pride themselves on having driven the NF from Britain's streets. While it is true that they provided visible opposition to the fascists at a time when the Labour government was shamefully silent, in truth the NF was fully capable of engineering its own demise. It never managed to provide proof that it was actually a party, as opposed to a mob. Its few genuine ideologues spent most of their time arguing with, or organizing coups against, one another. Ultimate ruin came when Tyndall, in a fit of hubristic megalomania, decided to stand 303 candidates at the 1979 general election, in order to give the impression that the NF was a significant political force. Most of the candidates were simply names on a ballot – they did no campaigning whatsoever. Tyndall promised that 'in some places we shall beat the Liberals', but that proved hollow. The NF garnered just 1.3 per cent of the national vote and lost all 303 deposits, pushing the party to the brink of bankruptcy.[13]

The main reason for the NF demise was Margaret Thatcher, whose rise brought racism back into the mainstream. In March 1977, she reflected that concerns about the racial integrity of the British people could only be addressed 'by holding out a clear prospect of an end to immigration'. For discontented Powellites, that seemed sufficient. They delighted when, the following year, Thatcher remarked: 'I think people are really rather afraid that this country might be rather swamped by people with a different culture.' That was essentially what Powell had said, minus the 'rivers of blood'. Disillusioned Tories who had once flirted with the NF saw Thatcher's election in 1979 as salvation. She offered the opportunity to turn anti-immigration sentiment into law, without the embarrassing spectacle of street violence. Her immediate introduction of stricter immigration controls demonstrated that she meant business. During the debate on these measures, the Tory MP Tony Marlow raised hardly a stir when he argued: 'People have criticised these measures because they say they are racialist, as if racialist is a word of abuse. What does racialist mean? It means tribal. After all, man is a tribal animal. We have a feeling of kith and kin for people like ourselves, with our own background and culture.'[14]

'What part of Africa do you come from?' Mrs Thatcher asked a black woman while campaigning in South London. 'Tooting,' came the reply. As that encounter made clear, assimilation would not be promoted by the Tories. What had once seemed distasteful was now mainstream – a case of Powellism without Powell. The Monday Club, one-time flirters with fascism, duly provided policy documents on the previously taboo subject of repatriation. Meanwhile, the ANL, satisfied that the NF had been defeated, disbanded. Members shifted their attention to new causes like CND and opposition to Tebbit's Law. As for the musicians who had once played at RAR gigs, their higher profile brought lucrative recording contracts.[15]

New York: Hardhats

On 4 May 1970, Sandy Scheuer was walking across the campus of Kent State University when she came within range of heavily armed National Guardsmen. They had been deployed on campus in response to the rising tide of student dissent following the invasion of Cambodia by US troops. Scheuer was not an anti-war activist, just an innocent student walking to class. Shot in the throat, she quickly bled to death. She was one of four students killed that day.

On the following day, another student was walking not far from Wall Street in New York. Unlike Scheuer, he was an anti-war protester, bound for a rally in protest against the Kent State killings. Quite suddenly, a construction worker from a nearby building site grabbed him. 'I was in Vietnam and I love to kill gooks,' the assailant shouted as he pummelled the protester.[16]

Similar incidents occurred the next day when medical students demonstrating in Battery Park were set upon by construction workers. On the 7th, with violence escalating, Mayor John Lindsay appealed for calm. 'The country is virtually on the edge of a spiritual – and perhaps physical – breakdown,' he lamented. He proposed that Friday, 8 May should be a 'day of reflection', when New York might mourn and then move on.[17]

Instead of reflection, Friday brought class war. As the radical attorney Charles Appel addressed a rally outside Federal Hall on Wall Street, a deafening cacophony of steel rose from an adjacent building site. Having roused themselves to a frenzy by banging girders, construction workers then went on a rampage, targeting anyone remotely resembling a student. 'They attacked us with lead pipes wrapped in American Flags,' one bloodied protester reported. Michael Belknap, a lawyer who stopped to help a bleeding youth, recalled hearing someone yell, 'He's a Commie bastard, we ought to kill him', before being punched and kicked.[18]

'These hippies are getting what they deserve,' John Halloran, a construction worker (or 'hardhat' as they came to be known) told a reporter. George Tangel, his hardhat emblazoned with an American flag, explained that he was beating up students 'because my brother got wounded in Vietnam, and I think this will help our boys over there by pulling this country together'. After making short work of the protesters, the mob marched on City Hall, where the flag had been placed at half-mast for the day of reflection. On the way, they shouted 'Lindsay is a queer'. Hardhats, already angry because of the mayor's apparent hostility toward the construction industry, could not stomach the way the Kent State dead were being honoured, while soldiers who had died in Vietnam received no similar ritual of mourning. On arriving at City Hall, they bullied a postal worker to raise the flag. The crowd cheered, some chanting 'Lindsay is a Red'. 'It was just like John Wayne taking Iwo Jima,' a delighted hardhat observed. As the flag rose, construction workers sang the Star Spangled Banner. Hardhats were removed and placed respectfully on hearts. 'Get your helmets off,' one worker shouted at policemen standing nearby. A few sheepishly complied.[19]

While the crowd sang, someone from City Hall rather bravely lowered the flag. Hardhats threatened to storm the building, causing Deputy Mayor Richard Aurelio to order the flag back up, so as to appease the mob. Meanwhile, fighting continued. Susan Harman, a Lindsay aide, witnessed hardhats randomly throwing punches, while yelling 'Get the hippie!' and 'Get the traitor!' When a construction worker armed with a large pair of pliers attacked a student near her, she tried to intervene. 'Let go of my jacket, bitch,' her assailant screamed, his fists flying. 'If you want to be treated like an equal, we'll treat you like one.' Suddenly, three men were punching her. 'My glasses were broken. I had trouble breathing, and I thought my ribs were cracked.' One workman found his colleagues' savagery perplexing. 'These are people I know well,' he said. 'They were nice, quiet guys until Friday. But I had to drag one fellow away from attacking several women. They became storm troopers.'[20]

At Pace College, a short distance away, another group, armed with wrenches, hammers and crowbars, stormed the administration building in search of students to attack. After forcing their way in, they rampaged through the building, throwing punches, breaking windows and smashing furniture. 'The whole thing was awfully fast and awfully brutal,' Dr Ivan Rohr recalled. Professor Melvyn Oremland, trapped in the Admissions Office by a vicious mob, found it 'the most frightening and horrible experience of my life'. 'What upset me to the point of physical sickness was the fact that the police stood there and didn't even attempt to help the students,' an administration official later testified. 'The . . . police on duty stood there like tin soldiers . . . While they were supposedly protecting City Hall, all the rioters were tearing up our campus and brutally beating the students.'[21]

Over subsequent days, complaints about police inaction poured into the mayor's office. '[The police] were mingling amiably on the steps of City Hall with the construction workers while the students were brutally beaten', a telegram from Deputy Manhattan Borough President Leonard Cohen complained. The New York Civil Liberties Union alleged that 'police stood around passively and, in some instances, joined in the assaults'. Statistics reinforce that allegation: despite over seventy people being treated for injuries, just six arrests were made, only two for assault. Lindsay, absent from City Hall on the day, was furious at the complicity of the police in the riot. At a subsequent press conference he expressed his disgust at the way the public had 'witnessed a breakdown of the police as the barrier between them and wanton violence'. The obvious went unmentioned: the police felt class solidarity with the hardhats and were disinclined to help students, the source of so much aggravation over the previous five years. This was payback for the riots at Columbia two years earlier.[22]

Trade union leaders, while officially condemning the violence, cleverly tried to exploit it. Chief among them was Peter Brennan, head of the Greater New York Building and Construction Trades

Council. Though he ridiculed allegations that employers had organized the riot, he made no secret of his support for hardhats, who were 'fed up with the violence by anti-war demonstrators, by those who spat at the American flag and desecrated it'. He warned that 'any child' who disparaged the United States should not be surprised if patriotic workers objected. 'Violence by [protesters] can bring violence by our people.'[23]

Brennan felt that 'a few ruffians [had] opened the door to some sanity'. He hoped for a backlash against Lindsay who, in conjunction with business leaders, building contractors and civil rights activists, had tried to increase opportunities for minorities within the construction industry. In 1967, the six most highly skilled building trades had minority membership of just 2 per cent. 'Why the hell should I work with spades', one worker asked rhetorically, 'when they are threatening to burn down my house?' That attitude prompted Lindsay to push through Executive Order 1971, requiring companies competing for municipal contracts to adopt affirmative action policies. The Nixon administration followed suit with the Philadelphia Plan, a scheme to increase minority membership in the skilled building trades to 20 per cent within five years. Brennan, uncertain how to stop these measures, was delighted when hardhats showed him the way.[24]

Brennan sensed that working-class political sympathies were shifting. The day after the riots the *New York Times* carried a photo of a construction worker and a stockbroker together chasing down a hippie – a neat encapsulation of that shift. Blue-collar workers, previously dedicated Democrats, had grown disenchanted with liberal politicians, who were blamed for civil rights legislation, welfare reforms and campus unrest. Workers felt marginalized by the alliance between poor blacks and liberal whites that had dominated politics in the 1960s. Lyndon Johnson's Great Society had not seemed great to them. As one observer of the New York riots proclaimed, ordinary workers 'are almost the only segment of the population the government hasn't paid much attention to . . . they [are] in a kind of limbo'.[25]

A chief complaint of the urban worker related to the money spent on welfare. At shipyards and construction sites, blue-collar workers listened in delight to Guy Drake's 'Welfare Cadillac' (1970), a hit song satirizing a benefit scrounger who, as a result of the generosity of the 'guvment', has enough spare cash to buy himself a brand-new luxury car. 'I'm working my ass off', one blue-collar worker complained, 'and I'm supposed to bleed for a bunch of people on relief?' The same contempt was directed against students who enjoyed generous scholarships but seemed to spend their time in constant complaint against their world. 'If I had a chance to get an education,' a worker remarked, 'I wouldn't be wasting my time on the streets.'[26]

Vietnam also rankled. While hardhat rhetoric suggests unwavering support for the war, the reality was more complicated. Throughout the war, the wealthy and educated were more likely to be supportive than those of low income and limited education. 'The whole goddamn country of South Vietnam is not worth the life of one American boy, no matter what the hell our politicians tell us,' one construction worker complained in 1970. 'I'm damn sick and tired of watching those funeral processions go by.' But disagreement with the war's purpose seldom extended to active protest. Most workers still adhered to the sacred tenet of 'my country, right or wrong'. What they objected to was the way their class had endured the lion's share of the fighting – and dying – without much recognition of their sacrifice. This explains their desperate desire to believe in Nixon's promise of peace with honour, which they hoped would give their sacrifices meaning. It also explains their anger toward privileged middle-class students who avoided military service *and* protested against the war. 'Here were these kids, rich kids,' one tradesman remarked, 'who didn't have to fight, they are telling you your son died in vain. It makes you feel like your whole life is shit, just nothing.'[27]

Blue-collar outrage was summarized in the 'America: Love It or Leave It' sticker pasted on bumpers and lunch pails. Displeasure was also manifested in the popularity of patriotic country music in outposts far beyond Nashville and the Southwest. Merle Haggard's attack upon the counterculture in 'Okie from Muskogee' (1969) was partly tongue in cheek, but it still harmonized perfectly with blue-collar indignation. Haggard followed up the success of 'Okie' with 'The Fightin' Side of Me', a suitably virile attack upon the 'squirrelly guys' who enjoy America's riches but disparage the way of life soldiers had fought to preserve. The song, released four months before the incidents in New York, provided the perfect backing track to hardhat violence.

Ronald Reagan had capitalized on blue-collar alienation in his brilliantly successful gubernatorial campaign in California in 1966, the first real indication that working-class support for the Democrats was haemorrhaging. A further hint that times were changing came in the 1968 presidential election, when the third party candidate George Wallace polled a surprising 13.5 per cent of the vote. While Wallace's support was concentrated in the Deep South, his bigoted conservatism had sufficient appeal among workers in the North and Midwest to scupper Hubert Humphrey's presidential bid.

Though Nixon lacked Reagan's populist charm, he was nevertheless determined to woo the 'forgotten Americans' who 'died to keep us free . . . give drive to the spirit of America . . . [and] give life to the American dream'. He directed the party faithful to go after the 'disaffected Democrats . . . blue-collar workers and . . . working-class white ethnics'. Courting the blue-collar vote, he understood, was time-consuming but not expensive. Workers who were already in stable jobs did not want costly federal programmes; they wanted economic stability instead and a reassurance that their taxes would not be wasted on welfare. They also wanted simple recognition of their sacrifices, particularly in Vietnam. Recognition of this sort came in Nixon's 'Silent Majority' speech of 3 November 1969. Drawing reference to a huge anti-war rally that took place nineteen days earlier, he divided the nation into those he could trust and those he could not. 'And so . . . to you, the great silent majority of my fellow Americans – I ask for your support,' he concluded. The *New York Times* correctly sensed that the speech had been written for a 'large and normally undemonstrative cross-section of the country that until last night refrained from articulating its opinions on the war'. In other words, Nixon had courted ordinary Americans simply by acknowledging their existence. After the speech, Gallup found that 75 per cent of those polled thought that the term 'silent majority' referred to those people who believed that 'protesters have gone too far'.[28]

A second large anti-war demonstration occurred on 15 November. Warming to his populist role, Nixon claimed that he hadn't noticed the protest because he was watching a football game. Toward the same end, he invited Haggard and Johnny Cash to the White House, though he insulted the latter by asking him to sing 'Welfare Cadillac'. In his efforts to achieve the common touch, Nixon was helped immensely by his pit-bull vice-president, Spiro Agnew, a man never fearful of sounding bigoted or stupid. 'The time has come', the vice-president remarked, 'for someone . . . to represent the workingmen of this country.' 'We must look to how we are raising our children,' he remarked after Kent State. 'They are, for the most part, the children of affluent, permissive, upper-middle-class parents who learned their Dr. Spock and threw discipline out the window – when they should have done the opposite.' At university, Agnew claimed, these coddled children encountered 'a smiling and benign faculty even less demanding than [their] parents'. Students inclined to violent protest, he concluded, belonged 'not in a dormitory, but in a penitentiary'.[29]

While Nixon and Agnew courted hardhats, Brennan courted Nixon and Agnew. To this end, he organized a pro-war march of around 100,000 construction workers and their supporters in New York on 20 May, a reiteration of hardhat patriotism without the confusing subtext of violence. Marchers carried banners that read: 'WE SUPPORT NIXON AND AGNEW', 'GOD BLESS THE ESTABLISHMENT', and the more colourful 'LINDSAY DROPS THE FLAG MORE TIMES THAN A WHORE DROPS HER PANTS'. A typical sentiment was voiced by John D'Anella, a RCA technician. 'Maybe the students are smarter than we are,' he told a reporter, 'but they have no right to burn down buildings. We love our flag. We love our country. If they destroy the flag, they are destroying our way of life.' Marching nearby was Mrs Allison Greaker and her two young children. 'We're part of the silent majority that's finally speaking,' she told a reporter. She thought the march provided the perfect reply 'to the creeps and the bums that have been hollering and marching against the President'. So, too, did the mere presence of her infant son – little Richard Nixon Greaker.[30]

'We're supporting the President and the country,' Brennan explained, 'not because he's for labor, because he isn't, but because he's our President, and we're hoping that he's right.' That sentiment delighted Agnew, who congratulated Brennan on 'a spirit of pride in country that seems to have become unfashionable'. Six days later, Brennan and his staff were guests at the White House, where they presented the president with a hardhat labelled 'Commander in Chief'. Accepting the gift, Nixon said that the hardhat had become 'a symbol, along with our great flag, for freedom and patriotism'. Nixon carefully explained to the group that the invasion of Cambodia had been necessary to protect 'our boys'. One Brennan aide, who had lost a son in Vietnam, responded: 'Mr. President, if someone would have had the courage to go into Cambodia sooner, they might have captured the bullet that took my son's life.' As Nixon aide Charles Colson recorded, 'The President was visibly moved.'[31]

After the visit, Colson, who had been placed in charge of attracting trade union support, predicted that workers would flock to Nixon in 1972. Unlike those workers, however, Brennan could not be bought with simple rhetoric. Assistant Labor Secretary Arthur Fletcher suspected that behind the 25 May demonstration lurked Brennan's cunning strategy to 'get inside the White House and be a formidable opponent to the Philadelphia plan'. That suspicion proved warranted. On Labor Day (7 September), Brennan returned to the White House for a private meeting with Nixon. A short time later, the New York Plan was announced – Lindsay's affirmative action goals for the construction industry were cut from 4,000 minority workers to just 800. In April 1972, Brennan offered another deal: he would mobilize hardhats in support of Nixon's re-election in exchange for nationwide implementation of the New York Plan. Nixon welcomed the offer, in part because of the disappointing Republican results in the mid-term elections of November 1970, which suggested that worker loyalty to the Democrats remained strong. After Nixon's landslide victory, Brennan was appointed Labor Secretary, a position he used to undermine affirmative action.[32]

The media had already sensed that a tectonic shift was occurring in American politics. A month before the 'Silent Majority' speech, *Newsweek* wrote:

> All through the skittish 1960s, America has been almost obsessed with its alienated minorities – the incendiary black militant and the welfare mother, the hedonistic hippie and the campus revolutionary. But now the pendulum of public attention is in the midst of one of those great swings that profoundly change the way the nation thinks about itself. Suddenly, the focus is on the citizen who outnumbers, outvotes, and could, if he chose to, outgun the fringe rebel. After years of feeling himself a besieged minority, the man in the middle – representing America's vast white middle class majority – is giving vent to his frustration, his disillusionment – and his anger.

On 5 January 1970, *Time* named the 'Middle Americans' its Men and Women of the Year. The magazine explained that 'In a time of dissent and "confrontation", the most striking new factor was the emergence of the so-called "Silent Majority" as a powerfully assertive force in U.S. society.' It noted how this group was suddenly throwing its weight around, either by demanding harsh punishments for student protesters, by defying the Supreme Court ban on prayer in schools, or simply by displaying a 'SPIRO IS MY HERO' bumper sticker. 'By their silent but newly felt presence, they influenced the mood of government and the course of legislation, and thus began to shape the course of the nation and the nation's course in the world.'[33]

'Who precisely are the Middle Americans?' *Time* asked. 'They are defined as much by what they are not as by what they are . . . Above all, Middle America is a state of mind, a morality, a construct of values and prejudices and a complex of fears.' In the weeks that followed the hardhat riots, an ordinary Joe – specifically the New York construction worker Joe Kelly – gave personality to the new ethos. The only thing unique about him was the fact that he courted attention. When asked whether most Americans supported hardhat violence, he replied that 'the large majority of people, going as high as 85 to 90 per cent, are more than happy. Not so much for the violence but for the stand we took . . . The construction worker is only an image that's being used. The hard hat is being used to represent all of the silent majority.' The media delighted in paying homage to this paragon of American ordinariness. 'Joe Kelly never thought the picture presented by his hardworking life would need any defense,' the *New York Times Magazine* gushed. 'There is his pretty blonde wife, Karen; two strawberry-blonde daughters, Robin Lynn . . . and Kerry Ann . . . and now a newborn son, James Patrick . . . There is also a collie named Missy and a newly bought brick-and-shingle, two-story, $40,000 house . . . tastefully furnished, with a modern kitchen, and a freshly sodded lawn on one of those breezy Staten Island streets.' His neighbours were a steamfitter, a bus driver, a policeman and a TV technician, all of whom 'have had too many peace protests, too many moratoriums, too many harsh laments and shouted obscenities against their country, too many rock throwings and strikes and fires on campuses . . . too many bombings and too many Vietcong flags . . . too many long haired youths and naked boys and girls, too many drugs, too much un-Americanism.'[34]

Nixon courted the Joe Kellys, and succeeded reasonably well, but it was always hard work. He had, after all, taken violin lessons as a young boy and had been encouraged to believe that he was special. Listening to Merle Haggard, or for that matter Spiro Agnew, was tough going. Not so Ronald Reagan, a more natural hero of middle America. For Reagan, 'Aw Shucks' was never artifice; bigotry was as comfortable as blue jeans. On 8 April 1970, Reagan had told reporters: 'if it takes a bloodbath' to silence student unrest, 'let's get it over with'. When, less than a month later, four students were killed at

Kent State, Reagan explained that 'bloodbath' had been 'a figure of speech'.[35] In truth, he needn't have bothered. The Joe Kellys were less inclined to sympathize with Sandy Scheuer than with those who shot her.[36]

Miami: Anita Bryant and the Moral Majority

Anita Bryant was America's sweetheart, a woman both sexy and pure. In 1958, she was crowned Miss Oklahoma and, the following year, was second runner-up in the Miss America pageant. Unlike most beauty queens, she possessed some talent, which she converted into a reasonably successful singing career. The big money, however, came from the Florida Citrus Commission. For most of the 1970s Bryant told Americans that, 'A day without orange juice is like a day without sunshine.' Then, quite suddenly, in 1977 Bryant came out – as a bigot.

Her bigotry was directed against gays, who were far too visible for her liking. The Stonewall riots of 1969 had encouraged a new confidence among gays, which had consequences both personal and political. Individually, they felt more confident to come out of the closet. Politically, their newfound solidarity inspired ever more strident demands for rights. Both these developments increased the unease felt among those uncomfortable with homosexuality. The greatest enemy of gay liberation was not the tiny group of extremists who considered homosexuality criminal, but the millions prepared to tolerate gays only if they remained invisible. 'As long as homosexuals do what they do in private, no problem,' remarked Shirley Spellerberg, a conservative radio and television commentator in South Florida in the 1970s. 'But when they start marching in the streets . . . that is too much.'[37]

After Stonewall, pressure from gay coalitions resulted in many cities passing legislation to protect the civil rights of homosexuals. In 1977, Dade County in Florida joined this bandwagon by introducing an amendment to outlaw discrimination on the basis of 'affectational or sexual preference'. The measure was sponsored by Ruth Shack, a county commissioner who had earlier achieved the impressive feat of gaining the endorsement of both Anita Bryant and the gay lobby. The former's support came mainly because Shack's husband was Bryant's agent.

The Metro Commission unanimously agreed to move Shack's amendment forward, which suggested that it would pass smoothly into law. Standing in the way, however, was Robert Brake, a retired legislator, who warned that schools would henceforth be obliged to hire openly homosexual teachers. He decided to force the amendment onto a ballot, a process which first required 10,000 names on a petition. A public meeting was called, at which hundreds of angry Miami residents gathered. Among those attending was Bryant, who felt betrayed by Shack. She delivered a short, rousing speech which convinced Brake that he had found the perfect person to front the campaign to kill the amendment.

Reverend William Chapman, pastor of the conservative Northwest Baptist Church, which Bryant attended, urged her to lead the fight. He publicly stated that he would burn down his parochial school 'rather than permit a homosexual to teach here'. As Bryant recalls, Chapman warned that 'special privileges' would be given to homosexuals. 'He noted the effect this ordinance would have on private and religious schools . . . The thought of known homosexuals teaching my children especially in a religious school bothered me.' Chapman told Bryant that God was summoning her. 'Our pastor said, "She's God's mother for America",' Bryant's husband, Bob Green, recalled. 'He firmly believed that Anita was sent by God, chosen, sent. He indicated to her that as a Christian mother and woman, this was her obligation.' She concluded: 'I couldn't say no to God when His Word is so plain.'[38]

Encouraged by Chapman, Bryant came to the conclusion that homosexuality was evidence of godlessness. 'Because he chooses to reject knowledge and suppress the truth and because he refuses to acknowledge that he is morally responsible to a holy God', she wrote, 'man falls into gross moral perversion, trampling upon the rights and welfare of others.' In her first broadside, she attacked the ordinance for 'infring[ing] upon my rights as a citizen and mother to teach my children and set examples of God's moral code as stated in the Holy Scriptures'. She promised that 'Before I yield to this insidious attack on God and his laws . . . I will lead a crusade to stop it as this country has never seen.'[39]

Within a few weeks, Bryant delivered a petition containing 64,304 signatures, forcing the amendment to a ballot. She had discovered a talent for rousing the rabble, and felt certain that she was indeed a soldier of the Lord. Audiences were repeatedly told that she felt a special duty because her twins, dangerously ill at birth, had been 'saved by the grace of God'. It therefore seemed a betrayal of his grace to expose them to homosexual teachers. 'This is not my battle,' she proclaimed. 'It's God's battle.' Echoing the familiar refrain, she claimed she had nothing against homosexuals per se, having worked with them in the entertainment industry, but she could not condone the permissiveness implicit in the amendment, which suggested that homosexuality was an acceptable way of life. 'If homosexuality were . . . normal', she argued, 'God would have made Adam and Bruce.'[40]

The Bryant team called their campaign 'Save Our Children', intentionally merging homosexuality and paedophilia. A contest originally about civil rights quickly morphed into one about child protection. The Dade amendment 'discriminates against my children's rights to grow up in a healthy decent community', Bryant argued. With intentionally overblown rhetoric, she played to irrational fears. 'Some of the stories I could tell you of child recruitment and child abuse by homosexuals would turn your stomach.' A newspaper ad read: 'recruitment of our children is absolutely necessary for the survival and growth of homosexuality – for since homosexuals cannot reproduce, they must recruit, must freshen their ranks . . . And who qualifies as a likely recruit: a 35-year-old father or mother of two . . . or a teenage boy or girl who is surging with sexual awareness?' An ad in the *Miami Herald* included a montage of stories about paedophiles, under which ran the message: 'THE OTHER SIDE

OF THE HOMOSEXUAL COIN IS A HAIR-RAISING PATTERN OF RECRUITMENT AND OUTRIGHT SEDUCTION AND MOLESTATION, A GROWING PATTERN THAT PREDICTABLY WILL INTENSIFY IF SOCIETY APPROVES LAWS GRANTING LEGITIMACY TO THE SEXUALLY PERVERTED.'[41]

The 'recruitment' issue caused the campaign to focus particularly on the teaching profession. Sharing a podium with Bryant, a prominent Catholic argued that to allow homosexuals to become teachers was akin to letting 'a fox in the chicken coop'. Gay teachers, Bryant maintained, posed a double threat. 'First, . . . [they] could encourage more homosexuality by inducing pupils into looking upon it as an acceptable life-style. And second, a particularly deviant-minded teacher could sexually molest children.'[42]

Bryant cleverly wove serious messages with flippant humour in order to encourage ridicule. 'If gays are granted rights,' she argued, 'next we'll have to give rights to prostitutes and to people who sleep with St. Bernards and to nailbiters.' Intoxicated by the approval of her adoring crowds, she grew increasingly malevolent. At one highly charged rally, she described gays as 'human garbage', who demand the right 'to have intercourse with beasts'. Lending support was the conservative firebrand Jerry Falwell, who warned that 'So-called gay folks would just as soon kill you as look at you.' Before long, every publicity-hungry bigot in Dade County was joining Bryant's choir. A local evangelist asserted that 'homosexuality is a sin so rotten, so low, so dirty that even cats and dogs don't practice it'.[43]

Bryant saw Miami as the first line of defence against the gay invasion. If the amendment won in Dade, that invasion would prove unstoppable. She warned that Congress was about to approve a 'national homosexuality bill' making it 'mandatory nationwide to hire known practicing homosexuals in public schools and in other areas'. That was wild exaggeration, but truth always came second to emotion. 'The hurt in my heart and the agony in my soul were of such intensity . . . when I heard . . . the news of a national homosexuality bill,' she told listeners. 'All I could do was cry.' Fanning the flames, the conservative columnist George Will warned that the

Miami ordinance meant 'the moral disarmament of society', with the right of homosexuals to marry coming next.[44]

Bryant proved an adept political campaigner – photogenic, confident and synthetically honest. Huge donations poured in, allowing her forces to run slickly produced television ads warning of a gay scourge. One in particular juxtaposed wholesome images of Miami's Orange Bowl parade with footage of a Gay Pride march in San Francisco. The narrator drove home the message: 'In San Francisco, when they take to the streets, it's a parade of homosexuals. Men hugging other men. Cavorting with little boys. Wearing dresses and makeup. The same people who turned San Francisco into a hotbed of homosexuality . . . want to do the same thing to Dade.'[45]

'The campaign', the *Miami Herald* remarked with disdain, 'has all the ingredients, from sex to religion to Anita Bryant bursting into the "Battle Hymn of the Republic", for a national media spectacular.' Ambitious right-wingers like Falwell, Jim Bakker, Pat Robertson, Senator Jesse Helms and Phyllis Schlafly boarded her bandwagon. In January, Bryant appeared on Bakker's nationally broadcast Christian television show, *The PTL Club*, and, in the following month, headlined Robertson's *700 Club*. Both appearances elicited the heaviest volume of positive mail ever experienced by either programme. Bakker called her 'the bombshell that exploded over America', while a *Newsweek* cover story titled 'Battle Over Gay Rights' had a montage of a fierce-looking Bryant against the backdrop of a gay rights parade. The suggestion was clear: she was defending America in a war against deviancy.[46]

'It breaks my heart', Shack confessed 'that we are sending people to the polls to decide whether or not we will discriminate against a segment of the community.' As a spokesperson for gay rights, she lacked Bryant's passion and had the disadvantage of being heterosexual. The media, craving flamboyance, wanted someone suitably outrageous to voice the gay argument. Into the fray stepped Bob Kunst, who ran a sexual awareness group called the Transperience Center. He perfectly embodied his own favourite slogan – 'Better blatant than latent'. To the frightened public, Kunst seemed proof of Bryant's warnings. She blamed Kunst's flamboyance on the fact that homosexuals like to swallow sperm, which is 'the concentrated form of life'.[47]

Shack watched in horror as an honest piece of liberal legislation was hijacked by two opposing sets of fundamentalists. 'I introduced this as an antidiscrimination ordinance,' she remarked ruefully; '[Kunst] turned it into a lifestyle discussion. It . . . [became] a discussion of sexuality and bestiality and pedophilia, as opposed to discrimination in the workforce.' Kunst nevertheless remains unrepentant. 'There's no other community in the world that had the debate about sexuality like we did,' he remarked on the thirtieth anniversary of the campaign. 'What did we do that was so wrong?' Blinded by television lights, he failed to notice the damage he caused.[48]

Lesbian and gay activists were slow to react to Bryant's offensive, for the simple reason that they found it so funny. Certain that the best response was ridicule, hundreds sent postcards to Bryant which read: 'We are switching to prune juice, and we will send you the results.' Experience had taught them that homophobics made lots of noise, but were generally unsuccessful in swaying public opinion. Miami, they felt confident, would not stoop to bigotry. That assumption was supported by an early poll showing 42 per cent in favour of the amendment, 33 per cent opposed, and the rest undecided. The National Gay Task Force decided not to join the fight, on the assumption that Bryant would hang herself. 'The feebleness of her arguments and the embarrassing backwardness of her stance both makes her attacks easier to counteract and tends to generate "liberal" backlash in our favor,' the group concluded. 'We can make her rantings work for us just as Sheriff Bull Connor's cattle prods and police dogs ultimately aided desegregation in the South.' The *Lesbian Tide* reflected:

> Bryant's image was not one to strike fear into the heart. Rivalling the Lennon Sisters for blandness, Anita Bryant seemed laughable when she started talking about 'men wearing dresses' teaching in public schools, and 'the devastation of the moral fibre of the youth of America'. Her ignorance of homosexuality was so complete, her

> prejudice so simplistic, she seemed a ludicrous parody of 1950s style American 'womanhood'; a sort of 'Ozzie and Harriet' gone mad.

What activists did not understand was that Bryant's ignorance harmonized perfectly with that of ordinary Americans. For them, homosexuality remained mysterious and threatening. It is well to bear in mind that, up until 1973, the American Psychiatric Association had classified homosexuality a mental disorder. The decision to remove that classification was reached only after acrimonious debate. At the APA annual meeting the previous year, a gay psychiatrist had worn a mask while giving a speech advocating reclassification, so that his identity would not be revealed and his career ruined.[49]

When the gay rights lobby finally recognized Bryant's danger, a more serious approach evolved. A fund-raising campaign was launched and activists, many from the Bay Area, rushed to Miami. Jim Foster, an aide to San Francisco Mayor George Moscone, soon came to the conclusion that an overtly gay rights campaign 'has no way of winning'. Focus was instead shifted toward the inviolable nature of freedom. 'A day without human rights is like a day without sunshine' became the motto. Echoing that sympathy, Shack argued that, 'Human rights are not gifts to be distributed to those who meet our approval and withheld from those with whom we disagree.'[50]

Logic, however, could not sway a public baying for blood. Bumper stickers read: 'KILL A QUEER FOR CHRIST'. Before long, local newspapers lined up behind Bryant. The *Miami News*, *Miami Beach Sun Reporter* and the Catholic *Miami Voice* abandoned moderation. They recycled old stories about gay sex crimes, stories which then made their way into Bryant's speeches. The *Herald* was initially more restrained, expressing guarded support for the ordinance. When popular opposition coalesced, however, the paper reversed its stance. An editorial signed by the executive editor, John McMullan, assured readers that the *Herald* 'opposed discrimination toward any group, including gays', but had no intention of 'endorsing homosexuality'. The furore, he argued, seemed unnecessary. The issue was 'manufactured . . . concocted, we suspect, by those more interested in flaunting their new deviate freedom than in preventing discrimination which . . . they had not experienced'. Shack's amendment, in other words, was a waste of money.[51]

Opponents of the ordinance were generally more emotionally motivated than supporters. Since backing for gay rights among heterosexuals was always lukewarm, the great difficulty lay in getting them to vote. As a result, the amendment was crushed, by a margin of 69 to 31 per cent, on 7 June. That result was probably not an accurate reflection of public sympathy, though it was an indication of Bryant's ability to rouse fear.

'Today, the laws of God and the cultural values of man have been vindicated,' Bryant declared. 'All America and all the world have heard the people of Miami.' Posing for photographers, her husband threw his arms around her, kissed her fully on the mouth and shouted: 'This is what heterosexuals do, fellas.' Bryant went on to reiterate that Miami was simply the first battle in a long crusade. She would take her show on the road.[52]

Thanks to Bryant, the idea that gays and lesbians habitually molested children was now commonly accepted. In response to the landslide, the Florida Legislature passed a new law prohibiting gays from adopting children or serving as foster parents. A nationwide Gallup poll found that while a majority believed in equal rights for homosexuals, 65 per cent thought they should be banned from teaching. The Miami campaign provided a template for anti-gay groups around the country. Over the next ten years, forty-four attempts were made to repeal similar antidiscrimination ordinances, with thirty-three successful.[53]

Bryant had succeeded beyond her wildest dreams. She had not simply overturned a local ordinance, she had also inspired a nationwide movement. The Dade result had demonstrated how a populist campaign based on bigotry and fear could motivate the otherwise apathetic to go to the polls. The chief beneficiary was Falwell, who quickly colonized the constituency Bryant had identified. At a meeting of like-minded conservatives in 1979, the campaigner Paul M.

Weyrich remarked: 'Jerry, there is in America a moral majority that agrees about the basic issues. But they aren't organized.' Weyrich felt that otherwise disparate individuals could be drawn together on the simple issue of morality, thus negating the doctrinal differences that had previously doomed attempts at uniting diverse evangelical groups. 'I was convinced', Falwell later wrote, 'that there was a "moral majority" out there . . . sufficient in number to turn back the flood tide of moral permissiveness, family breakdown and general capitulation to evil and to foreign policies such as Marxism-Leninism.' While holding aloft a Bible, Falwell shouted: 'If a man stands by this book, vote for him. If he doesn't, don't.' Within three years of its founding, the Moral Majority had a $10 million budget, 100,000 trained clergymen and several million volunteers. Once mobilized, this powerful political group could be delivered en bloc to approved political candidates. The goal was to 'get them saved, baptized and registered'. In truth, Falwell was tapping into the constituency already identified by Nixon. 'God', he proclaimed, 'is calling millions of Americans in the so-often silent majority to join in the moral-majority crusade to turn America around.'[54]

'We are fighting a holy war,' Falwell bellowed, 'and this time we are going to win.' He promised to turn America into a 'Christian republic'. 'The idea that religion and politics don't mix', he argued, 'was invented by the devil to keep Christians from running their own country.' Lending support, the evangelist James Robinson blasted those who called themselves 'pro-family' but refused to fight for family values: 'I'm sick and tired of hearing about all of the radicals, and the perverts and the liberals, and the leftists, and the communists coming out of the closet. It's time for God's people to come out of the closet, out of the churches, and change America.'[55]

There were, however, limits to what mobilized moral righteousness could achieve. A year after the Dade result, Bryant was in California, campaigning with Falwell on behalf of a ballot proposition that would ban gays and lesbians from teaching in public schools. That proved a bridge too far, as evidenced by the fact that opposition was voiced by both the arch-liberal Harvey Milk and the conservative Ronald Reagan. The former governor and would-be presidential candidate was happy to accept the support of the Christian right, but was reluctant to disturb his populist constituency by pushing through divisive legislation.

Bryant eventually discovered that she could not be both a conservative politician and a popular entertainer. Uncomfortable with controversy, the Florida Citrus Commission did not renew her contract. In quick succession, NBC replaced her as host of the Orange Bowl Parade and a planned television series was dropped because of 'the extensive national publicity arising from the controversial activities you have engaged in'. Her anti-gay campaign drew to a close in 1979 when her two organizations, Anita Bryant Ministries and Protect America's Children, collapsed due to mismanagement. The dream of fronting a nationwide campaign was never realized, due primarily to the fact that she lacked the emotional fortitude to handle the hatred she inspired. Addicted to love, she soon tired of politics, and tried instead to deliver her message by other means. A song called 'There's Nothing Like the Love Between a Man and a Woman' demonstrated, however, that bigotry put to music had limited appeal.[56]

Reacting to the demonization of Bryant, the *New York Times* lambasted 'Miami homosexualdom' for demonstrating 'how quickly a minority that had suffered discrimination of its own will use its newly won position to suppress and punish its critics'. Like so much of America, the paper preferred gays to be silent. But behind that broadside lay an important observation. Gays were speaking out, and they had Bryant to thank. 'It was the beginning of two movements, the Christian Coalition and gay rights,' Shack now feels. The Dade County debacle had starkly demonstrated that rights would not be granted without a fight. A more assertive and significantly more organized movement evolved. 'In a completely unintended way, Anita Bryant was about the best thing to happen to the gay rights movement,' feels John Coppola, a curator at the Stonewall Center. 'She and her cohorts were so over the top that it just completely galvanized the gay rights movement.' Among many homosexuals, Anita Bryant is affectionately remembered as the godmother of the gay rights movement.[57]

In Bed: Coming for Christ

In mid-Seventies America, good Christian women took to wrapping their naked bodies in cling film, the better to titillate their husbands. The idea was inspired by Marabel Morgan, whose answer to marital discontent was not to revolt but to submit. 'Wives, be subject to your husbands, as to the Lord,' she advised, quoting Ephesians. 'It is only when a wife surrenders her life to her husband, reveres and worships him, and is willing to serve him, that she becomes really beautiful to him . . . she becomes a priceless jewel, the glory of femininity, his queen.'[58]

While there was nothing particularly new about wifely submission within Christian fundamentalist circles, what made Morgan different was that thorny issue of sex. She was the freak offspring of two otherwise disparate movements: the conservative evangelical revival and the Sixties sexual revolution. Morgan advised discontented women to put 'sizzle back into your marriage' by 'plugging into God as the power source'. Religion offered a shining path to great sex and marital bliss.[59]

Morgan spoke from personal experience. In the mid-1960s, she was living her dream – nice home, loving husband, secure future. 'I played wife. It was fun cooking . . . folding his shirts, doing my little fairy tale stuff . . . life was strawberries for breakfast and lovin' all the time.' Then came the babies. 'Our lives became more complicated, and we gradually changed . . . I was helpless and unhappy.' She struggled with a 'nameless, intangible enemy that I could not define or fight' – a malaise not unlike the 'problem that has no name' Betty Friedan identified in *The Feminine Mystique*. Morgan's solution, however, was entirely different.[60]

At first, she tried assertiveness: she pursued her own interests, objected to her husband's dominance, argued, argued, argued. 'I really tried to insist on my rights and demand what I thought was due me.' Contentment remained elusive, however, and her marriage steadily unravelled. 'At the rate we were going, 10 years from now we would hate each other!' She then shifted focus. 'I'd tried to change Charlie, and that hadn't worked. Now I would have to change me.' Self-help books, bought in desperation, proved less useful than her own, irrepressible, can-do logic. 'A great marriage is not so much finding the right person', she decided, 'as *being* the right person.'[61]

The first step was to please Charlie sexually. '[He] was looking for me to make him happy when he came home, and I began to do it.' On Day One of the new Marabel, she finished her housework early, pampered herself with a bubble bath, slipped on a baby doll nightie and white go-go boots, put perfume in the right places and then awaited Charlie's return. 'My quiet, reserved, nonexcitable husband took one look, dropped his briefcase on the doorstep, and chased me around the dining room table. We were in stitches by the time he caught me, and breathless with that old feeling of romance.' The process was repeated over subsequent days, with costume changes keeping the adventure alive. Sex kitten morphed into pirate, then into cowgirl, then into harem slave. The 'super sex' brought instant rewards. A week into the new regime, 'I was stunned to see a truck pull up with a new refrigerator-freezer . . . Now, without being nagged, [Charlie] was beginning to give me what I yearned for.' He even let her redecorate the family room. 'I saw how hard she was trying,' he explained, 'and I couldn't help but respond.'[62]

Submission came easily because Morgan sincerely believed that God had 'planned for the woman to be under her husband's rule'. Though always religious, true fulfilment had come when she was born again. 'I asked him to take me and he took me. There was no bolt of lightning, only peace. I was tickled to death.' Her relationship with Christ had an erotic quality. 'Getting married or raising children doesn't completely fulfill a woman. [God] is the only One who can make you complete . . . A beautiful spiritual transaction occurs when a mortal woman tells an immortal Saviour what's bothering her . . .

He whispers in her mind, "Dare to trust Me." And timidly she assents *yes*, and peace comes.'[63]

Morgan's friends, intrigued by the change that had occurred, demanded to know the secret. 'At night women would call every half-hour until midnight,' Charlie recalled. 'I was about to go up the wall.' By 1971, she was giving Total Woman seminars around the country and was a frequent guest on the *Phil Donahue Show*. She franchised her method, training counsellors to teach submission at $15 per course. Among her students were Mrs Jack Nicklaus, Mrs Joe Frazier and Anita Bryant. 'Her enthusiasm is so contagious, so upbeat and optimistic,' Bryant remarked, 'I just knew all that womanliness was bound to rub off on me.'[64]

In 1973, her first book, *Total Woman*, was published. It was marketed by word of mouth and through the courses, for which it was required reading. To everyone's surprise, it became the most successful non-fiction title of 1974, outselling *All the President's Men*. Three other books quickly followed, including the *Total Woman Cookbook*, which included the 'You Tiger You' menu and the 'Reconcile Feast'. As a result of her success, *People* magazine named her one of the twenty-five 'most influential' Americans of 1975. 'What a gal!' wrote one (male) correspondent to *Time*. 'Her concerns, beliefs and fresh, wholesome image are a welcome relief from the hardcore, ego-stomping, stern-looking, rebellious feminists.'[65]

Total Woman reads like a neighbour's warm-hearted advice offered over the back fence. That perhaps explains its success. Homespun homilies blend with practical suggestions. 'A merry heart helps melt away the troubles,' Morgan advises. Harriet Habit and Phoebe Phobia – mortal enemies of marital harmony – are introduced. Another enemy is inefficiency: women who organize their days with military precision easily find time to seduce their husbands. A slovenly wife, on the other hand, is usually 'too tired to be available to him'.[66]

'A Total Woman is not a slave,' Morgan insists. 'She graciously chooses to adapt to her husband's way, even though at times she desperately may not want to. He in turn will gratefully respond by trying to make it up to her and grant her desires. He may even want to spoil her with goodies.' Submit, the book advises, or you might lose him. 'A man needs to be accepted as he is, just exactly as he is.' There was no secret in why men occasionally strayed. 'Many a husband rushes off to work leaving his wife slumped over a cup of coffee in her grubby undies. His once sexy bride is now wrapped in rollers and smells like bacon and eggs. All day long he's surrounded at the office by dazzling secretaries who emit clouds of perfume.' The book offers four simple steps to marital bliss – 'Accept Him, Admire Him, Adapt to Him, Appreciate Him'. The wife who baulks risks being cut adrift. Divorce lurks like a demon on every page. 'Carl has since found someone else to enjoy his exciting new way of life with him,' one parable concludes. 'In your marriage it only makes sense for both of you to paddle in the same direction. Otherwise, you'll only go in circles – or like Carl, he may pull out and go downstream.'[67]

Helpful hints are delivered in woodpecker rhythm: 'be touchable and kissable', 'remove all prickly hairs and be squeaky clean', keep your hands moving and moan a lot during intercourse, bolster a man's ego by letting him open jars, use dental floss, be ready for intercourse every night, put sexy notes in hubby's lunch box, call him at work and say 'I crave your body'. Variety is essential: have sex under the dining room table, on bales of hay, on the diving board or a trampoline; use lotions, candles, music and toys. Those too shy to buy nipple tassels should try using tea bags. Husbands also like partners driven ditzy by love. For instance, the wife should propose sex in a hammock. When he says: 'We don't have a hammock', she can then reply: 'Oh, darling, I forgot!'[68]

'It's a struggle to submit', Morgan admits, 'but it's worth it.' Husbands are by nature despots; whether they are benevolent depends on the wife. By submitting, women are rewarded with a comfortable home, a stable marriage, great sex and unexpected presents. 'He has never brought me a gift before', one satisfied student wrote, 'but this past week he bought me two nighties, two rose bushes, and a can opener!' Critics accused Morgan of turning marriage into a manipulative system of barter. 'The image of women . . . is an ultimately demeaning one,' wrote the journalist Joyce Maynard, 'it represents women as weak and empty-headed complainers, obsessed with material possessions.' One young woman, writing to *Time*, confessed that she found Morgan 'more dangerous to my liberty than either the Soviet Union or Communist China'. Unapologetic, Morgan countered: 'if I do something because I want to, because it gives joy, I'm not being manipulative at all'.[69]

Give and you shall receive, she insisted. After all, it was not just men who benefited from great sex. Orgasms were little gifts from God; sex was as 'clean and pure as . . . cottage cheese'. This advice departed sharply from traditional evangelicals who held that sex was devilish. 'Sexuality is nature's strongest competitor for . . . loyalty to Christ,' argued the fundamentalist Lewis Smedes. 'You cannot love God and sex.' Morgan, in contrast, argued that loving sex *was* loving God. Sex, as long as it occurred within marriage, was divine. Women might, however, have to teach their husbands a few things: 'Have him apply rhythmic pressure [to the clitoris] and don't give up.'[70]

Where Morgan led, others followed; top shelves at Christian bookshops were suddenly populated with titles like *Tough and Tender*, *Celebration in the Bedroom*, *The Gift of Sex* and *Intended for Pleasure*, all of which maintained that sex was holy. In *Do Yourself a Favor: Love Your Wife*, Pastor H. Page Williams urged husbands to discuss sex with their wives. 'It is in talking . . . that you let her take off your clothes, so to speak. She "talks off" your shirt of self-righteousness, your pants of self-sufficiency, your undershorts of self-pity. This is what stimulates her sexually.' 'Every wife has the right to be loved to orgasm,' advised Reverend Tim LaHaye, writing with his wife Beverley. He suggested that guidance on clitoral stimulation could be found in Song of Solomon and that penetration should be delayed in order to 'increase the possibility for both to experience orgasm'. Clifford and Joyce Penner promoted oral sex, while Reverend Charles Shedd and his wife Martha championed anal penetration. They were also rather fond of sex toys, boasting to Phil Donahue about their 'whole drawerful' of vibrators.[71]

Despite the acknowledgement of female sexual needs, these authors did not stray from the central premise that women should submit. Helen Andelin, a Mormon, argued that submission would give women a 'strange but righteous power over your man'. In her Fascinating Womanhood classes, students were encouraged to act and dress like little girls. One lesson focused on 'how to be cute, even adorable when you are angry'. 'Stomp your foot. Or, beat your fists on your husband's chest, pouting: "You hairy beast . . . How can a great big man like you pick on a poor little helpless girl? I'll tell your mother on you."' Therapists advised that the husband needed to feel superior, especially intellectually, even when he wasn't. 'There aren't many things more upsetting to the male ego than a female super-brain,' one book advised.[72]

In stark contrast to feminists, these advisers suggested that liberation would come through vulnerability. Beverley LaHaye urged wives to emulate Christ's 'willingness to be humbled, to be obedient unto death, and to be submissive . . . As the woman humbles herself (dies to self) and submits to her husband (serves him) she begins to find herself.' She related the joy she derived from tidying up after her husband. 'I was serving the Lord Jesus by doing this . . . It was almost a time of devotion each day as I lovingly picked up those blessed dirty socks.' When her husband began picking up his own socks she was distraught. 'Oh, how I missed those socks. I still get to take them from the clothes hamper and put them into the washing machine. May I do it heartily as unto the Lord!' Accepted wisdom held that women who refused to submit were asking to be abused. 'Wife-beating is on the rise because men are no longer leaders in their homes,' one minister argued. 'I tell the women they must go back home and be more submissive. I know this works, because the women don't come back.'[73]

The arguments of Morgan, LaHaye and others dovetailed nicely with the anti-feminist campaign conducted by Phyllis Schlafly. She was the Moral Majority's Wonder Woman – a hugely successful lawyer and politician who had never placed any of her six children in daycare. Feminists, she sneered, 'tell . . . women they are victims . . . Men are the enemy; if you go in the workforce, you will never be paid what you ought to be paid; and if you get married, your husband will probably beat you up.' In 1972 Schlafly published an article entitled 'What's Wrong with "Equal Rights" for Women?', which set in motion the nationwide campaign to defeat the Equal Rights Amendment (ERA). The ERA, which sailed through Congress in 1971, was making steady progress toward ratification by the individual states when the Schlafly juggernaut stopped it dead in its tracks.[74]

Schlafly began her attack with reference to biological inevitability. The position of women in society, she argued, 'is based on the fact of life – which no legislation or agitation can erase – that women have babies and men don't'. She then went on to argue that women, because of these biological differences, enjoyed special privileges. 'Our Judeo-Christian civilization has developed the law and custom that, since women must bear the physical consequences of the sex act, men must be required to bear the *other* consequences and pay in other ways.' Feminists, she warned, threatened to undermine that beautiful symbiosis. Equal rights would mean equal suffering; women would have to bear unpleasant burdens heretofore shouldered exclusively by men. 'Why should we lower ourselves to "equal rights" when we already have the status of special privilege?' If the ERA succeeded, Schlafly warned, women would lose the right to child support and alimony, they would be forced to serve in the military and they would lose their dower right to their husband's property in the event of divorce. Lending support, others argued that no-fault divorce made it easier for husbands to 'run off with their secretaries'. In other words, 'the women's movement is turning into men's liberation'.[75]

The family, Schlafly argued, 'gives a woman the physical, financial and emotional security of the home – for all her life'. Rather like Morgan, she argued that the home was not a pit of oppression, but a place where women could find fulfilment. Homes had become all the more idyllic because of the labour-saving devices produced by the 'inventive geniuses' (i.e. men) inspired by American free enterprise. 'The great heroes of women's liberation are not the straggly-haired women on television talk shows and picket lines, but Thomas Edison . . . or Clarence Birdseye . . . or Henry Ford.' Liberation came not through votes but vacuum cleaners.[76]

'Women's libbers', argued Schlafly 'are waging a total assault on the family, on marriage and on children.' Lending support, the child psychologist James Dobson advised that 'children need their mothers [at home] more than they do a newer car or a larger house'. Liberated women were, in other words, destroying the family, the very bedrock of American society. 'We are now raising a generation of children from broken homes', warned *Reader's Digest*, 'and creating a social time bomb.' Schlafly saw the campaign for equal rights as a conspiracy 'to make wives and mothers unhappy with their career, make them feel that they are "second-class citizens" and "abject slaves". Women's libbers are promoting free sex instead of the "slavery" of marriage. They are promoting Federal "day-care centers" instead of homes. They are promoting abortions instead of families.' Feminism, like communism, was 'godless'. The brilliance of Schlafly's campaign lay in its smooth transition from the particular to the general, household matters became national issues. By attacking feminism, she defended family *and* nation. The state, she argued, should buttress the family by outlawing abortion, making divorce difficult, restoring traditional educational standards, supporting prayer in schools, and by demonstrating its disapproval of homosexuality. In other words, government should go to war against 'deviancy', while leaving 'normal' people alone. 'The bottom line of the pro-family people', she stated, 'is to get the federal government off our backs.'[77]

'We're not trying to jam our moral philosophy down the throats of others,' argued Falwell. 'We're simply trying to keep others from jamming their amoral philosophies down our throats.' Anti-ERA activists argued that a 'tiny minority of dissatisfied, highly vocal, militant' feminists were trying to abolish the right of women to 'to stay at home, to rear your children, to be supported by your husband'. The 'war on the family', Schlafly maintained, 'deliberately degrades the homemaker'. 'There are sufficient men to be Presidents and not nearly enough women to be good mothers,' counselled Andelin. This line of argument exposed a significant weakness within the feminist movement, namely its inability to recognize that some women genuinely took pride in being good housewives and mothers.

Feminists of the 1970s tended to see the home as a prison that needed to be escaped if true liberation was to occur. In *Let Me Be a Woman*, evangelist Elisabeth Elliot countered that '"Equal opportunity" nearly always implies that women want to do what men do . . . which indicates that prestige is attached to men's work but not to women's. Women's work, particularly the task assigned by Creation exclusively to women, that of bearing and nurturing children, is regarded not only as of lesser value but even degrading.'[78]

'Women don't want to imitate the male pattern of obsessive work ending up with a heart attack and an engraved wrist watch,' wrote the feminist Gloria Steinem in 1971. 'We want to humanize the work pattern, to make new, egalitarian life-styles.' That might have been true in theory, but in practice feminists too often measured women's progress in relation to men, ignoring the fact that men's lives were far from perfect. As a result, women who either did not aspire to the male standard of success, or felt incapable of achieving it, had difficulty seeing what feminism could offer. No wonder, then, that Morgan became so popular; she gave these women the opportunity to feel pride in their accomplishments. 'So many women get "testy" when discussing [submission],' wrote Beverley LaHaye. 'All they can think of is their downtrodden rights. Has it ever occurred to you that God would never have asked you to submit to your husband unless he had a need for your respect and admiration?' Marriages were failing, argued Morgan, because the distinctions between men and women had become blurred. Women were seeking careers, rejecting motherhood, expecting equality. They were becoming too 'masculine'. 'God ordained man to be the head of the family, its president, and his wife to be the executive vice-president,' she wrote. By rededicating themselves to traditional roles, women would find marital harmony *and* empowerment. The husband, no longer feeling threatened, would learn to adore his wife.[79]

Thanks in large part to the efforts of Schlafly, the ERA eventually failed, falling three states short of ratification when the final deadline passed on 30 June 1982. While feminists cried foul, railing against a right-wing conspiracy of chauvinist men and quisling women, the failure had much to do with feminism itself. The movement of the 1970s never quite figured out how to recognize the dignity of motherhood, or the desire of some women to be homemakers. Central to the feminist thesis was the principle that 'a woman's role as a wife and as the socializer of children acts as a stunting influence on her creativity', or, as the feminist Laurel Limpus wrote: 'Men are encouraged to play out their lives in the realm of transcendence, whereas women are confined to immanence. This simply means that men work, create, do things, are in positions of authority, create their own histories; whereas women are confined to the home, where their function is not to create, but to maintain.' An assembly line worker would undoubtedly have been perplexed to discover that his job offered transcendence, just as a mother would be intrigued to find that rearing a child required no creativity. No wonder, then, that so many women found feminism threatening and so many men found it ridiculous. The futile campaign by radical feminists to make gender irrelevant would eventually inspire a new group to march in a different direction: the cultural feminists of the 1990s were essentialists who emphasized and celebrated female qualities. Morgan went down that road, but unfortunately brought with her the baggage of dependence and subservience.[80]

'I don't know why Total Woman should be a threat to feminists,' Morgan remarked, with that coy ingenuousness that Charlie loved. 'I'm for women's liberation in that it opens up more options. But marriage and children is also an option. When I share with other women what happened to me, I give them hope.' That was probably true. For many women, the simple solutions and limited empowerment offered by Morgan seemed a great deal more realistic (and a lot less scary) than the grandiose ambitions of feminists. 'You don't have to be a doormat anymore,' Mary Morris, the quintessential happy housewife, argued in the documentary *Who Will Save the Children?* 'That's not what submission means. It means we're equal but we each have certain things we do better than the other. Like diapers. I change diapers better than he does.' State legislators – the men who decided whether or not to ratify the ERA – interpreted the popularity of Morgan's advice as evidence that many women didn't want equal rights.[81]

This was a tale of 'do as I say, not as I do'. Schlafly became one of the most powerful women in America by telling women they did not need liberating. Morgan became a multimillionaire by teaching women to be submissive. Yet her peculiar brand of erotic domesticity had eventually to be sacrificed in favour of her career. 'I haven't had a bubble bath in years,' she complained in 1977. That was a lesson in itself. Perhaps without realizing it, Morgan had demonstrated the importance of women having a choice. 'After another long, depressing day as a secretary, my spirits were lifted by reading your article on the Total Woman,' one correspondent wrote to *Time*. 'I am no longer embarrassed that my goal in life is to be a wife and mother, rather than pound a typewriter or even be an executive. But I am also grateful to the women's liberation movement for allowing me the chance to choose.'[82]

7

FADS, FASHIONS AND CULTS

Colombia: Cocaine

Out in Homestead, in south Florida, a delicatessen sits by the marina. Back in the 1970s and 1980s, it sold bottles of ice-cold Dom Pérignon along with hot dogs and Reuben sandwiches. The bottles of premium bubbly walked off the shelves back when the marina was awash with cocaine money.

In the Sixties, drugs provided sensual pleasure and an avenue to rebellion. Smoking pot and dropping acid politicized a generation more than protest itself. 'LSD and pot signifies the total end of the Protestant Ethic,' proclaimed Jerry Rubin, with typical hyperbole. Getting stoned, he argued, offered a chance 'to free one's self from American society's sick notions of work, success, reward and status'. For the 'establishment', this rebellion seemed more threatening than the drugs themselves, especially since no one had proved conclusively that marijuana was actually harmful. The issue, in other words, wasn't dangerous drugs, but disobedient kids.[1]

Looking back on the Sixties and early Seventies, Peter Bourne, who would become Jimmy Carter's 'Drug Czar', felt that the government conducted a culture war but disguised it as a drug war. 'There was an effort to imply that marijuana was a public health problem, to justify the tough measures taken against those who experimented.

But it was really . . . very phoney.' Public health professionals, required to play along, felt uncomfortable giving scientific justification to what were in fact socio-cultural motives. According to Robert DuPont, director of the Narcotics Treatment Administration from 1970 to 1973, the 'drug problem' was contrived. 'It was . . . media hype, a bunch of know-nothings who were overreacting to a trivial blip.' Even notoriously thick-skinned politicians felt the twinge of hypocrisy. Bud Krogh, a Nixon aide, had a hard time justifying the administration's policy toward marijuana. 'I had just come out of school and a lot of my friends participated . . . and it was just not viewed by those of us on the staff as really the critical problem that we should be addressing.' Government unease leached down to law enforcement agencies. George Jung, a pot dealer, was once accidentally caught up in a heroin bust. 'We're sorry,' a contrite policeman explained, 'we really don't want to bust pot people but this is tied into a heroin operation and we have to arrest you.'[2]

Government hypocrisy encouraged distrust among the young. 'It reinforced the notion that . . . you can't believe what the government says,' Bourne feels. '[Young people] were saying it's some ulterior motive, because to say that smoking marijuana is dangerous is patently absurd . . . and therefore the government has to be lying.' By the same logic, pot dealers were turned into heroes for defying an iniquitous law. Jung saw himself as a reefer Robin Hood. 'I wasn't looked upon as the guy in the black hat in the Sedan hanging outside the schoolyard. In fact, I was welcomed. There were movie stars and rock stars. I became a pot star. I glorified in that.' As Rob Stoner, bass player for Bob Dylan, recalled, 'You were suspicious of anyone who *didn't* do drugs back then.'[3]

Nevertheless, in 1969 and 1970, more Americans died of drug overdoses than were killed in Vietnam. This statistic went unnoticed because the main culprit was heroin, the drug of the underclass. Policymakers took comfort in the assumption that neither heroin nor addiction were problems affecting white middle-class youths. That assumption ensured that a drug epidemic went unnoticed. From a base point in the 1960s, usage of all drugs – amphetamines, barbiturates, LSD, pot and heroin – rose steeply. 'What had started with the mantra of "Feed Your Head"', writes Bill Van Parys, 'progressed into a mainstream mandate and recreational drug use became (gasp!) almost Establishment.' Bill Alden, a former special agent for the Drugs Enforcement Agency, recalled how colleagues suddenly felt swamped. 'If you would have told me or my fellow agents back in the 1960s that there would be tons of drugs, and there would be millions and millions of people using drugs, we never would have believed it. When we started in the 1960s, most of the drug use was in the lower socio-economic pockets of the major metropolitan cities.' Jung remembers a dangerous atmosphere of unreality. 'People were basically looking the other way or just accepting it as kids will be kids and nobody really stood up to try to stop it. Nobody really came across and said it's evil. I don't think anybody . . . really knew what the hell was going on. It was just like a snowball coming down a mountain and when it got too big, then they didn't know what the hell to do with it.'[4]

Cocaine was a late arrival at the party, emerging in the early 1970s. 'It's a dynamite high,' confessed a Boston dealer. 'You feel like Adam, and God is blowing life into your nostrils.' Due to its expense, it became a drug of the middle class, which in turn meant that it seemed harmless. Krogh admits that complacency extended right to the White House. 'At that time, I don't think that cocaine was even on anybody's radar as something we needed to deal with.' Bourne, a highly respected drug expert, published 'The Great Cocaine Myth' in 1974, arguing that scare stories were entirely unfounded. To him, the drug seemed benign – it was difficult to get addicted and virtually impossible to overdose.[5]

'To snort cocaine is to make a statement,' wrote Robert Sabbag in his hip tale of the cocaine trade. 'It is like flying to Paris for breakfast.' Cocaine's popularity among wealthy, 'responsible' people seemed to confirm its harmlessness and also provided positive advertisement. For those addicted to glamour, cocaine was as indispensable as a Hermès bag or Bulgari watch. It was the first designer drug, its expense rendering it a symbol of success. One New York ad agency was rumoured to give free samples. In February 1979, five brokers were arrested for trading the drug on the floor of the Chicago Options Exchange. In Hollywood, producers added a hefty sum for cocaine to their budgets for blockbuster films, one editor explaining that 'people won't work without their wake-up calls'. Drug paraphernalia – nicely tooled mirrors and gold razor blades – reinforced the image of respectable rebellion. 'It became an accepted product,' Jung felt. 'If you were well to do and you were a jet-setter, it was okay to snort cocaine . . . everybody was snorting cocaine, everybody was laughing and having a good time and snorting cocaine.' At Studio 54, celebrities danced under a neon man in the moon snorting coke from a spoon. In the toilets, there were lines to do lines.[6]

By the end of the decade, it was estimated that 2 million Americans were spending $20 billion annually for 66,000 pounds of cocaine. The law provided little obstacle. 'There's a mindset in this country that it's okay for upper-class white America to do drugs,' Jung feels. 'Nobody ever stood up. Nobody ever said no.' Jung joined the gravy train, switching from pot to cocaine, which was easier to handle. 'It was unbelievable. To sell 50 or 100 kilos in a matter of a day was nothing.' The only problem was processing all that cash. 'It took hours upon hours and hours to count it and recount it and go over it and over it again. It was tedious as hell.'[7]

The cocaine came mainly from Colombia, where a few cartels, centred on Cali and Medellín, grew more powerful than the government itself. The dominant drug baron was Pablo Escobar, leader of the Medellín cartel, and arguably the most successful criminal in history. At its peak, his operation ran five flights loaded with cocaine into the US every day. Cocaine was an industry; the coca would come from producers in Peru or Bolivia and then get processed in huge factories hidden in the Colombian jungle. 'We conducted business, cocaine business,' Carlos Toro, essentially a PR agent for the Medellín cartel, reflects. 'Just like General Motors or IBM, we get orders that we have to fulfill . . . Under the contract with the cartel, we . . . were to move the cocaine at a certain frequency out of the country . . .

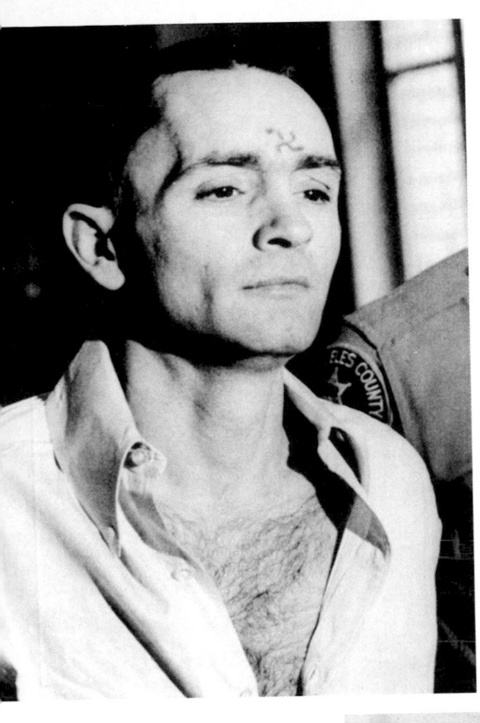

Charles Manson:
the death of trust.

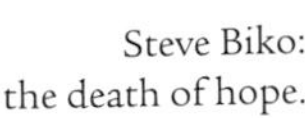

Steve Biko:
the death of hope.

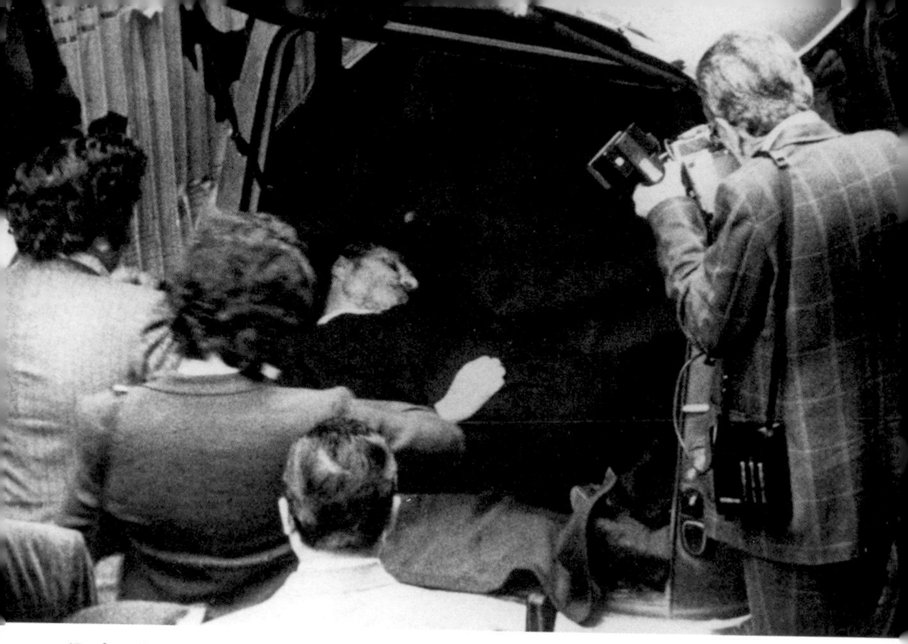

'Proletarian Justice': The body of Aldo Moro, found in the boot of a Renault in central Rome.

Terror Chic: Andreas Baader and Gudrun Ensslin.

Belfast on Bloody Sunday, 1972:
the Troubles begin.

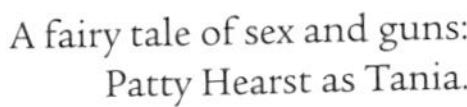

A fairy tale of sex and guns:
Patty Hearst as Tania.

Before the coup: Augusto Pinochet and Salvador Allende.

Looking in opposite directions: Generalissimo Franco and King Juan Carlos.

Successful submissive:
Marabel Morgan.

Skinheads:
not always racist.

Constructing a cliché:
Sid Vicious.

The psychopath of chess:
Bobby Fischer.

Sisterhood is strong:
Billie Jean King and Bobby Riggs.

Killer smile: Idi Amin.

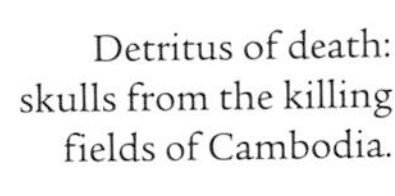

Detritus of death:
skulls from the killing
fields of Cambodia.

Nixon and Kissinger: the architects of so many Seventies problems.

Smiling for the camera: Menachem Begin, Jimmy Carter and Anwar Sadat at Camp David.

Margaret Thatcher: waving goodbye to an era.

We were the clearinghouse of the cocaine.' The business was impressively efficient, but not economically astute. Like the greedy monsters they were, cocaine barons mistakenly assumed that they could increase profits by increasing supply. The law of diminishing returns went unnoticed until it was too late. Eventually, the cartels found they had to sell an ever-greater amount simply to make the same income. 'Escobar basically had a Neanderthal ideology,' Jung concluded. 'He didn't understand supply and demand . . . if you flood the country with cocaine the price is going to go down and also it's going to expose everyone and bring in more people at greater threat of being arrested or caught.'[8]

Legal or moral issues were smothered under a blanket of money. 'I didn't pay a lot of attention to [the legality],' Juan Ochoa, an Escobar associate, admits. 'At that time, no one said anything about anything. It was so easy.' Drug barons could not believe their good fortune in tapping into wealthy Americans' insatiable appetite for cocaine. 'I've never understood what they liked in that substance,' Ochoa admits, 'because I don't think it has any positive effects . . . I think it's a really stupid thing.' Dealers derived perverse pleasure from messing with the minds of the American people and destabilizing their economy. For Carlos Lehder, of the Medellín cartel, the drug became an expression of his hatred of Americans. 'Carlos . . . wanted to flood the country with cocaine and destroy the political and moral structure of the United States,' Jung felt. 'As he stated, cocaine was the atomic bomb and he was going to drop it on America.'[9]

Drug barons were addicted to the life, if not the drug. Lehder bought an island called Norman's Cay in the Bahamas, to serve as a distribution centre for shipping cocaine into the United States. It was a sybarite's paradise. Toro recalls 'being picked up in a Land Rover with the top down and naked women driving to come and welcome me from my airplane. It was a Sodom and Gomorrah . . . Everybody was naked. You would find people in one corner having sex, people sleeping on the floor, plenty of food. I mean, you're talking about sin town . . . It's wonderful. Drugs, sex, there's no police. You own it, you made the rules, and it was just . . . fun.' Danger was also addictive. 'I have seen many people . . . go back to the drug business, not because of the money, but because of the excitement . . . knowing that somebody could . . . catch you – that you're going to spend the rest of your life in prison or . . . be killed,' Fernando Arenas confessed. 'We are . . . absolutely nutcases.'[10]

Money inevitably inspired violence. 'Any marijuana transaction I ever did with anyone, there were never any guns,' Jung maintains. 'It was simply . . . a handshake business and a trust factor.' With cocaine, however, the stakes were far too high. 'Suddenly everybody was carrying guns.' Escobar's hitmen would travel on motorbikes through the crowded streets of Medellín and Bogotá, seeking out enemies and gunning them down in broad daylight. 'The bloodshed . . . was not created by the cocaine itself,' Toro argued. 'The bloodshed and the violence and the assassinations and the . . . dead bodies and all these things . . . were a product of our doing . . . It was the law enforcement of collecting monies.' Oscar Toro, an industry minion who fell foul of his bosses, returned home to find his five-year-old son hanging from the rafters in his basement. His ten-year-old daughter and the family babysitter were later found brutally murdered in an abandoned building nearby.[11]

Escobar liked to eliminate an enemy's entire family, so as to underline his absolute power and strike fear into those tempted to defy him. Victims were sometimes tortured, partly to extract valuable information, but often simply to prolong their suffering. Steven Murphy, a DEA special agent in Medellín, recalls listening to an intercepted conversation between Pablo Escobar and his wife. 'In the background, while he was talking to his wife about family matters and things like that . . . screaming could be heard . . . Pablo put his hand over the receiver and turned around and asked whoever was committing this torture to please keep the guy quiet, that he was trying to talk to his family.' On one occasion, while Jung was enjoying a drink with Escobar at his ranch, a Chevy Blazer pulled up, two burly men got out and an individual was dragged from the back. '[Pablo] simply said "Excuse me". He walked over and executed the man and then he came back to the table. He simply looked at me and he said, "He betrayed me." . . . then he asked me what I'd like for dinner.'[12]

Among the barons, Escobar stood out because of the ferocity and breadth of his ambition. For him, cocaine was not simply a way to get rich. A freelance politician, he wanted to use the immense power of the business to bend the government to his will. This meant carefully cultivating a Robin Hood image. Schools, playgrounds and sports facilities were built, and a food distribution programme was established. Poor people loved him for his benificence, calling him El Patrón, and supporting him unquestioningly. Those immune to his largesse were brought round through intimidation. Politicians who refused bribes were offered a stark choice: 'I'm going to kill you, so what do you prefer? You prefer money or you prefer to be killed?' Those who summoned the courage to defy him did not live long. 'You couldn't confront Pablo Escobar, because you knew what would happen: you would die,' Jorge Ochoa recalled. '[He] . . . did whatever he wanted. He didn't consult with anyone . . . He intimidated everyone. It wasn't just us, but the rest of Colombia and all of the United States . . . He thought that whatever he wanted is the way it should be done, and he didn't ask anyone an opinion. He didn't take anyone into account.'[13]

The flood of cocaine swamped American law enforcement agencies. 'We are at almost a wartime status,' Coast Guard Admiral John Hayes admitted in 1979, 'but we are interdicting only about 10 per cent of the illegal drugs coming in.' Just 1 in 100 drug planes were intercepted, yet each of the 99 that got through carried perhaps 400 kilos. 'The business started growing like any business,' Jorge Ochoa recalled. 'It becomes like a ball of snow. It grows by itself, and demand makes it grow . . . It seemed like a game, and nobody paid any attention to it.' The biggest problem was laundering the money – hundreds of personnel in the US were assigned the sole task of thinking up clever ways to get cash back to Colombia without alerting federal agents. At first the job was easy, since banks were only too eager to assist. 'They used to help you set up accounts,' 'Mike', a money launderer, confessed. 'They would protect you, in a way.' Some banks offered advice on setting up bogus offshore companies. Mike McDonald, a drug agent in Florida, recalls a familiar scene in bank lobbies: '[You'd] see people standing in line with boxes of money on dollies and a deposit slip in their teeth . . . We had 12 individuals in Miami who were depositing $250 million or more annually into non-interest bearing checking accounts.' Bank officials knew they were breaking the law, but realized that if they refused the business, the launderers would simply find another willing bank.[14]

In 1979, a cash flow study by the Treasury revealed that billions of dollars were being drained out of the US economy through a sink-hole in south Florida. Treasury officials could not at first believe what their own statistics told them. But then came a moment of realization – as McDonald recalled: 'not "Ah ha" but "Oh, my God."' Even if the drug issue did not seem serious, the money issue did. More aggressive regulations were instituted, but they simply forced the launderers to get more creative.[15]

The cocaine explosion occurred against the backdrop of some real progress in combating hard drugs like heroin. The Nixon administration found itself confronted with two incontrovertible problems: firstly, the direct connection between addiction and crime, and secondly, the alarming statistics of usage among servicemen in Vietnam. The latter problem demanded sensitivity. As Bourne relates, 'when you had large numbers of GIs in Vietnam addicted to heroin, you couldn't attack them as moral reprobates. You had to say, "These poor fighting men have unfortunately become victims of heroin, and we've got to treat them in a very humane way."'[16]

What resulted was the most comprehensive drug strategy America had seen, one which concentrated not on enforcement but treatment. Struggling against his retributive instincts, Nixon reluctantly decided that no addict should be denied a place on a treatment programme. Federal spending on the drug problem rocketed from $80 million to over $600 million, with two-thirds going toward rehabilitation. 'We have never had that proportion of federal resources devoted to intervention on the demand side,' argues Jerome Jaffe, chief of the Special Action Office for Drug Abuse Prevention under Nixon. That approach inspired a steady chorus of public disapproval. Most people did not want treatment centres; they wanted a beefed up police force, tougher laws, larger prisons and longer sentences.[17]

Public disapproval was not, however, responsible for destroying Nixon's drug policy. Watergate was. After that scandal broke, every aspect of Nixon's administration came under attack. Within a year, Krogh was in prison, Jaffe had resigned and the whole programme was in tatters. At precisely this moment of chaos, cocaine appeared on the scene. The Ford administration was too preoccupied with trying to rescue the Republican party to pay much attention to a drug that didn't seem dangerous. A White Paper concluded that marijuana and cocaine were 'not serious' issues.

That logic continued after Carter became president. Malthea Falco, Assistant Secretary of State for International Narcotics Matters, admitted that 'The thrust of our policy . . . was to try to . . . reduce the availability of heroin . . . Cocaine was basically used by a relatively small number of very wealthy – you know, the jet set, the rock stars.' No wonder, then, that law enforcement agencies were not inclined to waste time on cocaine busts. Jim Kibble, a DEA agent, admitted that small-time dealers were essentially given free rein. 'You'd have an informant . . . say, "Hey, I got two kilos of coke." Unless the cocaine was sitting downstairs in a car with the bad guy outside the DEA office, you couldn't work it. They wanted no time expended. And this went on for a while. Nobody's going after the cocaine people. None of their people are getting arrested.' Those in the business took delight in making a mockery of the law. During a Florida muscular dystrophy telethon in 1979, Tracy and Darrell Boyd called in a donation of $10,000, calling themselves 'the blockade runners'.[18]

A monster grew, and no one noticed. 'It all happened so quick,' William Moran, a Miami lawyer who represented the drug traffickers, reflected. 'Nobody even knew what it was. It just went from a situation where people were importing marijuana into this country, and they used to add 10 kilos of cocaine in the shipment. And before you know it, it totally swallowed the business.' DuPont, author of the Ford White Paper, is now embarrassed by its naivety. His team easily convinced themselves that their ideas were progressive. 'Looking back on it, it's a terrible embarrassment, because [we] failed to understand the nature of addiction. [We] failed to understand not only the current status of the marijuana and cocaine problem, but the potential of those problems. And rather than being sophisticated, it just looks phenomenally dumb today.'[19]

The government's emphasis upon heroin angered suburban parents, for whom the real problem was marijuana. By 1978, surveys suggested that one in ten eighteen-year-olds were smoking pot every day, and 40 per cent indulged at least once a month. Parental dismay grew organized after Marsha Keith Schuchard witnessed pot being smoked at her thirteen-year-old daughter's birthday party. She complained directly to the White House and, before long, a parents' movement coalesced. Bourne's initial reaction was contempt: 'Quite frankly, Carter and I had regarded these people as pretty inconsequential gadflies . . . and we essentially ignored them.' That contempt proved costly, since those with political clout cared more about marijuana, not heroin. As the black comedian Richard Pryor said of the sudden shift of emphasis within the drug debate, 'We call it an epidemic now. That means white folks are doing it.' Ever the populist, Ronald Reagan understood precisely what middle-class parents wanted, and promised to get tough on drugs. Bourne, who had to watch his programme crumble under Reagan's onslaught, found the development deeply disturbing. 'It was a decision that people dying from drugs, or reducing the deaths, was not an important objective. The objective was, can you appeal to suburban voters who have this . . . irrational fear about their children smoking marijuana?'[20]

'I think this is one of the gravest problems facing us internally in the United States,' Reagan told the American people in 1981. He meant drugs in general, but drugs should never be approached 'in general'. The problem encompassed everything from suburban kids smoking reefer to inner-city addicts killing for a five-dollar fix. Reagan's tough talk was converted into tough policy, which in practice meant transforming drugs from a public health issue into a law enforcement matter. Cocaine consequently slipped through the net, since the government was not about to arrest Wall Street brokers, Hollywood producers and big time sports stars.[21]

While Reagan strutted, Americans snorted. The administration was powerless to stop the cocaine juggernaut. Eventually, the users, and those around them, began to feel uneasy. The wonderful drug proved a cruel tyrant. 'Everybody was starting to realize what the coke was all about and they were all starting to get lost,' Jung recalls. He experienced a personal epiphany. 'I began to wonder . . . what the hell it was really all about . . . It was insanity. The money meant nothing . . . I didn't have any friends, you know. I was just alone and I didn't even like myself.' Van Parys noticed a seismic shift in the culture of drug-taking, away from the camaraderie of pot. '[Cocaine] totally changed our behaviour toward one another. The dark suspicion that your drug partner might be a narc was replaced by the fear that he was holding and wasn't going to share. It hit home with me the night Whitney came by my house to ask me to steal syringes from my mom, a diabetic, so that he could shoot some cocaine . . . He didn't offer me any. Drugs were now a game of exclusivity, not democracy. I've got mine, you go get your own.' Cocaine was its own pusher: it lured users with promises of cheap paradise and, before they knew it, they found themselves trapped in a sordid slum of dependence. 'Everybody thought it was safe and easy fun,' recalls Jann Wenner. '[But] people got diverted by a lot of drug use. And people became very *unpleasant*.'[22]

'It got so that I couldn't imagine life without it,' a Boston real estate executive confessed in 1973. Those in the know say of cocaine: 'The problem is, that by the time you realize it's a problem, it's a problem.' That certainly applied to users, but even more fundamentally to the United States. For too long, the drug was ignored. By the time the government began to worry, cocaine was already an epidemic. In the meantime, the drug itself had morphed into crack – a more powerful, more addictive and much more dangerous substance than the stuff snorted up little silver straws. Because crack was cheaper than cocaine, it became a drug of the ghetto, tearing apart fragile families with an efficiency heroin never managed. 'Crack [could] destabilize whole neighborhoods,' Herbert Kleber recalled. 'We had not seen a drug that had that same kind of devastating impact . . . Because crack was also sold so cheaply, it made everything worth stealing. And most people stole where they lived . . . I've been in this field for over 35 years, and crack is the most devastating drug that I've ever encountered.' Bourne grew utterly demoralized. 'There was no effort made to find any effective treatment for cocaine addicts . . . Instead, you had a sort of inane policy of "Just Say No", which is like telling someone who's depressed, "Have a Nice Day."'[23]

In the end, some of the wisest reflections on the cocaine epidemic were uttered by those made rich from it. 'The responsibility belongs to all of us,' Jorge Ochoa remarked. 'This is not a problem that is only ours or of Colombia. It is also a problem of the Americans. And they have a great deal of responsibility . . . Of course you have to attack the problem and pursue it politically and all, but the people have to be educated as well. There is a need to try to stop the demand.' Jung, who witnessed how easy it was to pollute the mind of a nation, agreed: 'We have to come to the pool of self-reflection and . . . ask ourselves: was it the fact that Carlos [Lehder] and I had the courage to be bad or why did millions of Americans not have the courage to be good?'[24]

East London: Skinheads

Nidge Miller first encountered skinheads as a young teenager during a family holiday on the English coast. A gang of sharply dressed ruffians terrorized the town for no apparent purpose. They seemed utterly oblivious to authority. Miller was instantly smitten. 'A week later I had my head shaved, got my boots, my braces and a shirt.'[25]

Youth culture is often defined by sartorial styles – in Britain, a succession of Spivs, Bohemians, Beatniks, Teds, Mods, Rockers, Punks, Casuals and Hoodies have made their mark by what they wore. In the early 1960s, Mods ruled, causing journalists and politicians to predict the decline of civilization. By the middle of the decade, however, Mods were in retreat, largely because their style had been hijacked by Carnaby Street boutiques. When those dressed like Mods no longer *were* Mods, the jig was up.

Into the breach strode skinheads. They borrowed heavily from the Mod milieu, particularly the tight jeans and polo shirts. But the simmering menace of their look – underlined by shaved heads and Doc Marten boots – acted as a barrier to imitators. In other words, only those who genuinely aspired to be a skinhead, with the violence implied, actually dressed like one. More than just a look, skinhead was a defiant assertion of class pride. Emotions were worn like shirts, and the continued validitiy of those emotions has ensured the cult's survival. 'Skinheads . . . are too true,' one of the faithful insists. 'It wasn't a fashion . . . it's a way of life.'[26]

Skinhead started as an attempt to reclaim lost territory, a reassertion of culture. Those annoyed by the commercialization of Mod intentionally toughened the style, calling themselves 'hard' or 'gang' Mods, in contrast to the dandified 'peacock' Mods more interested in clothes than ethos. By 1968, hard Mods became known as skinheads in reference to their distinctive hairstyle, itself a macho riposte to the effeminate long hair of middle-class hippies. Hairstyle expressed class identity, since short hair was essential for anyone who had to hold down a job, and was mandatory for the machine-worker. The style's implied aggression indicated how marginalized working-class boys felt. 'It's . . . a mental state of being,' Rob Hingley believes. 'It's a proud badge of working class courage, that's how I see it.' The working class, excluded from the 1960s ethos, was fighting back. 'The dreamy, idealistic, liberal 1960s drew to an end,' recalls the former skinhead Chris Brown, and 'dear old Britannia, who had hitched up her skirt, kicked off her sandals and danced barefoot in the park with Timothy Leary's peace-loving hippies, suddenly received an abrupt dose of reality and a reminder that she was not quite ready to lose her head and her customs to a bunch of junkies from across the pond.'[27]

The clothes oozed machismo, but were never scruffy. Jeans were lovingly laundered; creases ironed with machine precision. Shirts, either Fred Perry or Ben Sherman polos, or American-style button-down Oxfords, were carefully pressed and worn tucked in. Braces, a Harrington coat and Crombie hat enhanced the image of a proud outlaw. 'For a finishing touch I rubbed some Brut into my neck and chest and behind my ears,' Martin King recalled. The defining feature was the boots, usually Doc Martens, with sixteen or twenty eyelets, polished to perfection. 'Putting those boots on was a big part of being a skinhead,' King reminisced. 'When you had them on you felt better equipped to deal with life on the streets. They made you feel ten times harder and meaner.'[28]

'Skinhead is basically a teenage thing,' argues McGinn. 'It gave you a sense of identity.' The implied power of the costume was particularly attractive to young boys in the turmoil of puberty who need a quick fix to problems of inferiority. McGinn, who grew up in Glasgow, underwent a rite of passage at the age of twelve, when he first put on the clothes. 'Big boots, cropped hair, a working class look. Young, aggressive . . . The first time I had a crop, I felt tremendous. A bovver boy. I thought, fucking great, look at the state of me!' Boys who grew up in rough neighbourhoods had to prove themselves early or face years of torment. 'With boots and a shaved head it's hard to look nice and quiet,' Big Iain feels. 'You look nasty whether you are or not. It's a predominantly violent look.'[29]

While clothes varied according to time and taste, the walk remained a constant. 'We walked in that distinctive way,' recalls Brown, 'the arrogant, bow-legged swagger, the arms thrust deep into pockets of short zip-up jackets or sheepskin coats, poking out at right angles, ready to annoy, aggravate, bovver anyone who dared to cross our paths . . . once I had mastered the all-important "fuck-off-outta-my-way" walk, I knew I had arrived.' Skinheads grew intoxicated by the terror they spread. 'We were absolutely vilified,' one former skinhead fondly recalled. Another remembered the visceral thrill that came from jumping on a train and watching a wave of fear pass through the carriage. 'That gave you a feeling of power.' A potent sense of freedom arose from being part of a mob beyond control. 'We didn't give a monkey's about anyone else,' one of the faithful boasted. 'We enjoyed ourselves, we did what we wanted. And bollocks to everyone else.'[30]

'What made us special was we stuck together,' Mick explained. Boys emerging from a culture of low self-esteem derived worth from belonging to a group so fearsome. 'You . . . really are your own little army,' Symond of Wycombe reflected. 'We knew that when violent situations did arise you would be together. There'd be at least five or six of you that would fight to the death, . . . because you were hated so much by everybody – by your parents, your school teachers, by the police, by everybody – it drew you so close together that you became as one.' For Ghane Chane, membership was a form of self-defence. 'Everybody was in a gang. Everybody . . . you were either in a gang or you were the victim.' Larry Jenkins was likewise comforted by mob mentality. 'It seemed like every shopping centre had a gang. So to protect yourself against other numbers, you had to congregate in numbers. It was pretty violent.'[31]

'You don't even think of yourself as a skinhead,' says Big Iain; 'it's just the way you live.' Gavin Watson, who joined a gang at the age of fourteen, feels that 'Ultimately, it's difficult to explain the attraction, as it is for anyone deeply passionate about music, style and fashion . . . It's like asking "Why do you love your wife?" There was a lot of love involved and a lot of passion involved . . . There was a spiritual and mystical part of being a skinhead that is unfathomable.' For 'Pan' the ethos was so strong that he never abandoned it. 'Skinhead's a way of life, a culture I live by,' he explains. 'It's about having pride in the way I look, it's about working for my living, earning everything I get. It's about the second family I have with my mates on the street, about being true to the values that I learned, the honour code that I learned . . . it's the truest culture because you're talking about the real people, the working people, the poor people.'[32]

The backing track to skinhead culture was initially Motown. Later, however, reggae's raw melodies took precedence – the sound seemed particularly suited to skinhead's rambunctiousness. 'Skinheads put reggae into the British charts,' a Ramsgate afficionado claims. 'If it wasn't for skinheads . . . I don't think reggae would have made it . . . Bob Marley wouldn't have got to where he got to if it wasn't for the white working class youth.' Chris Prete felt reggae the perfect expression of skinhead nation: 'You can't separate them. It's a basic music, simple and not complicated. It's got a hook with the bass beat, and once you start getting into the music, it's hard to walk away from it.'[33]

The love of black music seems strange, given the stereotyped racism of the skinhead. That stereotype, however, developed later. Skinhead's emergence coincided with an influx of Jamaican immigrants into London, causing a synthesis to develop. Skinheads adopted Jamaican rude boy culture, listened to reggae and ska, incorporated rasta slang and mannerisms, and frequented West Indian nightclubs. Membership was not defined by race, but rather by culture – it was perfectly possible, at first, to be a black or Asian skinhead. 'Our club . . . always used to stick together,' recalled Rikki, a Pakistani in the Glasgow Globetrotters gang. 'We had three Asians, the rest were white . . . but we were like a family.'[34]

Former skinheads who retain pride in their past blame the media for exaggerating the stereotype of social pariah. 'White working class males are an easy target,' Watson argues. 'The media just repeats that . . . stereotype of a muggy bonehead, glue sniffing, granny mugging thug,' another contends. 'It's a complete myth. A decent skinhead is someone who believes in himself, knows what he's looking for, knows what he wants, knows how to dress. Just someone who's well sussed, well clued up . . . No mugs.' The predilection for mindless mayhem nevertheless seems to justify the stereotype. Lee Thompson recalled doing 'stupid things like smashing windows and that. There was a bowling green next to us where old people used to enjoy their Sunday afternoons and one day we went over there with our steel combs and carved our names in the bowling pitch.' 'I don't say any of us are nice guys,' a skinhead proudly boasted to *Time* in 1970. 'We want to be "tasty" – y'know, big guys.'[35]

Nor was mayhem confined to petty vandalism; skinheads got the greatest thrill from grievous bodily harm. Jack Weeds, a train engineer, recalled being set upon by a skinhead pack baying for blood. 'I got boots in the back, in the guts, on the head, everywhere . . . These kids were actually skipping around with excitement.' A perfect night out usually included some aggro. 'Gigs were nearly always full of students who . . . are almost always commies, socialists, lefties or whatever,' recalls Mick White. 'Nearly every single week we used to smash the fuckers as they really got on our nerves.' Gangs would intentionally invade venues outside their turf, in search of confrontation. 'You were different, coming into their club, dancing to strange records, chatting their girls up, so it would always kick off,' Brian Kelson recollects. 'It was just a laugh, great fun. You'd always end up having a punch up. Everything would go flying, chairs and tables and whatever, you against them.' King recalls:

> Old Big Gob . . . started to call anyone who fancied a fight towards him. 'Come on . . .' he tried to say, but only the word 'come' made it out of his mouth as Jeff leapt on his back and someone else chucked a hot cup of tea in his face. At this we jumped and climbed all over him until he sank to his knees . . . He stopped struggling and fell forward as we gleefully kicked and stamped all over his body and head . . . I almost felt sorry for him but I quickly came to my senses.

One gangmember who belonged to 'the most violent firm of skinheads there was' recalled a never-ending sequence of fights. 'One day . . . a group of skinheads told us to stop getting us all barred from everywhere for fighting, and my brother . . . snapped back, "That's what being a skinhead's all about you dickheads and if you don't like fighting then you shouldn't fucking be one." That shut them up.' Brown agreed with that logic. 'To me, my hooliganism was a natural extension of the great strength of the British people, heroism in the face of adversity. It was lads just like me and my mates who had fought at Agincourt, Waterloo and the Somme and my allegiance and my pride was in myself, my football club and my country.'[36]

Skinhead began to decline around 1975 but then underwent a surge, perhaps because the ethos harmonized so well with the bleak second half of the decade, a time of economic blight and social tension. Skinhead's nihilism harmonized perfectly with the culture of hate that typified the late 1970s. While the merger of skinhead with neo-Nazi politics and football hooliganism was not automatic, it was entirely logical, since the three groups share a common constituency and certain core rituals. It's no wonder, then, that ultra-nationalist groups enjoyed conspicuous success recruiting discontented youths whose first port of call had been skinhead nation.

The original skinheads were perturbed when fascist thugs hijacked their culture, and made racism a defining feature. 'The multicultural thing was a big deal for us,' Chas Smash of Madness reflected. 'We felt we were part of a wave . . . its ideals were honourable and progressive.'[37] Equally disturbing was the emergence of punk, since surface similarities caused both groups to be deluged by the same torrent of outrage. Skinhead purists thought punks too dissolute. 'The clothes were just so scruffy and ill-fitting,' Kelson complained.

> The jeans would be skin tight and too short with great big boots, and the hair was shaven right off. They'd be taking drugs and sniffing glue, and you wouldn't have caught an original skinhead doing that – it was degrading. You were a working class bloke, proud of this great nation, and you wouldn't be seen dossing like a hippy. The public saw them as dirty, scruffy, bald-headed drug takers . . . To be brought up with such strong ideals about the movement and to see it taken over like that was worse than anything.[38]

In truth, the public's confusion was entirely understandable. By the late 1970s, British youth culture was a pit of writhing snakes, with similar strands of thought, music and behaviour intertwining but never completely amalgamating. As Brown writes, 'The word "diverse" was inadequate to describe the motley crew of teds, mods, skins, suedes, smoothies, punks, skunks, rude boys, soul boys and headbangers that filled Britain's streets, terraces and concert halls and who listened to a cacophony of music ranging from rockabilly to jazz funk by way of punk and ska.'[39] Separate cultures competed over the same raw material, namely alienated kids from tower blocks and council estates. Both punk and skinhead were attempts to assert identity amidst disintegrating working-class culture. If the picture of who belonged where seems confused, that is because the boys themselves were.

That confusion was reflected in the emergence of Oi!, a music that defied classification. For its practitioners and fans, it was a reaction to punk's poseurs, those whose badness was merely cosmetic. Oi! was the Doc Marten of sound, hard, often political lyrics backed by discordant angry noise. 'Oi! really was about the kids coming in off the streets, out of the tower blocks and the building sites and it was just for real,' Lol Pryor thought. Jon Richards, who still plays in the band Argy Bargy, sees the music as 'an attitude . . . It was that stand up for yourself, believe in yourself, fight for yourself attitude.' For Chas Smash, however, Oi! seemed like hatred and violence put to music. 'We weren't an Oi! band, we were happy, it was up, we were kids enjoying ourselves.' That distinction, however, was lost on the new skinheads, young kids who readily assigned their politics to the music they liked, regardless of what the original artist intended. 'It was depressing,' Chas Smash reflected,

> we were naive and just thought 'wow, loads of people!' Not thinking, 'ow, there's loads of right-wing skinheads' . . . that's the thing with right-wing organizations, they latch on. If there had been a couple of black people in our band, then maybe they wouldn't have . . . We used to have kids coming up to us in the early days . . . [of] the National Front, [with] a right-wing magazine, to autograph . . . There were all these rumours that we were funded by right-wing organizations. And it created a load of friggin trouble.

Kelson shared that disappointment with the way his ethos had been usurped. 'A lot of skinheads are from inner city areas and are unemployed. So I can see their point of view, but I still wish they'd get their own cult to voice it rather than taking our cult and using it!'[40]

In truth, racism had always been present within the movement, though it wasn't necessarily a defining feature. Ethnic hatred was focused in particular on Asian immigrants, who had not, it was argued, made enough effort to assimilate. Brown admits to beating up Asians in 1970, simply for the fun of it. 'They smell, don't they?' a skinhead told *Time* in June of that year. 'It's all that garlic. I mean, they've no right to be here.' He proudly described his 'Paki-bashing' technique: 'You go up to them and bump into them, and then you nut them right, and then you hit them, and as they go down you give them a kicking, bash them with an iron bar, and take their watches and rings and things like that.' In the month the *Time* article was published, more than 2,000 Pakistanis marched on Downing Street to protest against the rising tide of skinhead attacks.[41]

After 1976, 'Paki bashing' became as fashionable as boots and braces. 'It was the in thing to do,' one skinhead confessed. 'Have your hair cropped, get a pair of boots and go bash pakis.' Mick White, a member of the Tilbury gang responsible for racist riots in the Brick Lane area of London in 1977, explained the attraction for him was not the dress, or the music, but the opportunity to fight immigrants. 'Everyone knew skinheads didn't like pakis and I thought that's the one for me.' Meanwhile, ideologues hovered overhead, always ready to assign political meaning to racist violence. 'It's easy for an extreme party to grab hold of passionate kids,' one former member reckoned. 'Skinheads were very angry, and so for the extremists they were easy targets.' Membership in the British Movement or the National Front provided a sense of belonging to young boys desperate to inject meaning into their lives.[42]

Before long, social commentators carelessly lumped all skinheads into one far-right racist mob. In truth, it is difficult to discern what individual skinheads believed, and indeed whether beliefs, as opposed to emotions, were important. Chris Brown feels that violence was more important than racism. 'A lot of skinheads were just plain "bad lads" and the attacks and insults on lone Asians, like the assaults on lone greasers or homosexuals, were more about following the herd and proving one's so-called "hardness" than they were about making any kind of political statement.' Tilbury skinheads insisted that their group was apolitical – hatred was dispensed equally to Asians, glue sniffers, socialists, hippies and anyone who liked disco. One member of that gang recalled his disgust when a contingent of Nazis appeared at a concert. 'Although we hated pakis and sikhs and that, we also didn't like Nazis as our parents fought them in the war. We couldn't understand why skins should be connected to them as our idea of skinhead is to be British and proud of it, and all other cunts are the enemy, including Germans.' In a world packed with hatred, a skinhead did not have to look far to find an enemy. 'It wasn't just white kids bashing Asians,' Chris Prete insists. 'It was everybody bashing everybody to be top dog in the street.' 'There weren't too many Pakistanis in Henbury so we had to make do with queers,' recalls Brown.[43]

That same desire perhaps explains the appeal of football hooliganism, which reached epidemic proportions in the late 1970s. Hooligans boasted that the government ruled the country from Sunday to Friday, but they ruled on Saturdays. Kelson recalls attending a West Ham–Chelsea match, his first as a fully fledged skinhead. 'Everybody seemed to have crombies on . . . it was just electrifying . . . I remember sitting down at half time and there were four or five lads in front of us, pulling things out of their crombies, and they all had tools, knives and that.' Rob Hingley, a Plymouth Argyle fan, fondly recalled a holy ritual: 'On a Saturday you'd get dressed up, get the bus down to Plymouth to watch Argyle get mauled, try to get into the pubs, get thrown out, get beat up by the opposing teams' skinheads.' Meanwhile the rest of the nation shook its head in bewilderment. 'Those who wonder why people fight at football and then add, "It's only a game" are . . . totally missing the point,' argues George Marshall in *Skinhead Nation*. 'Football just happens to be the perfect arena for violence. The passion is certainly there and the football club acts as a focus for local pride and as a magnet for youths willing to defend its honour. Most importantly though, it offers the opportunity to travel all over the country to fight like-minded mobs.' For skinheads, hooliganism existed in a parallel universe with the game itself. 'Violence has home and away and even Cup fixtures,' Marshall explains. 'Getting a result is all important, losing face means anything from dropping a few points on a good day to being relegated or even put out of business on a bad one. There's even some movement between mobs, a sort of free transfer market.'[44]

After a Blackpool vs. Bristol Rovers match was repeatedly interrupted by crowd violence, the frustrated referee remarked: 'We are reaching the situation where it would be ideal to play matches in front of empty terraces.' Politicians, sociologists, psychiatrists and journalists struggled to understand, while populist firebrands demanded the return of national service. Chris Lightbrown offered his own explanation to the *Sun*:

> They will never stamp out football hooliganism. It is going to get more, rather than less. What's so marvellous is that these kids who are doing bum jobs and are said to be idiots, can get themselves organised like this and set up a fantastic military strategy that goes into battle. It is not as simple as it looks. Decoys are planted and flanks formed. It's great to see it. We have been brought up on war psychology so long that is has become part of our culture, and teenagers expect to be fighting. When there are no wars, there will be things like punch-ups at soccer matches.

'Violence is part and parcel of being young,' the former skinhead Paul Jameson explains, in a weak attempt at self-justification. Watford Jon agrees: 'You can't escape it, it's part of life.' That assumption is undoubtedly flawed, but it does perhaps explain the mindless nature of the violence. The leader of the Tilbury gang boasted: 'Pakis, blacks, Nazis, whoever got in our way, we'd bash. In them days we used to go out and have a fight or whatever, but now a few of us have got educated and now we work as nightclub bouncers . . . We still love violence.' Or, as Brown wrote of a former comrade: 'Benny joined the army. Carrying on being a hooligan and now getting paid for it. His predilection for queer bashing found greater rewards serving in Her Majesty's forces than it ever could on Civvy Street.'[45]

Jonestown: Dying for Dad

'I know that Pastor Jim Jones is God Almighty himself!' came a shout from the huge crowd gathered in a San Francisco gym on Sunday, 17 September 1972. 'You say I am God Almighty?' asked Jones. 'Yes, you are!' shouted another voice, and the crowd erupted.[46]

By the age of sixteen, Jones could already mesmerize a crowd. But while his passion was formidable, his belief frequently wavered – he struggled to understand how a loving God could allow widespread suffering. In the early 1950s, he drifted toward the Methodists, whose social conscience harmonized with his core beliefs. Established religion could not, however, contain an ego so large. Jones eventually set out on his own, taking his devoted followers into his 'People's Temple'.

At first, the Temple seemed a shining example of social awakening in 1960s Indiana. Jones preached racial brotherhood and communalism to a congregation consisting of middle-class whites angered by injustice and downtrodden blacks who suffered it. He campaigned not just for racial harmony, but also encouraged Christian charity toward the jobless, the ex-con, the single mother and the addict.

To many, he seemed a saint. Intelligent, charismatic and handsome, he attracted admirers even among those who rejected his religion. At the same time, however, his programme sparked fear among conservative Indianans, for whom socialism was taboo. Rumours circulated about his tyrannical powers and the sacrifices he demanded. Those who wanted to believe in Jones countered that prophets are frequently persecuted, as are socialists.

Jones, who confused criticism with harassment, sought a more welcoming home for his mission. He settled upon Ukiah, in northern

California, in part because caves in the area offered the perfect place for his Chosen to shelter from a nuclear apocalypse predicted to take place on 16 July 1967. In addition, his evangelical communalism seemed more likely to find acceptance in a state tolerant of eccentricity. In 1965, accompanied by 165 followers, Jones headed west.

The move was not immediately successful. Rumours (most of them true) circulated that he was a violent paranoiac, sexual predator and drug addict. By 1968, his congregation had dwindled to a few dozen. Jones responded by affiliating himself with the Disciples of Christ, a move which brought credibility, not to mention tax-exempt status. A monthly newsletter and regular radio broadcasts spread the word. By 1971, the Temple boasted 4,711 members, a number which, if slightly exaggerated, nevertheless demonstrated that a phoenix had risen. In addition to churches in Ukiah, San Francisco and Los Angeles, the Temple owned a forty-acre children's home, three convalescent centres, three dormitories and a heroin rehabilitation centre. The tireless Jones was also a part-time public schoolteacher and foreman of the Mendocino County Grand Jury.[47]

The People's Temple was not really a church, but a way of life to which one surrendered. New members were baptized 'in the holy name of socialism'. At services, which lasted up to six hours, the faithful sang hymns with lines like 'There's a highway to Utopia walking in a revolutionary way'. While the programme was undoubtedly attractive, even more so was the hypnotic power of Jones. In time, worship of God gave way to veneration of Pastor Jim. 'If you believe I am a son of God in that I am filled with love, I can accept that,' he told parishioners. 'I won't knock what works for you.' The faithful were occasionally told that he was the dual reincarnation of Jesus Christ and Karl Marx.[48]

'With over 4,000 members . . . we haven't had a death yet!' Jones boasted in October 1971. 'I am a prophet of God and I can cure both the illness of your body, as well as the illness of your mind.' His services provided miracles on demand, melting scepticism like butter. 'The reason I know it ain't fake,' Ann Moore explained to her worried sister, 'is how could it be if the leader can bring life to dead people, make the blind see, the lame walk, know the thoughts of your mind and the intents of your heart. I can tell a fake if I see one.' Among those convinced was Timothy Stoen, assistant prosecuting attorney of Mendocino County. In 1972, he told Lester Kinsolving, religious affairs reporter at the *Examiner*, that 'more than 40 persons have literally been brought back from the dead this year . . . I have seen Jim revive people stiff as a board, tongues hanging out, eyes set, skin graying, and all vital signs absent. Don't ask me how it happens. It just does . . . Jim will go up to such a person and say something like, "I love you" or "I need you" and immediately the vital signs reappear.'[49]

Jones could also apparently read minds; he recited information about a member's private life that only that individual could know. One new recruit was flabbergasted when Jones proceeded to identify 'all the names of her relatives, the brands in her refrigerator, the cost of her insurance policy, and the exact price – "*TO THE PENNY*" – of all the books she had purchased *years ago*!' This power enhanced his influence and made resistance futile. In truth, Jones had a bevy of loyal lieutenants who collected information through tapping phones, break-ins and sifting through the garbage of parishioners.[50]

The Temple was a trap that gently lured the innocent. It was, claimed Moore, 'a place where you'll never be lonely'. She found her own Utopia:

> the Temple is great . . . not just because Jim Jones can make people cough up cancers but because there is the largest group of people I have ever seen who are concerned about the world and are fighting for truth and justice . . . And all the people have come from such different backgrounds, every color, every age, every income group, and they have turned into constructive people from being dopers and thieves and being greedy . . . it's the only place I have seen real true Christianity being practiced.

For new members, financial contributions were entirely voluntary. In time, however, donations became a measure of faith. Once ensnared, the member might sign over 25 per cent of his income to the Church. Full commitment came when they renounced their former life by moving into Temple facilities and transfering all income, property and social security benefits to Jones. The deeper the commitment, the greater was the isolation from wider society, which validated the sense of being chosen.[51]

Control was tightened through complex behavioural manipulation. Members signed letters admitting to illegal and immoral acts that in fact had never happened. Others signed blank affidavits (which were filled in later) as evidence of their trust. At regular 'catharsis sessions', the faithful confessed misdeeds and dark thoughts. 'I don't respect Dad [Jones] the way I should,' one member admitted. 'Dad', another wrote, 'All I can say is that I am two people right now: one of them is a very humble and innocent person and the other is a cruel and insensitive person that goes around with bad thoughts on his mind.' Members dutifully reported those whose faith seemed to waver, thus contributing to an atmosphere of mistrust. Transgressions were brutally punished, with spouses forced to beat one another, and children encouraged to chastise wayward parents. 'The first forms of punishment were mental, where they would get up and totally disgrace and humiliate the person in front of the whole congregation,' Elmer Mertle recalled. 'Jim would then come over and put his arms around the person and say, "I realize that you went through a lot, but it was for the cause. Father loves you and you're a stronger person now. I can trust you more now that you've gone through and accepted this discipline."' By this means, confidence was continually undermined, isolation deepened and dependence reinforced.[52]

Sex was used to emasculate followers. A believer in marriage, Jones nevertheless argued that monogamy was reactionary and insisted that members should experiment. Catharsis sessions were often given over to sexual tittle-tattle designed to humiliate. Spouses complained openly about a partner's inadequacy. Those reluctant to experiment were brutally reprimanded and condemned as counter-revolutionary. Punishment took the form of forced congress, often of a homosexual nature.

Devotion was an investment and sacrifice its own reward. The faithful gave themselves to the People's Temple – spiritually, socially, sexually and financially. Since membership implied separation from normal society, belonging intertwined with isolation. Commitment was self-reinforcing, since to break with the church demanded an acknowledgement that all those sacrifices were meaningless. Thus, indoctrination had a ratchet effect – as time passed demands increased and breaking from the church grew more difficult. Those who lived in the compound effectively signed their lives over to the Temple, rendering it virtually impossible to start a new life outside. They were addicted to Jones and 'owned' by him.

California liberals supported Jones because of his considerable influence among the poor and his seemingly genuine desire to help the downtrodden. Jones cemented this affinity by contributing generously to sympathetic politicians. Those beholden to him were naturally inclined to believe the best of him, dismissing persistent rumours as McCarthyite persecution. The prominent state assemblyman Willie Brown described Jones as 'a combination of Martin Luther King, Angela Davis, Albert Einstein, and Chairman Mao'. He was 'a rare human being . . . [who] cares about people . . . who can be helpful when all appears to be lost and hope is just about gone'. In June 1977, Brown explained why Jones had enemies: 'When somebody . . . constantly stresses the need for freedom of speech and equal justice . . . that absolutely scares the hell out of most everybody.' He promised Jones that 'I will be here when you are under attack, because what you are about is what the whole system ought to be about!'[53]

'Can you win office in San Francisco without Jones?' a journalist asked Brown. He replied: 'In a tight race . . . forget it.' Proof came when George Moscone ran for mayor in 1974. Jones mobilized his disciples to canvass in the rougher precincts. After the election, which Moscone won by just 4,000 votes, allegations surfaced concerning thousands of People's Temple members voting where they were not registered. The reliability of the allegations was never adequately tested since the investigation was assigned to Stoen. Michael Prokes, a Jones adviser, privately boasted that 'Moscone acknowledges . . . that we won him the election'.[54]

Sympathetic insiders in the courts, politics and the civil service provided Jones with a shield against public scrutiny. 'We have won over the sheriff's office and the police department,' he openly boasted. Disciples working in the county welfare department streamlined the Temple's adoption of hundreds of young orphans. Those officials who could not be won over were incessantly bullied. Critics were threatened with legal action, popular disapproval or, in some cases, physical violence. In September 1971, the Baptist minister Richard Taylor of Ukiah warned the state attorney general, Evelle Younger, of 'the atmosphere of terror created in the community by so large and aggressive a group'. He demanded an investigation, but Younger refused. Around the same time, Kinsolving launched a series of exposés in the *Examiner*. After his third article, published on 19 September, Temple members picketed *Examiner* offices and ransacked Kinsolving's home. The series was cancelled, and Kinsolving officially reprimanded for failing to show 'charity, compassion or consideration'. His editor chastised him for being a 'bully and bigot'. Meanwhile, the *Chronicle*, the *Examiner*'s rival paper, courted favour with fulsome tributes written by the highly respected columnist Herb Caen. '[Jones] is in good company and obviously has many fine friends,' Caen wrote. 'The picture I get is of an intelligent and warm human, of which we have regrettably few these days.'[55]

As it turned out, a handful of critics had more effect upon Jones than a legion of docile admirers. 'He would not sleep for days at a time and [would] talk compulsively about . . . conspiracies against him,' Deborah Blakey recalled. 'As time went on, he appeared to become completely irrational.' An increasing amount of Temple income went toward a private army of heavily armed toughs. Driven by a deep paranoia that the CIA was out to destroy him, he made plans to quit America. In 1974, he obtained permission from the government of Guyana to build a settlement deep in the jungle. It would be called Jonestown.[56]

The breaking point came in 1977, when rumours surfaced of an exposé to be published in *New West* magazine. The publishers were bombarded with a fusillade of writs, pickets, threatening phone calls and angry letters. The article nevertheless went ahead, describing an atmosphere 'of Spartan regimentation, fear and self-imposed humiliation'. 'Please, please, please', a worried parishioner wrote to her father, 'do not get disturbed by the bad publicity . . . I am more convinced than ever of conspiratorial & political set-ups.' Jones escaped to Guyana, where 1,200 followers were already building Utopia.[57]

On the surface, Jonestown seemed impressive – an oasis of order in the middle of the jungle. 'The isolation of it was . . . beautiful,' a visiting journalist wrote. 'It was free of urban ill . . . When you saw the compound, you had to really be impressed by the labor and dedication that went into clearing this 2,700 acres – it was huge – and establishing crops and building structures . . . It looked really good on the surface.' Visitors from the Embassy saw efficiency, cleanliness and contentment, not to mention happiness. It seemed perfect. 'Dad,' wrote one newcomer, 'I would rather die than go back to the States as there is plenty of hell over there. I would give my body to be burned for the cause [rather] than be over there.'[58]

'Everything with me is going just fine,' Bruce Oliver assured his parents. 'I'm here in Jonestown and all I got to say is that you have to see it to believe it. It's the most beautiful place I've ever seen . . . This is the place I would want to spend the rest of my life.' For Jones, success was measured by glowing testimonials from those who called him Dad:

> 'I want to please you and one way I know is to please the family.'
> 'Father is wonderful, clean, straightforward and supernatural.'
> 'I know I still follow you because you have the gift to protect me.
> I like to look strong but I know I am weak.'

Ann Moore grew convinced that 'Jonestown was paradise . . . we could live together with our differences . . . we are all the same human beings.' Later, she reflected: 'The children loved the jungle, learned about animals and plants. There were no cars to run over them; no child-molesters to molest them; nobody to hurt them. They were the freest, most intelligent children I had ever known.'[59]

For others, paradise was prison. 'Rev. Jones' thoughts were made known to the population of Jonestown by means of broadcasts over the loudspeaker system,' wrote Blakey. 'When the Reverend was particularly agitated, he would broadcast for hours on end. He would talk on and on while we worked in the fields or tried to sleep.' Tracy Parks, a ten-year-old Jonestown survivor, recalled how, 'Children who said they were not happy and wanted to go away were severely beaten.' Others were dangled head first into a well. Defying Jones was unthinkable, escape virtually impossible. Even minor offences were punished by confinement underground in a small plywood box. 'Any disagreement with his dictates came to be regarded as "treason",' Blakey recalled. 'The Rev. Jones labelled any person who left the organization a "traitor" and "fair game". He steadfastly . . . maintained that the punishment for defection was death. The fact that severe corporal punishment was frequently administered . . . gave the threats a frightening air of reality.'[60]

For Jones, Utopia did not bring relief from his demons. Feverish paranoia encouraged contemplation of ultimate escape – mass suicide. 'Because our lives were so wretched anyway and because we were so afraid to contradict Rev. Jones, the concept was not challenged,' Blakey later testified. In frequent 'white night' exercises, the population 'would be awakened by blaring sirens. Designated persons, approximately fifty in number, would arm themselves with rifles, move from cabin to cabin, and make certain that all members were responding . . . we would be told that the jungle was swarming with mercenaries and that death could be expected at any minute.' On one occasion:

> we were informed that our situation had become hopeless and that the only course of action open to us was a mass suicide for the glory of socialism. We were told that we would be tortured by mercenaries if we were taken alive. Everyone, including the children,

> was told to line up. As we passed through the line, we were given a small glass of red liquid to drink. We were told that the liquid contained poison and that we would die within 45 minutes. We all did as we were told.

When death did not come, Jones calmly explained that the group had passed his test of loyalty. 'He warned us that the time was not far off when it would become necessary for us to die by our own hands.'[61]

On 13 November 1977 congressman Leo Ryan was alerted to the story of Bob Houston, who had died mysteriously the day after he left the People's Temple. Police judged the death an accident (he fell under the wheels of a train), but Houston's father suspected otherwise. Ryan began to investigate, and before long was inundated with letters from parents worried about children at Jonestown. Evidence surfaced of social security fraud, illegal adoptions and extreme cruelty. After Blakey, who had escaped, told of the 'white night' exercises, Ryan decided to travel to Guyana. Two assistants, nine journalists and eighteen concerned parents accompanied him.

By the time Ryan arrived, Jonestown was boiling with paranoia. 'It is hard to find a rational explanation for the continual press harassment,' Carolyn Moore Layton wrote to her parents. 'Maybe they just want to prove that you just can't be too successful a socialist group without being totally desecrated . . . [It] makes me wonder if we have tampered with someone's "master plan."' She had in mind the CIA, though she stressed that, if the agency intervened, 'we would never stand for it'. Despite the paranoia, residents managed to give the Ryan party a carefully rehearsed show about the joys of Jonestown. The performance was so convincing that Ryan began to wonder if he had been misled. Doubts began to surface, however, when two individuals secretly slipped him notes indicating their desire to leave. By the following morning, a dozen more had appealed for safe passage out.[62]

Jones went into meltdown. According to Charles Garry, the Reverend's lawyer who had accompanied Ryan, 'When 14 of his people decided to go out . . . Jim Jones went mad. He thought it was a repudiation of his work. I tried to tell him that 14 out of 1,200 was damn good. But Jones was desolate.' With the situation spiralling out of control, Ryan cut short his visit. He left in the afternoon, arriving at the nearby Kaituma airstrip along with fifteen defectors at 16.30. They then waited an agonizing forty-five minutes for a second plane to carry the additional passengers. As the group began to board, one of the 'defectors', Larry Layton, drew a gun and opened fire. At around the same time, a People's Temple vehicle approached Ryan's plane at speed. Three men inside raked the plane with rifle fire. When the shooting stopped, Ryan, three journalists and one defector were dead, while six others were seriously wounded.[63]

Back at Jonestown, calamity unfolded with the predictability of a carefully written script. Jones called together his flock. 'We've been so betrayed, we have been so terribly betrayed,' he cried, while confessing to a premonition that an attack would be made on Ryan. 'What's going to happen is that one of those people on the plane is going to shoot the pilot. I know that. I didn't plan it, but I know it's going to happen. And we better not have any of our children left when it's over.' He explained that enemies would shortly invade. Rather than await annihilation, he preferred 'revolutionary suicide'. 'Death is not a fearful thing,' he insisted. 'It's living that's treacherous.' With impressive efficiency, helpers brought large vats of Kool-Aid, laced with cyanide. 'So you be kind to the children and be kind to seniors,' he calmly told the faithful. 'Take the potion like they used to take in ancient Greece, and step over quietly, because we are not committing suicide – it's a revolutionary act . . . Lay down your life with dignity. Don't lay down with tears and agony . . . I don't care how many screams you hear; death is a million times preferable to spending more days in this life . . . Have trust. You have to step across. This world was not our home.'[64]

One single-minded woman, Christine Miller, openly questioned why fifteen defectors should be seen as a catastrophe. 'I think we all have the right to our own destiny as individuals!' she shouted at Jones. 'I look at all the babies and I think they deserve to live.' 'Guards with guns and bows and arrows pressed in on her,' one survivor recalled, 'and Jones tried to make her understand that she had to do it.' The crowd was warned that survivors would be castrated and tortured by the Guyanese army. If Jones had not managed to silence Miller, those desperate to die would have torn her apart.

Chaos reigned as frightened parishioners raced toward death. 'It's simple, it's simple!' Jones shouted as the poison was distributed. 'There's no convulsions with it, it's just simple, just please get it before it's too late.' Adults were given syringes to squirt poison into the mouths of young children, before they drank their own dose. 'There's nothing to worry about,' one of the women distributing the syringes shouted. 'Everybody keep calm and try and keep your children calm. And the oldest children can help love the little children and reassure them. They're not crying from pain. It's just a little bitter tasting but, they're not crying out of any pain.'[65]

Most parishioners willingly embraced death. 'We have pledged our lives to this great cause,' Richard Tropp wrote before he took his poison.

> We are proud to have something to die for. We do not fear death. We hope that the world will someday realize . . . the ideals of brotherhood, justice and equality that Jim Jones has lived and died for. We have all chosen to die for this cause. We know there is no way that we can avoid misinterpretation. But . . . Jim Jones and this movement were born too soon. The world was not ready to let us live . . . We did not want this kind of ending – we wanted to live, to shine, to bring light to a world that is dying for a little bit of love.

Some, however, found this one loyalty test too far. 'Babies were screaming, children were screaming,' a survivor recalled. With rebellion gathering, Jones made one final appeal:

> So be patient, be patient . . . I tell you I don't care how many screams you hear, I don't care how many anguished cries . . . death

> is a million times preferable to ten more days of this life. If you knew what was ahead of you, . . . you'd be glad to be stepping over tonight . . . Let's, let's be dignified. If you'll quit telling them they're dying, if you adults will stop some of this nonsense . . . Adults, adults, adults, I call on you to stop this nonsense. I call on you to quit exciting your children when all they're doing is going to a quiet rest.

Within a short time, 913 residents lay like shingles around the podium where Jones told them to die. Among the dead were at least 150 foster children who should never have been allowed to leave California. Jones himself was shot in the head, an apparent suicide. In his last recorded words, he told a dying crowd: 'We didn't commit suicide. We committed an act of revolutionary suicide protesting the conditions of an inhumane world.' Ann Moore, one of the last victims, wrote: 'We died because you would not let us live in peace.'[66]

A few days later, a *Time* reporter saw an eerie scene as his plane circled overhead. 'The large central building was ringed by bright colors. It looked like a parking lot filled with cars. When the plane dipped lower, the cars turned out to be bodies. Scores and scores of bodies – hundreds of bodies – wearing red dresses, blue T shirts, green blouses, pink slacks, children's polka-dotted jumpers. Couples with their arms around each other, children holding parents. Nothing moved.' Tim Chapman located the dead Jones. Something struck him, something about the way the bodies were arranged. Jones was on his back, while most of the others were on their stomachs, face down, their heads pointing toward their leader, in concentric arcs of death. 'I could tell that it wasn't their final statement,' Chapman remarked. 'It was Jones's.'[67]

'Gray skies dripped sadness and sorrow over San Francisco yesterday,' wrote Caen. 'Headlines told of tragedy and madness in steaming jungles . . . how to judge the insanity surrounding the end of Rev. Jim Jones . . . Who would have expected THIS?' In truth, some people had expected it, but they had been ignored, vilified or bullied. After the massacre, however, came a frenzy to explain. Pop psychologists readily provided theories explaining why so many people could have been so gullible. For others, incredulity fed suspicion. 'Until all the facts are in,' Jesse Jackson insisted, Jones would remain a man who 'worked for the people . . . I would hope that all of the good he did will not be discounted because of this tremendous tragedy.' Conspiracy theorists claimed that the CIA had been using Jonestown for mind control experiments, and that Jones was a victim as innocent as those who fell around him. Suspicion, which remains rife to this day, has been encouraged because Congress has refused to release in full the official investigation. In truth, however, government meddling in Jonestown was conspicuous by its absence. Jones got away with what he did because most government officials desperately wanted to be his friend.[68]

One-time allies frantically sought distance. In response to difficult questions, Moscone denied involvement, while Brown communicated in shrugs. In contrast to other politicians, he steadfastly refused to express regret. 'They all like to say, "Forgive me, I was wrong", but that's bullshit. It doesn't mean a thing now, it just isn't relevant.' That, however, was a hypocrite's lament. The behaviour of the press, of City Hall and of every prominent person who eagerly sought benediction from Jones was indeed relevant. Outside the offices of the San Francisco *Sun-Reporter*, as an angry crowd demanded explanation, one picket sign said it all: 'We had a madman in our midst and you told people he was a saint.'[69]

For the last thirty years, people have struggled to find explanation for why so many people followed Jones to doom. Refuge has been found in labelling those people kooks, weirdos, zombies. It is much harder to see them as products of American society, people who sought a peculiar escape from the common misery of their lives. Jonestown, wrote Tropp, 'was a monument to *life*, to the renewal of the human spirit, broken by capitalism, by a system of exploitation and injustice'. 'No matter what view one takes of the Temple,' Prokes argued, 'perhaps the most relevant truth is that it was filled with outcasts and the poor who were looking for something they could not find in our society. You just can't separate Jonestown from

America, because the Peoples Temple was not born in a vacuum, and despite the attempt to isolate it, neither did it end in one.' That argument was reiterated in an official statement read to a group of reporters in a hotel room in Modesto, California in March 1978:

> Beyond the satisfaction of their material needs, people found dignity and pride in the Temple that racism had previously denied them . . . And that's why so many chose to die in the end . . . [They] died . . . because they weren't allowed to live in peace. They died because they didn't want to be left with no choice but to come back to live in the rat-infested ghettoes of America. They died for all those who suffer oppression.

While that statement did not perhaps take sufficient account of the manipulative powers of Jones, it contained nevertheless a painful kernel of truth. For Prokes, at least, it seemed sufficient explanation. No more need be said. After delivering that statement, he got up, went to the bathroom, closed the door, turned on a faucet and shot himself in the head.[70]

On Stage: Punk

On 7 May 1977, the Clash were playing London's Rainbow Theatre. In the middle of 'White Riot', a white riot erupted. 'The audience . . . were the scariest I'd ever been in,' recalled Billy Bragg. 'They were punks and I'd never seen punks up close before – never been in an audience that was like being in a riot. They trashed the seats down at the front, threw them at the stage . . . Up in the balcony there were people just going mad!'[71]

Damage was estimated at £1,000. 'It was not malicious . . . just natural exuberance,' Allan Schaverian, the Rainbow's manager, told the *Sun*. 'The audience obviously got excited at the group's music. We expected some damage and arrangements were made to cover the cost.' In other words, CBS, producers of the Clash, wrote a cheque and everyone went home happy. 'We shall have more punk concerts soon,' promised an ecstatic Schaverian. Maurice Oberstein, managing director of CBS in Britain, shared his delight. 'Punk rock', he said, 'is perfectly harmless.'[72]

Punk was not supposed to be harmless. It was supposed to be revolutionary, violent, destructive of the status quo and certainly contemptuous of businessmen like Oberstein and Schaverian. Their approval is proof of punk's failure. At the back of the Rainbow two rows of seats remained untouched by the mayhem. They had been occupied by agents and managers – rock's moguls. As a metaphor, that perfectly illustrated the futility of punk's rebellion. The citadel would not crumble.

Punk has often been judged a limited genre – shallow, talentless rebels desperately striving to be despicable. In truth, however, the congregation is hugely diverse. Patti Smith is an immensely talented poet, while Sid Vicious was a violent lunatic with zero talent. Dee Dee Ramone conformed to the punk stereotype of average music and above average drug consumption, while Jonathan Richman – highly talented and strikingly sober – did not. The fact that all four are seen as archetypes of the genre reveals just how large the punk basket actually is.

The stereotype (personified by the Sex Pistols) is reductive to the point of triviality. Dress style was not uniform: Sid Vicious dressed like a caricature of a drug-addled hooligan, David Byrne like a schoolteacher, Richard Hell like a schoolteacher savaged by wolves. Nor is there a typical punk sound: Television sound nothing like the Buzzcocks, who in turn sound nothing like the Heartbreakers. 'The bands were held together by philosophy alone,' argues Lenny Kaye, guitarist for Patti Smith. 'They were hardly alike in style . . . The only time-share they cultivated was another way of looking at the world: good old Us versus Them.' Punk artists sought something raw; their music was an intentional counterpoint to the highly refined work of Seventies superbands like Led Zeppelin. Their songs were rebellion – a yearning to challenge, even destroy, the status quo, be it musical or political. 'We sing about the world that affects us,' claimed Joe Strummer of the Clash. 'We're not just another wank rock group like Boston or Aerosmith.' This also explains punk's demise, because when it ceased to challenge it withered and died.[73]

Punk was a musical coup, an attempt to reclaim rock from the polyester bands of the Seventies. 'I think that's what really created the anger,' Malcolm McLaren, producer of the Sex Pistols, reflected. 'The anger was simply about money, that the culture had become corporate, that we no longer owned it and everybody was desperate to fucking get it back.' Kaye felt a passionate sense of betrayal:

> The immediate gratification of rock & roll had been replaced by a workmanlike professionalism and studio sheen, a world away – or so it seemed – from the raw exuberance and spontaneous combustion of early rock. Slumbering singer/songwriters. Pyrite metal. Dinosaur bands lumbering under concept albums and pseudo-symphonies. The Sixties rock underground, now welcomed into the corridors of power, had made a collective bargain that, like most pacts with the Devil, gave it three wishes and took its soul. Confronted with a music that was smoothed and sated, we looked for the angularity, the jagged edges that could draw blood, the atonal skid-mark screech of our own rite of passage.

Guns were aimed at Prog rockers like Yes and Jethro Tull – the 'dinosaurs'. 'Our music is an answer to the early Seventies when artsy people with big egos would do vocal harmonies and play long guitar solos and get called geniuses,' Tommy Ramone explained. 'That was bullshit.' Punk sought to reinvigorate rock by injecting it with energy, excitement, grit and danger. 'That was the master plan,' claimed Scott Asheton of the Stooges: 'knock down the walls and blow people's shit away. All we wanted to do was make it different.' Iggy Pop 'wanted the music to come out of the speakers and just grab you by the throat and just knock your head against the wall and just basically kill you'. Richard Hell thought punk was 'an outlet for passions and ideas too radical for any other form'.[74]

'Music had become so bloated,' Hell thought. 'It was all these leftover sixties guys playing stadiums . . . it was all about the lights and the poses.' Punk pretended that the ever-widening gap between artist and audience could be closed, that performer and listener could become one. The audience was part of the carnival, as that night at the Rainbow demonstrates. Aficionados claim that the best punk has been lost because it was played live at small venues and never recorded. Concerts were not, however, lovefests – central to any performance was the contempt directed at audiences, sometimes expressed by spitting on those in the front row. As Strummer once shouted: 'We don't give a toss what you think, you pricks, this is what we like to play and this is how we're gonna play it.'[75]

The rebellious image was, however, somewhat contrived. 'We were almost Stalinist in the way that you had to shed all your friends, or everything that you'd known, or every way that you'd played before,' Strummer felt. 'We were guitar-playing drug addicts,' he admitted in a moment of honesty. 'I'd like to think the Clash were revolutionaries, but we loved a bit of posing as well. Where's the hair gel? We can't start the revolution 'til someone finds the hair gel!' The desire to smash rock's icons was nine-tenths artifice. 'I was into the Upstarts and everything in between, from Neil Young or Traffic to Stevie Wonder,' admitted Colin Newman of Wire. 'I was a total hippie,' Poly Styrene of X-Ray Spex confessed. 'I went to see Alan Ginsberg in Bath, I did that whole hippie thing for some time, and I did it for real: bathing in streams, living on ferns.'[76]

Nevertheless, while the rejection of other subcultures may have been contrived, the anger was not. 'I would like to know . . . the source of the deep rage that runs through this story like a razor-edged wire,' writes Charlotte Pressler in her memoir of the underground music scene in Cleveland. 'It wasn't, precisely, class-hatred; it certainly wasn't political; it went too deep to be accepting of the possibility of change . . . It was a desperate, stubborn refusal of the world, a total rejection; the kind of thing that once drove men into the desert . . . It should be remembered that we had all grown up with Civil Defense drills and air-raid shelters and dreams of the Bomb at night; we had been promised the end of the world as children, and we weren't getting it.' Punks assigned themselves the status of an underclass. 'We wanted to write songs about cars and girls,' Johnny Ramone remarked, 'but none of us had a car and no girls wanted to go out with us. So we wrote about freaks and mental illness instead.'[77]

Anger and alienation were particularly pronounced in Britain, where artists performed against a backdrop of a nation in decline. 'Britain's Not Working' roared the most famous Conservative poster of the 1979 election. Those three words perfectly summarized the mid-Seventies shambles that provided punk inspiration. Alienation was a safe harbour, a situation of complete separation from society that punksters achieved by being utterly offensive. Mainstream approval was the worst sort of failure. No greater praise could have been received than the explanation double-barrelled Bernard Brooke-Partridge, chairman of the GLC Arts Committee, gave for banning the Sex Pistols from London. 'I loathe and detest everything they stand for and look like. They are obnoxious, obscene and disgusting.'[78]

Long before the Sex Pistols were even an idea, punk bands were carving a niche for themselves in the United States, though primarily in the hothouse of New York, where weird was wonderful. New York clubs like CBGB's and Max's Kansas City provided artists like Television and Patti Smith an opportunity to play before live audiences. 'Word spread', writes Kaye, 'that a home for the disaffected had been founded on an avenue where many had traditionally come to lie in the gutter.' The genre was nevertheless quarantined within New York – the rest of America didn't really see the point.[79]

The phenomenon was noticed by McLaren, the business partner of Vivienne Westwood, who ran a boutique called SEX on the King's Road. Her shelves juxtaposed outrageous clothes with sex toys, the combined purpose being to shock. While in New York to promote Westwood's clothes, McLaren developed a taste for the New York Dolls and other groups playing at CBGB. 'The fact that they were so bad suddenly hit me with such force,' he later wrote. 'There was something wonderful. I thought how brilliant they were to be this bad.' On his return to London, he decided to start up a punk band to use as live advertisement for the boutique. The raw material stood in front of him – the yobs who lurked at SEX. Forming them into a band was a good way to keep them from nicking clothes. Steve Jones, Paul Cook and Glen Matlock had already dabbled in music, though not successfully. In need of a singer, McLaren chose John Lydon, who had the right looks and interesting dress sense, in particular a Pink Floyd T-shirt on which he had scrawled 'I HATE'. 'Can you sing?' McLaren asked. 'Like an outta tune violin,' Lydon snarled. His terrible voice suggested the perfect stage name – Johnny Rotten – while his deprived background provided suitable inspiration for songs. 'I learnt hate and resentment [at school],' he later explained. Lydon's friend John Ritchie, a psychopathic street urchin destined for prison or an early death, skulked nearby. Westwood, taken with his ugliness, brought him into the band. He became Sid Vicious, named after Lydon's pet hamster that had a tendency to bite. Like a mad scientist creating a monster, McLaren had concocted the Sex Pistols – 'Sex' as advertisement for the shop and 'Pistols' because it was both nasty and violent. McLaren later tried to provide method to the madness: 'I was taking the nuances of Richard Hell, the faggy, pop side of the New York Dolls, the politics of boredom, and mashing it all to make a statement, maybe the final statement, and piss off this rock and roll scene.'[80]

In truth, McLaren's creation was just slick marketing. 'The sort of people that get involved in band management, or clubs and promotions', explains the club owner Andy Czezowski, 'are able to see and exploit something coming along. People like Malcolm, who people may now revere as being The Man Who Invented Punk . . . was nothing of the sort: the man was nothing more than a t-shirt salesman. People coming through the shop, ideas bounced off and he was sufficiently aware and astute to realise that there might be an angle there somewhere.'[81]

'We were all extremely ugly people,' Lydon remarked. 'We were the outcasts, the unwanted.' 'They were terrible,' Bernard Sumner of Joy Division remarked. 'I thought they were great. I wanted to get up and be terrible too.' The rock establishment meanwhile struggled to comprehend the ugliness. Most traditionalists felt that punk ennobled incompetence. 'Punk hates talent' became a favourite expression of dismissal. 'Music is a wonderful, big world,' wrote George Martin, the Beatles' producer. '[But] what killed it, momentarily and inevitably, was the rise of punk rock – suddenly music became little boys dropping their trousers.' The rock critic Charles Young, writing in praise of the Ramones, remarked: 'their music derives much of its charm from . . . [their] instinctive understanding that great artistry can result from turning your liabilities into assets'. Confirming that appraisal, Debbie Harry confessed: 'We attracted the most fucked up and interesting people and had the cruddiest equipment.' Julie Burchill and Tony Parsons, on the other hand, found no joy in hideous mediocrity: 'The breakneck pace of the Ramones was indicative of nothing more than their utmost contempt for their music, their audience and, justifiably, themselves.'[82]

Sideburns, fanzine of the Stranglers, once carried three photos of finger positions for guitar chords. Under the photos ran the caption: 'This is a chord, this is another, this is a third, now form a band.' Punk musicians boasted that by lowering the talent standard they made music more democratic. 'To be a musician went against the whole idea,' Chrissie Hynde of the Pretenders argues. 'The minute anyone got serious about their musicality, they lost what was interesting about the punk scene. Not having a fucking clue and getting on stage and just doing it was what made it so exciting.' 'There was a lot of struggling with our instruments at the start,' Mick Jones of the Clash recalled. 'It was that struggling, learning to play, it made it alive, it made it real, it made it something that wasn't like anything else.'[83]

'Ideas were far more important than how well or badly you could play,' argued Marco Pirroni of Adam and the Ants. 'You could be as shitty as you wanted to. No one would like you if you were brilliant anyway.' Burchill and Parsons, however, found that pride in incompetence a bunch of pretentious nonsense. 'The mass of raw repressed energy', they argued, 'was never a genuine *movement* – it was just a collection of non-starter rat-racers who didn't lack the greed for fame and fortune so patently obvious in the idols they professed to despise, just the Old Guard's technical proficiency.' Unfortunately, the tendency to dismiss punk as a talent vacuum has meant that some genuinely gifted artists have been ignored or conveniently slotted into a different genre. The impressive talent of Elvis Costello, Blondie and Talking Heads has often disqualified them from punk identification. Nevertheless, while not all punk artists were devoid of ability, an impressive number were. 'Democratic' music lowered the talent bar sufficiently to allow a crowd of yobs to satisfy their dreams of becoming rock stars. As Burchill and Parsons wrote: 'punk required not virtuosity of music, but of attitude – the new wave's only revolutionary reform was that now *anyone* could become a tax-exile'.[84]

'Rock & roll is not just music,' said McLaren. 'You're selling an attitude too.' When attitudes become products, however, sincerity corrodes. Highbrow critics liked to portray the Pistols as Situationists with guitars, but in truth their politics was paper-thin and their emotion cleverly contrived. The socialist views of the Clash seem more genuine, but that did not prevent them from selling their political songs to CBS for a big advance. The Clash, write Burchill and Parsons, 'were the first band to use social disorder as a marketing technique to shift product – "I have gobbed in the eye of the whirlwind – please buy my record."' In any case, even blatantly political messages were susceptible to misinterpretation, amidst all that noise. One of the most memorable political Punk songs was 'Eton Rifles' by the Jam, which concerns a socialist Right to Work march heckled by pupils at Eton. The Tory leader David Cameron, a twelve-year-old Etonian when the song was released, recently claimed it as his favourite record. 'Which part of it didn't he get?' the Jam's Paul Weller asked. 'It wasn't intended as a fucking jolly drinking song for the cadet corps.'[85]

While it would be impossible to gather all punk artists into one political basket, they did share a common sense of doom. As the punk journalist Legs McNeil explained:

> Things had collapsed. We had lost the war in Vietnam, to a bunch of guys with sticks in black pyjamas. Vice President Spiro Agnew had to resign because he was caught taking bribes . . . And Richard Nixon had the Watergate burglars break into the Democratic national headquarters because he was so paranoid . . . So punk wasn't about decay, punk was about the apocalypse. Punk was about annihilation. Nothing worked, so let's get right to Armageddon. You know, if you found out the missiles were on their way, you'd probably start saying what you always wanted to, you'd probably turn to your wife and say, 'You know, I always thought you were a fat cow.' And that's how we behaved.

That reckless desire to offend perhaps explains the fondness for Nazi imagery. Swastikas were printed on T-shirts, worn on armbands, or drawn on faces. The Sex Pistols released a song called 'Belsen Was a Gas', which was supposed to be a joke, but turned out to be one irony too far. 'It was always very much an anti-mums and anti-dads thing,' Siouxsie Sioux explained of the swastikas. 'We hated older people – not across the board but particularly in suburbia – always harping on about Hitler . . . and that smug pride. It was a way of saying, "Well I think Hitler was very good actually": a way of watching someone like that go completely red-faced.' Her fellow band member Steve Severin confirmed that the swastikas 'weren't badges of intolerance, but symbols of provocation'. That was perhaps true, but symbols get misinterpreted by an audience immune to nuance. Siouxsie Sioux never quite realized that when she sang about 'too many Jews' (which she lamely explained as 'too many fat businessmen'), her words did not seem all that different from what the National Front was shouting about Zionist control of the economy. 'The swastika thing was past wrong,' the record dealer Don Hughes felt. 'And it got taken wrong by various football yobs and boneheads – they weren't going to understand talk about irony. To them it was a thumbs-up to racist thought.'[86]

The punk revolt was short-lived and ultimately ineffectual. It may have destabilized, but it never came close to destroying. Like all countercultures, it was eventually absorbed into the mainstream, defanged, and turned into commodity. 'It's good to know you've all been reading your News of the Worlds and you're all spitting like punks are supposed to,' sneered Jean-Jacques Burnel of the Stranglers during one of his live sets. The demise was clear to Lydon in early 1978. 'Punk was clichéd at that point. It was a joke on itself. Endless arseholes reading the Sun and the Daily Mirror and running out thinking that's what you needed to do: put some egg in your hair, wear a leather jacket, brothel creeps . . . A straitjacket mentality.' Billy Altman saw Lydon at CBGB in January 1978: 'Here he was, the most famous celebrity in punk, going completely unrecognized. I looked around . . . and realized precisely why that was. You see, there were at least two dozen people in the place who looked exactly like him.'[87]

Punk as commodity turned out to be much more successful than punk as rebellion – a few people got very rich indeed. 'No one's really very scared of punk, especially [not] the record companies,' the producer Sandy Pearlman told *Rolling Stone* in 1979. 'I'd seen Elvis and the Beatles on Ed Sullivan,' said Oberstein. 'It seemed perfectly natural; suddenly there was another bunch of screamers. The record companies are in business to make money, and I saw the potential that these artists had to be on our label rather than some other label . . . I wasn't interested in looking at the Clash as a social phenomenon; we were just making records.'[88]

Punk's main problem was that it was a giant contradiction. It was supposed to be all about hopelessness and despair, but there clearly was hope if a band like the Sex Pistols could make millions from being ugly and discordant. As one fan remarked: 'Everyone was going, "There's no future, there's no future", but at the same time by indulging in punk rock and everything surrounding it, they were creating a future for themselves.' 'Punk', wrote Burchill and Parsons, 'started off as a movement born out of No Fun and ended as a product whose existence was No Threat.' It was all over so quickly, dying young, rather like its iconic performer, Sid Vicious. In Britain, punk burst onto the scene in 1976 and was gone by 1979, disintegrating into hyphenated genres. The demise was predictable, since a movement built on chaos and incompetence and which celebrated failure could not really handle success. Punk was supposed to be played before live audiences in grotty theatres, not pressed onto discs marketed by CBS.[89]

Those discs nevertheless have achieved an acclaim disproportionate to the impact they had at the time. The inescapable fact of punk was that it was never very popular – concerts seldom sold out and most albums languished at the bottom of the charts. Now, however, punk albums pepper the 'all time greatest' lists. *Rolling Stone*'s '500 Greatest Albums of All Time', published in November 2003, included twenty-six punk albums. That acclaim, however, arises more from notoriety than excellence. Punk's capacity to inspire fear is fondly remembered. Sid Vicious, a pathetic creep and musical midget, somehow captured the zeitgeist because he became the perfect symbol of the sorry end to Western civilization. In that sense, the Sex Pistols provide a case study in marketing. McLaren presented them as a threat to society and the public obediently panicked.

Panic is not, however, enough to explain why the music seems 'great'. The best explanation lies in the genre's short life, the fact that it died young and remained, as a result, for ever new. Its status was enhanced by its unique nature – it remains easy to identify and chronicle. No song that came after sounds quite like 'Anarchy in the UK', or 'White Riot', or 'Search and Destroy'. Punk took music into a cul-de-sac; bands that came later, instead of continuing the challenge, turned back into safer thoroughfares. As a result, three decades on, punk remains undiluted, sounding neither stale nor jaded. 'Today, so many years later,' writes Griel Marcus, 'the shock of punk is that every good punk record can still sound like the greatest thing you've ever heard.' Those unable to appreciate its virtues, on the other hand, find that its repulsiveness does not mellow. 'It was all deliriously exciting', wrote Allan Jones after that fateful night at the Rainbow Theatre, 'but it has nothing to do with music, I fancy.'[90]

8

MORE THAN JUST A GAME

Beijing: Ping-Pong Diplomacy

Glenn Cowan was an ordinary American nineteen-year-old – a child of his time who liked rock music, soft drugs and casual sex. His only distinguishing feature was his passion for ping-pong, but that was hardly earth shattering. Then, one day, during a tournament in Japan, Cowan boarded a bus and changed the world.

Cowan was part of the American team attending the table tennis world championships in Nagoya, Japan in 1971. On 4 April, after finishing a practice session, he flagged down a tournament bus. To his surprise, the bus was occupied exclusively by Chinese players, coaches and officials, all flabbergasted by his sudden invasion. A Martian would have caused only slightly more shock. Cowan, who fancied himself a revolutionary, met stares with aplomb: 'I know all this . . . my hat, my hair, my clothes look funny to you. But there are many, many people who look like me and who think like me. We, too, have known oppression in our country and we are fighting against it. But just wait. Soon we will be in control because the people on top are getting more and more out of touch.' A tremor rippled through the bus as a translator struggled with the strange remark.[1]

Since 1949, there had been an embargo on civility between the

Chinese and Americans. The US pretended that the People's Republic did not exist, insisting that the exiled government in Taiwan was the true China. The Chinese, in turn, considered America the counter-revolutionary running dog – the epitome of capitalist evil. Then came Cowan.

Silent panic engulfed the bus as the flustered Chinese struggled to react. For the previous six years, China had refused to attend the world championships because, during the Cultural Revolution, international sporting competitions were derided as 'sprouts of revisionism'. By their mere presence, this team demonstrated that a semblance of normality was returning, but every player understood that the government still held a short leash. The decision to attend had been taken only after acrimonious meetings involving the Foreign Ministry and the State Commission for Physical Culture, chaired by Premier Zhou Enlai. The official aim was 'friendship first, competition second', but friendliness was not supposed to be extended to the Americans. 'During the contest, if we meet with officials of the US delegation', official guidelines advised, 'we do not take the initiative to talk or exchange greetings. If we compete with the US team, we do not exchange team flags.' Mao was blunter: 'Regard a Ping-Pong ball as the head of your capitalist enemy. Hit it with your socialist bat, and you have won the point for the fatherland.'[2]

That explains the consternation over Cowan. 'We were still in the Cultural Revolution,' Zhuang Zedong, the former world champion, recalls. 'Any exchange with Westerners would be [attacked] with vicious labels, such as "treason" or "spy". So when this American guy got on the bus, nobody dared talk to him.' Zhuang, however, felt torn between cultural conditioning and governmental stricture. Confucianism, burnt into the neurons of every Chinese person, taught politeness and harmony. 'I was thinking, China has been well-known as a country of hospitality for more than 5,000 years. If everyone ignores that American athlete, it would be ironic.' As the star of the Chinese team, Zhuang felt the need to set an example. 'I looked at him and thought, he's not involved in issuing policy. He's just an athlete, an ordinary person.' Much to the dismay of his teammates, Zhuang made his way up the aisle. A fellow player grabbed his sleeve, and the team manager blocked his way. 'Take it easy,' Zhuang retorted. 'As head of the delegation you have many concerns, but I am just a player.' He reached Cowan and, through an interpreter, welcomed him. 'Even now,' Zhuang recalls, 'I can't forget the naive smile on his face.'[3]

Zhuang wanted to give Cowan something, but most of the official gifts he had seemed too insignificant. 'Since he is an American athlete, I thought I should give him a bigger present.' He settled upon a silk embroidery of a Yellow Mountain scene, made in Hangzhou. The American, clearly taken aback by Zhuang's generosity, searched in his own bag, but could find only a comb. 'Jesus Christ, I can't give you a comb. I wish I could give you something, but I can't.' Cowan hesitated and then, with a wry smile, put the comb back. The interpreter, clearly bemused, asked if Cowan knew who had addressed him. 'Yes, the world champion Zhuang Zedong,' he replied. 'And I hope your team does well.'[4]

As the bus arrived at the main competition venue, photographers loitered, hoping for shots of those rare Chinese. Much to their surprise, Zhuang and Cowan disembarked together, wearing wide grins. The immense symbolism of that moment was lost on no one. Photographers pushed forward and reporters fired questions, but Zhuang was quickly hustled away and given a dressing down by Chinese officials. 'Chairman Mao told us we should differentiate between American policymakers and common people,' he retorted. 'What was wrong with my action?'[5]

The following day, Cowan found the perfect gift for his new friend. He returned to the arena, located Zhuang and, sensing a dramatic moment, pulled him in front of some television cameras. He presented him with a T-shirt in which an image blending the American flag and peace symbol was printed below the message 'LET IT BE'. Cowan then pulled from his bag the silk brocade picture, so that photographers got what looked like a spontaneous exchange of gifts. That image suggested that something very big was happening in Nagoya. 'Mr. Cowan, would you like to visit China?' a journalist shouted. 'Well, I'd like to see any country I haven't seen before – Argentina, Australia, China, . . . Any country I haven't seen before.' That wasn't the answer reporters wanted, so they tried again: 'But what about China in particular? Would you like to go there?' He hesitated, then replied: 'Of course.'[6]

Meanwhile, officials in Beijing frantically forged a response. A hastily convened meeting between the Foreign Ministry and the State Commission for Physical Culture drew up a report advising that the time was not yet ripe for an American team to visit China. That report was approved by Zhou, then sent to Mao, who took two days to concur. The Chinese were not, in principle, opposed to a visit, but they did not appreciate having their hands forced by athletes in Japan.

Photos of Zhuang and Cowan first hit the front pages of Japanese newspapers on the morning of 5 April. When the wire services picked up the story, it quickly circled the globe. The photos eventually made their way to Mao, who remarked: 'Zhuang Zedong is not only a good ping-pong player, but also a diplomat. He is quite politically sensitive.' On the evening of the 6th, after Mao had taken his customary heavy dose of sleeping pills and gone to bed, he had a sudden change of heart about an American visit. He instructed his nurse, Wu Xujun, to order the Foreign Ministry to extend a formal invitation. Pointing to the photo, he told Wu: 'The friendly Sino-American relationship is definitely the trend. Look, the encounter between Zhuang Zedong and Cowan is so natural. They bear no grudge against each other.' Wu, however, was under strict instructions not to act upon decisions made after the sleeping pills were administered. Mao nevertheless insisted, and forced himself to stay awake while the message was relayed to the Foreign Office.[7]

Keen to appear in control of events, the Foreign Ministry extended an invitation worded so as to cast the Americans as supplicants. 'Considering that the American team has made the request many times with friendly enthusiasm, it has been approved to invite it, including its leaders, to visit our country.' The Americans would be allowed to join an already scheduled tour that included teams from

Canada, Nigeria and Colombia. As an aside, the message added: 'If their traveling funds are insufficient, we can subsidize.'[8]

Back in the US, Vice-President Spiro Agnew provided his trademark knee-jerk response, dismissing the invitation as 'propaganda'. What Agnew didn't realize was that his boss, Richard Nixon, had been waiting anxiously for an opportunity of this sort. He immediately cabled back to Japan that the invitation must be accepted, and then told Agnew to shut up.

Prior to his election, Nixon had argued in *Foreign Affairs* that, 'There is no place on this small planet for a billion of its potentially most able people to live in angry isolation . . . we simply cannot afford to leave China forever outside the family of nations.' He reiterated that point when he told *Time* magazine that 'We must always seek opportunities to talk with [China] . . . If there is anything I want to do before I die, it is to go to China.' There were, however, a number of huge obstacles, among them the Vietnam War, the strident anti-communism of Nixon's own party, and American promises to Taiwan. These obstacles were so significant that, when Nixon raised the possibility with his national security adviser Henry Kissinger, the latter concluded: 'I think he has lost control of his senses.'[9]

Nixon nevertheless remained determined. For him, normalizing relations offered an opportunity to break a logjam in foreign policy. As William Smyser, a senior analyst at the National Security Council, recalls, the administration felt that 'we were stuck in a rut. We were stuck in a rut in Vietnam . . . we were stuck in a rut in the negotiations with the Soviet Union . . . We were also stuck in a rut with the American people, who were discouraged about whether foreign policy could ever produce anything good.' In Nixon's view, China offered the possibility of an end run – a chance to recast foreign affairs so profoundly that adversaries would be left flailing. Friendly relations with the Chinese would, it was anticipated, pressure the North Vietnamese to negotiate an end to the war. It would also, more importantly, drive a wedge between China and the Soviet Union, forcing the latter to make concessions, for instance at the Strategic Arms Limitation Talks. The idea also harmonized with the recently formulated Nixon Doctrine, which emphasized peaceful co-existence and disengagement in Asia. Since the US no longer felt obliged to roll back communism in every corner of the world, it no longer made sense to treat China like a pariah.[10]

An opportunity developed when festering Sino-Soviet border disputes destroyed once and for all the illusion of an impregnable communist bloc. Clandestine talks with the Chinese were held in Warsaw, but these stalled when the Americans invaded Cambodia in April 1970. Then, in October of that year, Nixon sent a message to the Chinese through a Pakistani intermediary, reiterating a willingness to talk. As a mark of his sincerity, at a banquet in honour of the Romanian leader Nicolae Ceaușescu, he used the term 'People's Republic of China' for the first time. Nixon realized that no one was better placed to pull off such a gambit. Liberal Democrats had long wanted better relations with China, but were not in a position to act on that desire, since to do so would provoke accusations of being soft on communism. Nixon, in contrast, was singularly well suited to open doors, since his anti-communist credentials were beyond dispute. As he later told Mao, 'Sometimes those on the right can do things which those on the left can only talk about.' He nevertheless realized that negotiations could be sabotaged if critics got wind of them at too early a stage. With typical secrecy, he instructed Kissinger to arrange back channel negotiations, while keeping the rest of his Cabinet, and the entire country, out of the loop.[11]

The Americans were pushing at an open door. The dispute with the Soviets had left the Chinese feeling deeply isolated. Like Nixon, Mao felt that something bold needed to be done to break the stalemate and allow China her rightful place on the world stage. Summoning four generals who had been disgraced during the Cultural Revolution, Mao asked for advice, making clear his desire for 'unconventional thoughts'. They unanimously came to the conclusion that, of her two main adversaries, the Americans posed the least threat. Among China watchers, a subtle change in attitude toward Nixon became apparent. While official propaganda continued to call him 'a gangster' with 'a blood-dripping butcher's knife', his conciliatory references to China were duly noted and sometimes reported in the press. On 18 December 1970, Mao told his old friend Edgar Snow that, if Nixon wanted to come to China, he would be welcome. 'I don't think I'll wrangle with him', he added, 'though I'll criticize him.'[12]

A mutual need to criticize proved the biggest obstacle. Neither side wanted to appear desperate for the other's good grace. Each felt the need to censure past transgressions. Negotiations therefore proceded as if through treacle. 'There had been about a year of back and forth,' Kissinger recalls. 'China had sent us a specific proposal to come to Beijing, and we were on course to answer favorably.' The ping-pong incident came at the perfect moment because it opened a door, without cumbersome diplomatic fanfare. It also offered the opportunity to sidestep hardliners at home, who could hardly object to an innocent sporting exchange. 'We wanted to play it all very low key,' Kissinger reflected. 'As it turned out, it worked out well for us.' He eventually concluded that the invitation was an intentional ploy by the Chinese to break the deadlock in the back channel talks. 'I think Zhou Enlai thought Westerners were slower than the Chinese in mental perception, and didn't think we had understood the message. So just as we were drafting a response to the message we had received, we heard he had invited the Ping-Pong team.' While that was probably true in principle, in fact the boldness came from Mao, not Zhou.[13]

On 10 April, nine players, two spouses and four officials crossed into the PRC. 'The American team could not have been more representative of the U.S. if the State Department had handpicked it,' John Roderick, the AP China correspondent, recalled. 'It was what foreigners often thought of Americans: friendly, racially diverse, individualistic.'[14] Suspicion and animosity were put on hold as both sides competed in a game of graciousness. The American public, for the most part, saw their table tennis team as intrepid explorers of a strange land. A fascination for all things Chinese suddenly developed. For the first time in over twenty years, polls showed a majority in favour of Chinese membership of the United Nations. As for the

Chinese, they treated the Americans like friendly extraterrestrials. 'We became VIPs from the moment we entered China,' the coach Jack Howard later remarked. 'Every meal had seven or eight courses with things I never saw before in my life . . . I think they were trying to kill us with kindness.' Matches were shown live on television – unusual in China at the time. 'If we were at a site like The Great Wall . . . they would all crowd around and look at us like we were from another planet,' Olga Soltesz recalls. The strangest guest of all was Cowan. His match with a middling Chinese player attracted a crowd of 18,000 at Beijing's Capital Stadium. 'The Chinese had never seen a person with long hair and hippie ways,' a fellow player recalled. 'Thousands of people would surround him in the streets. They loved him but were also a little terrified of him.'[15]

In order to make the games competitive the Americans were pitted against good club players, not the national team. They were, nevertheless, no match for their Chinese opponents. Keen not to humiliate, Chinese officials instructed players to go easy on their opponents. 'I knew they would be unlike any other games I'd ever played,' Zheng Minzhi, one of the Chinese players, recalled. 'I knew their significance and my responsibilities. I knew I was not only there to play, but more important, to achieve what cannot be achieved through proper diplomatic channels.' The games ironically mirrored the relationship the Chinese were trying to cultivate with America – one in which they were gracious but still in full control. Chinese self-regard was boosted when American players heaped praise on their country, much to State Department dismay. 'I like the way the Chinese people are united,' John Tannehill told reporters. 'In China there is no exploiting class. The workers have power. In the US, the workers are taken advantage of.' He added that Mao was 'the greatest moral and intellectual leader in the world today . . . he reaches most of the people. His philosophy is beautiful.' Another player, Judy Bochenski, proclaimed that women's liberation was far advanced in China because the women 'all wear trousers, they all have jobs, they all work like the men'.[16]

'Never before in history has a sport been used so effectively as a tool of international diplomacy,' Zhou announced. He stage-managed the spectacle perfectly, extracting maximum publicity. The climax came at a reception held at the Great Hall on 14 April. 'You have opened a new chapter in the relations of the American and Chinese people,' Zhou told his guests. 'I am confident that this beginning again of our friendship will certainly meet with majority support of our two peoples.' The only diversion from a carefully prepared script came when Cowan asked Zhou what he thought about hippies. The response was perfectly crafted: 'Young people ought to try different things. But they should try to find something in common with the great majority – remember that.' On learning of that exchange, Cowan's mother wrote to Zhou, thanking him for speaking sense to her son.[17]

A few hours after Zhou's speech, the Americans relaxed a twenty-year-old trade embargo with China. Confident of America's good intent, Zhou sent a message to Washington on the 29th, explaining that Mao would welcome 'direct conversations' with Nixon, and suggesting immediate exploratory talks. Nixon was beside himself with joy. 'This is the most important communication that has come to an American president since World War II,' he told Kissinger. He found some rare brandy that a supporter had sent after his election victory and toasted his good luck. On 17 May he formally accepted the Chinese invitation and named Kissinger as his preliminary representative.[18]

Kissinger's talks with Zhou were at times difficult, but too much had already been invested for either side to allow failure. Ritualized punches were traded, while the two boxers danced around the main issues of Vietnam and Taiwan. With respect to the former, Kissinger did not get Zhou to agree to pressure the North Vietnamese to end the war, but did get him to accept the sincerity of America's desire to disengage. On the subject of Taiwan, Kissinger, to Zhou's delight, made it clear that Nixon would not allow past loyalties to get in the way of new friendships.

'We were embarking', Nixon remembered, 'on a voyage of philosophical discovery as uncertain, and in some ways as perilous, as the voyages of geographical discovery of an earlier time.' Hyperbole aside, that was essentially true. Nixon's visit to China in February 1972 was important for the simple fact that it occurred more than for the detail of what was agreed. Both sides wanted a new era to begin. The visit's significance can be measured by the Soviets' panicked reaction. 'The news hit us like a bolt from the blue,' Georgii Arbatov, a senior adviser to Brezhnev, recalled. 'My colleagues said, "America will be China's ally . . . When Nixon visits Beijing, anything could happen. All this will make things very difficult for us. Where will it all end?"' One could argue that it ended with the demise of the Soviet Union in 1991. Rapprochement between China and the US meant that the Soviets were left to carry alone the burden of countering a rampant America. That burden eventually bankrupted her.[19]

Time magazine called it 'The ping heard round the world.' Granted, better relations between China and the US were inevitable. But they were undoubtedly helped along by a fortuitous encounter on a bus. In his memoirs, Kissinger praised the extraordinary proficiency of the Chinese in the game of power politics. Their skill came in making 'the meticulously planned appear spontaneous'. The perfect example, he feels, was the invitation to the American ping-pong team. 'Only Mao could have ordered this. And only Zhou could have orchestrated it.' While that is true to an extent, neither had the power to make Cowan board that bus, or to make Zhuang decide to be friendly. Those two men forced open a door that had been jammed for years. As Zhou once said, 'A ball bounced over the net and the whole world was shocked. The big globe was set in motion by a tiny globe – something inexplicable in physics but not impossible in politics.'[20]

Zhuang's life reveals in microcosm China's turbulent history. He spent much of the Cultural Revolution in prison, watching fellow players driven to suicide. Rehabilitation came when Mao decided that table tennis was useful on the world stage. As a reward for his gesture on that bus, he became a hero and was eventually made Minister for Physical Culture and Sport. After Mao's death, however, he again found himself caught in the crossfire of political rivalry. The former government minister became a street sweeper and was then thrown in jail for wearing a Swiss watch. Driven to despair, he tried to hang himself in 1977. When China returned to her senses in the 1980s, he enjoyed another rehabilitation and restoration of his heroic status.

Today, the collectivist Chinese celebrate the individual heroics of Zhuang. In contrast, in America, where celebrity worship is a religion, but fame often fleeting, Cowan was quickly forgotten. He did not take part in the return visit of the Chinese team to the US in 1972. That year, he was diagnosed as bipolar. The erratic behaviour that had once been his greatest asset became instead a dangerous liability. During the 1980s he drifted from job to job, eventually finding himself homeless. When he died of a heart attack in 2004 hardly anyone noticed. 'He was like a comet,' says Robert Lange, his former doubles partner. 'Flashed through the sky and then gone.' Quite understandably, he found it difficult to be a shoe salesman after he'd helped open the door to China. 'After China, everything seemed to be useless,' Tannehill feels. 'How could you do better than world peace?'[21]

Kinshasa: The Rumble in the Jungle

'I belong to the world, the black world,' Muhammad Ali once boasted. 'I'll always have a home in Pakistan, in Algeria, in Ethiopia.' Around the globe, blacks and whites bought that line. In the process, he became the most famous, and widely loved, sportsman in history. He was, as he claimed, 'the Greatest'.[22]

But what made him great? Boxing, yes, but also self-promotion. Ali was the king of hype, a man so skilled at selling himself that most people bought the pig without ever looking in the poke. As he grew older, he became immune to criticism, despite the profound contradictions in the saintly persona he constructed. No other hero has been so obsessed with the need to indulge in vulgar boasts about how many people love him.

By 1970, he was already a martyr – the cruel victim of American racism. He refused to serve in Vietnam supposedly because he was a pacifist, yet his pacifism was paper-thin. At one point he claimed that he should not have to serve since he was more valuable as a professional boxer than as a GI. 'I buy a lot of bullets, at least three jet bombers a year, and pay the salary of fifty thousand fighting men with the money they take from me after my fights.'[23] When he realized how selfish that line sounded, he abandoned it for an objection based on religion. His pacifism was opportunistic – he objected not to war, but to a specific war. His conscientious objection was an insult to those with a real conscience.

In 1967, Ali was banned from boxing because of his refusal to serve in Vietnam. Beaten by 'the system', he was widely reviled in his own country. Then, on 28 September 1970, a federal judge ordered that his boxing licence be restored. In the intervening period, America had turned against the war, rendering Ali's faux pacifism commendable. He emerged from purdah a hero.

A contest against Jerry Quarry was arranged for 26 October. 'I'm not just fighting one man,' Ali remarked. 'I'm fighting a lot of men, showing them here is one man they couldn't conquer. Lose this one, and it won't just be a loss to me. So many millions of faces throughout the world will be sad.' He did not lose.[24]

The title stripped from Ali had meanwhile been won by Joe Frazier. He was reluctant to fight Ali, but after the Quarry bout, could not refuse. Since Ali had identified himself as the champion of Black Power, that meant that Frazier could be cast as a traitor to blackness. 'Frazier's no real champion,' Ali claimed; '98 per cent of my people are for me. They identify with my struggle. Same one they're fighting every day in the streets. If I win, they win. I lose, they lose. Anybody black who thinks Frazier can whup me is an Uncle Tom.'[25]

Because Ali was the acknowledged champion of blacks around the world, to criticize him became politically unacceptable – the definition of racism. This gave him enormous freedom. He called Frazier 'an ignorant gorilla' – a statement which, uttered by anyone else, would have been condemned as racist or cruel. 'Joe Frazier is too ugly to be champ. Joe Frazier is too dumb to be champ. The heavyweight champion should be smart and pretty like me.'[26]

Frazier grew up in dire poverty in South Carolina. If the prerequisite to Black Pride was struggle, he was a card-carrying member of that club. Yet through no fault of his own, he became a pariah. Ali's glorious martyrdom had the unfortunate side-effect of blighting the career of a man who, under normal circumstances, would have been recognized as a decent man and a sublime boxer.

Having conquered the kingdom of blackness, Ali ruled it like a despot. Those who defied him were traitors. In *Sport Illustrated*, a rather brave Mark Kram commented:

> The disputation of the New Left comes at Frazier with its spongy thinking and push button passion and seeks to color him white, to denounce him as a capitalist dupe and a Fifth Columnist to the black cause . . . Among the blacks there is only a whisper of feeling for Frazier, who is deeply cut by their reaction. He is pinned under the most powerful influence on black thought in the country. The militants view Ali as the Mahdi, the one man who has circumvented what they believe to be an international white conspiracy.

Frazier later reflected: 'Calling me an Uncle Tom, calling me the white man's champion. All that was phoniness to turn people against me. He was helping himself, not black people. Ali wasn't no leader of black people.' He might as well have shouted into the wind. The all-powerful Ali had turned the contest into one of black vs. white. Those who hated Ali drifted to Frazier, including a sordid collection of bigots who still wanted Ali in army green.[27]

The only thing Ali could not control was what happened in the ring. On 8 March 1971, after fifteen punishing rounds, Frazier stood victorious. To many, that triumph seemed emblematic of the cynical Seventies, proof that the heavenly decade had passed. 'Joe Frazier, like Nixon, had finally prevailed for reasons that people like me refused to understand – at least not out loud,' wrote Hunter Thompson. By the same reasoning, revering Ali seemed one way to preserve a golden past. Thus, despite his failure, his reputation did not suffer. He still called himself the Greatest and the multitude bellowed agreement.[28]

Fourteen fights followed, only one of which Ali lost. Then, in January 1974, came a rematch with Frazier, a contest now lacking some of its lustre since Frazier had earlier lost his title to George Foreman. Ali won a unanimous decision after twelve rounds, thus opening the door to a match with Foreman. That fight promised to be so much more than a contest between two superb boxers. Every punch would carry a political message. Foreman, after all, had proudly waved an American flag after his victory in the 1968 Olympics, when other blacks had been demonstrably unpatriotic.

The Ali–Foreman fight was scheduled to take place on 30 October 1974 in Kinshasa, formerly Leopoldville, a place still haunted by the murder of President Patrice Lumumba, a Sixties socialist icon dwarfed only by Che. The Congo, now called Zaire, was ruled by Joseph Mobutu, the quintessential African despot and architect of Lumumba's demise. For him, the fight was an opportunity to shine a bright light on his fiefdom. Sporting events are often used as opportunities to swagger; Mobutu simply took that phenomenon and multiplied it exponentially. Sadly, the Rumble in the Jungle was a party Zaire could not afford. Every dollar paid to Ali and Foreman was stolen from the mouths of starving Congolese.

For many blacks, Zaire was sacred simply because it was Africa. 'The whole thing was being done by black people for black people, and Muhammad Ali was at the center of it all,' wrote Lloyd Price. 'It . . . [was] the perfect thing to do. Everything was starting to feel different. Black people were rising up and feeling proud.' Given that assumption, sordid details could be ignored. The fight was to be held in a huge, brutally ugly stadium, a testament to Mobutu's poisonous ego. In the basement below the ring were foetid cells in which political prisoners were mercilessly tortured. 'The floor beneath the floor', Norman Mailer admitted, 'was covered in blood.' If Ali was aware of that fact, one wonders why he agreed to the fight. If he was unaware, one wonders how he could claim to represent oppressed blacks everywhere. Ali would never have agreed to fight in South Africa, yet that regime's oppression was mild compared to Mobutu's. Ali seems to have been unaware that blacks can tyrannize blacks and that cruelty is not monochromatic. Ali was the master of profound political gestures, yet on this occasion he failed to use his celebrity to expose a tyrant.[29]

The fight also witnessed the emergence of the promoter Don King. After serving four years in prison for murder, King began systematically to impose his will on the sport of boxing, eventually dragging it into the gutter in which it wallows today. In promoting the fight, King brought together a rogues' gallery of investors, which included the Philippine dictator Ferdinand Marcos. The world got the fight it wanted, but the price was outrageous.

Foreman, a huge man, younger and more formidable than Ali, was the overwhelming favourite, making Ali an unaccustomed underdog. He took to that role with gusto. The old banter about how he was going to whup his opponent continued, but at the same time Ali felt safe in the knowledge that he did not have to win because he was not expected to do so. The match became one of the greatest moments in the history of sport because that is what everyone willed it to be. Ali was David to Foreman's Goliath, his reputation enhanced by the glow of martyrdom. As with Frazier, he attacked Foreman's blackness. Foreman was an interloper, a man who did not belong. 'He's in my country!' Ali shouted, and the adoring crowds bellowed approval.[30]

Most of the world had long revered Ali; most of America had recently joined the chorus. In this sense, the match was more than just a heavyweight championship; it was also an assertion of truths Americans now found evident, namely that blacks were oppressed and that the Vietnam War had been immoral. 'I'm not fighting for fame or money,' Ali claimed before the fight. 'I'm not fighting for me. I'm fighting for the black people on welfare, the black people who have no future, black people who are wineheads and dope addicts. I'm a politician for Allah.' The purse, by the way, was $10 million, split evenly. Justifying that amount, Ali quipped: 'Countries go to war to put their names on the map and wars cost a lot more than 10 million dollars.' Fans enthusiastically swallowed that huge plate of tripe.[31]

The way the match was fought lent credence to the epic scenario Ali had crafted: he suffered terribly for seven rounds, soaking up all the punishment Foreman could deliver. Midway through the eighth round, he went on the offensive, putting his tired and frustrated opponent on the canvas with a savage left-right combination. The fight was suddenly over, justice had been done, and Ali was again champion.

The world rejoiced. 'I think it was the sort of joyous reaction that comes with seeing something that suggests all things are possible,' wrote George Plimpton in *Sports Illustrated.* And

> the triumph of the underdog, the comeback from hard times and exile, the victory of an outspoken nature over a sullen disposition, the prevailing of intelligence over raw power, the success of physical grace, the ascendance of age over youth, and especially the confounding of the experts. Moreover, the victory assuaged the guilt feelings of those who remembered the theft of Ali's career.

What followed was both coronation and redemption. Americans, now hopelessly in love with Ali, celebrated him with an enthusiasm withheld when he first beat Sonny Liston in 1964. Guilt magnified adulation. Endorsement offers flooded in, as businesses suddenly abandoned scruples about black Muslims promoting their products. Nearly every periodical which had anything to do with sport (and a good number which didn't) named him person, boxer, or sportsman of the year.[32]

Ali is an empty vessel into which, over the years, have been poured the dreams of various constituencies. He did not change all that much between 1964, when he was a Muslim pariah, and 1974, when he became the hero of a nation. The United States, however, changed immensely during that period. It changed in a way that allowed accommodation and, in time, veneration of what had once seemed profane. By 1974, the race riots associated, rightly or wrongly, with

Ali's brand of Black Power were over. American participation in the war in Vietnam had also ended. The war itself was widely seen as a mistake. Those who had resisted the draft were folk heroes while those who had protested credited themselves with bringing the war to an end. Ali harmonized perfectly with the new zeitgeist. 'The Ali that America ended up loving was not the Ali I loved most,' the football star Jim Brown complained. 'The warrior I loved was gone. In a way, he became part of the establishment.'[33]

Ali became an icon because his features were so simply drawn; a more complicated individual would have revealed too many points of contradiction to satisfy such a large and varied constituency. He was a product of the media age, a hero of loud noise and beautiful presence but not a man of depth. He suited perfectly the simplification of politics and the shallow tendency to assign heroic status to the man who shouts the right lines loudest. Ali's admirers like to think that, in his heyday, the fighter reached beyond himself. He certainly made himself into a hero for oppressed people around the world. But a hero is a different thing than a leader. A leader would have confronted Mobutu by refusing to fight in his noxious fiefdom. The great problem with Ali was that it was a great deal easier to admire the man than to do something about the issues he supposedly symbolized. Loving Ali could be passed off as positive political action when it was nothing of the sort. That ultimately was the tragedy of the Rumble in the Jungle – a shallow and rather sordid boxing match marketed as a triumph of justice. No one bothered to look in the basement, where the blacks Ali claimed to represent were cruelly tortured, their screams muffled by the tumultuous ovation showered upon The Greatest.

Houston: The Battle of the Sexes

In the early spring of 1973, Margaret Court and Billie Jean King, the two dominant players on the women's tennis circuit, found themselves sharing a hotel elevator in Detroit. 'I'm going to play Bobby Riggs,' Court abruptly announced. King's jaw dropped.

Riggs was a fifty-five-year-old former Wimbledon champion. Over the previous year, he had openly derided women's tennis, underlining that derision by challenging top players to a match. A small man with a huge ego, he sought to humiliate them in order to cast a light upon himself. He ensnared Court by offering $10,000, win or lose. At a time when most players on the women's circuit had difficulty covering their expenses, it seemed like easy money. 'That's not enough,' King protested, 'and besides, this is not about tennis.' Court, a political novice, struggled to understand the fuss. 'Margaret,' King shouted, 'I'm just going to ask one thing of you: You have to win this match.' Court nodded. 'No, I mean it. You have to win this match. You have no idea how important it is.'[34]

Riggs's preferred opponent was King, the main object of his vitriol. An outspoken campaigner for women's rights, both on and off the court, she was instrumental in the founding of the Women's Tennis Association in 1973. In that same year, after considerable pressure from King, US Open officials had agreed to offer equal prize money to men and women. All this annoyed Riggs. Since he equated entertainment value with physical power, he could not accept that female players deserved equal shares. He sought to prove his point by showing that even a long-retired professional had more to offer than the best females. A match might, he hoped, embarrass and silence the annoying Billie Jean. Because she understood his intent precisely, she recognized its danger. 'Our reputation is at stake,' she told friends. 'We have nothing to gain.'[35]

King was a bulldog, Court a lamb – in this case one destined for slaughter. Politically conservative, deeply religious and astonishingly naive, she saw no need for feminism. 'I always felt your gift made room for you . . . I didn't feel you had to go over the top.' When King formed the breakaway Virginia Slims tour in order to gain a fair deal for female players, Court stayed put, arguing that tennis was sufficiently lucrative. Because she did not recognize discrimination, she did not understand the political significance of playing

Riggs. 'I am not carrying the banner for Women's Lib,' she insisted before the match. 'She didn't get it. She just didn't get it,' King later remarked. 'Margaret didn't see the big picture.'[36]

Riggs began his match long before the first serve, wearing Court down with a relentless psychological barrage. He boasted that he would beat her with cleverness – dinked serves, drop shots and lobs. His trademark sexist banter was interspersed with occasional asides about the importance of the match. 'Do you realize, Margaret, that this is the most important match ever played? Just think how many women are counting on you.' Never grasping how Riggs was manipulating her, Court failed to adapt an effective defence. 'With all the shouting and showbiz, I guess I was shocked,' she later admitted.[37]

The match was played at a country club near San Diego on 13 May 1973 – Mother's Day. By the second game, Riggs's psychological machinations and annoyingly effective tennis had reduced Court to an emotional wreck. 'I got her sidetracked,' he explained later. 'She was bewitched and bewildered.' Court unwittingly played the straight man to his comedy routine, which everyone dubbed the Mother's Day Massacre. The final score – 6–2, 6–1 – accurately reflected her humiliation. 'I didn't expect him to mix it up like that,' Court confessed. 'We girls don't play like that.' Riggs was not remotely surprised. 'It went exactly as I thought. The whole thing was pressure.' He added: 'Now I want King bad. I'll play her on clay, grass, wood, cement, marble, or roller skates. We got to keep this sex thing going. I'm a woman specialist now.'[38]

Watching the match, King felt her blood reach boiling point. All she had struggled for in women's tennis risked being destroyed by Riggs's mischief. She phoned her husband: 'That's it, I've got to play him. Larry, now we've got something to prove.'[39]

The Riggs cyclone arrived at a time of great turbulence in American gender relations. With dizzying quickness, feminism had changed from a noisy nuisance caused by a handful of rebels, to a mainstream movement posing painful questions for both sexes. Men found their patriarchal verities undermined, while women were confronted with injustice they had not heretofore noticed. For men in particular, but also for some women, Riggs represented a welcome reassertion of tradition. Those inclined to dismiss feminism as a load of nonsense saw him as their white knight, particularly because ridicule figured so prominently in his challenge. Cheers erupted when he argued 'Women who can, do. Those who can't become feminists.'[40]

Politics is usually not welcome in sport, but sport does provide an effective way to communicate political points to the unengaged masses. Riggs reduced a complicated gender issue to a simple contest. Though a match with King should not have had meaning beyond the tennis court, the context ensured that it did. The issue of women in sport had become highly contentious because of the passage of the Education Amendments Act in 1972. Title IX of that Act stipulated that no person could be excluded on the basis of gender from participating in any federally funded education programme. That clause was not originally intended to ensure greater participation of women in sport, but activists interpreted it that way. King, for instance, pointed out that, while she was at college, studies and tennis had to be shoehorned around the two jobs she needed to make ends meet. Her husband, in contrast, was given a tennis scholarship. Yet he was a very average player and she was already an international star. Giving teeth to Title IX, the Department of Health, Education and Welfare (HEW) proposed regulations requiring federally funded institutions to offer women facilities and programmes comparable to those men enjoyed. For traditionalists within American college sports, that spelled doom – many feared that money earmarked for football would go to synchronized swimming. Caspar Weinberger, the HEW secretary, ignored those objections and forced through the regulations. King was delighted, but feared the Riggs match might endanger that progress. 'I was nervous that maybe they would go back on Title IX if I lost that match. I know how things can change very quickly. And I knew the hearts and minds of people weren't matching Title IX.'[41]

Feminists were split over the importance of Title IX. Many argued that women gained nothing by entering the macho world of sport. Competition implied adopting the worst attributes of men. The strength issue meant they would always come second. King profoundly disagreed. She believed that the benefits derived from athletic competition (both physical and emotional) were massively important to female self-esteem. In any case, competition could not be willed away simply because it contradicted the feminist world-view. A very practical feminist, she also argued that beauty and sex were important tools of communication. The first priority for women was to get noticed. 'Sex is part of it . . . And it works in promoting sports. It's not demeaning if it's done with taste. It's how attention works.' While her ideas annoyed many feminists, they accorded with public opinion. At a time when most people were inclined to see feminists as dangerous rebels on the margins of society, King was busily mainstreaming gender issues. She was more interested in doors being opened than abstract principles being upheld.[42]

She was not, however, universally loved. Tennis fans preferred the dignified Court, or the charming Chris Evert. King's outspoken nature and her relentless success seemed too masculine. This was especially true in 1971, when she became the first female player to make more than $100,000 in a single season. While that was a huge sign of progress for women in sports, the money nevertheless made it harder for her to complain about iniquities in women's tennis, even though male players still earned more. As her star rose, so too did her vulnerability.

King and Riggs both understood the difficulties of fighting the tennis establishment. She campaigned against its sexism; he had fought its class snobbery. That struggle gave him the reputation of a battler, which he used to good effect. After his retirement, he satisfied his addiction to competition with huckstering – the naive were lured into bets they couldn't possibly lose, but usually did. 'Ride down the road with him', a *Time* reporter related,

> and he may bet you $100 that you would not jump out of the car and turn a quick somersault. Hole up in a hotel room with him and he will invent a betting game that involves tossing tennis balls over a curtain rod. Ask him to play golf with a tennis racket and

> he will not only oblige but win. Show up at one of his tennis matches and he may line you up for a side bet. Want to play him yourself? What kind of handicap do you want? A wet Bulgarian bear riding on his shoulders? A felled yak strapped to his side? One foot cemented to the court?

After retiring, Riggs briefly managed 'Gorgeous Gussy' Moran, the Anna Kournikova of the 1950s, famous for her frilly panties. Riggs lined up the less comely Pauline Betz to provide competition, but she proved too talented. Spectators felt cheated when Gorgeous Gussy was beaten. Riggs offered Betz a bribe to quit the tour, but she refused. When Riggs took a razor to Gussy's panties, in an attempt to increase their allure, the arrangement went sour. Her objections convinced him that she did not really understand the point of women's tennis. As Riggs saw it, the women's game could not be profitable unless it was decorative. Spectators who wanted action would surely prefer men.[43]

In a lament crafted for every hard-luck misogynist, Riggs alleged that his wife, Priscilla, had deserted him after she had been 'turned' by feminism. 'She began reading books about Women's Lib, and she had liberal friends. I began to get all that stuff about "I want to discover who I am."' Like much of what Riggs said, the story was nine-tenths fabrication, designed for middle-aged male fans. As he boasted, 'I've got Bobby's battalions all over the country, the over-45 guys who want to see one of their own make it big.' Sexist lines like 'Women should keep their biscuits in the oven and their buns in the bed' had precisely the same effect. The real Riggs was probably not quite that sexist, but the real Riggs stayed indoors. Since he lived life as a game, he seldom felt the need to be serious. He was, one reporter decided, 'the most notorious, obstreperous and . . . obnoxious 55-year-old adolescent in the land'.[44]

Riggs 'was a middle-aged divorced man who knew nothing about women's liberation', his son John admitted. 'He was rather simple-minded when it came to politics and world issues.' While he cleverly couched his challenge to King as a swipe at feminism, it was, in truth, all about himself. He was an attention junkie uncomfortable with growing old. 'He wanted to be important again,' his son admits. To that end, he tried to defy the ageing process by hooking up with a Hollywood nutrition specialist. The prescribed programme involved 450 pills a day. Prior to the Court match, he also adhered to a rigid training regime which included jogging and playing tennis six hours each day.[45]

'Riggs is the Muhammad Ali of the Geritol set,' the promoter Jerry Perenchio boasted. 'The Ali–Frazier fight was "The Fight". This is "The Match".' Perenchio was himself a measure of just how big the match was, since 'small' did not exist in his vocabulary. The president of Tandem Productions, he had earlier been involved in the Ali–Frazier fight and was a producer of *All in the Family*, *Sanford and Son* and *Maude*, three of television's biggest sitcoms. Perenchio persuaded ABC and UPI to pay $750,000 for the TV rights, fifteen times what NBC paid to cover the 1973 Wimbledon championships. Advertising went for $50,000 a minute. The purse was $100,000, winner take all, plus $150,000 to each player in ancillary rights. King demanded a five set match, partly to make a point about female strength, but also in the hope that her stamina would tell. That delighted ABC, since it meant more airtime.[46]

'I've played Billie Jean a dozen times in my mind,' Riggs boasted. 'Nothing she can do will be unexpected.' He delighted in his self-assigned role as a one-man wrecking ball out to destroy the reputation of women's tennis. 'After Billie Jean', he bragged, 'it'll be hot-and-cold running women, it'll be the Super Bowl or Rose Bowl of tennis, the Riggs spectacular once a year – the best woman player of the year, that's the one who'll have to play Bobby Riggs.' That, of course, all depended on beating King, but Riggs was supremely confident. He sounded exactly like Muhammad Ali:

> Billie Jean King is one of the all-time tennis greats, she's one of the superstars, she's ready for the big one, but she doesn't stand a chance against me, women's tennis is so far beneath men's tennis, that's what makes the contest with a 55-year-old man the greatest

> contest of all time . . . You may want to ask me if I have a game plan for Billie Jean. I don't need a game plan. I'll let her start something and I'll finish it. I have such a vast assortment of tennis weapons in my arsenal that I can handle anything she can throw at me. I'll psych her out a little bit. I'm psyching her out already, she won't admit it but I can see her coming apart at the seams already . . . She'll choke just like Margaret did.

'I was terrified,' King later admitted. While Riggs had endless fun, she was engaged in a deadly contest – sadly, the most important she would ever face. 'My stomach would be going in knots. Just to think about it, it was like whoa, in the bottom pit of your stomach. Oh my God. I can't lose. I've got to win.' She later reflected: 'It was not about tennis. It was about social change. It was about changing a way of thinking, about getting women athletes accepted.' To her intense dismay, she discovered that her comrades on the women's circuit, while vigorously voicing support, were quietly placing bets on Riggs.[47]

Court had remained polite, returning Riggs's banter with a smile. King was incapable of composure. 'He's not going to jive me,' she spat. 'If he gets too dirty, I can get tough too.' She gave the public the grudge match it wanted – a genuine battle of the sexes. 'That creep runs down women. That's why my feeling is like – hate . . . I hate him for putting down women, not giving us credit.' That took Riggs by surprise; no one had ever taken him so seriously. 'Please don't call me a creep. You don't mean it.' 'Creep,' she replied.[48]

King prepared obsessively, combining intense physical training with lengthy strategy sessions. Riggs, in contrast, had fun. For two months he held court at a friend's Beverly Hills mansion, a sybarite's paradise with wall-to-wall women. 'Instant fame has done a lot to improve my social life,' he remarked with a lascivious grin.[49] The house had a tennis court, but Riggs used it mainly for photo shoots. 'From the time he beat Margaret, he didn't pick up a racket for four months,' his son confessed. 'I said, "Dad, we need to practice." It was always, "I need to do this interview," or that "I need to do that

TV show." I kept telling him, "Dad, you're going to get killed." He kept saying, "I know what I'm doing."'[50] As a journalist noted, 'There were too many blondes to squeeze, too many reporters to hustle, too many products to hawk.' His confidence meanwhile remained high. 'I don't need to practice for Billie Jean King. She's terrible. She's got no forehand. She slices the ball, and comes to the net; I'll lob over her head. No problem.'[51]

King, like Riggs, understood that tennis, despite the political importance of this match, was still entertainment. She realized that she needed to impress the enormous number of viewers who had never watched a match before. A special dress, full of sequins, was ordered from the famous designer Ted Tinling, and blue suede tennis shoes were custom made by Adidas. When Perenchio suggested that she be brought to the court on a Cleopatra-style litter, complete with huge orange and red feathers and a gold lamé throne, carried by six muscle-bound athletes, she surprised him by agreeing. 'It was lights, showtime, and glitter. I loved that stuff.'[52]

On 20 September 1973, 30,492 fans flooded into the Houston Astrodome to watch the libber face the lobber. No larger crowd had ever attended a tennis match. The television audience was estimated at 90 million, also a record. ABC rolled out its big gun, Howard Cosell, the sportscaster made famous for his verbal jousts with Muhammad Ali and his idiosyncratic commentary on *Monday Night Football.* King's friend Rosie Casals, hired to play the shrew, flanked him. 'The producers told me exactly what to say . . . They wanted me to play a certain role.' The former tennis professional Gene Scott was, in contrast, brought along to provide calm, masculine solidity.[53]

King arrived on her litter, while Riggs was brought in on a glittering red rickshaw, surrounded by his aptly named Bosom Buddies. As arranged by Perenchio, he presented her with a giant Sugar Daddy lollipop; she gave him a piglet. In a pre-match interview, Riggs boasted: 'I'm going to try to win for all the guys around the world who feel, as I do, that the male . . . is supreme.' King was more restrained, mentioning that she was well-prepared and that Riggs probably was not. 'He's been living a pretty fast life.'[54]

The pattern of the match was clear by the fourth game. King unleashed a ferocious backhand down the line that Riggs just managed to reach but couldn't possibly control. That one shot proved that King would not be intimidated. At 4–4 in the first set, Riggs looked doomed. He had depended upon overwhelming King psychologically, yet that wasn't happening. His tricks weren't working. He needed a lopsided victory, but got a brawl. While the score suggested an evenly fought match, Riggs lacked the stamina for a long struggle. Looking crestfallen, he started making unforced errors, something he had depended on King to do. Serving to stay in the match at 4–5, he double faulted on set point. Instead of rattling King's nerves, he was unravelling.

The rest of the match proved a fait accompli. Riggs tried desperately to hang on, but found himself trying to board a train already gathering speed. The second set followed the pattern of the first, with Riggs losing 6–3. Cosell was perplexed:

> Funny, going into the telecast, one couldn't be sure how to treat it. Would it be high humour? Well, of course it couldn't be all that because too many women in this country were taking this match seriously in the wake of all of Bobby's talk and in the way he victimized Margaret Court. But it would seem there would be a mixture, some antics on the court by Bobby. None of this has so far eventuated. It has not been a comic night for Bobby.

Riggs found the gap steadily widening. Down 2–4 in the third set, he took an injury break in a last act of desperation. He frantically munched vitamins, gulped water and, ever the promoter, unwrapped a Sugar Daddy. None of that helped. The final score was again 6–3. It was, as *Time* remarked, 'a mixed singles mismatch between one excellent tennis player in her prime and another champion pathetically past his. To make matters worse . . . the psycher seemed to become the psychee.'[55]

'I underestimated you,' Riggs whispered when they shook hands at the net. That was true, but also irrelevant. One can speculate on what a fit Riggs, prepared as he had been for the Court match, might have achieved. But he wasn't fit, for the simple reason that it hadn't seemed necessary. 'It was like Bobby finally realized that the final exam was here and he hadn't studied for it,' his friend Lornie Kuhle remarked. Hubris had defeated him. That attribute was as relevant as his forehand or serve, since this was not just a contest between two tennis players, but between two agendas. His lack of preparation was typically male, a manifestation of his sense of entitlement As his son admitted: 'Bobby was perfect, perfect for Billie Jean King . . . The guy was a bigmouth and put his foot in it . . . Wouldn't train. Wouldn't work out. Overconfident. Played her in her backyard with her own balls, her own court. The idiot just stepped right into her trap.'[56]

Sports Illustrated captured the gravity of what had happened: 'What in the world kind of occasion was this in which the woman not only defeated the man but swamped him: outplayed and beat the living bejeezus out of him as well? Perhaps it was something like life. Or death.' 'How did Bobby play?' King was asked. 'He played like a woman – like a lot of the women I've beaten on tour.' For his part, Riggs had the good grace to turn off the hype: 'She was too good. She played too well. She was playing well within herself, and I couldn't get the most out of my game. It was over too quickly.'[57]

The match was a snapshot of the times. As *Time* commented: 'Five years ago these superheated matches could not have happened, and five years from now they would not mean anything.' So much of America was condensed into a single night at the Astrodome. Serious politics danced with garish spectacle. But, as the pragmatic King understood, the hype was essential because it drew attention to an important point. Glamour provided an exclamation point at the end of a sentence describing how the world had changed. 'What began as a huckster's hustle in defiance of serious athleticism', wrote Curry Kirkpatrick in *Sports Illustrated*, 'ended up not mocking the game of tennis but honoring it. This night King was both a shining piece of show biz and the essence of what sport is all about.'[58]

Donna de Varona, the Olympic swimming champion turned sports commentator, agreed: 'The guy was older and was this and that, but the truth is, it was a worldwide movement that needed a finishing sentence. And Billie Jean King gave it to us.' That took immense courage. Riggs could walk away having lost nothing, except perhaps the big paycheck he would have earned from playing Evert. King, however, had so much more at stake. 'You felt this was a symbolic match that was going to be used against women and to humiliate them if Billie Jean lost,' the feminist Gloria Steinem remarked. 'And for her to take that on, to put herself under that pressure, is the true meaning of heroism.' King's most important match was not about tennis at all. 'This was about history,' she remarked, 'getting us on to a more level playing field . . . all that was very close to my heart.' Reflecting on the match thirty years later, she found that the importance had not faded: 'The little boys that were watching, that are in their 40s now and early 50s, I call them the first generation of men of the women's movement. I can't tell you how many men have come up to me to tell me: "Billie, that match changed my life." These men are the first to insist that their daughters and sons have equal opportunities, and that's amazing.'[59]

Reykjavik: Fischer vs Spassky

According to the KGB, Bobby Fischer was a psychopath. Though that might have been an exaggeration, he was certainly mentally unstable, his psychosis contained by the sixty-four squares on a chess-board. Competitive chess, in other words, kept him sane. When he quit playing, madness descended. For a brief period in 1972, however, his mental instability proved useful to his country. Fischer became a Cold War hero.

He played like an assassin, combining cold logic with ruthless brutality. 'Chess is war over the board,' he once said. 'The object is to crush the opponent's mind.' He achieved this by scorning predictability – the unwritten rules of competitive chess were contemptuously broken. While opponents played for safe draws, he ferociously attacked, usually to good effect. At the board, he oozed disrespect, playing as if his opponent did not exist. 'I like the moment when I break a man's ego,' he sneered. Gary Kasparov called him a chess centaur – part human, part the very elements of the game. 'A loss to Fischer', wrote the *New York Times*, 'somehow diminishes a player. Part of him has been eaten, and he is that much less of a whole man.'[60]

Fischer's peculiar behaviour suggests a congenital disorder. At various times, he seemed a schizophrenic, a sociopath, or an autistic savant. Then again, his condition might have been acquired – he might have been driven mad. His neglectful mother, Regina, put her responsibility for saving the world above that of caring for her son. She was a communist and a Jew, characteristics enormously significant to her son's emotional development. His legal father was Hans-Gerhardt Fischer, a German biophysicist who abandoned his family before Bobby was born. His actual father was probably Paul Felix Nemenyi, a Hungarian Jewish physicist with whom Regina had an affair in 1942.

Nemenyi's probable parentage is ironic given Fischer's virulent anti-Semitism. He lived his life in revolt against his mother, particularly her Jewish roots and socialist politics. Indeed, his two hatreds – of communism and of Jews – eventually fused when he came to the conclusion that both were conspiring to take over the world. Soviet communism, he claimed, was 'basically a mask for Bolshevism, which is a mask for Judaism'.[61]

In 1949, at the age of six, Fischer was given a cheap chessboard bought from a corner shop. He taught himself to play, and before long his obsession with the game crowded out all other aspects of his life. He performed poorly at school, probably because he did not see the point of anything other than chess. When a psychiatrist was consulted about this obsession, Regina was told that her son seemed perfectly normal. At the age of seven Bobby joined the Brooklyn Chess Club, immediately finding that only the most gifted adult players could challenge him. He later moved to the Manhattan Chess Club, one of the best in the world, where the master John Collins briefly provided a fatherly influence. His effect on Fischer's game was, however, limited, since the young prodigy was already in a different orbit. 'Nobody taught Bobby,' Collins later admitted. 'Geniuses, like Beethoven, Shakespeare and Fischer come out of the head of Zeus . . . they seem to be genetically programmed, know before instructed.'[62]

At the age of thirteen came a quantum leap in ability, what Fischer called the moment he 'just got good'. In the Rosenwald Memorial Tournament, he beat the highly respected Donald Byrne, thirteen years his elder. *Chess Review* called it 'The Game of the Century'. Experts drooled over the unique fusion of relentless aggression and poetic grace. 'While we have learned to distrust superlatives, this is one game that deserves all the praise lavished on it,' wrote Fred Reinfeld. When word reached the Soviet Union, the reigning world champion Mikhail Botvinnik remarked: 'We will have to start keeping an eye on this boy.'[63]

By fourteen, he was US national champion, and a year later he became the youngest grandmaster in history. He continued attending school, but otherwise spent most of his time in the New York Public Library reading about chess. In 1959 he dropped out of school. 'All I want to do, ever, is play chess,' he explained. The deeper he became involved, the further he distanced himself from his mother. By 1962, he was living on his own, his mother preoccupied with her own obsession, a love affair with Russia.[64]

At the time of Fischer's emergence, thirty-three of the eighty-eight grandmasters were from the USSR, as had been every world champion since 1937. For the Soviets, chess was a sublime expression of revolutionary spirit – a contest which demanded iron determination, self-discipline and cold rationality. It was, according to Vasilyevich Krylenko, creator of the Red Army, 'a political weapon in the proletarian revolution'. Young prodigies were carefully groomed by grandmasters. Successful players became symbols of national pride and were given the sort of perks – high salaries, luxurious dachas, automobiles, food and clothing – usually reserved for atomic scientists, cosmonauts or senior military commanders.[65]

In the Soviet system, the team, not the individual, mattered. In tournaments, members cooperated to help a predetermined leader, rather like cyclists in the Tour de France. During the preliminary stages, they would erode the strength of outside challengers with long gruelling matches, in order to make life easier for their leader when he reached the final. Fischer, the lonely American, entered this milieu a solitary warrior fighting an entire army. He quickly grew disenchanted at having to endure a punishing sequence of contests, only to find a hand-picked champion waiting in the final, his strength still fresh because of matches arranged in his favour. To complain was to violate chess etiquette, yet complain Fischer did. 'The Russians have fixed world chess,' he told *Sports Illustrated* in 1962. His virulent hatred of communism was magnified by having to witness its cynical power first-hand. Individually, he insisted, 'they have nothing on me, those guys. They can't even touch me.' The Soviets in turn dismissed Fischer as *nyekulturni* – 'uncultured'. That criticism was appropriate, but so, too, was Fischer's complaint. Grandmasters from outside the USSR had long been aware of Soviet tactics, but to complain about the situation was like lying down in front of a Red Army tank.[66]

Despite his growing disillusionment, Fischer managed to carve a nice life for himself as a professional. Within his little world, he was a star. He did not, however, feel that his income matched his status. It seemed unfair that, despite being one of the best in the world at his game, he did not earn the kind of money champions in mainstream sports earned. Fischer wanted things: a Rolls-Royce, fancy clothes, a yacht, a private jet. He fantasized about owning a castle built to look exactly like a rook. When organizers refused his demands for more money, he grew increasingly bitter, and occasionally boycotted tournaments. 'Bobby . . . wanted money because to him it meant that people thought he was important,' the grandmaster Arnold Denker felt.[67]

A titan at the chessboard, Fischer was an emotionally stunted child away from it. 'If you were out to dinner with Bobby in the sixties, he wouldn't be able to follow the conversation,' a former friend remarked. 'He would have his little pocket set out and he'd play chess at the table. He had a one-dimensional outlook on life.' Holed up in his apartment, he would play chess matches with himself that lasted for days. A board next to his bed meant that chess was his last act at night, his first in the morning. When a journalist asked how he spent his time away from the board, he replied: 'There's really nothing for me to do. Maybe I'll study some chess books.' Aware of his social inadequacies, he grew ever more inclined to hide among chess pieces. 'Away from the board, Bobby suffered from a terrible inferiority complex,' Allan Kaufman, one-time director of the American Chess Foundation, recalled. 'In his mind he concocted lots of excuses: people were taking advantage of him; they were smarter than he was; if he had only had their education . . .'[68]

A tournament in Curaçao in 1962 reinforced his paranoia. After a series of gruelling round-robin matches, Fischer lost to Tigran Petrosian, chosen one of the Soviet team, and eventually finished a disappointing fourth. 'I'll never play in one of those rigged tournaments again,' Fischer spat. '[The Soviets] clobber us easy in team play. But man to man, I'd take Petrosian on any time.' Many years later, Nikolai Krogius, a Soviet grandmaster, admitted that Fischer's complaints were valid. 'There were some agreed draws at Curaçao.' But the American player Arthur Bisguier, who accompanied Fischer to Curaçao, thought his complaints 'absurd . . . just sour grapes'. During that trip, Bisguier witnessed Fischer passing time by systematically torturing insects. 'There were other things of this sort. And it was scary. If he wasn't a chess player, he might have been a dangerous psychopath.' Fischer's erratic behaviour also attracted the attention of the State Department, with questions raised about his suitability as a representative of America abroad.[69]

Angered by the Curaçao 'fix', Fischer retired from top-flight chess, switching to domestic events that he naturally dominated. His income plummeted, to the extent that he eventually took refuge at the YMCA. Removed from the controlled atmosphere of top-flight chess, he had time to indulge his delusions. His anti-Semitism grew more overt. 'There are too many Jews in chess,' he told *Harpers* magazine. 'They seem to have taken away the class of the game.' Late at night, according to Denker, he 'prowl[ed] parking lots, slipping white-supremacist pamphlets under windshield wipers'. He read *Mein Kampf, The Protocols of the Elders of Zion*, and other anti-Semitic texts. A one-time friend recalls accompanying Fischer to a documentary about Adolf Hitler. Afterwards, 'Bobby said that he admired Hitler. I asked him why, and he said, "Because he imposed his will on the world."'[70]

Fischer returned to top-flight chess in 1966, played with erratic brilliance for about two years, and then left again in a huff. The decision by FIDE, the governing body of chess, to change the format of championships from round robin to knockout eventually tempted the star out of exile. He displayed no ill-effects from his absence, sailing through the qualifying stages of the 1972 world championship, and at one stage winning a world record nineteen games in a row, a feat that brought personal congratulation from Richard Nixon. Ahead of him was a showdown with Boris Spassky, superman of Soviet chess and reigning world champion.

The 'clash of titans' caused the world's press to run short on hyperbole. Instead of a boring match between two Russians, the world would see the Cold War acted out on the chessboard, with ivory pieces becoming bombers and battleships. Fischer's virulent anti-communism suddenly found perfect validation. 'It is really the free world against the lying, cheating, hypocritical Russians,' he said. 'This little thing between Spassky and me. It's a microcosm of the whole world political situation.' For most Americans, those words were melody, the perfect expression of patriotism. But far from expressing love of country, Fischer was simply exercising the demons lurking inside his twisted mind.[71]

Fischer wanted the match to be played in Yugoslavia; Spassky preferred Iceland. Round one in the battle of wills went to the Russian when Reykjavik was selected. Fischer then threatened to pull out, on the grounds that the prize money of $125,000 seemed an insult. The contest tottered on the brink of collapse until the British chess enthusiast James Slater doubled the purse. Slater effectively challenged Fischer: 'If he isn't afraid of Spassky, then I have removed the element of money.' Further pressure was applied by Henry

Kissinger, who took time out from his troubles in Southeast Asia to remind Fischer of his duty. 'This is the worst player in the world calling the best player in the world,' Kissinger told Fischer. 'America wants you to go over there and beat the Russians.' 'I told Fischer to get his butt over to Iceland,' Kissinger subsequently boasted. Fischer, however, later maintained that Kissinger's pressure had no effect – he supposedly refused to take his call.[72]

The championship seemed to bring together two perfect archetypes. Spassky, a quiet, urbane intellectual, was presented as the product of a system – the exemplar of the Soviet communal approach. Fischer, on the other hand, was the rugged individualist, the self-made man. These caricatures delighted promoters and television producers alike, but were, in truth, mere spin. Fischer, driven by hate, cared only for himself. 'I am only interested in chess and money,' he confessed. Spassky, on the other hand, was a decent man who found himself in a cockfight. Neither blind patriot nor doctrinal communist, he was simply a brilliant chess player who wanted the world championship to be a sublime contest between two chess-masters, not some fundamentalist brawl.[73]

'Getting President Nixon and Mr Brezhnev together', remarked the *Guardian*, 'was child's play compared with the Fischer–Spassky chess summit.' After the wrangle over money was settled, Fischer fired complaints at tournament organizers like a mad sniper spraying bullets. The board was too shiny, the chairs too hard, the lights too bright, the cameras too close, the knight's nose too long. For a while, it seemed that the championship would crumble under this fusillade of complaint. Then, quite unexpectedly, the match began and Fischer, clearly unsettled, made a series of stupid moves, gifting Spassky a win.[74]

Another torrent of complaints followed, most of them pertaining to television cameras and intrusive spectators. Keen to impose his will upon the tournament, Fischer refused to play the second game unless his demands were met. To his surprise, the organizers ignored him, granting Spassky a win by forfeit. Pundits speculated that Fischer was playing a clever psychological game, designed to unsettle his opponent. 'I don't believe in psychology,' he countered. 'I believe in good moves.' That might have been true, but very few good moves had so far been played. If this was indeed a psychological gambit it was a very risky one, since Fischer was already down 2–0 against the best player in the world. The novelist Arthur Koestler, in Reykjavik to cover the match, coined the term 'mimophant' to describe Fischer. 'A mimophant is a hybrid species: a cross between a mimosa and an elephant. A member of this species is sensitive like a mimosa where his own feelings are concerned and thick-skinned like an elephant trampling over the feelings of others.'[75]

Keen to placate Fischer, Spassky consented to playing the next game behind closed doors. The Russian was flustered, evidence perhaps that Fischer's antics were wearing him down. Fischer won relatively easily, after which the match was moved back into the auditorium. Though the complaints did not stop, order had nevertheless been restored, with the result that the main news now concerned movements on the board. The world was captivated. In America, televised matches on PBS attracted the largest audiences the public network had ever enjoyed. A surprising proportion of the viewers were not chess players.

The *Daily Mail* called it 'SPASSKY SMASHKI'. With Fischer now winning, the Soviets took over the production of histrionics. Fischer, it was alleged, was being coached through a miniature radio receiver. Another variation on that theme came when it was claimed that the Americans were bombarding the room with radio impulses in order to scramble Spassky's brainwaves. The room was swept for bugs and the furniture X-rayed, but all that was found were two dead flies in a light fitting. A sample of Spassky's orange juice was sent to the Soviet Union to be tested for poisons. At one point a Soviet official circled the dais with an open plastic bag which was then carefully sealed, labelled 'air from stage' and sent for analysis.[76]

The sixth game was beautiful. Afficionados compared it to a classical symphony. Replay it today and even the novice can notice something decidedly strange. The game was supposed to pit two near-equals, but Spassky clearly seems at sea, while Fischer is in complete control, launching raid after audacious raid into the heart of the Russian's defence. Ripped to shreds, the gentleman Spassky acknowledged the presence of genius and graciously joined in the applause at the end of the match. Fischer, feeling decidedly uncomfortable, rushed from the room, unable to handle kindness from a man he needed to despise.

After that pivotal game, the outcome was inevitable. The Soviet fortress could do nothing to stop the American juggernaut. Fischer grew ever more confident and contemptuous. When one game was adjourned with Spassky in a seemingly unassailable position, Fischer's helper, Bill Lombardy, suggested that they meet back at the hotel to analyse possibilities for an escape. 'What do you mean, analyze,' Fisher spat. 'That guy's a fish. Let's go bowling.'[77]

Fischer won 12½–8½, a score that does not adequately reflect how comprehensively Spassky had been beaten. The Soviets were dumbfounded, unable to explain why the 'psychopath' had won. Dark allegations of dirty tricks were muttered. 'How come you yielded the crown to an American?' a suspicious interior minister asked the head KGB man in Reykjavik, Colonel Baturinsky. 'If I had my way, everyone who was . . . with Spassky would have been arrested.' A delighted Fischer confessed that he never thought 'there would come a day when chess would become headline news in our country and produce only a small comment in Pravda.' He readily offered a remark calculated to please American propagandists. 'The Russians had it all for 20 years. They talked of their military might and their intellectual might . . . It's given me great pleasure . . . as a free person . . . to have smashed this thing.' To believe that, however, required ignoring Fischer's massive character faults. As one correspondent to the *Washington Post* wrote: 'Fischer is the only American who can make everyone in the US root for the Russians.' In the closing ceremony in Reykjavik, he refused to thank his hosts or say kind words about his opponent. Instead, he tore open the envelope containing his winner's cheque, keen to make sure that the amount was correct.[78]

Fischer returned home a conquering hero, a man who, like Mark Spitz that same year, had demonstrated the superiority of the

American system. With defeat looming in Vietnam, the match provided a boost to battered American pride. America was suddenly in love with Bobby Fischer – and chess. He was flooded with lucrative product endorsement offers and invitations to talk shows. Women swooned over an oxymoron – a chess player with sex appeal. Fischer, however, grew increasingly uneasy, perhaps realizing how shallow was American love. 'The creeps are beginning to gather,' he complained. When Nixon invited him to the White House, Fischer declined. He refused, he told friends, 'because I found out that they wouldn't pay me anything for this visit'. Later, after the fog of madness descended, he complained: 'I was never invited to the White House . . . They invited that Olympic Russian gymnast – that little Communist, Olga Korbut.'[79]

Botvinnik once remarked that 'chess is an art which illustrates the beauty of logic'. In that sense, the game makes an imperfect metaphor for real life, which is neither beautiful nor logical. Chess has defined boundaries and strict rules; life does not. Once Fischer moved away from the board, he found himself checkmated by the capriciousness of his world and the instability of his psyche. Champion quickly morphed into madman and America's love dissolved.[80]

He retreated into the safe cloisters of the Worldwide Church of God, substituting fundamentalist religion for the certainties of chess. But the church was more interested in Fischer as poster boy than worshipper. They rewarded his celebrity with access to a private jet, a luxury apartment and fancy dinners, but the perks made it harder for Fischer to keep ugliness at bay. He'd craved escape from the creeps, but found creepiness multiplying exponentially. In 1977, he formally broke with the church, claiming that it was the tool of a 'satanical secret world government'. He later complained about being fleeced. He was referring specifically to money, but also felt that his soul had been stripped.[81]

The world chess champion became a hermit who had foresaken the game. FIDE found a challenger for the 1975 championship in the form of another Russian, Anatoly Karpov. Fischer, however, refused to play, dismissing the entire Russian team as 'the lowest dogs around'. Karpov consequently became champion by default. Those close to Fischer (and they were a diminishing number) desperately sought explanation for the forfeiture. 'Bobby was always afraid of losing,' Denker decided. 'I don't know why, but he was. The fear was in him.' Shelby Lyman felt that the explanation lay in Fischer's need to preserve unsullied a sublime moment in Reykjavik when he had single-handedly destroyed the Soviet chess machine. 'Hating to lose, and having the myth destroyed', Lyman felt, 'was a big part of him not playing.' Karpov offered his own explanation: 'I don't want to claim that Fischer was afraid of me. Most probably he was afraid of himself. He believed that the world champion has no right to make mistakes. But with such a belief you can't play chess, because you can't avoid mistakes.' In truth, however, it is probably futile to try to provide rational explanation for reasoning warped by paranoia, fear and hate.[82]

His income dwindling, he moved into seedy hotels, an existence suited to the hermit he wanted to be. He complained that dark forces were trying to pollute his precious bodily fluids and became a fanatical consumer of quack potions, which he kept in a locked case that never left his side. 'If the Commies come to poison me, I don't want to make it easy for them,' he explained. Each bizarre act was quickly trumped by behaviour even weirder. At one point, he had the fillings in his teeth removed, explaining, 'If somebody took a filling out and put in an electronic device, he could influence your thinking . . . I don't want anything artificial in my head.'[83]

Reporters who managed to contact Fischer discovered a man more interested in Jewish 'perfidy' than chess. Jews, he claimed, were kidnapping Christian children and using their blood for satanic rites. The Holocaust was invented to make Jews filthy rich. Jews were cheating him out of book royalties and stealing his patents. A reporter who tried to talk chess was told: 'We might as well get to the heart of the matter and then we can come back to chitchat . . . What is going on is that I am being persecuted night and day by the Jews!' Chess was dismissed as 'mental masturbation'. To the horror of his devoted fans, who still craved a god, he announced: 'Not only is the game dead, it's fixed.'[84]

A gaggle of Seventies tyrants, coveting the publicity a match would bring to their vile regimes, tried to lure Fischer out of retirement. Offers from Augusto Pinochet, the Shah of Iran and Ferdinand Marcos were all rejected. When a millionaire Francoist offered the unimaginable sum of $4 million for a match in Spain, Fischer scorned it as too little. Instead, he made ends meet by selling his celebrity like a street-corner hooker. A couple of thousand dollars could buy an hour on the phone with Bobby Fischer. A game cost $10,000. Fischer became the perfect gift for the person who had everything. Bob Dylan got an hour with the master as a gift from his manager.

In 1992, he agreed to a rematch with Spassky for the sum of $5 million. He won easily but incurred the wrath of the State Department by agreeing to play in Serbia. He became a fugitive from the law, a status perfectly suited to his persecution complex. Along with Jews and communists, Fischer now despised his native land. When Islamic terrorists attacked the World Trade Center on 11 September 2001, Fischer remarked: 'This is all wonderful news. I applaud the act. The U.S. and Israel have been slaughtering the Palestinians, just slaughtering them for years . . . Fuck the U.S. I want to see the U.S. wiped out . . . Death to the U.S.!'[85]

As the tirade continued, it became clear that the issue was not Palestine, Jews, or America, but Bobby Fischer. 'Nobody has single-handedly done more for the U.S. than me,' he spat. 'When I won the world championship, in 1972, the United States had an image of, you know, a football country, a baseball country, but nobody thought of it as an intellectual country. I turned all that around single-handedly . . . But I was useful then because there was the Cold War, right? But now I'm not useful anymore. You see, the Cold War is over and now they want to wipe me out, steal everything I have, and put me in prison.' The inclination to dismiss that statement as sheer lunacy is blocked by the bothersome germ of truth that lurks within.

Silicon Valley: Pong

'Entertainment has become a necessity,' proclaimed the *Annual Report* of Warner Communications in 1977. While that was a blatantly self-serving statement, it was inescapably true. Animal behaviourists have speculated that the otter's remarkable playfulness might arise from the fact that it does not have to spend every waking minute in search of food. The same can be said of humans, another species with a surplus of spare time. As Warner added: 'Having allowed technology to create the problem, man has begun using technology to redress it.' No wonder, then, that the computer's first direct intrusion into the lives of ordinary people came in the form of a game.[86]

Enter Nolan Bushnell – the perfect computer revolutionary. The new industry craved youth, and he was appropriately young. He also had a natural gift for electronics and the instincts of an explorer. While that suggests a typical computer nerd, Bushnell was not a typical member of the nerd-ocracy. What set him apart was business acumen – he was a natural entrepreneur who started in management at the age of fifteen when he was left to run the family business due to his father's death. 'It was extremely hard', he confessed, 'all of a sudden going from childhood to adulthood in 24 hours.'[87]

Bill Gates and Steve Jobs are credited with bringing computers to the masses. But their revolution did not take hold until the 1980s. The person who first put ordinary people in front of computers was Bushnell, through a rather simple game called Pong. His computer could do only one thing, but was no less remarkable for that limitation. Pong was the first successful venture in an industry that would eventually transform entertainment. Fifteen years after its arrival, Americans would spend more on Space Invaders than they spent on space exploration.

The idea originated in 1958 when Walter Higinbotham, a physicist and veteran of the Manhattan Project, was searching for a gimmick to spice up the annual open house at Brookhaven National Laboratory. He programmed a small analogue computer to graph the trajectory of a moving sphere, which was then displayed on an oscilloscope. The device, called 'Tennis for Two', proved a huge hit, with visitors paying little attention to other exhibits. An improved version was unveiled the following year, to even greater acclaim. Unlike Bushnell, however, Higinbotham was not an entrepreneur. To him, the game was too simple to be special. He neglected to patent it, and, by 1960, had moved on to other things.

The games bug then spread to MIT, where boffins developed a tennis simulation, an electronic maze, and a computerized version of Tic-Tac-Toe. The arrival of a brand new Digital Equipment Corporation PDP-1 magnified their ambition. Three members of the self-proclaimed Tech Model Railway Club – Wayne Witanen, J. Martin Graetz and Steve Russell – teamed up to develop Spacewar. 'We had this brand new PDP-1,' Russell recalls. 'It was the first minicomputer, ridiculously inexpensive for its time. And it was just sitting there . . . the obvious thing to do was spaceships.'[88]

Their game, featuring two spaceships in deadly battle, was unveiled at the 1962 MIT Open House. Like Tennis for Two, it was a huge hit. Witanen, Graetz and Russell refused to patent the invention, however, since to do so violated the nerd's moral code, which stipulated that ideas must be shared, to ensure development. In any case, Spacewar did not seem marketable, since it required a 'micro' computer the size of three refrigerators, which cost $120,000. Instead, the program was circulated around tech labs via ARPAnet, the precursor of the Internet. Hackers – as they proudly dubbed themselves – would improve the program and then pass it on. Before long, an electrical engineer at MIT developed an easy way of manoeuvring the spaceships with a device he called a joystick. 'The first few years of Spacewar at MIT were the best,' industry journalist Albert Kuhfeld reflected in 1971. 'The game was in a rough state, students were working their hearts out improving it, and the faculty was nodding benignly . . . The students [were] learning computer theory faster and more painlessly than they'd ever seen before.'[89]

Hackers might not have understood the consumer potential of their work, but Ralph Baer, a television engineer, did. In the early

1950s, he began thinking about how viewers might interact with television, instead of passively watching. His employers, however, pooh-poohed the idea, forcing Baer to confine his musings to his spare time. In 1966, he devised a single-purpose 'computer' which could be connected to a standard television set, allowing the viewer to play simulated ball games. Certain that his device would be compact and affordable enough for the general public, Baer applied for the first patent for a video game in 1968.

The major television manufacturers were at first sceptical. In 1971, however, Bill Benders, previously of RCA, joined Magnavox. He had witnessed a demonstration of Baer's toy at a trade fair and decided to gamble. Baer had originally envisaged a simple system retailing for around $20, in which two players manipulating controls would propel a ball around a TV screen. The games could be changed by placing mylar overlays on the screen, thus transforming the 'playing field' from tennis court to hockey pitch, etc. Magnavox called the game Odyssey, added scorecards, dice, playing cards, play money and a fancy box, and slapped on a price tag of $100.

Promoted by Frank Sinatra, the game did reasonably well in its first year, selling 100,000 units nationwide. Sales were, however, limited by the common assumption that a Magnavox television set was essential - a misconception the manufacturer encouraged. Sales declined drastically after the first year, but big money was still earned in licence fees and legal penalties imposed on firms that plagiarized the technology.

One such pirate was Bushnell. In 1962, he was studying electrical engineering at the University of Utah, while also selling advertising. Finding he still had some spare time, he took an evening job at an amusement park, where he learned the gaming industry. Before long, he started a business selling equipment for fairground games. 'It was kind of like an MBA, on-the-job training,' he recalled. His dream was to combine his knowledge of amusement parks with his computer expertise and work for Disneyland, but that never happened.[90]

The university had a PDP-1, which allowed Bushnell to play

Spacewar, an experience more formative than his actual studies. After leaving university, he embarked on a quest to adapt the concept onto a platform affordable as an arcade game. The big problem was not the technology, but attracting the financial backing. Investors seemed unaware that the computer age had arrived.

> You'd go to these . . . multimedia conferences. And they'd say, 'What's the killer app?' And I'd say: 'Guys, the killer app for multimedia is games . . .' And then they'd say: 'But what's really going to be important?' . . . People would look at you like you had three heads. 'You mean you're going to put the TV set in a box with a coin slot and play games on it? Oh, and then you're going to have people hook them up to their own TV set? Oh, I don't think so.'

Stifled by this lack of imagination, Bushnell took a job at Ampex, the company that invented videotape, in Sunnyvale, California. In his spare time he perfected his version of Spacewar, with help from his Ampex colleague Ted Dabney. A breakthrough came when he discovered how to translate a game designed for an expensive computer onto discreet logic chips assembled on a circuit board. This meant that the 'computer' would have just one task and therefore needed relatively simple circuitry. That logic had not previously occurred to computer engineers, who wanted machines that could do more, not less.[91]

Bushnell sold his device to Nutting Associates, an arcade game specialist, who called it Computer Space. Effectively the first coin-operated computer game, designed for bars and arcades, it was unveiled at a Chicago trade fair in 1971, to a lukewarm reception. This lack of enthusiasm was partly due to the fact that buyers had never seen a video game before, but was mainly caused by the game's complexity. Since the directions ran to a few pages and there were too many controls, it seemed beyond the capacity of the average bar-room customer.

Despite the failure of Computer Space, Nutting remained keen on Bushnell. In May 1972, they sent him to a trade show in

Burlingame, where Odyssey was unveiled. Though generally unimpressed, Bushnell was mildly charmed by the tennis game. His relations with Nutting subsequently broke down, however, convincing him to go it alone. He also left Ampex, taking Dabney with him. Both staked $500 in a new company called Syzygy, after the astronomical phenomenon in which the sun, moon and earth are in perfect alignment. That mouthful was jettisoned when Bushnell discovered that some hippies marketing candles had already claimed it. Syzygy became Atari, after a move in the Japanese board game Go.

Bushnell originally wanted Atari's first venture to be a game of similar complexity to Computer Space. In the meantime, however, he assigned Al Alcorn, an engineer poached from Ampex who was new to video games, a simple task, namely the tennis game witnessed at the Odyssey demonstration. That was technically product theft, but Bushnell wasn't worried. 'He figured we'd rip off the idea . . . but so what?' Alcorn recalls. 'It's no good, we're not going to sell it, we'll throw it away, so what harm is there, right?'[92]

Designing the game was easy. The difficulty lay in the detail, for instance showing the score on the screen, and adding sound. Bushnell wanted the roar of a crowd when a score occurred, but that proved too complex. Alcorn instead stuck with simple computer sounds that were already available and have since become iconic. He also added a speed function to make the ball gain pace, so that the game wouldn't become too easy. 'One of my lessons learned, is that if you can't fix it, call it a feature,' Alcorn reflected. 'The paddles on the original . . . didn't go all the way to the top. There was a defect in the [circuit] . . . I could have fixed it, but it turned out to be important, because if you get two good players they could just . . . play the game forever. And the game has to end in about three or four minutes otherwise it's a failure . . . So that gap at the top, again – a feature.'[93]

Within just three months, Alcorn created a beautifully simple and hopelessly addictive game. Bushnell was delighted. He put it in a wooden box, added a coin-operating facility, and called the game 'Pong' in imitation of its sound. In contrast to Computer Space,

Pong had six simple words of instruction: 'Avoid missing ball for high score'. The game was placed in Andy Capp's Tavern in Sunnyvale on 29 November 1972. Within a few days, the tavern manager phoned to report that the device had broken down. Bushnell investigated and found that the fault lay in the coin box which had overflowed with quarters.

That jammed coin box convinced Alcorn that a new age had dawned. 'When we first put it in I said, "Nolan, what if it's a good game, how will we know?" He said, "If it makes one hundred dollars a week that would be great." Well, it made that within the first two or three days.' In a stroke, they had created a new leisure pursuit and, arguably, a new addiction. 'It was sheer luck!' Alcorn feels. 'It was not like "Oh yeah, we're going to start a whole new industry."' He was flabbergasted: 'I mean, we're all 24 years old and have a tiger by the tail . . . We had no management experience, no business experience, we were just engineers, picking it up as we went along. To me personally, coming out of Berkeley in the 60s . . . I had no aspirations of being a capitalist pig or anything, but this was . . . fun.'[94]

Bushnell originally intended to sell the game to an established arcade game manufacturer. On the strength of that test run, however, he decided to do the manufacturing himself. He turned an old roller rink in Santa Clara into a factory and, within a year, sold 2,500 machines. Even though Pong was so much simpler than pinball machines already on the market, it seemed sophisticated and modern because it was electronic. That made it a huge hit in bars catering to students.

Pong's strength was also its weakness; its simplicity made it easy to imitate. Bushnell could not prevent interlopers from invading his market, and they often had better production capacity. Since the basic technology was easily adapted to different game formats, scores of versions were soon available. Adding to Bushnell's woes, Magnavox noticed the similarity to Odyssey. They sued, and Atari settled out of court, paying Magnavox $700,000.

Bushnell made huge mistakes, but still managed to make a living. Even though imitators poached his ideas, the market was big enough to accommodate a lot of manufacturers. Competitors could out-produce him, but he could out-develop them – they had the muscle, he the brains. Among the brains he hired was Steve Jobs, who, after hours, would sneak his friend Steve Wozniak into the factory to play the new games. Jobs tried to persuade Bushnell to enter the home computer market, but he declined. Before long, Jobs quit Atari and incorporated the lessons he had learned designing software and creating visually pleasing formats into his new company, Apple Computers, formed with Wozniak.

Production problems caused Atari to teeter on the edge of bankruptcy until 1975, with new games like Tank! and Breakout providing only brief rescue. A lifeline was thrown when the consumer giant Sears agreed to distribute Pong for the home market. The idea had earlier been offered to a number of big television manufacturers, but they were put off by the limited success of Odyssey. Tom Quinn, the buyer at Sears, initially ordered 50,000 units, but then increased that to 150,000 in time for Christmas 1975. The deal grossed $40 million in sales, with Atari earning $3 million. '[Sears] paid the bills, did all the advertising,' Alcorn recalled. 'It was the best thing that ever happened to us.'[95]

That success caught the attention of Time Warner, who bought the company in 1977 for $26 million. The original management team was left intact but, according to Alcorn, 'all creativity . . . ceased'. Alcorn grew disenchanted when the 'East Coast, effete intellectual people' took over. Fear of failure stifled imagination. 'They weren't Silicon Valley, they weren't start-up guys, they were not risk takers – so nothing came out!' Bushnell instinctively understood that imagination and a sense of adventure were essential in the computer business – be it in games, software or hardware. Since Time Warner lacked those qualities, before long Atari withered. Bushnell felt that the problem was a lack of vision:

> . . . no product looks like it's going to be a billion-dollar seller when you first enter the market. If you say, we're only going to market products that will sell $20 million or above, a lot of products

> don't look like that . . . So, [Time Warner] essentially wouldn't let anything out of the lab that didn't match an unrealistic hurdle rate. And so, as a result . . . if you're not introducing new stuff, you die. You wither. And it was really sad to see it.

Long before the demise, he jumped ship, a very rich man. He went on to found Chuck E. Cheese, one of the pioneers in the new field of entertainment restaurants designed for families.[96]

Meanwhile, the computer game industry took off, with fifty-three separate games released by fifteen companies in 1976. The growth was fuelled by Japanese manufacturers, who benefited from a huge demand in their home market. Japan's obsession with video games came close to an epidemic. The release of Space Invaders by Taito in 1978 virtually caused riots across Japan and saddled the Japanese Treasury with a brief shortage of coins. Distributed under licence by Midway, Space Invaders had only slightly less impact in America. It broke the mould, expanding the venue for games from pool halls, taverns and arcades to restaurants, department stores, airports and train stations. Wider availability brought new legitimacy and an entirely new constituency of players.

Close on the heels of the video game revolution came critics worried about social decay. There was indeed cause for worry, given the time and money that customers (mainly young men) spent at the machines. Content was also a problem – before long the seamier side of human imagination filtered into games. Ads promised that Watergate Caper would 'stimulate the larceny in all of us'. The leader in the bad taste stakes was Death Race 2000, a game inspired by the B-movie mogul Roger Corman. Players manoeuvred a vehicle which would chase down and run over tiny stick men, who, once hit, would be replaced by a little cross, which in turn became a new obstacle for the player. Sounds of screams added realism. The game appears tame by today's standards, but once seemed a giant step on the road to hell.[97]

'Ready or not, computers are coming to the people,' *Rolling Stone* proclaimed in 1972. 'That's good news, maybe the best since psychedelics.' The magazine attempted to calm the fears of those who dreaded a modern version of *Modern Times* – man falling victim to manipulative electronic machines. A new lexicon was unveiled: words like network, interface, hardware, software and hacker took on unaccustomed meaning. *Rolling Stone* liked computers because they were revolutionary at a time when the old revolutionaries of communes and college campuses had gone quiet. 'A young science travels where the young take it,' the magazine argued. This new science belonged to hackers. 'They are the ones who translate human demands into code that the machines can understand and act on. They are legion . . . A mobile new-found elite, with its own apparel, language and character, its own legends and humor. Those magnificent men with their flying machines, scouting . . . what's possible.'[98]

And what was possible? Hackers fantasized that someday all music could be stored on computer disk and accessed at will with 'essentially perfect fidelity'. They were already communicating electronically through the ARPAnet. Some were developing a program for 'processing' words, which could 'justify margins, incorporate corrections, handle illustrations, paging, footnotes, headings, indexing'. One young engineer fantasized about a 'hand-held' computer, which he called Dyna-Book. 'It's mostly high-resolution display screen, with a keyboard on the lower third and various cassette-loading slots, optional hook-up plugs, etc.' Hackers loved that word 'etc' – a large container holding their dreams.[99]

'Until computers come to the people', the magazine concluded, 'we will have no real idea of their most natural functions.' Thanks to Nolan Bushnell, that process had already begun. The world would eventually credit Bill Gates with bringing PCs into people's homes. But the fuse in this revolution was lit by Bushnell, who provided the first tiny hint of what a computer might do.[100]

9

WIZARDRY AND WOE

Detroit: 'The Pinto leaves you with that warm feeling'

On 28 May 1972, Lilly Gray paid dearly for buying American. On that day, accompanied by thirteen-year-old Richard Grimshaw, she was driving from Anaheim to Barstow, in Southern California. As she approached her exit on Interstate 15, she encountered heavy traffic, prompting her to decelerate. This caused the carburettor on her new Ford Pinto to malfunction, with the result that the engine stalled and the car coasted to a halt. The vehicle immediately behind the Pinto swerved, but the next car could not. It collided at a speed of between 28 and 37 miles per hour – not fast, but enough to transform the Pinto into a fireball. Lilly Gray died of severe burns a few days later. Richard Grimshaw miraculously survived, but required sixty-eight operations over ten years, and was left permanently disfigured.

The Gray/Grimshaw case was important because it was commonplace. Exploding Pintos seemed a frequent occurrence in the early 1970s, the result of a design fault that rendered the car vulnerable in rear-end collisions, even at low speeds. As fatal accidents and product liability suits mounted, J. Walter Thompson, Ford's ad agency, revised the car's campaign, removing the sentence 'Pinto leaves you with that warm feeling'.

The Pinto was Ford's answer to the Volkswagen Beetle, an attempt to make inroads into the subcompact market, heretofore dominated by European and Japanese manufacturers. Throughout the 1960s, Detroit had confidently assumed that Americans would always want large cars, equipped with gas-guzzling V-6 and V-8 engines. By the end of the decade, however, it became apparent that the market for compacts was growing. The shift was influenced partly by reasons of economy, but also by the success of the environmental movement in drawing attention to air pollution. Detroit, however, had difficulty responding quickly, given the considerable time necessary to design and develop new models.

Into the breach stepped Lee Iacocca, whose reputation at Ford had been enhanced by the enormous popularity of the sporty Mustang. Widely seen as a man with a Midas touch, he used his influence in 1968 to push for a subcompact. In his characteristically swashbuckling way, Iacocca demanded that the model be ready for the 1971 market, due to hit the showrooms in August 1970. That left just twenty-five months to develop the car, half the time usually necessary.

Iacocca wanted a car weighing less than 2,000 pounds and costing less than $2,000. The truncated development time meant that design and tooling had to be carried out simultaneously, rather than as part of an organic process. This meant that faults revealed during testing could not easily be corrected because tooling specifications were already set in stone.

Due to the rushed schedule, the Pinto that emerged was a four-wheeled bucket of trouble. Among its problems were a tendency to stall, gear slippage, sluggishness and poor fuel consumption. Most of these, however, fell into the category of annoying rather than dangerous. Not so the fuel tank. In most small cars, due to the truncated rear end, the tank is placed over the rear axle. The particular shape of the Pinto, however, meant that this would result in an unacceptably small cargo space, so it was pushed further back, less than ten inches from the flimsy rear bumper, in truth just a chrome strip. When it was pointed out that the design increased the risk of fire, a Ford engineer remarked: 'That's all true. But you miss the point entirely. You see, safety isn't the issue, trunk space is. You have no idea how stiff the competition is over trunk space. Do you realize that if we put a [safer] tank in the Pinto you could only get one set of golf clubs in the trunk?'[1]

All this meant that, in a rear-end collision caused by a car travelling at just 20 miles per hour, the Pinto's fuel tank would be pushed forward, into four sharp bolts protruding from the differential. Since that would almost inevitably mean rupture, all that was needed was a spark to produce an inferno. In 1977, the auto safety expert Byron Bloch, after a meticulous study of the fuel tank, concluded: 'It's a catastrophic blunder . . . Ford made an extremely irresponsible decision when they placed such a weak tank in such a ridiculous location in such a soft rear end. It's almost designed to blow up – premeditated.' Tests prior to the release of the model had uncovered the problem, but a re-design was vetoed due to the tight schedule. Asked whether these concerns were communicated to Iacocca, an engineer replied 'Hell no . . . That person would have been fired. Safety wasn't a popular subject around Ford in those days. With Lee it was taboo. Whenever a problem was raised that meant a delay on the Pinto, Lee would chomp on his cigar, look out the window and say "Read the product objectives and get back to work."' One industry executive assumed that concern about auto safety was like 'a hula hoop, a fad that will pass'.[2]

In truth, senior management was eventually alerted to the problem, but the holy writ of cost-benefit analysis dictated that it should be ignored. A number of low-cost solutions were available, among them inserting a rubber bladder into the fuel tank, or placing a plastic baffle between the tank and the differential housing. For the investment of less than $20 per car, the Pinto could have been rendered safe in collisions up to 45 miles per hour, thus exceeding safety standards. Indeed, investigation by Ford eventually revealed that calamities like the one that killed Lilly Gray could have been avoided at the cost of just $5.08 per car. While design changes were initially rejected because of the need to get the Pinto in the showrooms by

August 1970, in the long run Ford decided that, all things considered, a dangerous car promised more profits than a safe one.

Despite murmurings that the car was a lemon, the Pinto proved immensely popular. Americans wanted to buy domestic, and, given the opportunity, they did so. Sales were helped enormously when the Arab oil boycott, which began in October 1973, introduced Americans to the new phenomena of limited fuel supplies and higher cost. The frequency of fiery collisions nevertheless did not escape notice. Among the first to cause a stir was the consumer advocate Ralph Nader, followed closely by investigative journalists at *Mother Jones* magazine. Their exposé, published in August 1977, claimed that as many as 900 people had been killed in fires resulting from the defective fuel tank. Evidence then surfaced that Ford executives had made a conscious decision not to repair the fault. That story was taken up by Mike Wallace of CBS's *60 Minutes*. Keen on controversy, he exaggerated the casualty figures, confessing that he found it 'difficult to believe that top management at the Ford Motor Company [could] . . . sit there and say, "Oh, we'll buy 2,000 deaths, 10,000 injuries, because we want to make some money or we want to bring in a cheaper car."'[3]

All this negative publicity occurred simultaneously to the much-publicized Grimshaw case. That case hung on an internal Ford memo calculating that the risk of fuel tank fires could be reduced with the introduction of modifications costing $11 per vehicle. Such a modification, if introduced in 12.5 million vehicles, would cost Ford $137 million dollars. The memo further calculated that 180 fatalities and a similar number of serious burn injuries could be avoided as a result of the modification. Assuming a 'value per life' figure of $200,000 and per injury of $67,000, the company concluded that the total cost of not modifying the cars would be $49.5 million, or a savings of $87.5 million. The well-known trial lawyer Stuart Speiser called the memo 'possibly the most remarkable document ever produced in an American lawsuit'.[4]

On the strength of that powerful piece of evidence, the jury awarded the Gray family wrongful death damages of $560,000, while Grimshaw was given $2.5 million in compensatory damages and $125 million in punitive damages. The punitive damages award was later reduced by the judge to $3.5 million, but that still underlined Ford's faulty calculations of the value of human life.

Amidst the uproar over Ford's brutal pragmatism, nearly everyone missed the real story. Eventually, a powerful myth arose about the unique danger of the Pinto, which clouded the issue of Ford's liability and obscured a more general problem pertaining to the decline of the American auto industry. The notorious memo, it turns out, pertained not to the Pinto but to all Ford cars sold in a given year, and actually dealt with the risk of fire caused by rollover, not rear-end collision. Furthermore, the figure of $200,000 per life was not Ford's calculation but that devised by the National Highway Traffic Safety Administration for determining the cost of motor vehicle accidents.

It also transpired that Pinto fires resulted in not 'thousands' of deaths, but just twenty-seven in the years 1971 to 1977. Even that much reduced figure was probably an exaggeration given that it would have included high speed collisions, in other words, fatalities which would have resulted even if the fuel tank had been safer. Statistics eventually released by the Fatal Accident Reporting System (FARS) showed that the Pinto was in line with the national average in the frequency of fatal fires, though it was admittedly over double the average in fatal fires caused by rear-end collision.

The court in the Grimshaw case decided that 'Ford's institutional mentality was shown to be one of callous indifference to public safety.' That judgement harmonized with populist assumptions about the rapaciousness of corporate America. In fact, however, Ford's real error lay not in the application of cost-benefit analysis to human lives, but rather in allowing that analysis to enter the public domain, where it was judged by those unable to understand it. Every manufacturer makes similar calculations in designing products. As the *Mother Jones* article admitted, 'cost-valuing human life is not used by Ford alone . . . The process of wilfully trading lives for profits is built into corporate capitalism.' If the auto industry did not apply considerations of this sort, they would make tanks, not cars. Only a virtually indestructible car can avoid fatalities and a product liability case. Unfortunately, an indestructible car is also unaffordable. One of the reasons Americans got unsafe Pintos was because they demanded cheap cars.[5]

That, however, was not how Americans interpreted the scandal. Thanks to *Mother Jones*, Nader, Wallace and all the other critics eager to pour scorn, Americans blissfully assumed that the problem was exclusive to the Pinto and that, otherwise, nothing was rotten in the state of Michigan. In fact, during the Seventies the American car industry reached rock bottom. In terms of safety (or lack of it) the Pinto was about equal to its rivals, the Chevrolet Vega and the AMC Gremlin. In 1980, the NHTSA reported that ten out of twelve small cars failed basic safety standards when they crashed into a wall at 35 m.p.h. Bigger cars like the Mercury Monarch or Buick LeSabre were safer, but they were still dogs to drive. While America had demonstrated her technological prowess by landing on the moon, she had somehow forgotten how to make cars.[6]

The Japanese and the Europeans, on the other hand, had shown that they were rather good at building cars. By the end of the decade, around 30 per cent of the vehicles on American roads were foreign, an astonishing figure in a country where patriotism still influenced choice. Americans wanted to buy American cars, but Detroit was failing to provide what customers wanted. The industy's biggest failure came in its inadequate response to the Arab oil boycott and the cutting off of Iranian oil in 1978, both of which caused the demand for small cars to increase. Granted, part of the fault must go to the American government for preventing fuel prices from rising to their appropriate level, thus encouraging a dangerous complacency which prevails to this day. As Transportation Secretary Neil Goldschmidt complained in 1980, 'the U.S. Government allowed us to go from a nation importing a third of its oil to one importing almost 50 percent because there wasn't the political courage to deregulate the price of oil'.[7]

The main problem, however, was that Detroit failed to provide adequate choice when it came to fuel-efficient cars. Instead of responding to public demand, the auto industry concentrated on preserving the big car market by lobbying government to keep fuel prices low and by fighting the imposition of fuel efficiency and clean air standards. Industry executives assumed that the fad for small cars would pass and that the American demand for gas-guzzling behemoths would recover. While that proved a correct assumption in the long run, Detroit miscalculated the time necessary for that recovery to take place.

As a result, the car industry found itself on the brink of collapse by the end of the decade. Sales fell from 9.3 million in 1978 to just over 7 million in 1980. The bad news was dominated by Chrysler, which lost $2 billion in 18 months, in the process setting a record for the largest losses by any company in American history. The federal government was forced to step in with a $1.5 billion rescue package. That catastrophe obscured the serious problems of the other two major car manufacturers. In its North American market, Ford lost around $2 billion in 1980, while once mighty General Motors found itself in the red that year, the first time that had happened since 1921. The slump saw nearly 300,000 industry workers laid off, nearly a dozen plants closed and almost 1,500 dealerships shut.

The crisis was serious because of the central importance of the car to American culture. No other society was as dependent on automobiles, which made the failure of the industry to provide the cars Americans wanted all the more pathetic. The industry eventually responded by imitating the Japanese. Detroit began producing more and better small cars, but, more importantly, applied techniques perfected by Toyota and Datsun to the assembly line methods once synonymous with Henry Ford. In real terms, this increasingly meant that robots were building cars.

Efficiency measures eventually allowed a miraculous recovery in the 1980s. But just as the burning Pinto obscured the real problem of the auto industry in the 1970s, so too the dramatic recovery of Chrysler in the subsequent decade (a recovery engineered, ironically, by Iacocca) obscured much more serious problems in American transportation policy. The American love affair with the car remained a constant, and that meant a dangerous addiction to petroleum that the government was loath to address. 'Sometimes I feel like . . . there is no way you can change the . . . way people live,' one woman confessed. 'You can't just say look, you have to wake up and realize that you can't waste any more energy. You can't just drive your car to work everyday. People feel they deserve to be able to live this way. That they have worked hard to be able to live this way . . . I don't know if it will ever change.' That proved an accurate assessment, especially at a time when the government proved unwilling to make courageous decisions. When the oil supply recovered, so too did the American fondness for big cars. That fondness eventually led to the ridiculous epidemic of the SUV. The smoke from the Pinto fire obscured some painful truths about Americans and their cars. As it turned out, the real problem for America was not the few cars that exploded, but the millions that did not.[8]

Oldham: Test Tube Babies

In the beginning there was Bob. So goes the narrative popular within human fertility circles. Bob Edwards was a geneticist who believed that, under the right circumstances, a human egg could be fertilized outside the body and then re-introduced into the uterus of a woman, where it could develop to full maturity. That possibility provided immense hope to thousands of women who were infertile due to damaged Fallopian tubes. 'It was about more than infertility,' Edwards later remarked. 'It was also about issues like . . . the ethics of human conception. I wanted to find out exactly who was in charge, whether it was God Himself or whether it was scientists in the laboratory.'[9]

The first known case of embryo transplantation occurred in 1891, when Professor Walter Heape at the University of Cambridge harvested embryos from an angora rabbit and inserted them in the uterus of a recently mated Belgian hare. The resultant litter consisted of four Belgians and two angoras. That outcome set the tone for research in this field: scientists had repeatedly to answer complaints that they were tampering with nature. Nevertheless, when applied to humans, Heape's breakthrough seemed more than just the macabre fantasy of a mad scientist. Research was driven by the grief of millions of childless couples who just wanted a baby. 'Infertility is a disease, it is a real disease,' the fertility expert Jamie Grifo has remarked. 'It is a horrible disease and unless you have it, you don't know what it is like to have it . . . to have a child is not a cosmetic thing. It is a very important basic life event.' The dreaded word in gynaecological clinics was 'never'. As Patrick Steptoe recalled, 'That verdict of "never", though softly spoken, leaves the woman shaking, empty, her face too naked, her private grief too unconcealed. That word "never" is one I have heard . . . too often over the years. I have had to say it myself. Many times.'[10]

Salvation would come if Heape's research could be extended to a point where human embryos could be fertilized outside the body, allowed to mature, and then introduced into the uterus, to grow to full term. Among the pioneers was Dr Landrum Shettles, a maverick gynaecologist at Columbia Presbyterian Hospital in New York. He tried to force the pace of research in the 1960s, but was stopped by administrators who feared that his work would attract adverse attention and deter charitable funding. In truth, his limited understanding of cell biology would have proved a greater obstacle than the qualms of his administrators. Stated simply, he was a doctor, not a geneticist. Edwards, who first became interested in the topic in 1958, understood the science of reproduction intimately, and had managed to fertilize the embryos of rats, mice and rabbits outside the womb. He spent most of the 1960s trying to duplicate this success with humans, but failure proved persistent.

A breakthrough came in 1967 when Edwards happened across an article by Steptoe in the *Lancet*, discussing the potential for laparoscopy as a method for examining a woman's reproductive organs. The article mentioned that the laparoscope allowed access to the oviducts, which thrilled Edwards, since it suggested that egg collection could become easier. Gynaecologists warned that laparoscopy was dangerous, and Steptoe equally so, but Edwards ignored that advice. 'I needed Steptoe and Steptoe needed me,' he later admitted. The two had little in common – Steptoe was urbane, aloof, conservative and middle class; Edwards abrupt, fiercely socialist and decidedly working class. Their equally large egos did not bode well for working together, but they decided early on that their work was far too important to let personalities obstruct it. 'I can be damn difficult on occasions,' Edwards admitted. 'And I know Patrick could be difficult . . . we were probably both little prima donnas in our own way, but if there was any argument . . . we always went into a room together and sorted [it] out and agreed on what we would do.' For Edwards, working with Steptoe provided a direct connection to the human side of his research. 'It was Steptoe who really wetted me in to thinking like a doctor . . . They had a different outlook. They had a different ethics and I was learning fast, I was learning very fast.'[11]

The two explorers had to struggle against a crowd of colleagues willing them to fail, not to mention journalists who craved stories of science gone mad. 'The test tube time bomb is ticking away,' wrote William Breckon, who predicted 'shattering – and frightening – possibilities . . . among them, the possibility of producing hundreds of identical living organisms from just a single living organism'. In fact, for the first five years, obstacles proved more prominent than possibilities. Repeated failure demoralized the team and bolstered the legions of doubters. The problem of fertilizing an egg in vitro was quickly solved, as was that of keeping the fertilized egg alive to the point when it would, under normal circumstances, lodge itself in the uterus. The difficulty, however, lay in implantation. The first attempt in 1972 failed, as did every subsequent effort over the next three years. Implanted embryos invariably aborted well before the end of the first trimester. 'It was very hard to keep people's spirits up over such a length of time,' Muriel Harris, a senior member of the nursing team, recalled.[12]

An application for a major grant was rejected by the Medical Research Council because of 'serious doubts about ethical aspects'.

The team nevertheless struggled on, thanks to the generosity of sympathetic colleagues and funding provided by an American philanthropist. The work was made all the more complex because Edwards was based in Cambridge and Steptoe in Oldham, a two-hour drive away. Since Steptoe supplied the patients, that meant Edwards did the commuting. In an attempt to ease the pressure, Edwards helped Steptoe get a position at Newmarket General Hospital, just fifteen minutes from Cambridge, but the Medical Research Council vetoed the move on the grounds that laparoscopy was dangerous and in vitro fertilization held no promise. As a result, Edwards, who was so desperate to give parents the opportunity to have a child, had little time to spend with his own children. His schedule was determined entirely by the fertility cycles of Steptoe's patients. 'All too often I would see [my wife's] face cloud over as I had to disappoint the children or to cancel a party, a theatre outing, a dinner, at the last moment.'[13]

By 1977, it seemed that every option had been tried, yet success still proved elusive. More than simply an experiment falling short, each failure meant that a couple desperate for a child was left devastated. 'I had been frank with them all,' recalled Steptoe. 'They all knew that our approach was novel and unpredictable. But of course it did not help them when our method failed. We had to be successful. For their sake.' The next patient chosen, Lesley Brown, was a working-class woman from the Oldham area whose chances of conceiving were nil, since her Fallopian tubes had been removed. The team went back to basics. Instead of stimulating the production of eggs with hormones, they aspirated a single egg during her natural menstrual cycle. Edwards took it to Cambridge, where conception took place, then drove it back to Oldham. Departing from earlier practice, the team decided to return the fertilized embryo to the uterus earlier – at the eight-cell stage. 'That was a wonderful experience,' Brown exclaimed when her uncomfortable operation was completed. 'As soon as [it] was implanted, I felt as if I was in a cocoon,' she recalled. 'I was warm and comfortable, and I was sure. I always thought it would work.'[14]

From that point forward the pregnancy proved normal, but for relentless monitoring. Success seemed likely, yet the team had to keep quiet until the baby was born. At the back of everyone's minds was the possibility of some horrible deformity which would inevitably be blamed on the manner of conception. The Nobel laureate Max Perutz had warned of 'a new thalidomide catastrophe'. The press, alerted to the successful conception, circled the hospital like ravenous vultures. Payments were offered to hospital employees willing to divulge secrets. Some found the temptation too great, but Steptoe somehow managed to protect Brown's privacy.[15]

In the final weeks of the pregnancy, Brown developed toxcaemia, a not uncommon problem, but one which implied delivery by Caesarean section. The operation was carried out by Steptoe on 25 July 1978. 'Left hand under the buttocks and out she came,' he later wrote. 'Glorious. She was chubby, full of muscular tone . . . I held the head low and we sucked and cleared the mouth and throat. She took a deep breath. Then she yelled and yelled and yelled. I laid her down, all pink and furious, and saw at once that she was externally perfect and beautiful.' Reporters gathered in their hundreds outside the Oldham hospital. Steptoe's announcement was revolutionary because of its simplicity: 'All examinations showed that the baby is quite normal.' Baby Louise was a miracle for her parents and a gift of hope for the rest of the world. Edwards announced what so many couples were desperate to hear: 'This work may be developed in other respects. It may include the reversal of sterilization.'[16]

Louise Brown was probably the first working-class child famous just for being born. Her face was on the cover of virtually every newspaper and magazine around the world. 'How would you like to be the world's first test tube baby?' Johnny Carson asked in his opening monologue the day the news broke. 'What do you do on Father's day? Do you send a card to the Dupont Corporation? I understand that after the baby was conceived in the laboratory, a pair of beakers smoked a cigarette and stared at the ceiling!' Amid all the celebration, however, niggling doubts remained. Should man be tampering with conception? Was it morally wrong? Where would it lead?[17]

Steptoe and Edwards had broken the link between procreation and reproduction, a connection which seemed inviolate. They had literally made a human being. Something that was once sacred and mysterious had been reduced to a laboratory procedure and, worse, to a process able to be manipulated according to the whims of man. The next logical step was what seemed so frightening. The ability to manipulate procreation might lead to manipulating it for specific purpose – to make a better baby, or to avoid a flawed one. Edwards and Steptoe had celebrated Louise Brown as a solution to infertility, but was she also a harbinger of eugenics? When procreation becomes a process, do babies become a product to which quality standards can be applied?

Critics warned that a Pandora's Box had been opened. 'I have grave misgivings about the possible implications,' remarked the Archbishop of St-Andrews and Edinburgh, Cardinal Gordon Gray. The Vatican warned that Louise's birth would 'have very grave consequences for humanity'. Quite a few critics objected to the manner in which the sperm was harvested – namely by masturbation. From various quarters came muttered hopes for horrible problems so that the perpetrators of this gross experiment would learn not to tamper with nature. Some labelled Edwards the anti-Christ. Even James Watson, who helped unravel the mystery of DNA, argued that science had gone too far. Journalists, never given to celebration, were determined instead to explore the moral minefield, and did not lack for experts willing to stoke doubt. Martin Johnson, one of Edwards' research students, recalls a seemingly endless stream of phone calls from journalists who probed breaches in the team's moral defences. 'It was our little group against the world.'[18]

Unease was focused on two distinct implications: the first that embryo research would lead to cloning; the second that, in the process of research and treatment, fertilized embryos would be destroyed. The latter inspired renewed debate on the question of when life begins. Steptoe and Edwards had anticipated the outcry by bringing theologians and moral philosophers onto their team. What took them by surprise, however, was the venom with which criticism was delivered. That was all the more hurtful because they were utterly convinced that they were doing good. The theologian Gordon Dunstan, who helped Edwards prepare his defence, recalled him asking, after one particularly malicious attack: 'Why does he hate me so, he doesn't know what I do?'[19]

In response to critics who warned about where this research might lead, Steptoe argued that to stop the work because of a preoccupation with theoretical consequences would have been like stopping the Wright Brothers because their research might make aerial bombing possible. He kept repeating that he was interested only in allowing infertile women to have a baby. Lending support was Bishop Gordon Roe, who argued, with impeccable logic, that 'if the intent is . . . to help women to have babies . . . it can only be conformity with God's will because God in the first place created human beings to have children, to multiply and so on'. Steptoe came to a similar conclusion. Just before his death, he spoke with Roe about miracles and asked: 'Am I being presumptive in saying that miracles do still happen, that they work through the hands of people like me?' Roe concluded that it was entirely appropriate to think in such terms, that the team were 'assisting in God's creation, rather than interfering with it'.[20]

That same rationale was voiced by Georgeanna Jones, who reassured her husband: 'You must remember we are just helping, we are not doing anything that God himself isn't doing, we are his helper.' They found out about Louise Brown while moving into their retirement home in Norfolk, Virginia. As the most highly respected authorities on in vitro fertilization in America, they were naturally the first point of contact for inquisitive reporters. When asked if the same success could be achieved in America, Howard Jones replied: 'Yes, of course.' Could it be achieved in Norfolk? 'Yes.' What would you need? 'Money,' he replied. The next day came a call from an eager benefactor. 'How much do you want?' 'That was the first time in our entire professional career we had ever been asked how much money we wanted,' Jones reflected. The Joneses had not intended to open an in vitro fertilization clinic in Norfolk, but that is where the tide of events took them.[21]

The money was important because the outrage was greater in the United States than in Britain. That outrage made it difficult for legislators to pledge government funding. Eventually, the government, especially after Ronald Reagan became president, took the view that it would not block research, as long as it was funded privately. That had the unanticipated and rather sordid effect of turning fertility assistance into a business with profits a prime concern. 'The technology quickly fell into a corporate ethos,' Arthur Caplan, a professor of bioethics, remarks. 'It became something that was heavily marketed. It became something that was advertised, even for a time, with what I would describe as false advertising. People would say "We'll get you a baby" but they wouldn't say what their success rate was, or they wouldn't admit that they had a lot of failures.' American fertility experts who worried about government interference eventually found that their real problem was corporate interference.[22]

The day after Louise Brown's birth, enquiries from childless couples flooded into the offices of Steptoe and Edwards. They decided to form their own clinic, Bourn Hall, devoted to full-time research. Britain would remain the leader in this field, but successes would eventually occur around the world, because demand was universal. In time, the overwhelming support of ordinary people smothered the doubts of moral critics. Anti-abortionists had difficulty mustering opposition to a procedure so undeniably pro-life. 'No one, to my knowledge, has ever demonstrated, picketed, chained themselves to the doorway of an in vitro fertilization clinic,' remarks Caplan. The consensus held that while government should put obstacles in the way of cloning, it should not interfere with IVF.[23]

'This is life itself,' Edwards feels. 'When a baby is born, you have organised it all. That's a hell of an achievement . . . It's the magic of birth. The whole thing is incredible . . . just think of what it means to people. It's fantastic.' For those who benefited from the treatment, the personal bond with the IVF doctor seems more important than the sophisticated science. 'I remember women crying on the wards. The tears were awful,' Fiona Drewe, who had two boys through IVF, recalled. 'For some of the women, nothing could be done. But Patrick Steptoe was so sympathetic, and he never did it for the money.' Many children came to see their IVF doctor as an honorary grandparent. 'When dad told me Mr Steptoe had passed away, I broke down,' Louise Brown recalled. 'It was like losing a dear member of the family.' Writing in the *New York Times* on the death of Georgeanna Jones in 2005, Elizabeth Carr, America's first test tube baby, remarked: 'She wasn't special because she helped develop a reproductive technology. She was special because she helped my parents have me.'[24]

Cape Canaveral: Shuttle to Nowhere

The eminent physicist Ralph Lapp, a Manhattan Project veteran, was no great admirer of the Apollo mission. While Neil Armstrong and his crew were travelling to the moon in 1969, Lapp wrote that he and his fellow scientists were looking forward to a time when NASA might 'wind up its manned space spectaculars and get on with the job of promoting space science'. Apollo, he reminded readers, cost $25 billion. 'Yet manned space flights will have given scientists very little information about space. Man, himself, has been the main experiment. And man is the principal reason why Project Apollo has cost so much money.' He hoped that, on completion of the mission, President Nixon would say to NASA: 'In the name of all the people on this planet . . . I declare the senseless space race ended. And now, gentlemen, let us point our science and technology in the direction of man.'[25]

Lapp was no crank. His view was shared by a significant proportion of the scientific community, including a number of Nobel Prize winners. Many scientists objected to the way their budgets had been bled in order to fund a pointless race to the moon. While that race was being run, however, their protests were shouted into a vacuum. The mood changed when Apollo 11 splashed down. Since being first to the moon was the whole point, most Americans felt that no sequel was required. As the veteran news correspondent Eric Severeid accurately predicted: 'future flights will seem anti-climactic . . . and the pressure to divert these great sums of money to inner space, terra firma and inner man will steadily grow'.[26]

This attitude worried NASA. The agency understood that, unless it could produce a new goal to replace the moon, mediocrity threatened. NASA's role would be reduced to shooting rockets carrying satellites into inner space and perhaps sending the occasional probe to a distant planet. The man in space programme would wither and die, for the simple reason that it had no logic beyond beating the Russians. Yet, as Lapp understood, it was the presence of man in the space equation that had made it possible for NASA to attract big money.

Plagued by this dilemma, the NASA administrator Tom Paine decided, well before Armstrong's small step, that a new goal was needed, so that Apollo would seem like a beginning, not an end. On the eve of the Apollo 11 launch, he told reporters: 'While the Moon has been the focus of our efforts, the true goal is far more than being the first to land men on the Moon, as though it were a celestial Mount Everest . . . The real goal is to develop and demonstrate the capability for interplanetary travel.' The only logical destination was Mars. Paine instructed colleagues to prepare budget proposals on the assumption that a mission to the Red Planet would be launched as early as 1983. As had been the case with the moon, Mars was selected as the next destination not because it had any intrinsic worth, but simply because it was theoretically accessible.[27]

Paine's behaviour caused unease in the White House. The Nixon administration, rather like Lapp, was looking forward to clawing back NASA's huge budget. Nixon insisted that 'space expenditures must take their proper place within a rigorous system of national priorities'. The administration feared, however, that Nixon might be blackmailed into supporting an ambitious next step during the euphoria that would inevitably follow the moon landing. For this reason, Peter Flanigan, the White House liaison to NASA, told Paine 'to stop public advocacy of early manned Mars activity'. It was, he complained, 'causing trouble in Congress and restricting Presidential options'.[28]

Paine wanted $10 billion as a first instalment on a Mars mission. Robert Mayo, Nixon's budget director, had in mind a figure closer to $1.5 billion for the fiscal year of 1971, which would rule out anything ambitious. While Paine was effectively quarantined from the Oval Office, he did manage to work the old NASA voodoo on Vice-President Spiro Agnew, who responded by openly advocating a Mars mission during festivities surrounding the Apollo 11 launch. 'I was surprised at [Agnew's] obtuseness,' John Ehrlichman, Nixon's domestic affairs adviser, recalled. 'I had been wooed by . . . the Space Administration, but not to the degree to which they had made love to Agnew. He had been their guest of honor at space launchings, tours and dinners, and it seemed to me they had done a superb job of recruiting him to lead this fight to vastly expand their empire and budget.' On Nixon's instruction, Ehrlichman summoned Agnew to his office and told the vice-president to keep his mouth shut. 'There is no money,' he stressed. 'The President has already decided that.'[29]

Mayo thought the Mars proposals proof of NASA's talent for packaging selfish goals in patriotic wrapping. The goal, he felt, was 'much more beneficial to the space program than to the nation as a whole'. His report included a devastating critique of manned space travel, arguing that 'no defined manned project can compete on a cost-return basis with unmanned space flight systems . . . [Manned] missions . . . have little demonstrable economic or social return to atone for their high cost.' Mayo had also caught on to NASA's uncanny ability to justify future investment by reference to past expenditure. In other words, a mission to Mars, the agency had argued, would make the investment spent on going to the moon worthwhile. That, Mayo realized, was a clever way of endlessly spending money.

Nixon could not bring himself to be quite as tight-fisted as Mayo advocated. A NASA budget of $3.7 billion was sent to Congress, a figure that ruled out Mars, without insulting NASA. A disgusted

Paine warned that 'manned flight activity [will] end in 1972'. Locked in his world of adventure and fantasy, Paine did not remotely understand that most Americans wanted an even earlier end.

Congress, on the other hand, understood the American mood perfectly. Politicians sensed that while Americans celebrated Apollo 11, taxpayers would not for ever be willing to write blank cheques to NASA. Just after the landing, Gallup found that 53 per cent were opposed to a Mars mission, with 39 per cent in favor. More revealing was a *Newsweek* survey that showed 56 per cent wanted Nixon to spend less on space, while only 10 per cent wanted him to spend more. Congressman Olin Teague found that, after Apollo 11, 'the easiest thing on earth to vote against in Congress is the space program. You can vote to kill the whole space program tomorrow, and you won't get one letter.'[30]

Congress eventually settled on a budget of $3.269 billion. The budget would hover around that level until the mid-1980s, or, in real terms, one-third of its peak during the glory years of Apollo. In the Senate, Walter Mondale justified the cuts by arguing that 'It would be unconscionable to embark on a [Mars] project of such staggering cost when many of our citizens are malnourished, when our rivers and lakes are polluted, and when our cities and rural areas are dying. What are our values? What do we think is more important?' Senator William Fulbright summarized the congressional decision perfectly: 'We voted for sewers. Certainly sewers are more important than going to the moon.' Paine could not hide his disgust:

> One of the games that some people on the Hill might play would be to say, gee, let's hit the space program and wipe it out, and keep the sewers and so forth in. The idea was that, well, the reason the country was so crummy was because we went to the moon, and by God, if we had only spent that money on all these other things that we needed to do, then we would have a great country and a crummy space program. Wouldn't it be better than a great space program and a crummy country? This was the line of reasoning they slipped into.

Despite being hopelessly out of touch, Paine had managed to summarize American opinion perfectly.[31]

Stuck in his fantasies, Paine tried desperately to revive America's love affair with space. Shortly after the congressional decision, he organized a conference on the future of space travel, and invited the heroes of the glory days, including Werner von Braun, Arthur C. Clarke and Armstrong. Participants were encouraged to let their imaginations run wild. Paine wanted new rocket engines, new vehicles, and new destinations. He also promised wonderful spin-off technologies, including a rocket plane capable of travelling anywhere on earth in less than an hour, and foods made from fossil fuels which would 'free . . . man from his 5000 year dependence upon agriculture'. The new NASA, he promised, would be like 'Nelson's "Band-of-Brothers" – Sea Rovers – combining the best of naval discipline in some areas with freedom of action of bold buccaneers in others – men who are determined to do their individual and collective best to moving the planet into a better 21st Century'. Paine sent the report to the White House with a request for an immediate meeting. Nixon thanked him and filed the report.

The rock-collecting expeditions to the moon meanwhile continued. It is a measure of the short shelf life of Apollo that most Americans can only remember two missions – the first one and the nearly disastrous third one starring Tom Hanks. There were in fact five others. The later ones included a hugely expensive car that looked a lot like what Fred Flintstone once drove. It was driven for a few hours and then abandoned on the moon, much to the disgust of Americans who could only afford an inflammable Pinto. Apollo 14 is vaguely remembered, if only for a ridiculous stunt performed by golfer/astronaut Alan Shepard. In a subsequent *All in the Family* episode, Michael 'Meathead' Stivic (Rob Reiner) voiced a common disgust when he remarked: 'You don't think we got anything more important to do with twenty billion dollars than to send a guy up to the moon to hit a few golf balls?' During the next mission, one viewer phoned his local network to suggest that a large rock seen during the transmission should be named in honour of 'a taxpayer selected at random from the computers of the Internal Revenue Service'.[32]

Before disaster struck on Apollo 13, a scheduled live transmission from the capsule was cancelled by CBS in favour of the *Doris Day Show*. It was only after an explosion imperilled the crew that Americans started paying attention. Hardly anyone protested when coverage of Apollo 17, the last mission, was cut to a bare minimum. When CBS interrupted its hit show *Medical Center* to show the launch, viewers jammed telephone lines to complain. ABC shoehorned its coverage into the half time of a New York Jets–Oakland Raiders football game. Instead of showing the final steps of man on the moon, NBC broadcast a repeat of *The Tonight Show*.[33]

The waning of public enthusiasm did not stop hard-core space nuts from continuing to dream. Fantasies in fact proved much more exciting than the reality of repetitious lunar missions. Dreams did not need to obey the laws of economics or physics, which perhaps explains the popularity of *Star Trek*. A common feature among fantasists was the belief that a better life would evolve in space, as if man's beastliness was determined by gravity. Paine, for instance, insisted that utopia could be built on distant planets. 'As with the American experience of 1776,' he argued, 'founding a new society in a demanding environment will sweep aside old world dogmas, prejudices, outworn traditions, and oppressive ideologies. A modern frontier brotherhood will develop as the new society works together to tame its underdeveloped planet for posterity.'[34]

Gerard O'Neill, the popular space guru, thought that a perfect life could be realized in a space station, endlessly spinning in the ether. Space stations would bring 'perpetual plenty', thus solving the population crisis, the energy problem, poverty and even war itself. The first step toward this Utopia was a cosmic cruise liner he called Island One, which could supposedly be up and running before the end of the twentieth century, at a cost of only $31 billion. 'With an abundance of food and clean electrical energy, controlled climates and temperate weather, living conditions . . . should be much more pleasant than in most places on earth.' The station would be like 'a small, wealthy resort community on Earth: good restaurants, cinemas, libraries, perhaps small discotheques'. Playing to the environmental movement, he presented Island One as an eco-commune which would relieve pressure on Mother Earth. By 2050, he predicted, more people would be living in space than on terra firma. The planet could then recover from man's depredations, returning to a state of pastoral virginity. Fans of O'Neill shouted: 'Declare the Earth a wilderness area: if you love it, leave it.'[35]

A space station, or a ship capable of going to Mars, could not simply be placed on top of a Saturn V rocket and blasted into space, as had been the case with Apollo. Something that size would instead have to be constructed in orbit by astronauts bolting components together. O'Neill projected that hundreds of separate trips into near space would be necessary to construct Island One. Likewise, even the more modest ideas of Paine implied a schedule of flights that dwarfed Apollo. That kind of effort would be wasteful, costly and time-consuming if components were flown skyward in a disposable rocket like Saturn V. Much more sensible, it seemed, would be a reusable space ferry.

From this seed of fantasy, the idea of the Space Transportation System – commonly known as the Shuttle – grew. NASA loved the idea because it seemed a good way to keep manned space travel alive. Since something like a Shuttle was the necessary prelude to an ambitious mission to Mars or beyond, it seemed a step in the right direction. Nixon liked the idea for similar reasons. The president wanted to cut NASA's budget, but he did not want to surrender manned space spectaculars to the Soviets. He understood that, in order to remain interesting, space had to have a face.

The president and NASA therefore willingly colluded in a conspiracy to convince themselves, and the rest of the world, that the Shuttle was sensible. On the surface, the logic of a reusable spacecraft would seem unassailable. But the complicating factor was the crew. As Mayo and Lapp understood, the presence of human beings made spaceflight infinitely more complex and hugely more expensive. In a straightforward comparison, an unmanned disposable rocket would always be cheaper. In order to make the project seem a bargain,

NASA had to exaggerate the importance of man in the equation, and (in order to create an economy of scale) inflate the frequency of missions. To this end, NASA forecast 779 launches between 1978 and 1991, or more than 5 a month. At that rate, the total cost would be $50 billion, or $16 billion cheaper than the same number of flights with expendable rockets. But, critics asked, why were so many missions necessary if there were no plans to go to Mars? NASA replied that space needs would inevitably increase and that, in any case, surplus cargo room could be sold to private companies or to other nations, thus reducing the cost further. Besides (and this was said in a whisper), the military potential was enormous. Finally, the Shuttle was said to be essential to the construction of a space station, another example of NASA using one white elephant to justify the purchase of another.

The Shuttle sales pitch was based on the idea of space travel becoming mundane. 'Toward the end of the Seventies,' von Braun boasted, 'you will no longer have to go through gruelling years of astronaut training if you want to go into orbit. A reusable space shuttle will take you up there in the comfort of an airliner.' The use of the pronoun 'you' was intentional; space would be democratized. Congress, however, still baulked. Mondale and other critics quoted space heavyweights like James Van Allen, who was adamant that the US did not need a Shuttle. In order to gain congressional approval, NASA revised the plans in a way that cut the initial cost from $14 billion to $5.15 billion. 'That was one of the greatest mistakes,' an agency scientist later admitted. Reducing the cost had inevitable consequences for reusability and therefore profitability. In short, while the craft itself was cheaper, each mission became more expensive and the pre-flight preparation more complicated, rendering weekly missions pie in the sky. Out went the basic premise that a Shuttle would be cheaper than a disposable rocket, on which the entire project rested. But no one at NASA admitted that at the time. 'Every now and then I go back and look at those early projections and I have to close my eyes and shake my head,' the Shuttle planner Michael Weeks later confessed.[36]

As it turned out, the Shuttle was NASA's Pinto – badly designed and very dangerous. Two Shuttles have been lost, and fourteen crewmembers killed. Unlike the Pinto, however, the Shuttle is far from cheap. In 1993, a single launch cost $547 million, $180 million more than NASA had projected. Nor have the flights been nearly as frequent as NASA promised. Instead of 779 launches by 1992, NASA has managed just 124 by the end of 2008. The cost and unreliability have frightened away customers. In fact, the US has been placed in the embarrassing position of having to explain why countries wishing to put satellites in orbit often prefer the Russian or European space agencies.

'Apollo was a matter of going to the moon and building whatever technology could get us there,' writes the historian Walter McDougall; 'the Space Shuttle was a matter of building a technology and going wherever it could take us.' Armstrong's small step was the high point of America's brief love affair with space. At the time, anything seemed possible, and NASA promised that it was. Flying in space, experts predicted, would become as routine as jet travel. In fact, in 1968, PanAm began taking bookings for flights to the moon – the first scheduled for the year 2000. Governor Ronald Reagan reserved a seat. Executives at Hilton Hotels explored the possibility of constructing a lunar resort and the Catholic Church drew up plans for a chapel. Ever the optimist, Paine predicted that 'by 1984 a round trip, economy-class rocket-plane flight to a comfortably orbiting space station can be brought down to a cost of several thousand dollars', while a trip to the moon would run in 'the $10,000 range'. 'By the time I'm 40,' the Kiss guitarist Ace Frehley remarked, 'inter-planetary travel will be common . . . I'm gonna be on Mars.' He turned forty in 1991.[37]

The dream died because manned space travel failed to produce a return to justify the massive expense. Unlike the explorers of the fifteenth and sixteenth centuries, astronauts brought back neither gold, nor spices, nor even potatoes. The best they could manage was rocks. The landing itself was enough to justify Apollo 11, but subsequent missions made NASA look like a one-trick pony. Soon after the euphoria of the moon landing dissipated, NASA lost the ability to charm (and fool) the American people. The agency's capacity to dream up new adventures never waned, but the public's tolerance for adolescent fantasy had ended.

Seveso: Who Knows?

On a cold morning in early February 1980, Paolo Paoletti left his home in Monza, near Milan, bound for work. As he strode across a courtyard to his car, he noticed four strangers approach, all carrying weapons. He quickly ran back toward his home, but was gunned down on his front step. The killers escaped in a Fiat parked nearby.

Paoletti's death was tragic but not extraordinary. He was the eighth victim of terrorists in Italy that year. This is not, however, another story about Seventies terrorism, in this case spilling over into a new decade. It is instead a tale of environmental disaster, since Paoletti was killed in revenge for an accident at the ICMESA chemical plant where he worked. In 1976, the plant released a cloud of dioxin-laced gas over the nearby town of Seveso. The terrorists, members of a group called Prima Linea, had executed Paoletti for 'provoking the dioxin to crush the proletariat'.[38]

Around lunchtime on 10 July 1976, a reactor at the ICMESA plant in Meda, 20 kilometres north of Milan, overheated, causing a dioxin release. The cloud travelled in a southwesterly direction, contaminating roughly six square kilometres with one of the most toxic chemicals known to man. Dioxin was already notorious as a component of Agent Orange, the herbicide used with devastating effect in Vietnam. Seveso, a town of 17,000 people, received the brunt of the contamination, but nearby Meda, Desio and Cesano Maderno were also affected.

ICMESA was owned by Givaudan, a subsidiary of the Swiss firm Hoffmann-La Roche. Officials at all levels of the company reacted with stony silence, hoping the problem would go away. Residents, however, soon realized something was amiss. 'I couldn't breathe,'

Vinicio Lazzaretti recalled. 'It made my eyes water. The next day all the leaves and plants and flowers were riddled with small holes, as if they had been struck with tiny hailstones.' A few days later, locals noticed how the ground was littered with dead birds, rats, mice and lizards. Dogs and cats started to bleed from the nose and mouth, then dropped dead. Scare stories circulated on a rising wind of panic. One farmer told how he watched his cat suddenly collapse. When he went to pick the animal up, its tail fell off. He claimed that, when he exhumed the body to show it to investigators, only the skull remained.[39]

The day after the accident, ICMESA managers admitted that a cloud of herbicide had been released which might cause minor damage to agriculture, but otherwise posed no risk. They advised local residents not to eat vegetables from their gardens. Government officials, inclined to trust ICMESA, relayed that advice the following day, but were otherwise reluctant to probe further. Five days after the release, town administrators declared an area of 12 hectares, containing some 200 people, contaminated, but did not order an evacuation. Lacking guidance from health officials, people stayed put, continuing to drink water from taps and milk from their cows. Some even ate the chickens that had mysteriously died.

After the initial panic, residents seemed determined to downplay the problem. Most had migrated from Sicily, Calabria and the Veneto to take jobs at ICMESA – thus moving from Italy's poorer regions to one of her wealthiest. Delighting in unaccustomed job security, they bought homes and easily adjusted to a better life. They therefore desperately hoped this problem would dissipate as quickly as the wind that had brought it. Occasional illness from chemical poisoning was fatalistically accepted as the price of a better life.

Ignoring the problem proved difficult, however, when children began exhibiting pustular eruptions, called chloracne, and adults developed liver and kidney ailments. ICMESA, meanwhile, steadfastly refused to acknowledge a problem. On Day 6, officials told the Seveso town council that they were as yet unsure of the nature of the emission, but felt confident that no danger existed. The factory operated virtually as normal, though workers grew restless. Not until 18 July did investigating magistrates rule that Building B, where the accident had occurred, should be sealed. The mayor of Meda promptly extended that order to the entire factory.

Givaudan's stone wall came tumbling down on the 19th, when officials were forced to admit that dioxin had been found in samples taken from the factory vicinity. A public statement released in Geneva the following day prompted huge headlines in Italian newspapers on the 21st. On that same day, Herwig von Zwehl, the plant's technical director, and Paoletti, director of production, were arrested. The Milan prefecture decided that a meeting to discuss health issues was necessary, but, rather bizarrely, delayed that meeting until the 24th. By this stage, the number of children suffering from chloracne had approached 200, and over 3,000 animals had died.

Evacuation was finally ordered on the 24th, but was not effected until two days later, when 170 people from Seveso and 55 from Meda were moved from the area deemed heavily contaminated. New laboratory results subsequently predicated enlargement of the danger zone and evacuation of an additional 511 people. A slaughter of animals was also ordered, eventually resulting in 78,000 being culled.

After anguished debate, a decision was made on 2 August to allow 'therapeutic' abortions for pregnant women in the first trimester living within the area of maximum contamination. That decision provoked predictable outrage from the Catholic Church. Cardinal Colombo, Archbishop of Milan, urged women considering an abortion to continue their pregnancy, since he was confident that families willing to adopt malformed children could be found. The first three abortions were carried out on 13 August, two by Professor G.B. Candiani of Milan, an outspoken critic of abortion who cooperated only after being told by health officials that there was significant risk to the health of the mother. At the same time, the government advised that women in the area of heaviest contamination should avoid becoming pregnant for at least three months. This provoked another outcry from the church, since strictures prohibiting birth control had to be relaxed.

Finally alerted to the seriousness of the crisis, Italians promptly panicked. Lacking real knowledge about dioxin, they freely indulged in alarmist hearsay. Dioxin took on the character of a modern plague, caused by man's enslavement to science. Papers carelessly labelled Seveso 'Italy's Hiroshima'. The communist newspaper *L'Unita* consulted a Vietnamese expert on dioxin poisoning, who predicted an epidemic of liver cancer and hepatitis and warned that the poison would be carried through rivers and streams as far as the sea. A retrospective study of the crisis, published in 1978, found that 'the mass media seemed to suggest that . . . small children burnt by the cloud . . . could be met at every street corner'. It was not just the area that was seen as contaminated, but the people themselves and everything they produced. For months, Italians refused to buy or handle any goods even remotely associated with Seveso.[40]

The only group managing to remain relatively calm was the people of Seveso, since they could see that effects were localized and that no one, as yet, had died. That said, the papers tried their best to foil their efforts to maintain composure. According to a post-crisis study, 'Daily assemblies with large audiences at the local level were never able to counteract efficiently the influence of the mass media, where miraculous solutions and reassuring statements alternated with catastrophic perspectives and declarations of impotence.'[41]

On 11 August, Hoffmann-La Roche took the extraordinary step of admitting blame and promising full compensation. Dr Adolf Jann told a news conference that 'from the moment the extent of the danger was appreciated, the company's first priority [has] been to save lives, [and] avoid organic damage to the health of people'. However disingenuous that claim might have been, the company's decision had the beneficial effect of kickstarting the process of recovery, since a culprit had been identified and compensation promised without a bitter legal battle.[42]

An investigation nevertheless ensued, with the aim of identifying individuals responsible. It quickly became apparent that Hoffmann-La Roche's equivocation over the first two weeks of the crisis was not simply a panicked reaction but consistent with a long-term pattern of behaviour. A 1978 study concluded that, 'The production and diffusion of the toxic cloud . . . was more than an accident. It was the logical, though casual, fallout of a production process where controls and safeguards were practically nonexistent, and which had been modified over the years to maximize output.' This raised serious questions about possible dioxin release over the three decades prior to the accident. ICMESA had consistently blocked attempts by local authorities to monitor its discharge of effluents. Residents recalled incidents of animals mysteriously dying, for which compensation was quietly paid. The legal investigation eventually led to five ICMESA employees being convicted in 1983 for 'negligently causing . . . a disaster'. They were given prison sentences ranging from four to five years, but an appeals court reversed their convictions two years later.[43]

The legal investigation exposed an extraordinary level of contempt shown by Hoffmann La-Roche toward the local community. The firm seemed to think that secrecy and subterfuge were perfectly acceptable, despite the fact that the plant was handling some of the most dangerous chemicals known to man. Local residents, up to and including government officials, were kept entirely in the dark about what was actually made at the plant, rendering the formulation of emergency plans difficult. Investigators also discovered that 'changes had been made in plant or processes which compromised the safety of the facilities but were not communicated to authorities responsible for public health and safety'.[44]

Due to the lethality of dioxin, decontamination proved hugely difficult. As early as 16 August, Hoffmann-La Roche urged Italian officials to adopt a 'scorched earth' approach, namely dismantling the factory, burning all vegetation and removing up to 30 centimetres of topsoil from the contaminated area. Local officials were, however, understandably reluctant to take such drastic steps. Recovery was therefore slowed by government infighting and interminable debates over appropriate procedure.

Decontamination began in January 1977, with demolition of affected buildings (including the factory) following ten months later. The most seriously contaminated material was sealed in containers and exported to unknown destinations. Hoffmann-La Roche claimed that barrels were sent (appropriately) to Switzerland, but subsequent revelations suggested otherwise.

In 1992, an article in *Corriere della Sera* revealed that 150 metric tons of heavily contaminated substances, in containers innocuously labelled 'sodium chloride', had ended up at a dump in East Germany. Revelations that some of the material might have gone to France led to a bomb attack upon a Hoffmann-La Roche office in Paris. When asked where precisely barrels had been sent, an official at Hoffmann-La Roche pleaded ignorance. 'That was part of the contract with the disposal firm,' he explained. 'They were anxious that no one should know, including ourselves and the Italian authorities. Obviously, they feared that if the location became known there might be difficulties.'[45]

Two years after the crisis, the most heavily contaminated sector, an area of 90 hectares, continued to stymie clean-up efforts. 'It may be a wasteland forever – we just don't know what to do,' one official complained. Eventually, topsoil to a depth of 40 centimetres was removed. This was placed in huge concrete holding vessels constructed on site, along with other contaminated material. The vessels were then covered with soil brought from outside the region and a large park was built. To locals, that seemed an appropriate memorial. 'This place was a desert,' park administrator Antonio Mambriani remarked in 1999. 'Now, you see it is covered with trees. If anything good came of dioxin, it was probably this park and the green it gave Seveso.' Thanks to the thoroughness of clean-up efforts, the town now has a lower level of residual dioxin than most of the rest of Italy. Decontamination was not just physical, but also spiritual: the removal of affected buildings and millions of cubic metres of soil allowed the community to feel cleansed, thus aiding recovery.[46]

Seveso, it seems, was a disaster without devastation. The only clearly identifiable fatality was Paoletti who, most Italians felt, got what he deserved. As for the rest of the community, life returned to normal, or, in many cases, better than normal, much more quickly than most people expected. Evacuees first began returning in October

1977. Those whose homes had to be demolished were given new houses of equal or greater value. Former factory workers were all found new jobs. Children affected by chloracne got free holidays and other compensation.

Public health was carefully monitored, to the point where Seveso became the most systematically studied case of dioxin contamination in history. The health effects have not lived up to the biblical plague so often predicted. Anecdotal evidence pointed to an unusual incidence of some cancers and other ailments, but statistics proved inconclusive despite the determination of investigators to uncover every stone. Nor were an unusual number of malformed babies born. The only identifiable medical effect over the short term was a skewed gender ratio among infants born in the area during the first seven years after the accident. Baby girls outnumbered boys by forty-six to twenty-eight, a disproportion consistent with dioxin.

The most important consequence of Seveso, it seems, was not illness, but resolve, represented most profoundly by the European Community's Seveso Directive. The EC, slowly inching toward regulation of dangerous industries due to accidents at Flixborough in the UK in 1974, Beek in the Netherlands in 1975 and Manfredonia in Italy in 1976, acted with atypical urgency after Seveso. A strict system of regulation and monitoring was instituted, but the most impressive aspect of the directive was the way it addressed the contempt shown by Hoffmann-La Roche toward the local population. The EC established a 'need to know' principle, which stipulated that local residents and industrial workers must be informed about the hazards of an industry. While this falls short of the 'right to know' principle common in the United States, in the sense that 'experts' determine 'need', it was a massive step forward.

Therein lies the paradox of Seveso. Instead of hundreds of malformed children and horrible deaths, we have what appears to be a safer world resulting from a disaster that did not happen. Instead of despair, Seveso symbolizes recovery. This image is, however, dangerous as it encourages a false sense of security about the ability of modern industrial societies to act in their own best interest. In the early 1990s, for instance, Seveso was used by officials in Arkansas not as an example of the risks of dioxin poisoning, but of the safety of production processes. Critics of a proposed toxic waste incinerator were bombarded with evidence from Seveso (of which there is so much) supposedly demonstrating that risks would be minimal. The evidence that Seveso seems to present, namely that low level dioxin contamination is not dangerous, has encouraged a complacency toward the chemical, thus impeding efforts to find a safer alternative. By the same token, the remarkable recovery of Seveso has been used as justification for limited liability on the part of polluters, thus affecting assessments of damage and levels of compensation.

Regulations like those enshrined in the Seveso Directive reinforce the belief that all will be well. Ironically, however, it was the absence of regulations that facilitated Seveso's miraculous recovery. The process of healing was quickened because the most heavily contaminated materials were packed up and exported to destinations unknown, just the sort of clandestine operation which new regulations render impossible. Further, it is well to bear in mind that Seveso's recovery was aided profoundly by the fact that there was never any doubt about culpability, which meant that a bruising legal fight was avoided. Recompense was offered with unusual speed. Had Hoffmann-La Roche been able to argue that it had complied with safety regulations, the firm would have been less likely to cooperate in the process of recovery. Regulations do not just protect the public, they also protect industrial firms from those seeking recompense.

Seveso's legacy is therefore difficult to assess. Over the years, it has evolved into an example of how modern industrial societies cope with and adjust to ecological threats. It has reinforced confidence that tree-hugging doom merchants can be ignored – that ecological crises are never as bad as predicted. Yet that is whistling in the dark. Seveso is a typical Seventies ecological disaster. The plethora of such disasters, including, perhaps most notoriously, that of Love Canal in Niagara Falls, New York, has encouraged the belief that environmental safety declined during the decade, when in fact the opposite is true. These disasters are notorious precisely because awareness of environmental issues rose significantly during the decade, as did the public's assertion of its right to a cleaner environment. 'Twenty years ago we just accepted our lot,' an ordinary Welsh housewife who led a protest against a polluting factory confessed in 1972. 'We wouldn't have thought about protesting, but things have changed and we won't stand for it any longer.' The decade was one of enormous environmental progress, symbolized most profoundly by the first Earth Day on 22 April 1970. But awareness did not necessarily lead to good practice. Seveso illustrates the prevalent 'What can we get away with?' attitude that typifies the approach to environmental questions. There has been a tendency to address the effects of high-growth, high-consumption habits without questioning the assumed right to live that way. This has meant piling up problems for the future, but also, in many cases, exporting unpleasant production processes (or effluents) to countries too poor to enjoy the luxury of high environmental standards. As Gladwyn Hill wrote in the *New York Times*, on the occasion of the first Earth Day, what was needed was 'a sudden, remarkable, spontaneous rebellion not of one group against another so much as of everybody against the physical conditions to which two centuries of promiscuous "progress" have brought us'.[47]

Seveso also illustrates precisely how dangerous the short-term mentality typical of so much environmental concern can be. The community seems to have recovered miraculously and the ill-effects have supposedly been minor. Recent studies, however, suggest something different. On 1 August 2008, researchers at the University of Milan revealed that a study of 1,772 women who lived in the contaminated zone were six times more likely than a similar control group to give birth to babies with altered thyroid function, a condition which can lead to reduced growth and retarded intellectual development. 'Our findings', the study concluded, 'indicate that maternal exposure to persistent environmental contaminants such as [dioxin] produces effects on neonatal thyroid function that may occur far apart in time from the initial exposure.' In other words, the most profound effect of Seveso might be felt by a generation born twenty or thirty years after the disaster. And what about the children of those children, as yet unborn? Perhaps the wisest comment on Seveso was uttered two years after the accident by Ugo Basilico, a local builder who, along with his wife, decided not to have a second child. 'Even the professors don't know,' he remarked. 'They forecast. They warn. They show concern. But they don't know.'[48]

Three Mile Island: Meltdown

On 16 March 1979, *The China Syndrome* premiered in the United States. In the film, a reporter, played by Jane Fonda, asks a nuclear power expert what the consequence of a meltdown at a nuclear plant might be. He replies that it would 'render an area the size of Pennsylvania permanently uninhabitable'. Twelve days later, life imitated art. A meltdown occurred at Three Mile Island – in Pennsylvania.[49]

In the years after Hiroshima, America fell in love with the atom. Physicists boasted that electricity would become so cheap to produce that there would be no point in metering it – it could be given away. Experts, convinced of their own invincibility, condescendingly dismissed fears about safety. The attractiveness of nuclear power increased after the Arab oil boycott, the mighty atom providing the perfect response to OPEC's stranglehold. Nuclear generation also seemed clean, an important point at a time of growing eco-awareness.

Basking in public goodwill, utility companies laid down plans for scores of nuclear plants. 'We had no control over the number,' Harold Denton, chief of reactor operations at the Nuclear Regulatory Commission, admits. The rate of approval led critics to conclude that the NRC had abandoned regulation in favour of the rubber stamp. That unease was shared by insiders. Peter Bradford, an NRC Commissioner, saw quite a few colleagues leave in the mid-1970s over concerns that safety was being neglected. The official position seemed to be 'that everything was safe enough already'. As a result, 'anyone who wanted to raise a new concern, anyone who was sceptical that a particular plant should be licensed, had an immensely heavy burden . . . Because nothing, nothing serious had happened yet.' An inquiry after the accident would severely criticize the NRC for being 'an agency hypnotized by equipment'.[50]

The nuclear plant at Three Mile Island in Pennsylvania was located on a sandbar on the Susquehanna River, just 10 miles from Harrisburg, the state capitol. Reactor No. 2 had gone into operation on the very last day of 1978, so that its owners, Metropolitan Edison, could benefit from tax credits totalling $40 million. That decision to go live was probably hasty. During the period between 28 March 1978, when the chain reaction started, and the commencement of power generation on 31 December – a total of 274 days – malfunctions forced shutdowns on 195 days. The shutdowns were caused by problems similar to those which eventually led to the worst nuclear accident in American history.

The first hint of a crisis came at 04.00 on 28 March 1979. Two bursts of a klaxon tore through the control room after the main feedwater pumps mysteriously stopped. As per the established protocol, both the turbine and the reactor automatically shut down. This, however, led to a build-up of pressure in the containment vessel, which triggered an automatic valve to open. Once the pressure was released, the valve should have closed. Unbeknownst to the operators, it failed to do so. Cooling water drained from the system, causing the nuclear core to overheat. In an instant, a minor problem became a major calamity.

In the control room, a technician witnessed 'Bells . . . ringing, lights . . . flashing, and everybody . . . grabbing and scratching.' Up to this point, every action had been programmed, automatic responses to clear signals. Suddenly, however, human beings, with fickle judgement, intervened. Lacking a reliable indicator of the coolant level, technicians surmised that the containment vessel must be flooding, when it fact it was draining. They therefore reacted precisely in the opposite way to what was demanded – they shut off the emergency water system. Left alone, it would have cooled the dangerously overheating core. Fuel rods were consequently exposed and meltdown began.[51]

Inside the control room, the cacophony of lights, klaxons and sirens increased. 'The place was swarming with white hats,' an operator recalled. Despite the hullabaloo, engineers remained convinced that meltdown was impossible. 'Most of us who had spent our lives in this business didn't believe that could happen,' Bob Long recalled. 'We had a mindset that . . . we had these marvellous safety systems which had back-ups of back-ups . . . That . . . made it hard for people to really come to grips with the reality that severe damage had occurred.' In fact, by dawn the core had reached 4,300 degrees – true meltdown would occur at 5,200 degrees. That could, in turn, lead to 'China syndrome', when the core burns its way through the concrete base of the plant, superheating the groundwater underneath and causing fissures to spider in all directions. Highly radioactive geysers of steam would then erupt, causing a deadly radiation shower.[52]

At 06.15, a new alarm sounded, this time indicating radiation in the control room. Technicians had suddenly to accept that foolproof safety systems were not coping. Supervisor Gary Miller immediately issued a general emergency declaration, a situation unprecedented in the American nuclear industry. Emergency services were consequently mobilized, a development inevitably noticed by journalists. Mike Pintek, a local reporter, phoned the plant, somehow got through to the control room and, to his immense surprise, was told of the crisis. Pintek then relayed this information to his radio listeners, triggering panic. By 09.06 the Associated Press was reporting the accident nationwide. Reporters flocked to the plant.

'I knew we were in another dimension,' Governor Dick Thornburgh felt when alerted to the situation. 'My first thought was that . . . no accident at a nuclear plant could be anything but serious.' He immediately mobilized the state's emergency council, chaired by William Scranton, the lieutenant governor. Scranton contacted MetEd, who insisted there was no cause for alarm. 'We are not in a China Syndrome situation,' David Klucsick, a company spokesman insisted. That confidence was quickly relayed to journalists at an impromptu press conference. 'Everything is under control,' Scranton announced. 'There is and was no danger to public health and safety.' Before long, Scranton discovered that he had inadvertently colluded in subterfuge. 'The indignation that welled up within me was memorable. I still haven't gotten over that.'[53]

That afternoon, MetEd held its own press conference. The company chose as their official spokesman Jack Herbein, a boorish nuclear engineer with no public relations experience. His first mistake was to refer to the morning's events as an 'accident', a word he attempted to swallow between the 'd' and the 'e'. The word he preferred – 'incident' – then shot from his mouth like a watermelon seed. That shaky start permanently destroyed his credibility; his dishonesty was as obvious as a long wooden nose. Herbein's credibility suffered further when he came up with the quintessential engineer's euphemism, calling the problem 'a normal aberration'. Reporters, feeding on the carrion of catastrophe, refused to swallow Herbein's cosy fibs. 'I didn't buy it and there were quite a few other people that didn't buy it,' Robert Reid, mayor of nearby Middletown recalled. He was especially annoyed by Herbein's condescending replies, as if he, the expert, should not have to answer ignorant questions. Interviewed later in the day, Scranton was unable to disguise his distrust of MetEd. The situation, he admitted, was 'more complex than the company first led us to believe'.[54]

A new player now entered the fray, in the form of the Nuclear Regulatory Commission in Bethesda, Maryland. A crisis team was mobilized, and experts sent to Three Mile Island. Initially at least, the NRC shared MetEd's confidence. 'I thought it had been a small loss-of-coolant accident,' Denton recalled. His natural instinct was to assume that the problem would quickly be solved by the plant's built-in safety measures. 'It was . . . the Titanic sort of mentality that this plant was so well designed that . . . you couldn't possibly have a serious core damage.' Experts, however, soon received a crash course in fallibility. 'The collective feelings', an engineer related, 'went from: a. bravado and disbelief; to b. caution in jumping to conclusions; to c. grudging admission that maybe something was wrong; to d.

realization that it was, indeed, a real accident; to e. apprehension that the reactor really might melt; and, finally, to a feeling of awe and humility that the technology that we had thought was foolproof wasn't.'[55]

Jim Higgins, among the first NRC experts to arrive at Three Mile Island, encountered a scene from the Twilight Zone – the plant was virtually deserted but for some personnel in full radiation suits and respirator masks. 'It gave the impression like, there is something very wrong here.' Respirators made communication hugely difficult, a problem compounded by the fact that there were only two telephone lines into the plant, and they were quickly overloaded. 'There was just a terrible communications problem,' Denton confessed. 'You got only bits and pieces.' Information was instead passed by a system of runners using walkie-talkies, with the inevitable result that vital statistics were garbled on the bush telegraph. Not until the evening was Babcock & Wilcox, the designers of the plant, able to communicate the vital instruction to pump water into the containment vessel. That seemed to stabilize the situation. The core temperature began to drop, and the crisis seemed to pass.[56]

That was the message Walter Cronkite conveyed on the *CBS Evening News* when he described the crisis as just 'the first step in a nuclear nightmare . . . no worse than that'. That impression was confirmed when Scranton visited the next day. Though unnerved by having to don heavy protective gear, and by encountering contaminated water, he went away feeling calm. MetEd officials had, meanwhile, begun an aggressive public relations campaign. Appearing on ABC's *Good Morning America*, president Walter Creitz assured viewers that the problem had been brought under control without injury to anyone.[57]

The NRC did not share Creitz's confidence and was, in fact, growing increasingly annoyed by MetEd complacency. From the beginning, NRC staff had advocated limited evacuation, an option Thornburgh resisted. 'No matter how well planned,' he later explained, 'evacuations had the potential to kill or injure people.' On the 30th, however, a new revelation seemed to justify NRC pessimism. In the early morning, technicians reported that a large cloud of radioactive gas had escaped. When pressed for hard figures on the size of the release, Creitz replied: 'I'll be honest . . . I don't know.' Nor could he promise that the problem would not recur. Under renewed pressure, Thornburgh stubbornly resisted evacuation. An exasperated Joseph Hendrie, the NRC commissioner, vented his frustration to his staff: 'We are operating almost totally in the blind, [Thornburgh's] information is ambiguous, mine is non-existent . . . it's like a couple of blind men staggering around making decisions.' Denton, agreeing with Hendrie, argued that 'the important thing . . . is to get a start rather than sitting here waiting to die. Even if we can't minimize the individual dose, there might still be a chance to limit the population dose.'[58]

An evacuation of everyone in a 5-mile radius of the plant would have involved 24,522 people. Double the radius and the number increased six-fold. Double it again and over 635,000 people would require moving. Evacuation plans were sketchy, having been devolved to the various counties and towns. A local authority lawyer, who was tasked with improvizing plans after the accident had already occurred, confessed that he felt let down by the failure of state and federal authorities to provide guidance. 'I don't know what they assumed, but if they assumed the counties knew [what to do] then they shouldn't have done that. They shouldn't have assumed anything. Because counties didn't plan for nuclear accidents. Nobody planned for nuclear accidents.' Oren Henderson, head of the Pennsylvania civil defence authority, later admitted feeling completely overwhelmed. 'We lacked so much knowledge about what was going on.' To his horror, Thornburgh discovered that plans called for Dauphin County, on one side of the river, and Cumberland County, on the other, to evacuate in convergent directions. In other words, two crowds would collide on a bridge over the Susquehanna.[59]

Thornburgh compromised by urging everyone within a 10-mile radius to stay indoors until further notice. One resident recalled how the sense of crisis descended at his elementary school:

> We came back inside from a recess and the teachers seemed very nervous and kept us in our rooms. Periodically the teacher would come in to the room and say, 'Johnny, your mother is here' and the child would leave. At first we didn't know what was going on and the departures only made those of us remaining even more scared. At some point, the teachers told us about the accident and the possibility that the area would be too dangerous to live in for 40 years if the worst happened. The world seemed a very chaotic, scary thing . . . that day.

An enterprising Harrisburg official came up with the bright idea of using air raid sirens to drive home Thornburgh's message. A full-blown panic inevitably resulted. 'People in Harrisburg are running around like crazy,' a news cameraman noted.[60]

Lacking firm guidance from government, residents took matters into their own hands. 'You hear one thing from the utility,' Suzanne Machita complained in the midst of packing her car. 'Then one thing from the Government, another thing from Harrisburg and something else from civil defense. I don't know what to believe, what to do, so I guess the best thing is to go. It's better than doing nothing.' Robin Stuart received a panicked phone call from her sister in California. 'Get out!' she cried. 'Get out. Hurry up and get out.' Before long, the phone started ringing non-stop with friends around the country shouting the same message. Marsha McHenry found her neighbours in a determined mood. '[They said] that I was to come down to their house, they had guns and they had a chainsaw and a big truck and they would get up on the highway, cut down any barriers that were there and fight their way through.' Reid watched in horror as the roads out of Middletown became hopelessly clogged with overloaded cars.[61]

At a press conference on Friday, Herbein openly questioned the advice to stay indoors: 'It's certainly the civil defense's prerogative to take those steps, but we don't think it . . . necessary. If the civil defense chooses to tell inhabitants of Middletown to keep their windows and doors shut, that's their prerogative. We have our windows and doors open.' He added, for good measure, that consumers would have to absorb the multimillion dollar cost of decontamination. Journalists revolted. 'Mr. Herbein,' someone interjected, 'is your plant a lemon?' Frustration led to journalistic meltdown. 'I live a mile from the plant,' one reporter shouted. 'What are you going to be doing to protect my family?' Another calmly asked: 'Mr. Herbein, don't you feel a responsibility to a million people living around the plant to keep them informed?' Wounded by having his authority questioned, Herbein stuttered: 'I don't know why, I don't know why we need to, we need to tell you each and every thing that we do.' Pintek shot back: 'Well, why not, Jack? You know, we only live here, and you may kill us here before you're all finished.' Pintek later reflected: 'I was angry . . . in fact, I'm still angry. I was just upset with the way things were being handled and the way we were lied to.' Finally, with television cameras capturing the moment, a clearly rattled Herbein shouted: 'We didn't injure anybody. We didn't overexpose anybody. We didn't kill a single soul. The release of radioactivity off-site was minimal.'[62]

Pintek found that his job had suddenly become personal. A group of professional journalists had morphed into a mob frightened for their lives. 'I shouted a question to Jack Herbein . . . along the lines of, "You started to melt that thing down, didn't you, didn't you?" . . . at that moment I was not a journalist any more, . . . I lived here and I was mad. I was angry.' Amidst the tumult, few grasped the import of Herbein's rather nonchalant announcement that a bubble of hydrogen gas was building up in the reactor core. 'It's serious,' he remarked, 'but not to the extent that we have to evacuate the citizenry.' After all, what could be more harmless than a bubble?[63]

Thornburgh, reassured by MetEd confidence, remained convinced that he could get away with limited evacuation. He asked Hendrie for advice, and the reply seemed to contradict that confidence. 'If my wife were pregnant and we had small children in the area,' Hendrie replied, 'I would get them out, because we don't know what's going to happen.' Pregnant women and pre-school age children living within a 5-mile radius were therefore urged to leave. Since the governor had essentially admitted that there was a health risk, the exodus quickened, with some 140,000 people eventually leaving. 'The moment that's so crystal clear in my mind is driving on the highway and trying to imagine what would happen to this area,' McHenry recalled. 'All of this beautiful countryside would be destroyed. It would be so contaminated that nobody could be there for hundreds of years. I looked as hard as I could at everything, and tried to burn it into my mind, what everything looked like, because I wasn't going to see it again.'[64]

Thornburgh was buffeted between MetEd's equivocation and journalists' trepidation. 'We worked hard to preserve our credibility by releasing only such information as we were confident in and by correcting any misleading information,' he reflected. 'This effort was frustrating in the extreme due to the wide variety of sources, many of which were ill-informed or uninformed.' In desperation, he asked President Carter to send an overseer he could trust. Carter immediately dispatched Denton. '[That] proved to be a turning point,' Thornburgh concluded. '[Denton] was able to translate nuclear jargon into plain English and earned the confidence of me and my staff, the news media, and the general public.' Pintek echoed that appraisal: 'He's kind of this slow talking . . . southern-sounding kind of guy who automatically puts you at ease . . . That's kind of how it felt: Finally someone is here that we can trust.'[65]

Denton issued an immediate statement: 'We've assured ourselves that there is no imminent danger to the public as a result of the way the core is being cooled.' Beneath that calm, anxieties lurked. 'I was dealing with absolute chaos,' he recalled. 'They (MetEd) were fighting fires. They were trying to cope with all the demands being placed on them and they didn't have enough staff.' He decided to take matters out of the hands of MetEd and to make all crucial decisions himself. His immediate concern was the hydrogen bubble. Estimates put it at 1,000 cubic feet. Two possibilities existed, both catastrophic. The worst was that the bubble would continue to grow and force coolant out of the reactor, causing the core to speed back towards meltdown. Slightly less serious was the possibility that a spark would cause the bubble to explode, blowing the top off the containment vessel. A Princeton scientist calculated that the bubble contained energy equivalent to three tons of TNT. After that revelation, panic quickly descended. 'How the hell do we get the bubble out of there?' Denton's assistant Roger Mattson shouted. He sensed a race with death which made Thornburgh's reluctance to evacuate seem stupid. 'Got to say it . . . I don't know what we are protecting at this point. I think we ought to be moving people.'[66]

News broadcasts freely used the word 'meltdown', thus fuelling panic. 'The world has never known a day quite like today,' Cronkite remarked that Friday. 'It faced the considerable uncertainties and dangers of the worst nuclear power plant accident of the atomic age. And the horror tonight is that it could get much worse. The potential is there for the ultimate risk of a meltdown.' Thornburgh was outraged by the reckless irresponsibility of that statement. 'One could almost feel the collective shudder going through central Pennsylvania.' Reporting on something they did not remotely understand, journalists were forced to trust 'experts', who were themselves flummoxed. Journalists feasted on predictions of doom. Jim Hill, a local reporter, later remarked: 'After three days feeding on the carcass of Three Mile Island, I was beginning to feel as ugly as what I ate. There was nothing delicious about this story.'[67]

Overfed on rumour, residents feared the worst. 'I had an image of the whole valley being completely devastated and people just falling over,' one housewife later told an interviewer. 'There would be no place to go to escape it . . . The whole thing seemed so futile to me that I just couldn't think about it. You couldn't eat, you couldn't drink . . . There was just nothing you could do.' The helplessness felt by ordinary people was exacerbated by conflicting signals from those in authority. Reports from the NRC seemed grave, while those from MetEd remained upbeat. Herbein told reporters on Friday night that the bubble had shrunk from 1,000 to 800 cubic feet, adding that 'I personally think the crisis is over'. Around the same time, Mattson was approaching panic. He had been thinking of a crisis coming within days, but suddenly decided that an explosion could occur at any moment. In contrast, another NRC engineer, Victor Stello, argued that there was little danger of explosion – the problem would correct itself. In other words, the situation was either catastrophic or harmless, with nothing in between.[68]

At 21.00 on Saturday, the Associated Press reported that the bubble was 'showing signs of becoming potentially explosive, complicating decisions on whether to mount a risky operation to remove the gas'. Officials surmised that 'tens of thousands of people might have to be evacuated if engineers decided to try to remove the bubble, operations that could risk a meltdown'. After that announcement, Paul Critchlow, the governor's press secretary, faced a near riot. 'About 20 or 30 reporters burst through the door of this office. They said: "We want to know if our lives are in danger. What the hell's going on here? We want to know if we have to get out." . . . They were pale. They were frightened. At that point, they had lost interest in the story they were supposed to be covering.' 'It's Saturday night,' Pintek recalls thinking. 'I'm saying to myself, my life, at about 27 years old, is going to be over, because these – these arrogant utility operators have allowed this thing to run out of control and they're going to kill us.' At 23.00, Denton tried to calm nerves. 'We see no possibility of hydrogen explosions in either the containment or the reactor vessel in the near term,' he told reporters. That, however, did not rule out an explosion in the long term. Journalists uneasily speculated on Denton's definitions of 'near' and 'long'.[69]

President Carter was fuming, annoyed not just by the crisis, but by how poorly the news had been handled. 'There are too many people talking,' he complained to his press secretary Jody Powell. 'And my impression is that half of them don't know what they are talking about . . . Get those people to speak with one voice.' That, however, was impossible. 'That AP piece was the crowning blow,' a White House aide later remarked. 'The president felt that the information . . . was frightening a lot of people. He wanted to show the public that it was not dangerous.' An aide suggested that Carter should go to Three Mile Island. When Powell raised this possibility with Denton, the latter was enthusiastic. 'Yes,' he replied, 'I think it would be a great help.'[70]

On Sunday morning, Stello went to mass. To his astonishment, the priest offered the congregation general absolution, the sacrament given when death is imminent. Only then did it dawn on Stello how the crisis was affecting ordinary people, who had no knowledge of nuclear power and no standard by which to judge massively conflicting reports. 'What we had done to these people [was] just outrageous,' he reflected. 'We had frightened them so bad . . . they thought they were gonna die.'[71]

Carter's visit was taking place at the same time as Hendrie's announcement that residents within a radius of 20 miles should prepare to evacuate. Since that was the largest evacuation yet suggested, it implied a crisis spiralling beyond control. As Carter flew into the complex, he contemplated the possibility that the reactor might explode at any moment. On the ground, the two principal protagonists in the bubble scare, Stello and Mattson, were at each other's throats. Stello berated Mattson for spreading unwarranted fear, while Mattson criticized Stello for complacency. Meanwhile, Denton briefed Carter, without being fully certain which of his two deputies was right. Carter realized that he had no choice but to follow through with the visit; since his only purpose was to calm fears, he would cause a stampede if he shied away. The moment demanded that he act presidential.

Stello worked frantically to turn conjecture into fact. He sensed there was something wrong with Mattson's calculations, but couldn't quite put his finger on it. When realization dawned, it proved embarrassingly simple: hydrogen needs oxygen to explode, and there was not enough oxygen in the containment vessel. The bubble had probably never been a threat.

Carter's visit calmed nerves. Fred Lynch, who helped direct traffic for the visit, remarked: 'The president of the United States doesn't just walk into a danger area. It kind of makes you feel comfortable.' The crisis was not yet over, but panic cooled at the same rate as the core. In the end, the danger to the general public had been tiny, or so it seems. Because vent monitors malfunctioned, there is no reliable documentation of the actual radiation released. Those in the area who subsequently lost loved ones to cancer believe the plant was to blame. Most epidemiologists are equally certain that it was not. In 1996, a federal judge dismissed damage claims by more than 2,000 residents, citing a 'paucity of proof'.[72]

Residents could not, however, easily forget their terror. One Harrisburg housewife compared the situation to when Hurricane Agnes hit central Pennsylvania in 1972. 'There was fear then, but nothing like in 1979. We could see the floodwaters, but we knew that in a few days or weeks, we could start rebuilding our lives. With Three Mile Island, we couldn't see the danger, but we knew that if this "flood" hit, we could never come back. Many people I know still have not forgiven MetEd, and never will, for what they did to us.' Thornburgh agreed that the disaster was made much worse by the ham-fisted public relations of MetEd. 'It first seemed to speak with many voices, and then with none at all.'[73]

Three years would pass before engineers could discern precisely how serious the crisis had been. As it turned out, journalists were perfectly entitled to use the term 'meltdown' since that is precisely what had occurred. A camera lowered into the core revealed that 50 per cent had melted down, or 20 tons of uranium had been turned into a molten mass. 'It was not the China Syndrome,' Mattson remarked, 'but we melted the core down . . . No question about it.'[74]

At the Middletown Elks Club, the cheeseburger was renamed 'The Meltdown' and a bowl of beans became the 'bubble buster'. A local radio station offered a mock weather forecast: 'Partly cloudy tomorrow with a 40 percent chance of survival.' 'What's the five-day forecast for Harrisburg?' a DJ asked. 'Two days.' Jack Baker, who ran a shop in Middletown, made a killing on T-shirts that read 'Happiness is a cool reactor' and 'Hell no, we won't glow'. Humour, however, was a thin veneer applied over a dense core of anguish. For a few days, panic had been entirely warranted. The crisis had been compounded by the abject failure of the authorities to cope. 'I don't see how you could ever erase the memories of frustration, of uncertainty . . . punctuated by moments of stark terror that attach to an incident like Three Mile Island,' Thornburgh reflected. America's love affair with the atom subsequently went into meltdown. 'If our faith in MetEd is shaken', wrote the Middletown *Press and Journal* in a front-page editorial, 'our belief in the entire nuclear power industry also rides on thin ice.' After Three Mile Island, no new plants were ordered in the United States. 'This is the end of nuclear power,' one expert predicted. 'From now on in, it's going to be coal city.'[75]

10

TYRANTS

Uganda: Big Daddy Amin

Idi Amin was responsible for the deaths of probably 300,000 Ugandans. The cream of society – academics, lawyers, clerics, doctors, scientists – were murdered, along with countless common people. During eight years in power, he destroyed a thriving economy, so much so that it took over thirty years for GDP to return to where it had been when he took power. 'He will never be rehabilitated', writes the Africanist Richard Dowden, 'but to this day when you mention his name many Ugandans laugh rather than weep.'[1]

Amin often provoked laughter. On the occasion of the Silver Jubilee in 1977, he asked Queen Elizabeth for some of her twenty-five-year-old underwear. When informed that the British economy was in crisis, he launched a 'Save the British Fund' which raised 43,000 East African shillings, not to mention tons of bananas, coffee and vegetables. A lover of Scottish pipe music, he once offered to lead the Scots in a war of independence. In 1971, in an attempt to mend fences with Tanzanian president Julius Nyerere, he confessed: 'I love you very much and if you had been a woman I would have considered marrying you . . . But as you are a man that possibility does not arise.'[2]

In truth, Amin was as funny as a laughing hyena. He used humour to disarm opponents, intentionally cultivating the image of a buffoon and taking advantage of those who fell for it. Many saw him as a not-very-noble savage, the perfect embodiment of every white assumption of what a black man should be. As Yasmin Alibhai-Brown, who grew up in Uganda, wrote, Amin 'is *the* monster that has long dwelt in the Western imagination – very black, colossal, sexually insatiable, brutal, easily aroused to fury and intemperate acts yet gullible like a child, covetous, power crazy, cannibalistic, corrupt and so on . . . Some white people felt oddly comforted by this archetype who so fitted what they thought they knew about black men; they were sure they could control and manage such beasts.'[3]

Amin's father was a poor Kakwa peasant from the north of Uganda, his mother a witch doctor – a fact which might explain the significance her son assigned to dreams and omens. He received some schooling at the local mission, though probably not much, given that he was essentially illiterate. What he lacked in brainpower, he made up in physicality: he was six feet, four inches tall, weighed 300 pounds, was immensely strong, ruggedly handsome, and possessed a 200-watt smile. He was also a superb athlete – his prowess at boxing, rugby and running delighted his sports-mad colonial masters.

Soldiering offered the best escape from rural poverty, and also the opportunity to use his physique to good advantage. In expeditions against marauders in northern Uganda, Amin impressed his British officers with bravery and brute strength. His rise was consequently rapid; in 1959 he was one of the first Ugandans promoted to 'effendi', a non-commissioned rank reserved for native soldiers who possessed leadership potential. Three years later, as a lieutenant posted to the Northern Frontier of Kenya, his barbarism surfaced. A minor cattle rustling problem was used as excuse for slaughter – villagers were tortured, beaten to death and buried alive. By this stage, however, Ugandan decolonization was too far advanced for the British to court-martial a black lieutenant they had singled out for stardom. The incident was quietly buried, except by Amin, who incorporated it into his personal folklore.

Amin seemed symbolic of the new, independent Uganda –

unrefined, immensely strong and hugely optimistic. His star rose when he came under the wing of Prime Minister Milton Obote, who, like others, assumed that this simple soldier could easily be controlled. The two were made for each other. Both were crooks, fully prepared to fleece their country. Over the next seven years, they found plenty of opportunity for thievery and for consolidating their respective power. Obote had in mind a classic autocracy, unfettered by parliamentary procedure. That meant that he needed the brute force Amin could provide. Amin was generously rewarded, eventually gaining complete control of the military and police. As he gained power, however, the acolyte turned on his master. A regular sequence of assassination attempts, though never conclusively linked to Amin, had his fingerprints everywhere. By the end of 1970, Obote was searching for a way to rid himself of his troublesome general.

In January 1971, Obote made the mistake of leaving the country in order to attend a Commonwealth summit. Before leaving, he challenged Amin to account for huge sums missing from the defence budget. Amin, sensing a 'now or never' moment, had his soldiers occupy key points in Kampala. Obote, told that he would not be allowed to return to Uganda, denounced Amin as 'the greatest brute an African mother has ever brought to life'.[4]

Amin cast himself as a reluctant coupmaster, an unselfish patriot interested only in saving Uganda. He was, he claimed, a simple soldier without political ambition. Judging by the raucous celebrations, most Ugandans believed him. 'Amin told us many times', Henry Kyemba, a former aide, recalled, 'that the traditional political life of Uganda would reassert itself, that elections would be held, that the civil service would not be interfered with, that the country would soon get back on an even keel. Because Obote had been so unpopular, Amin was acclaimed as a hero.' He was the perfect populist – a giant of a man with an incandescent smile who walked through crowds without bodyguards, telling jokes, kissing babies, slapping backs. 'The first time I saw Idi Amin was when . . . he leapt on to a platform in my local town to address the people,' Dowden recalls. '"I am one of you, I know you, we are going to make life better" [he shouted] . . . I was swept along by Amin's ebullient enthusiasm, joining the crowd to shout a huge "O ye" in answer to his . . . If he had offered me a job at that moment . . .' That scene was repeated in village after village, where all were implored to work for Uganda. Asians, who numbered more than 50,000, were told that they would always be welcome, though they were politely encouraged 'to socialise and co-operate with your brother Africans. Marriages can unite Ugandans together.'[5]

Intrigued by developments, Donald Slater, the British high commissioner in Kampala, found that Colonel Baruch Bar-Lev, the Israeli defence attaché, had helped engineer the coup. Bar-Lev informed Slater that 'all potential foci of resistance, both up-country and in Kampala, ha[s] been eliminated'. Being intimately familiar with the violent nature of Ugandan politics, Slater understood precisely what that meant. He explained to the Foreign Office that Israeli interest in Uganda arose from a desire to make life difficult for Sudan, as payback for supporting Egypt in the Six Day War. Amin had earlier cooperated with the Israelis by funnelling arms to Anya-Nya rebels in Sudan, much to Obote's dismay. As Slater explained: '[The Israelis] do not want the rebels to win. They want to keep them fighting.' Amin was not particularly interested in Sudanese politics; he simply wanted the perks that friendship with Israel could bring. It's no coincidence, then, that his first state visit as Ugandan leader was a shopping trip to Tel-Aviv. That visit gave the Israelis their first real glimpse of the friend they had bought. Shocked by Amin's greed, Golda Meir refused to give him everything he demanded, but did transfer some tanks, an assortment of small arms and a personal jet.[6]

The British, who had come to despise Obote, celebrated Amin's arrival. The *Daily Telegraph*, always appreciative of obedient Africans, called him 'a welcome contrast to other African leaders and a staunch friend of Britain'. Echoing that sentiment, a Foreign Office memo proclaimed: 'General Amin has certainly removed from the African scene one of our most implacable enemies in matters affecting Southern Africa.' It seemed politic to 'take prompt advantage' of this fortuitous development. 'Amin needs our help.' To that end,

Slater was instructed 'to get as close to Amin as you can and see whether you can . . . feed a certain amount of advice'.[7]

Slater, burdened by a swollen conscience, counselled circumspection. That brought a mild rebuke from the foreign minister Sir Alec Douglas-Home, who reminded Slater that 'The PM will be watching this and will, I am sure, want us to take quick advantage of any opportunity of selling arms. Don't overdo the caution.' In early April a Foreign Office minister, Lord Boyd, travelled to Kampala and reported that Amin wanted a signed portrait of the Queen and a state visit to Britain as soon as possible. The FO could hardly contain its delight.[8]

Slater eventually warmed to the man. 'He has earned a great deal of popularity by mixing freely, driving his own jeep, ignoring security precautions,' one report contended. 'I believe him sincere in his wish to hold elections.' Despite rumours of ethnic massacres, assassinations and kidnappings, Amin was invited to London. The highlight of the trip came when he got to ride with the Queen in an open carriage, and dine at Buckingham Palace. After inspecting military bases, he asked for armoured cars and aircraft – preferably the new Harrier jump jet. Much to the dismay of the Ministry of Defence, the Foreign Office was in favour of selling Amin everything he wanted. The reasoning went: if the British did not do so, some other country would.[9]

Meanwhile, the true nature of Amin's statecraft was emerging. He had almost no understanding of government, but was intimately familiar with the military. The mysterious was therefore transformed into the familiar – Uganda became a military state, right down to renaming Government House 'the Command Post'. Soldiers were installed as political advisers and military tribunals replaced civil courts. Veteran civil servants were told that henceforth they would be subject to military discipline. The government, recalled Moses Ali, a former aide, became dominated by 'illiterates and sycophants . . . They could not even read maps, they excelled in praising him, they were no better than Amin himself.' Out in the hinterlands, local government was divested to army commanders who established individual fiefdoms streamlined for terror and larceny.[10]

'The second day Amin was in power, people started dying,' a former aide revealed. 'He . . . is a man of death, and this satisfies him. "I am power" I have heard him say . . . The important thing to him is to survive – and thus to eliminate all opposition. To kill a wife, to kill a son – it doesn't concern him.' Removing opposition was a huge task, since enemies were everywhere. Amin established the Public Safety Unit and the State Research Bureau, overlapping agencies specializing in espionage and terror. A facility for interrogation, torture and execution was established at Nakasero, where inmates were given hammers or clubs and ordered to bludgeon one another to death. Some had nails hammered in their skulls. At Mugire Prison in Kampala, execution was swift but brutal. 'You would hear a short cry and then sudden silence,' a former prisoner described. 'I think they were being strangled and then had their heads smashed. Next day the floors of . . . the elimination chambers . . . were littered with loose eyes and teeth.'[11]

An indication of Amin's power came shortly after the coup when an explosion at Makindye Prison killed thirty-two army officers, most of them from the Acholi and Langi tribes loyal to Obote. Around two-thirds of the army, or about 6,000 soldiers, were executed during his first year in power. The decimation of officer ranks opened the way for rapid promotion. Corporals become colonels virtually overnight. Amin's air force commander, Smuts Guweddeko, was plucked from a telephone exchange, while his chief henchman, Major Malyamungu, had previously been a night watchman.

Loyalty was a commodity subject to steep inflation. A huge proportion of the Ugandan national income went toward buying the allegiance of soldiers. A regular 'whisky run' would leave Entebbe airport and fly to Stansted, where planes would be loaded with booze, electrical goods, jewellery and perfume for distribution to officers and troops. All this booty bankrupted Uganda. When money ran short, Amin ordered more to be printed.

By 1972, the once charming smile looked menacing. Amin

remained popular by appealing to base emotions – xenophobia, paranoia and greed. Ugandans were encouraged to turn against the Asians among them, who became 'parasites'. Most Asians were third- or fourth-generation émigrés, whose ancestors had been brought to Uganda by the British to provide an entrepreneurial class. In September 1972, Amin, acting upon an order from God communicated in a dream, ordered them out. They were allowed to take only what they could carry. Ordinary Ugandans, told that Asian wealth would be redistributed, welcomed the expulsion. In truth, however, there was hardly anything left after the army swept it up like locusts. Amin failed to realize that Asian businesses were the bedrock of the Ugandan economy. Since these businesses could not run themselves, they quickly disappeared. Construction ground to a halt, shops closed and factories went quiet.

The Ugandan growth rate, which had been rising at a yearly average of 4.6 per cent before Amin took power, went into freefall, hitting -11.9 per cent in 1980. During the first five years of Amin's rule, sugar production declined by 83 per cent, tobacco by 28 per cent and coffee by 22 per cent. A great deal of produce went unsold, since transport was perpetually in chaos. By 1977, only one in twenty trucks registered in Uganda actually worked. 'They can still grow export crops', a UN agronomist remarked, 'but uncertain delivery dates and past failure to live up to contracts have turned buyers off.' Foreign investment evaporated as financiers deserted a country that no longer worked. Amin had come to power promising to make all Ugandans rich, yet during his reign basic commodities like sugar, salt, cooking oil and soap were affordable only to those able to pay extortionate black market prices. Smuggling was the sole sector of the economy in growth. That said, black market traders took huge risks. The standard punishment for holding contraband salt was to force the culprit to eat his entire stock. Even animals suffered – elephants were poached for ivory, hippos shot for meat. Crocodiles, on the other hand, fared well, feasting on a steady supply of corpses dumped in the Nile.[12]

Terror, too, was a growth area. With little system, but great energy,

Amin slaughtered the cream of Ugandan society – doctors, engineers, poets, artists, teachers, judges and journalists – and took enormous pleasure in doing so. A former aide described the state of fear: 'You are walking, and any creature making a step on the dry grass behind you might be an Amin man. Whenever you hear a car speeding down the street, you think it might suddenly come to a stop – for you. I finally fled, not because I was in trouble or because of anything I did, but out of sheer fear. People disappear. When they disappear, it means they are dead.' Omnipresent lawlessness gave petty criminals freedom to rape, steal and murder at will. While a massacre of the peasantry was never Amin's aim, he created the conditions for it to happen.[13]

Bodies floating in the Nile provided demonstration of Amin's capricious power. As a method of control, fear proved as effective as violence itself. Amin took delight in announcing disappearances on the radio before the individual in question was actually grabbed. In 1977, after the Church of Uganda complained about army behaviour, Amin targeted the much-respected Archbishop Janan Luwum. Ugandans were told that Luwum had died in an auto accident, when in fact he had been shot, almost certainly by Amin himself. The clumsiness of the cover-up was probably intentional – Amin was sending a message that those with absolute power did not need to construct a good story. Equally contemptuous was the murder of High Court Judge Benedicto Kiwanuka, who was bundled from his courtroom moments before a trial was to begin. Thugs dragged him to a car, removed his shoes, and stuffed him in the trunk. The shoes were then neatly placed on the pavement as a symbolic assertion of Amin's ability to make people disappear.

The outside world was slow to react, perhaps because most Westerners expected Africans to behave this way, and because they still found it difficult to take Amin seriously. He was a sick joke; tales of his perversity were eagerly traded. Stories that he kept the heads of his victims in his freezer and occasionally ate his enemies fed a macabre appetite for horror. Myth eventually smothered the man; bizarre tales obstructed comprehension that Amin was a real person who carried out real murders. Refuge was sought in simple explanations: it was widely believed that Amin was suffering from advanced syphilitic insanity or that he consumed several bottles of whisky a day. Both explanations promised a quick demise, without need of intervention.

Foreign opposition nevertheless mounted. Human rights activists pushed for a ban on Ugandan coffee, apparently unaware that, thanks to Amin, very little coffee was being produced. The criticism caused Amin to turn against his former friends. The expulsion of Asians was a calculated act of malice toward the British – an attempt to flood the UK with refugees. British stock fell further when they refused to provide the arms Amin demanded. In 1975, he threatened to execute Denis Hills, a British resident in Uganda who had called him a 'village tyrant'. The death sentence was lifted only after the foreign secretary, James Callaghan, went to Kampala and made a humiliating plea for mercy. After that victory, Amin added a Victoria Cross to a tunic already crowded with decorations. He became 'His Excellency President for Life, Field Marshal Al Hadji Doctor Idi Amin, VC, DSO, MC, Lord of All the Beasts of the Earth and Fishes of the Sea, and Conqueror of the British Empire in Africa in General and Uganda in Particular'.

In 1972, the United States cut off aid. In a memo to the State Department, the American ambassador Thomas Melady described the Ugandan regime as 'racist, erratic and unpredictable, brutal, inept, bellicose, irrational, ridiculous, and militaristic', not to mention 'xenophobic'. Reacting to American disdain, Amin made overtures to the Soviets and began threatening the few remaining US citizens in Uganda. The national security adviser, Henry Kissinger, suggested breaking off diplomatic relations, but Secretary of State William Rogers warned that this might make matters worse. Ties had to be maintained, he argued, because Amin 'is crazy and we have to recognize it'. The Americans did eventually close their embassy, but then watched helplessly as Amin drew closer to the Arabs. When a plane carrying 112 American Peace Corps volunteers stopped at Entebbe airport on its way to Zaire, Amin had the group detained on suspicion of mercenary activity. They were eventually released, but a point had been made.[14]

Playing the Americans like a puppeteer, Amin then announced that he was no longer interested in Soviet aid. 'They wanted me to become a socialist in return for two squadrons of MIGs, but I refused.' Taking the bait, some State Department officials pressed for a resumption of relations, arguing that Amin was likely to be around for a long time. The election of Jimmy Carter, however, brought rapprochement to an abrupt halt. Uganda seemed a good test case for Carter's human rights principles. In one of his first foreign policy pronouncements, the president proclaimed that the Amin regime 'disgusted the entire civilised world' and called upon the UN to 'go into Uganda to assess the horrible murders that apparently are taking place'. Amin responded by announcing the detainment of 200 Americans still resident in Uganda. When reporters asked Paul Chepkwurui, the Ugandan chargé d'affaires, the reason for the detainment, he replied: 'There are some bad people in Uganda, and maybe if some of these missionaries tried to leave on their own, they might be harassed or something.' Once again, Big Daddy had made fools of those who thought they could control him. 'He always acts the same way,' a Ugandan exile remarked. 'He threatens a group of foreigners, and then he says everything is O.K. Then he threatens them again, and then he says everything is O.K. The foreign government dances back and forth – and everyone forgets about the thousands of Ugandans who are dying.'[15]

After peace was restored to Sudan in 1972, Israel lost interest in Uganda. When their benificence dried up, so too did their welcome. Some 500 Israeli advisers were sent packing, and Amin suddenly started shouting about Zionist conspiracy. He shifted from pro-Israeli to pro-Arab overnight, in the process rediscovering an Islamic heritage and developing an enthusiasm for building mosques. Muammar Gaddafi of Libya became his new best friend. Meanwhile, Amin sent a telegram to UN Secretary General Kurt Waldheim, praising Hitler and the German people who 'knew that the Israelis are not people who are working in the interest of the people of the world, and that is why they burnt the Israelis alive with gas'. On 27 June 1976, terrorists from the Popular Front for the Liberation of Palestine, in conjuction with the Baader–Meinhof gang, hijacked an Air France flight from Tel Aviv and landed at Entebbe, with Amin's permission. Almost all of the non-Jewish passengers were released, leaving about 100 hostages, who were offered in exchange for 50 Palestinian prisoners, most of whom were held in Israel. In the midst of the crisis, seventy-five-year-old Dora Bloch was taken to a Ugandan hospital for emergency medical treatment. On 4 July, Israeli commandos staged a daring rescue, freeing the hostages. Three were killed, along with one Israeli soldier, all of the hijackers and forty-five Ugandan soldiers. On hearing of the raid, Amin took out his rage on Bloch. She was dragged from her hospital bed and beaten to death.[16]

By the end of the decade, Amin gradually ran out of things to destroy. In 1979, he threw his corpulent army across the border into Tanzania, as part of a long-running attempt to humiliate Nyerere. On this occasion, most of his soldiers were too drunk to fight, or too distracted by pillage. When Nyerere counter-attacked with his much more disciplined force, Ugandan resistance melted. Before long, Tanzanian tanks, backed by disgruntled Ugandan exiles, were entering Kampala, cheered on by locals. Gaddafi briefly offered help, but then wisely backed away. The coup had a foreign cast, but in truth Amin was brought down by the lunacy of his own febrile ambition.

Amin, along with four wives and more than thirty children, escaped Kampala just as Tanzanian forces were circling the city. He went first to Tripoli, then to Saudi Arabia, where he was offered asylum on the condition that he keep quiet. Under the circumstances, that was an onerous condition – silence never suited Amin.

The BBC correspondent Brian Barron followed the Tanzanian tanks into Kampala. 'We . . . immediately went to the headquarters of his secret police, the State Research Bureau . . . We stumbled down the stairs of the empty building into a charnel house. The floor was awash with blood, the bodies of the SRB's last victims lying in the darkness in their concrete dungeons.' The carnage, it seemed, was over. Back came Obote, who killed more Ugandans than the inefficient Amin ever managed. The thievery also continued, which meant that Uganda's economic devastation only worsened. But because Obote killed quietly, most people forgot about Uganda.[17]

Manila: Ferdinand and Imelda

Ferdinand Marcos was a brilliant lawyer, military hero and gifted politician who rose from humble beginnings to become president of the Philippines. Actually, none of that is true, except for the part about being president. The rest is fabrication, a carefully constructed screen behind which a ruthless thief hid.

During the Second World War, Marcos served in the Battle of Bataan, an experience mined for heroic tales. Numerous decorations for valour, including the Congressional Medal of Honor, were claimed, almost all without substance. In 1949, his fabricated war record proved useful in gaining a seat in the Philippines House of Representatives. Ten years later, a further inflated record helped in his successful Senate race. In the meantime, he married the former beauty queen Imelda Romualdez, history's most famous lover of shoes, and a liar in his same galaxy. Since the Romualdez clan was one of the most powerful in the Philippines, she was the perfect complement to the ambitious Marcos.

Ever since the Spanish-American War, the United States had governed the Philippines with tolerant suzerainty, leaving day-to-day administration to a cabal of rich Filipino landowners whose perfidy was ignored as long as they protected American interests. That arrangement continued after the Second World War when America morphed from colonial to neocolonial power. Because Marcos was closely connected to the network of families with whom Americans did business, he was perfectly situated to benefit from the relationship. He was a devout believer in democracy and capitalism – or, to be precise, the theory of the former and the reality of the latter. That proved enough for the Americans, who needed a reliable ally during the Cold War. His thievery was ignored. 'Marcos . . . has always been corrupt by American standards,' the American ambassador admitted. 'But by Filipino standards he is no better or no worse than other Filipino politicians.'[18]

In 1964, Marcos ran for president. A consummate marketer, he paid the journalist Hartzell Spence to produce a biography that further embroidered already fabricated tales of heroism. Spence's *For Every Tear a Victory* turned the Bataan experience into a comic book adventure. The CIA, recognizing Marcos's value, vouched for his lies. American newspapers obediently printed whole sections of the book verbatim, thus enhancing his credibility. For years, a US army investigation exposing the 'criminal' fabrications in the Marcos story was quarantined by dark forces in Washington.[19]

With American help, and his own immense wealth, Marcos won the election by 670,000 votes. To ordinary Filipinos, he was their John Kennedy, a handsome man of youthful vigour who promised new frontiers and seemed genuinely interested in helping the poor. Ambitious public works schemes during his first term confirmed that impression. What Filipinos did not see, however, were the bribes and kickbacks which allowed Marcos to grow richer as he grew more popular. Those projects also camouflaged his failure to act upon his main campaign promise – land reform. He was not about to alienate his wealthy partners in crime.

Lyndon Johnson, keen for Philippine support in the Vietnam War, was generous with aid. Marcos played Johnson liked a fiddle, expressing warm support for American efforts in Indochina, but never providing real help. The US nevertheless took solace in the knowledge that the Philippines remained stable. As for the corruption, Americans were fatalistic. 'Marcos is a product of the political system . . . not the cause of that system,' wrote Ambassador Henry Byroade. 'The whole atmosphere has been one of public expectancy that anyone able to move through these ranks would capitalize financially on their positions – and anyone who did not would be considered naive indeed – if not down-right incapable.'[20]

Marcos's performance during his first term would easily have been enough to win re-election, but, rather like Nixon, he wanted a landslide. To that end, he engineered the most corrupt election in Filipino history. Bribes were freely distributed and black propaganda liberally spread. His opponent, Sergio Osmeña, was accused of being a CIA stooge – an ironic charge given the help Marcos received from American friends. 'We were helping him get re-elected,' Paul Kattenburg, director of Philippine affairs at the State Department, later admitted. 'How we specifically did it, whether we just put money in there, or whether we printed things or helped him stuff the boxes or God knows what, I just don't know. But . . . the election was crooked as hell.'[21]

To bolster his campaign, Marcos commissioned a film of his wartime exploits. Rejecting a boring documentary, he demanded a Hollywood-style epic. Top of his wish list was a buxom American starlet to play his wartime lover. According to Byroade, Marcos's biggest weakness was women – 'he liked American blondes'. Those prepared to pimp for him were generously rewarded. 'No . . . price is too high to pay . . . [in] satisfying the presidential genitals,' his former aide Primitivo Mijares admitted. Procurers could expect 'a fat governmental contract, an unsecured multi-million peso loan, or anything of [value]'. On this occasion, a crony was sent to Hollywood to find suitable candidates. He returned with two, Joyce Reese and Dovie Beams.[22]

Marcos chose Beams, whom he made his mistress, showering her with presents, holidays and bundles of money. In return, she occasionally took briefcases full of cash to foreign banks for deposit. On one of these trips, she bought a small tape recorder, supposedly for recording language lessons Marcos provided, in preparation for her role in the film. The lessons were frequently interrupted with spontaneous lovemaking and Beams sometimes 'forgot' to turn off the recorder. Before long, she had a large store of incriminating material. The sounds of lovemaking were scandalous enough, but even more inflammatory was presidential pillow talk, in which he openly discussed rigging the election. At one point, he revealed plans for manufacturing an internal communist threat so serious that it would allow him to declare martial law.

Money and violence were twin pillars of the Marcos campaign. Vigilante gangs terrorized Osmeña supporters and intimidated voters. On the island of Batanes, the heavily armed Suzuki boys murdered public officials and took over radio stations, telegraph offices and polling stations. Elsewhere, another group of thugs, 'The Monkees', received training in vote rigging and intimidation from the Special Constabulary. The military, assigned the task of collecting ballot boxes from outlying islands, were ordered to burn those from areas unsympathetic to Marcos and replace them with pre-stuffed boxes. In one precinct in southern Cebu, votes for Marcos outnumbered registered voters by 2,000.

Osmeña was 'outspent, outshouted, and outgunned', Eduardo Lachica of the *Philippines Herald* remarked. While Filipinos were accustomed to fraud, never before had they witnessed an election so lopsided. Marcos won by 1.7 million votes, gaining 74 per cent, and dominating congressional races. Osmeña rightly complained that 'democracy was raped'. The margin of victory made it impossible for Marcos even to pretend that the election had been fair. Fraud on such a grand scale also proved enormously expensive. Marcos spent around $168 million, over five times the amount expended eight years earlier by all parties in the election. The money came not from his personal fortune, but from the Treasury. Whenever money ran dry, pesos were printed, causing skyrocketing inflation. By 1970 the country teetered on the verge of economic collapse, forcing Marcos to seek a $100 million loan from the US. After the IMF stepped in to stabilize the peso, the Philippines underwent a forced devaluation of 50 per cent, which devastated the 27 million citizens who made less than $200 a year.[23]

After the election, many Filipinos gave up on Marcos. He was now the unpopular president of a nation caught in a spiral of decline. His butchering of the economy caused crime rates to soar and civil unrest to spread. All this breathed life into the communist movement, which had been moribund prior to his arrival. Formally established in 1968, the Communist Party of the Philippines (CPP) was headquartered in Tarlac Province, north of Manila, where its military arm, the New

People's Army, conducted insurgency operations. Meanwhile, on Mindanao, the Moro National Liberation Front (MNLF), a Muslim separatist group, began a low level war of liberation.

As revelations of thievery and corruption emerged, public discontent grew and moves were made to impeach Marcos. He responded by promising to give away everything he owned. In fact, his wealth was 'given' to the Marcos Foundation, where it was sheltered from do-gooders. Amid tight security at his inauguration, Marcos assumed a new guise, that of humble penitent. 'Our people have come to a point of despair,' he solemnly admitted. 'I know this for . . . I have heard the cries of thousands and clasped hands in brotherhood with millions of you. I know the face of despair and I know the face of hunger.' The people, he claimed, had been betrayed. 'Our government is gripped in the iron hand of venality, its treasury is barren, its resources are wasted, its civil service is slothful and indifferent, its armed forces demoralized and its councils sterile.' He promised a crusade against corruption. 'Our society must chastise the profligate rich who waste the nation's substance . . . on personal comforts and luxuries.'[24]

Those not fooled by the charade took to the streets in protest. On 26 January, during ceremonies surrounding his State of the Nation address, Marcos listened in silent rage as Father Pacifico Ortiz drew attention to the 'growing fears, the dying hopes, the perished longings and expectations of a people who had lost their political innocence'. Those people, Ortiz added, 'know that salvation, political or economic, does not come from above, from any one man or party or foreign ally . . . salvation can only come from below – from the people themselves, firmly united . . . to stand for their rights whether at the polls, in the market place or at the barricades'. Four days later, in what was called the 'Battle of Mendiola', the discontented stormed the presidential palace, colliding head on with the new, American-trained Metrocom paramilitary security force. The worst political violence in Philippine history saw six student protesters gunned down and hundreds injured.[25]

Marcos meanwhile sought solace with Dovie. She assiduously

recorded lovemaking sessions, afterwards posting the tapes to friends in the States. When Marcos announced that he was dissatisfied with the rough cuts of her film and might cancel it, she fled to Los Angeles vowing revenge. Seven months later she returned, telling anyone who would listen that Marcos was a philandering liar. Wind of the scandal reached the papers, where journalists, no longer inclined to cooperate in mythmaking, decided to publish the story, though always in hooded language. Imelda found out about the affair by reading her morning paper. 'It had reached the point where even the angels in heaven were beginning to hold their noses,' said her bodyguard.[26]

Fearing for her life, Dovie sought protection from the US Embassy. American officials, however, were disinclined to intervene, given their need to remain friendly with Marcos. Byroade offered her a bribe, funded by Imelda, in exchange for silence. Those negotiations broke down when she revealed the existence of the tapes. In desperation, she called a press conference, where one of the tapes was played. Thanks to an enterprising reporter, a pirate copy was slipped to student protesters, who played it from campus loudspeakers. Passers-by listened to their president begging Dovey for a blowjob.

The crisis spurred Imelda into action. In public, she covered for her husband, spreading rumours that Dovey was a CIA agent. Dovey was spirited out of the country, escorted by Delfin Cueto, the first lady's favourite assassin. She, however, managed to give him the slip in Hong Kong and returned safely to the US. Marcos meanwhile poured scorn on Dovie's allegations, claiming that she was psychologically disturbed. That prompted her to release more tapes, in addition to clippings of his pubic hair, originally offered as a token of his love.[27]

Imelda turned humiliation into opportunity. 'It was the girls that did it,' a former CIA agent reflected. 'That gave Imelda her power, her hold over Marcos . . . It put her out of his control.' She briefly toyed with running for president, but decided instead on monetary compensation. In order to ensure her continued support, he signed over a sizeable chunk of the nation's wealth, including shares in gold mines and the newly built San Juanico Bridge. She was also made Governor of Metro Manila and Minister of Human Settlements, two fiefdoms useful for larceny. A one-time friend of the family reflected: 'In the Philippines, a philandering husband has to pay for the rest of his life. Marcos just used our taxes.'[28]

Philippine law prevented a president from serving more than two terms. Marcos, however, was not about to allow the law to get in the way of his thievery. In 1972, by careful use of bribes and intimidation, he managed to get that ban nullified, thus allowing a third term. His re-election, however, was by no means certain, given the damage his reputation had suffered. Senator Benigno 'Ninoy' Aquino had capitalized on the public's disgust by putting himself forward as the only man capable of cleaning up politics.

Since the possibilities for stealing the election were greatly reduced, Marcos decided that martial law offered more promise. This necessitated manufacturing an internal threat to justify the suspension of civil liberties. The rather meagre danger of communist revolution was therefore carefully magnified through bogus crises. One of these involved a fishing trawler, the *Karagatan*, which ran aground off Luzon, supposedly with 3,500 rifles, 80 rockets and 160,000 rounds of ammunition on board. The strength of the NPA was inflated to 1,000 men, a ten-fold increase on previous estimates. Marcos warned of the 'imminent danger' of communist revolution, and complained that Philippine society was 'sick, so sick that it must . . . be cured now'. The CIA, though never inclined to underestimate a communist threat, on this occasion struggled to find evidence of one.[29]

The US realized that the crisis was manufactured, but was disinclined to protest. As early as 15 September 1971, Nixon advised Byroade that the US would back Marcos 'to the hilt' if he declared martial law. The president explained:

> We would not support anyone who was trying to set himself up as a military dictator, but we would do everything we could to back a man who was trying to make the system work and to preserve

> order. Of course, we understood that Marcos would not be entirely motivated by national interests, but this was something which we had come to expect from Asian leaders. The important thing was to keep the Philippines from going down the tube, since we had a major interest in the success or the failure of the Philippine system. Whatever happens, the Philippines was our baby.

That message was reiterated in the summer of 1972, when the State Department officially confirmed that 'in the event of serious insurgency problems the United States would [extend] support'. Marcos responded by assuring Nixon that American interests would not be imperilled and that opposition figures would be given an opportunity to leave the country.[30]

With all his actors on stage, Marcos felt confident for the performance to begin. On 22 September a number of bombs rocked the Philippines. Blame was laid at the feet of the NPA, even though no arrests were made. Later that evening, a motorcade carrying Defence Minister Juan Ponce Enrile was sprayed with gunfire, all the shots conveniently hitting the wrong car. (Enrile later admitted that the ambush had been staged.) Shortly after that incident, Marcos declared martial law. The NPA's actions, he claimed, 'have assumed the magnitude of an actual state of war'. He directed his armed forces to 'prevent or suppress all forms of lawless violence as well as any act of insurrection or rebellion and to enforce obedience to all the laws and decrees, orders and regulations promulgated by me'.[31]

Troops took control of the media, communications facilities, universities, trade unions and opposition parties. Around 30,000 people were placed in concentration camps, including prominent politicians, journalists, student leaders and union officials. The process was carried out with surprisingly little outcry. For Aquino, this came as no surprise. 'The people are now ready for leadership,' he told a reporter. 'They will accept a diminution of civil liberties . . . You can cut corners now.' Byroade likewise noted that 'A rather surprising number of people seem to be in the mood of letting Marcos go ahead and take over . . . This does not mean any great shift of popularity . . . Rather it is more a philosophical resignation to "Who else is there?"' Rafael M. Salas, a former executive secretary, felt that events clearly demonstrated Marcos's acute understanding of his country. 'He knows the average Filipino . . . [He knows] to what degree [a Filipino] can be scared, what are the limits before he becomes violent. Within these limits, he will apply any sort of artifice.'[32]

Ever the lawyer, Marcos called his regime 'constitutional authoritarianism'. He insisted it would be administered by civilians, not the military. 'This is martial law as conceived by a constitution,' he proudly boasted. 'It is not the offensive type of martial law . . . Anything illegal would be anathema, contrary to everything we are fighting for.' Within one year, he promised, order would be restored and democracy would return. Having been warned of imminent revolution, Filipinos breathed a sigh of relief when nothing of the sort materialized. Crime disappeared, mainly because journalists were prevented from reporting it. 'There is calm and even rejoicing among the people now,' Marcos claimed. On that subject, at least, he wasn't lying.[33]

The Marcos kleptocracy would remain in power until 1986. His 'inoffensive' form of martial law resulted in 3,257 'extra-judicial' deaths, 35,000 cases of torture and 70,000 political prisoners. In the mid-1980s, Imelda openly boasted that 'we own practically everything in the Philippines'. Marcos eventually accumulated assets valued at between $5 billion and $10 billion, making him, in financial terms, the second most corrupt leader in history. The US cooperated fully. As one Senate report admitted, US policy was guided by the realization 'that we need the Philippines more than they need us'. Marcos understood that need perfectly, and exploited it with ruthless efficiency.[34]

Phnom Penh: Pol Pot

Like Idi Amin, Pol Pot had a lovely smile. Boyhood friends found him good company – quiet but fun. 'He never said very much,' one friend fondly recalled. 'He just had that smile of his. He liked to joke, he had a slightly mischievous way about him.' Others described him as an 'adorable child' who 'wouldn't hurt a chicken'. In the 1960s, when the child became a communist revolutionary, he adopted the alias 'Pouk', the Khmer word for 'mattress', because he was good at smoothing conflict. Only later, when skulls were stacked like cans on shelves, did the mattress become a bed of nails. Only then did the smile seem sinister.[35]

It is easy to blame the Cambodian killing fields on Pol Pot. The label 'psychopath' provides a reassuring way of imposing quarantine on evil. But that's too simple. Pol Pot was definitely one of the most malevolent men in history, but he did not by himself fashion the barbarity.

Why, then, did a beautiful country of gentle people descend into utter madness? Perhaps because the image itself deceives. Cruelty and violence were endemic in Cambodian society long before Pol Pot. The educational system relied heavily on rote learning, producing a population overly respectful of authority and disinclined to introspection. The Khmer, unlike their Vietnamese and Chinese neighbours, were not heavily influenced by Confucianism, which holds that the errant individual can be reformed. They believed instead that enemies, being irredeemable, had to be eliminated. It was not uncommon for murder to be followed by a symbolic act of cannibalism – the liver cut out and eaten in order to underline the subjugation.

Cultural factors tending toward barbarity were magnified by external pressure peculiar to the 1970s. Cambodia, supposedly a neutral country, was in truth a slave nation ruthlessly exploited by the Chinese, the Americans and the Vietnamese. The Ho Chi Minh trail ran through Cambodia, thus allowing Vietnamese communists to smuggle arms southward through an area sheltered from American interdiction. Viet Cong units slipped into Cambodia whenever the tide of conflict shifted unfavourably. The port of Sihanoukville became an increasingly important conduit for VC supplies. Fearful of angering communists in his own country, Prince Norodom Sihanouk, the Cambodian leader, did not resist these incursions. Though not technically at war, Cambodia was a battlefield.

Hanoi's exploitation of Cambodia angered Pol Pot, leader of the Kampuchean Communist Party (KCP). On that foundation, he built a successful revolution. His rabid nationalism delighted the Chinese, who welcomed disunity among Indochinese communists, the better to limit their influence. The success of the KCP, particularly in the north-western provinces, disturbed Sihanouk's carefully cultivated neutrality. Mistakenly assuming that Pol Pot was a puppet of Hanoi, Sihanouk courted the United States, a move that delighted Nixon. Before his inauguration, he had advised Kissinger that 'a very definite change of policy toward Cambodia should be one of the first orders of business'. The president hoped that a freer hand in Cambodia would lead to success in Vietnam.[36]

Nixon's friendship was expressed with bombs. 'I want a plan where every god-damn thing that can fly goes into Cambodia and hits every target that is open,' he told Kissinger. On 18 March 1969, the US began pounding Cambodia, the aim being to cut the Ho Chi Minh Trail, destroy supplies destined for the VC, and eliminate guerrilla bases. Under 'Operation Menu', a greater payload was dropped on Cambodia in fourteen months than fell on Japan during the entire Second World War. The operation was kept secret (except from those underneath the bombs) because, according to Kissinger, Sihanouk would otherwise have been forced to reveal his complicity.[37]

The B-52s failed to eliminate the Vietnamese threat, but did succeed in further destabilizing Cambodia. A year after the bombing began, Sihanouk was ousted by his own ministers. The new government, under General Lon Nol, immediately demanded that all Vietnamese troops leave, much to Nixon's delight. Nixon's good fortune was, however, destined to be short-lived, since Lon Nol was even weaker than his predecessor. The ultimate benefactor was Pol Pot, whose insurrection thrived on government fragility. By May 1970 Khmer Rouge troops had captured most of the countryside, forcing Lon Nol's forces into urban areas.

With the situation steadily worsening, Nixon decided to invade.

Fifteen thousand American and ARVN troops crossed the border on 1 May 1970. 'Cambodia . . . has sent out a call to the United States . . . for assistance,' Nixon subsequently claimed. That was a lie: Lon Nol was not fully informed beforehand and the operation was designed to bolster American efforts in Vietnam, not to aid the struggle against the Khmer Rouge. Nixon admitted as much when he angrily asserted that his 'legal justification' was 'the right of the President of the United States . . . to protect the lives of American men'. In Kissinger's view, 'Cambodia could not be considered a country separate from Vietnam'.[38]

Pol Pot could not have asked for a better recruiter than Nixon. Peasants whose lives were torn apart by American action proved particularly susceptible to KCP propaganda. 'The bombers may kill some Communists, but they kill everyone else, too,' a disgruntled villager complained. 'The ordinary people . . . sometimes literally shit in their pants when the big bombs and shells came,' a former KCP leader recalled. 'Their minds just froze up and they would wander around mute for three or four days. Terrified and half-crazy, the people were ready to believe what they were told . . . That was what made it so easy for the Khmer Rouge to win the people over.' Nixon achieved what had heretofore seemed impossible, namely harmony between Pol Pot and Sihanouk. A new alliance called the National United Front for Kampuchea (FUNK) was formed, in which Sihanouk provided political credibility and Pol Pot brute force.[39]

The United States, having intervened solely for selfish reasons, was not about to make a long-term commitment. When the Americans eventually left, the main obstacle to a Khmer Rouge victory was removed. The country nevertheless still had to endure three more years of brutal civil war. On 17 April 1975, the revolution was complete – the US watched helplessly as Khmer Rouge troops entered Phnom Penh and swept Lon Nol aside.

Year Zero in the new Democratic Republic of Kampuchea began. Pol Pot was a man in a hurry. 'To win such a big victory in just five years is extremely fast,' he proclaimed. 'The party has thus ordered that the national construction efforts to be carried out from now should be fulfilled rapidly so that ours will rapidly become a prosperous country with an advanced agriculture and industry and so that our people's standard of living will be rapidly improved.' Shortly after the victory, Sihanouk accompanied Khieu Samphan and Khieu Thirith, two rabid KCP ideologues, on a visit to Zhou Enlai, who warned against a quick conversion to communism. Sihanouk recalls how his two colleagues 'just smiled an incredulous and superior smile'. They later boasted: 'We will be the first nation to create a completely communist society without wasting time on intermediate steps.'[40]

The striking feature of Cambodian communism was its utter simplicity. Party documents read like primary school summaries of Marxist thought. 'The masses are a grouping of individuals en masse and they are the ones who create a society,' a Party Congress paper stated.

> They are the laborers who are the producers, the workers who are cleaner than other classes . . . the petty-bourgeoisie, the exploiting feudalists, and capitalists 'do not belong to the masses' . . . If we look back to ancient times, we see that at that time, there were slaves and masters; and later on, there were feudalists governing but they were all defeated by the craftsmen. Then, Marx found out the facts and encouraged struggle to fight against the capitalists and build socialism.

Simple theory inspired simple solutions, encouraging the assumption that change could occur rapidly. Literally overnight, old Cambodia was destroyed: the KCP abolished the law courts, the postal system, religion and money. Pagodas were destroyed. In their place came barren wooden barns where the religion of revolution was preached.[41]

Class divisions were eradicated by turning everyone into workers. To this end, urban areas were evacuated. Cambodia underwent a forced migration of between 2 and 3 million people. Not surprisingly, the death toll was prodigious. Hospitals were emptied, with the very ill transported to the countryside on beds, most dying en route. Richard Dudman, one of the few Westerners to gain access to Phnom Penh after the evacuation, found 'the eerie quiet of a dead place – a Hiroshima without the destruction, a Pompeii without the ashes'. The people were told that evacuation was necessary to protect them from American bombing and because food shortages were severe. In truth, the real aim was to obliterate the urban bourgeoisie. 'The city is bad', an official explained, 'for there is money in the city. People can be reformed, but not cities. By sweating to clear the land, sow and harvest crops, men will learn the real value of things. Man has to know that he is born from a grain of rice.' The eradication of decadent cities was designed to protect the purity of the peasant, who was identified as the real Cambodia. 'Our traditional mentality, mores, traditions, literature, and arts and culture and tradition were totally destroyed by U.S. imperialism . . . Our people's traditionally clean, sound characteristics and essence were . . . replaced by imperialistic, pornographic, shameless, perverted, and fanatic traits.' Party documents railed against the 'overwhelming unspeakable sight of long-haired men and youngsters wearing bizarre clothes' – evidence of corrupt American influence in urban areas. One refugee recalled how, during the evacuation, 'I saw the Khmer Rouge arrest about twenty young men with long hair. They shot them before our eyes.'[42]

'The party opposes independent-mindedness,' went one proclamation. That simple statement validated incredible brutality. Schools were closed, libraries ransacked and books burnt in order to destroy independent thought. Holidays, music, entertainment and romance were banned. Contentment would come through uniformity: everyone would wear the same clothes, eat the same food, and even chew in a communist manner. Children were encouraged to turn on their parents, the better to destroy romantic notions of family. Near Phnom Thom, children were forced to watch as their bourgeois parents were systematically executed. 'Why are you crying over enemies?' an official shouted as the pile of corpses grew. 'If you don't stop we'll kill you too!'[43]

Migrants to the countryside were 'new people', automatically suspicious because of their corrupt origins. They were given the hardest labour in the worst conditions and were forced to undergo incessant political indoctrination. Those seen as particularly dangerous, like schoolteachers, doctors, lawyers and anyone educated, were simply executed. Professionals and intellectuals who returned from exile in France in order to do their bit for the new Cambodia were met at the airport by Khmer Rouge goons, taken away, tortured and killed. Death sentences were meted out to those who complained about conditions, grieved over the death of relatives, engaged in religious worship, stole food, wore jewellery, or engaged in unauthorized sexual relations.

The ill or disabled, an unaffordable burden, were often murdered. Meanwhile, all those identified as 'mongrels', i.e. not pure Khmer, were forced to leave. Since Cambodia was a multi-ethnic society with large concentrations of Chinese, Vietnamese and Thai who had lived in the country for generations, the social disruption was immense. Perhaps the worst sufferers were the Cham, an ethnic minority who arrived from Vietnam in the fifteenth century. A pogrom killed 90,000, half their number.

'Money is a tool of dictatorship of the capitalist class,' a party document proclaimed. Elementary logic concluded that abolishing money would solve the problem. 'We won't use money again, and will never ever think about re-circulating currency . . . The more we forget about money, the happier we feel; not using money is good and comfortable.' While the abolition did not completely eradicate capitalism, it did remove a major manifestation of freedom, namely the ability to purchase. It also meant that work, being unpaid, became indistinguishable from slavery. The government's assertion that there was no unemployment was true, since nearly everyone was a slave.[44]

'Within Cambodian society', a party document boasted, 'there is equality without rich or poor, and there are no longer capitalists, feudalists or petty-bourgeoisie, only workers and farmers.' Everyone was supposed to be equal, but that was a typical communist con. Cadres always managed to find food, despite widespread starvation. In the wake of the evacuation of urban areas came a horde of party hacks, looting in the name of class struggle. Nor was cronyism absent, despite claims to ideological purity. A niece of a prominent government official was given a prestigious job as an English translator for Radio Phnom Penh, despite knowing hardly any English.[45]

The journalist Elizabeth Becker was shocked by the drastic transformation of Cambodia. 'Although the terrain was achingly familiar, the people . . . seemed alien . . . The few peasants I saw wore rags. No one was allowed to talk to me freely . . . Cambodians . . . answered my questions from official translators with blank faces or occasional expressions of fear.' Becker was one of the few Western journalists allowed an audience with Pol Pot. She met him in a huge receiving room, the elegance of which contrasted sharply with the suffering outside. 'Pol Pot [was] seated like a king . . . Here was the man who had committed some of the worst crimes in modern history and he was not what I had expected . . . He was actually elegant – with a pleasing smile and delicate, alert eyes . . . his gestures nearly dainty.' Instead of an interview, Becker got a lecture. For over an hour, 'in the softest voice', he railed against the violation of his country by the Americans, Soviets and Vietnamese. 'I left convinced he was insane.'[46]

The revolution adopted a mantra justifying murder – 'If you keep these people there is no profit, if they go there is no loss.' Every Cambodian dreaded the capricious utterance of those words. 'We search for the microbes within the party,' Pol Pot told cadres in 1976. 'As our socialist revolution advances . . . seeping into every corner . . . we can locate the ugly microbes.' Schools, no longer necessary for education, were turned into torture chambers where 'microbes' were first forced to confess and then were executed for imaginary crimes. At the school in Tuol Sleng, 'classrooms were converted into prison cells and the windows were fitted with bars and barbed wire. The classrooms on the ground floor were divided into small cells, 0.8m x 2m each, designed for single prisoners, who were shackled with chains fixed to the walls or floors.' Kang Khek Leu managed Tuol Sleng, where 17,000 people died. 'I and everyone else who worked in that place knew that anyone who entered had to be psychologically demolished . . . given no way out . . . Nobody who came to us had any chance of saving himself.' In each cell a long list of rules validated cruelty. 'If you disobey any . . . regulation, you shall get either ten lashes or five shocks of electric discharge.' Even suffering was regulated. 'While getting lashes or electrification you must not cry.' Torturers were sometimes as young as twelve, since the very young proved easy to indoctrinate. Children learned the trade by tormenting animals. Those who performed well were then let loose on humans.[47]

'We saw enemies, enemies, enemies everywhere,' Kang Khek Leu confessed. Since party paranoia was boundless, so too was killing. A party congress in January 1977 noted that much progress had been made in purifying the country, but the slaughter would still have to continue.

> Our enemies are now weakening and are going to die. The revolution has pulled out their roots, and the espionage networks have been smashed; in terms of classes, our enemies are all gone. However, they still have the American imperialists, the revisionists, the KGB, and Vietnam. Though they have been defeated, they still go on. Another thing is that the enemies are on our body, among the military, the workers, in the cooperatives and even in our ranks. To make Socialist Revolution deeply and strongly, these enemies must be progressively wiped out.

When Dudman asked Ieng Sary, number three in the KCP hierarchy, about the killings, the latter did not deny them. He questioned, however, why the West was so worried about the fate of a few rich Cambodians and so uninterested in how the lot of the poor had improved. In view of the 'complicated situation' after the war, the KCP deserved credit for 'solv[ing] the problem in good condition' and 'avoid[ing] many more killings'. Sary seems to have believed his own propaganda. 'Basically, the . . . situation is good,' he told his diary in 1976. 'So far, we have used a short-cut, but it is the very correct path. In the (outside) world, socialist revolutions have spilled a great deal of blood, but we have not spilled much blood. But for taking this path, we would have experienced much bloodshed.' As it happened, one-quarter of the Cambodian population was slaughtered. That seemed an affordable loss, since, as party slogans starkly proclaimed, 'One or two million young people are enough to make the new Kampuchea.'[48]

In an interview in 1997, Pol Pot remarked: 'I came to carry out the struggle, not to kill people.' His aim, he insisted, had been 'to stop Kampuchea becoming Vietnamese. For the love of the nation and the people it was the right thing to do.' Ironically, the policies designed to make Cambodia resistant to Vietnamese interference in fact rendered her more susceptible to conquest. When Vietnamese troops invaded on 25 December 1978, they found a people devastated by hunger, savagery, social distintegration and murder. Within two weeks Phnom Penh was conquered, sending Pol Pot scurrying into the hinterland.[49]

The Chinese, driven by hatred of the Vietnamese, continued to support the Khmer Rouge and insisted that the UN should recognize Pol Pot's exiled regime as the legitimate government. For geopolitical reasons, the US played along, in order to impress their new friends, the Chinese. In any case, still smarting from their defeat in Vietnam, the Americans were not about to back Hanoi. The principle of 'my enemy's enemy is my friend' passed for intelligent foreign policy. Kissinger explained that 'the Chinese want to use Cambodia to balance off Vietnam . . . We don't like Cambodia, for the government in many ways is worse than Vietnam, but we would like it to be independent. We don't discourage . . . China from drawing closer to Cambodia.' That warped policy continued for the rest of the decade, even after Jimmy Carter's election supposedly brought greater attention to human rights. 'I encouraged the Chinese to support Pol Pot,' Carter's national security adviser Zbigniew Brzezinski later confessed. 'Pol Pot was an abomination. We could never support him, but China could.' The US, he admitted, 'winked publicly' as China continued to arm the Khmer Rouge.[50]

Nixon, Ford, Kissinger and Brzezinski tacitly supported the Khmer

Rouge, for purely cynical reasons. In contrast, leftist intellectuals in the West, including Noam Chomsky, openly supported Pol Pot for sublime ideological reasons. The hard left salivated at the way the communist experiment was implemented with such alacrity. Doctrine – and distance – ensured blindness toward human suffering. Leftists swallowed every last line of KCP propaganda and begged for more, while openly rejecting evidence of brutality. The British academic Laura Summers could find 'little evidence of famine', even though she did not visit the country. She admitted that, 'Life is without doubt confusing and arduous . . . but current hardships are probably less than those endured during the war.' She and her friends blithely concluded that a communist omelette necessitated breaking a few eggs. Malcolm Caldwell argued that, 'The forethought, ingenuity, dedication and eventual triumph of the liberation forces in the face of extreme adversity and almost universal foreign scepticism, detachment, hostility and . . . sabotage ought to have been cause for worldwide . . . congratulation rather than the disbelief and execration with which it was in fact greeted.' The world, he felt, had much to learn from Pol Pot. The revolution heralded 'the great . . . and necessary change beginning to convulse the world', which would 'shift it from a disaster-bound course to one holding out promise of a better future for all'. To all that, an angry François Ponchaud, author of *Cambodia: Year Zero*, replied: 'How many of those who say they are unreservedly in support of the Khmer revolution would consent to endure one hundredth part of the present sufferings of the Cambodian people?'[51]

When fantasy finally yielded to truth, Summers and her friends indulged in some impressive logical contortions. Khmer Rouge crimes, they argued, demonstrated that the regime was fascist, not communist, since true communists are incapable of such cruelty. Caldwell, who accompanied Becker on the trip to Phnom Penh in 1978, seems to have been limbering up for a somersault of just this sort. 'If it is true that Pol Pot has . . . killed Khmer peasants, I have to make a different evaluation of Kampuchea's development . . . Killing an innocent peasant is a token of fascism.' That equivocation proved fatal. The Khmer Rouge could not afford to have their most outspoken cheerleader switch sides. Shortly after his audience with Pol Pot, Caldwell was murdered.[52]

Pol Pot accepted that perhaps 800,000 Cambodians died as a result of his experiment. More reliable estimates set that figure at 1.7 million. Recent studies have suggested a figure exceeding 2.2 million. Before his death in 1998, Pol Pot admitted that 'our movement made mistakes'. They weren't, however, his mistakes, but those of followers who misunderstood instructions. 'There were people to whom [I] . . . felt very close and . . . trusted . . . completely. Then in the end they made a mess of everything.' While his attempt to evade blame suggests a cowardly rat, Pol Pot was right about one thing, namely the matter of collective responsibility. His people did make a mess of things. His skill came in moulding them into killers by playing upon their fear, racism, class bigotry and hunger for violence. 'Pol Pot', Kang Khek Leu recalled, 'said you always had to be suspicious, to fear something.' The desire to survive inspired a willingness to kill.[53]

Death was ubiquitous, but killing was inefficient. Cambodia was a poor country unable to afford instruments of mass extermination. The people died not in huge gas chambers or in front of individual machine gunners. In most cases, Cambodians killed other Cambodians, individually, by beating them to death. 'It is important to do torture by hand,' a Tuol Seng handbook proclaimed. 'When the enemies respond in a way that fits with . . . our questions, we get so happy we laugh and have a good time.' The people willingly joined in the slaughter. They could have stopped Pol Pot, but they chose not to do so.[54]

Rhodesia: From Smith to Mugabe

On 11 November 1965, Ian Smith, prime minister of the British colony of Rhodesia, unilaterally declared independence. 'There can be no happiness in a country', he argued, 'where people, such as ourselves, who have ruled themselves with an impeccable record for over forty years, are denied what is freely granted to other countries.'[55]

The Unilateral Declaration of Independence, or UDI, was a desperate attempt to stop Father Time. White Rhodesians, who constituted just 5 per cent of the population, could not accept the logic of decolonization, namely that power would eventually be transferred to the black majority. Nearly six years earlier, the then British prime minister, Harold Macmillan, had warned the South African parliament that a 'wind of change is blowing through this continent, and whether we like it or not, this growth of national consciousness is a political fact'. Whites in neighbouring Rhodesia foolishly thought that by taking control of their own affairs they could shelter from the wind.[56]

Smith was a man enslaved to fantasy. His Rhodesian Front (RF) had been formed with one essential purpose: to preserve white rule. Harold Wilson, the British prime minister, thought Smith 'a confused and unhappy man' held captive by deluded supporters. 'He has been in these last weeks under intolerable pressure from his colleagues and from unreasoning extremists . . . But it must not be forgotten that it was Mr. Smith who called the Rhodesian Front into existence.' In Wilson's view, 'reason had fled the scene and . . . emotions, unreasoning racialist emotions at that, had taken command'.[57]

The British had felt inclined to grant independence, but were not enthusiastic about black majority rule. Many MPs, especially within the Conservative Party, considered surrendering power to blacks in Rhodesia an abomination. Nevertheless, in the face of worldwide condemnation of Smith's action, the British obligingly protested. Wilson argued that UDI was 'an act of rebellion against the Crown . . . and actions taken to give effect to it will be treasonable'. Tough words were not, however, the prelude to tough action. Downing Street resisted pressure, mainly from African nations, to use force. Wilson opted instead for economic sanctions, hoping gradually to wear down Smith's resistance. Most of the world followed suit, but Portugal and South Africa did not. As a result, triangular trade patterns evolved, allowing many countries to maintain a moral stand without having to suffer for their principles. By 1972, trade with Rhodesia was healthier than before UDI. The white standard of living rose significantly, thus encouraging a new influx of settlers who were eager to live like colonials in the supposedly post-colonial era.[58]

The black population felt let down by Britain, but they were accustomed to that. 'Mr Smith has won,' one black Rhodesian told *The Times* on the day UDI was declared. 'I don't hear Mr Wilson's aeroplanes.' Not all blacks were that fatalistic, however. The nationalist group ZANU (Zimbabwe African National Union) had made its feelings clear well before UDI. 'We do not trust you', a telegram to Wilson read. 'We will not rely on you in future. We the people of Zimbabwe, shall fight through our own way until we liberate ourselves. It is abundantly clear to us that you and your government do not want African majority rule.' Many blacks saw no difference between rule by Smith or rule by London. 'The position of the Africans is still the same,' Edward Ndlovu, deputy secretary of the rival nationalist group ZAPU (Zimbabwe African People's Union), argued. 'Apartheid has always been in Rhodesia.' The only solution, it seemed, was armed struggle.[59]

Britain tried to negotiate with Smith but he grew more intransigent. A deal tabled in 1966 would have delayed majority rule past the year 2000, but he declined it, as he did an even better offer the following year. He had quite clearly decided that the British could be ignored. In 1969 he pushed through a new constitution, promising that it would 'entrench government in the hands of civilised Rhodesians for all time'. Then, on 2 March 1970, Rhodesia perfunctorily declared itself a republic, severing all links with the Crown. The move, Smith explained, 'was forced upon us'. He assumed that Western nations would be forced to accept the fait accompli, and would react by lifting sanctions and extending diplomatic recognition forthwith. Both Britain and the United States, however, immediately insisted that they would not recognize the new republic.[60]

Smith had so far handled the independence issue with consummate dexterity. Just when things were going well for him, however, circumstances beyond his control rendered Rhodesia's security much more precarious. In neighbouring Mozambique, gains made by Liberation Front of Mozambique (FRELIMO) guerrillas threatened Portugal's hold over her colony. That success allowed ZANU, beginning in 1972, to use areas under FRELIMO control as forward bases for launching raids into north-eastern Rhodesia. Matters worsened in April 1974 with the end of the Salazar regime in Portugal. Salazar, a loyal ally, had helped Smith sidestep sanctions. The new government in Lisbon quickly withdrew from Mozambique, effectively handing the country over to FRELIMO. This meant that the 760-mile eastern border with Rhodesia was open to infiltration by ZANU at any point.

Cuban forces, which had been helping the insurgents in Angola, found themselves under-occupied after the Portuguese pulled out. Castro, rather than bringing his forces home, decided to see what mischief they might make in Rhodesia. Other communist countries, including Russia and China, likewise funnelled an ever-increasing supply of modern weaponry to ZAPU and ZANU. Especially worrying for Smith was the influx of Soviet SAM missiles, a counterweight to his monopoly of air power.

These developments caused the mood to change in Pretoria. Rhodesia, Angola and Mozambique had provided South Africans with a buffer zone between themselves and black-controlled Africa. For that reason, South Africa had assiduously supported white governments in those countries. But the departure of Portugal from Angola and Mozambique blew that cordon sanitaire to smithereens. Once an asset, Rhodesia suddenly became a liability. John Vorster, the South African premier, came to the conclusion that a stable black regime offered more security than an embattled white one. 'As the South Africans see it, beyond the short run the Rhodesian position is hopeless,' *The Times* reported. 'The net has now tightened.'[61]

Vorster pressured Smith to make a deal with opposition forces in his country, in order to ensure a smooth transition to black rule. Backing him was Zambia's Kenneth Kaunda, who was tired of having his country used as a base for ZAPU insurgents. The first fruits of this pressure was Smith's agreement to release the nationalist leaders, Joshua Nkomo of ZAPU and Robert Mugabe of ZANU, both of whom had been in prison for more than ten years.

While Smith seemed doomed, it was not clear which nationalist group would inherit Rhodesia. Bishop Abel Muzorewa, leader of the African National Council, provided the most moderate option, but his desire for peace implied inflated consideration to white interests. Both ZANU and ZAPU judged the plan an insult to the black population. 'Muzorewa's . . . surrender of the principle of "one man one vote" and his unprincipled flirtation with Ian Smith represent a radical and dangerous deviation from the correct line of the masses,' ZAPU officially declared. Despite the bluster, Nkomo was ready to bargain with Smith, in the interests of a quick end to the costly war. Had Smith grasped that nettle, he might have been able to retain a vestige of power. Pragmatism, however, was not a distinguishing feature of his regime.[62]

Mugabe, in contrast, considered negotiation an abomination. He did not, in any case, think it necessary, certain as he was that Smith would eventually be strangled by his own intransigence. Resigned to the long game, Mugabe sought majority rule without diluting conditions. Promises of Marxism and land redistribution were designed not only to inspire followers, but also to incense white Rhodesians, making them ever more intractable. As he saw it, victory would be won through armed struggle and would, therefore, be total. 'ZANU has been committed to a policy of violent revolution in order to change totally and completely the existing social and political system,' a party document proclaimed. 'There won't be a ceasefire until there is a definite programme to transfer power to the African people of Zimbabwe.'[63]

As events quickly demonstrated, Mugabe was right about Smith's intransigence. In August 1975, talks with Muzorewa, organized after pressure from Vorster and Kaunda, were abandoned after just one day because Smith would not allow immunity to be given to nationalist leaders in order to attend. 'It would involve people who are well-known terrorist leaders who bear responsibility for . . . murders and other atrocities,' he explained. A meeting with Nkomo in December proved similarly unproductive. Smith was shackled by his own remit, which was to prevent majority rule. 'We are prepared to bring black people into our government', he conceded, 'but I don't believe in majority rule, black majority rule, ever in Rhodesia, not in a thousand years.'[64]

Mugabe, meanwhile, was consolidating his guerrilla army at bases in Mozambique. 'I am going to war,' he told his mother, adding that he did not know 'whether I shall return or not'. Emboldened by the arrival of their leader, ZANU forces intensified their raids, attacking white homesteads in Eastern Rhodesia. At the same time, in response to the failure of talks between Smith and Nkomo, ZAPU, operating from bases in Zambia and Botswana, also went on the offensive. Smith now faced a two-front war of frightening intensity. Whites watched as their paradise crumbled. Faced with the daily threat of ambush, they turned their farms into mini-fortresses. Many simply left – either to escape the danger, or to avoid being drafted into military service.[65]

The escalation of the conflict, and Mugabe's Marxism, alarmed Henry Kissinger. He feared that Rhodesia would become another Angola – in other words, a magnet for Soviet meddling. Vorster, increasingly impatient with Smith's obduracy, shared Kissinger's concerns. Together, they sought to force Smith to accept majority rule. South Africa cut supplies of fuel and arms, while Kissinger reminded Smith that it was foolish to alienate Americans. At a meeting in Pretoria in September 1976, he shoved in front of Smith a five-point programme for a settlement based on black majority rule 'within two years'. Under the plan, an interim government consisting of equal numbers of white and black representatives would forge a new constitution. Elections would then follow. As a sweetener, sanctions would end immediately and 'substantial economic support would be made available'. Smith nevertheless felt betrayed. 'You want me to sign my own suicide note,' he snarled.[66]

Desmond Frost, the Rhodesian Front chairman, lambasted the United States for seeking to 'spend . . . thousands of millions of dollars in literally buying the white man out of Rhodesia'. As Smith recognized, however, complaining would not make the deal go away. 'It was made abundantly clear to me', he told his people, 'that as long as present circumstances in Rhodesia prevailed, we could expect no help or support from the free world. On the contrary, the pressures on us . . . would continue to mount.' While isolation had once inspired fierce intransigence, Smith was now resigned to defeat. 'Dr Kissinger assured me that we share a common aim and a common purpose, namely to keep Rhodesia in the free world and to keep it from communist penetration.' It therefore seemed necessary to accept the offer, since further struggle would only result in even more ignominious terms. 'Clearly, this agreement does not give us the answer which we would have liked. However, it does present . . . an opportunity . . . [for] Rhodesians to work out amongst themselves, without interference from outside, our future constitution.'[67]

While Smith claimed that he had no option but to accept Kissinger's deal, that did not stop him from undermining it. While going through the motions of implementing the plan, he plotted with Muzorewa, in the hope of finding an alternative that might neuter black resistance, satisfy whites, and placate Kissinger and Vorster. A deal was reached in March 1978, and, thirteen months later, the ANC easily won elections, largely because ZANU and ZAPU boycotted them. Muzorewa became prime minister of the new nation, called Zimbabwe-Rhodesia, but the civil service and military remained in the hands of whites, and Smith was still in the government. He justified the arrangement on the grounds that, if power were to be distributed solely on the basis of skin colour, 'Rhodesia would . . . develop into a kind of banana republic where the country would in no time be bankrupt.' The arrangement nevertheless destroyed Muzorewa's already threadbare credibility; Nkomo and Mugabe dismissed him as a puppet.[68]

The guerrilla war continued, spreading throughout rural areas. The agricultural community was devastated, with schools closed, the health service in tatters and ambushes a daily threat. All this caused the white exodus to quicken. With the situation spiralling out of control, Britain made one last attempt at a negotiated settlement by inviting black leaders to London. Muzorewa and Nkomo accepted, but Mugabe demurred, in fear that a settlement would dilute his revolution. That intransigence drew the wrath of Kaunda and Samora Machel, president of Mozambique, both of whom wanted the suffering in their countries to stop. Mugabe was bluntly told that if he refused to attend, all aid would cease. Incandescent with rage, he accused his allies of selling out. 'The frontline states said we *had* to negotiate, we *had* to go to this conference,' he recalled. 'Why should we be denied the ultimate joy of having militarily overthrown the regime here?' Since he could not defy Kaunda and Machel, he went to London determined to wreck the conference.[69]

While in London, Mugabe discovered the limits of his power. Despite his hostility, an agreement for a ceasefire was forged. When he refused to accept it, Machel reiterated that Mozambique would no longer provide sanctuary to ZANU guerrillas. Though he felt robbed of ultimate victory, Mugabe eventually accepted the need to cooperate. Under the terms of the Lancaster House agreement, signed on 21 December 1979, Zimbabwe briefly reverted to colonial status, until a new government could be elected.

In January 1980, Mugabe returned home for the first time in five years. The huge crowd greeting him was an indication of the militant mood he had successfully fostered. Thousands of youths, their emotions swinging wildly between jubilation and anger, provided a clear hint that violence would figure prominently in the upcoming election. They carried banners and wore T-shirts celebrating the paraphernalia of their war – land mines, rockets, Kalashnikovs. Mugabe was inclined to encourage their militancy, but Machel told him to behave. He warned that if Mugabe played the role of Marxist demagogue, whites would leave Zimbabwe in droves and economic ruin would result. Heeding that warning, Mugabe offered a convincing display of moderation. 'Stay with us,' he told whites, 'please remain in this country and constitute a nation based on national unity.' He further promised: 'We will not seize land from anyone who has a use for it. Farmers who are able to be productive and prove useful to society will find us co-operative.'[70]

While Mugabe feigned civility, his followers wreaked havoc. For them, violence was a legitimate tool of electoral campaigning. Eastern Rhodesia, Mugabe's stronghold, became a no-go area for supporters of Muzorewa and Nkomo. 'The word *intimidation* is mild,' Nkomo complained. 'People are being terrorised. It's *terror*. There is fear in people's eyes.'[71]

The result was a landslide. ZANU won 63 per cent of the vote, and 57 of the 80 seats set aside for blacks (whites were guaranteed 20 seats). Nkomo got just 24 per cent and 20 seats, while Muzorewa was annihilated, earning just 8 per cent and 3 seats. The result suggests that ZANU intimidation was highly effective, but that explanation is perhaps too simple. In truth, a significant proportion of voters supported Mugabe not because they liked him, nor because they were frightened into doing so, but because they wanted an end to the war. They rightly concluded that, if Mugabe failed to win, the armed struggle would continue. Zimbabweans voted for peace and got Mugabe.

'You have inherited a jewel,' Julius Nyerere of Tanzania told Mugabe. 'Keep it that way.' Apparently mindful of that warning, he sought to allay the fears of those whites inclined to leave. 'If yesterday I fought you as an enemy, today you have become a friend and ally with the same national interest, loyalty, rights and duties as myself,' he told them on the eve of independence.

> If yesterday you hated me, you cannot avoid the love that binds you to me and me to you . . . The wrongs of the past must now stand forgiven and forgotten. If ever we look to the past, let us do so for the lesson the past has taught us, namely that oppression and racism are inequalities that must never find scope in our political and social system. It could never be a correct justification that because the whites oppressed us yesterday when they had power, the blacks must oppress them today because they have power. An evil remains an evil whether practiced by white against black or black against white.

Iron had been turned into gold. Even Smith expressed delight at this feat of political alchemy. Whites who were hastily preparing to leave the country unpacked their bags. The charm offensive continued when Mugabe offered Nkomo a place in his new government and announced that white representatives would also be given posts, 'so as to bring about a government that will be reassuring to all people of Zimbabwe'. In newspapers around the world, Mugabe was acclaimed a hero.[72]

'I don't know why a lot of people in the West don't like me,' Mugabe remarked in 1978. He surmised it was because they found his Marxism frightening. 'Western society claims to be pursing Christian principles. Is there anything to beat the principle of social togetherness, justice to the whole people, rather than justice to a few, such as Rockefeller and Ford? . . . If we are poor together then that's acceptable. But if we are poor because a few individuals are rich then obviously I cannot accept that system.' Mugabe's interviewer on that occasion was not entirely convinced. The big question, Lawrence Pintak concluded, was 'whether Mr Mugabe is sincere in his desire to build a society based on equality and justice for all, or if he is the potential tyrant that so many believe'.[73]

Tehran: Islamic Revolution

In early 1975, Amnesty International announced that Iran was one of the world's 'worst violators of human rights'. A few years earlier, President Richard Nixon voiced a different opinion. In a conversation with Imelda Marcos, he remarked that 'while perhaps Iran's formal government did not meet the idealistic criteria of many critics, it was perhaps the best system for Iran'. He praised the Shah – 'a strong and selfless leader who was a great favorite . . . and who had generously and progressively . . . distributed Iran's great oil revenues to the benefit of his people'.[74]

There was a small grain of truth to what Nixon said. The transformation under the Shah had been astounding. 'When I left [in

1960] . . . this was still a backward country,' an academic remarked after a decade abroad. 'Only a few cities . . . had running water . . . Most industry was handicrafts, and about eighty percent of the people still lived in rural villages . . . when I came back, it was a different country. All the young people . . . were going to school. There are a hundred thousand university graduates now and almost two hundred thousand people in universities.' Between 1960 and 1979, a rural agrarian country changed into an urban industrialized one. Tehran's population more than doubled, coal and cement output trebled, and production of iron ore increased from 2,000 to 900,000 tons. In order to service this modern economy, railways, roads and ports were developed. The transformation was funded by oil revenues, which rose from $285 million in 1960 to $20 billion in 1976.[75]

The 'White Revolution', however, seriously destabilized society – something Nixon chose to ignore. The effect could be seen in Isfahan, once a paradise. 'Five years ago, there were five hundred and sixty thousand people . . . and this was one of the most beautiful cities in the world,' a local official remarked in 1978.

> Then the Shah . . . put a steel mill here . . . Naturally, foreign companies followed suit . . . Now we have more than a million people. The doubling in five years of a population that had been stable for three hundred years has changed everything. This used to be an educational center, with a university, many religious schools, and lots of music. Now it is an industrial town. Over three hundred thousand workers have come in from the countryside . . . They live five or six to a room . . . They make good wages . . . but . . . they're miserable.

'I could cry about what has happened here,' a *bazaari* complained. 'It used to be a paradise of water and gardens and beautiful buildings. Now the town is full of strangers.'[76]

Land reform was central to the White Revolution. Large estates were bought up and redistributed, thus transferring power from landowners to the state and neutralizing a group that stood as an obstacle to modernization. Landowners had, however, provided a stabilizing influence by acting as a source of authority in the countryside. Without them, the people were cut adrift, desperately seeking stability in an uncertain world.

New welfare agencies, designed to promote progressive ideas, were set up to replace the authority of landowners. These agencies, or corps, dealt with literacy, health, religion, development, etc., and were staffed by university graduates loyal to modernization. Being outsiders, they were greeted with suspicion in the hinterlands. This was especially true of the religious corps, drawn from theology graduates from secular universities, rather than from the more conservative and traditional *madrasas*, or colleges of Islamic education.

The Shah envisaged a modern utopia – a 'great civilisation' inspired by central government, with Japan as its model. Opposition was not tolerated. When the parliament, or *Majlis*, proved uncooperative, the Shah neutralized it, turning Iran into a one-party state. Iranians found this denial of basic freedoms intolerable, but worse still was the way their culture was obliterated in the rush to modernize. 'In his enthusiasm to build the country, [he] . . . ignored the people in it,' an Isfahan academic remarked. 'The masses were left out of his development program. The bazaari were left out. The mullahs were left out.' Much to the people's dismay, the new wealth was unevenly distributed. A handful of families became very rich through lucrative contracts and corruption. As a result, the further change progressed, the more enemies the Shah created.[77]

One common complaint related to the role women played in the White Revolution. A general liberation meant veils were removed and Western dress became common. Co-ed schools were encouraged. 'I do not want co-education,' the Ayatollah Shariatmadari objected. 'I want to separate the schools of learning from the schools of flirting . . . in co-educational schools there is a corruption of moral values . . . The girls . . . have illegitimate children, and others have abortions. The girl loses her self-respect and her status in society. Either she suffers a great personal loss or she takes up another way of life – prostitution.' Young males from conservative families found the female invasion distressing. 'They don't know how to deal with the young women sitting next to them in their classes,' the Isfahan *bazaari* complained. 'In the past, they had never seen any women . . . not wearing a veil. Now they see miniskirts and bare arms and bare legs. They say to me, "What do they want, these women? What are they trying to do to me?"'[78]

The *ulema*, graduates of the *madrasa*, posed the greatest threat to the White Revolution. According to Islamic custom, government belonged to the Imam, or his representative, the *mujtahid*. A secular government was accepted on sufferance – the ruler tolerated only if he respected Sharia law. Since the Shah's reforms seriously undermined Sharia, he found himself on a collision course with religious authority. As change gathered pace, the *ulema*, symbolic of stability, found their popularity grew. They opposed the Shah not only because he represented corrupt modernism, but also out of self-protection. *Ulema* had depended on charitable endowments, or *waqf*, which usually meant land. This arrangement had allowed most to live a comfortable life. Land reform, however, undermined that system, at the same time that it supplanted religious authority in the countryside. The *ulema*'s hardships also ironically improved their reputation, since their wealth had once rendered them suspect.

Among the *mujtahid*, the Ayatollah Khomeini stood out because of his willingness to involve himself in secular politics. The Shah, he argued, was seeking 'to spread . . . colonial culture to the remotest towns and villages and pollute the youth of the country'. Khomeini's opposition was formidable because it was based not just on religion but also, fundamentally, on nationalism. The Shah was chastised for selling Iran's soul to the corrupt West. This explains Khomeini's power: while other religious critics focused on narrow issues like land reform or the status of women, he concentrated on matters of nationalist import. The Shah, unable to tolerate opposition of this sort, exiled Khomeini to Turkey in 1964. The following year he moved to Najaf in Iraq, where he became a focal point of anti-government agitation.[79]

With secular modes of political expression stifled by the centralization of power, Khomeini became the most important outlet for discontent. 'We want Khomeini,' one worker told a journalist. 'He will take power from the rich and give it to us.' According to Shapur Bakhtiar, the Shah's last prime minister, Iranians decided that Khomeini had a divine mission. 'People . . . thought he would create a paradise.' Somewhat surprising was the way Khomeini appealed to young urban intellectuals, those educated under the White Revolution. Their discontent was partly economic. 'Students have grown up under the Shah, and they don't know what things were like before development started,' the Isfahan official explained. 'All they know is that the Shah promised that Iran was going to be like France or Germany. That isn't happening.' As a result of their disappointment, they were 'turning back to the old days, and pursuing an idealized version of what things were like then. They are pushing the mullahs to go back and re-create the wonderful past.' The problem was compounded because many students came from poor, rural families of conservative religious background. Going to university was a rude awakening; they often felt polluted by Western values, what became known as 'Westoxication'. The very people who the Shah hoped would provide the backbone of a new, progressive culture abandoned him in favour of an aged, reactionary cleric.[80]

Intellectual justification for the marriage of secular radicalism with conservative Islam was provided by Dr Ali Shariati, who argued that a moral revolution based on Shi'ite custom was the essential precursor to socialist transformation. He also believed that 'revolutionary leadership is incompatible with democracy', an idea that dovetailed nicely with Khomeini's autocratic nature. Meanwhile, some Islamic fundamentalists looked to Marxism for political guidance. The Ayatollah Motahari, ideological architect of the Islamic Revolution, rejected Marx's atheism, but saw value in his ideas about the eradication of social injustice and anti-imperialism. As one closet Marxist confessed, '[Marx] exposes the imperialists and their rape of all the countries of the Third World, including Iran.' Thus, two seemingly antithetical strains of opposition, namely traditional Shi'a culture and radical Marxism, became fused in the person of Khomeini, the figurehead of 'Islamic Marxism'. The radical left allied themselves with Khomeini in order to destroy the secular progressives who wanted neither the Shah, nor religious fundamentalism, nor Marxism. They did not, however, understand that they were being used. After taking from them what he needed, Khomeini crushed them.[81]

An economic downturn added new grievances to simmering discontent. Fuelled by oil and fantasy, the White Revolution paid scant attention to the need to build a stable economy. Between 1973 and 1976, Iran literally overdosed on spending. Oil revenue went toward development projects that had little justification beyond display. As a result, the economy overheated and inflation skyrocketed, with rents in Tehran trebling. The government responded by slamming on the brakes, instituting an austerity policy that froze growth and increased unemployment. Those still waiting for the benefits of the economic miracle joined the swelling ranks of the discontented.

'Inflation', *The Economist* reported, 'reached such alarming proportions that the Shah, who tends to look at economic problems in military terms, declared war on profiteers.' That was not strictly true, since the very rich were left alone in favour of an offensive against the *bazaaris*. 'Inspectorate teams', in truth vigilante gangs, were sent into the bazaars to root out those deemed to have betrayed the people's trust. Guild courts, masterminded by the ruthless security service SAVAK, imposed some 250,000 fines, banned 23,000 traders and sent 8,000 shopkeepers to prison. One shopkeeper rightly complained that 'the bazaar was being used as a smokescreen to hide the vast corruption rampant in the government'.[82]

Beginning around 1977, a liberalization of sorts occurred within Iran, partly because of the worldwide attention paid to human rights abuses. This liberalization meant that the discontented grew more assertive. The National Front, first active in the 1950s, was revived to give focus to secular opposition, and the Tudeh Party, a Marxist group operating underground since 1953, also underwent a resurgence. Neither group, it should be stressed, advocated an Islamic republic, though both were prepared to work with the mullahs.

Discontent boiled into protest in May 1977 when middle-class intellectuals began challenging the government through letter-writing campaigns, radical pamphlets and poetry readings. When police tried to break up a peaceful reading at Aryamehr University on 19 November, students took to the streets, colliding head-on with SAVAK. One student was killed and over seventy injured, leading to a rash of sympathy protests. Religious dissidents then joined the protest. On 7 January 1978, riots broke out in Qom after a government-controlled newspaper clumsily accused Khomeini of a wide range of sins, among them spying for the British and writing erotic poetry. Seminaries and bazaars emptied as angry citizens demanded an official apology. Security forces again reacted with unwarranted force, resulting in a number of deaths. In Tehran, *bazaaris* closed their shops as a mark of respect for the Qom martyrs. The fact that the *bazaaris* and the *ulema* were now working in concert was a worrying development for the Shah.

Iran, remarked Shariatmadari, 'is erupting like a volcano, and, like a volcano, after building up pressure for years and years it is impossible to stop'. The Shah refused at first to respond to the tremors, seeing them as a harmless manifestation of the liberalization he had allowed. He thought the demonstrations would, like a safety valve, release pressure. While that indeed happened, the security forces had not properly adjusted to liberalization. They reacted in character, namely with violence and torture. Iran found herself in a situation where the people were more inclined to protest and were daily supplied with reasons for doing so.[83]

In August 1978, Jafar Sharif-Emami was appointed prime minister with a view to placating religious opposition. 'I'm a patient man,' he claimed. 'I do not intend to leave this office until there is calm in Iran.' To this end, he reinstated the Islamic calendar and closed casinos and nightclubs. Concessions, however, simply made the discontented more confrontational. A schoolteacher was openly scornful: 'We're given to understand that the ruling clique is talking about religion now, and putting on a turban and the white garments of holiness. But that is a mere pretense. Even a child can see through that.'[84]

Reeling from the protests, the government declared martial law on 7 September 1978. In a stroke, Sharif-Emami's efforts to appease were negated by General Gholam Ali Oveissi, the new military governor of Tehran. Widely reviled as the 'butcher of Iran' after his vicious response to riots in 1963, Oveissi lived up to his reputation. On the 8th, thousands took to the streets, many unaware that martial law had been declared. Their ignorance proved fatal. Oveissi's goons, confident that they could now exercise maximum force, fired indiscriminately, killing a hundred protesters and wounding many more. The worst violence occurred in Jaleh Square, where a peaceful demonstration met a hail of bullets. 'Black Friday', as it became known, proved a point of no return.

Khomeini's greatest ally was the Shah, whose insensitive governance inspired inexhaustible displeasure. There was nothing inevitable about the Ayatollah's remarkable rise; at various stages, political subtlety might have ensured a more moderate outcome. For instance, it is difficult to understand the logic behind the Shah's decision to ask Saddam Hussein to expel Khomeini from Iraq. That simply fuelled the indignation felt by religious protesters, while failing to limit the Ayatollah's influence. In fact, the opposite occurred. Khomeini ended up in France, where he used the modern media to communicate with his people more effectively than had been possible from Najaf.

Government efforts to cut inflation provided new reasons for unrest. Price controls annoyed the *bazaaris*, as did the fall in the inflation rate, since they liked to pay back loans in inflated money. The growth rate, which had been hovering around 15 per cent, suddenly fell to 2 per cent in 1978, causing contracts to dry up and unemployment to rise. The effect was particularly noticeable in the construction industry, where a shortage of workers turned into a surplus virtually overnight. Take-home pay fell by around 30 per cent, cancelling out the fall in inflation. In October the heretofore quiet workers joined protests by downing tools.

Unable to restore order, Sharif-Emami resigned on 5 November. Senior military commanders, concerned about the spiralling chaos, demanded a military government. The Shah complied, but intentionally blunted its ferocity by putting at its head General Gholam Reza Azhari, who lacked Oveissi's ruthlessness. General Nasser Moghadam, head of SAVAK, complained that 'the government is not strong enough. We in the security forces . . . feel handcuffed.' Meanwhile, the Shah tried desperately to court public favour. 'The revolution of the Iranian people cannot fail to have my support as the monarch of Iran and as an Iranian,' he proclaimed. 'I have heard the revolutionary message of you, the people . . . Remember that I stand by you in your revolution against colonialism, oppression and corruption.' Iranians struggled to understand what precisely the Shah meant. Khomeini rejected the speech outright, correctly judging it an act of desperation. 'This is the end for the Shah,' he remarked. 'The monarchy will be eradicated. Pahlavi forced himself upon the Iranian people; no one wanted him.'[85]

In early December came the holy month of Moharram, which would climax with festivals commemorating the martyrdom of Imam Hussein, the Prophet's grandson. The government tried to take control of celebrations, but soon found itself overwhelmed by the people's desire for a huge demonstration of rejection. Some 2 million people took part in protests on 9 and 10 December, the largest in Iranian history. The protests were notable for their peacefulness, due in large part to the desire of both lay and religious leaders to avoid bloodshed. Both had come to the conclusion that the will of the people would soon overwhelm the Shah. 'The national movement should not assume the form of an armed struggle,' Khomeini had insisted. The effect was clear to a reporter from the *Christian Science Monitor*, who saw 'A giant wave of humanity [sweep] through the capital declaring louder than any bullet or bomb . . . the clear message, "the Shah must go".'[86]

In one last desperate move, the Shah asked Bakhtiar to be prime minister on 4 January. Despite the disapproval of his National Front colleagues, Bakhtiar accepted. 'I tried to act as a statesman, to avoid catastrophe,' he later explained. In doing so, he incurred the wrath of Khomeini, who had proclaimed on 3 November that cooperation with the Pahlavi regime was, by definition, treasonous. Bakhtiar convinced the Shah to leave Iran, which he did on the 16th. Political prisoners were released, SAVAK dissolved, censorship relaxed and elections promised. The moves, though well-intentioned, were futile. National Front colleagues continued to spurn Bakhtiar and Khomeini called him a traitor. Bakhtiar's decision to allow Khomeini to return to Iran was understandable, but also fatal. 'I knew Khomeini was a crook,' Bakhtiar explained, 'but I was still not prepared to stop him from returning.' The Ayatollah arrived on 1 February, and four days later Bakhtiar left office. He fled the country on the 11th.[87]

After Bakhtiar's departure, a provisional government headed by Mehdi Bazargan was installed, but in truth the unstoppable Khomeini was in charge. On his direction, revolutionary committees took control of mosques and factories. In Tehran, a revolutionary council, hand-picked by Khomeini, insinuated itself into the nation's governance. At the end of March, a referendum expressed overwhelming support for an Islamic Republic. What that meant, however, was not entirely clear. Bazargan envisaged a parliamentary democracy conducting government on Islamic principles. Radical clerics, however, had different ideas. They wanted power vested in the *ulema*, who would govern through the revolutionary council and whose authority revolutionary guards would enforce. An Assembly of Experts, dominated by radical *ulema*, rejected Bazargan's model.

The new constitution, promulgated in November 1979, maintained the customary structure of President, Cabinet and Parliament, but otherwise differed markedly from the modern conception of a republic. Government would henceforth 'extend the sovereignty of God's law throughout the world'. Civil law would be derived from Islamic doctrine. The authority of secular institutions was severely curtailed by the power vested in the Revolutionary Guard and by a council of twelve guardians, who could veto legislation if it contradicted Islamic doctrine. Finally, a supreme guide, or *vali faqih*, would oversee all aspects of governance. That role went to Khomeini, appointed for life.[88]

The rest of the world struggled to understand. The revolution had once seemed familiar to observers, be they conservative, liberal or Marxist. Iran seemed a classic case of democratic will overcoming autocracy. Then, however, the religious element, which most Westerners blithely assumed to be incidental, imposed its character upon the revolution, producing something altogether alien. 'The notion of a popular revolution leading to the establishment of a theocratic state seemed so unlikely as to be absurd,' one White House aide noted. Quite how absurd would be revealed very quickly.[89]

11

BEGINNINGS

Camp David: Accord?

Prior to the Yom Kippur War, Israel treated Egypt with contempt. That changed on 6 October 1973, when Egyptian forces swarmed across the Suez Canal. They were eventually driven back, but that was immaterial. 'No matter what happens,' Anwar Sadat told his people, 'there has been a victory which cannot be erased . . . Our wounded nation has restored its honor and the political map of the Middle East has been changed.'[1]

Despite his triumph, Sadat remained in a precarious position. Egyptians grew impatient with undelivered promises of economic prosperity. Violent riots over food prices placed enormous pressure on him to cut his military budget and channel money to the poor. That, however, was only possible if peace with Israel could be forged. Sadat hoped to use Egypt's new prestige to broker agreement, but Israel proved unwilling in the turmoil following the war. Golda Meir, her reputation damaged, resigned in June 1974. In her place came Yitzhak Rabin, a man disinclined to take risks at a time of oil crisis and world recession. Despite Sadat's genuine desire to move the peace process forward, the period from December 1973 to January 1977 was characterized by persistent stalemate.

The Sinai I and II agreements allowed the disengagement of forces and the re-opening of the Suez Canal, but that was a far cry from long-term peace. Kissinger tried to forge a settlement based on UN Resolution 242 – the idea that Israel would exchange the occupied territories for peace – but Israel found that distasteful. The biggest stumbling block was the West Bank, where settlements were being established as a calculated snub to Palestinian demands for self-determination.

The situation changed in 1977, when new actors took the stage. The election of Jimmy Carter in November 1976 offered a stark contrast to Kissinger's cynicism. Carter's peace credentials were beyond dispute; he was motivated by morality, not opportunism. Less than a month after assuming office, he wrote to Sadat confessing that he would 'count heavily on your advice as we begin to find ways to make significant progress . . . toward a just and lasting peace'. Sincerity was his strength, but also his weakness, since he could not hide his sympathy for the Palestinians. Trouble erupted when he mentioned the idea of a Palestinian 'homeland' to Rabin, who was contemplating a withdrawal to defensible borders. That poor choice of words scuppered further progress.[2]

Opportunity arose anew when Rabin resigned on 22 April 1977. At the subsequent election, Labour was defeated, with Likud, a coalition led by Menachem Begin, forming the new government. On the surface, Likud's rigidly ideological foreign policy seemed to rule out compromise with Egypt. The principle of a Jewish homeland was inviolate, with any surrender of occupied territories seen as a betrayal of the 6 million victims of the Holocaust. A central plank in Likud's campaign had been the right of Jews to settle in the West Bank, Gaza and Sinai.

Begin's pedigree perfectly embodied Likud ideology. One of his brothers and both parents died in the Holocaust. After the war, he became leader of Irgun, the Zionist terrorists responsible for the King David Hotel bombing in 1946. Personal struggles shaped his view of Israel – adversity was met with relentless aggression and uncompromising belief. 'From my early youth', he remarked, 'I had been taught by my father, who went to his death at Nazi hands voicing his faith in God . . . that we Jews were to return to the land of Israel – not go, travel or come, but return.' In real terms, this meant that the status of the West Bank and Gaza was non-negotiable. They were part of the ancient realm of King David that Zionists were pledged to recreate – a place not 'occupied', but 'liberated'. Begin insisted on referring to the West Bank by the ancient biblical names, Judea and Samaria. Likud policy was acted out in the new settlements established in the occupied territories. The day after his election victory, Begin visited the Elon Moreh settlement and declared: 'We stand on the land of liberated Israel. There will be many Elon Morehs. There will be many, many settlements in the coming weeks.'[3]

Begin derided suggestions that Egypt might formally recognize the existence of Israel, a massive step for an Arab nation. 'My dear Egyptian friends,' he replied, 'we have existed . . . without your recognition for 3,700 years. We never asked your President or government to recognize our right to exist.' All this suggested that the peace process would be put on hold for the term of Begin's ministry. Begin, however, delighted in wrong-footing his critics. Discussions were soon opened with Carter and Sadat. It quickly became apparent, however, that Begin's notions of security and sovereignty remained huge obstacles.[4]

Sadat responded to Begin's intransigence with an outrageous gamble. On 9 November 1977, he told the Egyptian National Assembly: 'You heard me saying that I am prepared to go to the ends of the earth if . . . doing so will prevent any of my officers or men being killed or wounded. I really am ready to go to the ends of the earth and Israel will be amazed to hear that . . . I am prepared to go to their very home, to the Knesset itself and discuss things with them.'[5]

The risks involved in that declaration were too huge for its sincerity to be doubted. At a stroke, Sadat had proven his credentials as a peacemaker. That forced Begin to respond positively, otherwise his peace feelers would have been exposed as fraudulent. Offering an invitation to Sadat nevertheless felt like swallowing poison. 'We, the

Israelis', he replied, 'stretch out our hands to you. It is not, as you know a weak hand. If attacked, we shall always defend ourselves . . . But . . . it will be a pleasure to welcome your President.'[6]

When Begin met Sadat at Ben-Gurion airport on 19 November he combined welcome with warning: 'I am waiting for you, Mr. President, and all the ministers are waiting for you.' Sadat began by telling the Knesset that he wanted to save 'my Egyptian Arab people and the pan-Arab nation from the horrors of . . . destructive wars'. There followed eloquent oration on the theme that 'no one can build his happiness . . . [on] the misery of others'. That implied a need to abandon old verities. Egypt would offer Israel recognition. 'I declare it to the whole world, that we accept to live with you in permanent peace based on justice.' Israelis, however, would have to recognize that 'you have to give up once and for all the dreams of conquest and give up the belief that force is the best method for dealing with the Arabs'. That meant, specifically, not just an Israeli withdrawal from Sinai, but recognition of the rights 'of the people of Palestine for . . . a state on their land'. Refusing to mince his words, he concluded: 'You have to face reality bravely, as I have done . . . Peace cannot last if attempts are made to impose fantasy concepts on which the world has turned its back.'[7]

Sadat's speech was eloquent and optimistic, Begin's reply stern and mean-spirited. Balloons of hope were punctured or tethered firmly to earth. If Sadat's speech suggested a new and promising future, Begin's evoked a familiar and depressing past. There were inevitable references to the Holocaust and to the bloody struggle for a Jewish homeland – a struggle of 'few against the many, weak against the strong'. He railed against those who wished 'to choke and destroy the . . . last hope of the Jewish nation', reminding Sadat that on four occasions Israel had been forced to fight for her survival. 'We have sworn an eternal vow, this entire generation . . . We shall never again place our nation in such danger.' While he did not reject the offer of peace, he emphasized that peace could not compromise security or heritage. He claimed that everything was open to negotiation, but conspicuously omitted mention of Palestine.[8]

The different tone of the two speeches was subsequently echoed in different approaches to negotiation. Sadat insisted that he was not interested in 'a partial peace, mainly to terminate the state of belligerency'. Yet Begin sought nothing more. He offered a partial withdrawal from Sinai, but simultaneously encouraged new Jewish settlements there, not to mention in the West Bank and Gaza. His obstinacy put Sadat in a difficult position. As all Egyptians understood, the risk he had taken would be worthwhile only if it produced something sublime, especially since talking to Israel imperilled Arab unity. If nothing wonderful resulted, his detractors would dismiss him as weak – an appeaser, if not a traitor.[9]

'It is possible to establish a peace in hours,' Sadat complained. 'The only obstacle is Mr. Begin.' He hinted that unless significant progress was achieved before October 1979, he might cancel the Sinai Disengagement Agreement. The next step, everyone understood, might be another war. That worried Carter, as did the very real possibility that if Sadat failed, an anti-American extremist would take his place. Carter was not prepared to allow the breakthrough achieved at the Knesset to be squandered. 'It is imperative', he wrote to Sadat on 3 August 1978, 'that every effort be made to capitalize on this unprecedented opportunity . . . for a comprehensive and permanent peace agreement.' An identical letter was sent to Begin. In his own version of the bold move, Carter invited both men to Camp David to 'search for additional avenues toward peace'.[10]

The two leaders arrived on 5 September. Camp David was perfectly suited for Carter's purposes. Since it is, in the fullest sense, a retreat, the summit could be conducted in an atmosphere of isolation, relaxation and informality. While it was impossible for an intruder to get in, it was also difficult for a guest to leave. The best way out was success. For two weeks, Carter politely kept the Israelis and Egyptians captive, in what Begin called an 'elegant jail'. The unstated premise was that they would stay until they reached agreement.

Unlike most high-level negotiations, this one came without a previously agreed script. One American official called it a 'virginal experience' – nothing was agreed beforehand because nothing could be agreed. Begin arrived with the confidence of a man who had nothing to lose. He knew that he could return home empty-handed and still earn the admiration of his people, especially since many did not want him to succeed. That confidence encouraged intransigence. 'We cannot sacrifice our security for the sake of Sadat's prestige,' he warned Carter. 'We leaders of Israel cannot betray our children.'[11]

Since Begin had something concrete to offer, namely land, he had immense power. Sadat, in contrast, could offer only ethereal promises of peace. Unlike Begin, he faced ignominy if he went home empty-handed. Carter was likewise in a precarious position. The summit, he admitted, was 'a very high-risk thing for me politically'. Widely seen as a lightweight, he desperately needed a success to bolster his lacklustre presidency. Beyond Carter's personal risk, failure threatened to destroy America's prestige with Arab nations, which was built on the shaky premise that she alone could influence Israeli policy.[12]

Two basic issues were at stake. The first was peace between Israel and Egypt. That hinged on the Sinai question. The second issue was the broader matter of a Middle East peace, which pivoted on Palestine. The status of Palestine was the glue holding Arab states together – a collective responsibility. The nature of the peace was therefore wholly dependent on that issue, yet settling it was virtually impossible. Begin would not budge on the right of Jews to live on their 'sacred lands'. The solution that gradually evolved was to decouple Palestine from the more finite aim of peace between Israel and Egypt. That meant dismantling the notion of a single Arab nation.

After customary pleasantries on the first day, the delegations got down to business on the 6th with Begin and Sadat carefully setting out their stalls. Disagreements, though apparent, did not erupt. On the 7th, however, the knives came out. Sadat insisted that the Israelis withdraw from the Sinai, and Begin flatly refused. 'Jimmy . . . said the meeting was *mean*,' Rosalynn Carter noted. 'I had heard raised voices from the bedroom where I was working. They were brutal with each other, personal, and he had had to break into arguments . . . when their words became too heated.'[13]

Begin's intransigence over the land issue nearly caused the talks to collapse. 'Sadat announced angrily that a stalemate had been reached,' Carter recalled. 'He saw no reason for the discussions to continue.' As Begin and Sadat made for the door, 'I got in front of them to partially block the way. I urged them not to break off their talks . . . Begin agreed . . . Sadat nodded his head. They left without speaking to each other.' The same stalemate was apparent the following day. 'Begin is not ready for peace,' Sadat complained. In his diary, Zbigniew Brzezinski, the national security adviser, noted: 'Carter doubtless agreed with Sadat, but he admirably maintained his position as a conciliator.'[14]

Like a disappointed schoolmaster, Carter scolded his charges: 'The atmosphere between the two of you is not conducive to any agreement.' Abandoning three-way discussions, he decided instead to act as go-between. By working out a proposal with one leader and then taking it to the other for amendment, he tried to assemble an accord from 'bite-size' agreements. Some progress was made, but Begin remained firmly entrenched on key issues. 'My right eye will fall out, my right hand will fall off before I ever agree to the dismantling of a single Jewish settlement,' he declared. An angry Carter countered that Begin was throwing away peace for 'a few illegal settlers on Egyptian land'. With no prospect of breaking the stalemate, Sadat announced on the 15th: 'We can go no further.' He requested a helicopter out. Carter's response laced flattery with threat: 'I explained . . . the extremely serious consequences . . . that his action would harm the relationship between Egypt and the United States, he would be violating his personal promise to me . . . [and] damage one of my most precious possessions – his friendship and our mutual trust.' Decoded, that meant that American aid to Egypt would be cut if Sadat left.[15]

Somehow, the logjam broke. After securing Sadat's agreement to stay, Carter offered to build new airfields for the Israelis and guaranteed them access to oilfields on the peninsula. In exchange, Begin would be required to relent on the settlements. He continued to protest, but finally agreed to submit the question to the Knesset.

That, for the time being, proved acceptable to Sadat. On 17 September, the Camp David Accords were signed. On the following day, Kissinger telephoned with a simple message for Carter: 'Hate to say: "You've not only done as well as I could have – but better."'[16]

A limited deal had been struck: Israel and Egypt agreed on the principle of land for peace, with the details to be worked out later. While there is no doubting the importance of the agreement, the Accords are measured by what they neglected, namely Palestine. A 'transfer of authority' was mentioned, and the possibility of a 'self-governing authority . . . in the West Bank and Gaza' mooted, but this was simply verbiage. 'Camp David is a dirty deal,' the PLO leader Yasser Arafat shouted. As the weeks passed, events proved that assessment correct. Both Carter and Sadat thought that Begin had promised that no more settlements would be built on the West Bank during the five-year transition period set aside for the negotiation of Palestine's future. Begin, however, insisted that no such moratorium had been established. Before long, new settlements were being built, with his enthusiastic encouragement.[17]

The other neglected issue was Jerusalem. Sadat insisted that 'Legal and historical Arab rights in the city must be respected and restored.' He wanted East Jerusalem to be under Arab sovereignty and insisted that the city's holy places should be administered by their respective religious groups. Begin vetoed all that, arguing that 'Jerusalem is one city indivisible, the capital of the State of Israel'. The issue was resolved by ignoring it – Jerusalem was absent from the agreement.[18]

On 27 September, after strident debate, the Knesset approved the Accords by a vote of 84 to 19, with 17 abstentions. Seven months and much argument later, the details of a settlement were finally resolved. Israel agreed to a staged withdrawal from 80 per cent of Sinai, which meant abandoning settlements. For that sacrifice, she received an Egyptian pledge to peace and a UN commitment to buttress the newly agreed borders, not to mention a lot of American money. The agreement was formally signed at the White House on 26 March 1979. Carter predicted that it would become 'the cornerstone of a comprehensive settlement, one that can bless with peace all the peoples who have suffered from the conflict in the Middle East'. For their efforts, Begin and Sadat were awarded the Nobel Peace Prize in 1978. Sadat openly regretted that Carter had not also been honoured, since 'It was [his] patience, persistence, and understanding which have made possible the progress thus far achieved.'[19]

Begin fared well as a result of the Accords. Some conservatives objected to the abandonment of Sinai settlements, but on the whole Israelis welcomed the step toward peace and the international approval that went with it. To those of a pragmatic bent, the fact that Israel's southern frontier was now secure made it easier to deal with problems in the north. The invasion of the Lebanon in 1982 might not have occurred had the Israelis had to worry about Egypt. Likewise, Israeli actions against the PLO did not provoke a meaningful response from Cairo. Egypt looked the other way as Israel consolidated her hold upon the West Bank and Golan Heights through the relentless establishment of settlements.

'This is certainly one of the happiest moments of my life,' Sadat confessed on 26 March 1979. In contrast to Begin, however, he gained little from his gamble. Peace proved lonely. Arabs everywhere condemned the abandonment of the Palestinians. Syrians lambasted 'Sadat the traitor', while their president, Hafez Assad, argued that 'Time will prove that the Middle East will still be in a state of war.' *Al Thawra*, Iraq's government paper, condemned Sadat for 'continuing his cooperation in imperialist-Zionist plans' and immediately called for 'punishment' in the form of an economic boycott. Eventually, eighteen Arab nations imposed sanctions and Egypt was expelled from the Arab League.[20]

The peace dividend never really materialized, despite an increased flow of American aid. Feeling cheated, Egyptians took their anger into the streets. Unrest was met with a combination of concession and repression, with the balance tilting increasingly toward the latter. Admired abroad, Sadat was despised at home. In September 1981, when a coup threatened, he arrested over 1,000 of his political enemies. The next month, during a parade to celebrate the anniversary of the Yom Kippur War, he was assassinated by a Muslim extremist.

For Carter, Camp David was a lonely triumph in a presidency crowded with failure. 'We have won, at least, the first step of peace – a first step on a long and difficult road,' he remarked at the White House signing ceremony. He accepted that 'Differences still separate the signatories to this treaty from each other and also from some of their neighbors who fear what they have done.' But the important point was that peace had replaced war. 'The soil of the two lands is not drenched with young blood. The countrysides of both lands are free from the litter and carnage of a wasteful war. Mothers in Egypt and Israel are not weeping today for their children fallen in senseless battle . . . Peace has come.'[21] For Carter, it was a triumph achieved because of qualities personal to him. 'Carter's control of the environment so that his special dimensions of personality and persuasion were most effective was masterly,' wrote the highly respected journalist Hugh Sidey. 'He did not sermonize or drop new proposals like bombs. He took ideas from both men, combined them with his own, then carried them back as if they were the inspirations of his guests. Such subtle flattery got him almost everything.' For a brief moment, Carter's goodness unravelled bitterness and distrust.[22]

The peace was popular in the West because it seemed the product of goodness. For that reason, too, Sadat was widely admired. Within that admiration, however, lies a clue to the limitations of what had been achieved. The West admired him because he did not act according to type. He was not a typical Arab, whatever that was supposed to be. His ability to cross cultures seemed reason for optimism in a desert otherwise devoid of hope. But that which made him a hero in the West made him a traitor in the Middle East. A comprehensive and meaningful peace could not be built on the expectation that other Arab leaders would be willing to sacrifice their reputations and abandon so much in order to satisfy the West.

Washington: Not Enough Bombs

The Cuban Missile Crisis of 1962 seemed proof that nuclear deterrence worked. John Kennedy and Nikita Khrushchev, faced with Armageddon, backed away from confrontation. In consequence, the world learned to stop worrying, even if it did not love the bomb. That sense of well-being was, however, based on the strategy of Mutually Assured Destruction, or MAD, in which security rested on the ability to destroy an enemy many times over. By 1969 the US and USSR were together spending more than $50 million a day on nuclear armaments. Eventually, both powers had more weapons than they had targets. Russian shoe factories were included on the American target list, on the grounds that Russians need shoes. The guiding principle, one analyst confessed, was to 'go . . . after what the adversary values. If he values his grandma, we . . . target grandmas.'[23]

Though arsenals continued to grow, so too did a willingness to negotiate. The Limited Test Ban Treaty (1963) was followed closely by the Hotline Agreement (1963), the Outer Space Treaty (1967) and the Sea Bed Treaty (1971). None of these affected the size of arsenals, but they did underline that the superpowers were talking. Détente was buttressed by essentially meaningless agreements.

MAD did not mean parity. While both superpowers expanded arsenals during the 1960s and early 1970s, the US stayed comfortably ahead. That lead did not, however, provide much advantage, since America did not possess a first-strike capability – in other words, the ability to deliver instantaneous destruction of a magnitude ruling out retaliation. Robert McNamara, Kennedy's secretary of defense and originator of the MAD idea, learned that supremacy was essentially worthless in the nuclear age. During the Cuban Missile Crisis, he reflected,

> The United States . . . had approximately five thousand strategic warheads, compared to the Soviet's three hundred. Despite an advantage of seventeen to one in our favor, President Kennedy and

> I were deterred from even considering a nuclear attack on the USSR by the knowledge that, although such a strike would destroy the Soviet Union, tens of their weapons would survive to be launched against the United States. These would kill millions of Americans. No responsible political leader would expose his nation to such a catastrophe.

That realization did not, however, prevent arsenals from expanding. In 1968, McNamara admitted that American nuclear superiority was 'both greater than we had originally planned and more than we require'. This had happened because caution always ruled: 'a strategic planner . . . must prepare for the worst plausible case and not be content to hope and prepare for the most probable'. America's consistent lead unsettled the Soviets, who genuinely feared that the US sought a first-strike capability. That fear caused the USSR to expand its arsenal, so as to retain a second-strike capability. 'Clearly the Soviet buildup is in part a reaction to our own buildup since the beginning of the 1960s,' McNamara admitted. Soviet expansion in turn prompted American response. And so on, and so on.[24]

In 1969, Kissinger told Congress that the Nixon administration had no desire to expand the American nuclear arsenal, because there was no need. Kissinger, like McNamara, took comfort in MADness. 'With no advantage to be gained by striking first and no disadvantage to be suffered by striking second,' he explained, 'there will be no motive for surprise or pre-emptive attack. Mutual invulnerability means mutual deterrence. It is the most stable position.' The number of weapons was not, however, the only factor in the security equation. New methods of delivery could upset the apple cart. Thus, even though Kissinger was happy with his arsenal when Nixon entered office, there was little likelihood he would remain so. The US and the USSR were two greyhounds chasing a mechanical rabbit called security they could never possibly catch.[25]

MAD presumed that an attack would always succeed, that nothing could prevent warheads from hitting targets. An anti-ballistic missile

(ABM) system, however, upset that presumption. 'We can hit a fly in space,' Khrushchev boasted. While that boast was entirely hot air, nuclear planners never gamble – as McNamara made clear. Every threat, no matter how bogus, required a response. Since an ABM system would increase the chances of the Soviets surviving a nuclear war, that constituted an effort to achieve first-strike capability by other means. MAD was undermined because destruction would be neither assured nor mutual. The only sensible response to a Soviet ABM system was to inundate it with more weapons than it could possibly handle – in other words, to build more bombs.[26]

A new generation of Intercontinental Ballistic Missiles (ICBM) was designed to address the new threat. Multiple Re-Entry Vehicles, or MRV, started as one missile, but then broke into separate warheads which would scatter in different directions, thus overwhelming any missile defence. That idea was improved further with MIRV, or Multiple Independently targeted Re-entry Vehicles, wherein each warhead carried its own guidance system. Not satisfied with that bit of wizardry, engineers then developed MARV, or Manoeuvrable Re-entry Vehicles, which allowed warheads to change course according to necessity, for instance, to avoid ABM defences.

These developments ensured that advantage remained with the attacker. Since MAD was based precisely on that premise, a sense of security was restored. As a result, the Soviet Union and the United States agreed that ABM was pointless and, being pointless, could be outlawed. The entire panoply of MRV was nevertheless retained, even though ABM was its raison d'être. As Robert Oppenheimer, father of the Bomb, once remarked, weapons are developed not because they are useful but because they are possible. MRVs were possible, ABM was not. ABM was therefore outlawed, while MRV was not. The failure to limit MRVs meant that, from 1972 to 1982, the US and USSR added 12,000 warheads to their arsenals, despite Kissinger's claim in 1969 that no more weapons were needed.

America's talent for making smaller weapons meant that they did not originally need hugely powerful rockets for their ICBMs. The

Soviets, in contrast, had initially needed to build bigger rockets to transport heavier weapons. In time, they developed lighter warheads, but still retained their powerful rockets. With the advent of MRV, those rockets gave them an advantage, since they could mount more warheads on each missile than the Americans could manage. Nixon seems to have walked blindly into this trap; he should have sought to ban MRVs, since they gave the Soviets an advantage. 'I would say in retrospect that I wish I had thought through the implications of a MIRVed world more . . . than I did,' Kissinger later admitted. The new wrinkle in the atomic equation eventually allowed the Soviets to move ahead in the number of actual ICBM warheads, even though there was little disparity in the number of missiles. This would prove crucial during the Carter presidency, when American military 'weakness' became controversial.[27]

While the two sides steadily expanded arsenals, they also negotiated their limitation. The Strategic Arms Limitation Talks (SALT), which began in 1969, sought to reduce the pace of arms expansion. The biggest obstacle in the way of agreement was that neither side wanted to compromise strength. For this reason, the aim was limitation, not reduction. Growth would be regulated, but shrinkage was taboo. Both sides sought nothing more than the definition of a comfortable equilibrium. An agreement was reached in 1972 that did not reduce the ability of both sides to destroy the world. The chief benefit was a slight reduction in expenditure, not to mention the fact that enemies had come to an agreement.

'The greatest paradox of the nuclear age,' Kissinger once stated, is the fact that while 'power has never been greater; it has also never been less useful.' Frustration with nuclear impotence had long inspired strategists to look for ways to break the stranglehold of MAD – in other words, to use the power without suffering the consequences. This dilemma motivated American consideration of the neutron bomb, an idea that surfaced in 1977. The goal was a small nuclear device which killed people, but did not destroy buildings, effectively a 'dirty bomb' that releases lethal radiation but does not explode. Such a weapon, it was thought, would prove useful in a

European war as an effective counterweight to the numerically superior Red Army. It would enable NATO to stop Soviet forces without destroying all of Central Europe.[28]

The idea provoked immense moral outrage. Critics complained that the neutron bomb was the ultimate manifestation of the capitalist ethic in that buildings were valued more than people. That distaste deeply affected President Carter, who confessed that he 'did not wish the world to think of him as an ogre'. His national security adviser Zbigniew Brzezinski recalled that Carter 'had a queasy feeling about the whole thing' and eventually decided 'that he would like to find a graceful way out'. An escape was found, but it was hardly graceful. Carter laid himself open to criticism that he did not have the stomach to protect his country.[29]

Like McNamara, Kissinger and Nixon before him, Carter was not comfortable with the endless expansion of arsenals. 'By enjoining sovereign nations to forgo nuclear weapons', he argued in 1976, 'we are asking for a form of self-denial that we have not been able to accept ourselves.' It behoved the superpowers, therefore, to 'get down to . . . the actual negotiation of reductions in strategic forces'. Despite that hint of promise, Carter, once he became president, found himself shackled by the same dilemma that had plagued his predecessors. MAD seemed the only option and security could not be compromised. As a result, Carter deployed new cruise missiles in Europe, commissioned the first Trident submarine and doubled the number of warheads targeted at the Soviet Union. Yet despite that massive escalation of America's arsenal, Carter was eventually crucified for being weak on defence.[30]

In 1978, Congress discovered that America's arsenal was larger than was necessary. If the Russians launched a surprise attack, congressmen surmised, the US could still depend upon having 4,900 thermonuclear warheads to fire back. If, on the other hand, America received adequate warning of a Soviet attack, some 7,500 warheads would be available for retaliation. If those weapons were deployed, it would result in the destruction of 90 per cent of Soviet military targets, 80 per cent of industrial targets, all government facilities and 90 million people. In a first strike, the US would be able to destroy all but 400 Soviet nuclear warheads.

That study should have provided reassurance that MAD remained stable. A group of professional worriers, however, worked diligently to undermine equanimity. In 1972, the veteran foreign policy adviser Paul Nitze revived his Committee on the Present Danger, a think tank first established twenty-two years earlier when the Soviets exploded their first atomic weapon. The new CPD included old-timers like Nitze and Eugene Rostow, in addition to a new generation of anti-Soviet hardliners who would figure prominently in the Reagan era. 'By its continuing strategic nuclear buildup', the group warned, 'the Soviet Union demonstrates that it does not subscribe to American notions of nuclear sufficiency and mutually assured deterrence. Soviet nuclear offensive and defensive weapons are designed to enable the USSR to fight, survive and win an all-out nuclear war.'[31]

In an article published in *Foreign Affairs* in 1976, Nitze accused the Soviets of preparing for nuclear blackmail. According to his scenario, the advantage that the Soviets possessed in ICBM warheads as a result of MRV would allow them to launch a devastating first strike which would eliminate most American missiles. The Americans would then be left with their submarine-launched missiles and bombers. At this point the 'shelter gap' – the Soviet ability to protect a far higher percentage of their citizens – would come into play. 'As the Soviet civil defense program becomes more effective', Nitze wrote, 'it tends to destabilize the deterrent relationship' because the US can 'no longer hold . . . the Soviet population . . . hostage to deter a Soviet attack'. Nitze estimated that the American second strike would kill only 3 per cent of the Soviet population (a mere 7.5 million people), an entirely acceptable level of loss for them. The Soviets would then respond by hitting American cities, causing a much higher level of loss, due to the American failure to build shelters. An American president, realizing this likely sequence of events beforehand, would suffer a 'paralysis of will' and decide not to use his weapons at all. In other words, by mere threat of attack the Soviets could bend the Americans to their will, since an attack would not bring mutual destruction.[32]

On another front, Nitze and his merry band of doom-mongers raised the old dilemma of nuclear impotence. Deterrence, they argued, gave a natural advantage to the Soviets, who possessed much larger conventional forces. Back in the 1950s a gaggle of nuclear strategists, led by Herman Kahn, had struggled with this dilemma, to no avail. The acceptance of MAD in the early 1960s was essentially an acknowledgement that the problem was insoluble. In the 1970s, however, a new generation began once more to think the unthinkable. Consideration of nuclear war required redefining standards of survivability, a redefinition that some hardliners easily managed. 'If we have to start over again with Adam and Eve,' argued Senator Richard Russell of Georgia, 'I want them to be Americans.'[33]

The SALT II Agreements of June 1979 added fuel to the pyre on which the CPD would burn Carter. Under the terms of the treaty each side could add an additional 4,000 warheads to their armouries by 1985. In addition, each superpower was allowed to deploy one new weapon system over the subsequent five years, without those weapons counting in the 4,000 warhead limit. Nitze and his friends objected that SALT II institutionalized an American disadvantage and was therefore equivalent to surrender to nuclear blackmail. They argued that Carter, by signing SALT II and rejecting the neutron bomb, had given the Soviets the keys to the world. The committee talked loudly of a 'Vietnam syndrome' which rendered Americans fearful about using their rightful power. One member, Jeanne Kirkpatrick, argued that failure in Vietnam had fostered a 'culture of appeasement, which finds reasons not only against the use of force, but denies its place in the world'.[34]

In 1980, Carter ran for re-election against Ronald Reagan, the darling of the CPD. Reagan won the election by a landslide. He thought MAD was madness – 'the craziest thing I ever heard of'. It reminded him of 'two westerners standing in a saloon aiming their guns at each other's head – permanently'. In searching for an alternative, he was prepared to contemplate a nuclear holocaust. His team of advisers included thirty-two members of the CPD, individuals who had also embraced the idea of Armageddon. 'Every day I think that time is running out,' the new defence secretary, Caspar Weinberger, confessed. Reagan's vice-president, George H.W. Bush, politely explained how a nuclear war might be won. '[If] you have survivability of command and control, survivability of industrial potential, protection of a percentage of your citizens, and you have a capability that inflicts more damage on the opposition than it can inflict on you. That's the way you can have a winner.' The world started to worry again.[35]

Afghanistan: Trapping the Bear

In the 'Great Game' of the nineteenth century, Britain and Russia vied for control of Afghanistan. The game ended in 1907 when the two adversaries formally agreed not to argue. Then, in the mid-1970s, a new 'Great Game' began, with the Americans replacing the British. In the sequel, the object was changed. While the British had once tried to keep the Russians out of Afghanistan, the Americans now tried to draw them in – the aim being to create a Russian Vietnam.

During the reign of King Mohammad Zahir Shah (1933–73), Afghanistan was reasonably stable, at least in comparison to the situation before or since. Stability began to unravel when the Afghans were drawn into Cold War rivalries. Mohammed Daoud Khan, cousin of the king and prime minister from 1953–63, willingly courted the Soviets, in an attempt to counterbalance American friendliness toward Iran and Pakistan. In 1955, he refused to join the Baghdad Pact, essentially an anti-communist, pro-Western pledge by Central Asian states, and instead reached agreement with the Soviets on a package of military and economic aid.

In 1964, the establishment of a constitutional monarchy paved the way to genuine political parties. Within a year, the People's Democratic Party of Afghanistan (PDPA) was founded, with Soviet assistance. Party harmony was, however, difficult to maintain amidst ethnic and clan rivalries. By 1966, the PDPA had split into two factions, Khalq and Parcham. The former, led by Nur Mohammed Taraki, advocated the abolition of the monarchy and the immediate establishment of a radical socialist state. Parchamites, led by Babrak Karmal, were gradualists who contended that Afghanistan, lacking a true proletariat, was not yet ready for Marxist revolution.

On 17 July 1973, Daoud, supported by Parchamites, led a coup against his cousin, proclaiming Afghanistan a republic and naming himself president. The coup left Taraki and his Khalq colleagues out in the cold. Increasingly bitter factionalism worried the Soviets, who instructed their ambassador to warn Taraki and Karmal that prolonged 'internal strife' would endanger socialist transformation. The Soviets wanted a stable, modern Afghanistan modelled on their central Asian republics. They feared that PDPA disunity would be exploited by conservative Afghans and by their supporters in Pakistan, Iran and the United States.[36]

Mismanagement, rivalry and controversy dogged the Daoud government, which meant that those wishing it ill grew in number with each passing month. Of particular concern was the emergence of an Islamic fundamentalist opposition, mirroring developments in Iran. Islamic factions, collectively known as 'mujahedeen', opposed Daoud's progressivism. This alarmed the Soviets, who feared that an Islamic resurgence might sweep across their central Asian republics.

Aware of the unpopularity of Marxism among Afghan traditionalists, Daoud began to distance himself from the PDPA, eventually establishing a government distinctly his own, administered through his National Revolutionary Party. He also cut ties with the Soviet Union and made overtures toward non-communist countries like Pakistan, Iran, Saudi Arabia and the United States. The Soviets, fearful of losing a solid ally, reacted by attempting to broker rapprochement between Khalq and Parcham. That proved easier once Daoud excluded Parchamites from his government. A fragile unity was achieved after the murder in April 1978 of Mir Akbar Khyber, a prominent Parchamite. At his funeral on 19 April some 20,000 mourners witnessed the strange spectacle of Taraki and Karmal speaking from the same podium.

That unity, flimsy though it was, frightened Daoud. He reacted by arresting PDPA leaders on suspicion that they were plotting against him, which in fact they were. That, however, proved insufficient. The PDPA, backed by a fresh shipment of Soviet arms, launched a coup on 27 April, easily overwhelming the presidential guard. On the following day, Daoud and his family were shot and thrown into a mass grave. Taraki went from prison to presidency in one quick leap. While the coup wasn't exactly engineered by the Soviets, many Afghans saw it that way. Airstrikes against Daoud's forces were carried out with a level of precision that suggested the pilots might be Russian. According to an Afghan journalist, 'anyone who believed that Soviets were not involved in the 1978 coup, was either uninformed . . . or was confirming Lenin's assessment that there will always be useful idiots who . . . inadvertently support the Communist cause'.[37]

The 'Saur' or 'Red' revolution at first seemed popular. The *New York Times* found that 'nearly every Afghan . . . said [they were] delighted by the coup', while the *Wall Street Journal* reported that '150,000 persons . . . marched to honor the new flag . . . the participants appeared genuinely enthusiastic'. The show of support gave Taraki the confidence to embark upon Marxist revolution. Helped by Soviet advisers, his government instituted a wholesale transformation of Afghan society, based on universal education, nationalization of assets, political indoctrination and land reform. The custom of arranged marriage and dowries was attacked, as was the usurious Islamic lending system. To leftists in the West, the abolition of brutal, often misogynistic Afghan customs seemed a positive example of what Soviet imperialism could achieve.[38]

Since Karmal and his followers had never supported Taraki's plans for rapid socialist transformation, PDPA unity quickly disintegrated. Parchamites were excluded from the new government and, in keeping with the Afghan fondness for purges, many were murdered. The resumption of violent factionalism worried Moscow. As one official report declared, 'repressions have taken on mass proportions, are being carried out without regard to law, and are directed not only at class enemies of the new regime . . . but also at persons who could be used for revolutionary interests'. This policy, the Soviets feared, 'brings out discontent among the populace, undermines the authority of the revolutionary government and leads to the weakening of the new regime'. Taraki's supporters defended the purge, arguing that Parchamites threatened the socialist transformation. In truth, Taraki coveted the efficiency of a one-party state. 'We respect the experience of a multi-party system in some socialist countries,' he remarked, 'but we prefer to follow the example of the USSR. What is happening in Afghanistan is the beginning of the dictatorship of the proletariat, based on the Soviet model.' As for the Parchamites, Taraki added: 'Lenin taught us to be merciless towards the enemies of the revolution.'[39]

The Soviets felt that Taraki's haste endangered the stability of the revolution. 'The leadership of Afghanistan . . . [does] not sufficiently appreciate the role of Islamic fundamentalists,' Dimitri Ustinov warned his Politburo colleagues on 18 March. As Ustinov understood, Taraki's reforms, though humane and progressive, trampled on sacred Islamic customs. Secular, class-based goals were given priority over Sharia law. Land reform, as was the case in Iran, undermined the authority of large landowners and mullahs. Likewise, the liberation of women insulted the core values of many Afghans. The popularity of the Saur revolution that Western journalists had noticed arose not from the fact that it was progressive, but because it had toppled the widely despised Daoud. Many Afghanis now worried that Taraki would turn Afghanistan into a Soviet colony. At the back of everyone's mind was the warning given by King Abdur Rahman Khan in 1901: 'My last words . . . are: Never trust the Russians.' Mohammed Sharif, an Afghan journalist, felt that 'except for a small number of socialist intellectuals and Soviet-trained officials in the capital, the rest of . . . Afghan society remained very hostile toward the Soviets. An average Afghan views the Soviet Union as an expansionist empire committed to the destruction of Islam.'[40]

While Taraki was oblivious to the sensitivities of his people, the Soviets were not. 'It is completely clear to us that Afghanistan is not ready . . . to resolve all of the issues it faces through socialism,' the KGB chairman Yuri Andropov told the Politburo on 17 March. 'The economy is backward, the Islamic religion pre-dominates, and nearly all of the rural population is illiterate. We know Lenin's teachings about a revolutionary situation. Whatever situation we are talking about in Afghanistan, it is not that type of situation.' As Andropov understood, this was not a good time to alienate Islamic fundamentalists. Their power was painfully obvious from events in Iran. One of Khomeini's first acts on seizing control was to warn Taraki that, if he trampled on Islam, he would suffer the same fate as the Shah.[41]

Evidence that the fundamentalist contagion was spreading came on 12 March 1979, when the National Islamic Liberation Front, a loose collection of mujahedeen based in Pakistan, called for a jihad or holy war against the Taraki government and its supporters. In Herat, the jihad was launched by Ismail Khan, an Afghan Army captain who led a mutiny at the local garrison, targeting Soviet advisers. Around thirty were killed, their bodies displayed on pikes around the city.

Taraki, meanwhile, was behaving like a puppet who had cut his strings. In a fit of panic, he warned the Soviet premier Alexei Kosygin on 18 March that 'The situation [in Herat] is bad and getting worse.' When Kosygin asked what should be done, Taraki demanded heavy weaponry. Oblivious to the impact a Soviet involvement of this sort might have on world opinion, Taraki suggested 'that [if] you place Afghan markings on your tanks and aircraft . . . no one will be any the wiser'. Kosygin disagreed. 'I do not want to disappoint you, but it will not be possible to conceal this. Two hours later the whole world will know about this. Everyone will begin to shout that the Soviet Union's intervention in Afghanistan has begun.' Oblivious to that warning, Taraki then added that he was also short on soldiers skilled in heavy weaponry. 'We want you to send us Tajiks, Uzbeks, and Turkmens,' he told Kosygin. 'They could drive tanks, because we have all these nationalities in Afghanistan. Let them don Afghan costume and wear Afghan badges and no one will recognize them.'[42]

In view of what happened later, it is interesting to note just how adamantly Soviet leaders opposed invasion at this time. At a meeting on 20 March, Kosygin expressed the view that 'There would be huge minuses for us. A whole bouquet of countries would quickly come out against us. And there are no pluses for us at all.' Foreign Minister Andrei Gromyko echoed that view, adding that it would be 'a nice gift for China'. Andropov admitted that it might be possible to 'suppress a revolution in Afghanistan . . . with . . . bayonets', but to do so would be 'entirely inadmissible'.[43]

The Afghan Army took ten days to recapture Herat. Airstrikes by Soviet-supplied bombers killed more than 20,000 residents, a toll which increased when government forces then indulged in brutal reprisals. The carnage, designed to intimidate mujahedeen supporters, had precisely the opposite effect. Every new act of brutality increased the people's susceptibility to mujahedeen logic. That logic was attractive not simply because it was rooted in Islamic tradition, but also because it was genuinely nationalist. Taraki's reliance upon outside help to deal with an internal threat only served to increase doubts about his regime's legitimacy. As Soviet officials noted, 'The situation in . . . Afghanistan . . . continues to deteriorate . . . The reactionary clergy is intensifying anti-government and anti-Soviet agitation and in this regard preaching the idea of creating a "free Islamic republic" . . . similar to Iran's.' The inability of Taraki to retain the loyalty of his people can be measured by the flood of desertions within the Afghan Army. Many soldiers, following Ismail Khan's example, simply switched to the mujahedeen.[44]

The discomfiture of Taraki and his Soviet backers delighted Washington. Adhering to the dubious strategy of 'my enemy's enemy is my friend', the CIA in early March urged President Carter to back the mujahedeen. The agency suggested that supplies and money could be transferred through Pakistan's Inter-Services Agency, which was already involved in this 'good cause'. The US found themselves in a somewhat ironic position: having recently watched Islamic fundamentalists drive their great friend the Shah out of Iran, the

Americans were now hoping to use a similar group of fundamentalists to do their dirty work in Afghanistan. This meant getting friendly with the odious Pakistani dictator Zia-ul-Haq, thus contradicting Carter's much-trumpeted emphasis upon human rights. In exchange for Pakistani help, the US also turned a blind eye toward Zia's clandestine nuclear weapons programme.

The US, of course, did not remotely care about what was best for the Afghan people, their only concern was to make life difficult for the Soviets. Under-Secretary of Defense Walter Slocumbe openly discussed the possibility of 'sucking the Soviets into a Vietnamese quagmire'. Taken with the idea, Carter on 3 July officially sanctioned the CIA to funnel around $500,000 to the Afghan rebels. In the following month, the ambassador in Kabul frankly admitted that America's 'larger interests . . . would be served by the demise of the [PDPA government], despite whatever setbacks this might mean for future social and economic reforms in Afghanistan'. Americans harboured no illusions about the barbarism of their new ally. In May 1979, the *Washington Post* reported that the mujahedeen liked to 'torture victims by first cutting off their noses, ears, and genitals, then removing one slice of skin after another'. One of America's new friends was the mujahedeen warlord Gulbuddin Hekmatyar, a brutal sadist and opium dealer whose trademark was throwing acid in the faces of women who refused to wear the veil.[45]

Meanwhile, the Afghan tail continued to wag the Soviet dog. The Russians found themselves tied to a dangerously unstable regime, in the form of Taraki and his deputy Hafizullah Amin. 'Afghanistan's difficulties are becoming more intense,' a Politburo report warned. 'In the Party and the government a collegial leadership is lacking, all power in fact is concentrated in the hands of . . . Taraki and . . . Amin.' Their knee-jerk response to each crisis was to demand more Russian help. 'The arrival of Soviet troops will significantly raise our moral spirit, will inspire even greater confidence and calm,' they assured Moscow in early August. When the Soviets expressed concern about how intervention might be viewed in the wider world, Amin insisted that 'we are a sovereign and independent state and solve all our problems independently. Your troops will not participate in combat actions. They will be used only in moments that are critical for us.' He promised that, with sufficient help, his government could eradicate the mujahedeen by early spring.[46]

To make matters worse, Taraki and Amin were now arguing, each blaming the other for the worsening situation. On 9 September, the Politburo asked their ambassador in Kabul, Alexandre Puzanov, to impress upon them that 'a rift in the leadership would be fatal to the revolutionary cause'. Little, however, could be done, since Amin had already launched a coup. On the 14th, his goons seized control of the presidential offices and arrested Taraki, who was later executed. On the following day, a worried Gromyko advised his team in Kabul that they should try 'to restrain . . . Amin from repressions of supporters of . . . Taraki and other people . . . who are not enemies of the revolution'. That plea was about as effective as an umbrella in a tornado, since a purge had already begun. Watching from the sidelines, KGB agents grew convinced that the American-educated Amin was about to switch sides. These fears spread to the Politburo when his purge eliminated those whom the Soviets considered good communists. According to KGB General Leonid Shebarshin, the Politburo feared that Amin was preparing to '[do] a Sadat on us'.[47]

Now desperate, the Soviets decided to throw their weight behind Karmal, who had earlier escaped to Czechoslovakia. A deal was struck whereby he would request Soviet help to restore order, thus allowing the USSR to invade. Selling this plan to Brezhnev on 1 December, Andropov advised that two Soviet battalions already in Kabul would be 'entirely sufficient', but additional forces might be necessary 'in the event of unforeseen complications'. Andropov felt certain that active intervention 'would allow us to decide the question of defending the gains of the April revolution, establishing Leninist principles in the party and state leadership of Afghanistan, and securing our positions in this country'. General Nikolai Ogarkov, chief of the general staff, however, had deep misgivings. At a meeting with Brezhnev on 10 December, he argued that 'the Afghan problem should be decided by political means, instead of relying on . . . force'.

'The Afghan people . . . [have] never tolerated foreigners on their soil,' he warned. Brezhnev sympathized, but, his options running out, reluctantly sided with Andropov.[48]

On 24 December Soviet troops moved on targets in Kabul and other cities. Four days later, the Politburo announced that Afghanistan had been 'liberated' and Amin executed. Karmal was formally installed as the new prime minister, whereupon he confirmed that the invasion had been his idea. In a message to Russia's allies, the Politburo explained that invasion had been necessary because of the 'sharp deterioration of the situation', caused by the 'gross interference on the part of several powers into the affairs of Afghanistan'. Even the dim-witted recognized the reference to the United States. Soviet leaders genuinely believed that right was on their side. According to the former KGB general Oleg Kalugin, everyone agreed that 'Afghanistan [was] . . . a country within our sphere of interest, and we . . . had to do whatever possible to prevent the Americans and the CIA from installing an anti-Soviet regime there'.[49]

Since this was a Cold War conflict, rhetoric could be recycled. 'The Soviet attack on Afghanistan and the ruthless extermination of its government', Carter argued, 'have highlighted in the starkest terms the darker side of their policies – going well beyond competition and the legitimate pursuit of national interest, and violating all norms of international law and practice.' The clandestine support for the mujahedeen was turned into official policy. 'It is essential that Afghanistan's resistance continues,' Brzezinski told Carter. 'This means more money as well as arms shipments to the rebels, and some technical advice . . . we should make Soviet involvement as costly as possible.' On that score, the Carter administration succeeded. Within a month, the Soviets had 85,000 troops in Afghanistan. Their standing commitment would eventually expand to 105,000, with over 600,000 troops serving in total. Brzezinski was quite proud of the way he had helped to lure the Soviets into a trap. 'We didn't push the Russians to intervene, but we knowingly increased the probability that they would,' he later boasted. 'The day that the Soviets officially crossed the border, I wrote to President Carter: "We now have the opportunity of giving to the Soviet Union its Vietnam War."' Carter said essentially the same thing to his wife: 'We will help to make sure that Afghanistan will be their Vietnam.'[50]

Over the next twelve years, the US would channel around $3 billion dollars in cash and military hardware to the mujahedeen, far more than was actually needed in their war with the Soviets. Brzezinski has no regrets about his Faustian deal. 'That secret operation was an excellent idea,' he later insisted. 'What is most important to the history of the world? The Taliban or the collapse of the Soviet empire? Some stirred-up Moslems or the liberation of Central Europe and the end of the cold war?'[51]

That statement was made in 1998. Four years later, American troops, deployed in Afghanistan to fight those 'stirred-up Moslems', discovered for themselves what had become of all that weaponry the US had given to their friends the mujahedeen.

Downing Street: Maggie Knows Best

To the British of the mid-Seventies, she was 'Mrs Thatcher, Milk Snatcher'. Margaret Thatcher's defining moment came in 1971 when, as education secretary in Edward Heath's government, she abolished the provision of free school milk for children aged seven to eleven. Never mind that Labour had previously done the same for secondary school pupils. Never mind that kids seldom drank the milk, which was usually curdled by the time it was distributed. The point was that Thatcher's mean-spirited cut had set down a marker by demonstrating that she held no sentimental attachment to the welfare state. The fact that it was a woman who had taken milk from the mouths of babes made the act seem that much more ruthless, more foreboding. Though not everyone realized it, the age of consensus was dead. Its executioner was a woman.

Thatcher was born in 1925 in Grantham. Her father, Alfred Roberts, was a grocer, self-made man, alderman and lay Methodist preacher – characteristics that shaped Margaret. 'I . . . owe almost everything to my father', she confessed after her triumphant election in 1979, 'and . . . the things that I learned in a small town, in a very modest home, are just the things that I believe have won the election.' She inherited his belief in hard work, Christian morality and the idea that one gets what one deserves. A scholarship allowed entry to Oxford, where she was president of the university's Conservative Association, only the third woman to hold that post. She graduated in 1947, married a wealthy man in 1951, gave birth to twins two years later, and then embarked upon a crusade.[52]

In 1958, she was chosen as parliamentary candidate for the safe Conservative seat of Finchley in North London. That campaign provided a clear indication of her philosophy. 'Don't be scared of the high-flown language of economists and cabinet ministers,' she told a ladies luncheon. 'Think of politics at our own household level. After all, women live in contact with food supplies, housing shortages and the ever-decreasing opportunities for children, and we must therefore . . . remember . . . that as more power is taken away from the people, so there is less responsibility for us to assume.' The *Finchley Press* admired how she 'weighed up Russia's propagandist moves with the skill of a housewife measuring the ingredients in a familiar recipe, pinpointed Nasser as the fly in the mixing bowl, switched swiftly to domestic problems . . . then swept her breathless audience into a confident preview of Conservatism's dazzling future.'[53]

She won comfortably and, in parliament, quickly established a reputation as a high flyer. Though loyal to her party, she was never prepared to compromise rigid principles. In 1961, she defied the whip by supporting the reintroduction of corporal punishment. Misguided humanitarian concerns had, she felt, caused the country to '[lose] sight of the . . . true aims of punishment . . . [which] should be . . . the protection of the community'. That suggested an uncompromising conservatism, as did her support for capital punishment and her opposition to the liberalization of divorce laws. She was, however, one of the few Tories to support the decriminalization of male homosexuality, and also backed the legalization of abortion.[54]

Religion infused her politics, but only to a limited extent. She was devout, but not fundamentalist, and was by no means softened by Christian charity. 'Even the Good Samaritan had to have money to help, otherwise he too would have had to pass on the other side,' she famously remarked. Faith provided moral foundation for her vision of society. 'I believe that by taking together . . . key elements from the Old and New Testaments, we gain . . . a proper attitude to work and principles to shape economic and social life. We are told we must work and use our talents to create wealth. "If a man will not work he shall not eat", wrote St. Paul to the Thessalonians. Indeed, abundance rather than poverty has a legitimacy which derives from the very nature of Creation.' That was essentially her father's lesson; it did not require Christian reinforcement, but was stronger because of it. In line with these beliefs, she attacked Labour policy as 'a step not merely towards Socialism but towards Communism'. The Labour prime minister Harold Wilson, she argued in 1966, was 'an apostle of change, a change to more power for politicians over people and their pockets. I reject that kind of change; we are more interested in progress than in change, progress through increased personal responsibility and increased personal endeavour.' All that suggested a very hard-hearted woman, but she insisted she possessed a soft core. 'I'm a romantic at heart', she insisted; 'there are times when I get home at night, and everything has got on top of me, when I shed a few tears silently, alone.' In the absence of witnesses, many people doubted that revelation.[55]

In the Conservative leadership contest of 1964, Thatcher supported Ted Heath, and was rewarded with a leg up the ministerial ladder. She entered the Shadow Cabinet in 1967, moving quickly from Fuel to Environment to Education. She became, during this period, a devout supporter of the monetarist theories espoused by Milton Friedman and F.A. Hayek, in opposition to Keynesian gospel. Within the Tory party, the guru of monetarism was Sir Keith Joseph, social security minister in the government of 1970–4. For Thatcher, monetarism was instinctive; it harmonized with her housewife's ethic of self-reliance and fiscal responsibility. 'Any woman who understands the problems of running a home', she argued, 'will be nearer to understanding the problems of running a country.' It did not worry her that monetarism favoured those with greater means, since she had nothing against wealth, as long as it came from hard work. 'Pennies do not come from heaven,' she maintained. 'They have to be earned here on earth.'[56]

The Tories' Selsdon Park declaration of January 1970 seemed to promise a full conversion to monetarism – Thatcherism before Thatcher. Government intervention was declared taboo, and ailing industries would not be rescued simply out of sentiment. Heath's heart, however, wasn't in it, as a series of U-turns eventually made clear. This alienated Conservative rightwingers, who gave up on him long before the country did.

When the Conservatives failed to hold on to power in the election of February 1974, Thatcher and Joseph sharpened their knives. A second defeat in October settled the matter – Heath had to go. In between those two elections, Joseph delivered a speech outlining monetarist policy and offering a clear alternative to Heath. The number one danger facing the country, he argued, was inflation, on which he outlined three 'truths': 'First that inflation at its present pace cannot be abated entirely painlessly. Secondly, the cure by gradual abatement would be infinitely less painful than what would happen if we reflate . . . Thirdly, there is one thing worse – far worse – than stopping inflation, and that is not stopping it.' The message was clear: there is no alternative. That message was so often trumpeted it became known as 'TINA'. 'We need a government with strong nerves to set broad policy lines and stick to them,' Joseph insisted. 'Then we can recover our footing, and . . . the soundness of our economy . . . will be restored.'[57]

Joseph was proposing a revolution, one he briefly thought he might lead. He was, however, a rather scary figure who brought Rasputin to mind. His hopes for the leadership were dashed when a speech in Birmingham in October 1974 carried a hint of eugenics. Wisely withdrawing from the race, he passed the monetarist baton to Thatcher. A perfect partnership evolved: he provided the intellectual weight, she the ruthlessness of a Rottweiler.

Had Heath done the decent thing and resigned after the second election defeat, Thatcher might never have become prime minister. His incorrigible vanity, however, rendered it impossible to accept rejection. Because he did not resign, the mainstream candidates – William Whitelaw, James Prior and Sir Geoffrey Howe – held to party etiquette and did not challenge him when a leadership contest was held on 4 February 1975. Thatcher was seen as a stalking horse who would gauge party interest in a genuine challenge. Contrary to expectation, however, the stalking horse proved a thoroughbred – she polled 130 votes, Heath 119. Now the frontrunner, she proved impossible for Whitelaw, Howe or Prior to overtake. On the second ballot a week later, she secured 146 votes out of 279 cast – the necessary majority. The MP Julian Critchley rightly called it a 'peasants' revolt' – the party peons had expressed their displeasure with an elitist leadership by electing a grocer's daughter. The grandees had not supported her and none expected her to last.

That expectation might have been fulfilled, if not for the cooperation of the 1974–9 Labour government. Its misfortune was her blessing; had she been forced to fight the next election against a popular Labour prime minister, her tenure as leader might have been compared to that of William Hague or Michael Howard, the hapless victims of Tony Blair. Unlike them, however, she had the good fortune to become leader at a time when the country seemed to be falling apart. Because the disintegration seemed serious, Thatcher's radicalism gained credibility.

Thatcher was also helped by the mysterious resignation of Wilson, until then the most formidable leader in Labour's history. James Callaghan, who took over in April 1976, had immense ministerial experience, but lacked the fortitude essential for the top job. Not long after he entered Downing Street, Britain plunged into its worst economic crisis since 1931. The pound went into freefall, with government efforts to halt the slide serving only to spread panic. By May, with the pound at $1.70, Britain was forced to seek help from foreign banks. A line of credit was secured only on the condition that public spending be cut by $1 billion. This alienated the party's left wing, who thought the 'capitalist crisis' was caused not by too much socialism, but by not enough.

With the pound continuing to fall, the government prepared for an appeal to the International Monetary Fund, a move that would necessitate further cuts. The annoyance of leftwingers erupted at the party's Blackpool conference in September. The MP Judith Hart urged Callaghan to 'tell the IMF that we do not agree with the pre-Keynesian classical economics that dominate the IMF . . . tell them that there are . . . other solutions. Let us convince the international field that our answers are right.' Stuck in Cloud Cuckooland, the left pushed for the nationalization of the banks and increases in welfare spending. Callaghan responded with his New Realism. 'We used to think that you could spend your way out of a recession and increase employment by cutting taxes and boosting government spending,' he told a chamber disinclined to recognize reality. 'I tell you in all candour that that option no longer exists, and that, in so far as it ever did exist, it only worked . . . by injecting a bigger dose of inflation into the economy, followed by a higher level of unemployment . . . that is the history of the last twenty years.' To Labour supporters, that sounded painfully like Mrs Thatcher. In fact, it was precisely what Thatcher thought, but her solution was a great deal more brutal than what Callaghan had in mind.[58]

When sterling fell to $1.50, the chancellor Denis Healey presented his party with a stark choice: either the IMF or the Tories. The latter, he warned, would mean 'massive new cuts in the public expenditure, unemployment in the low millions, and a return to the confrontation between a British government and the working people of this country'. The party reluctantly came round. The terms, agreed in October, involved the IMF loaning $3.9 billion, in exchange for an agreement that the government would cut public spending by $2.5 billion, sell £500 million worth of BP shares and maintain stringent controls on the money supply. In other words, in order to stay in office, Labour underwent a forced conversion to monetarism. Thatcher made much of her opponents' predicament. 'People do not have to get into the hands of international bankers if they run their affairs in such a way that they do not need to go for loans,' she argued with characteristic homespun logic. Sticking the knife in further, she taunted Labour: 'Nothing I can say about the Chancellor of the Exchequer is half as damning as the judgement he passed on himself . . . when he . . . [said] that the alternative to another loan would be economically savage and would produce riots in the streets. What an account of one's stewardship to say . . . that there will be riots in the streets unless the capitalist countries bail one out!'[59]

By-election losses were meanwhile slowly eroding Labour's majority in the Commons. A shabby deal with the Liberals, agreed on 23 March 1977, allowed the government to remain in power, much to Thatcher's disgust. 'Mr. Callaghan and his Labour Government have not been reprieved,' she snarled. 'They have secured a stay of execution but they are still under sentence of death.' Contrary to expectations, however, Labour's medicine began to work. The pound edged toward $2.00, inflation and unemployment fell, and early repayments on the IMF loan were made. 'Is this the Labour miracle?' the *Sunday Times* asked. Polls suggested a dead heat between Labour and the Tories.[60]

Sustaining the miracle, however, depended upon the cooperation of the trade unions, who had shelved wage demands while the government fixed the economy. In January 1978, Callaghan asked for restraint to continue. The TUC, however, rejected his plea, signalling open war in the autumn. Gambling on the workers' good sense, Callaghan assumed that, when crunch time came, they would forgo a pay rise in order to ensure a Labour victory at the next election. That proved misguided. At the Labour conference, the TUC outlook prevailed. What resulted was double-digit wage demands during what came to be known as the Winter of Discontent. Trade unions queued up to pummel the government, downing tools without any effort at negotiation. The issue was not pay, but vengeance; the government was being punished for supposedly losing touch with the working man. Callaghan's great mistake came in trying to govern in the interests of the country, rather than the workers. What followed was the worst period of industrial unrest since the General Strike of 1926. Hospital operations were cancelled, rubbish went uncollected, essential services were curtailed, and the dead went unburied.

The workers won, but the reputation of the trade union movement was shredded. So, too, was the idea of worker solidarity. 'Nobody is in favour of somebody else's strike,' remarked the trade union leader Clive Jenkins, 'but they're always in favour of their own.' Organized labour came to be seen as a dragon in need of St George. 'Each night the television screens carried film of bearded men in duffle coats huddled around braziers,' recalled Healey. 'Nervous viewers thought the Revolution had already begun.' One poll in January 1979 suggested that 51 per cent of the people believed the unions were under communist control. Worse still, the unions had managed to alienate their most loyal supporters – 83.4 per cent of Labour voters wanted a ban on secondary picketing. Frank Chapple of the Electricians Union found the madness bewildering: 'Whether the wildcat strikers in the vanguard were politically motivated, misled, sick-minded or just plain stupid, it was all far removed from [the] trade unionism . . . I could remember.' 'This shambles was of course a triumph for Mrs Thatcher,' Healey reflected. 'The cowardice and irresponsibility of some union leaders in abdicating responsibility . . . guaranteed her election; it left them with no grounds for complaining about her subsequent action against them.'[61]

When Labour's precarious hold on government slipped away on 28 March 1979, the country faced the most momentous election since 1945. Thatcher spoke in apocalyptic tones appropriate to turbulent times. The election, she suggested, was the last opportunity to stave off complete collapse. On every soapbox, she reiterated her personal 'vision': 'a man's right to work as he will, to spend what he earns, to own property, to have the state as a servant and not as master: these are . . . the essence of a free country, and on that freedom all our other freedoms depend'.[62]

On 3 May, the Tories gained 43.9 per cent of the vote, Labour 36.9 and the Liberals 13.8. Under Britain's peculiar electoral system, that was enough to give the Tories a majority of 70 seats over Labour, and 43 overall. It was by no means a mandate for the kind of radicalism Thatcher presented, but that hardly mattered to her.

Around 1975, a sense of confusion and malaise settled upon Britain. Wilson's 'White Heat' gave way to a cold winter of discontent. The hope that once fuelled the 1960s seemed cruelly mistaken. 'All over the country', wrote Margaret Drabble, 'people blamed other people for the things that were going wrong – the trades unions, the present government, the miners, the car workers, the seamen, the Arabs, the Irish, their own husbands, their own wives, their own idle good-for-nothing offspring, comprehensive education. Nobody knew whose fault it really was, but most people managed to complain fairly forcefully about somebody.' A revolution had occurred and Thatcher, though not its author, was its beneficiary. The turbulence of the 1960s had frightened ordinary people. They reacted by circling the wagons and taking refuge in the family – the only institution that still offered stability. Traditional values like individualism, morality and hard work took centre stage, as Thatcher understood. Politicians on the left struggled to come to terms with this resurgence of beliefs once derided as bourgeois. Those still stuck in the 1960s ethos of progressivism fought this new conservativism by contemptuously deriding it. This explains why Labour in Britain and the Democrats in America lost touch with their blue-collar bases. Disenchanted with the left, the working class shifted allegiance to those once seen as oppressors. That shift was not, however, inevitable: in New Zealand, Australia, France, Italy and Spain, the left adjusted to the political trend and rode it, in the process avoiding the right-wing fundamentalism that characterized Britain and America in the 1980s. The British Labour Party, in contrast, would take until 1997 to accept that the people did not actually want socialism. There was no more potent sign of a party out of touch than Labour delegates stubbornly singing the 'Red Flag' and calling each other 'comrade' at party conferences throughout the 1980s.[63]

The fact that Thatcher had won a landslide with less than 44 per cent of the vote did not trouble her, since she was convinced that she alone understood what ailed Britain. She was the stern governess who would correct Britain's self-indulgent ways, with monetarism her cod liver oil. Hers would be, as she promised, 'a conviction government', which was really just a polite way of saying 'Maggie knows best'. The fact that she did not care about being popular gave her enormous power. Consensus, that noble goal of previous prime ministers, was, she argued, 'the process of abandoning all beliefs, principles, values and policies . . . it is something in which no one believes and to which no one objects'. Those who sought consensus were 'quislings' and 'traitors'.[64]

On entering 10 Downing Street the morning after her election, Thatcher quoted St Francis of Assisi: 'Where there is discord, may we bring harmony. Where there is error, may we bring truth. Where there is doubt, may we bring faith. And where there is despair, may we bring hope.' Hollower words had seldom been spoken. Synthetic sincerity would become a Thatcher trademark. The message sounded fine, but the face said: 'I don't really care if you believe me.' There had indeed been discord, error, doubt and despair. In time, however, the Seventies would seem like a quaint period of social harmony compared to the strife that followed.[65]

EPILOGUE

'I can't believe Ronald Reagan is president'

The favourite pronoun of the Sixties generation was 'we', as in 'We can change the world'. In the 1970s, that same generation favoured the pronoun 'they', as in 'They killed the revolution' or 'I just knew they would fuck it all'. 'They' remained conveniently undefined, an omnibus enemy. In the preferred mythology, the Sixties was something the people made happen, the Seventies something that happened to the people.

The tendency to dismiss the Seventies as an alien force, authoritarian conspiracy or even a black hole arises out of the desire to venerate the Sixties, to preserve it as a time when change seemed possible and hope transcendent. The Heavenly Decade is seen as 'natural', typified by flowers, soulful music, naked bodies and the emphasis upon 'free'. The Polyester Decade, on the other hand, is artificial and contrived – man-made fabrics, processed music, authoritarian rule and technology out of control. The greater the contrast, the more beautiful the Sixties becomes.

Time, however, does not leap. Every decade is the evolutionary product of the era that precedes it; the present is child of the past. And, while it might be comforting to talk in terms of 'they', it is delusion to dismiss an ethos as conspiracy – the product of cruel 'other'. Hard as it might be to accept, the vast majority wanted the Sixties over. In the Seventies, Kenneth Keniston wrote, frustrated radicals came painfully to the realization that 'a great many young people . . . are primarily motivated by a desire to take part in the

American system, rather than to change it'. That rude awakening was not confined to the United States, as the failure of the Angry Brigade and Red Army Fraction demonstrated. In this sense, the demise of rebellion might simply have been the inevitable consequence of a generation's eventual maturity. Baby boomers were growing up.[1]

As was mentioned at the beginning of this book, during the course of my research violence emerged as the predominant theme of the Seventies. That, too, seems like stark contrast to the decade of peace and love. Yet we so often fail to realize that in the Sixties 'peace and love' was more demand than defining feature. The slogan is best seen as a pained lament to a time of hate and war. Hack away the flowers and the violence of the Sixties is starkly revealed. The barbarity of the Seventies was, in other words, the continuation of a well-established trend.

The violence of those times obscures another dominant theme of the 1970s, that of family. Terror and uncertainty inspired an entirely understandable turn inward, toward the home. In that sense, the 'me' of the 'me decade' was an act of self-defence, an attempt to turn away from horror and focus on things small and controllable. Leaving aside her bizarre methods of seducing her husband, there is no denying that Marabel Morgan was trying to create a better family. The emphasis upon kith and kin was not, however, exclusively conservative, nor did those on the right alone feel the pull. Battered by the struggles of the Sixties, Tom Hayden realized in late 1969 that he desperately wanted a home. Linda LeClair did not want a husband in the strictest sense, but she did want a family. The same desire motivated skinheads. Likewise, Jonestown was an attempt to escape the horrors of the world and create an extended family. The dreadful ending to that story should not obscure the fact that the community was built by lost souls desperate for a loving person to call 'Dad'.

Even science got in on the act. The greatest scientific breakthrough of the Seventies was, arguably, the test tube baby, an attempt to give the childless an opportunity to make families of their own. The one glaring mistake of the Christian Right was its knee-jerk attempt to apply rigid moral doctrine to a development so clearly pro-family.

In other ways, however, the right rode the family wave with impressive dexterity. Phyllis Schlafly and Jerry Falwell cleverly hijacked a desire and turned it into a movement – family values. They managed, cynically but brilliantly, to establish the maxim that protection of the family was synonymous with morality and therefore conservatism. It was not that the left denigrated the family – by no means. Unfortunately, however, many left-wing causes, including gay rights, feminism and sexual liberation, could be presented as a threat to the family, as Anita Bryant demonstrated. Nor did it help that a few prominent Sixties radicals had once urged the young to kill their parents and smash monogamy. The left had difficulty digging itself out of that hole. They started the game of 'Happy Families' five cards down.

Ronald Reagan and Margaret Thatcher turned the pro-family movement into a machine for winning elections. 'We must mobilize every asset we have – spiritual, moral, educational, economic and military – in a crusade for national renewal,' Reagan proclaimed early in his presidency. 'We must restore to their place of honor the bedrock values handed down by families to serve as society's compass.' Thatcher presented the family as fortress, a battered but still formidable institution evoking the sublime values of the past and offering the best hope for the future. While Reagan's image of the family was cosy and warm, hers was stern and disciplined – the embodiment of Alderman Roberts. 'We are reaping what was sown in the Sixties,' she repeatedly argued during her 1979 election campaign. 'Fashionable theories and permissive claptrap set the scene for a society in which old values of discipline and restraint were denigrated.' Social welfare, she argued, 'undercut the family unit'. She built a formidable populist movement by convincing the British electorate that the simple verities of the home provided the perfect philosophy for the world.[2]

In early 1981, the BBC's *Not the Nine O'Clock News* included a satirical skit in which the cast (Pamela Stephenson, Griff Rhys Jones, Mel Smith and Rowan Atkinson) sang around a campfire dressed like cowboys. Every line of the song began 'I believe' and every belief was preposterous. ('I believe Nixon is not a crook.' 'I believe JR really loves Sue Ellen.' 'I believe the Ayatollah tells a good knock-knock joke.') The last line was delivered with bitter irony: 'But I can't believe that Ronald Reagan is president.' To many observers, the Reagan presidency seemed proof that America had gone mad. In retrospect, however, his election seems entirely logical – the plausible outcome of the 1970s, and as such emblematic of popular reaction to the previous two decades. Reagan had already established himself as the spokesperson for the conservative counter-revolution that had emerged from the 1960s, one which fed off the excesses of that decade. He then drew enormous political capital out of the domestic and international problems of the Seventies – the 'decline' of the family, the drug problem, the oil crisis, humiliation in Iran, the SALT II 'sell-out', Nicaragua and Afghanistan.

The journalist Bill Moyers would later remark, 'We didn't elect this guy because he knew how many barrels of oil are in Alaska. We elected him because we want to feel good.'[3] The power of the Reagan–Thatcher revolution arose from the desire of so many people to see the new leaders as their salvation. Thatcher promised 'harmony, truth, faith and hope', Reagan a 'new American Revolution'. 'We have every right to dream heroic dreams,' he proclaimed during his Inaugural Address on 20 January 1981. As he later told Congress, 'All we need to begin with is a dream that we can do better than before, all we need to have is faith, and that dream will come true.' Thatcher's dreams were embedded in the past – a return to 'Victorian values'.[4]

Reagan and Thatcher dominated the 1980s and, in consequence, have monopolized analysis of the period. Their ascendancy has encouraged a careless assumption, namely that their radicalism was the inevitable response to Sixties excesses and Seventies turbulence. Or, as Thatcher so frequently proclaimed, 'there is no alternative'. The experience elsewhere, however, demonstrates otherwise. In Canada, France, Australia and, especially, in Spain during the 1980s necessary adjustments were made without the noise and strife evident in Britain and America. Yet while the approach in those countries was different, the result was fundamentally the same. The Sixties and Seventies were everywhere put to bed. Left-wing radicalism was vanquished, socialism neutered, and the ascendancy of wealth restored. Money could suddenly be discussed without guilt or embarrassment. And, across the world, family was seen as the most dependable and secure fortress against evil and uncertainty. While governments certainly encouraged that retreat into the home, it was in truth voluntary. The baby boomers were now middle-aged and had families of their own. As the Weatherman Billy Ayers once confessed: being parents 'gave us something to think about besides our fucked-up selves'.[5]

Human beings are constantly inspired by belief in renewal, a belief that is most powerful at the end of a decade. Thus, New Year's Eve, 1979, witnessed a widespread sense of relief that a horrible era was over. Popular will demanded that the Eighties would be different. Ray Bollig, a reveller in Times Square, confessed that he had come into the city to say goodbye to the 'depressing 1970s': 'No more oil crisis, no more Irans – the 70s are dead!' That, of course, seems cruelly ironic today. The passage of time would reveal that the ugliness of the 1970s could not so easily be willed away. The tone of the new decade was different, but its underlying nature was not. There was no expiry date on the problems the Seventies had revealed. Nor could the honeyed words of Reagan make them disappear.[6]

Perhaps, then, the Seventies is despised because of its dismal familiarity. The Sixties, in contrast, is worshipped because the myth of change predominates, effectively camouflaging the ugliness of those times. The difference appears stark: the 'dressed up' version of the heavenly decade offers a glorious alternative to our constraining present. The Seventies, on the other hand, seems terrible because reality predominates – we see the decade for what it was. The violence, thievery, mendacity and cynicism are painfully familiar, given the world we live in now. While the Sixties seems like our innocent and hopeful past, the Seventies is depressingly like the present – and probably the future.

ACKNOWLEDGEMENTS

I would like to thank Christopher Hill, Gavin Cooke and Barbara Neeson for helping with research. Will Skjott, Russ Coombes and Megan Stahl provided useful references. Finally, thanks to my darling daughter Natalie for helping with the footnotes, bibliography and photographs.

NOTES

INTRODUCTION

1 Coe, p.176.
2 Perlstein, pp.416, 455; Haslam, p.193; Salisbury, p.221.
3 Haslam, pp.133–4.

CHAPTER ONE

1 *NME*, 29 August 1992; Bugliosi and Gentry, p.102.
2 *Mojo*, September 1999.
3 Ibid.; 'Charles Manson', chemistrydaily.com.
4 Schulman interview with Manson, *Today Show,* 1987, youtube.com.
5 *Mojo*, September 1999; Perlstein, p.443; Hoskyns, p.96.
6 *Collusion*, February 1982.
7 Salisbury, p.231.
8 *Independent*, 12 July 2003.
9 Hoskyns, pp.95–6; *Rolling Stone*, 9 May 1974.
10 *Mojo*, September 1999; Hayden, p.379.
11 *Mojo*, September 1999.
12 Ibid.
13 Ibid.
14 Ibid.
15 Powers, *Diana*, p.126; H. Jacobs, p.202; *The Militant,* 16 January 1970; Collier and Horowitz, p.96; *Mojo*, September 1999; Hayden, p.359.
16 *Mojo*, September 1999; Hoskyns, p.97; Salisbury, p.230.
17 *Mojo*, September 1999.
18 Hoskyns, p.97.
19 A quick Google search reveals around fifteen websites containing that statement, or a close variation thereof.
20 Henderson, p.440.
21 *Independent*, 31 May 2009; thehendrixcollection.gobot.com.

22 Chenoweth, pp.26, 31.
23 *Rolling Stone*, 1 April 1971; *Melody Maker*, 26 September 1970; Cross, p.313.
24 *Rolling Stone*, 15 November 1969; *Let It Rock*, February 1974; *Q*, June 1992.
25 Cross, p.248; *Sunday Times*, 9 September 2006; *Let It Rock*, February 1974; Neville, *Hippie*, p.222.
26 *NME*, 20 September 1975.
27 Ibid.; Green, *Days in the Life*, pp.282, 310.
28 *Observer*, 23 April 2006.
29 *Rolling Stone*, 4 February 1971.
30 Cross, p.337.
31 Salisbury, p.231.
32 *Rolling Stone*, 29 October 1970.
33 M. Lydon, p.171.
34 Salisbury, p.229.
35 BBC, 12 May 1971.

CHAPTER TWO

1 Communiqué 8, recollectionbooks.com/siml/library/AngryBrigade.
2 Jean Weir, 'An Introduction to the Angry Brigade', lib.com.org.
3 Haslam, p.180.
4 Time.com, 13 November 2006.
5 Turner, *Biba*, jacket blurb.
6 Booker, p.295.
7 Ibid., p.18; Green, *All Dressed Up*, p.72.
8 *Rolling Stone*, 4 Feburary 1971.
9 Communiques 6 and 7, recollectionbooks.com/siml/library/AngryBrigade; *Observer*, 3 February 2002, 23 April 2006.
10 Communiques 13 and 5, recollectionbooks.com/siml/library/AngryBrigade.
11 *Observer*, 3 February 2002; Green, *Days in the Life*, p.356; Weir, lib.com.org.
12 Communiqués 13 and 9, recollectionbooks.com/siml/library/AngryBrigade.
13 *Observer*, 3 February 2002.
14 Ibid.
15 *Black Flag*, February 1983.
16 Turner, *Crisis?*, p.63; *Observer*, 23 April 2006.
17 recollectionbooks.com/siml/library/AngryBrigade.
18 Harriman, p.91.
19 Linder, p.1.
20 'A Statement from Yip', personal collection; 'Testimony of Ed Sanders', law.umkc.edu/faculty/projects/ftrials/chicago7.
21 Linder, p.3.

22 Schneir, pp.114–15, 120–1, 149.
23 Hayden, p.350.
24 Hayden, p.381; R. Jacobs, p.22; Lucas, p.224.
25 Trial transcript, law.umkc.edu/faculty/projects/ftrials/chicago7.
26 Mailer testimony, law.umkc.edu/faculty/projects/ftrials/chicago7; Perlstein, p.447.
27 Hayden, p.410; 'A Trial Account', law.umkc.edu/faculty/projects/ftrials/chicago7.
28 'The Chicago Seven: 1960s Radicalism in the Federal Courts', Federal Judicial Center, fjc.gov/history/chicago7.nsf.
29 Closing argument of Thomas Foran, law.umkc.edu/faculty/projects/ftrials/chicago7; Perlstein, p.450; Peter Coyote interview, 12 January 1989, diggers.org.
30 Schneir, pp.151, 156.
31 Rosenberg, p.5.
32 *Time*, 26 April 1968.
33 Farber, p.190; *Time*, 10 May 1968.
34 Farber, p.193.
35 *Columbia Spectator Online*, 27April 2008.
36 *Columbia Spectator Online*, 27April 2008; *Time*, 26 April 1968.
37 Farber, p.189.
38 *Time*, 26 April 1968; Farber, p.190.
39 *Columbia Spectator Online*, 27 April 2008; *Time*, 13 September 1968.
40 *Columbia Spectator Online*, 27 April 2008; *National Review*, 21 May 1968; *New York Post*, 17 April 1968.
41 *Life*, 31 May 1968; Farber, p.192.
42 Kahn, p.54; Ward Elliott, 'Sexual Revolutions, Great and Small', claremontmckenna.edu/govt/welliott/Sexrevns.htm.
43 Green, *Days in the Life*, p.424; *Guardian*, 18 March 1993.
44 *Time*, 26 April 1968.
45 *Ramparts*, August 1971; DeMott, p.70.
46 Hayden, pp.378, 425; Green, *Days in the Life*, pp.407–8.
47 U.S. Census Bureau, 'Marital Status of the Population 15 Years and Over, by Sex and Race: 1950 to Present', 2001; Cherlin, p.13.
48 Schulman and Zelizer, p.16; Ehrenreich, Chapter 5, www3.niu.edu/~td0raf1/history468/Fundamentalist%20sex.htm.
49 http://althouse3.blogspot.com; *Columbia Spectator Online*, 27 April 2008.
50 Diane Ravitch, review of *Family Circle: The Boudins and the Aristocracy of the Left* by Susan Braudy, internet.
51 *Nation*, 18 December 2003.
52 'Tales from the Underground', *Online Newshour*, 22 August 1996; Collier and Horowitz, p.102.

53 *Hard Times*, 23 March 1970; *I.F. Stone's Bi-Weekly*, 23 March 1970.
54 Collier and Horowitz, p.108.
55 R. Jacobs, p.54; Collier and Horowitz, p.116; 'Tales from the Underground'.
56 Collier and Horowitz, p.107.
57 *Observer*, 21 September 2003.
58 'Tales from the Underground'.
59 *New York Times*, 11 September 2001; Ayers, preface.
60 *Democracy Now!* broadcast, 2 January 2005; *New York Times*, 11 September 2001.
61 *Online Newshour*, 22 August 1996; Collier and Horowitz, pp.117–18; *Observer*, 21 September 2003; Mark Rudd, 'How a Movie Changed My Life', markrudd.com; Hayden, p.360.
62 *Online Newshour*, 22 August 1996; *New York Times*, 11 September 2001.
63 Kathy Boudin, Parole Hearing Statement, brynmawr.edu/Alumnae/bulletin/letsu01.htm.

CHAPTER THREE

1 Library of Congress, *A Country Study: Bangladesh*, memory.loc.gov.
2 Ibid.; *New York Times*, 11 November, 1970.
3 *A Country Study: Bangladesh*.
4 Payne, p.50; *Daily Telegraph*, 29 March 1971.
5 Mascarenhas, pp.116–17; Rummel, p.335.
6 *Washington Post*, 10 January 1972; *Time*, 12 April 1971; *The Times*, 13 April 1971; interview with Ferdousi Priyabhashinee, 14 July 2003, drishtipat.org.
7 *Newsweek*, 19 July 1971; *Z Magazine*, Sept. 1991; *New York Times*, 7 May 1971.
8 *Z Magazine*, Sept. 1991; *International Herald Tribune*, 6 July 1971; *Washington Post*, 10 January 1972.
9 Afsan Chowdhury, 'The Bewas village'; interview with Geoffrey Davis, 1 June 2002, both drishtipat.org.
10 Brownmiller, pp.80–1.
11 Priyabhashinee interview.
12 Dallek, p.336; Consul-General (Dacca) to Secretary of State, 28 March, 6 April 1971, National Archives.
13 Dallek, pp.337–8; Foreign Relations, 1969–1976, Volume E-7, Documents on South Asia, 1969–1972; *International Herald Tribune*, 1 July 1971.
14 *Sunday Telegraph*, 5 December 1971; *New York Times*, 19 December 1971.
15 Priyabhashinee interview.
16 *Irish News*, 25 April 1967.
17 David Trimble, Nobel acceptance speech, 10 December 1998, nobel.org.
18 Eamonn McCann interview, nd, bbc.co.uk.

19 *The Times*, 24 April 1967; *Nusight Magazine*, September 1969.
20 Ann Hope interview, nd, bbc.co.uk.
21 Munck, p.217.
22 *Irish Times*, 8 February 1967.
23 *Protestant Telegraph*, 1 August 1970.
24 *Irish News*, 7 October 1968.
25 *Irish News*, 16 August 1969; *Guardian*, 19 August 1969.
26 Daithi O'Conaill interview, nd, bbc.co.uk.
27 *Belfast Telegraph*, 9 August 1971.
28 *Times of India*, 1 February 1972.
29 Salisbury, p.145.
30 *Time*, 29 October 1973.
31 *Time*, 19 October 1981.
32 Memorandum of Conversation [Memcon] between Muhammad Hafez Ismail and Kissinger, 20 May 1973, National Security Archives (hereafter NSA); William Burr, 'The October War and US Policy', NSA, 7 Ocober 2003; *Al-Ahram Weekly On-line*, 8–14 October 1998.
33 Zeira, p.80; Ben-Porat, p.61; Kumaraswamy, p.4.
34 Commission of Inquiry, Vol. 1, p.71; Rabinovich, pp.51–7.
35 Rabinovich, p.89; Memcon between Simcha Dinitz and Kissinger, 7 October 1973, NSA; Sachar, p.755.
36 Memcon between Simcha Dinitz and Kissinger, 7 October 1973, NSA.
37 ariel-sharon-life-story.com.
38 *Time*, 22 October 1973.
39 Memcon between Meir and Kissinger, 22 October 1973, NSA.
40 *Time*, 22 October 1973.
41 U.S. Embassy Soviet Union Cable 13148 to Department of State, 21 October 1973, NSA.
42 Memcon between Meir and Kissinger, 22 October 1973, NSA; Memcon between Kissinger, Meir, Dinitz and General Yariv, 1 November 1973, NSA.
43 Kissinger to Ismail, 21 October 1973, NSA; Sadat to Nixon, 23 October 1973, NSA.
44 Brezhnev Hotline Message, 23 October, NSA; Message from Brezhnev to Nixon, 24 October 1973, NSA; Dallek, p.529.
45 Dallek, p.530.
46 Stein, np.
47 Dallek, p.531; Transcript, 'Secretary's Staff Meeting', 23 October 1973, NSA.
48 Memcon between Kissinger, Meir, Dinitz and General Yariv. 1 November 1973, NSA; Memcon between Meir, Nixon and Kissinger, 1 November 1973, NSA; Memcon between Kissinger, Meir and Party, 3 November 1973, NSA.
49 ariel-sharon-life-story.com.

50 Transcript, 'Secretary's Staff Meeting', 23 October 1973, NSA.
51 *Time*, 29 October 1973.
52 Isaacs, p.489; Salisbury, p.325.
53 Del Vecchio, np; Duiker, p.219.
54 Duiker, p.225.
55 McMahon, pp.443–5.
56 Nixon, *RN*, p.349; Dallek, p.126; Haldeman, p.81.
57 Nixon, *RN*, pp.393–4; Haldeman, p.83.
58 Johnson, p.65.
59 McMahon, p.449.
60 Richard Nixon, 'Silent Majority' speech, 3 November 1969, americanrhetoric.com; Dallek, p.163.
61 *Time*, 15 January 1979; Kolko, pp.378, 381; Lewy, pp.166–7.
62 Hanhimäki, p.73; Blum, p.367.
63 Kolko, pp.388–9; Hunt, p.236.
64 McMahon, p.456.
65 Dallek, p.261.
66 'The Week that Changed the World – Nixon, Mao and the "Opening to China"', ABC.com.
67 Nixon, *RN*, pp.606–7; Dallek, p.372; Herring, p.247.
68 Tran Van Don, p.208; Nixon, *RN*, p.733; Anderson, pp.159–60.
69 Harrison, p.287; Nixon, *RN*, p.734.
70 Kahn, pp.79, 83.
71 *Washington Post*, 7 January 1973; Dallek, p.441; Nixon, *RN*, p.738; Baritz, p.213.
72 *Time*, 15 January 1979; McMahon, pp.557–8, 562.
73 Truong Nhu Tang, p.215; Dallek, p.455.
74 *Newsweek*, 5 February 1973.
75 *Independent*, 12 September 2007; Biko, p.48.
76 Barney Pityana, 'Steve Biko: An Enduring Legacy', sahistory.org; Woods, p.65.
77 Biko, pp.15, 91; *Independent*, 12 September 2007.
78 Biko, pp.29, 30, 48; *Independent*, 12 September 2007.
79 Bennie Khoapa, 'The New Black', in B. S. Biko, ed, *Black Viewpoint* (1972), np, sahistory.org; *Boston Globe*, 25 October 1977; Biko, p.21.
80 Biko, p.21; Khoapa, np.
81 Biko, p.23.
82 Woods, p.185; Biko, p.127; Bernstein, p.8.
83 Woods, p.100; *New York Times*, 14 September 1977.
84 *New York Times*, 14 September 1977; BBC, 2 December 1977.
85 BBC, 2 December 1977; Woods, p.210; *New York Times*, 14 September 1977.
86 Truth and Reconciliation Committee Report, info.gov.za/otherdocs/2003/trc.

87 Nelson Mandela, 'We Remember Steve Bantu Biko', nelsonmandela.org.
88 Ibid.; Moore, p.40.

CHAPTER FOUR

1 Reeve, p.29.
2 Ibid., pp.24–5.
3 Ibid., p.38; *Time*, 25 August 2002.
4 *Time*, 25 August 2002.
5 Ibid.
6 *Sports Illustrated*, 18 September 1972; Reeve, p.55.
7 Reeve, p.79.
8 CBS.com, 5 September 2002.
9 *Time*, 25 August 2002, Reeve, p.90.
10 '5 Questions for Jim McKay', americansportscastersonline.com; UPI.com, 7 September 1972; Reeve, p.115.
11 *Los Angeles Times*, 8 September 1972; *Daily Telegraph*, 5 August 2002; *Sports Illustrated*, 5 August 1996.
12 *Sports Illustrated*, 20 August 2002; 'Tit for Tat', Channel4.com; palestinefacts.org.
13 Meir, p.385; 'Tit for Tat'; *Boston Herald*, 28 January 2006.
14 *Boston Herald*, 28 January 2006; *Time*, 25 August 2002; *Sports Illustrated*, 20 August 2002; Reeve, p.124.
15 CBS.com, 5 September 2002.
16 *Sports Illustrated*, 18 September 1972, 5 August 1996.
17 *Washington Post*, 4 March 2007.
18 'Baader-Meinhof: In Love with Terror', BBC4, 2008.
19 Ibid.; J. Becker, *Hitler's Children*, p.56.
20 'Baader-Meinhof', BBC4.
21 Ibid.; J. Becker, *Hitler's Children*, p.162.
22 J. Becker, *Hitler's Children*, p.82; 'Build Up the Red Army!', 5 June 1970, home.att.net/~rw.rynerson/rafgrund.htm.
23 'Build Up the Red Army!'; 'Baader-Meinhof', BBC4.
24 'Baader-Meinhof', BBC4; RAF, 'The Urban Guerrilla Concept', April 1971, scribd.com/doc/14881947/The-Urban-Guerilla-Concept; J. Becker, 'The Red Army Faction: Another Final Battle on the Stage of History', libertarian.co.uk; J. Becker, *Hitler's Children*, p.162.
25 'The Urban Guerrilla Concept'.
26 'Baader-Meinhof', BBC4.
27 Ibid.
28 Ibid.

29 Ibid.
30 J. Becker, 'The Red Army Faction'.
31 'Baader–Meinhof', BBC4.
32 J. Becker, *Hitler's Children*, p.173.
33 'Baader–Meinhof', BBC4; J. Becker, *Hitler's Children*, p.240.
34 *The First Post*, 13 February 2007; 'Baader–Meinhof', BBC4; RAF communiqué, 20 April 1998, germanguerilla.com/red-army-faction/documents/98_03.html.
35 *Observer*, 28 September 2008.
36 RAF communiqué, 20 April 1998, germanguerilla.com/red-army-faction/documents/98_03.html; A. Grossman, '"State-Fetishism": some remarks concerning the Red Army Faction', n.d. (circa 1979), lib.com.org; 'Baader–Meinhof', BBC4.
37 'Baader–Meinhof', BBC4.
38 *Guerrilla: The Taking of Patty Hearst*, PBS, 2004.
39 *Guerrilla*; 'The Symbionese Liberation Army', black-dahlia.org/sla.html.
40 pbs.org/wgbh/amex/guerrilla/index.html; *Rolling Stone*, 23 October 1975; Graebner, pp.14–15; *Guerrilla*.
41 'The Symbionese Liberation Army', *Guerrilla*.
42 *Guerrilla*.
43 pbs.org/wgbh/amex/guerrilla/index.html.
44 Ibid.
45 *Guerrilla*; Graebner, p.12; 'The Symbionese Liberation Army'.
46 *Rolling Stone*, 23 October 1975.
47 Graebner, p.17; *Guerrilla*.
48 *Guerrilla*.
49 Ibid.
50 *Guerrilla*; Graebner, p.35.
51 *Guerrilla*.
52 Ibid.; *Rolling Stone*, 23 October 1975.
53 *Rolling Stone*, 23 October 1975.
54 *Guerrilla*.
55 Ibid.; *Rolling Stone*, 23 October 1975.
56 *Guerrilla*.
57 Ibid.
58 Ibid.
59 Ibid.
60 Ibid.; *Rolling Stone*, 20 November 1975.
61 McLellan and Avery, pp.481–3.
62 Sfgate.com, 23 January 2001.
63 *Guerrilla*; Graebner, p.49.
64 Graebner, pp.19, 63.

65 *Guerrilla.*
66 Ibid.
67 *Todo Modo*, Cinevera, 1976.
68 *Time*, 24 May 1976.
69 Ibid.; *Guardian*, 26 March 2001.
70 *New Criterion*, 1 November 1998.
71 *Guardian*, 26 March 2001, 14 January 2008.
72 *Nation*, 9 March 2005.
73 *Daily Telegraph*, 16 March 2008.
74 *Direland*, 16 March 2008.
75 Sciascia, p.34; *New York Times*, 23 April 1994.
76 *Nation*, 9 March 2005; Sciascia, p.78; *New York Times*, 23 April 1994.
77 Judith Harris, 'Aldo Moro 30 Years On', wantedinrome.com, 30 April 2008.
78 Drake, p.251.
79 *National Catholic Reporter*, 17 March 2008; *Direland*, 26 March 2008; euro.news.net, 9 May 2008.
80 *British Church Newspaper*, 10 November 2006; *New York Times*, 23 April 1994.
81 *New York Times*, 23 April 1994.
82 Ibid.
83 *National Catholic Reporter*, 17 March 2008; *British Church Newspaper*, 10 November 2006.
84 *Direland*, 16 March 2008.
85 *British Church Newspaper*, 10 November 2006.
86 euro.news.net, 9 May 2008; Drake, p.254.
87 Tremlett, p.304; *Slate*, 15 March 2004.
88 flashpoints.info/CB-Basque%20Spain.htm.
89 *Le Monde Diplomatique*, February 1998.
90 Ercegovac, np.
91 Lezra, pp.178–9.
92 Ibid., p.182.
93 Ibid.; Preston, p.49.
94 *Time*, 13 October 1975.
95 Ercegovac, n.p.
96 Clark, p.74.
97 *Time*, 10 August 1981.
98 Ibid.; *Le Monde Diplomatique*, February 1998.
99 Ercegovac, np; *Time*, 10 August 1981.
100 *Time*, 10 August 1981.

CHAPTER FIVE

1 Congress of Linares (July 1965); Congress of Chillán (November 1967); *Revista Punto Final* (22 November 1967), josepinera.com.
2 *El Mercurio*, 28 November 1999, josepinera.com.
3 Kissinger/Helms telecon, 12 September 1970; Nixon/Kissinger telecon, 12 September 1970, NSA archives; Dallek, p.233.
4 Kissinger/Rogers telecon, 14 September 1970, NSA archives.
5 Blum, p.385.
6 Kristian Gustafson, 'CIA Machinations in Chile in 1970: Reexamining the Record', Walter L. Pforzheimer Award article, 2002, cia.gov; *Commentary*, 10 November 2003.
7 Gustafson.
8 Ibid.; Dallek, p.235.
9 *Commentary*, 10 November 2003; Gustafson.
10 Gustafson.
11 *Commentary*, 10 November 2003.
12 Gustafson.
13 Ibid.; Dallek, p.239.
14 Gustafson.
15 Ibid.
16 *Commentary*, 10 November 2003.
17 *The Times*, 19 September 2005.
18 *Commentary*, 10 November 2003.
19 Don Mabry, 'Chile: Allende's Rise and Fall', historicaltextarchive.com; José Pinera, 'The Chamber of Deputies Resolution of August 22, 1973', josepinera.com.
20 *The Times*, 19 September 2005; Nixon/Kissinger telecon, 4 July 1973, NSA archives.
21 Pinera, 'The Chamber of Deputies'.
22 Ibid.
23 Ibid.
24 *Guardian*, 14 September 1973.
25 Ibid., 11 October 1999; *Los Angeles Times*, 11 September 2008.
26 *Time*, 23 October 1972; White House tapes, 1 July, 13 September 1971, 15–16 May 1972, nixon.archives.gov.
27 Kahn, p.106; *Washington Post*, 17 June 1997; Blum, p.373; White House tapes, 1 July 1971.
28 Patterson, *Grand Expectations*, p.761.
29 Kahn, p.128; White House tapes, 21 March 1973.
30 Blum, p.421.
31 Ibid., p.423; White House tapes, 19 July 1972.

32 White House tapes, 23 June 1972.
33 Blum, p.425.
34 Ibid., pp.423, 438; White House tapes, 23 March 1973.
35 White House tapes, 21 March 1973.
36 Kahn, p.108.
37 McQuaid, p.204; Nixon press conference, 30 April 1973, Nixon.archives.gov.
38 White House tapes, 15 August 1972; *Washington Post*, 18 November 1973.
39 *Time*, 12 November 1973.
40 Nixon, State of the Union Address, 30 January 1974, americanrhetoric.com; McQuaid, p.260.
41 Blum, p.468.
42 Nixon Farewell Address, 9 August 1974, americanrhetoric.com.
43 *Time*, 19 August 1974; Patterson, *Grand Expectations*, p.779.
44 Patterson, *Grand Expectations*, pp.782–3.
45 *Athens News*, 20 April 1997.
46 Ibid., 16 July 2004; *Time*, 5 August 1974.
47 Salisbury, p.155.
48 Ibid., p.142.
49 Ioannis Tzortzis, 'The *Metapolitefsi* that Never Was: a Re-evaluation of the 1973 "Markezinis Experiment", unpublished paper, University of Birmingham, nd, web.archive.org.
50 *Time*, 15 October 1973.
51 Tzortzis; *Time*, 15 October 1973.
52 *Time*, 15 October 1973; Tzortzis.
53 *Athens News*, 17 November 1999.
54 Ibid., 16 July 2004.
55 Tzortzis; BBC, 25 November 1973.
56 Tzortzis.
57 BBC, 25 November 1973.
58 Tzortzis.
59 BBC, 23 July 1974.
60 *Time*, 5 August 1974; *Athens News*, 23 July 2004.
61 *Time*, 5 August 1974.
62 Ibid., 15 October 1973.
63 Ibid., 19 February 1973; Snepp, p.65.
64 Williams, p.309.
65 Young, p.290.
66 Werner and Huynh, pp.206–7; Harrison, *The Endless War*, pp.291, 293.
67 Snepp, p.44.
68 Kolko, pp.468, 525.
69 Anderson, p.189.
70 Butler, pp.102, 120.

71 Davidson, p.779; *Time*, 15 January 1979.
72 Anderson, p.194.
73 Ibid., pp.196–9; *Time*, 24 April 1995, 24 April 2000; Snepp, p.337.
74 *Time*, 24 April 1995; Snepp, pp.304–5.
75 Kahn, p.156; Pimlott, p.180; Anderson, p.199; *Time*, 24 April 1995.
76 *Time*, 24 April 1995; Snepp, pp.542–3, 563.
77 Pimlott, p.187; Ehrhart, p.49.
78 Carr, p.157; Romero Salvadó, p.159.
79 Carr, p.169.
80 Bernecker, pp.66–7.
81 Ibid., p.69; Tremlett, p.70.
82 Romero Salvadó, p.162.
83 Bernecker, p.69; *Newsweek*, 3 November 1975.
84 Carr, p.174.
85 Tremlett, p.76.
86 Bernecker, p.69.
87 Coverdale, p.622.
88 Tremlett, pp.66–7, 71, 76, 94.
89 Mallin, p.22.
90 SI.com, 10 April 2006.
91 Gilbert, p.21; B. Marcus, p.105.
92 *Time*, 8 January 1973; Mallin, pp.4, 27.
93 SI.com, 10 April 2006.
94 *New Internationalist*, October 1979.
95 *Time*, 14 March 1977; Schulman and Zelizer, pp.250, 257.
96 FSLN National Directorate, np.
97 *El Pais*, 8 June 1978.
98 Gilbert, p.38.
99 FSLN National Directorate, np; Harvey, p.317.
100 *New York Times*, 28 June 1987.

CHAPTER SIX

1 Enoch Powell, speech, 20 April 1968, telegraph.co.uk.
2 Ibid.
3 *Birmingham Post*, 22 April 1968.
4 Ponting, p.331; Foot, p.181.
5 *New African*, 1 October 2004; Crossman, Vol. 1, pp.149–50; Ponting, p.331.
6 *Skinhead Nation*, np, thelastgriffin.multiply.com; Brown, pp.172, 208.
7 *Skinhead Nation*; Brown, p.206.

8 *Observer*, 14 October 2007; Barry, p.91; *Sounds*, 9 October 1976; *Melody Maker*, 9 December 1978.
9 Sounes, p.252; Haslam, p.235; Barry, p.90; David Renton, 'The Anti-Nazi League', d.k.renton.co.uk.
10 'The Anti-Nazi League'.
11 Haslam, pp.156, 278; *Green Left*, 20 August 1997; *Socialist Worker*, 14 July 2007; 'The Anti-Nazi League'.
12 'The Anti-Nazi League'; *Spiked*, 29 April 2008.
13 Christopher Husbands, 'A Century of British Fascism', searchlight-magazine.com.
14 Miles and Phizacklea, p.106; Haslam, p.277; *Hansard*, 10 March 1980.
15 Haslam, p.278.
16 *New York Times*, 6 May 1970.
17 Carroll, p.56.
18 *Wall Street Journal*, 11 May 1970.
19 *Wall Street Journal*, 11 May 1970; *Washington Star*, 17 May 1970; *New York Times*, 8 May 1970.
20 *Nation*, 15 June 1970; *Wall Street Journal*, 11 May 1970.
21 'The Hard Hat Riots', chnm.gmu.edu/hardhats/homepage.html.
22 *Wall Street Journal*, 11 May 1970; *New York Times*, 10 May 1970.
23 *New York Post*, 9 May 1970; *New York Times*, 20 May 1970.
24 *New York Times*, 20 May 1970; Carroll, p.60.
25 Carroll, p.58.
26 Ibid., p.59.
27 Ibid.; Freeman, p.735.
28 Blum, pp.310–11, 372; Nixon, 'Acceptance Speech', 8 August 1968, watergate.info; *New York Times*, 5 November 1969; Nixon, 'Silent Majority' speech, 3 November 1969, americanrhetoric.com; *San Francisco Chronicle*, 26 November 1969.
29 Carroll, p.60; *Time*, 11 May 1970.
30 *Time*, 25 May 1970.
31 Ibid.; *Nation*, 15 June 1970; *New York Times*, 27 May 1970; Carroll, p. 57; Memorandum, Charles W. Colson for the President's File, 'Building and Construction Trades Meeting with the President', 26 May 1970, National Archives.
32 *St Louis Post-Despatch*, 27 May 1970.
33 *Newsweek*, 6 October 1969; *Time*, 5 January 1970.
34 *Time*, 5 January 1970; *New York Times Magazine*, 28 June 1970.
35 *Nation*, 10 January 2000.
36 *Berkeley Daily Gazette*, 9 April 1970.
37 MiamiHerald.com, 9 June 2007.
38 *Time*, 13 June 1977; MiamiHerald.com, 9 June 2007; Blount, p.130.

39 Bryant, *Anita Bryant Story*, p.51; Chapman, pp.145–7.
40 Chapman, pp.146, 148; 'Days Without Sunshine', stonewall-library.org.
41 Schulman and Zelizer, p.24; Blount, p.133; Clendinen, p.310; D'Emilio and Freedman, np.
42 Chapman, p.146; Blount, p.131.
43 *Pensito Review*, 4 June 2007; *Gay City News*, 17 May 2007; D'Emilio and Freedman, np.
44 Blount, p.131; D'Emilio and Freedman, np.
45 Blount, p.133.
46 MiamiHerald.com, 9 June 2007.
47 Chapman, p.147; *Phoenix*, 5 August 2008.
48 MiamiHerald.com, 9 June 2007.
49 Chapman, p.149; Blount, p.133; Clendinen, pp.300–1.
50 'Days Without Sunshine'.
51 *Time*, 13 June 1977; MiamiHerald.com, 9 June 2007.
52 Chapman, p.150.
53 *Phoenix*, 5 August 2008.
54 *New York Times*, 16 May 2007; Schulman and Zelizer, p.26.
55 D'Emilio and Freedman, np; Ehrenreich, np; Schulman and Zelizer, p.14.
56 Chapman, p.147.
57 'Days Without Sunshine'; MiamiHerald.com, 9 June 2007; *Pensito Review*, 4 June 2007.
58 Ehrenreich, np.
59 *Time*, 14 March 1977.
60 Ibid.; Morgan, *Total Woman*, pp.17–19.
61 *Time*, 14 March 1977; *People*, 7 April 1975; Ehrenreich, np.; Heller, p.76.
62 *People*, 7 April 1975; *Time*, 14 March 1977; Morgan, *Total Woman*, p.25.
63 *Time*, 14 March 1977; Morgan, *Total Joy*, pp.190–1.
64 *Time*, 14 March 1977; Bryant, *Bless This House*, p.44.
65 *Time*, 4 April 1977.
66 Morgan, *Total Woman*, p.29.
67 Ibid., pp.50, 71, 75, 92.
68 *Time*, 14 March 1977.
69 Ibid.; *Atlantic*, January/February 2003; Ehrenreich, np; *Time*, 14 March, 4 April 1977.
70 Ehrenreich, np.
71 Ibid.
72 Ibid.; *Time*, 10 March 1975.
73 Ehrenreich, np.; LaHaye, pp.63–4.
74 *Washington Times*, 7 October 2005.
75 Levy, pp.221, 222, 224; Schulman and Zelizer, p.23.
76 Levy, pp.222–3.

77 Ibid.; Schulman and Zelizer, pp.19–20, 25–6, 80.
78 Schulman and Zelizer, p.22; *Time*, 10 March 1975; Elliott, pp.159–60.
79 Salisbury, p.77; LaHaye, p.79; Morgan, *Total Woman*, pp.69–70.
80 DeMott, p.43.
81 *Time*, 14 March 1977; Ehrenreich, np.
82 *Time*, 14 March, 4 April 1977.

CHAPTER SEVEN

1 Lucas, p.220.
2 Interviews with Peter Bourne, Robert DuPont, Bud Krogh, George Jung, 'Frontline: Drug Wars', PBS.org.
3 Bourne; Jung, Sounes, p.242.
4 Kahn, p.256; Jung, Bill Alden interview, 'Frontline'.
5 *Time*, 16 April 1973; Krogh.
6 *Time*, 29 January 1979; Jung, 'Drug Wars', Part One, PBS.org.
7 Jung, 'Drug Wars', Part One.
8 Ibid.
9 Jung, Juan Ochoa interview, 'Drug Wars', Part One.
10 'Drug Wars', Part One; Fernando Arenas interview, 'Frontline'.
11 *Time*, 29 January 1979; Jung, 'Drug Wars', Part One.
12 Jung, 'The Godfather of Cocaine', PBS.org.
13 Jorge Ochoa interview, 'Frontline'; 'The Godfather of Cocaine', PBS.org.
14 *Time*, 29 January 1979; 'David' (money launderer) interview; Mike McDonald interview, 'Frontline'.
15 McDonald.
16 Bourne.
17 'Drug Wars', Part One; Jerome Jaffe interview, 'Frontline'.
18 *Time*, 29 January 1979; 'Drug Wars', Part One.
19 DuPont; 'Frontline: Inside the Cartel', PBS.org.
20 Bourne; 'Drug Wars', Part One.
21 'Drug Wars', Part One.
22 Kahn, pp.257–8; Jung; Sounes, p.257.
23 *Time*, 16 April 1973. Bourne; Robert Stutman, Herbert Kleber interviews, 'Frontline'.
24 *Time*, 29 January 1979; Jung, Jorge Ochoa Interview.
25 *Skinhead Nation*, thelastgriffin.multiply.com.
26 Ibid.
27 Ibid.; Brown, p.1.
28 King, p.19.
29 *Skinhead Nation*.

30 Brown, p.2; BBC.co.uk, 12 April 2007; 'The Sharpies', ABC.net; *Skinhead Nation*.
31 *Skinhead Nation*; 'The Sharpies'.
32 *Skinhead Nation*; BBC.co.uk, 12 April 2007.
33 *Skinhead Nation*.
34 Ibid.
35 Ibid.; *Time*, 8 June 1970.
36 *Time*, 8 June 1970; King, p.69; *Skinhead Nation*; Brown, p.158.
37 Interview with Chas Smash, 16 August 1999.
38 *Skinhead Nation*.
39 Brown, p.236.
40 Bob Timm, 'Smiling Smash', www.madnesstradingring.com; *Skinhead Nation*.
41 *Time*, 8 June 1970
42 *Skinhead Nation*.
43 Ibid.; Brown, p.19.
44 *Skinhead Nation*.
45 Haslam, p.193; Brown, pp.37, 60; *Skinhead Nation*.
46 *San Francisco Examiner*, 18 September 1972.
47 *Examiner*, 17 September 1972.
48 Lester Kinsolving, 'Sex, Socialism and Child Torture with Rev. Jim Jones', unpublished, Jonestown Apologists Alert website, jonestownapologistsarticlearchive.blogspot.com (hereafter JAA); *Examiner*, 18 September 1972.
49 Ann Moore to Rebecca Moore, 2 December 1972, jonestown.sdsu.edu; JAA; *Examiner*, 17 September 1972.
50 *Examiner*, 19 September 1972.
51 Ann Moore to Rebecca Moore, 3 September, 2 December 1972.
52 *Idea*, 1 September 1996; *New West*, 1 August 1977.
53 Kinsolving Family Report, JAA.
54 Ibid.; *New West*, 1 August 1977.
55 *Examiner*, 17 September 1972; Kinsolving Family Report.
56 Blakey affidavit, June 1978, jonestown.sdsu.edu.
57 *New West*, 1 August 1977; Pat Katsaris to her father, n.d., jonestown.sdsu.edu.
58 Kahn, p.266; *Palladium-Item*, 16 November 2003.
59 Bruce Oliver to his parents, n.d., jonestown.sdsu.edu; Ann Moore suicide note, jonestown.sdsu.edu; *Time*, 11 December 1978.
60 CNN.com, 18 November 1998; Blakey affidavit.
61 Blakey affidavit.
62 Carolyn Moore Layton to her parents, 19 August 1977, jonestown.sdsu.edu.
63 *Time*, 4 December 1978.
64 Jonestown Death Tape, jonestown.sdsu.edu.
65 Ibid.

66 Tropp suicide note; Ann Moore suicide note; Death Tape; *Time*, 4 December 1978.
67 *Time*, 4 December 1978.
68 Kinsolving Family Report.
69 Ibid.
70 Tropp suicide note; Prokes to Herb Caen, n.d. (March 1979); Prokes statement, March 1979, jonestown.sdsu.edu.
71 *Q*, June 2002.
72 *Sun*, 11 May 1977.
73 Kahn, p.162; *Rolling Stone*, 8 March 1979.
74 Kahn, p.162; McNeil and McCain, pp.50, 304–5; Haslam, p.185; *Rolling Stone*, 12 August 1976.
75 McNeil and McCain, p.148; Sounes, p.292.
76 *Mojo*, November 1999; *Westway to the World*, Don Letts, dir. (3DD Entertainment, London, 2000) [documentary]. Robb, pp.27, 37.
77 Pressler, np; Sabin, p.164.
78 *Rolling Stone*, 20 October 1977.
79 Kahn, p.163.
80 G. Marcus, *Lipstick*, p.49; Sounes, p.286; Haslam, pp.13, 190.
81 Gray, p.131.
82 Massey, p.75; *Rolling Stone*, 12 August 1976; G. Marcus, *Lipstick*, p.7; Haslam, pp.184, 196; Burchill and Parsons, p.65.
83 *Westway to the World*; Savage, p.281; J. Lydon, p.185.
84 J. Lydon, pp.220–1; Burchill and Parsons, p.49.
85 *Rolling Stone*, 20 October 1977; *Sunday Times*, 18 May 2008; Burchill and Parsons, p.54.
86 McNeil and McCain, p.318; Savage, p.241; J. Lydon, p.182; Sabin, p.208; Strongman, p.207.
87 The Stranglers, 'Do You Wanna?/Death and Night and Blood' on *Live (X Cert)*; Robb, p.405; Kahn, p.211.
88 *Rolling Stone*, 8 March 1979; Savage, p.304.
89 Haslam, p.242; Burchill and Parsons, p.88.
90 G. Marcus, *Lipstick*, p.80; *Melody Maker*, 14 May 1977.

CHAPTER EIGHT

1 Tim Boggan, 'Ping Pong Oddity', usatt.org/articles/ppoddity01.shtml.
2 Macmillan, p.176; SI.com, 11 June 2008.
3 Macmillan, p.177; SI.com, 11 June 2008.
4 Boggan; SI.com, 11 June 2008.
5 SI.com, 11 June 2008.

6 Boggan.
7 Hong and Sun, p.437; SI.com, 11 June 2008.
8 'China Through a Lens', China.org; Hong and Sun, p.438.
9 *Foreign Affairs*, October 1967; 'China Through a Lens'; 'The Week that Changed the World – Nixon, Mao and the "Opening to China"', ABC.com.
10 'The Week that Changed the World'.
11 Ibid.
12 Ibid. 'China Through a Lens'.
13 SI.com, 11 June 2008; *New York Times*, 26 July 1997.
14 SI.com, 11 June 2008.
15 *Newsweek*, 26 April 1971; *Palm Beach Post*, 23 July 2008; SI.com, 11 June 2008.
16 *New York Times*, 26 July 1997; *Washington Post*, 13, 18 April 1971.
17 'Ping-Pong Diplomacy', PBS.org; SI.com, 11 June 2008.
18 'The Week that Changed the World'.
19 Ibid.
20 SI.com, 11 June 2008; *Smithsonian* magazine, April 2002; 'China Through a Lens'.
21 SI.com, 11 June 2008.
22 Marqusee, p.175.
23 Ibid.
24 Ibid., p.254.
25 Ibid., p.258.
26 Ibid.
27 Ibid., p.259; Riess, p.394.
28 Thompson, p.12.
29 Kahn, p.150; *When We Were Kings*, Leon Gast, dir. (New York, 1996) [film].
30 Kahn, p.148.
31 *When We Were Kings*.
32 Riess, pp.196–7.
33 Marqusee, p.278.
34 Roberts, p.16.
35 Ibid., p.17.
36 Ibid., pp.10, 15–16, 20.
37 Ibid., p.21.
38 *Associated Press*, 18 September 2003; Roberts, p.24.
39 Roberts, p.24.
40 Ibid., p.19.
41 *Associated Press*, 18 September 2003.
42 Roberts, p.211.
43 *Time*, 10 September 1973.

44 Ibid.; Roberts, p.104.
45 Roberts, pp.15, 17.
46 *Time*, 10 September 1973.
47 *Time*, 10 September 1973; Roberts, pp.92, 99; *St Petersburg Times*, 12 December 1999.
48 Roberts, p.94; *Time*, 10 September 1973.
49 Roberts, p.106.
50 *Associated Press*, 18 September 2003.
51 *Time*, 1 October 1973; Roberts, p.104.
52 Roberts, p.110.
53 Ibid., p.124.
54 Ibid., p.122.
55 *Time*, 1 October 1973; Roberts, p.129.
56 *Time*, 1 October 1973; Roberts, p.135.
57 *Sports Illustrated*, 1 October 1973; Roberts, p.133.
58 *Time*, 10 September 1973; *Sports Illustrated*, 1 October 1973.
59 Roberts, p. 131; *The Tennis Channel*, 10 September 2003.
60 *Independent*, 19 January 2008; *Atlantic Monthly*, December 2002; *New York Times*, 19 January 2008; Edmonds and Eidinow, pp.217–18.
61 *Atlantic Monthly*, December 2002.
62 *Daily Telegraph*, 19 January 2008.
63 *Atlantic Monthly*, December 2002.
64 Ibid.
65 *The Times*, 19 January 2008.
66 *Atlantic Monthly*, December 2002.
67 Ibid.
68 Ibid.
69 Edmonds and Eidinow, pp.10, 12; *Atlantic Monthly*, December 2002.
70 *Atlantic Monthly*, December 2002.
71 *The Times*, 19 January 2008.
72 Edmonds and Eidinow, pp.126, 131; *Atlantic Monthly*, December 2002.
73 Edmonds and Eidinow, p.26.
74 Ibid., p.202.
75 *New York Times*, 19 January 2008; Edmonds and Eidinow, p.21.
76 Edmonds and Eidinow, p.201.
77 *Atlantic Monthly*, December 2002.
78 *Sunday Times*, 20 January 2008; Edmonds and Eidinow, p.237.
79 *Atlantic Monthly*, December 2002; *Sunday Times*, 20 January 2008.
80 *Independent*, 20 January 2008.
81 *Atlantic Monthly*, December 2002.
82 Ibid.; *Independent*, 20 January 2008.
83 *Atlantic Monthly*, December 2002.

84 Ibid.
85 Ibid.
86 G. Marcus, *Lipstick*, p.43.
87 'An Interview with Nolan Bushnell', nd, thetech.org/exhibits/online/revolution/bushnell.
88 *Rolling Stone*, 7 December 1972.
89 Ibid.
90 Bushnell interview.
91 Ibid.
92 'Interview with Al Alcorn', IGN.com.
93 Ibid.
94 Ibid.
95 DeMaria and Wilson, p.28.
96 Bushnell interview; Alcorn interview.
97 Watergate Caper flyer, arcadeflyers.com.
98 *Rolling Stone*, 7 December 1972.
99 Ibid.
100 Ibid.

CHAPTER NINE

1 *Mother Jones*, September/October 1977.
2 Ibid.
3 Owen, p.2.
4 G. Schwartz, p.1020.
5 Ibid., p.1036; *Mother Jones*, September/October 1977.
6 *Time*, 8 September 1980.
7 Ibid.
8 'Interview with Homemaker No. 1', 1 August 1979, threemileisland.org.
9 *The Times*, 24 July 2003.
10 Jamie Grifo, in Tim Appleton, 'Conversations with Fertility Experts', ifcresourcecentre.co.uk/Tim_appleton/Interview_rame.htm; Edwards and Steptoe, p.2.
11 Robert Edwards, in Appleton.
12 BBC Radio 4, 27 July 2003; Edwards and Steptoe, p.89.
13 Edwards and Steptoe, pp.105, 115.
14 Ibid., pp.163, 170; *Observer*, 27 July 2003.
15 Edwards and Steptoe, p.129.
16 Edwards and Steptoe, p.204; 'On this Day', 25 July 1978; bbc.co.uk BBC Radio 4, 27 July 2003.
17 *American Experience*: *Test Tube Babies*, PBS.org.

18 'On this Day', 25 July 1978; *The Times*, 24 July 2003; bbc.co.uk BBC Radio 4, 27 July 2003.
19 Gordon Dunstan, in Appleton.
20 *New York Times*, 23 March 1988; Bishop Gordon Roe, in Appleton.
21 Howard Jones, in Appleton.
22 'Ethical Questions', *American Experience*: *Test Tube Babies.*
23 Ibid.
24 *The Times*, 24 July 2003; bbc.co.uk, 24 July 2003; *Observer*, 27 July 2003; *New York Times*, 25 December 2005.
25 *New York Times*, 17 July 1969.
26 Hogan, p.35.
27 Turnill, pp.221–2.
28 Statement by President Nixon on the Space Program, 7 March 1970, NASA History Office; Heppenheimer, np.
29 Ehrlichman, pp.144–5.
30 NASA History Office, Folder 6716, 'Public Opinion 1967–69', Heppenheimer, np.
31 *Congressional Record*, 6 July 1970; Heppenheimer, np.
32 *All in the Family*, CBS Television, 1972; *Washington Star*, 8 May 1975.
33 *New York Times*, 11 December 1972; Cernan, p.340.
34 D. Carter, p.200.
35 Benjamin, pp.20, 127, 131; McCurdy, p.151.
36 Klerkx, p.168; Burrows, pp.519, 526.
37 McDougall, p.423; McCurdy, p.202; Haslam, p.126.
38 *The Times*, 6 February 1980.
39 *Time*, 16 August 1976.
40 Bonnacorsi, et al, p.237.
41 Ibid., p.235.
42 *The Times*, 12 August 1976.
43 Bonnacorsi et al., p.234; Gerber and Jensen, p.259.
44 Mitchell, np; unu.edu/unupress/unupbooks/uu21le/uu21le00.htm.
45 *The Times*, 7 April 1983.
46 *Time*, 14 August 1978; Mick Corliss, 'Dioxin: Seveso disaster testament to effects of dioxin', 6 May 1999, getipm.com/articles/seveso-italy.htm.
47 Haslam, pp.34–5; DeMott, p.62.
48 Baccarelli, et al., np; *Time*, 14 August 1978.
49 *China Syndrome.*
50 *American Experience: Meltdown at Three Mile Island*, PBS.org (hereafter *Meltdown*); *Time*, 24 March 1980.
51 washingtonpost.com, 27 March 1999.
52 Ibid.; *Meltdown.*
53 *Time*, 9 April 1979; washingtonpost.com; *Meltdown.*

54 *Time*, 9 April 1979; *Washington Post*, 28 March 1989.
55 washingtonpost.com, 27 March 1999; *Meltdown*.
56 *Meltdown*; Washingtonpost.com, 27 March 1999.
57 *Meltdown*.
58 Thornburgh, Address to Dickinson College, September 1999, threemileisland.org/; Washingtonpost.com, 27 March 1999.
59 'Interview with attorney', 7 July 1979, threemileisland.org; *Time*, 9 April 1979; Washingtonpost.com, 27 March 1999.
60 Washingtonpost.com, 27 March 1999.
61 *Time*, 9 April 1979; *Meltdown*.
62 *Meltdown*; *Time*, 9 April 1979.
63 *Meltdown*; Washingtonpost.com, 27 March 1999.
64 Thornburgh, Address to Dickinson College; *Meltdown*.
65 *Meltdown*; washingtonpost.com, 29 March 1999.
66 *Meltdown*; Washingtonpost.com, 27 March 1999.
67 Thornburgh, Address to Dickinson College; *Meltdown*; Washingtonpost.com, 27 March 1999.
68 'Interview with Homemaker No. 1', 1 August 1979, threemileisland.org; Washingtonpost.com, 27 March 1999.
69 *Meltdown;* Washingtonpost.com.
70 Washingtonpost.com, 27 March 1999.
71 *Meltdown*.
72 Civil Action No. 1: CV-88-1452, United States District Court for the Middle District of Pennsylvania; *Washington Post*, 24 February 1997.
73 Thornburgh, Address to Dickinson College; Washingtonpost.com, 27 March 1999.
74 *Meltdown*.
75 Washingtonpost.com, 27 March 1999; *Time*, 24 March, 16 April 1980.

CHAPTER TEN

1 *Independent*, 16 January 2007.
2 Ibid., 18 August 2003.
3 Ibid.
4 *New York Times*, 18 August 2003.
5 *New Vision*, 11 April 1999; *Independent*, 16, 18 August 2003.
6 *Independent*, 16 January 2007; *Monitor*, 31 March 2002.
7 *Monitor*, 31 March 2002.
8 *Independent*, 16 January 2007.
9 Ibid.
10 *Monitor*, 30 April 1999.

11 *Time*, 7 March 1977.
12 Ibid.
13 Ibid.
14 Melady to Dept. of State, 2 January 1973; Kissinger to Nixon, 22 March 1973. Both in *Foreign Relations, 1969–1976*, Volume E-6, Documents on Africa, 1973–1976, state.gov/r/pa/ho/frus/nixon/e6/66834.htm.
15 *Time*, 7 March 1977; American Embassy Kinshasa to Secretary of State, 2 November 1975, *Foreign Relations, 1969–1976*, Volume E-6; Carter news conference, 23 February 1977, presidency.ucsb.edu.
16 *Guardian*, 18 August 2003.
17 bbc.co.uk, 16 August 2003.
18 Henry Byroade to Richard Nixon, 13 May 1970, history.state.gov/historicaldocuments/frus1969-76v20.
19 Seagrave, p.5.
20 Henry Byroade to Richard Nixon, 13 May 1970.
21 Bonner, p.77.
22 Ellison, pp.104–5.
23 Seagrave, p.256.
24 Inaugural Addresses, 30 December 1969, marcospresidentialcenter.com.
25 Seagrave, pp.258–9.
26 Ellison, p.106.
27 *Daily Telegraph*, 19 June 2001.
28 Ellison, p.103; Seagrave, p.266.
29 Seagrave, p.285; *Time*, 12 April 1971.
30 Memorandum of a Conversation between Nixon and Byroade, 15 January 1971, history.state.gov/historicaldocuments/frus1969-76v20; Kessler, p.52.
31 Martial law decree, marcospresidentialcenter.com.
32 *Economic and Political Weekly*, 14 October 1972; Telegram, Byroade to State Department, 15 September 1972, history.state.gov/historicaldocuments/frus1969-76v20; Wurfel, p.28.
33 *Economic and Political Weekly*, 14 October 1972.
34 Alfred McCoy, 'Dark Legacy: Human rights under the Marcos regime', lecture, 20 September 1999, hartford-hwp.com/archives/54a/062.html; Salonga, p.8; Kessler, p.52.
35 Short, pp.28–34.
36 Page, p.252.
37 Kiernan, p.16; Head and Grinter, p.130.
38 Nixon, *New Road*, pp.675, 683; Blum, p.366.
39 Werner and Huynh, pp.222–5; Duiker, p.231.
40 *New York Times*, 17 April 1998; 'A Country Study: Cambodia', memory.loc.gov.
41 Ieng Sary Diary, 10 July 1976, yale.edu/cgp/iengsary.htm.

42 *Time*, 8 January 1979; Harvey, pp.150, 152; Jackson, p.44.
43 Ieng Sary Diary, frontispiece; Harvey, p.151.
44 Ieng Sary Diary, 14 July 1976.
45 Ibid., 10 July 1976.
46 BBC News, 20 April 1998, bbc.co.uk.
47 E. Becker, p.260; *New York Times*, 17 April 1998; *Independent*, 11 February 2008; Cambodian Communities out of Crisis website, cambcomm.org.uk.
48 *Independent*, 11 February 2008; Ieng Sary Diary, 14 July 1976, 18 January 1977; *Time*, 8 January 1979; Harvey, p.151.
49 *Far Eastern Economic Review*, 30 October 1997.
50 Kiernan, pp.17–18.
51 Summers, p.4; Caldwell, *Kampuchea*, pp.91, 109; Ponchaud, p.193; Ear, ff.
52 Caldwell, *Malcolm Caldwell's South-East Asia*, p.8.
53 *New York Times*, 17 April 1998; *Independent*, 11 February 2008.
54 E. Becker, p.295.
55 'On this Day', 11 November 1965, bbc.co.uk.
56 Harold Macmillan, 'Winds of Change' speech, southafrica.to/history/WindsOfChange.htm.
57 *Hansard*, 11 November 1965.
58 *Hansard*, 11 November 1965.
59 *The Times*, 24 April 1965; 23 June 1969; 18 March 1976.
60 Meredith, p.320; 'On this Day', 2 March 1970, bbc.co.uk.
61 *The Times*, 18 March 1976.
62 George Silundika interview, nd, rhodesian.net.
63 *Zimbabwe News*, December 1974, rhodesian.net.
64 'On this Day', bbc.co.uk, 26 August 1975; Meredith, p.323.
65 Meredith, p.323.
66 Ibid., p.324; *The Times*, 25 September 1976.
67 *The Times*, 16, 25 September 1976.
68 'On this Day', 1 June 1979, bbc.co.uk.
69 Meredith, p.325.
70 'On this Day', 27 January 1980, bbc.co.uk.
71 Meredith, p.327.
72 Meredith, p.328; Raftopoulos and Savage, pp.x–xi; 'On this Day', 4 March 1980, bbc.co.uk.
73 *The Times*, 26 September 1978.
74 Abrahamian, *Iran Between Two Revolutions*, p.499; 'Memorandum for the President's File', 22 October 1971, history.state.gov/historicaldocuments/frus1969-76v20.
75 *New Yorker*, 18 December 1978; Yapp, pp.330–1.
76 *New Yorker*, 18 December 1978.
77 Ibid.
78 Ibid.

79 Arjomand, p.99.
80 Abrahamian, 'Iran in Revolution', p.3; Bakhtiar and Halliday, p.11; *New Yorker*, 18 December 1978.
81 Abrahamian, 'Iran in Revolution', p.6; *New Yorker*, 18 December 1978; Ansari, pp.200–1.
82 Abrahamian, *Iran Between Two Revolutions*, p.497; *New York Times*, 17 December 1978.
83 *New Yorker*, 18 December 1978.
84 Ibid.
85 Ibid.; *New York Times*, 7 November 1978; Ansari, p.207.
86 Ansari, p.209; *Christian Science Monitor*, 12 December 1978.
87 Bakhtiar and Halliday, p.13.
88 Bakhash, p.233.
89 Arjomand, p.3.

CHAPTER ELEVEN

1 *Time*, 29 October 1973.
2 Carter to Sadat, 14 February 1977, Carter Library, jimmycarterlibrary.org.
3 *New York Times*, 9 March 1992.
4 *Time*, 11 September 1978.
5 Schulze, p.110.
6 Address by Menachem Begin to the Egyptian People, 11 November 1977, Carter Library.
7 *New York Times*, 9 March 1992; Anwar Sadat, 'Peace with Justice', speech to the Knesset, 20 November 1977, Carter Library.
8 *New York Times*, 21 November 1977.
9 Sadat, 'Peace with Justice'.
10 *Time*, 11 September 1978; Carter to Begin, 3 August 1978; Carter to Sadat, 3 August 1978, Carter Library.
11 *Time*, 11 September 1978, 19 March 1979.
12 *Time*, 11 September 1978.
13 'Thirteen Days After Twenty-Five Years', Carter Library.
14 Carter, p.344; 'Camp David Negotiations', Camp David website, ibiblio.org/sullivan/CampDavid.
15 'Camp David Accords 25th Anniversary'; 'Camp David Negotiations'.
16 Kissinger phone message, 18 September 1978, Carter Library.
17 *Time*, 2 October 1978.
18 Sadat to Carter, 17 September 1978; Begin to Carter, 17 September 1978, Carter Library.
19 Presidential statement, 14 March 1979; American Embassy Cairo to Secretary of State, 27 October 1978, Carter Library.

20 *Time*, 19 March 1979, 19 October 1981.
21 Carter speech, 26 March 1979, Carter Library.
22 *Time*, 2 October 1978.
23 Nolan, pp.30, 44–5.
24 McNamara, *Blundering*, pp.44–5, 96–7.
25 Ibid., p.71.
26 Bethe, p.134.
27 McNamara, *Blundering*, p.66.
28 Cox, p.101.
29 Brzezinzki, pp.302–5.
30 Cox, p.185.
31 McNamara, *Blundering*, p.48.
32 Nitze, p.33.
33 Salisbury, p.177.
34 Schulman and Zelizer, p.269.
35 Fischer, p.104; Boyer, pp.151–4; *New York Times*, 30 May 1982.
36 'Decree of the Secretariat of the CC CPSU – An Appeal to the Leaders of the PDPA Groups "Parcham" and "Khalq"', 8 January 1974, Cold War International History Project, Woodrow Wilson Center, wilsoncenter.org (hereafter CWIHP).
37 Payind, p.118.
38 Pilger, pp.153–4; *New York Times*, 6 May 1978; *Wall Street Journal*, 6 January 1979.
39 Memo from Soviet Central Committee to Erich Honecker, 13 October 1978, CWIHP; Vasiliy Mitrokhin, 'The KGB in Afghanistan', Working Paper No. 40, Woodrow Wilson Center (February 2002), pp.40–1.
40 Transcript of CPSU CC Politburo Discussions on Afghanistan, 17 March 1979, CWIHP; Payind, pp.107–8.
41 Transcript of CPSU CC Politburo Discussions on Afghanistan, 17 March 1979, CWIHP.
42 Transcript of Kosygin–Taraki phone conversation, 18 March 1979, CWIHP.
43 *Cold War International History Project Bulletin*, Issue 4 (Fall 1994), pp.70–1.
44 Gromyko-Andropov-Ustinov-Ponomarev Report to CPSU CC on the Situation in Afghanistan, 28 June 1979, CWIHP.
45 Coll, p.46; Holmes and Dixon, p.27; *Washington Post*, 11 May 1979; Pilger, p.156.
46 Gromyko-Andropov-Ustinov-Ponomarev Report to CPSU CC on the Situation in Afghanistan, 28 June 1979; Conversation of the chief of the Soviet military advisory group in Afghanistan, Lt. Gen. Gorelov, with H. Amin, 11 August 1979, CWIHP.
47 CPSU CC Politburo Decisions on Afghanistan, 13 September 1979; Cable from Soviet Foreign Minister Gromyko to Soviet Representatives in Kabul, 15 September 1979; Wolf, p.10.

48 Personal memorandum from Andropov to Brezhnev, 1 December 1979, CWIHP; Sotiropoulos, p.65.
49 Payind, p.121; Wolf, p.17.
50 Schulman and Zelizer, pp.265, 282; Coll, p.51; *Le Nouvel Observateur*, 21 January 1998.
51 *Le Nouvel Observateur*, 21 January 1998.
52 Margaret Thatcher quotes, igreens.org.uk/margaret_thatcher_quotes.htm.
53 Young, pp.31, 39–40.
54 *Hansard*, 14 February 1961.
55 Young, p.64; *Scotsman*, 22 May 1988; Margaret Thatcher, speech to Conservative Party Conference, 12 October 1966, margaretthatcher.org; *Time*, 14 May 1979.
56 Thatcher quotes, igreens.org.uk/margaret_thatcher_quotes.htm.
57 Sir Keith Joseph, 'Inflation is caused by governments', Preston, 5 September 1974, margaretthatcher.org.
58 Rosen, pp.349–50.
59 Rosen, p.353; *Hansard*, 11 October 1976.
60 *Sunday Express*, 27 March 1977; Derbyshire and Derbyshire, p.76.
61 Haslam, p.298; Healey, pp.462–3; Chapple, p.150.
62 Young, pp.103–4.
63 Drabble, pp.59–60.
64 *Observer*, 25 February 1979; *Brussels Journal*, 13 October 2005; Thatcher quotes, igreens.org.uk/margaret_thatcher_quotes.htm.
65 'On this Day', 4 May 1979, bbc.co.uk.

EPILOGUE

1 Salisbury, p.218.
2 Reagan, speech at Kansas State University, 9 September 1982, presidency.ucsb.edu/ws/index.php?pid=42945; Haslam, pp.307–8.
3 Patterson, *Restless Giant*, p.159.
4 Ronald Reagan, Inaugural Address, 20 January 1981, bartleby.com/124/pres61.html; Speech to Joint Session of Congress, 28 April 1981, presidency.ucsb.edu/ws/index.php?pid=43756.
5 'Tales from the Underground', *Online Newshour*, 22 August 1996.
6 Sounes, p.408.

BIBLIOGRAPHY

Abrahamian, Ervand, *Iran Between Two Revolutions*. Princeton, NJ, 1982.

Abrahamian, Ervand, 'Iran in Revolution: The Opposition Forces', *MERIP Reports*, March–April, 1979.

Ali, Muhammad and Richard Durham, *The Greatest: My Own Story*. Chicago, 1976.

Ali, Tariq, *Street Fighting Years: An Autobiography of the Sixties*. London, 1987.

Allyn, David, *Make Love Not War*. New York, 2000.

Anderson, David L., *Shadow on the White House*. Lawrence, Kans.,1993.

Andrew, John, *The Other Side of the Sixties: Young Americans for Freedom and the Rise of Conservative Politics*. New Brunswick, NJ, 1997.

Ansari, Ali. *Modern Iran Since 1921*. Harlow, 2003.

Arjomand, Said, *The Turban for the Crown*. Oxford, 1988.

Ayers, William, *Fugitive Days*. New York, 2001.

Baccarelli, Andrea et al., 'Neonatal Thyroid Function in Seveso 25 Years after Maternal Exposure to Dioxin'. *PLoS Medicine*, 2008.

Bakhash, Shaul, *Reign of the Ayatollahs*. New York, 1990.

Bakhtiar, Shahpur and Fred Halliday, 'Shahpur Bakhtiar: "The Americans Played a Disgusting Role"', *MERIP Reports*, March–April, 1982.

Ball, Moya, *Vietnam-on-the-Potomac*. New York, 1992.

Baritz, Loren, *Backfire*. New York, 1985.

Barrett, David, *Uncertain Warriors*. Lawrence, Kans., 1993.

Barry, Lee, *John Martyn*. London, 2006.

Baskir, Lawrence and William Strauss, *Chance and Circumstance*. New York, 1978.

Becker, Elizabeth, *When the War was Over: Cambodia's Revolution and the Voices of its People*. New York, 1987.

Becker, Jillian, *Hitler's Children: The Story of the Baader–Meinhof Terrorist Gang*. London, 1989.

Beckett, Clare, *Margaret Thatcher*. London, 2006.

Ben-Porat, Yoel, 'The Yom Kippur War: A Mistake in May Leads to a Surprise in October'. *IDF Journal* (Summer 1986).

Benjamin, Marina, *Rocket Dreams*. New York, 2003.

Berger, Dan, *Outlaws in America*. Oakland, Calif., 1996.

Bergerud, Eric, *The Dynamics of Defeat*. Boulder, Colo., 1991.

Bernecker, Walther, 'Monarchy and Democracy: The Political Role of King Juan Carlos in the Spanish *Transicion*'. *Journal of Contemporary History*, 1998.
Bernstein, Hilda, *Steve Biko*. London, 1978.
Bethe, Hans, *The Road From Los Alamos*. New York, 1991.
Biko, Steve, *I Write What I Like*. London, 1987.
Blount, Jackie M., *Fit to Teach: Same Sex Desire, Gender, and School Work in the Twentieth Century*. New York, 2004.
Blum, John, *Years of Discord*. New York, 1991.
Bonnacorsi, Aurora et al., 'In the Wake of Seveso'. *AMBIO*, 1978.
Bonner, Raymond, *Waltzing With a Dictator: the Marcoses and the Making of American Policy*. New York, 1987.
Booker, Christopher, *The Neophiliacs*. London, 1970.
Booth, John, *The End and the Beginning: the Nicaraguan Revolution*. Boulder, Colo., 1985.
Boyer, Paul, *Fallout*. Columbus, Ohio, 1998.
Boyne, W.J., *The Yom Kippur War and the Airlift that Saved Israel*. New York, 2002.
Bregman, Ahron, *A History of Israel*. London, 2003.
Brown, Chris, *Bovver*. London, 2001.
Brownmiller, Susan, *Against Our Will: Men, Women and Rape*. New York, 1975.
Bryant, Anita, *Bless This House*. Old Tappan, NJ, 1972.
Bryant, Anita, *The Anita Bryant Story: The Survival of Our Nation's Families and the Threat of Militant Homosexuality*. Grand Rapids, Mich., 1977.
Brzezinski, Zbigniew, *Power and Principle*. New York, 1983.
Bugliosi, Vincent and Curt Gentry, *Helter-Skelter*. London, 1975.
Burchill, Julie and Tony Parsons, *The Boy Looked at Johnny: The Obituary of Rock and Roll*. London, 1978.
Burrows, William, *This New Ocean*. New York, 1999.
Butler, David, *The Fall of Saigon*. New York, 1985.
Caldwell, Malcolm, *Kampuchea: Rationale for Rural Policy*. Hyderabad, 1979.
Caldwell, Malcolm, *Malcolm Caldwell's South-East Asia*. Townsville, Queensland, 1979.
Capps, Walter, *The Vietnam Reader*. New York, 1991.
Carr, Raymond, *Modern Spain*. London, 1980.
Carroll, Peter, *It Seemed Like Nothing Happened: America in the 1970s*. Piscataway, NJ, 1990.
Carter, Dale, *The Final Frontier*. London, 1988.
Carter, Jimmy, *Keeping Faith: Memoirs of a President*. London, 1982.
Cavallo, Dominick, *A Fiction of the Past: The Sixties in American History*. New York, 1999.
Cernan, Eugene, *The Last Man on the Moon*. New York, 1999.
Chang, Jung and Jon Halliday, *Mao: The Unknown Story*. London, 2006.
Chapman, Thomas, 'Constructing the Moral Landscape through Anti-Discrimination

Law: Discourse, Debate, and Dialogue of Sexual Citizenship in Three Florida Communities'. Unpublished Ph.D. thesis, Florida State University, 2007.

Chapple, Frank, *Sparks Fly!* London, 1984.

Chenoweth, Lawrence, 'The Rhetoric of Hope and Despair: A study of the Jimi Hendrix Experience and Jefferson Airplane'. *American Quarterly*, 1971.

Cherlin, Andrew, *Marriage, Divorce, Remarriage.* Cambridge, Mass., 1981.

Clark, Robert, *Negotiating with ETA: Obstacles to Peace in the Basque Country, 1975–1988*. Reno, Nev., 1990.

Clendinen, Dudley, et al., *Out for Good: The Struggle to Build A Gay Rights Movement in America.* New York, 2001.

Coe, Jonathan, *The Rotters' Club.* London, 2001.

Coll, Steve, *Ghost Wars: The Secret History of the CIA, Afghanistan, and Bin Laden.* London, 2004.

Collier, Peter and David Horowitz, *Destructive Generation*. New York, 1990.

Commission of Inquiry, *The Yom Kippur War, An Additional Partial Report: Reasoning and Complement to the Partial Report of April 1, 1974.* Jerusalem,1974.

Coverdale, John, 'Spain from Dictatorship to Democracy'. *International Affairs*,1977.

Cox, John, *Overkill.* London, 1971.

Coyote, Peter, *Sleeping Where I Fall.* Washington, DC, 1998.

Cross, Charles, *Room Full of Mirrors: A Biography of Jimi Hendrix.* London, 2005.

Crossman, Richard, *Diaries of a Cabinet Minister,* Vol. 1. London, 1975.

Crow, Barbara. *Radical Feminisim: A Documentary Reader.* New York, 2000.

D'Emilio, John and Estelle Freedman. *Intimate Matters: A History of Sexuality in America.* New York, 1988.

Dallek, Robert, *Nixon and Kissinger: Partners in Power.* London, 2008.

Davidson, Phillip, *Vietnam at War.* Oxford, 1988.

DeGroot, Gerard, *A Noble Cause?: America and the Vietnam War.* London, 1999.

DeGroot, Gerard, *Dark Side of the Moon: The Magnificent Madness of the American Lunar Quest.* New York, 2007.

DeGroot, Gerard, *Student Protest: The Sixties and After*. London, 1998.

DeGroot, Gerard, *The Bomb: A Life.* London, 2004.

DeGroot, Gerard, *The Sixties Unplugged: A Kaleidoscopic History of a Disorderly Decade.* London, 2008.

Del Vecchio, John, 'The importance of story: Individual and cultural effects of skewing the realities of American involvement in Southeast Asia for social, political and/or economic ends'. Vietnam Symposium, Texas Tech University, 1996.

DeMaria, Rusel and Johnny Wilson, *High Score!: The Illustrated History of Electronic Games.* New York, 2003.

DeMott, Benjamin, *Surviving the 70s.* New York, 1972.

Derbyshire, Ian and J. Denis Derbyshire, *Politics in Britain: From Callaghan to Thatcher.* London, 1990.

Dickstein, Morris, *Gates of Eden: American Culture in the Sixties*. New York, 1977.

Diederich, Bernard, *Somoza and the Legacy of U.S. Involvement in Central America*. New York, 1981.

Drabble, Margaret, *The Ice Age*. New York, 1977.

Drake, Richard, *The Aldo Moro Murder Case*. Cambridge, Mass., 1995.

Duiker, William, *Sacred War*. New York, 1995.

Duncanson, Dennis, *Government and Revolution in Vietnam*. New York, 1968.

Ear, Sophal, 'The Khmer Rouge Canon 1975–1979: The Standard Total Academic View on Cambodia', unpublished Ph.D. thesis, University of California, Berkeley, 1995.

Edmonds, David and John Eidinow, *Bobby Fischer Goes to War*. London, 2004.

Edwards, Robert and Patrick Steptoe. *A Matter of Life: The Story of a Medical Breakthrough*. Glasgow, 1981.

Ehrenreich, Barbara, *Re-making Love: The Feminization of Sex*. New York, 1986.

Ehrhart, William, *In the Shadow of Vietnam: Essays, 1977–1991*. Jefferson, NC, 1977.

Ehrlichman, John, *Witness to Power*. New York, 1982.

Elliott, Elisabeth, *Let Me Be a Woman: Notes to My Daughter on the Meaning of Womanhood*. Wheaton, Ill., 1981.

Ellison, Katherine, *Imelda, Steel Butterfly of the Philippines*. New York, 1989.

Ercegovac, Peter, 'Competing National Ideologies, Cyclical Responses: The Mobilisation of the Irish, Basque and Croat National Movements to Rebellion Against the State', unpublished Ph.D. thesis, University of Sydney, 1999.

Farber, David, *The Sixties: From Memory to History*. Durham, NC, 1994.

Fischer, Beth, *The Reagan Reversal: Foreign Policy and the End of the Cold War*. Columbia, Mo., 1997.

Foot, Paul, *Immigration and Race in British Politics*. London, 1965.

Freeman, Joshua, 'Hardhats: Construction Workers, Manliness, and the 1970 Pro-War Demonstrations'. *Journal of Social History*, 1993.

FSLN National Directorate, *On the General Political-Military Platform of the Struggle of the Sandinista Front for National Liberation*. Oakland, Calif., 1977.

Gates, Robert, *From the Shadows: the Ultimate Insider's Story of Five Presidents and How They Won the Cold War*. New York, 1997.

Gerber, Jurg and Eric Jensen, *Encyclopedia of White Collar Crime*. London, 2006.

Gilbert, Dennis, *Sandinistas*. Oxford, 1988.

Gitlin, Todd, *The Sixties: Years of Hope, Days of Rage*. New York, 1987.

Goodson, Larry, *Afghanistan's Endless War: State Failure, Regional Politics, and the Rise of the Taliban*. Seattle, Wash., 2001.

Goodwin, Richard, *Remembering America: A Voice from the Sixties*. New York, 1989.

Graebner, William, *Patty's got a Gun: Patricia Hearst in 1970s America*. Chicago, 2008.

Gray, Marcus, *The Clash: Return of the Last Gang in Town*. London, 2001.

Green, Jonathan, *All Dressed Up: The Sixties and the Counter Culture*. London, 1999.

Green, Jonathan, *Days in the Life*. London, 1988.

Gustainis, Justin J., *American Rhetoric and the Vietnam War*. Westport, Conn., 1993.

Haldeman, H. R., *The Ends of Power*. New York, 1989.

Hanhimäki, Jussi, *The Flawed Architect: Henry Kissinger and American Foreign Policy*. Oxford, 2004.

Harriman, Robert, *Popular Trials: Studies in Rhetoric and Communication*. Tuscaloosa, Ala., 1993.

Harrison, James, *The Endless War*. New York, 1989.

Harvey, Robert, *Comrades: The Rise and Fall of World Communism*. London, 2003.

Haslam, David, *Young Hearts Run Free: The Real Story of the 1970s*. London, 2007.

Hauser, Thomas, *Muhammad Ali: His Life and Times*. New York, 2004.

Hayden, Tom, *Reunion*. New York, 1988.

Head, William and Lawrence Grinter, eds., *Looking Back on the Vietnam War*. Santa Barbara, Calif., 1993.

Healey, Denis, *The Time of My Life*. London, 1990.

Hebdige, Dick, *Subculture: The Meaning of Style*. London, 2002.

Heineman, Kenneth, *Campus Wars*. New York, 1993.

Heller, Jennifer, 'Marriage, Womanhood, and the Search for "Something More": American Evangelical Women's Best-selling "Self-Help" Books, 1972–1979'. *Journal of Religion and Popular Culture*, 2002.

Henderson, David, *'Scuse Me While I Kiss The Sky: The Life of Jimi Hendrix*. London, 2003.

Heppenheimer, T. A., *The Space Shuttle Decision*. Washington, DC, 1999.

Herring, George C., *America's Longest War*. New York, 1986.

Hitchcock, William I., *The Struggle for Europe: The History of the Continent Since 1945*. London, 2003.

Hobsbawm, Eric, *Interesting Times: A Twentieth Century Life*. London, 2002.

Hoffman, Abbie, *Revolution for the Hell of It*. New York, 1968.

Hogan, Alfred, 'Science on the Set', unpublished Ph.D. thesis, University of Maryland, 1986.

Holloway, David, 'Soviet Nuclear History', *Cold War International History Project Bulletin*. Fall, 1994.

Holloway, David, *The Soviet Union and the Arms Race*, New Haven, Conn., 1984.

Holmes, David and Norm Dixon, *Behind the US War in Afghanistan*. Sydney, 2001.

Hong, Zhaohui and Yi Sun, 'The Butterfly Effect and the Making of "Ping-Pong Diplomacy"', *Journal of Contemporary China*, 2000.

Hoskyns, Barney, *Hotel California*. London, 2005.

Hunt, Richard, *Pacification*. Boulder, Colo., 1995.

Isaacs, Arnold, *Without Honor: Defeat in Vietnam and Cambodia*. Baltimore, Md., 1998.

Isserman, Maurice and Michael Kazin, *America Divided: the Civil War of the 1960s*. New York, 2000.

Jackson, Karl, ed., *Cambodia: 1975–1978*. Princeton, NJ, 1989.
Jacobs, Harold, *Weatherman*. Berkeley, Calif., 1970.
Jacobs, Ron, *The Way the Wind Blew*. New York, 1997.
Johnson, George, ed., *The Nixon Presidential Press Conferences*. New York, 1978.
Kahn, Ashley, et al., *Rolling Stone: The Seventies—A Tumultuous Decade Reconsidered*. Boston, Mass., 1998.
Kakar, M. Hassan, *Afghanistan: The Soviet Invasion and the Afghan Response, 1979–1982*. Berkeley, Calif., 1995.
Kaplan, Fred, *The Wizards of Armageddon*. Stanford, Calif., 1983.
Karnow, Stanley, *Vietnam: A History*. London, 1993.
Katsiaficas, George, *The Imagination of the New Left*. New York, 1987.
Kessler, Richard J., 'Marcos and the Americans', *Foreign Policy*, Summer, 1986.
Kiernan, Ben, 'Coming to Terms with the Past: Cambodia', *History Today*, September, 2004.
King, Martin, *A Boy's Story: The Revelations and Wild Times of a Young Skin*. Edinburgh, 2000.
Klatch, Rebecca, *A Generation Divided: The New Left, the New Right, and the 1960s*. Berkeley, Calif., 1999.
Klerkx, Greg, *Lost in Space*. London, 2004.
Kolko, Gabriel, *Anatomy of a War*. New York, 1994.
Krepinevich, Andrew, *The Army and Vietnam*. Baltimore, Md., 1986.
Kumaraswamy, P.R., *Revisiting the Yom Kippur War*. London, 2000.
Kuzmiak, D.T., 'The American Environmental Movement', *The Geographical Journal*, 1991.
LaHaye, Beverly, *The Spirit-Controlled Woman*. New York, 1995.
Launius, Roger and Howard McCurdy, eds., *Spaceflight and the Myth of Presidential Leadership*. Urbana, Ill., 1997.
Levin, Bernard, *The Pendulum Years*. London, 1989.
Levy, Peter, *America in the Sixties: Left, Right and Center*. Westport, Conn., 1998.
Lewy, Guenter, *America in Vietnam*. Oxford, 1978.
Lezra, Jacques, 'The Ethic of Terror in Radical Democracy', *Arizona Journal of Hispanic Cultural Studies*, 2003.
Liang Heng and Judith Shapiro, *After the Nightmare*. New York, 1986.
Linder, Douglas. 'The Chicago Seven Conspiracy Trial', <http://www.law.umkc.edu/faculty/projects/ftrials/Chicago7/Account.html>.
Logsdon, John, *The Decision to Go to the Moon*. Chicago, 1970.
Lucas, J. Anthony, *Don't Shoot—We Are Your Children*. New York, 1968.
Lydon, John, *Rotten: No Irish, No Blacks, No Dogs*. London, 1994.
Lydon, Michael, *Flashbacks*. New York, 2003.
McCurdy, Howard, *Space and the American Imagination*. Washington, DC, 1997.
Macdonald, Ian, *Revolution in the Head: The Beatles' Records and the Sixties*. London, 1995.

McDougall, William A., *The Heavens and the Earth: A Political History of the Space Age*. Baltimore, Md., 1997. Macmillan, Margaret, *Nixon and Mao: The Week That Changed the World*. London, 2008.

McLellan, Vin and Paul Avery, *The Voices of Guns. The Definitive and Dramatic Story of the Twenty-Two Month Story of the Symbionese Liberation Army*. New York, 1977.

McMahon, Robert, *Major Problems in the History of the Vietnam War*. Lexington, Mass., 1990.

McNamara, Robert, *Blundering into Disaster*. New York, 1986.

McNamara, Robert, *In Retrospect*. New York, 1995.

McNeil, Legs and Gillian McCain, *Please Kill Me: The Uncensored Oral History of Punk*. London, 1996.

MacPherson, Myra, *Long Time Passing*. New York, 1984.

McQuaid, Kim, *The Anxious Years: America in the Vietnam-Watergate Era*. New York, 1989.

Maitland, Sara, *Very Heaven: Looking Back at the 1960s*. London, 1998.

Mallin, Jay, *The Great Managuan Earthquake*. New York, 1974.

Marcus, Bruce, ed., *Nicaragua: The Sandinista People's Revolution*. New York, 1985.

Marcus, Eric, *Making History: The Struggle for Gay and Lesbian Equal Rights, 1945–1990*. New York, 1992.

Marcus, Greil, *Lipstick Traces: A Secret History of the Twentieth Century*. New York, 1990.

Marcus, Greil, *The Dustbin of History*. New York, 1995.

Marqusee, Mike, *Redemption Song, Muhammad Ali and the Spirit of the Sixties*. London, 2005.

Marshall, George, *Skinhead Nation*. London, 1996.

Mascarenhas, Anthony, *The Rape of Bangla Desh*. Delhi, 1972.

Massey, Howard, ed., *Behind the Glass: Top Record Producers Tell How They Craft Their Hits*. San Francisco, 2000.

May, Elaine Tyler, *Homeward Bound*. New York, 1988.

Meir, Golda, *My Life*. New York, 1975.

Meredith, Martin, *The State of Africa: A History of Fifty Years of Independence*. London, 2006.

Michener, James, *Kent State: What Happened and Why*. New York, 1971.

Miles, Barry, *Hippie*. London, 2003.

Miles, Robert and Annie Phizacklea, *Racism and Political Action in Britain*. London, 1979.

Miller, James, *'Democracy is in the Streets': From Port Huron to the Siege of Chicago*. New York, 1987.

Mitchell, James K., ed., *The Long Road to Recovery: Community Responses to Industrial Disaster*. Tokyo, 1996.

Moore, Basil, ed., *Black Theology, The South African Voice*. London, 1973.

Morgan, Marabel, *The Total Woman*. London, 1975.

Morgan, Marabel, *Total Joy*. London, 1977.
Munck, Ronaldo, *Ireland: Nation, State, and Class Struggle*. London, 1985.
Neville, Richard, *Hippie Hippie Shake*. London, 1995.
Neville, Richard, *Playpower*. London, 1971.
Nitze, Paul, 'Assuring Strategic Stability in an Era of Détente', *Foreign Affairs*, January, 1976.
Nixon, Richard M., *A New Road for America: Major Policy Statements, March 1970 to October 1971*. New York, 1972.
Nixon, Richard M., *RN: The Memoirs of Richard Nixon*. New York, 1978.
Nolan, Janne, *An Elusive Consensus: Nuclear Weapons and American Security After the Cold War*. Washington, DC, 1999.
Owen, David, 'Problems in Assessing Punitive Damages Against Manufacturers of Defective Products', *The University of Chicago Law Review*, Winter, 1982.
Page, Caroline, *US Official Propaganda During the Vietnam War, 1965–1973*. New York, 1996.
Patterson, James, *Grand Expectations: The United States, 1945–1974*. Oxford, 1997.
Patterson, James, *Restless Giant: The United States from Watergate to Bush v. Gore*. New York, 2005.
Payind, Alam, 'Soviet-Afghan Relations from Cooperation to Occupation', *International Journal of Middle East Studies*, 1989.
Payne, Robert, *Massacre*. London, 1972.
Perlstein, Rick, *Nixonland: The Rise of a President and the Fracturing of America*. New York, 2008.
Pike, Douglas, *PAVN: People's Army of Vietnam*. Novato, Calif., 1986.
Pike, Douglas, *Viet Cong: The Organization and Techniques of the National Liberation Front of South Vietnam*. Cambridge, Mass., 1966.
Pilger, John, *The New Rulers of the World*. London, 2002.
Pimlott, John, *Vietnam: The Decisive Battles*. London, 1990.
Ponchaud, François, *Cambodia: Year Zero*. New York, 1978.
Ponting, Clive, *Breach of Promise: Labour in Power, 1964–70*. London, 1989.
Powers, Thomas, *Diana: The Making of a Terrorist*. New York, 1971.
Powers, Thomas, *Vietnam: The War at Home*. Boston, Mass., 1984.
Pressler, Charlotte, *Those Were Different Times*. New York, 1979.
Preston, Paul, *The Triumph of Democracy in Spain*. London, 1986.
Rabinovich, Abraham, *The Yom Kippur War: The Epic Encounter That Transformed the Middle East*. New York, 2005.
Raftopoulos, Brian and Tyrone Savage, *Zimbabwe: Injustice and Political Reconciliation*. Harare, 2004.
Reagan, Ronald, *An American Life*. New York, 1990.
Reeve, Simon, *One Day in September*. London, 2000.
Riess, Steven, ed., *Major Problems in American Sport History*. Boston, Mass., 1997.
Robb, John and Oliver Craske, *Punk Rock: An Oral History*. London, 2006.

Roberts, Selena, *A Necessary Spectacle: Billy Jean King, Bobby Riggs and the Tennis Match that Leveled the Game*. New York, 2005.

Romero Salvadó, Francisco, *Twentieth-Century Spain*. London, 1999.

Rosen, Greg, *Old Labour to New*. London, 2005.

Rosenberg, Rosalind, 'The Women Question at Columbia: From John W. Burgess to Judith Shapiro', Columbia University Seminar on the History of the University, 17 February 1999.

Ross, S., *The Middle East Since 1945*. London, 2004.

Rubin, Barnett, *The Fragmentation of Afghanistan*. New Haven, Conn., 1995.

Rubin, Jerry, *Do It!* New York, 1970.

Rubin, Jerry, *Growing Up at Thirty-Seven*. New York, 1976.

Rudd, Mark, 'How a Movie Changed my Life', *Heartland Journal*, Summer, 2005.

Rummel, R.J., *Death by Government: Genocide and Mass Murder since 1900*. London, 1997.

Rutledge, Leigh, *The Gay Decades: From Stonewall to the Present*. New York, 1992.

Sabin, Roger, ed., *Punk Rock: So What?* London, 1999.

Sachar, Howard M., *A History of Israel from the Rise of Zionism to Our Time*. New York, 2007.

Salisbury, Harrison, ed., *The Eloquence of Protest: Voices of the 70's*. Boston, Mass., 1972.

Salonga, Jovito R., *Presidential Plunder: The Quest for the Marcos Ill-Gotten Wealth*. Manila, 2000.

Sandbrook, Dominic, *White Heat*. London, 2006.

Savage, Jon, *England's Dreaming: Sex Pistols and Punk Rock*. London, 2005.

Schneir, Walter, ed., *Telling It Like It Was: The Chicago Riots*. New York, 1969.

Schulman, Bruce and Julian Zelizer, *Rightward Bound: Making America Conservative in the 1970s*. New York, 2008.

Schulze, Kirsten, *The Arab–Israeli Conflict*. London, 2008.

Schwartz, Gary, 'The Myth of the Ford Pinto Case'. *Rutgers Law Review*, 1991.

Schwartz, Richard, *Cold War Culture*. New York, 1998.

Sciascia, Leonardo, *The Moro Affair*. New York, 2004.

Seagrave, Sterling, *The Marcos Dynasty*. London, 1989.

Sevy, Grace, ed., *The American Experience in Vietnam*. Norman, Okla., 1989.

Sheehan, Neil, *A Bright Shining Lie*. London, 1990.

Short, Philip, *Pol Pot: The History of a Nightmare*. London, 2004.

Sick, Gary, *All Fall Down: America's Tragic Encounter with Iran*. New York, 1985.

Sked, Alan and Chris Cook, *Post-War Britain: A Political History*. London, 1979.

Smith, Hazel, *Nicaragua: Self-determination and Survival*. London, 1993.

Snepp, Frank, *Decent Interval*. New York, 1977.

Sotiropoulos, Ioannis, 'The Decisive Factors that Influenced the Soviet Decision-Making Process for the Invasion of Afghanistan', *Defensor Pacis*, September, 2007.

Sounes, Howard, *Seventies: The Sights, Sounds and Ideas of a Brilliant Decade*. London, 2007.

Spicer, Al, *The Rough Guide to Punk*. London, 2006.

Steigerwald, David, *The Sixties and the End of Modern America*. New York, 1995.

Stein, Kenneth, 'The October 1973 War: Super-Power Engagement and Estrangement', *Zmanim*, 2003.

Stine, Peter, *The Sixties*. Detroit, 1995.

Strongman, Phil, *Pretty Vacant: A History of Punk*. London, 2007.

Summers, Laura, 'Cambodia: Consolidating the Revolution', *Current History*, December, 1975.

Suri, Jeremi, *Henry Kissinger and the American Century*. Cambridge, Mass., 2007.

Teodori, Massimo, *The New Left: A Documentary History*. New York, 1969.

Thompson, Hunter S.. *Fear and Loathing in Las Vegas*. London, 1993.

Tran Van Don, *Our Endless War*. Novato, Calif., 1978.

Tremlett, Giles, *Ghosts of Spain*. London, 2006.

Truong Nhu Tang, *A Vietcong Memoir*. San Diego, 1985.

Turner, Alwyn, *Crisis? What Crisis?* London, 2009.

Turner, Alwyn, *The Biba Experience*. London, 2005.

Turnill, Reginald, *The Moonlandings*. Cambridge, 2003.

Unger, Irwin and Debi Unger, eds., *The Times Were a Changin': The Sixties Reader*. New York, 1998.

Varon, Jeremy, *Bringing the War Home: The Weather Underground, the Red Army Faction and Revolutionary Violence in the 1960s and 1970s*. Berkeley, Calif., 2004.

Wells, Tom, *The War Within*. Berkeley, Calif., 1994.

Werner, Jayne and Luu Doan Huynh, eds., *The Vietnam War: Vietnamese and American Perspectives*. Armonk, NY, 1993.

Wiener, Jon, *Professors, Politics and Pop*. New York, 1991.

Williams, Robert and Philip Cantelon, eds., *The American Atom*. Philadelphia, 1984.

Williams, William Appleman, et al., eds., *America in Vietnam: A Documentary History*. New York, 1975.

Wills, Garry, *Reagan's America*. New York, 1988.

Witcover, Jules, *The Year the Dream Died*. New York, 1997.

Wolf, Matt, 'Stumbling Towards War: The Soviet Decision to Invade Afghanistan'. *Past Imperfect*, 2006.

Woods, Donald, *Biko*. London, 1987.

Wurfel, David, 'Martial Law in the Philippines'. *Pacific Affairs*, 1977.

Yapp, M.E., *The Near East Since the First World War*. Harlow, 1996.

Young, Hugo, *One of Us*. London, 1993.

Zeira, Eli, *The October 73 War: Myth Against Reality*. Tel Aviv, 1993.

INDEX